CASSELL MULTILINGUAL DICTIONARY OF LOCAL GOVERNMENT AND BUSINESS

CASSELL MULTILINGUAL DICTIONARY OF LOCAL GOVERNMENT AND BUSINESS

The European Language Initiative

Edited by Clive Leo McNeir

CASSELL

Cassell
Villiers House
41/47 Strand
London
WC2N 5JE

387 Park Avenue South
New York
NY 10016-8810

First published 1993

British Library Cataloguing-in-Publication Data
A catalogue entry for this book is available from the British Library

Library of Congress Cataloging-in-Publication Data
is available from the Library of Congress

ISBN 0-304-32715-8

Printed in Great Britain by Bookcraft (Bath) Ltd, Midsomer Norton, Avon

Contents

Foreword

I am happy to be able to support The European Language Initiative as an imaginative and important use of Community funds to support language training.

Helping communication between local authorities in different member states is an essential part of building the Community. The Community is not just the concern of governments; its aim, clearly set out in the founding treaty, is 'the ever-closer union of the peoples of Europe'.

In supporting The European Language Initiative through the Lingua Programme, the Commission has wished to recognize and encourage the Association of District Secretaries and the Union des Dirigeants Territoriaux de l'Europe as they strengthen the channels of communication between them and their partners in other member states. I believe that initiatives such as these are of great importance for the Community, and I wish it every success in the future.

The Right Honourable Sir Leon Brittan QC
Vice-President of the European Commission

Avant-Propos

Les travaux menés par l'Union des Dirigeants Territoriaux de l'Europe (UDITE) ont montré la complexité et les difficultés des terminologies administratives employées par les autorités locales.

En effet il ne suffit pas de traduire une loi, un concept, une organisation; faut-il encore que chacun mette le même contenu aux mots employés.

De ce fait le projet de dictionnaire de The European Language Initiative (TELI) est très important pour l'ensemble des collectivités et des entreprises européennes. La volonté de l'UDITE est d'améliorer les relations entre les collectivités de la Communauté grâce à une meilleure communication entre les associations constitutives.

Je remercie The Association of District Secretaries (ADS) qui, au nom de l'ensemble des participants à l'UDITE, a bien voulu diriger le travail réalisé.

Je considère qu'avec le travail technique réalisé sur le droit comparatif et les finances locales européennes, le dictionnaire est un excellent exemple de collaboration entre toutes les associations.

Je salue et félicite TELI pour cette brillante initiative et je suis fier de m'y être associé et d'avoir encouragé ce projet.

Je suis persuadé que tous les professionnels qui estiment que la connaissance réciproque est le meilleur moyen de bâtir l'Europe de demain réserveront dans chaque pays un accueil particulièrement favorable à ce projet.

Gérard Combe
Président de l'UDITE

Preface

The European Language Initiative, of which this dictionary is the first tangible product, is one of the largest and most important language projects currently in progress in the European Community. Little did I realize, when my colleagues and I first set out to devise a solution to the language problem confronting us, that in such a short space of time we would be involved in so ambitious a venture.

The need for understanding between local government officers and elected members in the EC member states is vital as our countries grow more closely together. Contacts take place at many levels and on many issues, and we discovered at an early stage that we have more in common than we had initially imagined. Despite some differences in policies and structures, we find that we share common goals and standards. In seeking to understand each other's problems, we seek to help in identifying solutions. To achieve this, we must be able to communicate clearly with one another, using the language of local government.

Similarly, if we are to support the business sector, we must have the means of understanding the language of commerce and industry, just as they must have the opportunity to become familiar with our domain. This is a major part of the task that we have set ourselves and is a key element in our contribution to the development of a more integrated Europe.

Personally, I am delighted that the initiative is being spearheaded by my professional body, the Association of District Secretaries, on behalf of the Union des Dirigeants Territoriaux de l'Europe, which unites officers in local government throughout the European Community. This is a clear indication of the benefits that can arise from close co-operation with our colleagues on the Continent and it is a privilege to be part of this important work.

Marilyn Hayward
Chairman of The European Language Initiative
and former President of the Association of District Secretaries

Introduction

This dictionary, like all others, should probably carry the equivalent of a government health warning. This would not assert that dictionaries may be harmful to your health, far from it, but that they can be misleading if the reader assumes translations of terms to be absolutely accurate and valid in all situations. In many cases a dictionary can only indicate the nearest equivalent term, so that the user gains an understanding of what a word means which is as close to reality as is reasonably possible.

The Question of Equivalents

The fact is that, even at the simplest of levels, words are not exact equivalents when compared with their counterparts in other countries. Thus, though the word 'house' may be accurately translated between languages, the object itself may vary significantly in style and structure between countries or even between regions of the same country.

Nowhere is this difficulty more clearly illustrated than in the field of specialist technical language, as exemplified in this dictionary. Numerous terms are quoted, for which the nearest equivalent word is given as translation, since that is the object of the exercise. However, a distinction must be drawn between identifying the best available translation and claiming that one term is the exact equivalent of the other.

Users are asked to bear in mind that the structures and practices of local government and business vary sometimes quite markedly from one country to another. This has, of course, a direct bearing on the language used in different countries. A term which has an obvious translation may in reality have a quite different meaning from the one assumed, because of the dissimilar context in which it is used.

A schools 'inspector' in Britain is manifestly not the same in terms of rôle and powers as an 'inspecteur' in France or an 'Aufsichtsbeamter' in Germany. In order to clarify these differences it would be necessary to produce a textbook of practice rather than a mere dictionary. To multiply all the detailed explanations required by the various languages would create an unwieldy and unusable volume.

For these practical reasons alone, it has been decided to aim at the nearest equivalent translation, with an asterisk (*) to indicate where care must be taken in using a given term. Users are advised to refer to other sources for a more detailed description and explanation of how different terms are employed in a particular country. Some of the sources are listed in the brief bibliography on page 222.

The Selection of Terms

The sheer range and diversity of local government makes any selection process a major task. Local democracy embraces many disciplines and its activities impact on all our lives in a great variety of ways. In compiling this dictionary the aim has been to try to reflect this range and give a reasonable coverage over all the areas of responsibility exercised by local authorities.

At the same time several hundred business terms have been included. Local government finds itself increasingly involved with the business community in matters such as attracting inward investment, promoting tourism, joint public–private sector ventures, etc. Both sectors are learning each other's language and in so doing are arriving at a greater understanding of each other's strengths and needs. For this reason the rôle and contribution of both parties in the development of the Single European Market should be understood. This is particularly important in respect of small and medium-sized enterprises (SMEs).

If a smaller company wishes to expand its activities beyond its national boundaries it is likely to contact two organizations in the area chosen: the local chamber of commerce and the local authority. It is vitally important that all the parties involved should be able to communicate with each other to mutual benefit. This dictionary and the supporting products and activities of The European Language Initiative (TELI) seek to contribute to this development.

Change, Growth and Flexibility

Local government and the business world are accustomed to operating in a climate of change. In commerce and industry, markets may be influenced by a considerable variety of forces. Similarly, local government finds itself having to respond to changing conditions and priorities, not to mention political fluctuations and the occasional reorganization. Language is equally susceptible to change.

This dictionary should be regarded as a starting-point. It covers a wide range of activities but it cannot cover them all. Language changes to meet new circumstances and a number of terms included here have only recently appeared. Words that are now commonplace may, surprisingly, have been coined only a few years ago. A word such as 'informatique' is typical of the terms derived from the revolution in information technology that have been assimilated into everyday working life.

With this in mind, we have included a number of blank pages at the end of the text so that the user can add new words and expressions as they are encountered over time. This is essentially a working manual designed to grow in step with the experience and expertise of the user.

Clive Leo McNeir
Director of The European Language Initiative

Acknowledgments

Thanks are due to many parties for their rôle in producing this dictionary. Financial support has been given by a consortium of organizations, as follows:

Municipal Journal
Association of District Secretaries
Society of County Secretaries
Society of County Treasurers
Local Government Management Board
The Lingua Bureau of the European Commission
Cassell plc
Association of Chief Technical Officers
Society of Information Technology Managers
Institution of Economic Development Officers

We gratefully acknowledge the advice, guidance and support of our parliamentary adviser, Anthony Simpson MEP, who has freely given of his time and energies since the inception of the initiative. Thanks are also due to Doug Hoyle MP for his active help and encouragement which have been a considerable support throughout the project.

We further acknowledge with thanks the invaluable assistance of local authorities and professional organizations. The lead rôle has been taken from the start by the Association of District Secretaries (ADS) on behalf of the Union des Dirigeants Territoriaux de l'Europe (UDITE). The management committee of the project has been chaired by the initiative's instigator, Marilyn Hayward, former president of ADS. The work has enjoyed the personal support of the president of UDITE, Gérard Combe.

The compilation of terms could not have proceeded without the willing cooperation of the officers of local authorities in France (Besançon, Calais, Grenoble, Toulon, Yvelines), Germany (Brühl) and Britain (Cotswold, Dover, Enfield), with further assistance from the Syndicat National des Secrétaires Généraux et Directeurs Généraux in France, the Deutsche Städte- und Gemeindebund in Germany and the Local Government International Bureau in London. Considerable assistance was provided by Eric Gaskell, Head of the Library of the Commission of the European Communities, and the London Research Centre, Research Library.

The production team comprised Clive Leo McNeir, director of The European Language Initiative, Neil Morris, Roswitha Morris, Leslie Weatheritt and Cassandra Williams, with contributions from Geoff Scaplehorn and Roger Everest-Phillips.

How to use this Dictionary

This dictionary has been designed for easy use. It contains nearly 3,500 terms or words, organized in alphabetical order and accessible in any of the three languages.

Access

If, for example, you wish to learn the meaning of 'Tagesordnung' in German, you will find the word in the 'T' section, translations given in English and French:

Tagesordnung (f) *De*
agenda *En*
ordre (m) du jour *Fr*

Similarly, if you wish to know the French equivalent of an English term, you access the English term according to its first letter. The translation will be found in French and German:

pie chart *En*
camembert (m) *Fr*
Kreisdiagramm (nt) *De*

Note: the languages are indicated as follows:
En for English
Fr for French (Français)
De for German (Deutsch)

Grammatical Information

The amount of grammatical information given with each entry has been kept to the minimum consistent with clarifying your understanding and use of the term.

For nouns, the gender is given in French and German and both masculine and feminine forms are shown, where this is required. Plurals are given only if there is a specific reason for doing so, such as an irregular form.

Examples:

doctor *En*
médecin (m) (f = femme médecin) *Fr*
Arzt/Ärztin (m/f) *De*

Hochhaus (nt) *De*
highrise block *En*
gratte-ciel (m) (pl. les grattes-ciel) *Fr*

Other parts of speech are given as follows:

(adj) adjective
(adv) adverb
(noun)
(vb) verb

Genders are given as follows:

(f) feminine
(f.pl) feminine plural
(m) masculine
(m.pl) masculine plural
(nt) neuter
(nt.pl) neuter plural

(pl) where no gender is applicable, eg
Kosten (pl) *De*
Finanzen (pl) *De*
Spesen (pl) *De*

Local Government Departments

Responsibilities for local services and operations vary between countries, and even departments which share similar titles may differ quite markedly in terms of the functions they perform. The list which follows is intended as an approximate guide to main service activities and the senior officers in the departments which manage them. The inclusion of departments in the list does not imply that their rôles are directly comparable. It should also be noted that titles of functions, officers and departments are not uniform between authorities. Those listed below are for guidance only. Individual local authorities decide for themselves how they organize and name their services and the units and staff who perform them.

En **Functions** **(Official Job Title)**	**Fr** **Responsabilités** **(Titre de la fonction occupée)**	**De** **Funktionen** **(Berufsbezeichnung)**
Chief Executive	Secrétaire Général (commune)/Directeur Général (département)	Kreisdirektor/Landdirektor/Stadtdirektor/Verwaltungsleiter
Architecture (Chief Architect)	Direction des bâtiments (Responsable des bâtiments)	Architektur und Bauwesen (Leitender Architekt)
Economic Development (Economic Development Officer)	Développement économique (Responsable du développement économique)	Wirtschaftliche Entwicklung (Leiter des Amtes für Wirtschaftsförderung)
Education & Training (Chief Education Officer)	Education et formation (Responsable de l'éducation)	Erziehung und Ausbildung (Leiter der Abteilung Erziehung und Ausbildung)
Environmental Control (Chief Environmental Health Officer)	Service de l'hygiène (Directeur de l'hygiène)	Umweltschutz (Leiter des Umweltamtes)
European Liaison (European Officer)	Affaires européennes (Responsable des affaires européennes)	Europafragen (Europabeauftragter)
Finance (Borough/City/County/District Treasurer)	Direction des affaires financières (Adjoint finances)	Finanz (Kämmerer)

Housing (Director of Housing)	Office communale: HLM (Directeur de l'Office Publique: HLM)	Städtebau (Leiter des Bauordnungsamtes)
Libraries and Arts (Chief Librarian)	Bibliothèques et culture (Directeur des affaires culturelles)	Bibliothek und Kultur (Leitender Bibliothekar)
Personnel (Chief Personnel Officer)	Relations humaines (Directeur des relations humaines)	Personal (Leiter des Personalamtes)
Planning (Director of Planning)	Programmation et urbanisme (Directeur de la programmation; Directeur de l'urbanisme)	Stadtplanung (Leiter des Planungsamtes)
Public Relations (Press Officer and Director of Public Relations)	Relations publiques (Responsable des relations publiques)	Presseamt (Leiter des Presseamtes)
Recreation and Public Parks (Chief Leisure Officer)	Loisirs/parcs et jardins (Directeur des parcs et jardins)	Öffentliche Grünanlagen (Chefingenieur)
Refuse Collection and Street Cleaning (Chief Engineer)	Ramassage des ordures/ nettoyage des rues (Directeur de la propreté)	Abfallbeseitigung/ Straßenreinigung (Chefingenieur)
Social Services (Director of Social Services)	Direction des affaires sociales (Directeur des affaires sociales)	Sozialhilfe/ Gesundheitswesen (Leiter des Sozialdezernats)
Technical Services (Director of Technical Services)	Services techniques (Directeur des services techniques)	Technische Dienste (Chefingenieur)
Trading Standards (Chief Trading Standards Officer)	Normes de conformité (Directeur de la consommation et de la répression des fraudes)	–
Transport & Highways (Director of Highways and Transportation)	Ponts et chaussées (Ingénieur en chef/ Directeur de la voirie)	Verkehr (Leiter des Verkehrsamtes)

à qui de droit *Fr*
an alle, die es angeht *De*
to whom it may concern *En*

abaissement (m) (du terrain) *Fr*
Senkung (f) *De*
subsidence *En*

abatement (m) personnel (sur l'impôt) *Fr*
Steuerfreibetrag (m) *De*
personal allowance *En*

abattage (m) (des arbres) *Fr*
Baumfällung (f) *De*
tree felling *En*

abattement (m) d'impôt *Fr*
steuerliche Vergünstigung (f) *De*
tax benefit/concession/relief *En*

abattement (m) personnel (sur l'impôt) *Fr*
Steuerfreibetrag (m) *De*
tax allowance *En*

Aberkennung (f), Deprivation (f) *De*
deprivation *En*
privation (f) *Fr*

Abfall (m), Müll (m) *De*
waste *En*
déchets (m.pl) *Fr*

Abfallbeseitigung (f) *De*
refuse disposal *En*
décharge (f) des ordures *Fr*

Abfallbeseitigung (f) *De*
waste disposal *En*
élimination (f) des déchets *Fr*

Abfälle (m.pl) *De*
litter *En*
détritus (m) *Fr*

Abfalleimer (m) *De*
litter bin *En*
boîte (f) à ordures *Fr*

Abfallrückgewinnung (f) *De*
waste recovery *En*
récuperation (f) des déchets *Fr*

(Abfall)wiederaufbereitung (f); Recycling (nt) *De*
waste recycling *En*
recyclage (m) des déchets *Fr*

Abfindung (f) *De*
redundancy payment *En*
indemnité (f) de licenciement *Fr*

Abfindung (f) *De*
severance pay *En*
compensation (f) pour perte d'emploi *Fr*

Abflußgraben (m) *De*
storm drain *En*
fossé (m) d'évacuation *Fr*

Abflußrohr (nt) *De*
soil pipe *En*
conduit (m) d'effluent *Fr*

Abgaskontrolle (f) *De*
emission control *En*
contrôle (m) d'émission *Fr*

Abgeordnete(-r) (m/f) *De*
Member of Parliament *En*
député (m) *Fr*

abgestuftes Sozialrentensystem (nt) *De*
graduated pension scheme *En*
retraite (f) des cadres *Fr*

abhängige Angehörige (pl) *De*
dependants *En*
charges (f.pl) de famille *Fr*

abhängige Kinder (nt.pl) *De*
dependent children *En*
enfants (m/f. pl) à charge *Fr*

Abkommen (nt) *De*
agreement (in writing) *En*
convention (f) (par écrit) *Fr*

Ablage (f) *De*
filing *En*
classement (m) (de documents) *Fr*

ablegen (vb) *De*
file (vb) *En*
classer (vb) *Fr*

Ablehnung (f); Verweigerung (f) *De*
refusal *En*
refus (m) *Fr*

Abnehmerverein (m) *De*
consumer group *En*
groupe (m) consommateur *Fr*

abnormal load *En*
convoi (m) exceptionnel *Fr*
Schwertransport (m) mit Überbreite *De*

abolir (vb) *Fr*
abschaffen (vb) *De*
abolish (vb) *En*

abolish (vb) *En*
abolir (vb) *Fr*
abschaffen (vb) *De*

abolition *En*
abolition (f) *Fr*
Abschaffung (f) *De*

abolition (f) *Fr*
Abschaffung (f) *De*
abolition *En*

above-mentioned (adj) *En*
susmentionné (adj) *Fr*
obenerwähnt (adj) *De*

Abrechnungstag (m) *De*
account day *En*
jour (m) de liquidation *Fr*

abri (m) anti-atomique *Fr*
Atombunker (m) *De*
fallout shelter *En*

Abriß (m) *De*
abstract *En*
résumé (m) *Fr*

*** see/siehe/voir: Introduction page IX**

Absatzforschung (f) *De*
field survey *En*
levé (m) du terrain *Fr*

Absatzübereinkommen (nt) De
marketing agreement *En*
accord (m) de commercialisation *Fr*

abschaffen (vb) *De*
abolish (vb) *En*
abolir (vb) *Fr*

Abschaffung (f) *De*
abolition *En*
abolition (f) *Fr*

Abschluß (m) der Sekundarstufe *De*
general certificate of secondary education *En*
certificat (m) de fin d'études du premier cycle *Fr*

Abschlußklasse (f) *De*
sixth form *En*
classes (f.pl) terminales *Fr*

abschreiben (vb), (Schulden, Verlust) *De*
write off (vb) (a debt, a loss) *En*
amortir (vb) (une dette, une perte) *Fr*

Abschreibtypistin (f) *De*
copy typist *En*
dactylo copiste (f) *Fr*

absentéisme (m) scolaire *Fr*
unentschuldigtes Fernbleiben (nt); Schuleschwänzen (nt) *De*
truancy *En*

absetzbar (adj); steuerlich —. *De*
tax deductible (adj) *En*
déductible des impôts (adj) *Fr*

Absicherung (f) von Risiken *De*
risk management *En*
gestion (f) des risques *Fr*

abstain (vb) *En*
s'abstenir (vb) *Fr*
sich der Stimme enthalten (vb) *De*

Abstimmung (f) *De*
ballot *En*
scrutin (m) *Fr*

Abstimmung (f), Wahl (f) *De*
poll *En*
scrutin (m) *Fr*

abstract *En*
résumé (m) *Fr*
Abriß (m) *De*

(ab)stützen (vb) *De*
underpin (vb) *En*
étayer (vb) *Fr*

Abteilung (f) *De*
department *En*
service (m) *Fr*

Abteilung (f) *De*
section *En*
section (f) *Fr*

Abteilungsleiter/-in (m/f) *De*
head of department *En*
chef (m) de service *Fr*

Abteilungsleiter/-in (m/f) *De*
section head *En*
chef (m) de section *Fr*

abus (m) d'autorité *Fr*
Amtsmißbrauch (m) *De*
abuse of authority *En*

abus (m) de dissolvants *Fr*
Lösungsmittelmißbrauch (m) *De*
solvent abuse *En*

abus (m) des narcotiques *Fr*
Drogenmißbrauch (m) *De*
drug abuse *En*

abuse of authority *En*
abus (m) d'autorité *Fr*
Amtsmißbrauch (m) *De*

Abwasser (nt) *De*
effluent *En*
effluent (m) *Fr*

Abwasser (nt) *De*
liquid waste *En*
déchets (m.pl) liquides *Fr*

Abwasser (nt) *De*
sewage *En*
effluent (m) *Fr*

Abwasserbeseitigung (f) *De*
effluent disposal *En*
dispositif (m) d'évacuation des eaux usées *Fr*

Abwasserkanal (m) *De*
sewer *En*
égout (m) *Fr*

Abwasserklärung (f) *De*
sewage treatment *En*
épuration (f) des eaux usées *Fr*

abziehbare Unkosten (pl) *De*
allowable expense *En*
dépense (f) déductible *Fr*

accéder (vb) à *Fr*
zugreifen auf (vb) *De*
access (vb) *En*

accept (vb) an offer *En*
accepter (vb) une offre *Fr*
ein Angebot annehmen (vb) *De*

accepter (vb) une offre *Fr*
ein Angebot annehmen (vb) De
accept (vb) an offer En

access (vb) *En*
accéder (vb) à *Fr*
zugreifen (vb) auf *De*

access road *En*
route (f) d'accès *Fr*
Zufahrtsstraße (f) *De*

access to information *En*
droit (m) à l'information *Fr*
Zugang (m) zu Informationen *De*

accident (m) de la route *Fr*
Verkehrsunfall (m) *De*
road accident *En*

accident (m) du travail *Fr*
Arbeitsunfall (m) *De*
industrial accident *En*

accident rate *En*
taux (m) d'accidents *Fr*
Unfallziffer (f) *De*

accidents (m.pl) du travail *Fr*
Arbeitsverletzung (f) *De*
industrial injury *En*

accommodate (vb) *En*
loger (vb) *Fr*
unterbringen (vb) *De*

accommodation *En*
logement (m) *Fr*
Unterkunft (f) *De*

accommodation agency *En*
agence (f) immobilière *Fr*
Wohnungsvermittlung (f) *De*

accord (m) de commerce bilateral *Fr*
bilateraler Handelsvertrag (m) *De*
bilateral trade agreement *En*

accord (m) de commercialisation *Fr*
Absatzübereinkommen (nt) *De*
marketing agreement *En*

*** see/siehe/voir: Introduction page IX**

accord (m) mutuel *Fr*
gegenseitiges Einvernehmen (nt) *De*
mutual agreement *En*

accord (m) restrictif *Fr*
einschränkender Vertrag (m) *De*
restrictive covenant *En*

accorder (vb) les frais et dépens *Fr*
Kosten erstatten (vb) *De*
award (vb) costs *En*

accorder (vb) un permis *Fr*
lizensieren (vb) *De*
license (vb) *En*

accorder (vb) une augmentation de salaires *Fr*
eine Lohnerhöhung gewähren (vb) *De*
award (vb) a wage increase *En*

accotement (m) (de la route) *Fr*
Bankette (f) *De*
verge *En*

accotement (m) *Fr*
Randstreifen (m) *De*
hard shoulder *En*

account *En*
compte (m) *Fr*
Konto (nt); Rechnung (f) *De*

account day *En*
jour (m) de liquidation *Fr*
Abrechnungstag (m) *De*

account executive *En*
chef (m) de comptes client *Fr*
Kontaktgruppenleiter (m) *De*

account overdrawn *En*
compte (m) découvert *Fr*
Konto (nt) überzogen *De*

account rendered *En*
compte (m) rendu *Fr*
zur Begleichung vorgelegte Rechnung (f) *De*

accountability *En*
responsabilité (f) *Fr*
Verantwortlichkeit (f) *De*

accountable (adj) *En*
responsable (adj) *Fr*
verantwortlich (adj) *De*

accountancy/accounting *En*
comptabilité (f) *Fr*
Buchhaltung (f) *De*

accountant *En*
comptable (m) *Fr*
Buchhalter/Buchhälterin (m/f) *De*

accredited agent *En*
agent (m) accrédité *Fr*
Handelsbevollmächtigte(r) (m) *De*

accroissement (m) démographique *Fr*
Bevölkerungszuwachs (m) *De*
population growth *En*

accueil (m) *Fr*
Rezeption (f) *De*
reception area *En*

accusé (m) de réception *Fr*
Empfangsbestätigung (f) *De*
acknowledgment of receipt *En*

accusé (m) mineur *Fr*
jugendliche(r) Straftäter/-in (m/f) *De*
juvenile offender *En*

accuser (vb) réception (de) *Fr*
Empfang bestätigen (vb) *De*
acknowledge (vb) receipt (of) *En*

achat (m) à crédit *Fr*
Ratenkauf (m) *De*
hire purchase *En*

achat (m) du logement *Fr*
Hauskauf (m) *De*
house purchase *En*

acheteur (m) (-euse f.) *Fr*
Käufer/-in (m/f) *De*
shopper *En*

aciérie (f) *Fr*
Stahlwerk (nt) *De*
steelworks *En*

Ackerland (nt) *De*
agricultural land *En*
terre (f) agricole *Fr*

Ackerland (nt) *De*
farmland *En*
terre (f) agricole *Fr*

acknowledge (vb) receipt (of) *En*
accuser (vb) réception (de) *Fr*
Empfang bestätigen (vb) *De*

acknowledgment of receipt *En*
accusé (m) de réception *Fr*
Empfangsbestätigung (f) *De*

acquisition (f) (par la personne) publique *Fr*
öffentliche Beschaffung (f) *De*
public procurement *En*

Acronym *En*
sigle (m) *Fr*
Akronym (nt) *De*

Act of Parliament *En*
loi (f) *Fr*
Parlamentsakte (f) *De*

acte (m) *Fr*
Urkunde (f) *De*
deeds *En*

acte (m) de décès *Fr*
Todesschein (m) *De*
death certificate *En*

acte (m) de mariage *Fr*
Trauschein (m) *De*
marriage certificate *En*

acte (m) de naissance *Fr*
Geburtsurkunde (f) *De*
birth certificate *En*

actif et passif (m) *Fr*
Aktiva und Passiva (nt.pl) *De*
assets and liabilities *En*

action (f) *Fr*
Aktie (f) *De*
share *En*

action (f) communautaire *Fr*
Gemeinschaftsaktion (f) *De*
community action *En*

action (f) pour combler le retard scolaire *Fr*
Förderunterricht (m) *De*
remedial education *En*

action (f) réciproque *Fr*
Interaktion (f) *De*
interaction *En*

action (f) sociale *Fr*
Gemeindefürsorge (f) *De*
community care *En*

action (f) sociale *Fr*
Pflegeleitung (f) *De*
care management *En*

action group *En*
groupe (m) d'action *Fr*
Initiative (f) *De*

action plan *En*
plan (m) d'action *Fr*
Aktionsprogramm (nt) *De*

*** see/siehe/voir: Introduction page IX**

action research *En*
recherche (f) appliquée *Fr*
Handlungsforschung (f) *De*

actionnaire (m/f) *Fr*
Aktionär/-in (m/f) *De*
shareholder *En*

activated sludge *En*
boue (f) activée *Fr*
Belebtschlamm (m) *De*

actuaire (m) *Fr*
Aktuar (m) *De*
actuary *En*

actual cost *En*
prix (m) de revient effectif *Fr*
Gestehungskosten (pl) *De*

actuary *En*
actuaire (m) *Fr*
Aktuar (m) *De*

acute health care *En*
service (m) de soins intensifs *Fr*
Intensivkrankenpflege (f) *De*

adaptation (f) des maisons *Fr*
Wohnungsanpassung (f) *De*
housing adaptation *En*

adapted building *En*
bâtiment (m) adapté *Fr*
angepaßte Bauweise (f) *De*

added value *En*
valeur (f) ajoutée *Fr*
Mehrwert (f) *De*

addressing machine *En*
machine (f) à imprimer les adresses *Fr*
Adressiermaschine (f) *De*

adjudicataire (m) *Fr*
Auftragnehmer/-in (m/f) *De*
contractor *En*

adjuger (vb) des dommages-intérêts *Fr*
Schadenersatz zugestehen (vb) *De*
award (vb) damages *En*

administer (vb) *En*
administrer (vb) *Fr*
verwalten (vb) *De*

administrateur (m) délégué *Fr*
Geschäftsführer/-in (m/f) *De*
managing director *En*

administrateur (m) des finances *Fr*
Finanzbeamte(r)/-in (m/f) *De*
finance officer *En*

administrateur (m) *Fr*
Verwaltungsbeamte(r)/-beamtin (m/f) *De*
administrator *En*

administration *En*
administration (f) *Fr*
Verwaltung (f) *De*

administration (f) *Fr*
Behörden (f.pl) *De*
authorities *En*

administration (f) *Fr*
Verwaltung (f) *De*
administration *En*

administration (f) de l'école *Fr*
Schulleitung (f) *De*
school management *En*

administration (f) du bureau *Fr*
Büroleitung (f) *De*
office management *En*

administration (f) publique *Fr*
öffentliche Verwaltung (f) *De*
public administration *En*

administrative law *En*
loi (f) de l'administration *Fr*
Verwaltungsrecht (nt) *De*

administrator *En*
administrateur (m) *Fr*
Verwaltungsbeamte(r)/-beamtin (m/f) *De*

administrer (vb) *Fr*
verwalten (vb) *De*
administer (vb) *En*

admission (f) des jeunes au travail *Fr*
Anstellung (f) Jugendlicher *De*
youth employment *En*

adolescent (m) (-ente f.) (de 13 à 19 ans) *Fr*
Teenager (m) *De*
teenager *En*

adopt (vb) (minutes of council) *En*
approuver (vb) le procès-verbal d'une séance du conseil *Fr*
zustimmen (vb) *De*

adopted road *En*
rue/route (f) entretenue par la municipalité *Fr*
öffentliche Straße (f) *De*

adopted sewer *En*
égout (m) entretenu par la municipalité *Fr*
öffentlicher Abwasserkanal (m) *De*

adoption (of council minutes) *En*
approbation (f) du procès-verbal d'une séance du conseil *Fr*
Zustimmung (f) *De*

adoption (of road by council) *En*
prise (f) en charge d'une rue par la municipalité *Fr*
Übernahme (f) *De*

Adressenkartei (f) *De*
mailing list *En*
liste (f) de diffusion *Fr*

Adressiermaschine (f) *De*
addressing machine *En*
machine (f) à imprimer les adresses *Fr*

adult education *En*
enseignement (m) des adultes *Fr*
Erwachsenenbildung (f) *De*

adult literacy campaign *En*
campagne (f) contre l'analphabétisme *Fr*
Kampagne (f) gegen das Analphabetentum *De*

adult training *En*
formation (f) pour adultes *Fr*
Erwachsenenbildung (f) *De*

adult training centre *En*
centre (m) de formation pour adultes *Fr*
Ausbildungszentrum (nt) für Erwachsene *De*

adult training strategy *En*
programme (m) de formation pour adultes *Fr*
Erwachsenenbildungsprogramm (nt) *De*

advance payment *En*
paiement (m) par anticipation *Fr*
Vorauszahlung (f) *De*

advertisement *En*
annonce (f) *Fr*
Anzeige (f) *De*

advertising campaign *En*
campagne (f) de publicité *Fr*
Werbekampagne (f) *De*

advertising *En*
publicité (f) *Fr*
Werbung (f) *De*

advice centre *En*
service (m) conseil *Fr*
Beratungsstelle (f) *De*

advice note *En*
lettre (f) d'avis *Fr*
Anzeige (f) *De*

advisory body *En*
conseil (m) consultatif *Fr*
Beratungsgremium (nt) *De*

advisory service *En*
service (m) consultatif *Fr*
Beratungsdienst (m) *De*

aerial survey *En*
inspection (f) aérienne *Fr*
Luftbildmessung (f) *De*

affaires (f.pl) *Fr*
Geschäft (nt), Betrieb (m), Unternehmen (nt) *De*
business *En*

affaires (f.pl) de la place *Fr*
örtliches Gewerbe (nt) *De*
local business *En*

affordable housing *En*
logement (m) à loyer modéré *Fr*
erschwingliche Wohnungen (f.pl) *De*

affordable rent *En*
loyer (m) de faible montant *Fr*
erschwingliche Miete (f) *De*

affranchisement (m) *Fr*
Emanzipation (f) *De*
emancipation *En*

age distribution *En*
distribution (f) par âge *Fr*
Altersverteilung (f) *De*

age group *En*
classe (f) *Fr*
Altersgruppe (f) *De*

âge (m) de fin de scolarité *Fr*
Schulabgangsalter (nt) *De*
school leaving age *En*

âge (m) de la retraite *Fr*
Renten-, Pensionsalter (nt) *De*
retirement age *En*

âge (m) de retraite *Fr*
Renten-, Pensionsalter (nt) *De*
pension age *En*

âge (m) scolaire *Fr*
Schulalter (nt) *De*
school age *En*

agence (f) d'aménagement territorial *Fr*
örtliche Planungsorganisation (f) *De*
local development agency *En*

agence (f) de promotion de l'entreprise *Fr*
Unternehmerorganisation (f) *De*
enterprise agency *En*

agence (f) immobilière *Fr*
Immobilienmakler/-in (m/f) *De*
estate agency *En*

agence (f) immobilière *Fr*
Wohnungsamt (nt) *De*
housing agency *En*

agence (f) immobilière *Fr*
Wohnungsvermittlung (f) *De*
accommodation agency *En*

agence (f) pour la promotion de l'entreprise locale *Fr*
örtlicher Unternehmerverband (m) *De*
local enterprise agency *En*

agenda *En*
ordre (m) du jour *Fr*
Tagesordnung (f) *De*

agenda (m) *Fr*
Terminkalender (m) *De*
diary *En*

agenda item *En*
question (f) à l'ordre du jour *Fr*
Punkt (m) auf der Tagesordnung *De*

agent (m) accrédité *Fr*
Handelsbevollmächtigte(r) (m) *De*
accredited agent *En*

agent (m) attitré *Fr*
Handelsvertreter (m) *De*
appointed agent *En*

agent (m) de police *Fr*
Polizeibeamte(r)/-in (m/f) *De*
police officer *En*

agent (m) de police *Fr*
Polizist/-in (m/f) *De*
constable *En*

agent (m) de pollution de l'air *Fr*
Luftschadstoff (m) *De*
air pollutant *En*

agent (m) de poursuites *Fr*
Gerichtsvollzieher (m) *De*
bailiff *En*

agent (m) de probation *Fr*
Bewährungshelfer/-in (m/f) *De*
probation officer *En*

agglomération (f) *Fr*
geschlossene Ortschaft (f) *De*
built up area *En*

aggregate economic activity *En*
ensemble (m) des activités économiques *Fr*
Gesamtwirtschaft (f) *De*

aggregate finance *En*
finances (f.pl) communales/départementales/régionales *Fr*
Gesamtfinanzen (pl) *De*

aggregates (civil eng.) *En*
granulats (m.pl) *Fr*
Zuschlagstoffe (m.pl) *De*

Agrarpolitik (f) *De*
agricultural policy *En*
politique (f) agricole *Fr*

agreement (in writing) *En*
convention (f) (par écrit) *Fr*
Abkommen (nt) *De*

agreement (legal) *En*
convention (f) *Fr*
(rechtliche) Vereinbarung (f) *De*

agréments (m.pl) d'une région/ville *Fr*
öffentliche Anlagen/Einrichtungen (f.pl) *De*
amenities of a region/town *En*

agricultural land *En*
terre (f) agricole *Fr*
Ackerland (nt) *De*

agricultural policy *En*
politique (f) agricole *Fr*
Agrarpolitik (f) *De*

agricultural waste *En*
déchets (m.pl) agricoles *Fr*
landwirtschaftlicher Abfall (m) *De*

agriculture *En*
agriculture (f) *Fr*
Landwirtschaft (f) *De*

*** see/siehe/voir: Introduction page IX**

agriculture (f) *Fr*
Landwirtschaft (f) *De*
agriculture *En*

agriculture (f) *Fr*
Landwirtschaft (f) *De*
farming *En*

aide (f) au logement *Fr*
Wohnungbauzuschuß (m) *De*
housing grant *En*

aide (f) d'adulte handicappé *Fr*
Pflegegeld (nt) für Erwerbsunfähige *De*
invalid care allowance *En*

aide (f) financiaire à l'aménagement *Fr*
Entwicklungshilfe (f) *De*
development grant *En*

aide (f) financière *Fr*
Finanzhilfe (f) *De*
financial assistance *En*

aide (f) initiale financiaire *Fr*
Anstoßfinanzierung (f) *De*
pump-priming *En*

aide (f) judiciaire *Fr*
Prozeßkostenhilfe (f) *De*
legal aid *En*

aide (f) médicale gratuite *Fr*
Krankengeld (nt) *De*
medical benefit *En*

aide (f) personalisée au logement (A.P.L.) *Fr*
gesichertes Mietverhältnis (nt) *De*
regulated tenancy *En*

aide (f) personnalisée au logement *Fr*
Wohngeld (nt) *De*
housing benefit *En*

aide (f) sociale *Fr*
Familienpflege (f) *De*
family care/support/welfare *En*

aides (f.pl) régionales *Fr*
Gebietshilfe (f) *De*
regional aid *En*

aims and objectives *En*
but (m) *Fr*
Ziele (nt.pl) *De*

air monitoring *En*
contrôle (m) de l'air *Fr*
Luftqualitätskontrolle (f) *De*

air pollutant *En*
agent (m) de pollution de l'air *Fr*
Luftschadstoff (m) *De*

air pollution *En*
pollution (f) de l'air *Fr*
Luftverschmutzung (f) *De*

air quality *En*
qualité (f) de l'air *Fr*
Luftqualität (f) *De*

air transport *En*
transport (m) aérien *Fr*
Luft(fracht)verkehr (m) *De*

aire (f) de services (au bord d'une autoroute) *Fr*
Autobahnraststätte (f) *De*
motorway service area *En*

aire (f) de stationnement *Fr*
Park-, Rastplatz m *De*
parking area; layby *En*

aire (f) de stationnement pour nomades *Fr*
Zigeunerlager (nt) *De*
gipsy site *En*

airport capacity *En*
capacité (f) d'accueil d'un aéroport *Fr*
Flughafenkapazität (f) *De*

Akronym (nt) *De*
Acronym *En*
sigle (m) *Fr*

Akte (f) *De*
file (noun) *En*
dossier (m) (documents) *Fr*

(Akten usw) zirkulieren lassen (vb) *De*
circulate (vb) papers etc *En*
distribuer (vb) les papiers etc *Fr*

Aktenschrank (m) *De*
filing cabinet *En*
classeur (m) *Fr*

Aktie (f) *De*
share *En*
action (f) *Fr*

Aktienbesitz (m) *De*
shareholding *En*
possession (f) d'actions *Fr*

Aktiengesellschaft (AG) (f) *De*
public limited company (plc) *En*
Société (f) anonyme (SA) *Fr*

Aktionär/-in (m/f) *De*
shareholder *En*
actionnaire (m/f) *Fr*

Aktionsprogramm (nt) *De*
action plan *En*
plan (m) d'action *Fr*

Aktiva und Passiva (nt.pl) *De*
assets and liabilities *En*
actif et passif (m) *Fr*

aktualisieren (vb) *De*
update (vb) *En*
tenir (vb) qn au courant *Fr*

Aktuar (m) *De*
actuary *En*
actuaire (m) *Fr*

alderman *En* *
échevin (m) (Belg.) *Fr*
Alderman (m), Stadtrat (m) *De*

Alderman (m), Stadtrat (m) *De* *
alderman *En*
échevin (m) (Belg.) *Fr*

alerte (f) aux crues *Fr*
Flutwarnung (f) *De*
flood warning system *En*

aliéné(e) (adj) *Fr*
geisteskrank (adj) *De*
mentally ill (adj) *En*

alignement (m) de la route *Fr*
Straßenausrichtung (f) *De*
road alignment *En*

alimentation (f) électrique *Fr*
Elektrizitäts-, Stromerzeugung (f) *De*
electricity generation *En*

alimentation (f) en énergie *Fr*
Energieversorgung (f) *De*
energy supply *En*

Alkohol (m) am Steuer *De*
drink driving *En*
conduite (f) en état d'ivresse *Fr*

allégement (m) des impôts *Fr*
Ermäßigung (f) der Gemeindeabgaben *De*
rate relief *En*

allégement (m) des intérêts *Fr*
Zinsfreibetrag (m) *De*
interest relief *En*

*** see/siehe/voir: Introduction page IX**

allgemeine Wahlen (f.pl) *De*
general election *En*
élections (f.pl) législatives *Fr*

Allgemeinmedizin (f) *De*
general practice *En*
médecine (f) générale *Fr*

allocation (f) à laquelle on a droit *Fr*
Anspruch (m) *De*
entitlement *En*

allocation (f) d'adulte handicappé *Fr*
Erwerbsunfähigkeits-, Invalidenrente (f) *De*
disablement benefit *En*

allocation/indemnité (f) de maladie *Fr*
Krankengeld (nt) *De*
sick pay; sickness benefit *En*

allocation (f) familiale *Fr*
Kindergeld (nt) *De*
child benefit *En*

allocation (f) familiale *Fr*
Kindergeld (nt) *De*
family allowance *En*

allocation (f) parent isolé (API) *Fr*
Haushaltsfreibetrag (m) für Alleinerziehende *De*
one parent family benefit *En*

allocation of resources *En*
répartition (f) des moyens *Fr*
Zuweisung (f) der Mittel *De*

allocations (f.pl) familiales *Fr*
Familienzulage (f) *De*
family income supplement/support *En*

allowable expense *En*
dépense (f) déductible *Fr*
abziehbare Unkosten (pl) *De*

Alten- Altersheim (nt) *De*
community home *En*
résidence (f) pour personnes âgées *Fr*

Alten-, Altersheim (nt) *De*
old people's home *En*
maison (f) de retraite *Fr*

Altenpflege (f) *De*
care of the aged *En*
soins (m.pl) des personnes âgées *Fr*

Alter (nt) *De*
third age *En*
troisième age (m) *Fr*

ältere Menschen (m.pl) *De*
elderly people *En*
personnes (f.pl) agées *Fr*

alternative economic strategy *En*
politique (f) économique alternative *Fr*
Alternativwirtschaftsprogramm (nt) *De*

alternative use *En*
transformation (f) d'utilisation *Fr*
Alternativmöglichkeit (f) *De*

Alternativmöglichkeit (f) *De*
alternative use *En*
transformation (f) d'utilisation *Fr*

Alternativplan (m) *De*
contingency plan *En*
programme (m) pour l'imprévu *Fr*

Alternativwirtschafts-programm (nt) *De*
alternative economic strategy *En*
politique (f) économique alternative *Fr*

(Alters)rente (f), Pension (f) *De*
retirement pension *En*
pension (f) de retraite *Fr*

Altersgruppe (f) *De*
age group *En*
classe (f) *Fr*

Altersrente (f) *De*
old age pension *En*
pension (f) de retraite *Fr*

Altersverteilung (f) *De*
age distribution *En*
distribution (f) par âge *Fr*

am Apparat bleiben, bitte (Telefon) *De*
hold the line, please (telephone) *En*
ne quittez pas (téléphone) *Fr*

amalgamation *En*
unification (f) *Fr*
Vereinigung (f) *De*

ambassade (f) *Fr*
Botschaft (f) *De*
embassy *En*

amélioration (f) de la route *Fr*
Straßenerneuerung (f) *De*
road improvement *En*

amélioration (f) des grandes routes *Fr*
Straßenausbau (m) *De*
highway improvement *En*

amélioration (f) du logement *Fr*
Verbesserung (f) der Wohnverhältnisse *De*
housing improvement *En*

amélioration (f) en matière d'environnement *Fr*
Umweltverbesserung (f) *De*
environmental improvement *En*

amélioration (f) *Fr*
Verbesserung (f) *De*
improvement *En*

améliorer (vb) (l'environnement etc) *Fr*
(Umgebung usw) verschönern (vb) *De*
enhance (vb) (environment etc) *En*

améliorer (vb) un batiment *Fr*
verbessern, ausbauen (vb) *De*
upgrade (vb) (building) *En*

aménagement (m) autorisé *Fr*
genehmigter Wohnbau (m) *De*
permitted development *En*

aménagement (m) cohérent *Fr*
relevante Entwicklung (f) *De*
relevant development *En*

aménagement (m) d'un quartier *Fr*
Stadtteilentwicklung (f) *De*
neighbourhood development *En*

aménagement (m) d'une maison *Fr*
Umbau (m) *De*
house conversion *En*

aménagement (m) des campagnes *Fr*
Landesplanung (f) *De*
country planning *En*

aménagement (m) des campagnes *Fr*
ländliche Planung (f) *De*
rural planning *En*

*** see/siehe/voir: Introduction page IX**

aménagement (m) du paysage *Fr*
Landschaftsplanung (f); Landschaftsgestaltung (f) *De*
landscape planning; landscaping *En*

aménagement (m) du terrain *Fr*
Grund-und-Bodenerschließung (f) *De*
land development *En*

aménagement (m) mixte *Fr*
Mischform (f) *De*
mixed development *En*

aménagement (m) régional *Fr*
Regionalplanung (f) *De*
regional development *En*

aménagement (m) rural *Fr*
ländliche Entwicklung (f) *De*
rural development *En*

aménagement (m) territorial *Fr*
örtliche Entwicklung (f) *De*
local development *En*

aménagement (m) urbain et rural *Fr*
Stadt- Landschafts- planung (f) *De*
town and country planning *En*

aménagement (m) urbain *Fr*
Wohnsiedlung (f) *De*
residential development *En*

amende (f) *Fr*
Geldstrafe (f) *De*
fine *En*

amenities of a region/town *En*
agréments (m.pl) d'une région/ville *Fr*
öffentliche Anlagen/Einrichtungen (f.pl) *De*

amenity centre *En*
centre (m). de récréations *Fr*
Freizeitzentrum (nt) *De*

ameublement (m) *Fr*
Einrichtungsgegenstände (m.pl) *De*
furnishings *En*

amortir (vb) (une dette, une perte) *Fr*
(Schulden, Verlust) abschreiben (vb) *De*
write off (vb) (a debt, a loss) *En*

amour (m) du bien public *Fr*
Gemeinsinn (m) *De*
public spirit *En*

amtlich (adj) *De*
official (adj) *En*
officiel (adj) *Fr*

amtliches Kennzeichen (nt) *De*
registration number (vehicle) *En*
numéro (m) d'immatriculation *Fr*

Amtsarzt/Amtsärztin (m/f) *De*
Medical Officer *En*
médecin-directeur (m) *Fr*

Amtsleiter (m) *De*
chief officer *En*
chef (m) de service *Fr*

Amtsmißbrauch (m) *De*
abuse of authority *En*
abus (m) d'autorité *Fr*

Amtsvergehen (nt) *De*
malpractice *En*
négligence (f) *Fr*

Amtszeit (f) *De*
tenure *En*
(periode de) jouissance (f) *Fr*

an alle, die es angeht *De*
to whom it may concern *En*
à qui de droit *Fr*

Analphabetentum (nt) *De*
illiteracy *En*
analphabétisme (m) *Fr*

analphabétisme (m) *Fr*
Analphabetentum (nt) *De*
illiteracy *En*

analyse (f) d'un fichier *Fr*
Klumpen-, Sammelanalyse (f) *De*
cluster analysis *En*

analyse (f) *Fr*
Analyse (f) *De*
analysis *En*

analyse (f) *Fr*
Programmanalyse (f) *De*
programme analysis *En*

Analyse (f) *De*
analysis *En*
analyse (f) *Fr*

analyse (f) de chemin critique *Fr*
kritische Pfadanalyse (f) *De*
critical path analysis *En*

analyse (f) de l'existant *Fr*
Lagebericht (m) *De*
position statement *En*

analyse (f) de la demande *Fr*
Nachfrageanalyse (f) *De*
demand analysis *En*

analyse (f) de la fonction *Fr*
Arbeitsplatzstudie (f)/-bewertung (f) *De*
job analysis/evaluation *En*

analyse (f) de marché *Fr*
Marktanalyse (f) *De*
market analysis *En*

analyse (f) de systèmes *Fr*
Systemanalyse (f) *De*
systems analysis *En*

analyse (f) démographique *Fr*
demographische Analyse (f) *De*
demographic analysis *En*

analyse (f) des coûts et rendements *Fr*
Kosten-Nutzen-Analyse (f) *De*
cost benefit analysis *En*

analyse (f) des coûts *Fr*
Kostenanalyse (f) *De*
cost analysis *En*

analyse (f) des données *Fr*
Datenanalyse (f) *De*
data analysis *En*

analyse (f) des facteurs *Fr*
Faktorenanalyse (f) *De*
factor analysis *En*

analyse (f) des performances *Fr*
Leistungsbeurteilung (f) *De*
performance appraisal/evaluation *En*

analyse (f) des résultats (d'une politique/action etc) *Fr*
Wirkungsanalyse (f) *De*
impact analysis *En*

analyse (f) des risques *Fr*
Risikoanalyse (f) *De*
risk analysis *En*

analyse (f) des sols *Fr*
Bodenanalyse (f) *De*
soil testing *En*

analyse (f) du réseau *Fr*
Netzanalyse (f) *De*
network analysis *En*

*** see/siehe/voir: Introduction page IX**

analyse (f) économique *Fr*
Wirtschaftsanalyse (f) *De*
economic analysis *En*

analyse (f) statistique *Fr*
statistische Analyse (f) *De*
statistical analysis *En*

analyser (vb) *Fr*
überprüfen (vb) *De*
vet (vb) *En*

analysis *En*
analyse (f) *Fr*
Analyse (f) *De*

analyste (m/f) de systèmes *Fr*
Systemanalytiker (m) *De*
systems analyst *En*

Anbau (m) *De*
house extension *En*
extension (f) d'une maison *Fr*

ancient monument *En*
monument (m) historique *Fr*
historisches Denkmal (nt) *De*

ancillary staff *En*
personnel (m) auxiliaire *Fr*
Hilfspersonal (nt) *De*

Änderungsauftrag (m) *De*
variation order *En*
changement (m) d'instructions *Fr*

anfechten (vb); eine Entscheidung *De*
challenge (vb) a decision *En*
porter (vb) une réclamation contre une decision *Fr*

Anforderung (f) *De*
requisition *En*
demande (f) *Fr*

Anfrage (f) *De*
enquiry *En*
enquête (f) *Fr*

Angaben (f.pl); Beschreibung (f) *De*
specification *En*
descriptif (m) *Fr*

Angebot (nt) *De*
form of tender *En*
modèle (m) de soumission *Fr*

Angebot (nt) an Arbeitskräften *De*
labour supply *En*
offre (f) de main-d'oeuvre *Fr*

Angebot (nt) und Nachfrage (f) *De*
supply and demand *En*
offre (f) et la demande *Fr*

Angebotsaufforderung (f) *De*
invitation to tender *En*
mise (f) d'un travail en adjudication *Fr*

Angeklagte(-r) (m/f) *De*
defendant *En*
défendeur (m) (-eresse f.) *Fr*

angelernt (adj) *De*
semi skilled *En*
semi-qualifié (-ée f.) (adj) *Fr*

angemessene Miete (f) *De*
fair rent *En*
loyer (m) raisonnable *Fr*

angepaßte Bauweise (f) *De*
adapted building *En*
bâtiment (m) adapté *Fr*

Angestellte(-r) (m/f), Arbeitnehmer/-in (m/f) *De*
employee *En*
employé (m) (-ée f.) *Fr*

Angestellte(-r) (m/f) eines Wahlvorstands *De*
poll clerk *En*
secrétaire (m/f) du scrutin *Fr*

Anlagevermögen (nt) *De*
fixed assets *En*
immobilisations (f.pl) *Fr*

Anleitung (f) *De*
guidance note *En*
circulaire (m) d'application *Fr*

année (f) budgétaire *Fr*
Rechnungsjahr (nt) *De*
fiscal year *En*

annehmen (vb); ein Angebot *De*
accept (vb) an offer *En*
accepter (vb) une offre *Fr*

annonce (f) *Fr*
Anzeige (f) *De*
advertisement *En*

annuaire (m) des téléphones *Fr*
Fernsprechbuch (nt) *De*
telephone directory; phone-book *En*

annual accounts *En*
bilan (m) annuel *Fr*
Jahresabschluß (m) *De*

annual basis *En*
annuellement (adv) *Fr*
Jahresbasis (f) *De*

annual budget cycle *En*
cycle (m) budgétaire annuel *Fr*
Haushaltskreislauf (m) *De*

annual general meeting (shareholders) *En*
assemblée (f) d'actionnaires annuelle *Fr*
Jahreshauptversammlung (f) *De*

annual report *En*
rapport (m) annuel (de gestion) *Fr*
Jahresbericht (m) *De*

annuellement (adv) *Fr*
Jahresbasis (f) *De*
annual basis *En*

annuité (f) *Fr*
Rechnungsjahr (ht) *De*
financial year *En*

annuler (vb) *Fr*
annullieren (vb) *De*
cancel (vb) *En*

annullieren (vb) *De*
cancel (vb) *En*
annuler (vb) *Fr*

anpassungsfähige Arbeitsweise (f) *De*
flexible working *En*
mobilité (f) horaire *Fr*

Anreizsystem (nt) *De*
incentive scheme *En*
système (m) d'incitations monétaires *Fr*

Anspruch (m) *De*
entitlement *En*
allocation (f) à laquelle on a droit *Fr*

ansteckende Krankheit (f) *De*
infectious disease *En*
maladie (f) contagieuse *Fr*

Anstellung (f) Jugendlicher *De*
youth employment *En*
admission (f) des jeunes au travail *Fr*

Anstoßfinanzierung (f) *De*
pump-priming *En*
aide (f) initiale financiaire *Fr*

*** see/siehe/voir: Introduction page IX**

Antrag (m) auf Bauerlaubnis *De*
planning application *En*
demande (f) d'autorisation de construire *Fr*

Antrag (m) auf Zuschuß *De*
grant application *En*
demande (f) d'allocation *Fr*

Antragsformular (nt) *De*
application form *En*
formulaire (m) de demande *Fr*

Antragsformular (nt) *De*
application form *En*
bulletin (m) de souscription *Fr*

Antragssteller/-in (m/f) *De*
claimant *En*
réclamant (m) *Fr*

Antwortsrate (f) *De*
response rate *En*
taux (m) de réponse *Fr*

Anwalt/Anwältin (m/f) *De*
counsel *En*
avocat (m) *Fr*

Anwaltschaft (f) *De*
legal profession *En*
droit (m) *Fr*

Anweisungen (f.pl) *De*
terms of reference *En*
mandat (m) *Fr*

Anweisungen geben, unterweisen (vb) (Architekt usw.) *De*
brief (vb) (an architect etc) *En*
donner (vb) des instructions (à un architecte etc) *Fr*

Anzeige (f) *De*
advertisement *En*
annonce (f) *Fr*

Anzeige (f) *De*
advice note *En*
lettre (f) d'avis *Fr*

appartement (m) duplex *Fr*
Maison(n)ette (f), zweistöckige Wohnung (f) *De*
maisonette *En*

appartement (m) *Fr*
Mietshaus (nt) *De*
tenement *En*

appartement (m) *Fr*
Wohnung (f) *De*
flat *En*

appeal (noun, legal) *En*
appel (m) *Fr*
Einspruch (m) *De*

appeal (vb) against a decision *En*
porter (vb) une réclamation contre une décision *Fr*
Einspruch gegen eine Entscheidung einlegen (vb) *De*

appeals procedure *En*
procédure (f) d'appel *Fr*
Einspruchsverfahren (nt) *De*

appear (vb) (in court) *En*
comparaître (vb) en justice *Fr*
vorgeladen werden; auftreten (vb) *De*

appel (m) *Fr*
Einspruch (m) *De*
appeal (noun, legal) *En*

appelant (m) *Fr*
Berufungskläger/-in (m/f) *De*
appellant *En*

appellant *En*
appelant (m) *Fr*
Berufungskläger/-in (m/f) *De*

application (f) de la loi *Fr*
Durchführung (f) (des Gesetzes) *De*
law enforcement *En*

application form *En*
bulletin (m) de souscription *Fr*
Antragsformular (nt) *De*

application form *En*
formulaire (m) de demande *Fr*
Antragsformular (nt) *De*

appoint (vb) *En*
nommer (vb) *Fr*
ernennen (vb) *De*

appointed agent *En*
agent (m) attitré *Fr*
Handelsvertreter (m) *De*

appointment (job) *En*
nomination (f) (emploi) *Fr*
Ernennung (f) (Stelle) *De*

appointment (meeting) *En*
rendez-vous (m) *Fr*
Termin (m) *De*

apporter (vb) des réformes au gouvernement local *Fr*
Kommunalverwaltungsreformen durchsetzen (vb) *De*
reform (vb) local government *En*

apportionment *En*
partage (m) *Fr*
Zuteilung (f) *De*

appraisal *En*
évaluation (f) *Fr*
Beurteilung (f) *De*

appréciation (f) de valeur professionnelle *Fr*
Personalbeurteilung (f) *De*
staff appraisal/assessment *En*

appréciation (f) des investissements *Fr*
Investitionsabschätzung (f) *De*
investment appraisal *En*

appréciation (f) des risques *Fr*
Risikoeinschätzung (f) *De*
risk assessment *En*

apprenti (m) *Fr*
Lehrling (m) *De*
apprentice *En*

apprentice *En*
apprenti (m) *Fr*
Lehrling (m) *De*

apprenticeship *En*
apprentissage (m) *Fr*
Lehre (f) *De*

apprentissage (m) *Fr*
Lehre (f) *De*
apprenticeship *En*

approach road *En*
route (f) d'accès *Fr*
Zufahrtsstraße (f) *De*

approbation (f) du procès-verbal d'une séance du conseil *Fr*
Zustimmung (f) *De*
adoption (of council minutes) *En*

appropriation *En*
appropriation (f) *Fr*
Besitzergreifung (f) *De*

appropriation (f) *Fr*
Besitzergreifung (f) *De*
appropriation *En*

approuver (vb) le procès-verbal d'une séance du conseil *Fr*
zustimmen (vb) *De*
adopt (vb) (minutes of council) *En*

appuyer (vb) (une proposition) *Fr*
(einen Antrag) unterstützen (vb) *De*
second (vb) (a motion) *En*

*** see/siehe/voir: Introduction page IX**

aptitude (f) à lire et écrire ***Fr***
Lese- und Schreibfertigkeit (f) *De*
literacy *En*

aptitude (f) professionnelle ***Fr***
(fachliche) Qualifikation (f) *De*
professional qualification *En*

Arbeit (f), Beschäftigung (f) ***De***
employment *En*
emploi (m) *Fr*

Arbeit (f) ***De***
labour *En*
travail (m) *Fr*

Arbeit (f) ***De***
work *En*
travail (m) *Fr*

Arbeiter/-in (m/f) ***De***
blue collar worker *En*
ouvrier (m) (-ière f.) *Fr*

Arbeiter/-in (m/f) ***De***
Worker *En*
ouvrier (m) (-ière f.) *Fr*

Arbeitermobilität (f) ***De***
labour mobility *En*
mobilité (f) de la main-d'oeuvre *Fr*

Arbeiterrechte (nt.pl) ***De***
workers' rights *En*
droits (m.pl) de la main-d'oeuvre *Fr*

Arbeiterschaft (f), Belegschaft (f) ***De***
work force *En*
main-d'oeuvre (f) *Fr*

Arbeiterschaft (f) ***De***
labour force *En*
main-d'oeuvre (f) *Fr*

Arbeitgeber/-in (m/f) ***De***
employer *En*
patron (m) (-onne f.) *Fr*

Arbeitnehmer/-in (m/f); Angestellte (-r) (m/f) ***De***
employee *En*
employé (m) (-ée f.) *Fr*

Arbeitsamt (nt) ***De***
job centre *En*
bureau (m) de placement *Fr*

Arbeitsbedingungen (f.pl) ***De***
conditions of employment *En*
définition (f) d'un emploi *Fr*

Arbeitsbedingungen (f.pl) ***De***
conditions of service *En*
conditions (f.pl) de service *Fr*

Arbeitsbedingungen (f.pl) ***De***
employment conditions *En*
conditions (f.pl) d'emploi *Fr*

Arbeitsbedingungen (f.pl) ***De***
working conditions *En*
conditions (f.pl) de travail *Fr*

Arbeitsbeschaffung (f) ***De***
employment creation *En*
création (f) d'emploi *Fr*

Arbeitsbeschaffungsmaßnahmen (f.pl) ***De***
job creation programme *En*
programme (m) de création de l'emploi *Fr*

Arbeitsbeschaffungsprogramm (nt) ***De***
employment initiative *En*
programme (m) de création d'emploi *Fr*

Arbeitsbeschreibung (f) ***De***
job specifications *En*
données (f.pl) d'exécution *Fr*

Arbeitsblatt (nt), Tabellenkalkulation (f) ***De***
spreadsheet *En*
tableur (m) *Fr*

Arbeitserfahrung (f) ***De***
work experience *En*
stage (m) de pratique professionnelle *Fr*

Arbeitsgericht (nt) ***De***
industrial tribunal *En*
tribunal (m) industriel *Fr*

Arbeitsgruppe (f) ***De***
working party *En*
groupe (m) de travail *Fr*

Arbeitshygiene (f) ***De***
occupational health/hygiene *En*
hygiène (f) du travail *Fr*

Arbeitskonflikt (m) ***De***
industrial dispute *En*
conflit (m) du travail *Fr*

Arbeitskosten (pl) ***De***
labour costs *En*
prix (m) de la main-d'oeuvre *Fr*

Arbeitskräfte (f.pl) ***De***
manpower *En*
main-d'oeuvre (f) *Fr*

Arbeitskräftenachfrage (f) ***De***
labour demand *En*
demande (f) de main-d'oeuvre *Fr*

Arbeitslast (f) ***De***
workload *En*
programme (m) de travail *Fr*

Arbeitsleistung (f) ***De***
industrial performance *En*
production (f) industrielle *Fr*

arbeitslos (adj) ***De***
unemployed; unwaged (adj) *En*
en chômage (adj) *Fr*

Arbeitslose(r) (m/f) ***De***
unemployed/unwaged person *En*
chômeur (m) *Fr*

Arbeitslosengeld (nt) ***De***
unemployment benefit *En*
indemnité (f) de chômage *Fr*

Arbeitslosigkeit (f) ***De***
unemployment *En*
chômage (m) *Fr*

Arbeitsmarkt (m) ***De***
job market *En*
marché (m) du travail *Fr*

Arbeitsmarkt (m) ***De***
labour market *En*
marché (m) du travail *Fr*

Arbeitsmarktpolitik (f) ***De***
employment policy *En*
politique (f) de l'emploi *Fr*

Arbeitsplanung (f) ***De***
employment planning *En*
programmation (f) de l'emploi *Fr*

Arbeitsplatz (m) ***De***
work station *En*
station (f) de travail *Fr*

Arbeitsplatzflexibilität (f) ***De***
job mobility *En*
mobilité (f) de l'emploi *Fr*

Arbeitsplatzstudie (f)/ -bewertung (f) ***De***
job analysis/evaluation *En*
analyse (f) de la fonction *Fr*

Arbeitsplatzverlust (m) ***De***
job loss *En*
perte (f) de l'emploi *Fr*

Arbeitsrecht (nt) ***De***
employment law *En*
statut (m) de la fonction publique territoriale; code (m) du travail (secteur privé) *Fr*

*** see/siehe/voir: Introduction page IX**

Arbeitsrecht (nt) *De*
labour law *En*
législation (f) du travail *Fr*

Arbeitsschutz (m) *De*
employment protection *En*
sécurité (f) de l'emploi *Fr*

Arbeitsschutz (m) *De*
occupational safety *En*
sécurité (f) au travail *Fr*

Arbeitsstudie (f) *De*
work study *En*
étude (f) du travail *Fr*

Arbeitsstunden (f.pl) *De*
hours of work *En*
heures (f.pl) de présence *Fr*

Arbeitsunfall (m) *De*
industrial accident *En*
accident (m) du travail *Fr*

Arbeitsunterricht (m) *De*
industrial training *En*
formation (f) industrielle *Fr*

Arbeitsverletzung (f) *De*
industrial injury *En*
accidents (m.pl) du travail *Fr*

Arbeitsvertrag (m) *De*
contract of employment *En*
contrat (m) d'emploi *Fr*

Arbeitswoche (f) *De*
working week *En*
semaine (f) de travail *Fr*

Arbeitszeit (f) *De*
working hours *En*
heures (f.pl) de travail *Fr*

arbitrage (m) *Fr*
Schlichtung (f) *De*
arbitration *En*

arbitration *En*
arbitrage (m) *Fr*
Schlichtung (f) *De*

archéologie (f) de sauvegarde *Fr*
Denkmalschutz (m) *De*
rescue archaeology *En*

architect *En*
architecte (m/f) *Fr*
Architekt/-in (m/f) *De*

architecte (m/f) *Fr*
Architekt/-in (m/f) *De*
architect *En*

architecte (m.) expert *Fr*
Gutachter (m) *De*
surveyor (of property) *En*

architecte (m/f) paysagiste *Fr*
Landschaftsarchitekt/-in (m/f) *De*
landscape architect *En*

architect's department *En*
service (m) d'architecture *Fr*
Bauaufsichtsamt (nt) *De*

architectural (adj) *En*
architectural (adj) *Fr*
architektonisch (adj) *De*

architectural (adj) *Fr*
architektonisch (adj) *De*
architectural (adj) *En*

architecture *En*
architecture (f) *Fr*
Architektur (f) *De*

architecture (f) *Fr*
Architektur (f) *De*
architecture *En*

architecture (f) de paysage *Fr*
Landschaftsgestaltung (f) *De*
landscape architecture *En*

architecture (f) domestique *Fr*
inländische Architektur (f) *De*
domestic architecture *En*

architecture (f) intégrée *Fr*
Lokalarchitektur (f) *De*
community architecture *En*

architecture (f) urbaine *Fr*
Städtebau (m) *De*
urban design *En*

Architekt/-in (m/f) *De*
architect *En*
architecte (m/f) *Fr*

architektonisch (adj) *De*
architectural (adj) *En*
architectural (adj) *Fr*

Architektur (f) *De*
architecture *En*
architecture (f) *Fr*

Archiv (nt) *De*
archives *En*
archives (f.pl) *Fr*

archivage (m) *Fr*
Aufzeichnung (f) *De*
record keeping *En*

Archivar/-in (m/f) *De*
archivist *En*
archiviste (m/f) *Fr*

archives *En*
archives (f.pl) *Fr*
Archiv (nt) *De*

archives (f.pl) *Fr*
Archiv (nt) *De*
archives *En*

archivist *En*
archiviste (m/f) *Fr*
Archivar/-in (m/f) *De*

archiviste (m/f) *Fr*
Archivar/-in (m/f) *De*
archivist *En*

Archivkraft (f) *De*
filing clerk *En*
documentaliste(m/f) *Fr*

Area Of Outstanding Natural Beauty *En*
région (f) naturelle remarquable *Fr*
Landschaftsschutzgebiet (nt) *De*

area team *En*
équipe (f) régionale *Fr*
Regionalgruppe (f) *De*

Armut (f) *De*
poverty *En*
pauvreté (f) *Fr*

arrêté (m) d'interdiction *Fr*
Verbotsbestimmung (f) *De*
prohibition order *En*

arrêté (m) municipal *Fr*
Verordnung (f) *De*
byelaw *En*

arriéré (m) d'emprunt *Fr*
Hypothekenschulden (f.pl) *De*
mortgage arrears *En*

arriéré (m) d'impôts locaux *Fr*
Kommunalsteuerschulden (f.pl) *De*
rate arrears *En*

arriérés (m.pl) de loyer *Fr*
Mietschulden (f.pl) *De*
rent arrears *En*

arrivée (f) d'eau chaude *Fr*
Warmwasserversorgung (f) *De*
hot water supply *En*

arterial road *En*
grande voie (f) de communication *Fr*
Hauptverkehrsstraße (f) *De*

articulated vehicle *En*
semi-remorque (f) (pl. semi-remorques) *Fr*
Gelenkfahrzeug (nt) *De*

artisan (m) *Fr*
Handwerker (m) *De*
craftsman *En*

*** see/siehe/voir: Introduction page IX**

arts centre *En*
maison (f) de culture *Fr*
Kulturzentrum (nt) *De*

arts policy *En*
politique (f) culturelle *Fr*
Kulturpolitik (f) *De*

Arzt/Ärztin (m/f) *De*
doctor *En*
médecin (m) (f = femme médecin) *Fr*

ärztliche Behandlung (f) *De*
medical treatment *En*
traitement (m) médical *Fr*

ärztliche Untersuchung (f) *De*
medical examination *En*
examen (m) médical *Fr*

asile (m) assuré *Fr*
sichere Unterrkunft (f) *De*
secure accommodation *En*

asile (m) de nuit *Fr*
Nachtasyl (nt) *De*
night shelter *En*

asile (m) pour femmes *Fr*
Frauenhaus (nt) *De*
women's refuge *En*

asphalt *En*
asphalte (m) *Fr*
Asphalt (m) *De*

Asphalt (m) *De*
asphalt *En*
asphalte (m) *Fr*

asphalte (m) damé *Fr*
gewalzter Asphalt (m) *De*
rolled asphalt *En*

asphalte (m) *Fr*
Asphalt (m) *De*
asphalt *En*

assainissement (m) du terrain *Fr*
Geländeentwässerung (f) *De*
land drainage *En*

assemblée (f) d'actionnaires annuelle *Fr*
Jahreshauptversammlung (f) *De*
annual general meeting (shareholders) *En*

assemblée (f) générale extraordinaire *Fr*
außerordentliche Generalversammlung (f) *De*
extraordinary general meeting *En*

assessment of potential (staff) *En*
évaluation (f) du potentiel (personnel) *Fr*
Potentialbeurteilung (f) (Personal) *De*

assessment of property *En*
évaluation (f) de propriété *Fr*
Grundvermögensbewertung (f) *De*

assets *En*
avoirs (m.pl) *Fr*
Vermögen (nt) *De*

assets and liabilities *En*
actif et passif (m) *Fr*
Aktiva und Passiva (nt.pl) *De*

assignation (f) *Fr*
Verfügung (f) *De*
writ *En*

assignation (f); faire (vb) une - à quelqu'un *Fr*
jmdm eine Vorladung zustellen (vb) *De*
summons (vb); to serve a summons (noun) *En*

assistance (f) à domicile *Fr*
Hauspflege (f) *De*
domiciliary care *En*

assistance (f) individuelle *Fr*
Sozialarbeit (f) *De*
casework *En*

assistance (f) sociale *Fr*
Sozialarbeit (f) *De*
welfare work *En*

assistant (m) (-ante f.) social(e) *Fr*
Sozialarbeiter/-in (m/f) *De*
social worker *En*

assistant (m) (-ante f.) social(e) *Fr*
Sozialarbeiter/-in (m/f) *De*
welfare worker *En*

assistant (m) (-ante f.) social(e) *Fr*
Sozialberufler/-in (m/f) *De*
community worker *En*

assistante (f) maternelle *Fr*
Tagesmutter (f) *De*
child minder *En*

assisted area *En*
zone (f) subventionnée *Fr*
Subventionsgebiet (nt) *De*

association (f) *Fr*
Partnerschaft (f) *De*
partnership *En*

association (f) communautaire *Fr*
Kommunalverband (m) *De*
community association *En*

association (f) de locataires *Fr*
Mieterausschuß (m) *De*
tenants' association *En*

association (f) de parents d'élèves *Fr*
Elternbeirat (m) *De*
parent teacher association (PTA) *En*

association (f) de propriétaires/locataires *Fr*
Interessengemeinschaft (f) von Benachbarten *De*
residents' association *En*

association (f) des collectivités territoriales *Fr*
Kommunalbehördenausschuß (m) *De*
local authority association *En*

association (f) locale *Fr*
Bürgergemeinschaft (f) *De*
community group *En*

association (f) professionnelle *Fr*
Berufsorganisation (f) *De*
professional association *En*

association (f) projetée *Fr*
Joint-Venture-Projekt (nt) *De*
joint venture project *En*

associé (m) *Fr*
Partner/-in (m/f) *De*
partner *En*

assurance (f) *Fr*
Versicherung (f) *De*
insurance *En*

assurance (f) au tiers *Fr*
Haftpflichtversicherung (f) *De*
third party insurance *En*

assurance (f) d'état *Fr*
staatliche Versicherung (f) *De*
national insurance *En*

assurance (f) d'un service *Fr*
Dienstleistungen (f.pl) *De*
service delivery/provision *En*

*** see/siehe/voir: Introduction page IX**

assurance (f) maladie privée *Fr*
private Krankenkasse (f) *De*
private health insurance *En*

assurance (f) médicale *Fr*
Krankenversicherung (f) *De*
medical insurance *En*

assurance (f) professionnelle *Fr*
Berufsabsicherung (f) *De*
professional indemnity *En*

assurances (f.pl) sociales *Fr*
Sozialversicherung (f) *De*
national insurance *En*

atelier (m) *Fr*
Industrieanlage (f) *De*
industrial unit *En*

atelier (m) *Fr*
Werkstatt (f) *De*
workshop *En*

atelier (m) pour les handicapés *Fr*
beschützende Werkstätte (f) *De*
sheltered workshop *En*

atmosphärische Verschmutzung (f) *De*
atmospheric pollution *En*
pollution (f) atmosphérique *Fr*

atmospheric pollution *En*
pollution (f) atmosphérique *Fr*
atmosphärische Verschmutzung (f) *De*

Atombunker (m) *De*
fallout shelter *En*
abri (m) anti-atomique *Fr*

Atomenergie (f) *De*
atomic energy *En*
énergie (f) atomique *Fr*

atomic energy *En*
énergie (f) atomique *Fr*
Atomenergie (f) *De*

Atommüll (m) *De*
nuclear waste *En*
déchets (m.pl) nucléaires *Fr*

atomwaffenfreie Zone (f) *De*
nuclear free zone *En*
zone (f) non nucléaire *Fr*

attainment target *En*
évaluation (f) de progrès *Fr*
Ziele (nt.pl) *De*

attendance allowance *En*
frais (m.pl) de déplacement *Fr*
Pflegegeld (nt) *De*

attroupement (m) *Fr*
verbotene Versammlung (f) *De*
unlawful assembly *En*

au delà des pouvoirs (adj) *Fr*
ultra vires (adj) *De*
ultra vires (adj) *En*

auction sale *En*
vente (f) aux enchères *Fr*
Versteigerung (f) *De*

audience (f) *Fr*
Verhandlung (f) *De*
hearing (court) *En*

audio-typist *En*
dictaphoniste (f) *Fr*
Audiotypistin (f) *De*

Audiotypistin (f) *De*
audio-typist *En*
dictaphoniste (f) *Fr*

audit *En*
vérification (f) de comptes *Fr*
Rechnungsprüfung (f) *De*

audit (vb) *En*
vérifier et certifier (vb) *Fr*
prüfen (vb) *De*

audited accounts *En*
comptes (m.pl) vérifiés et certifiés *Fr*
geprüfte Geschäftsbücher (nt.pl) *De*

auditor *En*
commissaire (m) de comptes *Fr*
Rechnungsprüfer/-in (m/f) *De*

auditor's report *En*
rapport (m) des vérificateurs des comptes *Fr*
Bericht (m) des Abschlußprüfers *De*

Aufgabe (f); Pflicht (f) *De*
duty *En*
devoir (m) *Fr*

Aufgaben (f.pl) *De*
duties (professional) *En*
fonctions (f.pl) *Fr*

aufgeschloßen (adj) *De*
responsive (adj) *En*
sensible (adj) *Fr*

aufgeschüttete Straße (f) *De*
elevated road *En*
route (f) surélevée *Fr*

Auflösung (f) *De*
liquidation *En*
liquidation (f) *Fr*

Aufriß (m) *De*
elevations *En*
élévation (f) *Fr*

aufsetzen (vb); einen Vertrag (usw) —. *De*
draw up (vb) (contract etc) *En*
préparer (vb) le projet d'un contrat *Fr*

Aufsicht (f) *De*
supervision *En*
direction (f) (d'une entreprise) *Fr*

Aufsichtsbeamte (-r)/-in (m/f)*De* *
inspector *En*
inspecteur (m) (-trice f.) (d'Académie/de l'Education Nationale) *Fr*

Aufsichtspersonal (nt) *De*
supervisory staff *En*
cadre (m) de maitrise *Fr*

Aufsichtspflicht (f) *De*
supervision order *En*
mandat (m) de surveillance *Fr*

aufsteigende Feuchtigkeit (f) *De*
rising damp *En*
humidité (f) qui monte du sol *Fr*

Auftragnehmer/-in (m/f) *De*
contractor *En*
adjudicataire (m) *Fr*

Auftragsreinigung (f) *De*
contract cleaning *En*
nettoyage (m) au contrat *Fr*

Aufwertung (f) *De*
revaluation *En*
révalorisation (f) *Fr*

Aufzeichnung (f) *De*
record keeping *En*
archivage (m) *Fr*

Aufzeichnung (f) *De*
records management *En*
gestion (f) des archives *Fr*

augmentation (f) de loyer *Fr*
Mieterhöhung (f) *De*
rent increase *En*

*** see/siehe/voir: Introduction page IX**

Ausbesserungszuschuß (m) *De*
repair grant *En*
subvention (f) de réhabilitation *Fr*

ausbilden (vb) *De*
train (vb) *En*
former (vb) *Fr*

Ausbildung (f) *De*
training *En*
formation (f) *Fr*

Ausbildung (f) für Behinderte u. Schwererziehbare *De*
special education *En*
éducation (f) spécialisée *Fr*

Ausbildungskrankenhaus (nt) *De*
teaching hospital *En*
centre (m) hospitalier universitaire *Fr*

Ausbildungsoffizier (m) *De*
training officer *En*
responsable (m/f) de la formation *Fr*

Ausbildungspolitik (f) *De*
training policy *En*
politique (f) de formation *Fr*

Ausbildungsprogramm (nt) *De*
training scheme *En*
programme (m) de formation *Fr*

Ausbildungsprogramm (nt) für Jugendliche *De*
youth training scheme *En*
éducation-formation (f) des jeunes *Fr*

Ausbildungszentrum (nt) *De*
training centre *En*
centre (m) de formation *Fr*

Ausbildungszentrum (nt) für Erwachsene *De*
adult training centre *En*
centre (m) de formation pour adultes *Fr*

Auschußbeschluß (m) *De*
committee resolution *En*
voeux (m.pl) du comité *Fr*

Außenarbeiten (f.pl) *De*
external works *En*
travaux (m.pl) extérieurs *Fr*

außerordentliche Generalversammlung (f) *De*
extraordinary general meeting *En*
assemblée (f) générale extraordinaire *Fr*

Ausgaben (f.pl) *De*
spending *En*
dépense(s) (f) *Fr*

Ausgaben (f.pl) *De*
expenditure *En*
dépense (f) *Fr*

Ausgaben kürzen (vb) *De*
limit (vb) expenditure *En*
limiter (vb) les dépenses *Fr*

Ausgaben (f.pl); nach eigenem Ermessen verfügbare —. *De*
discretionary spending *En*
dépenses (f.pl) discrétionnaires (par le conseil municipal) *Fr*

Ausgabenkürzung (f) *De*
expenditure cut *En*
réduction de la dépense *Fr*

ausgeben (vb) *De*
spend (vb) *En*
dépenser (vb) *Fr*

Ausgrabung (f) *De*
excavation *En*
excavation (f) *Fr*

Aushilfe (f), Aushilfskräfte (f.pl) *De*
temporary staff *En*
personnel (m) (à titre) provisoire *Fr*

Auskunft (f) *De*
information *En*
renseignements (m.pl) *Fr*

Auskunftsbeamte(r)/-beamtin (m/f) *De*
information officer *En*
informaticien (m) (-ienne f.) *Fr*

Auskunftsbüro (nt) *De*
information centre *En*
bureau (m) de renseignements *Fr*

Auskunftsdienst (m) *De*
information service *En*
service (m) (de l') informatique *Fr*

ausländische Direktinvestition (f) *De*
inward investment *En*
implantation (f) d'une société étrangère *Fr*

Auslandsgeschäft (nt) *De*
foreign trade *En*
commerce (m) extérieur *Fr*

Auslandsinvestition (f) *De*
foreign investment *En*
investissement (m) extérieur *Fr*

Ausräucherung (f) *De*
fumigation *En*
désinfection (f) *Fr*

aussagen (vb) *De*
give (vb) evidence *En*
porter (vb) témoignage *Fr*

ausschlaggebende Stimme (f) *De*
casting vote (of chairman) *En*
voix (f) prépondérante du président *Fr*

Ausschreibung (f) *De*
competitive tendering *En*
mise (f) d'un travail en adjudication *Fr*

Ausschußbericht (m) *De*
committee report *En*
rapport (m) au comité *Fr*

Ausschußsekretär/-in (m/f) *De*
committee clerk *En*
secrétaire (m/f) de séance *Fr*

Ausschußsitzung (f) *De*
committee meeting *En*
réunion (f) d'un comité *Fr*

Ausschußvorsitzende(r) (m/f) *De*
committee chair(man) *En*
président (m) (-ente f.) d'un comité *Fr*

Aussendienstzulage (f) *De*
subsistence allowance *En*
indemnité (f) journalière *Fr*

ausserhalb der normalen Arbeitszeiten (f.pl) *De*
unsocial hours *En*
heures (f.pl) indues *Fr*

Ausstellungsgelände (nt) *De*
exhibition centre *En*
salon (m) d'exposition *Fr*

austreten (vb) *De*
opt out (vb) *En*
se retirer (vb) *Fr*

Auswanderer/-in (m/f) *De*
emigrant *En*
émigrant (m) *Fr*

*** see/siehe/voir: Introduction page IX**

Auszahlungen (f.pl) *De*
disbursements *En*
dépenses (f.pl) *Fr*

Auszahlungskonto (nt) *De*
disbursements account *En*
compte (m) des dépenses *Fr*

authorities *En*
administration (f) *Fr*
Behörden (f.pl) *De*

Autobahn (f) *De*
motorway *En*
autoroute (f) *Fr*

Autobahn (f) um eine Stadt *De*
orbital motorway *En*
autoroute (f) périphérique *Fr*

Autobahnplanung (f) *De*
motorway planning *En*
programmation (f) des autoroutes *Fr*

Autobahnraststätte (f) *De*
motorway service area *En*
aire (f) de services (au bord d'une autoroute) *Fr*

autocritique (f) *Fr*
Selbstbeurteilung (f) *De*
self appraisal *En*

Autonomie (f) *De*
autonomy *En*
autonomie (f) *Fr*

autonomie (f) *Fr*
Autonomie (f) *De*
autonomy *En*

autonomie (f) locale *Fr*
Kommunalautonomie (f) *De*
local autonomy *En*

autonomy *En*
autonomie (f) *Fr*
Autonomie (f) *De*

autorisation (f)/permis (m) de construire *Fr*
Baugenehmigung (f) *De*
planning consent/permission *En*

autorisation (f) quasi-effective *Fr*
durchdachte Zustimmung (f) *De*
deemed consent *En*

autorité (f) de justice *Fr*
gerichtliche Verfügung (f) *De*
court order *En*

autorité (f) publique *Fr*
gesetzgebende Körperschaft (f) *De*
statutory authority/body *En*

autoroute (f) *Fr*
Autobahn (f) *De*
motorway *En*

autoroute (f) périphérique *Fr*
Autobahn (f) um eine Stadt *De*
orbital motorway *En*

auxiliary staff *En*
personnel (m) auxiliaire *Fr*
Hilfspersonal (nt) *De*

avancement (m) *Fr*
Verbesserung (f); Beförderung (f) *De*
upgrading *En*

avancement (m) (personnel) *Fr*
Beförderung (f) *De*
promotion (staff) *En*

avancer (vb) (personnel) *Fr*
befördern (vb) *De*
upgrade (vb) (staff) *En*

avec effet rétrospectif (adj) *Fr*
rückwirkend (adj) *De*
retrospective (adj) *En*

avis (m) *Fr*
Mitteilung (f) *De*
notification *En*

avis (m) d'application (d'une loi etc) *Fr*
Vollstreckungsbenachrichtigung (f) *De*
enforcement notice *En*

avis (m) d'imposition *Fr*
Kommunalsteuerbescheid (m) *De*
rate bill/demand *En*

avis (m) d'imposition *Fr*
Prinzip (nt) der Gemeindeabgaben *De*
rate precept *En*

avis (m) de crédit *Fr*
Gutschriftanzeige (f) *De*
credit note *En*

avis (m) de non-accomplissement de contrat *Fr*
Verletzung (f) einer Hauptpflicht *De*
breach of condition notice *En*

avocat (m) *Fr*
Anwalt/Anwältin (m/f) *De*
counsel *En*

avocat (m) *Fr*
Rechtsanwalt/-anwältin (m/f) *De*
barrister *En*

avoir un personnel trop nombreux *Fr*
Überbesetzung (f) *De*
overmanning *En*

avoirs (m.pl) *Fr*
Vermögen (nt) *De*
assets *En*

award (vb) a wage increase *En*
accorder (vb) une augmentation de salaires *Fr*
eine Lohnerhöhung gewähren (vb) *De*

award (vb) costs *En*
accorder (vb) les frais et dépens *Fr*
Kosten erstatten (vb) *De*

award (vb) damages *En*
adjuger (vb) des dommages-intérêts *Fr*
Schadenersatz zugestehen (vb) *De*

*** see/siehe/voir: Introduction page IX**

B

background information *En*
données (f.pl) de base *Fr*
Hintergrundinformation (f) *De*

bad debts *En*
mauvaises dettes (f.pl) *Fr*
uneinbringliche Schulden (f.pl) *De*

bail (m) *Fr*
Pacht-, Mietvertrag (m) *De*
lease *En*

bail (m) à long terme *Fr*
langfristiger Mietvertrag (m) *De*
long lease *En*

bail (m) commercial (pl. baux commerciaux) *Fr*
Ladenmiete (f) *De*
shop rent *En*

bailiff *En*
agent (m) de poursuites *Fr*
Gerichtsvollzieher (m) *De*

bailleur (m) bailleresse (f) *Fr*
Verpächter/-in (m/f) *De*
lessor *En*

baisse (f) démographique *Fr*
Bevölkerungsschwund (m) *De*
population decline *En*

balance (f) commerciale *Fr*
Handelsbilanz (f) *De*
trade balance *En*

balance (f) des paiements *Fr*
Zahlungsbilanz (f) *De*
balance of payments *En*

balance of payments *En*
balance (f) des paiements *Fr*
Zahlungsbilanz (f) *De*

balance sheet *En*
bilan (m) *Fr*
Bilanz (f) *De*

balance (vb) the budget *En*
équilibrer (vb) le budget *Fr*
bilanzieren (vb) *De*

balanced council *En*
conseil (m) où aucun parti n'a la majorité absolue *Fr*
Rat (m) mit Kräftegleichgewicht *De*

balayeur (m) de rues (personne) *Fr*
Straßenfeger (m) *De*
street sweeper (person) *En*

balayeuse (f) de rues (machine) *Fr*
Straßenkehrmaschine (f) *De*
street sweeper (machine) *En*

ballot *En*
scrutin (m) *Fr*
Abstimmung (f) *De*

ban (noun) *En*
proscription (f) *Fr*
Verbot (nt) *De*

ban (vb) *En*
interdire (vb) *Fr*
verbieten (vb) *De*

band (vb) *En*
répartir (vb) les élèves en sections de force homogène *Fr*
einstufen (vb) *De*

bank account *En*
compte (m) en banque *Fr*
Bankkonto (nt) *De*

bank balance *En*
solde (m) en banque *Fr*
Bankguthaben (nt) *De*

bank charges *En*
frais (m.pl) bancaires *Fr*
Bankspesen (pl) *De*

bank holiday *En*
fête (f) légale *Fr*
gesetzlicher Feiertag (m) *De*

bank loan *En*
prêt (m) bancaire *Fr*
Bankdarlehen (nt) *De*

bank rate *En*
taux (m) officiel de l'escompte *Fr*
Diskontsatz (m) *De*

bank statement *En*
relevé (m) de compte *Fr*
Kontoauszug (m) *De*

Bankauftrag (m) *De*
banker's order *En*
ordre (m) bancaire *Fr*

Bankdarlehen (nt) *De*
bank loan *En*
prêt (m) bancaire *Fr*

banker's draft *En*
traite (f) bancaire *Fr*
Banktratte (f) *De*

banker's order *En*
ordre (m) bancaire *Fr*
Bankauftrag (m) *De*

banker's reference *En*
référence (f) de banquier *Fr*
Bankzeugnis (nt) *De*

Bankett (nt) *De*
footing *En*
base (f) (en béton) *Fr*

Bankette (f) *De*
verge *En*
accotement (m) (de la route) *Fr*

Bankguthaben (nt) *De*
bank balance *En*
solde (m) en banque *Fr*

Bankkonto (nt) *De*
bank account *En*
compte (m) en banque *Fr*

Bankrott (m) *De*
bankruptcy *En*
faillite (f) *Fr*

bankrupt *En*
failli (m) *Fr*
Gemeinschuldner (m) *De*

*** see/siehe/voir: Introduction page IX**

bankrupt (to go) (vb) ***En***
faire (vb) faillite *Fr*
Pleite machen (vb) *De*

bankruptcy ***En***
faillite (f) *Fr*
Bankrott (m) *De*

Bankspesen (pl) ***De***
bank charges *En*
frais (m.pl) bancaires *Fr*

Banktratte (f) ***De***
banker's draft *En*
traite (f) bancaire *Fr*

Banküberweisung (f) ***De***
credit transfer *En*
transfert (m) de fonds *Fr*

Bankzeugnis (nt) ***De***
banker's reference *En*
référence (f) de banquier *Fr*

banlieue (f) ***Fr***
Vorort (m); Vororte (m.pl) *De*
suburb/suburbia *En*

(de) banlieue (adj) ***Fr***
Vorort— *De*
suburban (adj) *En*

banque (f) commerciale ***Fr***
Handelsbank (f) *De*
merchant bank *En*

banque (f) de données ***Fr***
Datenbank (f), -bestand (m) *De*
data bank/base *En*

banque (f) de virement ***Fr***
Girobank (f) *De*
clearing bank *En*

Banque (f) Européenne d'Investissement ***Fr***
Europäische Investitionsbank (f) *De*
European Investment Bank *En*

Bargeldauszahlungsautomat (m) ***De***
cash dispenser *En*
distributeur (m) d'argent comptant *Fr*

barrage ***En***
barrage (m) *Fr*
Staustufe (f) *De*

barrage (m) ***Fr***
Staustufe (f) *De*
barrage *En*

barrage (m) contre les inondations ***Fr***
Hochwasserbarriere (f) *De*
flood barrier *En*

barrage (m) de la route ***Fr***
Straßensperrung (f) *De*
road closure *En*

barrière (f) commerciale ***Fr***
Handelsschranke (f) *De*
trade barrier *En*

barrister ***En***
avocat (m) *Fr*
Rechtsanwalt/-anwältin (m/f) *De*

base (f) (en béton) ***Fr***
Bankett (nt) *De*
footing *En*

Basisdemokratie (f) ***De***
grassroots democracy *En*
populisme (m) *Fr*

bâtiment (m) ***Fr***
Gebäude (nt) *De*
building *En*

bâtiment (m) ***Fr***
Bauindustrie (f) *De*
building industry *En*

bâtiment (m) ***Fr***
Bauindustrie (f) *De*
construction industry *En*

bâtiment (m) à structure discontinue ***Fr***
Tragkonstruktion (f) *De*
framed construction *En*

bâtiment (m) adapté ***Fr***
angepaßte Bauweise (f) *De*
adapted building *En*

bâtiment (m) administratif ***Fr***
Bürohaus (nt), -gebäude (nt) *De*
office block/building *En*

bâtiment (m) bas ***Fr***
Gebäude (nt) mit wenigen Stockwerken *De*
low rise building *En*

bâtiment (m) classé d'intérêt historique ou architectural ***Fr***
Gebäude (nt) unter Denkmalschutz *De*
listed building *En*

bâtiment (m) en état d'abandon ***Fr***
verfallenes Gebäude (nt) *De*
derelict building *En*

bâtiment (m) en surnombre ***Fr***
unbenutztes Gebäude (nt) *De*
redundant building *En*

bâtiment (m) isolé thermiquement ***Fr***
energiesparende Bauweise (f) *De*
low energy building *En*

bâtiment (m) municipal ***Fr***
Bürgerbau (m) *De*
municipal building *En*

bâtiment (m) partagé ***Fr***
Zweizweckgebäude (nt) *De*
dual use building *En*

bâtiment (m) préfabriqué ***Fr***
Fertigbau (m) *De*
prefabricated building *En*

bâtiment (m) public ***Fr***
öffentliches Gebäude (nt) *De*
public building *En*

bâtiment (m) sans étage ***Fr***
eingeschoßiges Gebäude (nt) *De*
single storey building *En*

bâtiments (m.pl) aménagés ***Fr***
Umbauten (m.pl) *De*
converted buildings *En*

Bauabteilung (f) ***De***
planning department *En*
service (m) d'urbanisme *Fr*

Bauarbeiten (f.pl) ***De***
housing repair *En*
réparations (f.pl) du logement *Fr*

Bauaufsicht (f) ***De***
planning control *En*
service (m) d'autorisation et droit des sols *Fr*

Bauaufsichtsamt (nt) ***De***
architect's department *En*
service (m) d'architecture *Fr*

Baubeschränkung (f) ***De***
planning restraint *En*
limiter (vb) l'urbanisation *Fr*

Baudenkmal (nt) ***De***
historic building *En*
monument (m) historique *Fr*

Bauentwurf (m), Bauplan (m) ***De***
building design *En*
dessein (m) de construction *Fr*

Baugenehmigung (f) ***De***
planning consent/permission *En*
autorisation (f)/permis (m) de construire *Fr*

*** see/siehe/voir: Introduction page IX**

Bauindustrie (f) De
building industry *En*
bâtiment (m) *Fr*

Bauindustrie (f) De
construction industry *En*
bâtiment (m) *Fr*

Bauingenieur/-in (m/f) De
civil engineer *En*
ingénieur (m) constructeur *Fr*

(Bau)inspektion (f) De
survey (noun) (construction) *En*
levé (m) *Fr*

Bauinspektion (f) De
site inspection *En*
reconnaissance (f) du terrain *Fr*

Bauinspektor (m) De
building inspector *En*
inspecteur (m) de la construction *Fr*

Baukontrolle (f), Bauaufsicht (f) De
building control *En*
contrôle (m) de construction *Fr*

Baukosten (pl) De
building costs *En*
coût (m) de construction *Fr*

Baukostenkalkulation (f) De
quantity surveying *En*
métrage (m) *Fr*

Baukostenkalkulator/-in (m/f) De
quantity surveyor *En*
métreur (m) vérificateur *Fr*

Bauland (nt) De
building land *En*
terrain (m) constructible *Fr*

Bauleiter/-in (m/f) De
clerk of works *En*
conducteur (m) des travaux *Fr*

Baulückenschließung (f) De
infill; infilling *En*
urbanisation (f) contrôlée *Fr*

Baumaschinen (f.pl) für Erdarbeiten De
earth-moving equipment *En*
engins (m.pl) de chantier *Fr*

Baumfällung (f) De
tree felling *En*
abattage (m) (des arbres) *Fr*

Baumpflanzung (f) De
tree planting *En*
plantage (m) (des arbres) *Fr*

Baumschutzanweisung (f) De
tree preservation order *En*
protection (f) réglementaire (d'un arbre) *Fr*

Bauordnung (f) De
building regulations *En*
règlements (m.pl) de construction *Fr*

(Bau)planungsausschuß (m) De
planning & development committee *En*
commission (f) d'urbanisme *Fr*

Bauplanungseinspruch (m) De
planning appeal *En*
recours (m) contre un acte d'urbanisme *Fr*

Bauplatz (m) im Grünen De
green field site *En*
terrain (m) vièrge *Fr*

Baupolitik (f) De
planning policy *En*
politique (f) d'urbanisme *Fr*

Bausparkasse (f) De
building society *En*
société (f) immobilière *Fr*

Baustelle (f) De
building/construction site *En*
chantier (m) de construction *Fr*

Bauunternehmer (m) De
developer *En*
lotisseur (m) *Fr*

Bauvertrag (m) De
building contract *En*
contrat (m) de bâtiment *Fr*

Bauvorschrift (f) De
planning regulation *En*
règlements (m.pl) d'urbanisme *Fr*

Beamte(-r)/-in (m/f) De
(executive) officer *En*
rédacteur (m) *Fr*

Beamte(-r)/-in (m/f) im Umweltamt De
environmental health officer *En*
inspecteur (m) (-trice f.) de la salubrité publique *Fr*

Beamte(-r)/-in (m/f) der Gesundheitsbehörde De
public health officer *En*
inspecteur (m) (-trice f.) de salubrité *Fr*

beantragen (vb) De
claim (vb) *En*
réclamer (vb) *Fr*

beaufsichtigen (vb) De
supervise (vb) *En*
diriger (vb) (une entreprise) *Fr*

Bebauungsplangebiet (nt) De
simplified planning zone *En*
zone (f) d'aménagement concerté (ZAC) *Fr*

bed and breakfast establishment En
hôtel (m) garni *Fr*
Frühstückspension (f) *De*

befördern (vb) De
upgrade (vb) (staff) *En*
avancer (vb) (personnel) *Fr*

Beförderung (f) De
promotion (staff) *En*
avancement (m) (personnel) *Fr*

Beförderung (f), Transport (m) De
transport *En*
transport (m) *Fr*

Beförderungs-, Transportkosten (pl) De
transport costs *En*
frais (m.pl) de transport *Fr*

Beförderungspolitik (f) De
transport policy *En*
politique (f) de transport *Fr*

befreien (vb) De
exempt (vb) *En*
exempter (vb) *Fr*

Befreiung (f) De
exemption *En*
exemption (f) *Fr*

Befreiung (f) von der Mehrwertsteuer De
zero rating *En*
imposition (f) nulle *Fr*

Begrenzung (f) öffentlicher Ausgaben De
capping of public expenditure *En*
limitation (f) des dépenses publiques *Fr*

Begutachtung (f), Gutachten (nt) De
survey (for rating) *En*
cadastre (m) *Fr*

*** see/siehe/voir: Introduction page IX**

behalf; on — of *En*
de la part de *Fr*
für *De*

Behinderte (m/f.pl) *De*
handicapped people *En*
personnes (f.pl) handicapées *Fr*

Behinderte(-r) (m/f) *De*
disabled person *En*
personne (f) handicappée *Fr*

behinderte Kinder (nt.pl) *De*
handicapped children *En*
enfants (m/f.pl) handicapés *Fr*

Behinderung (f) *De*
disability *En*
incapacité (f) *Fr*

Behinderung (f) *De*
handicap *En*
handicap (m) *Fr*

Behörden (f.pl) *De*
authorities *En*
administration (f) *Fr*

(Beihilfe) auszahlen (vb) *De*
pay out (vb) benefits *En*
verser (vb) les prestations *Fr*

Beihilfe (f) für unter Denkmalschutz stehendes Gebäude *De*
conservation grant *En*
participation (f) à la maintenance d'un bâtiment historique *Fr*

Beitrag (m) zur Rentenversicherung *De*
superannuation contribution *En*
retenue (f) pour la retraite *Fr*

Belästigung (f); (sexuelle) —. *De*
(sexual) harrassment *En*
harcèlement (m) (sexuel) *Fr*

Belebtschlamm (m) *De*
activated sludge *En*
boue (f) activée *Fr*

benachteiligt, depriviert (adj) *De*
deprived (adj) *En*
privé (adj) *Fr*

Benachteiligte (pl) *De*
disadvantaged group *En*
groupe (m) désavantagé *Fr*

benchmark *En*
repère (m) *Fr*
Höhenmarke (f) *De*

bénéfice (m) brut *Fr*
Bruttogewinn (m) *De*
gross profit *En*

bénéfice (m) marginal *Fr*
Gewinnspanne (f) *De*
marginal profit *En*

benefit *En*
indemnité (f) *Fr*
Sozialhilfe (f) *De*

benutzerfreundlich (adj) *De*
user friendly (adj) *En*
à la portée de l'utilisateur/ "facilement utilisable" *Fr*

beratender Ausschuß (m) *De*
consultative committee *En*
comité (m) consultatif *Fr*

Berater/-in (m/f) *De*
consultant *En*
expert-conseil (m) *Fr*

Berater/-in (m/f) *De*
counsellor *En*
conseiller (m) (-ère f.) *Fr*

Beratung (f); Beratungsbüro (nt) *De*
consultancy *En*
cabinet (m) d'experts-conseils *Fr*

Beratung (f) *De*
consultation *En*
consultation (f) *Fr*

Beratungsdienst (m) *De*
advisory service *En*
service (m) consultatif *Fr*

Beratungsdienst (m) *De*
counselling service *En*
service (m) conseil *Fr*

Beratungsgremium (nt) *De*
advisory body *En*
conseil (m) consultatif *Fr*

Beratungsstelle (f) *De*
advice centre *En*
service (m) conseil *Fr*

Berechtigung (f) *De*
eligibility *En*
éligibilité (f) *Fr*

Bericht (m) *De*
working paper *En*
document (m) de travail *Fr*

Bericht (m) des Abschlußprüfers *De*
auditor's report *En*
rapport (m) des vérificateurs des comptes *Fr*

Bericht erstatten (vb); einem Ausschuß — —. *De*
report (vb) to committee *En*
présenter (vb) un rapport en commission *Fr*

Berichterstattung (f) *De*
report writing *En*
rédaction (f) de rapports *Fr*

Beruf (m), Tätigkeit (f) *De*
occupation *En*
métier (m) *Fr*

berufene(-r) Sachkundige(-r) (m/f) *De*
co-opted member (of council) *En*
membre (m) coopté du conseil *Fr*

berufliche Entwicklung (f) *De*
career development *En*
développement (m) de la carrière *Fr*

berufliches Verhalten (nt) *De*
professional conduct *En*
déontologie (f) *Fr*

Berufsabsicherung (f) *De*
professional indemnity *En*
assurance (f) professionnelle *Fr*

Berufsbeamtentum (nt) *De*
careers service *En*
service (m) d'orientation professionnelle *Fr*

Berufsberater/-in (m/f) *De*
careers officer *En*
conseiller (m) (-ère f.) d'orientation *Fr*

Berufsberatung (f) *De*
vocational guidance *En*
orientation (f) professionnelle *Fr*

Berufsberatungsstelle (f) *De*
careers office *En*
bureau (m) d'orientation professionnelle *Fr*

Berufschulerziehung (f) *De*
non advanced further education *En*
formation (f) continue *Fr*

Berufserziehung (f)/ -ausbildung (f) *De*
vocational education/training *En*
éducation (f) professionnelle *Fr*

Berufserziehung (f) *De*
occupational training *En*
éducation (f) professionnelle *Fr*

Berufsethos (nt) *De*
professional ethics *En*
déontologie (f) professionnelle *Fr*

*** see/siehe/voir: Introduction page IX**

Berufskrankheit (f) *De*
occupational disease *En*
maladie (f) professionnelle *Fr*

Berufsorganisation (f) *De*
professional association *En*
association (f) professionnelle *Fr*

Berufsrisiken (nt.pl) *De*
occupational hazards *En*
risques (m.pl) du travail *Fr*

berufstätige Frau (f) *De*
working woman *En*
femme (f) professionnelle *Fr*

Berufsunfallversorgung (f) *De*
industrial injuries benefit *En*
indemnité (f) pour accidents du travail *Fr*

Berufungsgericht (nt) *De*
court of appeal *En*
cour (f) d'appel *Fr*

Berufungskläger/-in (m/f) *De*
appellant *En*
appelant (m) *Fr*

Berufungsrecht (nt) *De*
right of appeal *En*
droit (m) d'appel *Fr*

Beschäftigung (f) in beschützenden Werkstätten *De*
sheltered employment *En*
emplois (m.pl) réservés *Fr*

Beschäftigungslosigkeit (f) *De*
redundancy *En*
licenciement (m) *Fr*

Beschäftigungspolitik (f) *De*
manpower policy *En*
politique (f) d'emploi *Fr*

beschließen (vb); (Debatte usw) *De*
wind up (vb) (debate etc) *En*
résumer (vb) (un débat etc) *Fr*

beschließen, zu empfehlen (vb) *De*
resolve (vb) to recommend *En*
donner (vb) un avis *Fr*

beschlußfähige Anzahl (f) *De*
quorum *En*
quorum (m) *Fr*

Beschlußfassung (f) *De*
decision-making *En*
prise (f) de décision *Fr*

beschützende Werkstätte (f) *De*
sheltered workshop *En*
atelier (m) pour les handicapés *Fr*

Beschwerde (f) *De*
grievance *En*
grief (m) *Fr*

Beschwerdeverfahren (nt) *De*
complaints procedure *En*
procédure (f) pour porter plainte *Fr*

besetzen (vb); ein Haus *De*
squat (vb) *En*
s'établir (vb) comme squatter dans une maison inoccupée (sans titre) *Fr*

Besitz (m); Amtszeit (f) *De*
tenure *En*
(période de) jouissance (f) *Fr*

Besitz (m), Immobilie (f) *De*
property *En*
propriété (f) *Fr*

Besitzergreifung (f) *De*
appropriation *En*
appropriation (f) *Fr*

besoin (m) d'emprunt *Fr*
Kreditbedarf (m) *De*
borrowing requirement *En*

besoin (m) en éducation spécialisée *Fr*
Sonderlernanspruch (m) *De*
special educational need *En*

besoin (m) en logement *Fr*
Wohnungsnot (f) *De*
housing need *En*

bestellen (vb) *De*
order (vb) *En*
commander (vb) *Fr*

Bestellung (f) *De*
order (noun) *En*
commande (f) *Fr*

besteuern (vb) *De*
tax (vb) *En*
imposer (vb) *Fr*

Besteuerung (f) *De*
taxation *En*
imposition (f) *Fr*

Besuchsrecht (nt); Wegerecht (nt) *De*
right of access *En*
droit (m) d'accès *Fr*

Beteiligungs-, Risikokapital (nt) *De*
venture capital *En*
capitaux (m.pl) spéculatifs *Fr*

béton (m) armé *Fr*
Stahlbeton (m) *De*
reinforced concrete *En*

béton (m) malaxé *Fr*
Fertigbeton (m) *De*
ready-mixed concrete *En*

béton (m) précontraint *Fr*
Spannbeton (m) *De*
prestressed concrete *En*

béton (m) prémoulé *Fr*
vorgefertigter Beton (m) *De*
precast concrete *En*

Betreuung (f) *De*
caretaking *En*
gardiennage (m) *Fr*

Betriebsaltersversorgung (f) *De*
occupational pension scheme *En*
retraite (f) des cadres *Fr*

(betriebseigene) Kinderkrippe (f) *De*
workplace nursery *En*
crèche (f) au lieu de travail *Fr*

Betriebsförderungsprogramm (nt) *De*
business expansion scheme *En*
programme (m) d'expansion commerciale *Fr*

Betriebsführer (m), kaufmännischer Direktor (m) *De*
business manager *En*
directeur (m) commercial *Fr*

Betriebsgelände (nt) *De*
business park *En*
centre (m) d'affaires *Fr*

Betriebskapital (nt) *De*
working capital *En*
fonds (m.pl) de roulement *Fr*

Betriebskosten (pl) *De*
operating cost *En*
frais (m.pl) d'exploitation *Fr*

Betriebskosten (pl) *De*
running cost *En*
frais (m.pl) d'exploitation *Fr*

Betriebssicherheit (f) *De*
industrial safety *En*
sécurité (f) industrielle *Fr*

Betrug (m) *De*
fraud *En*
fraude (f) *Fr*

betrügerisch (adj) *De*
fraudulent (adj) *En*
frauduleux (-euse f.) (adj) *Fr*

betterment levy *En*
impôt (m) sur les plus-values *Fr*
Wertzuwachsabgabe (f) *De*

Beurteilung (f) *De*
appraisal *En*
évaluation (f) *Fr*

Beurteilung (f) sozialer Bedürftigkeit *De*
needs assessment *En*
évaluation (f) du quotient familial *Fr*

Beurteilungsaufgaben (f.pl) *De*
standard assessment tasks *En*
tâches (f.pl) évaluées (à l'école en GB) *Fr*

Bevölkerung (f) *De*
population *En*
population (f) *Fr*

Bevölkerungsdichte (f) *De*
density of population *En*
densité (f) de la population *Fr*

Bevölkerungsdichte (f) *De*
population density *En*
densité (f) de la population *Fr*

Bevölkerungsprognose (f) *De*
population forecast/projection *En*
prévision (f) démographique *Fr*

Bevölkerungsschätzung (f) *De*
population estimate *En*
population (f) estimative *Fr*

Bevölkerungsschwund (m) *De*
population decline *En*
baisse (f) démographique *Fr*

Bevölkerungsstatistik (f) *De*
population statistics *En*
statistiques (f.pl) démographiques *Fr*

Bevölkerungstrend (m) *De*
demographic trend *En*
mouvement (m) démographique *Fr*

Bevölkerungsüberschuß (m) *De*
overspill *En*
déversement (m) de population *Fr*

Bevölkerungsverteilung (f) *De*
population distribution *En*
répartition (f) de la population *Fr*

Bevölkerungswandel (m) *De*
population change *En*
évolution (f) démographique *Fr*

Bevölkerungszuwachs (m) *De*
population growth *En*
accroissement (m) démographique *Fr*

Bewährung (f) *De*
probation *En*
probation (f) *Fr*

(auf) Bewährung (f) *De*
on probation *En*
en liberté (f) surveillée *Fr*

(auf) Bewährung Freigelassene(-r) (m/f) *De*
probationer *En*
jeune délinquant (m) (-ante f.) en liberté surveillée *Fr*

Bewährungsdienst (m) *De*
probation service *En*
comité (m) de probation *Fr*

Bewährungshelfer/-in (m/f) *De*
probation officer *En*
agent (m) de probation *Fr*

bewilligen (vb) *De*
grant aid (vb) *En*
subventionner (vb) *Fr*

bewilligen (vb); das Budget *De*
pass (vb) the budget *En*
voter (vb) le budget *Fr*

Bewohner/-in (m/f) *De*
resident *En*
habitant (m) (-ante f.) *Fr*

Bewohnung (f) *De*
occupancy *En*
occupation (f) *Fr*

bezahlter Urlaub (m) *De*
holiday with pay *En*
congé (m) payé *Fr*

bezahlter Urlaub (m) *De*
paid holidays *En*
congés (m.pl) payés *Fr*

Bezahlung (f) *De*
remuneration *En*
rémunération (f) *Fr*

Beziehungen (f.pl) zwischen Arbeitgebern und Gewerkschaften *De*
industrial relations *En*
relations (f.pl) humaines dans l'entreprise *Fr*

Beziehungen (f.pl) zwischen den Rassen *De*
race relations *En*
rapports (m.pl) entre les races différentes *Fr*

Beziehungen zwischen Arbeitgebern und -nehmern *De*
labour relations *En*
rapports (m.pl) du travail *Fr*

Bezirk (m) *De*
district *En*
district (m) *Fr*

Bezirks/Stadtteil/-entwicklungsplan (m) *De*
borough (development) plan *En*
plan (m) de développement de la municipalité *Fr*

bezirksgebundene/stadtteilge-bundene Einteilung (f) *De*
zoning (school catchment areas) *En*
sectorisation (f) *Fr*

Bezirksgesundheitsamt (nt) *De*
community health service *En*
service (m) de santé communautaire *Fr*

Bezirksgesundheitspflege (f) *De*
community health care; medecine *En*
service (m) de santé *Fr*

Bezirksschätzer (m), Taxator (m) *De*
district valuer *En*
inspecteur (m) des domaines *Fr*

Bezirksstrukturplan (m) *De*
county structure plan *En*
plan (m) d'ensemble du comté/département *Fr*

Bezirksverwaltungsplan (m) *De*
district plan *En*
plan (m) d'aménagement urbain *Fr*

*** see/siehe/voir: Introduction page IX**

bezugsfertig (adj) *De*
(with) vacant possession *En*
libre possession (*Fr*)

bibliobus (m) *Fr*
Fahrbücherei (f) *De*
mobile library *En*

bibliothécaire (m/f) *Fr*
Bibliothekar/-in (m/f) *De*
librarian *En*

Bibliothek (f) *De*
library *En*
bibliothèque (f) *Fr*

Bibliothekar/-in (m/f) *De*
librarian *En*
bibliothécaire (m/f) *Fr*

Bibliotheksamt (nt) *De*
libraries department *En*
bibliothèque (f) *Fr*

bibliothèque (f) d'ouvrages de référence *Fr*
Präsenzbibliothek (f) *De*
reference library *En*

bibliothèque (f) *Fr*
Bibliothek (f) *De*
library *En*

bibliothèque (f) *Fr*
Bibliotheksamt (nt) *De*
libraries department *En*

bibliothèque (f) municipale *Fr*
öffentliche Bücherei (f) *De*
public library *En*

bien (m) public *Fr*
das öffentliche Wohl (nt) *De*
public good *En*

biens (m.pl) de consommation durables *Fr*
langlebige Konsumgüter (nt.pl) *De*
consumer durables *En*

biens (m.pl) de consommation *Fr*
Konsumgüter (nt.pl) *De*
consumer goods *En*

bilan (m) *Fr*
Bilanz (f) *De*
balance sheet *En*

bilan (m) annuel *Fr*
Jahresabschluß (m) *De*
annual accounts *En*

Bilanz (f) *De*
balance sheet *En*
bilan (m) *Fr*

bilanzieren (vb) *De*
balance (vb) the budget *En*
équilibrer (vb) le budget *Fr*

bilateral trade agreement *En*
accord (m) de commerce bilateral *Fr*
bilateraler Handelsvertrag (m) *De*

bilateraler Handelsvertrag (m) *De*
bilateral trade agreement *En*
accord (m) de commerce bilateral *Fr*

Bildschirmgerät (nt) *De*
visual display unit (VDU) *En*
unité (f) de visualisation *Fr*

bill of exchange *En*
lettre (f) de change *Fr*
Wechsel (m) *De*

bill of rights *En*
déclaration (f) des droits des citoyens *Fr*
Bill of Rights (f) *De*

Bill of Rights (f) *De*
bill of rights *En*
déclaration (f) des droits des citoyens *Fr*

bills of quantities *En*
devis (m) *Fr*
Kostenvorschläge (m.pl) *De*

bindender Vertrag (m) *De*
binding agreement *En*
convention (f) irrévocable *Fr*

binding agreement *En*
convention (f) irrévocable *Fr*
bindender Vertrag (m) *De*

Binnenmarkt (m) *De*
internal market *En*
marché (m) intérieur *Fr*

birth certificate *En*
acte (m) de naissance *Fr*
Geburtsurkunde (f) *De*

bitume (m) *Fr*
Bitumen (nt) *De*
bitumen *En*

bitumen *En*
bitume (m) *Fr*
Bitumen (nt) *De*

Bitumen (nt) *De*
bitumen *En*
bitume (m) *Fr*

blocage (m) des salaires *Fr*
Lohnstopp (m) *De*
wage freeze *En*

block grant *En*
subvention (f) de l'Etat *Fr*
Pauschalsubvention (f) *De*

block of flats *En*
immeuble (m) *Fr*
Wohnblock (m) *De*

blue collar worker *En*
ouvrier (m) (-ière f.) *Fr*
Arbeiter/-in (m/f) *De*

board meeting *En*
réunion (f) du conseil *Fr*
Vorstandssitzung (f) *De*

board of directors *En*
conseil (m) d'administration *Fr*
Vorstand (m) *De*

Bodenanalyse (f) *De*
soil testing *En*
analyse (f) des sols *Fr*

Bodenangebot (nt) *De*
land availability *En*
disponibilité (f) de terrain *Fr*

Bodennutzung (f) *De*
land use *En*
utilisation (f) des terrains *Fr*

Bodenpolitik (f) *De*
land policy *En*
politique (f) foncière *Fr*

Bodenpreis (m) *De*
land price *En*
prix (m) du terrain *Fr*

Bodenschwelle (f) *De*
sleeping policeman *En*
ralentisseur (m); "gendarme (m) couché" *Fr*

boîte (f) à ordures *Fr*
Abfalleimer (m) *De*
litter bin *En*

boîte (f) à ordures *Fr*
Mülltonne (f) *De*
refuse bin *En*

bollard *En*
borne (f) *Fr*
Poller (m) *De*

bonus scheme *En*
prime (f) *Fr*
Prämiensystem (nt) *De*

*** see/siehe/voir: Introduction page IX**

book cost *En*
prix (m) de revient comptable *Fr*
Buchwert (m) der Einkäufe (f) *De*

bookkeeper *En*
commis-comptable (m) *Fr*
Buchhalter (m) *De*

bookkeeping *En*
tenue (f) des livres *Fr*
Buchhaltung (f) *De*

bordereau (m) de livraison *Fr*
Lieferschein (m) *De*
delivery note *En*

borne (f) *Fr*
Poller (m) *De*
bollard *En*

borough *En* *
ville; municipalité (f) *Fr*
(Stadt)gemeinde (f), Bezirk (m) *De*

borough council *En* *
conseil (m) municipal *Fr*
Stadtverwaltung (f), Gemeinderat (m) *De*

borough (development) plan *En*
plan (m) de développement de la municipalité *Fr*
Bezirks/-Stadtteilentwicklungsplan (m) *De*

borrowing requirement *En*
besoin (m) d'emprunt *Fr*
Kreditbedarf (m) *De*

Börse (f) *De*
stock exchange *En*
bourse (f) *Fr*

Börsenmakler (m) *De*
stockbroker *En*
courtier (m) en bourse *Fr*

borstal *En*
école (f) de redressement pour jeunes gens *Fr*
Jugendstrafanstalt (f) *De*

Botschaft (f) *De*
embassy *En*
ambassade (f) *Fr*

bouche-trou (m) *Fr*
Notbehelf (m) *De*
stop-gap *En*

boue (f) activée *Fr*
Belebtschlamm (m) *De*
activated sludge *En*

boueur (m) *Fr*
Müllwerker (m), -mann (m) *De*
dustman *En*

boulevard (m) périphérique *Fr*
Umgehungsstraße (f) *De*
ring road *En*

boundary *En*
frontière (f) *Fr*
Grenze (f) *De*

boundary change *En*
modification (f) des circonscriptions électorales *Fr*
Grenzänderung (f) *De*

bourse (f) *Fr*
Börse (f) *De*
stock exchange *En*

bourse (f) *Fr*
Stipendium (nt) *De*
bursary *En*

bourse (f) *Fr*
(Studien)beihilfe (f); Zuschuß (m); Subvention(f) *De*
grant (noun) *En*

bourse (f) d'entretien *Fr*
Unterhaltsbeihilfe (f) *De*
maintenance grant *En*

bourse (f) d'études *Fr*
Studienbeihilfe (f) *De*
student grant *En*

Brand (m) *De*
fire *En*
incendie (m) *Fr*

Brandgefahr (f) *De*
fire risk *En*
risque (m) d'incendie *Fr*

breach of condition notice *En*
avis (m) de non-accomplissement de contrat *Fr*
Verletzung (f) einer Hauptpflicht *De*

breach of contract *En*
rupture (f) de contrat *Fr*
Vertragsbruch (m) *De*

break-even point *En*
point (m) de seuil *Fr*
Rentabilitätsgrenze (f) *De*

Breitenbeschränkung (f) *De*
width restriction *En*
limitation (f) de largeur *Fr*

Brenn-, Kraftstoff (m) *De*
fuel *En*
combustible (m) *Fr*

Brennstoffkosten (pl) *De*
fuel cost/price *En*
prix (m) du combustible *Fr*

Brennstoffleistung (f) *De*
fuel efficiency *En*
rendement (m) énergétique *Fr*

Brennstoffsteuer (f) *De*
fuel tax *En*
impôt (m) sur le combustible *Fr*

Brennstoffverbrauch (m) *De*
fuel consumption *En*
consommation (f) de combustible *Fr*

bridging loan *En*
crédit (m) provisoire *Fr*
Vorschußkredit (m) *De*

bridle Path/bridleway *En*
sentier (m) pour cavaliers *Fr*
Reitweg (m) *De*

brief (vb) (an architect etc) *En*
donner (vb) des instructions (à un architecte etc) *Fr*
Anweisungen geben, unterweisen (vb) (Architekt usw.) *De*

briefing meeting (with chairman) *En*
réunion (f) préparatoire (avec le président) *Fr*
Einsatzbesprechung (f) *De*

Brückenwaage (f) *De*
weighbridge *En*
pont-bascule (m) (pl.ponts-bascules) *Fr*

Bruttogewinn (m) *De*
gross profit *En*
bénéfice (m) brut *Fr*

Bruttoinlandsprodukt (nt) *De*
gross domestic product *En*
produit (m) national brut *Fr*

Buchhalter (m) *De*
bookkeeper *En*
commis-comptable (m) *Fr*

Buchhalter/Buchhälterin (m/f) *De*
accountant *En*
comptable (m) *Fr*

Buchhaltung (f) *De*
accountancy/accounting *En*
comptabilité (f) *Fr*

*** see/siehe/voir: Introduction page IX**

Buchhaltung (f) *De*
bookkeeping *En*
tenue (f) des livres *Fr*

Buchwert (m) der Einkäufe (f) *De*
book cost *En*
prix (m) de revient comptable *Fr*

budget *En*
budget (m) *Fr*
Budget (nt), Haushaltsplan (m) *De*

budget (m) *Fr*
Budget (nt), Haushaltsplan (m) *De*
budget *En*

budget (m) adaptable *Fr*
elastischer Etat (m) *De*
flexible budget *En*

budget (m) de programme *Fr*
Programmbudget (nt) *De*
programme budget *En*

budget (m) prévisionnel avec décisions modificatives *Fr*
Nettobudget (nt) *De*
net budget *En*

Budget (nt), Haushaltsplan (m) *De*
budget *En*
budget (m) *Fr*

budget policy *En*
politique (f) budgétaire *Fr*
Haushaltspolitik (f) *De*

(Budget usw) festlegen (vb) *De*
fix (vb) the budget *En*
établir (vb) le budget *Fr*

budgetary control *En*
contrôle (m) budgétaire *Fr*
Budgetkontrolle (f) *De*

budgétisation (f) à base zéro *Fr*
auf Null basierender Haushalt (m) *De*
zero based budgeting *En*

Budgetkontrolle (f) *De*
budgetary control *En*
contrôle (m) budgétaire *Fr*

Budgetüberweisung (f) *De*
virement *En*
virement (m) *Fr*

Budgetunterschreitung (f) *De*
underspending *En*
dépenses (f.pl) en dessous des chiffres prévus dans le budget *Fr*

building *En*
bâtiment (m) *Fr*
Gebäude (nt) *De*

building contract *En*
contrat (m) de bâtiment *Fr*
Bauvertrag (m) *De*

building control *En*
contrôle (m) de construction *Fr*
Baukontrolle (f), Bauaufsicht (f) *De*

building costs *En*
coût (m) de construction *Fr*
Baukosten (pl) *De*

building design *En*
dessein (m) de construction *Fr*
Bauentwurf (m), Bauplan (m) *De*

building industry *En*
bâtiment (m) *Fr*
Bauindustrie (f) *De*

building inspector *En*
inspecteur (m) de la construction *Fr*
Bauinspektor (m) *De*

building land *En*
terrain (m) constructible *Fr*
Bauland (nt) *De*

building regulations *En*
règlements (m.pl) de construction *Fr*
Bauordnung (f) *De*

building society *En*
société (f) immobilière *Fr*
Bausparkasse (f) *De*

building stock *En*
parc (m) de bâtiments *Fr*
Gebäudebestand (m) *De*

building/construction site *En*
chantier (m) de construction *Fr*
Baustelle (f) *De*

built up area *En*
agglomération (f) *Fr*
geschlossene Ortschaft (f) *De*

bulletin (m) (d'informations) *Fr*
Rundschreiben (nt) *De*
newsletter *En*

bulletin (m) de souscription *Fr*
Antragsformular (nt) *De*
application form *En*

Bundes- *De*
federal (adj) *En*
fédéral (adj) *Fr*

Bundesregierung (f) *De*
federal government *En*
gouvernement (m) fédéral *Fr*

bureau (m) *Fr*
Büro (nt) *De*
office *En*

bureau (m) *Fr*
Schreibtisch (m) *De*
desk *En*

bureau (m) d'études *Fr*
Entwurfsbüro (nt) *De*
design office *En*

bureau (m) d'études *Fr*
Konstruktionsbüro (nt) *De*
drawing office *En*

bureau (m) d'orientation professionnelle *Fr*
Berufsberatungsstelle (f) *De*
careers office *En*

bureau (m) de placement *Fr*
Arbeitsamt (nt) *De*
job centre *En*

bureau (m) de placement *Fr*
Stellenvermittlung (f) *De*
employment agency/office *En*

bureau (m) de poste *Fr*
Post (f) *De*
post office *En*

bureau (m) de renseignements *Fr*
Auskunftsbüro (nt) *De*
information centre *En*

bureau (m) de vote *Fr*
Wahllokal (nt) *De*
polling station *En*

bureau (m) des contributions *Fr*
Finanzamt (nt) *De*
tax office *En*

bureau (m) du cadastre *Fr*
Grundbuchamt (nt) *De*
land registry *En*

bureau (m) électronique *Fr*
elektronisches Büro (nt) *De*
electronic office *En*

bureau (m) pour la prévention de la délinquance *Fr*
Jugendamt (nt) *De*
juvenile bureau *En*

*** see/siehe/voir: Introduction page IX**

bureau (m) sans cloisons *Fr*
Großraumbüro (nt) *De*
open plan office *En*

bureaucracy *En*
bureaucratie (f) *Fr*
Bürokratie (f) *De*

bureaucratic *En*
bureaucratique (adj) *Fr*
bürokratisch (adj) *De*

bureaucratie (f) *Fr*
Bürokratie (f) *De*
bureaucracy *En*

bureaucratique (adj) *Fr*
bürokratisch (adj) *De*
bureaucratic *En*

Bürger/-in (m/f) *De*
citizen *En*
citoyen (-enne f.) *Fr*

Bürgerbau (m) *De*
municipal building *En*
bâtiment (m) municipal *Fr*

Bürgerberatungsstelle (f) *De* *
citizens advice bureau *En*
conciliateur (m) *Fr*

Bürgergemeinschaft (f) *De*
community group *En*
association (f) locale *Fr*

bürgerliche Freiheit (f) *De*
civil liberty *En*
liberté (f) civile *Fr*

Bürgermeister (m) *De* *
mayor *En*
maire (m)/bourgmestre (m) (Belg.) *Fr*

Bürgerrechte (nt.pl) *De*
civil rights *En*
droits (m.pl) civiques *Fr*

Bürgersteig (m) *De*
pavement *En*
trottoir (m) *Fr*

Bürgerwehr (f) *De*
neighbourhood policing *En*
îlotage (m) *Fr*

Büro (nt) *De*
office *En*
bureau (m) *Fr*

Büroangestellte(-r) (m/f) *De*
office worker *En*
employé (m) (-ée f.) de bureau *Fr*

Büroarbeit (f) *De*
clerical work *En*
travail (m) de bureau *Fr*

Bürobedarf (m), -maschinen (f.pl) *De*
office equipment/machinery *En*
matériel (m) de bureau *Fr*

Büroerweiterung (f) *De*
office development *En*
développement (m) tertiaire *Fr*

Bürohaus (nt), -gebäude (nt) *De*
office block/building *En*
bâtiment (m) administratif *Fr*

Bürokratie (f) *De*
bureaucracy *En*
bureaucratie (f) *Fr*

bürokratisch (adj) *De*
bureaucratic *En*
bureaucratique (adj) *Fr*

Büroleitung (f) *De*
office management *En*
administration (f) du bureau *Fr*

Büromiete (f) *De*
office rent *En*
loyer (m) commercial *Fr*

Büropersonal (nt) *De*
clerical staff *En*
personnel (m) d'exécution *Fr*

Büropersonal (nt) *De*
office staff *En*
personnel (m) de bureau *Fr*

Büroräume (m.pl) *De*
office accommodation *En*
locaux (m.pl) pour bureaux *Fr*

Bürosäuberung (f) *De*
office cleaning *En*
nettoyage (m) de bureau *Fr*

Bürostunden (f.pl) *De*
office hours *En*
heures (f.pl) de bureau *Fr*

bursary *En*
bourse (f) *Fr*
Stipendium (nt) *De*

Busbahnhof (m) *De*
coach station *En*
gare (f) routière *Fr*

business *En*
affaires (f.pl) *Fr*
Geschäft (nt), Betrieb (m), Unternehmen (nt) *De*

business advice *En*
conseil (m) commercial *Fr*
geschäftlicher Ratschlag (m) *De*

business card *En*
carte (f) d'affaires *Fr*
Visitenkarte (f) *De*

business community *En*
monde (m) des affaires *Fr*
Geschäftskreise (m.pl), Geschäftswelt (f) *De*

business development *En*
développement (m) commercial *Fr*
Geschäftsentwicklung (f) *De*

business expansion scheme *En*
programme (m) d'expansion commerciale *Fr*
Betriebsförderungsprogramm (nt) *De*

business manager *En*
directeur (m) commercial *Fr*
Betriebsführer (m), kaufmännischer Direktor (m) *De*

business park *En*
centre (m) d'affaires *Fr*
Betriebsgelände (nt) *De*

business plan *En*
plan (m) d'aménagement *Fr*
Geschäftsplan (m) *De*

business rate *En*
taxe (f) professionnelle *Fr*
Gewerbesteuer (f) *De*

but (m) *Fr*
Ziele (nt.pl) *De*
aims and objectives *En*

buts (m.pl) *Fr*
Ziele (nt.pl) *De*
objectives *En*

by-election *En*
élection (f) partielle *Fr*
Nachwahl (f) *De*

by-pass *En*
route (f) d'évitement *Fr*
Umgehungsstraße (f) *De*

byelaw *En*
arrêté (m) municipal *Fr*
Verordnung (f) *De*

*** see/siehe/voir: Introduction page IX**

C

cabinet *En*
cabinet (m) *Fr*
Kabinett (nt) *De*

cabinet (m) d'experts-conseils *Fr*
Beratung (f); Beratungsbüro (nt) *De*
consultancy *En*

cabinet (m) *Fr*
Kabinett (nt) *De*
cabinet *En*

cabinet (m) particulier *Fr*
privates Büro (nt) *De*
private office *En*

cadastre (m) *Fr*
Begutachtung (f), Gutachten (nt) *De*
survey (for rating) *En*

cadastreur (m) *Fr*
Vermessungsingenieur/-in (m/f) *De*
chartered surveyor *En*

cadre (m) de maitrise *Fr*
Aufsichtspersonal (nt) *De*
supervisory staff *En*

cadre (m) supérieur *Fr*
höherer Beamter/höhere Beamtin (m/f) *De*
senior officer *En*

cadres (m.pl) moyens *Fr*
Middlemanagement (nt) *De*
middle management (public sector) *En*

cahier (m) des charges *Fr*
Vertragsbedingungen (f.pl) *De*
conditions of contract *En*

caisse (f) d'épargne *Fr*
Sparkasse (f) *De*
savings bank *En*

caisse (f) de retraite *Fr*
Pensionsfonds (m) *De*
pension fund *En*

caisse (f) des retraités *Fr*
Rentenfonds (m) *De*
superannuation fund *En*

calculator *En*
machine (f) à calculer *Fr*
Rechenmaschine (f) *De*

camembert (m) *Fr*
Kreisdiagramm (nt) *De*
pie chart *En*

camion (m) lourd *Fr*
Schwerlastwagen (m) *De*
heavy lorry *En*

campagne (f) contre l'analphabétisme *Fr*
Kampagne (f) gegen das Analphabetentum *De*
adult literacy campaign *En*

campagne (f) de commercialisation *Fr*
Werbekampagne (f) *De*
marketing campaign *En*

campagne (f) de publicité *Fr*
Werbekampagne (f) *De*
advertising campaign *En*

campus *En*
campus (m) *Fr*
Campus (m) *De*

Campus (m) *De*
campus *En*
campus (m) *Fr*

campus (m) *Fr*
Campus (m) *De*
campus *En*

campus (m) scientifique *Fr*
Technologiepark (m) *De*
science park *En*

campus (m) technologique *Fr*
Technologiepark (m) *De*
technology park *En*

cancel (vb) *En*
annuler (vb) *Fr*
annullieren (vb) *De*

candidat (m) *Fr*
Kandidat/-in (m/f) *De*
candidate *En*

candidate *En*
candidat (m) *Fr*
Kandidat/-in (m/f) *De*

canvass (vb) (vote etc) *En*
solliciter (vb) (la voix etc) *Fr*
werben (vb) *De*

capacité (f) d'accueil d'un aéroport *Fr*
Flughafenkapazität (f) *De*
airport capacity/volume *En*

capacité (f) d'écoulement de trafic *Fr*
Verkehrsaufkommen (nt) *De*
traffic capacity/volume *En*

capacité (f) des grandes routes *Fr*
Straßenauslastung (f) *De*
highway capacity *En*

capacité (m) de trafic de la route *Fr*
Straßenauslastung (f) *De*
road capacity *En*

capital accounting/budget *En*
section (f) d'investissement dans le budget *Fr*
Kapitalkontrolle (f) *De*

capital allowance *En*
déductions (f.pl) fiscales sur les investissements *Fr*
Vermögenszuteilung (f) *De*

capital cost *En*
coût (m) d'investissement *Fr*
Kapitalkosten (pl) *De*

capital expenditure *En*
charges (f.pl) d'investissement *Fr*
Kapitalaufwendungen (f.pl) *De*

capital expenditure *En*
immobilisations (f.pl) *Fr*
Kapitalauslagen (f.pl) *De*

capital finance *En*
investissement (m) *Fr*
Vermögensfinanzierung (f) *De*

capital funding *En*
financement (m) d'investissement *Fr*
Kapitalanlage (f) *De*

capital gains tax *En*
impôt (m) sur la plus-value *Fr*
Steuer (f) auf Kapitalgewinn *De*

capital grants *En*
subventions (f.pl) spécifiques *Fr*
Investitionszuschüsse (m.pl) *De*

capital programme *En*
programme (m) d'investissement *Fr*
Investitionsprogramm (nt) *De*

capital spending *En*
dépenses (f.pl) d'investissement *Fr*
Kapitalaufwand (m) *De*

capitation (f) *Fr* *
Kopfsteuer (f) *De*
poll tax *En*

capitaux (m.pl) spéculatifs *Fr*
Beteiligungs-, Risikokapital (nt) *De*
venture capital *En*

capitaux (m.pl) spéculatifs *Fr*
Risikokapital (nt) *De*
risk capital *En*

capping of public expenditure *En*
limitation (f) des dépenses publiques *Fr*
Begrenzung (f) öffentlicher Ausgaben *De*

car (m) scolaire *Fr*
Schulbus (m) *De*
school bus *En*

caractère (m) confidentiel *Fr*
Vertraulichkeit (f) *De*
confidentiality *En*

care management *En*
action (f) sociale *Fr*
Pflegeleitung (f) *De*

care of the aged *En*
soins (m.pl) des personnes âgées *Fr*
Altenpflege (f) *De*

care order *En*
ordonnance (f) de placement en maison d'enfants *Fr*
Jugendfürsorgeanordnung (f) *De*

care proceedings *En*
procédure (f) d'ordonnance de placement *Fr*
Fürsorgeerziehungsverfahren (nt) *De*

career break *En*
interruption (f) dans la carrière *Fr*
Unterbrechung (f) der Berufstätigkeit *De*

career development *En*
développement (m) de la carrière *Fr*
berufliche Entwicklung (f) *De*

careers office *En*
bureau (m) d'orientation professionnelle *Fr*
Berufsberatungsstelle (f) *De*

careers officer *En*
conseiller (m) (-ère f.) d'orientation *Fr*
Berufsberater/-in (m/f) *De*

careers service *En*
service (m) d'orientation professionnelle *Fr*
Berufsbeamtentum (nt) *De*

caretaker *En*
concièrge (m/f) *Fr*
Hausmeister (m) *De*

caretaking *En*
gardiennage (m) *Fr*
Betreuung (f) *De*

caring services *En*
service (m) des soins *Fr*
Fürsorge (f) *De*

carrefour (m) *Fr*
Kreuzung (f) *De*
intersection *En*

carrefour (m) *Fr*
Kreuzung (f) *De*
junction *En*

carrefour (m) *Fr*
Straßenkreuzung (f) *De*
road junction *En*

carriage free (adj) *En*
franco (adj) *Fr*
frachtfrei (adj) *De*

carriageway *En*
chaussée (f) *Fr*
Fahrbahn (f) *De*

carte (f) d'abonnement *Fr*
Dauerkarte (f) *De*
season ticket *En*

carte (f) d'affaires *Fr*
Visitenkarte (f) *De*
business card *En*

carte (f) d'identité *Fr*
Personalausweis (m) *De*
identity card *En*

carte (f) de crédit *Fr*
Kreditkarte (f) *De*
credit card *En*

case conference *En*
réunion (f) de concertation *Fr*
Fallbesprechung (f) *De*

case law *En*
jurisprudence (f) *Fr*
Fallrecht (nt) *De*

case study *En*
étude (f) individuelle *Fr*
Fallstudie (f) *De*

casework *En*
assistance (f) individuelle *Fr*
Sozialarbeit (f) *De*

cash dispenser *En*
distributeur (m) d'argent comptant *Fr*
Bargeldauszahlungsautomat (m) *De*

cash flow *En*
cash-flow (m) *Fr*
Cash-flow (m) *De*

cash limit *En*
plafond (m) du budget *Fr*
Kreditbegrenzung (f) *De*

Cash-flow (m) *De*
cash flow *En*
cash-flow (m) *Fr*

cash-flow (m) *Fr*
Cash-flow (m) *De*
cash flow *En*

casier (m) judiciaire *Fr*
Vorstrafen (f.pl) *De*
police record *En*

casting vote (of chairman) *En*
voix (f) prépondérante du président *Fr*
ausschlaggebende Stimme (f) *De*

catchment area *En*
secteur (m)/réseau (m) de ramassage (des écoliers) *Fr*
Einzugsgebiet (nt) *De*

*** see/siehe/voir: Introduction page IX**

cédule (f) d'impôts locaux *Fr*
Kommunalsteueraufstellung (f) *De*
schedule of rates *En*

census *En*
recensement (m) *Fr*
Volkszählung (f), Zensus (m) *De*

census data *En*
résultats (m.pl) du recensement *Fr*
Zensusdaten (nt.pl) *De*

census of population *En*
recensement (m) de la population *Fr*
Volkszählung (f) *De*

central business district *En*
zone (f) centrale de commerce *Fr*
Geschäftszentrum (nt) *De*

central government *En*
gouvernement (m) central *Fr*
Zentralregierung (f) *De*

central (m) téléphonique *Fr*
Femmeldeamt (nt) *De*
telephone exchange *En*

central purchasing office *En*
centrale (f) d'achats *Fr*
Haupteinkaufsabteilung (f) *De*

central service *En*
service (m) central *Fr*
Hauptbetrieb (m) *De*

centrale (f) atomique *Fr*
Kern-, Atomkraftwerk (nt) *De*
nuclear power station *En*

centrale (f) d'achats *Fr*
Haupteinkaufsabteilung (f) *De*
central purchasing office *En*

centrale (f) électrique *Fr*
Elektrizitätswerk (nt) *De*
electrical power station *En*

centrale (f) électrique *Fr*
Kraftwerk (nt) *De*
power station *En*

centralization *En*
centralisation (f) *Fr*
Zentralisierung (f) *De*

centralisation (f) *Fr*
Zentralisierung (f) *De*
centralization *En*

centre (m) civique *Fr*
Verwaltungszentrum (nt) (einer Stadt) *De*
civic centre *En*

centre (m) commercial *Fr*
Einkaufszentrum (nt) *De*
shopping area/centre/mall *En*

centre (m) commercial *Fr*
Handelszentrum (nt) *De*
commercial centre *En*

centre (m) d'accueil *Fr*
Durchgangslager (nt) *De*
reception centre *En*

centre (m) d'affaires *Fr*
Betriebsgelände (nt) *De*
business park *En*

centre (m) de conférences *Fr*
Konferenzzentrum (nt) *De*
conference centre *En*

centre (m) de conseil résidentiel *Fr*
Wohnberatungsbüro (nt) *De*
housing advice centre *En*

centre (m) de formation *Fr*
Ausbildungszentrum (nt) *De*
training centre *En*

centre (m) de formation *Fr*
Fachzentrum (nt) *De*
skill centre *En*

centre (m) de formation pour adultes *Fr*
Ausbildungszentrum (nt) für Erwachsene *De*
adult training centre *En*

centre (m) de la ville *Fr*
Innenstadt (f) *De*
city centre *En*

centre (m) de loisirs *Fr*
Freizeitzentrum (nt) *De*
recreation centre *En*

centre (m) de protection maternelle et enfantile *Fr*
Kinderabteilung (f) im Gesundheitsamt *De*
child welfare centre *En*

centre (m) de récréations *Fr*
Freizeitzentrum (nt) *De*
amenity centre *En*

centre (m) de récréations *Fr*
(städtisches) Freizeitzentrum (nt) *De*
civic amenity centre *En*

centre (m) de responsabilité *Fr*
Kostenstelle (f) *De*
cost centre *En*

centre (m) de soins gynécologiques *Fr*
Frauenklinik (f) *De*
well woman clinic *En*

centre (m) de traitement de l'information *Fr*
Zentrum (nt) für Informationstechnik *De*
information technology centre *En*

centre (m) hospitalier universitaire *Fr*
Ausbildungskrankenhaus (nt) *De*
teaching hospital *En*

centre (m) médical *Fr*
Poliklinik (f) *De*
health centre *En*

centre (m) social *Fr*
Freizeitzentrum (nt) *De*
leisure centre *En*

centre (m) social *Fr*
Gemeindehalle (f) *De*
community hall *En*

centre (m) social *Fr*
Gemeindezentrum (nt) *De*
drop-in centre *En*

centre (m) social *Fr*
Gemeinschaftszentrum (nt) *De*
community centre *En*

centre (m) urbain *Fr*
Stadtmitte (f) *De*
urban centre *En*

centre (m) ville *Fr*
Innenstadt (f), -bezirk (m) *De*
inner city *En*

centre (m) ville *Fr*
Stadtmitte (f) *De*
town centre *En*

certificat (m) *Fr*
Zeugnis (nt), Bescheinigung (f) *De*
certificate *En*

certificat (m) d'assurance *Fr*
Versicherungsschein (m) *De*
insurance certificate *En*

certificat (m) d'assurance *Fr*
Versicherungsurkunde (f) *De*
certificate of insurance *En*

certificat (m) de fin d'études du premier cycle *Fr*
Abschluß (m) der Sekundarstufe *De*
general certificate of secondary education *En*

*** see/siehe/voir: Introduction page IX**

certificat (m) de tenue au feu *Fr*
feuerpolizeiliches Zeugnis (nt) *De*
fire certificate *En*

certificate *En*
certificat (m) *Fr*
Zeugnis (nt), Bescheinigung (f) *De*

certificate of insurance *En*
certificat (m) d'assurance *Fr*
Versicherungsurkunde (f) *De*

chair/chairman/ chairperson *En*
président (m) (-ente f.) *Fr*
Vorsitzende(r) (m/f) *De*

chairmanship *En*
présidence (f) *Fr*
Vorsitz (m) *De*

challenge (vb) a decision *En*
porter (vb) une réclamation contre une decision *Fr*
eine Entscheidung anfechten (vb) *De*

chamber of commerce/trade *En*
chambre (f) de commerce *Fr*
Handelskammer (f) *De*

chambre (f) de commerce *Fr*
Handelskammer (f) *De*
chamber of commerce/trade *En*

champs (m.pl) communs *Fr*
Gemeindeland (nt) *De*
common land *En*

champs (m.pl) communs *Fr*
Kommunalgrundstück (nt) *De*
community land *En*

Chancengleichheit (f) *De*
equal opportunities *En*
chances (f.pl) égales *Fr*

Chancengleichheit (f) *De*
equality of opportunity *En*
égalité (f) des chances *Fr*

chances (f.pl) égales *Fr*
Chancengleichheit (f) *De*
equal opportunities *En*

change of use *En*
changement (m) d'usage *Fr*
Gebrauchsänderung (f) *De*

changement (m) d'implantation *Fr*
Industrieverlegung (f) *De*
industrial relocation *En*

changement (m) d'instructions *Fr*
Änderungsauftrag (m) *De*
variation order *En*

changement (m) d'usage *Fr*
Gebrauchsänderung (f) *De*
change of use *En*

changement (m) de politique *Fr*
Richtungswechsel (m) *De*
policy change *En*

changement (m) économique *Fr*
Strukturwandlung (f) *De*
economic change *En*

changements (m.pl) technologiques *Fr*
technische Veränderungen (f.pl) *De*
technological change *En*

channel link/tunnel *En*
tunnel (m) trans-Manche *Fr*
Kanaltunnel (m) *De*

chantier (m) de construction des navires *Fr*
Werft (f) *De*
dockyard *En*

chantier (m) de construction *Fr*
Baustelle (f) *De*
building/construction site *En*

chantier (m) naval (pl. chantiers navals) *Fr*
Werft (f) *De*
shipyard *En*

charge capping *En*
limitation (f) des impôts locaux par le gouvernement central *Fr*
Höchstgrenze (f) für Kommunalabgaben *De*

charges (f.pl) d'investissement *Fr*
Kapitalaufwendungen (f.pl) *De*
capital expenditure *En*

charges (f.pl) de famille *Fr*
abhängige Angehörige (pl) *De*
dependants *En*

charitable trust *En*
organisme (m) charicatif *Fr*
Stiftung (f) *De*

charité (f) *Fr*
Wohltätigkeit (f) *De*
charity *En*

charity *En*
charité (f) *Fr*
Wohltätigkeit (f) *De*

Charta (f), Gründungsurkunde (f) *De*
charter *En*
charte (f) (d'une ville) *Fr*

charte (f) (d'une ville) *Fr*
Charta (f), Gründungsurkunde (f) *De*
charter *En*

charter *En*
charte (f) (d'une ville) *Fr*
Charta (f), Gründungsurkunde (f) *De*

chartered surveyor *En*
cadastreur (m) *Fr*
Vermessungsingenieur/-in (m/f) *De*

château (m) d'eau *Fr*
Wasserturm (m) *De*
water tower *En*

chauffage (m) solaire *Fr*
Sonnenheizung (f) *De*
solar heating *En*

chauffage (m) urbain *Fr*
Sammelheizung (f) *De*
group heating *En*

chaussée (f) *Fr*
Fahrbahn (f) *De*
carriageway *En*

chaussée (f) *Fr*
Straße (f); Fahrbahn (f) *De*
roadway *En*

check (vb) draft minutes/report *En*
vérifier (vb) un projet de procès-verbal/rapport *Fr*
Entwürfe überprüfen (vb) *De*

chef (m) *Fr*
Führer/-in (m/f) *De*
leader *En*

chef (m) de comptes client *Fr*
Kontaktgruppenleiter (m) *De*
account executive *En*

chef (m) de section *Fr*
Abteilungsleiter/-in (m/f) *De*
section head *En*

*** see/siehe/voir: Introduction page IX**

chef (m) de service ***Fr***
Abteilungsleiter/-in (m/f) *De*
head of department *En*

chef (m) de service ***Fr***
Amtsleiter (m) *De*
chief officer *En*

chef (m) du personnel ***Fr***
Personalleiter/-in (m/f) *De*
personnel manager *En*

chef (m) du service exportation ***Fr***
Exportabteilungsleiter (m) *De*
export manager *En*

chef-lieu de comté/département ***Fr***
Grafschaftshauptstadt (f) *De*
county town *En*

chemical waste ***En***
déchets (m.pl) chimiques *Fr*
chemische Abfälle (m.pl) *De*

chemin de fer (m) à voie étroite ***Fr***
Personenverkehr (m) *De*
light rail transit *En*

chemin (m) de desserte ***Fr***
Entlastungsstraße (f) *De*
relief road *En*

chemin (m) de fer ***Fr***
Eisenbahn (f) *De*
railway *En*

chemin (m) de fer souterrain; métro (m) ***Fr***
Untergrundbahn; U-bahn (f) *De*
underground railway *En*

chemin (m) privé ***Fr***
Privatstraße (f) *De*
private road *En*

chemin (m) privé ***Fr***
Privatweg (m), -straße (f) *De*
unadopted road *En*

chemische Abfälle (m.pl) ***De***
chemical waste *En*
déchets (m.pl) chimiques *Fr*

chèque (m) de voyage ***Fr***
Reisescheck (m) *De*
traveller's cheque *En*

chèque (m) postal ***Fr***
Giro (nt), Postscheck (m) *De*
giro *En*

chief architect ***En***
directeur (m) de l'architecture *Fr*
leitender Architekt (m) *De*

chief constable ***En*** *
commissaire (m) de police *Fr*
Polizeipräsident (m) *De*

chief education officer ***En*** *
responsable (m/f) de l'éducation *Fr*
Stadtschulrat (m) *De*

chief executive (city/borough/town) ***En*** *
secrétaire -général (m) (commune)/secrétaire-communal (m) (Belg.) *Fr*
Hauptverwaltungsbeamte(-r)/-beamtin (m/f)/Stadtdirektor/-in(m/f) *De*

chief executive (county) ***En***
directeur-général (m) (région, département) *Fr*
Hauptverwaltungsbeamte(-r)/-in (m/f) *De*

chief officer ***En***
chef (m) de service *Fr*
Amtsleiter (m) *De*

chiffre (m) d'affaires ***Fr***
Umsatz (m) *De*
turnover *En*

child abuse ***En***
violence (f) contre les enfants *Fr*
Kindesmißhandlung (f) *De*

child benefit ***En***
allocation (f) familiale *Fr*
Kindergeld (nt) *De*

child care ***En***
soin (m) des enfants *Fr*
Kinderfürsorge (f) *De*

child minder ***En***
assistante (f) maternelle *Fr*
Tagesmutter (f) *De*

child welfare centre ***En***
centre (m) de protection maternelle et enfantile *Fr*
Kinderabteilung (f) im Gesundheitsamt *De*

child welfare ***En***
protection (f) de l'enfance *Fr*
Kinderfürsorge (f) *De*

children at risk ***En***
enfance (f) en danger *Fr*
gefährdete Kinder (nt.pl) *De*

children in care ***En***
enfants (m/f.pl) placés *Fr*
Kinder (nt.pl) in Pflege *De*

children's home ***En***
home (m) d'enfants *Fr*
Kinderheim (nt) *De*

chômage (m) ***Fr***
Arbeitslosigkeit (f) *De*
unemployment *En*

chômage; en-(adj) ***Fr***
arbeitslos (adj) *De*
unemployed; unwaged (adj) *En*

chômage (m) de longue durée ***Fr***
Langzeitarbeitslosigkeit (f) *De*
long term unemployment *En*

chômage (m) des jeunes ***Fr***
Jugendarbeitslosigkeit (f) *De*
youth unemployment *En*

chômage (m) partiel ***Fr***
Kurzarbeit (f) *De*
short time working *En*

chômage (m) saisonnier ***Fr***
saisonabhängige Arbeitslosigkeit (f) *De*
seasonal unemployment *En*

chômeur (m) ***Fr***
Arbeitslose(r) (m/f) *De*
unemployed/unwaged person *En*

ci-joint (adv) ***Fr***
hiermit (adv) *De*
herewith (adv) *En*

circonscription (f) électorale ***Fr***
parlamentarischer Wahlkreis (m) *De*
parliamentary constituency *En*

circonscription (f) électorale ***Fr***
Wahlbezirk (m) *De*
electoral ward *En*

circonscription (f) électorale ***Fr***
Wahlbezirk (m) *De*
ward (constituency) *En*

circonscription (f) électorale ***Fr***
Wahlkreis (m) *De*
constituency *En*

circulaire (m) d'application ***Fr***
Anleitung (f) *De*
guidance note *En*

*** see/siehe/voir: Introduction page IX**

circular *En*
lettre (f) circulaire *Fr*
Rundbrief (m) *De*

circulate (vb) papers etc *En*
distribuer (vb) les papiers etc *Fr*
(Akten usw) zirkulieren lassen (vb) *De*

circulation (f) directe *Fr*
Durchgangsverkehr (m) *De*
through traffic *En*

circulation (f) intense *Fr*
starker Verkehr (m) *De*
heavy traffic *En*

circulation (f) routière *Fr*
Straßenverkehr (m) *De*
road traffic *En*

circulation (f) (routière) *Fr*
Verkehr (m) *De*
traffic *En*

citation (f) *Fr*
Vorladung (f) *De*
summons *En*

cité-jardin (f) *Fr*
Gartenstadt (f) *De*
garden city *En*

citer (vb) (quelqu'un à comparaître) *Fr*
(gerichtlich) vorladen (vb) *De*
summons (vb) (to appear in court) *En*

citizen *En*
citoyen (m) (-enne f.) *Fr*
Bürger/-in (m/f) *De*

citizens advice bureau *En* *
conciliateur (m) *Fr*
Bürgerberatungsstelle (f) *De*

citoyen (m) (-enne f.) *Fr*
Bürger/-in (m/f) *De*
citizen *En*

city centre *En*
centre (m) de la ville *Fr*
Innenstadt (f) *De*

City Council *En*
conseil (m) municipal *Fr*
Stadtrat (m) *De*

city *En*
(grande) ville (f) *Fr*
(Groß)stadt (f) *De*

City Hall *En*
hôtel (m) de ville *Fr*
Rathaus (nt) *De*

civic amenity centre *En*
centre (m) de récréations *Fr*
(städtisches) Freizeitzentrum (nt) *De*

civic centre *En*
centre (m) civique *Fr*
Verwaltungszentrum (nt) (einer Stadt) *De*

civic duties *En*
devoirs (m.pl) civiques *Fr*
staatsbürgerliche Pflichten (f.pl) *De*

civic occasions *En*
occasions (f.pl) civiques *Fr*
(offizielle) Stadtanlässe (m.pl) *De*

civil defence *En*
protection (f) civile *Fr*
Zivilschutz (m) *De*

civil engineer *En*
ingénieur (m) constructeur *Fr*
Bauingenieur/-in (m/f) *De*

civil engineering *En*
travaux (m.pl) publics *Fr*
Hoch- und Tiefbau (m) *De*

civil law *En*
droit (m) civil *Fr*
Zivilrecht (nt) *De*

civil liberty *En*
liberté (f) civile *Fr*
bürgerliche Freiheit (f) *De*

civil rights *En*
droits (m.pl) civiques *Fr*
Bürgerrechte (nt.pl) *De*

civil servant *En*
fonctionnaire (m/f) *Fr*
(Staats)beamte(-r)/-beamtin (m/f) *De*

claim (vb) *En*
réclamer (vb) *Fr*
beantragen (vb) *De*

claimant *En*
réclamant (m) *Fr*
Antragssteller/-in (m/f) *De*

classe (f) *Fr*
Altersgruppe (f) *De*
age group *En*

classement (m) (de documents) *Fr*
Ablage (f) *De*
filing *En*

classer (vb) *Fr*
ablegen (vb) *De*
file (vb) *En*

classes (f.pl) terminales *Fr*
Abschlußklasse (f) *De*
sixth form *En*

classeur (m) *Fr*
Aktenschrank (m) *De*
filing cabinet *En*

classroom *En*
salle (f) de classe *Fr*
Klassenzimmer (nt) *De*

clause (f) pénale (de dommages-intérêts) *Fr*
Strafklausel (f) *De*
penalty clause *En*

clavier (m) *Fr*
Tastatur (f) *De*
keyboard (computer) *En*

cleaner *En*
nettoyeur (m)/ nettoyeuse (f) *Fr*
Raumpfleger/-in (m/f) *De*

cleaning *En*
nettoyage (m) *Fr*
Reinigung (f), Putzen (nt) *De*

cleansing service *En*
service (m) d'assainissement *Fr*
Reinigungsdienst (m) *De*

clearing bank *En*
banque (f) de virement *Fr*
Girobank (f) *De*

clearway *En*
(grande) route (f) à stationnement interdit *Fr*
Straße (f) mit Halteverbot *De*

clerical staff *En*
personnel (m) d'exécution *Fr*
Büropersonal (nt) *De*

clerical work *En*
travail (m) de bureau *Fr*
Büroarbeit (f) *De*

clerk of works *En*
conducteur (m) des travaux *Fr*
Bauleiter/-in (m/f) *De*

clerk to the council *En* *
secrétaire-général (m) *Fr*
(Gemeinde)schriftführer (m) *De*

client *En*
client (m) *Fr*
Kunde/Kundin (m/f) *De*

*** see/siehe/voir: Introduction page IX**

client (m) *Fr*
Kunde/Kundin (m/f) *De*
client; customer *En*

client group *En*
clientèle (f) *Fr*
Kundschaft (f) *De*

client; customer *En*
client (m) *Fr*
Kunde/Kundin (m/f) *De*

clientèle (f) *Fr*
Kundschaft (f) *De*
client group *En*

clinic *En*
dispensaire (m) *Fr*
Klinik (f) *De*

clinical (adj) *En*
clinique (adj) *Fr*
klinisch (adj) *De*

clinique (adj) *Fr*
klinisch (adj) *De*
clinical (adj) *En*

clinique (f) du planning familial *Fr*
Familienberatungsstelle (f) *De*
family planning clinic *En*

clinique (f) privée *Fr*
privates Pflegeheim (nt) *De*
private home *En*

cluster analysis *En*
analyse (f) d'un fichier *Fr*
Klumpen-, Sammelanalyse (f) *De*

coach station *En*
gare (f) routière *Fr*
Busbahnhof (m) *De*

coal industry *En*
industrie (f) houillère *Fr*
Kohle(n)industrie (f) *De*

coal mine *En*
mine (f) de charbon *Fr*
Kohlenbergwerk (nt) *De*

coal mining *En*
exploitation (f) de la houille *Fr*
Kohlenbergbau (m) *De*

coalfield *En*
région (f) carbonifère *Fr*
Kohlenrevier (nt) *De*

coalition *En*
coalition (f) *Fr*
Koalition (f) *De*

coalition (f) *Fr*
Koalition (f) *De*
coalition *En*

coalition (to form a) (vb) *En*
se coaliser (vb) *Fr*
eine Koalition bilden (vb) *De*

code (m) de construction et d'urbanisme *Fr*
Eigentumsrecht (nt) *De*
property law *En*

code (m) de déontologie *Fr*
Verhaltenskodex (m) *De*
code of conduct *En*

code (m) du travail (secteur privé); statut (m) de la fonction publique territoriale *Fr*
Arbeitsrecht (nt) *De*
employment law *En*

code (m) postal *Fr*
Postleitzahl (f) *De*
postcode *En*

code of conduct *En*
code (m) de déontologie *Fr*
Verhaltenskodex (m) *De*

coffrage (m) (du béton) *Fr*
Schalung (f) *De*
shuttering *En*

collective bargaining *En*
convention (f) collective *Fr*
Tarifverhandlungen (f.pl) *De*

collectivité (f) territoriale *Fr*
Kommunalbehörde (f) *De*
local authority *En*

collège (m) *Fr*
Gesamtschule (f) *De*
comprehensive school *En*

collège (m) *Fr*
Oberschule (f) *De*
high school *En*

collège (m) (classique/moderne/techni-que) *Fr*
höhere Schule (f) *De*
secondary school *En*

collège (m) privé *Fr*
Privatschule (f) *De*
public school *En*

collège (m) subventionné par l'Etat (en GB) *Fr* *
subventionierte Schule (f) (in GB) *De*
grant maintained school (GB) *En*

collège (m) technique; lycée (m) technique *Fr*
Fachhochschule (f) *De*
technical college *En*

college of education *En*
école (f) normale *Fr*
Pädagogische Hochschule (f) *De*

college of higher education *En* *
école (f.) professionnelle d'enseignement supérieur *Fr*
Hochschule (f.) *De*

coloured people *En*
gens (m.pl) de couleur *Fr*
Farbige (pl) *De*

combustible (m) *Fr*
Brenn-, Kraftstoff (m) *De*
fuel *En*

comité (m) consultatif de consommateurs *Fr*
Konsumgenossenschaft (f) *De*
consumer council *En*

comité (m) consultatif *Fr*
beratender Ausschuß (m) *De*
consultative committee *En*

comité (m) de direction *Fr*
Hauptausschuß (m) *De*
management committee *En*

comité (m) de direction *Fr*
Lenkungsausschuß (m) *De*
steering committee *En*

comité (m) de probation *Fr*
Bewährungsdienst (m) *De*
probation service *En*

Comité (m) des Régions *Fr*
Regionalausschuß (m) *De*
Committee of the Regions *En*

commande (f) *Fr*
Bestellung (f) *De*
order (noun) *En*

commande (f) par correspondance *Fr*
Mail-order (f), Versandhandel (m) *De*
mail order *En*

commander (vb) *Fr*
bestellen (vb) *De*
order (vb) *En*

commerçant (m) (-ante f.) au détail *Fr*
Einzelhändler (m) *De*
retailer *En*

*** see/siehe/voir: Introduction page IX**

commerçant (m) (-ante f.) *Fr*
Ladenbesitzer/-in (m/f) *De*
shopkeeper *En*

commerce *En*
commerce (m) *Fr*
Handel (m) *De*

commerce (m) *Fr*
Handel (m) *De*
commerce *En*

commerce (m) *Fr*
Handel (m); Gewerbe (nt) *De*
trade *En*

commerce (m); faire (vb) le - (de /en qch, avec qn) *Fr*
Handel treiben (vb) *De*
trade (vb) *En*

commerce (m) au détail *Fr*
Einzelhandel (m) *De*
retail industry *En*

commerce (m) en gros *Fr*
Großhandel (m) *De*
wholesale trade *En*

commerce (m) extérieur *Fr*
Auslandsgeschäft (nt) *De*
foreign trade *En*

commercial centre *En*
centre (m) commercial *Fr*
Handelszentrum (nt) *De*

commercial development *En*
développement (m) commercial *Fr*
wirtschaftliche Entwicklung (f) *De*

commercial improvement area *En*
zone (f) d'amélioration commerciale *Fr*
wirtschaftliches Entwicklungsgebiet (nt) *De*

commercial premises *En*
locaux (m.pl) commerciaux *Fr*
Geschäftsräume (m.pl) *De*

commercial rate *En*
taxe (f) professionnelle *Fr*
Handelsrate (f) *De*

commercial transport *En*
transport (m) routier *Fr*
Fracht (f) *De*

commercial viability *En*
viabilité (f) commerciale *Fr*
wirtschaftliche Lebensfähigkeit (f) *De*

commercialisation (f)/techniques (f.pl) commerciales *Fr*
Marketing (nt) *De*
marketing *En*

commis-comptable (m) *Fr*
Buchhalter (m) *De*
bookkeeper *En*

commissaire (m) de comptes *Fr*
Rechnungsprüfer/-in (m/f) *De*
auditor *En*

Commissaire (m) de la République *Fr*
Staatsanwalt (m) *De*
Procurator Fiscal (Scotland) *En*

commissaire (m) de police *Fr* *
Polizeipräsident (m) *De*
chief constable *En*

commission (f) d'enquête *Fr*
Untersuchungsausschuß (m) *De*
committee of enquiry *En*

commission (f) d'urbanisme *Fr*
(Bau)planungsausschuß (m) *De*
planning & development committee *En*

Commission (f) des Communautés Européennes *Fr*
Europäische Kommission (f) *De*
European Commission *En*

commission (f) des finances *Fr*
finance/policy and resources committee *En*
Grundsatz-und-Ressourcenausschuß (m) *De*

committee chair(man) *En*
président (m) (-ente f.) d'un comité *Fr*
Ausschußvorsitzende(r) (m/f) *De*

committee clerk *En*
secrétaire (m/f) de séance *Fr*
Ausschußsekretär/-in (m/f) *De*

committee cycle *En*
période (f) de session *Fr*
Sitzungsturnus (m) *De*

committee meeting *En*
réunion (f) d'un comité *Fr*
Ausschußsitzung (f) *De*

committee of enquiry *En*
commission (f) d'enquête *Fr*
Untersuchungsausschuß (m) *De*

Committee of the Regions *En*
Comité (m) des Régions *Fr*
Regionalausschuß (m) *De*

committee report *En*
rapport (m) au comité *Fr*
Ausschußbericht (m) *De*

committee resolution *En*
voeux (m.pl) du comité *Fr*
Auschußbeschluß (m) *De*

common agricultural policy *En*
politique (f) agricole commune *Fr*
gemeinsame Agrarpolitik (f) *De*

common land *En*
champs (m.pl) communs *Fr*
Gemeindeland (nt) *De*

common law *En*
droit (m) coutumier *Fr*
Gewohnheitsrecht (nt) *De*

common market *En*
marché (m) commun *Fr*
Gemeinsamer Markt (m) *De*

communal (adj) *Fr*
kommunal (adj) *De*
communal *En*

communal *En*
communal (adj) *Fr*
kommunal (adj) *De*

Communauté (f) Economique Européenne *Fr*
Europäische Wirtschaftsgemeinschaft (f) *De*
European Economic Community *En*

communauté (f) *Fr*
Gemeinschaft (f) *De*
community *En*

communauté (f) rurale *Fr*
Landgemeinde (f) *De*
rural community *En*

commune *En*
commune (f) *Fr*
Kommune (f) *De*

commune (f) *Fr*
Kommune (f) *De*
commune *En*

*** see/siehe/voir: Introduction page IX**

communication *En*
communication (f) *Fr*
Kommunikation (f) *De*

communication (f) *Fr*
Kommunikation (f) *De*
communication *En*

communiqué (m) de presse *Fr*
Presseinformation (f) *De*
press release *En*

communism *En*
communisme (m) *Fr*
Kommunismus (m) *De*

communisme (m) *Fr*
Kommunismus (m) *De*
communism *En*

community *En*
communauté (f) *Fr*
Gemeinschaft (f) *De*

community action *En*
action (f) communautaire *Fr*
Gemeinschaftsaktion (f) *De*

community architecture *En*
architecture (f) intégrée *Fr*
Lokalarchitektur (f) *De*

community association *En*
association (f) communautaire *Fr*
Kommunalverband (m) *De*

community care *En*
action (f) sociale *Fr*
Gemeindefürsorge (f) *De*

community centre *En*
centre (m) social *Fr*
Gemeinschaftszentrum (nt) *De*

community charge *En*
impôts (m.pl) locaux *Fr*
Gemeindesteuer (f) *De*

community charge register *En*
liste (f) des contribuables *Fr*
Gemeindesteuerverzeichnis (nt) *De*

community development *En*
développement (m) communautaire *Fr*
Gemeindeentwicklung (f) *De*

community education *En*
éducation (f) civique *Fr*
Gemeinschaftskunde (f) *De*

community enterprise *En*
société (f) d'économie mixte *Fr*
Kommunalunternehmen (nt) *De*

community group *En*
association (f) locale *Fr*
Bürgergemeinschaft (f) *De*

community hall *En*
centre (m) social *Fr*
Gemeindehalle (f) *De*

community health care/ medecine *En*
service (m) de santé *Fr*
Bezirksgesundheitspflege (f) *De*

community health service *En*
service (m) de santé communautaire *Fr*
Bezirksgesundheitsamt (nt) *De*

community home *En*
résidence (f) pour personnes âgées *Fr*
Alten- Altersheim (nt) *De*

community initiative *En*
initiative (f) communautaire *Fr*
Kommunalinitiative (f) *De*

community land *En*
champs (m.pl) communs *Fr*
Kommunalgrundstück (nt) *De*

community policing *En*
maintien (m) de l'ordre locale *Fr*
Kommunalüberwachung (f) *De*

community relations *En*
intégration (f) sociale locale *Fr*
Verhältnis (nt) zwischen Bevölkerungsgruppen *De*

community service *En*
Travaux (m.pl) d'Intérêt Général (TIG) *Fr*
Sozialdienst (m) *De*

community work *En*
oeuvres (f.pl) sociales *Fr*
Sozialarbeit (f) *De*

community worker *En*
assistant (m) (-ante f.) social(e) *Fr*
Sozialberufler/-in (m/f) *De*

commuter *En*
personne (f) qui fait un long trajet journalier entre résidence et travail *Fr*
Pendler/-in (m/f) *De*

company *En*
société (f) *Fr*
Gesellschaft (f) *De*

company law *En*
droit (m) commercial *Fr*
Gesellschaftsrecht (nt) *De*

comparaître (vb) en justice *Fr*
vorgeladen werden; auftreten (vb) *De*
appear (vb) (in court) *En*

compensation (f) pour perte d'emploi *Fr*
Abfindung (f) *De*
severance pay *En*

competition *En*
concurrence (f) *Fr*
Wettbewerb (m) *De*

competitive tender *En*
soumission (f) compétitive *Fr*
konkurrenzfähiges Angebot (nt) *De*

competitive tendering *En*
mise (f) d'un travail en adjudication *Fr*
Ausschreibung (f) *De*

complaints procedure *En*
procédure (f) pour porter plainte *Fr*
Beschwerdeverfahren (nt) *De*

complément (f) de revenu *Fr*
zusätzliche Hilfe (f) zum Lebensunterhalt *De*
income support *En*

compléments (m.pl) de salaire en nature *Fr*
zusätzliche Leistungen (f.pl) *De*
fringe benefits *En*

complex (m) sportif *Fr*
Sportzentrum (nt) *De*
sports centre *En*

composition (f) de la famille *Fr*
Haushaltsstruktur (f) *De*
household composition/structure *En*

comprehensive school *En*
collège (m) *Fr*
Gesamtschule (f) *De*

comptabilité (f) en monnaie constante *Fr*
laufende Betriebskostenrechnung (f) *De*
current cost accounting *En*

comptabilité (f) *Fr*
Buchhaltung (f) *De*
accountancy/accounting *En*

*** see/siehe/voir: Introduction page IX**

comptable (m) ***Fr***
Buchhalter/Buchhälterin (m/f) *De*
accountant *En*

compte (m) ***Fr***
Konto (nt); Rechnung (f) *De*
account *En*

compte (m) de provisions ***Fr***
Einnahmebuch (nt) *De*
receipts account *En*

compte (m) découvert ***Fr***
Konto (nt) überzogen *De*
account overdrawn *En*

compte (m) des dépenses ***Fr***
Auszahlungskonto (nt) *De*
disbursements account *En*

compte (m) en banque ***Fr***
Bankkonto (nt) *De*
bank account *En*

compte (m) rendu ***Fr***
zur Begleichung vorgelegte Rechnung (f) *De*
account rendered *En*

comptes (m.pl) consolidés ***Fr***
konsolidierter Kontenabschluß (m) *De*
consolidated accounts *En*

comptes (m.pl) de gestion ***Fr***
Geschäftsbilanz (f) *De*
management accounts *En*

comptes (m.pl) vérifiés et certifiés ***Fr***
geprüfte Geschäftsbücher (nt.pl) *De*
audited accounts *En*

compteur (m) à eau ***Fr***
Wasserzähler (m), -uhr (f) *De*
water meter *En*

compteur (m) à gaz ***Fr***
Gaszähler (m) *De*
gas meter *En*

compulsory competitive tendering ***En***
mise (f) d'un travail en adjudication obligatoire *Fr*
Pflichtausschreibung (f) *De*

compulsory purchase ***En***
expropriation (f) *Fr*
Enteignung (f) *De*

compulsory purchase order (CPO) ***En***
contrat (m) d'expropriation *Fr*
Enteignungsbeschluß (m) *De*

Computer (m) ***De***
computer *En*
ordinateur (m) *Fr*

computer ***En***
ordinateur (m) *Fr*
Computer (m) *De*

computer aided design ***En***
dessein (m) assisté par ordinateur (DAO) *Fr*
computergestützter Entwurf (m) *De*

computer control ***En***
gestion (f) par ordinateur *Fr*
Computersteuerung (f) *De*

computer graphics ***En***
graphique (f) *Fr*
Computergraphik (f) *De*

computer industry ***En***
industrie (f) informatique *Fr*
Computerindustrie (f) *De*

computer printout ***En***
sortie (f) sur imprimante *Fr*
Computerausdruck (m) *De*

computer program ***En***
programme (m) machine *Fr*
(Computer)programm (nt) *De*

(Computer)programm (nt) ***De***
computer program *En*
programme (m) machine *Fr*

computer programmer ***En***
programmeur (m) *Fr*
Programmierer (m) *De*

computer programming language ***En***
langage (m) machine *Fr*
Programmiersprache (f) *De*

computer service ***En***
service (m) informatique *Fr*
Computerdienst (m) *De*

computer software ***En***
logiciel (m) *Fr*
Software (f) *De*

computer suite ***En***
salle (f) informatique *Fr*
Computerbüro (nt) *De*

Computerausdruck (m) ***De***
computer printout *En*
sortie (f) sur imprimante *Fr*

Computerbüro (nt) ***De***
computer suite *En*
salle (f) informatique *Fr*

Computerdienst (m) ***De***
computer service *En*
service (m) informatique *Fr*

computergestützter Entwurf (m) ***De***
computer aided design *En*
dessein (m) assisté par ordinateur (DAO) *Fr*

Computergraphik (f) ***De***
computer graphics *En*
graphique (f) *Fr*

Computerindustrie (f) ***De***
computer industry *En*
industrie (f) informatique *Fr*

computerization ***En***
informatisation (f) *Fr*
Computerisierung (f) *De*

Computerisierung (f) ***De***
computerization *En*
informatisation (f) *Fr*

Computersteuerung (f) ***De***
computer control *En*
gestion (f) par ordinateur *Fr*

comté (m) (en GB) ***Fr***
Grafschaft (f) (in GB) *De*
county (GB) *En*

conception (f) des grandes routes ***Fr***
Straßenplanung (f) *De*
highway design *En*

concession (f) ***Fr***
Lizenz (f) *De*
franchise (business) *En*

concession (f) de services publics ***Fr***
Ermöglichung (f) *De*
enabling role *En*

concessionary fare ***En***
tarif (m) réduit *Fr*
ermäßigter Tarif (m) *De*

concessionnaire (m) ***Fr***
Konzessionär (m) *De*
distributor *En*

concièrge (m/f) ***Fr***
Hausmeister (m) *De*
caretaker *En*

*** see/siehe/voir: Introduction page IX**

conciliateur (m) *Fr*
Bürgerberatungsstelle (f) *De*
citizens advice bureau *En*

conciliation *En*
conciliation (f) *Fr*
Schlichtung (f) *De*

conciliation (f) *Fr*
Schlichtung (f) *De*
conciliation *En*

concurrence (f) *Fr*
Wettbewerb (m) *De*
competition *En*

condamnation (f) avec sursis *Fr*
Strafe (f) mit Bewährung *De*
suspended sentence *En*

condition (f) des maisons *Fr*
Wohnbedingungen (f.pl) *De*
housing condition *En*

conditions (f.pl) d'emploi *Fr*
Arbeitsbedingungen (f.pl) *De*
employment conditions *En*

conditions (f.pl) de paiement *Fr*
Zahlungsbedingungen (f.pl) *De*
terms of payment *En*

conditions (f.pl) de service *Fr*
Arbeitsbedingungen (f.pl) *De*
conditions of service *En*

conditions (f.pl) de travail *Fr*
Arbeitsbedingungen (f.pl) *De*
working conditions *En*

conditions of contract *En*
cahier (m) des charges *Fr*
Vertragsbedingungen (f.pl) *De*

conditions of employment *En*
définition (f) d'un emploi *Fr*
Arbeitsbedingungen (f.pl) *De*

conditions of service *En*
conditions (f.pl) de service *Fr*
Arbeitsbedingungen (f.pl) *De*

conducteur (m) des travaux *Fr*
Bauleiter/-in (m/f) *De*
clerk of works *En*

conduit (m) d'effluent *Fr*
Abflußrohr (nt) *De*
soil pipe *En*

conduite (f) d'eau *Fr*
Hauptwasserleitung (f) *De*
water main *En*

conduite (f) en état d'ivresse *Fr*
Alkohol (m) am Steuer *De*
drink driving *En*

conference *En*
congrès (m) *Fr*
Konferenz (f) *De*

conférence (f) *Fr*
Vorlesung (f) *De*
lecture *En*

conférence (f); faire (vb) une —. *Fr*
eine Vorlesung halten (vb) *De*
lecture (vb) *En*

conference centre *En*
centre (m) de conférences *Fr*
Konferenzzentrum (nt) *De*

conférence (f) de presse *Fr*
Pressekonferenz (f) *De*
press conference *En*

confiance (f) publique *Fr*
Vertrauen (nt) der Öffentlichkeit *De*
public confidence *En*

confidentiality *En*
caractère (m) confidentiel *Fr*
Vertraulichkeit (f) *De*

conflict of interest *En*
heurt (m) d'intérêts *Fr*
Interessenkonflikt (m) *De*

conflit (m) du travail *Fr*
Arbeitskonflikt (m) *De*
industrial dispute *En*

confrontation *En*
confrontation (f) *Fr*
Konfrontation (f) *De*

confrontation (f) *Fr*
Konfrontation (f) *De*
confrontation *En*

congé (m) *Fr*
Kündigung (f) *De*
notice to quit *En*

congé (m) de maladie *Fr*
Krankenurlaub (m); Krankengeld (nt) *De*
sick leave/sickness benefit *En*

congé (m) de maternité *Fr*
Mutterschaftsurlaub (m) *De*
maternity leave *En*

congé (m) de paternité *Fr*
Vaterschaftsurlaub (m) *De*
paternity leave *En*

congé (m) payé *Fr*
bezahlter Urlaub (m) *De*
holiday with pay *En*

congé (m) statutaire *Fr*
Urlaubanspruch (m) *De*
holiday entitlement *En*

congédier (vb) *Fr*
entlassen (vb) *De*
dismiss (vb) *En*

congrès (m) *Fr*
Konferenz (f) *De*
conference *En*

congés (m.pl) payés *Fr*
bezahlter Urlaub (m) *De*
paid holidays *En*

conjoncture (f) du marché *Fr*
Kräfte (f.pl) des freien Markts *De*
market forces *En*

conseil (m) commercial *Fr*
geschäftlicher Ratschlag (m) *De*
business advice *En*

conseil (m) consultatif *Fr*
Beratungsgremium (nt) *De*
advisory body *En*

conseil (m) d'administration d'un hôpital (en GB) *Fr* *
Krankenhaustreuhandgesellschaft (f) (in GB) *De*
hospital trust (in GB) *En*

conseil (m) d'administration *Fr*
Managementteam (nt) *De*
management team *En*

conseil (m) d'administration *Fr*
Vorstand (m) *De*
board of directors *En*

conseil (m) d'administration *Fr*
Vorstand (m) *De*
governing board/body *En*

conseil (m) départemental/général *Fr*
Grafschaftsrat (m) *De*
county council *En*

conseil (m) en gestion *Fr*
Unternehmensberater (m) *De*
management consultant *En*

*** see/siehe/voir: Introduction page IX**

conseil (m) financier *Fr*
Finanzberatung (f) *De*
financial advice *En*

conseil (m) judiciaire *Fr*
juristischer Rat (m) *De*
legal advice *En*

conseil (m) municipal (d'une petite commune) *Fr*
Gemeinderat (m) *De*
parish council *En*

conseil (m) municipal *Fr*
Gemeinderat (m) *De*
local council *En*

conseil (m) municipal *Fr* *
Kreisausschuß (m), Kreisrat (m) *De*
district council *En*

conseil (m) municipal *Fr*
Stadtrat (m) *De*
City Council *En*

conseil (m) municipal *Fr*
Stadtrat (m) *De*
town council *En*

conseil (m) municipal *Fr* *
Stadtverwaltung (f), Gemeinderat (m) *De*
borough council *En*

conseil (m) où aucun parti n'a la majorité absolue *Fr*
Rat (m), in dem keine Partei die absolute Mehrheit hat *De*
hung council *En*

conseil (m) où aucun parti n'a la majorité absolue *Fr*
Rat (m) mit Kräftegleichgewicht *De*
balanced council *En*

conseil (m) qui a le droit de prendre des décisions *Fr*
Entscheidungsträger (m) *De*
decision-making body *En*

conseil (m) régional *Fr*
Regionalausschuß (m), Gemeinderat (m) *De*
regional assembly/council *En*

conseiller (m) (-ère f) *Fr*
Berater/-in (m/f) *De*
counsellor *En*

conseiller (m) (-ère f.) à la chambre régionale des comptes *Fr*
Rechnungsprüfer (m) *De*
district auditor *En*

conseiller (m) (-ère f.) d'orientation *Fr*
Berufsberater/-in (m/f) *De*
careers officer *En*

conseiller (m) général *Fr* *
Grafschaftsverordnete(r) (m/f) *De*
county councillor *En*

conseiller (m) (-ère f.) juridique *Fr*
Rechtsberater/-in (m/f) *De*
law officer *En*

conseiller (m) (ère f.) /membre (m) du conseil *Fr*
Stadtverordnete(r) (m/f) *De*
councillor *En*

conseiller (m) (-ère f.) municipal(e) *Fr*
Gemeinderat/Gemeinderätin (m) *De*
local councillor *En*

consent *En*
consentement (m) *Fr*
Zustimmung (f) *De*

consentement (m) *Fr*
Zustimmung (f) *De*
consent *En*

consequential loss *En*
perte (f) indirecte *Fr*
Folgeschaden (m) *De*

conservateur (m) (-trice f.) *Fr*
Konservative(-r) (m/f) *De*
conservative *En*

conservateur(m) (-trice f.) *Fr*
Tory (m), Konservative(-r) (m/f) *De*
tory *En*

conservation (f) *Fr*
Erhaltung (f) *De*
preservation *En*

conservation area *En*
zone (f) protégée *Fr*
Naturschutz-, Landschaftsschutzgebiet (nt) *De*

conservation (f) de l'eau *Fr*
Wasserschutz (m) *De*
water conservation *En*

conservation (f) de la nature *Fr*
Naturschutz (m) *De*
nature conservation *En*

conservation grant *En*
participation (f) à la maintenance d'un bâtiment historique *Fr*
Beihilfe (f) für unter Denkmalschutz stehendes Gebäude *De*

conservationist *En*
partisan (m) (-ane f.) de la conservation *Fr*
Umweltschützer/-in (m/f) *De*

conservative *En*
conservateur (m) (-trice f.) *Fr*
Konservative(r) (m/f) *De*

conservative estimate *En*
évaluation (f) prudente *Fr*
vorsichtige Schätzung (f) *De*

consignment *En*
expédition (f) *Fr*
Versendung (f) *De*

consolidated accounts *En*
comptes (m.pl) consolidés *Fr*
konsolidierter Kontenabschluß (m) *De*

consolidation (f) *Fr*
Fundierung (f) *De*
funding *En*

consolider (vb) *Fr*
finanzieren (vb) *De*
fund (vb) *En*

consommateur (m) (-trice f.) *Fr*
Verbraucher/-in (m/f) *De*
consumer *En*

consommation (f) d'énergie *Fr*
Energieverbrauch (m) *De*
power consumption *En*

consommation (f) de combustible *Fr*
Brennstoffverbrauch (m) *De*
fuel consumption *En*

consommation (f) de l'électricité *Fr*
Stromverbrauch (m) *De*
electricity consumption *En*

consortium *En*
consortium (m) *Fr*
Konsortium (nt) *De*

consortium (m) *Fr*
Konsortium (nt) *De*
consortium *En*

*** see/siehe/voir: Introduction page IX**

constable ***En***
agent (m) de police *Fr*
Polizist/-in (m/f) *De*

constituency ***En***
circonscription (f) électorale *Fr*
Wahlkreis (m) *De*

constituent ***En***
électeur (m) (-trice f.) *Fr*
Wähler/-in (m/f) *De*

constitution ***En***
constitution (f) *Fr*
Verfassung (f) *De*

constitution (f) ***Fr***
Verfassung (f) *De*
constitution *En*

constitutional law ***En***
droit (m) constitutionnel *Fr*
Verfassungsrecht (nt) *De*

constitutional reform ***En***
réforme (f) constitutionnelle *Fr*
Verfassungsreform (f) *De*

construction (f) dangereuse ***Fr***
gefährliche Konstruktion (f) *De*
dangerous structure *En*

construction (f) des grandes routes ***Fr***
Straßenbau (m) *De*
highway construction *En*

construction (f) du terrain ***Fr***
Geländeerschließung (f) *De*
site development *En*

construction (f) navale ***Fr***
Schiffbau (m) *De*
shipbuilding *En*

construction (f) routière ***Fr***
Straßenbau (m) *De*
road building/construction *En*

construction industry ***En***
bâtiment (m) *Fr*
Bauindustrie (f) *De*

constructions (f.pl) mécaniques ***Fr***
Maschinenbau (m) *De*
mechanical engineering *En*

construit en vue d'un usage déterminé (adj) ***Fr***
speziell gebaut; Zweck- *De*
purpose-built (adj) *En*

consulat (m) ***Fr***
Konsulat (nt) *De*
consulate *En*

consulate ***En***
consulat (m) *Fr*
Konsulat (nt) *De*

consult (vb) ***En***
consulter (vb) *Fr*
sich beraten, konsultieren (vb) *De*

consultancy ***En***
cabinet (m) d'experts-conseils *Fr*
Beratung (f); Beratungsbüro (nt) *De*

consultant ***En***
expert-conseil (m) *Fr*
Berater/-in (m/f) *De*

consultation ***En***
consultation (f) *Fr*
Beratung (f) *De*

consultation (f) ***Fr***
Beratung (f) *De*
consultation *En*

consultative committee ***En***
comité (m) consultatif *Fr*
beratender Ausschuß (m) *De*

consulter (vb) ***Fr***
sich beraten, konsultieren (vb) *De*
consult (vb) *En*

consumer ***En***
consommateur (m) (-trice f.) *Fr*
Verbraucher/-in (m/f) *De*

consumer council ***En***
comité (m) consultatif de consommateurs *Fr*
Konsumgenossenschaft (f) *De*

consumer durables ***En***
biens (m.pl) de consommation durables *Fr*
langlebige Konsumgüter (nt.pl) *De*

consumer goods ***En***
biens (m.pl) de consommation *Fr*
Konsumgüter (nt.pl) *De*

consumer group ***En***
groupe (m) consommateur *Fr*
Abnehmerverein (m) *De*

consumer law ***En*** *
droit (m) du consommateur *Fr*
Konsumgesetz (nt) *De*

container ***En***
conteneur (m) *Fr*
Container (m) *De*

Container (m) ***De***
container *En*
conteneur (m) *Fr*

container terminal ***En***
port (m) pour conteneurs *Fr*
Containerterminal (nt) *De*

containerization ***En***
conteneurisation (f) *Fr*
Verpackung (f) in Container *De*

Containerterminal (nt) ***De***
container terminal *En*
port (m) pour conteneurs *Fr*

contamination (f) de la nourriture ***Fr***
Lebensmittelverseuchung (f) *De*
food contamination *En*

contempt of court ***En***
outrage (m) au tribunal *Fr*
Ungebühr (f) vor Gericht *De*

conteneur (m) ***Fr***
Container (m) *De*
container *En*

conteneurisation (f) ***Fr***
Verpackung (f) in Container *De*
containerization *En*

continental (adj) ***En***
continental (adj) *Fr*
kontinental (adj) *De*

continental (adj) ***Fr***
kontinental (adj) *De*
continental (adj) *En*

contingency plan ***En***
programme (m) pour l'imprévu *Fr*
Alternativplan (m) *De*

contingency reserve ***En***
provision (f) *Fr*
Sonderrücklage (f) *De*

continuing education ***En***
éducation (f) permanente *Fr*
Fortbildung (f) *De*

contract ***En***
contrat (m) *Fr*
Vertrag (m) *De*

contract cleaning ***En***
nettoyage (m) au contrat *Fr*
Auftragsreinigung (f) *De*

contract compliance ***En***
exécution (f) de contrat *Fr*
Vertragseinhaltung (f) *De*

contract law ***En***
droit (m) des obligations *Fr*
Vertragsrecht (nt) *De*

contract management ***En***
gestion (f) de contrat *Fr*
Projektmanagement (nt) *De*

*** see/siehe/voir: Introduction page IX**

contract of employment *En*
contrat (m) d'emploi *Fr*
Arbeitsvertrag (m) *De*

contract out (vb) *En*
renoncer (vb) par contrat *Fr*
nicht beitreten (vb) *De*

contract regulations *En*
dispositions (f.pl) d'un contrat *Fr*
Vertragsvorschriften (f.pl) *De*

contractant (m) privé *Fr*
privater Auftragnehmer (m) *De*
private contractor *En*

contractor *En*
adjudicataire (m) *Fr*
Auftragnehmer/-in (m/f) *De*

contractual claim *En*
créance (f) contractuelle *Fr*
vertraglicher Anspruch (m) *De*

contractuel (m) (-elle f.) *Fr*
Hilfspolizist/-in (m/f); Politesse (f) *De*
traffic warden *En*

contrainte (f) sur les salaires *Fr*
Zurückhaltung (f) bei Lohnforderungen *De*
wage restraint *En*

contrat (m) *Fr*
Vertrag (m) *De*
contract *En*

contrat (m) à durée déterminée *Fr*
Fixvertrag (m) *De*
fixed term contract *En*

contrat (m) d'emploi *Fr*
Arbeitsvertrag (m) *De*
contract of employment *En*

contrat (m) d'expropriation *Fr*
Enteignungsbeschluß (m) *De*
compulsory purchase order (CPO) *En*

contrat (m) de bâtiment *Fr*
Bauvertrag (m) *De*
building contract *En*

contrat (m) de location *Fr*
Mietvertrag (m) *De*
tenancy agreement *En*

contrat (m) de service *Fr*
Dienstleistungsvertrag (m) *De*
service (level) agreement *En*

contrat (m) gouvernemental *Fr*
Regierungsauftrag (m) *De*
government contract *En*

contremaître (m) *Fr*
Vorarbeiter (m) *De*
foreman *En*

contribuable (m/f) à l'impôt local *Fr*
Kommunalsteuerzahler/-in (m/f) *De*
ratepayer *En*

contribuable (m/f) *Fr*
Steuerzahler/-in (m/f) *De*
taxpayer *En*

contributions (f.pl) directes *Fr*
direkte Steuern (f.pl) *De*
direct taxation *En*

contributions (f.pl) foncières *Fr*
Grundsteuer (f) *De*
land tax *En*

contributions (f.pl) indirectes *Fr*
indirekte Steuern (f.pl) *De*
indirect taxation *En*

contrôle (m) budgétaire *Fr*
Budgetkontrolle (f) *De*
budgetary control *En*

contrôle (m) d'émission *Fr*
Abgaskontrolle (f) *De*
emission control *En*

contrôle (m) de construction *Fr*
Baukontrolle (f), Bauaufsicht (f) *De*
building control *En*

contrôle (m) de gestion *Fr*
Geschäftsrechnungsprüfung (f) *De*
management audit *En*

contrôle (m) de l'air *Fr*
Luftqualitätskontrolle (f) *De*
air monitoring *En*

contrôle (m) de l'aménagement *Fr*
Erschließungskontrolle (f) der Entwicklung *De*
development control *En*

contrôle (m) de l'environnement *Fr*
Umweltkontrolle (f) *De*
environmental control *En*

contrôle (m) de l'immigration *Fr*
Einwanderungskontrolle (f) *De*
immigration control *En*

contrôle (m) de la circulation *Fr*
Verkehrskontrolle (f) *De*
traffic control *En*

contrôle (m) de la pollution *Fr*
Verschmutzungskontrolle (f) *De*
pollution control/monitoring *En*

contrôle (m) de qualité *Fr*
Qualitätsgarantie (f), -kontrolle (f) *De*
quality assurance/control *En*

contrôle (m) des changes *Fr*
Devisenkontrolle (f) *De*
currency control *En*

contrôle (m) des changes *Fr*
Devisenkontrolle (f) *De*
exchange control *En*

contrôle (m) des coûts *Fr*
Kostenkontrolle (f) *De*
cost control *En*

contrôle (m) des finances *Fr*
Finanzkontrolle (f) *De*
financial control *En*

contrôle (m) des poids-lourds *Fr*
Lastkraftwagenkontrolle (f) *De*
lorry control *En*

contrôle (m) des stocks *Fr*
Warenbestandkontrolle (f) *De*
stock control *En*

contrôle (m) du projet *Fr*
Projektaufsicht (f) *De*
project control *En*

contrôle (m) externe *Fr*
externe Rechnungsprüfung (f) *De*
external audit *En*

contrôle (m) interne *Fr*
innerbetriebliche Rechnungsprüfung (f) *De*
internal audit *En*

contrôle (m) politique *Fr*
politische Kontrolle (f) *De*
political control *En*

contrôleur (m) des contributions directes *Fr*
Steuerinspektor/-in (m/f) *De*
inspector of taxes *En*

controlled tenancy *En* *
loyers (m.pl) soumis à réglementation HLM *Fr*
Mietpreisüberwachnung (f) *De*

controversial issues *En*
questions (f.pl) controversables *Fr*
strittige Fragen (f.pl) *De*

conurbation *En*
conurbation (f) *Fr*
Konurbation (f) *De*

conurbation (f) *Fr*
Konurbation (f) *De*
conurbation *En*

convention (f) collective *Fr*
Tarifverhandlungen (f.pl) *De*
collective bargaining *En*

convention (f) *Fr*
(rechtliche) Vereinbarung (f) *De*
agreement (legal) *En*

convention (f) irrévocable *Fr*
bindender Vertrag (m) *De*
binding agreement *En*

convention (f) (par écrit) *Fr*
Abkommen (nt) *De*
agreement (in writing) *En*

converted buildings *En*
bâtiments (m.pl) aménagés *Fr*
Umbauten (m.pl) *De*

conveyancing *En*
rédaction (f) des actes translatifs de propriété *Fr*
(Eigentums)übertragung (f) *De*

convoi (m) exceptionnel *Fr*
Schwertransport (m) mit Überbreite *De*
abnormal load *En*

coopérative (f) industrielle *Fr*
gewerbliche Genossenschaft (f) *De*
industrial co-operative *En*

coopérative (f) ouvrière de production (COOP) *Fr*
Produktivgenossenschaft (f) *De*
worker co-operative *En*

cooptation (f) *Fr*
Kooptation (f) *De*
co-option *En*

co-opted member (of council) *En*
membre (m) coopté du conseil *Fr*
berufene(-r) Sachkundige(-r) (m/f) *De*

co-option *En*
cooptation (f) *Fr*
Kooptation (f) *De*

coordination (f) des projets *Fr*
Unternehmensbewertung (f) *De*
project co-ordination *En*

co-ordinator *En*
coordonnateur (m) (-trice f.) *Fr*
Koordinator/-in (m/f) *De*

coordonnateur (m) (-trice f.) *Fr*
Koordinator/-in (m/f) *De*
co-ordinator *En*

copie (f) pour information *Fr*
Kopie (f) zur Information *De*
copy for information *En*

copy for information *En*
copie (f) pour information *Fr*
Kopie (f) zur Information *De*

copy typist *En*
dactylo copiste (f) *Fr*
Abschreibtypistin (f) *De*

corbeille (f) à papiers *Fr*
Papierkorb (m) *De*
waste paper basket *En*

coroner *En*
coroner (m) *Fr*
Coroner (m) *De*

Coroner (m) *De*
coroner *En*
coroner (m) *Fr*

coroner (m) *Fr*
Coroner (m) *De*
coroner *En*

corporate image *En*
image (f) de marque de la firme/de l'organisation *Fr*
Firmenimage (nt) *De*

corporate management *En*
management (m) *Fr*
Firmenleitung (f) *De*

corporate plan *En*
plan (m) d'ensemble *Fr*
Korporationsplan (m) *De*

corporate policy *En*
politique (f) de la firme *Fr*
Geschäftspolitik (f) *De*

corporate responsibility *En*
responsabilité (f) corporative *Fr*
Gesamtverantwortung (f) *De*

corporate strategy *En*
stratégie (f) corporative *Fr*
Unternehmensstrategie (f) *De*

corporation tax *En*
impôt (m) sur le revenu des sociétés *Fr*
Körperschaftssteuer (f) *De*

corps (m) d'inspecteurs *Fr*
Inspektion (f) *De*
inspectorate *En*

corps (m) de sapeurs-pompiers *Fr*
Feuerwehr (f) *De*
fire brigade/service *En*

corps (m) électoral *Fr*
Wähler (pl), Wählerschaft (f) *De*
electorate *En*

corps (m) enseignant *Fr*
Lehrberuf (m) *De*
teaching profession *En*

correspondance(f) *Fr*
Korrespondenz (f) *De*
correspondence *En*

correspondence *En*
correspondance(f) *Fr*
Korrespondenz (f) *De*

cost analysis *En*
analyse (f) des coûts *Fr*
Kostenanalyse (f) *De*

cost benefit analysis *En*
analyse (f) des coûts et rendements *Fr*
Kosten-Nutzen-Analyse (f) *De*

cost centre *En*
centre (m) de responsabilité *Fr*
Kostenstelle (f) *De*

cost control *En*
contrôle (m) des coûts *Fr*
Kostenkontrolle (f) *De*

cost cutting *En*
réduction (f) des coûts *Fr*
Kostenverringerung (f) *De*

cost effectiveness *En*
rapport (m) qualité-prix *Fr*
Rentabilität (f) *De*

cost of living allowance *En*
maintien (m) du pouvoir d'achat *Fr*
Zuschuß (m) zu den Lebenshaltungskosten *De*

cost of living *En*
coût (m) de la vie *Fr*
Lebenshaltungskosten (pl) *De*

*** see/siehe/voir: Introduction page IX**

cost planning *En*
programmation (f) des dépenses *Fr*
Kostenplanung (f) *De*

cost-effectiveness *En*
coût (m) et efficacité (f) *Fr*
Wirtschaftlichkeit (f) *De*

costing *En*
évaluation (f) du coût *Fr*
Kostenberechnung (f) *De*

costs *En*
prix (m.pl) de revient *Fr*
Kosten (pl) *De*

coucher (vb) sur la dure *Fr*
(im Freien) schlafen (vb) *De*
sleep (vb) rough *En*

council chamber *En*
salle (f) du conseil *Fr*
Sitzungssaal (m) des Rats *De*

council dwelling/flat/house *En*
habitation (f) à loyer modéré (HLM) *Fr*
Sozialwohnung (f) *De*

council estate *En*
groupe (m) de HLM *Fr*
Wohnviertel (nt) mit Sozialwohnungen *De*

council house sales *En* *
vente (f) des HLM *Fr*
Verkauf (m) von Sozialwohnungen *De*

council meeting *En*
réunion (f) du conseil *Fr*
Ratssitzung (f) *De*

council member *En*
membre (m) du conseil *Fr*
Gemeinderats-, Stadtratsmitglied (nt) *De*

council tax *En* *
impôt (m) local *Fr*
Gemeindesteuer (f) *De*

councillor *En*
conseiller (m) (-ère f.)/membre (m) du conseil *Fr*
Stadtverordnete(-r) (m/f) *De*

counsel *En*
avocat (m) *Fr*
Anwalt/Anwältin (m/f) *De*

counselling service *En*
service (m) conseil *Fr*
Beratungsdienst (m) *De*

counsellor *En*
conseiller (m) (-ère f.) *Fr*
Berater/-in (m/f) *De*

country planning *En*
aménagement (m) des campagnes *Fr*
Landesplanung (f) *De*

county (GB) *En*
comté (m) (en GB) *Fr*
Grafschaft (f) (in GB) *De*

county council *En* *
conseil (m) départemental/général *Fr*
Grafschaftsrat (m) *De*

county councillor *En* *
conseiller (m) général *Fr*
Grafschaftsverordnete(r) (m/f) *De*

county court *En* *
tribunaux (m.pl) de première instance *Fr*
Grafschaftsgericht (nt) *De*

county hall *En*
hôtel (m) du département *Fr*
Kreishaus (nt) *De*

county structure plan *En*
plan (m) d'ensemble du comté/département *Fr*
Bezirksstrukturplan (m) *De*

county town *En* *
chef-lieu de comté/département *Fr*
Grafschaftshauptstadt (f) *De*

coupure (f) de journal *Fr*
Zeitungsausschnitt (m) *De*
press cutting *En*

cour (f) d'appel *Fr*
Berufungsgericht (nt) *De*
court of appeal *En*

cour (f) de justice *Fr*
Gerichtsgebäude (nt) *De*
law court *En*

cour (f) de récréation *Fr*
Freizeitgelände (nt) *De*
recreation area *En*

cour (f) de récréation *Fr*
Spielplatz (m) *De*
play area/ground *En*

courrier (m) *Fr*
Post (f) *De*
mail *En*

courrier (m) électronique *Fr*
elektronische Post (f) *De*
electronic mail *En*

cours (m) du change *Fr*
Wechselkurs (m) *De*
exchange rate *En*

cours (m) de perfectionnement (à l'établissement où on travaille) *Fr*
innerbetriebliche Fortbildung (f) *De*
in-service training/INSET *En*

court *En*
tribunal (m) *Fr*
Gericht (nt) *De*

court of appeal *En*
cour (f) d'appel *Fr*
Berufungsgericht (nt) *De*

court order *En*
autorité (f) de justice *Fr*
gerichtliche Verfügung (f) *De*

court terme; à — — (adj) Fr
kurzfristig (adj) De
short term (adj) En

courtier (m) en bourse *Fr*
Börsenmakler (m) *De*
stockbroker *En*

coût (m) d'investissement *Fr*
Kapitalkosten (pl) *De*
capital cost *En*

coût (m) de construction *Fr*
Baukosten (pl) *De*
building costs *En*

coût (m) de l'unité *Fr*
Kosten (pl) pro Einheit *De*
unit cost *En*

coût (m) de la vie *Fr*
Lebenshaltungskosten (pl) *De*
cost of living *En*

coût (m) et efficacité (f) *Fr*
Wirtschaftlichkeit (f) *De*
cost-effectiveness *En*

coût (m) foncier *Fr*
Erschließungswert (m) *De*
development value *En*

coût (m) marginal *Fr*
Grenzkosten (pl) *De*
marginal cost *En*

coût (m) variable *Fr*
variable Kosten (pl) *De*
variable cost *En*

*** see/siehe/voir: Introduction page IX**

Craft Design and Technology CDT *En*
technologie (f) et travaux (m.pl) manuels *Fr*
Werken (nt), Gestaltung (f) und Technologie (f) *De*

craftsman *En*
artisan (m) *Fr*
Handwerker (m) *De*

crash barrier *En*
glissière (f) *Fr*
Leitplanke (f) *De*

créance (f) contractuelle *Fr*
vertraglicher Anspruch (m) *De*
contractual claim *En*

créancier (m) *Fr*
Gläubiger/-in (m/f) *De*
creditor *En*

création (f) d'emploi *Fr*
Arbeitsbeschaffung (f) *De*
employment creation *En*

crèche (f) *Fr*
Kinderkrippe (f) *De*
creche *En*

creche *En*
crèche (f) *Fr*
Kinderkrippe (f) *De*

crèche (f) au lieu de travail *Fr*
(betriebseigene) Kinderkrippe (f) *De*
workplace nursery *En*

crèche (f) collective *Fr*
Kindertagesheim (nt), Kindertagesstätte (f) *De*
day nursery *En*

credit *En*
crédit (m) *Fr*
Kredit (m) *De*

crédit (m) *Fr*
Kredit (m) *De*
credit *En*

credit card *En*
carte (f) de crédit *Fr*
Kreditkarte (f) *De*

crédit (m) provisoire *Fr*
Vorschußkredit (m) *De*
bridging loan *En*

credit note *En*
avis (m) de crédit *Fr*
Gutschriftanzeige (f) *De*

credit transfer *En*
transfert (m) de fonds *Fr*
Banküberweisung (f) *De*

crédit-bail (m) *Fr*
Leasing (nt) *De*
leasing *En*

creditor *En*
créancier (m) *Fr*
Gläubiger/-in (m/f) *De*

crime rate *En*
taux (m) du crime *Fr*
Kriminalitätsrate (f) *De*

criminal court *En*
tribunal (m) criminel *Fr*
Strafgericht (nt) *De*

criminal law *En*
droit (m) criminel *Fr*
Strafrecht (nt) *De*

crise (f) du logement *Fr*
Mangel (m) an Häusern/Wohnungen *De*
housing shortage *En*

crise (f) économique *Fr*
Depression (f) *De*
slump *En*

crise (f) économique *Fr*
Wirtschaftskrise (f) *De*
depression *En*

critical path analysis *En*
analyse (f) de chemin critique *Fr*
kritische Pfadanalyse (f) *De*

croissance (f) économique *Fr*
Wirtschaftswachstum (nt) *De*
economic growth *En*

cross-curricular *En*
à travers le programme d'études *Fr*
quer durch das Pensum (nt) *De*

cultural policy *En*
politique (f) culturelle *Fr*
Kulturpolitik (f) *De*

currency *En*
unité (f) monétaire *Fr*
Währung (f) *De*

currency control *En*
contrôle (m) des changes *Fr*
Devisenkontrolle (f) *De*

current cost accounting *En*
comptabilité (f) en monnaie constante *Fr*
laufende Betriebskostenrechnung (f) *De*

current expenditure *En*
dépenses (f.pl) de fonctionnement *Fr*
laufende Ausgaben (f.pl) *De*

curriculum *En*
programme (m) d'études *Fr*
Lehrplan (m) *De*

curriculum development *En* *
développement (m) du plan d'études *Fr*
Lehrplangestaltung (f) *De*

customer care *En*
soins (m.pl) du client *Fr*
Kundenbetreuung (f) *De*

customer relations *En*
relations (f.pl) avec la clientèle *Fr*
Kundenbeziehungen (f.pl) *De*

customer service *En*
service (m) de la clientèle *Fr*
Kundendienst (m) *De*

customs *En*
douane (f) *Fr*
Zoll (m) *De*

customs clearance *En*
dédouanement (m) *Fr*
Zollabfertigung (f) *De*

cutback *En*
réduction (f) *Fr*
Kürzung (f) *De*

cycle facilities *En*
pistes (f.pl) cyclables *Fr*
Verkehrseinrichtungen (f.pl) für Radfahrer *De*

cycle lane/path *En*
piste (f) cyclable *Fr*
Radweg (m), Fahrradspur (f) *De*

cycle (m) budgétaire annuel *Fr*
Haushaltskreislauf (m) *De*
annual budget cycle *En*

cyclic (adj) *En*
cyclique (adj) *Fr*
zyklisch (adj) *De*

cyclique (adj) *Fr*
zyklisch (adj) *De*
cyclic (adj) *En*

cyclist *En*
cycliste (m/f) *Fr*
Radfahrer/-in (m/f) *De*

cycliste (m/f) *Fr*
Radfahrer/-in (m/f) *De*
cyclist *En*

*** see/siehe/voir: Introduction page IX**

dactylo copiste (f) *Fr*
Abschreibtypistin (f) *De*
copy typist *En*

dactylo(graphe) (m/f) *Fr*
Schreibkraft (f) *De*
typist *En*

dactylographie (f) *Fr*
Maschineschreiben (nt) *De*
typing *En*

damages *En*
dommages-intérêts (m.pl) *Fr*
Schadenersatz (m) *De*

dangerous structure *En*
construction (f) dangereuse *Fr*
gefährliche Konstruktion (f) *De*

dangerous substance *En*
matière (f) dangereuse *Fr*
gefährlicher Stoff (m) *De*

dangerous waste *En*
déchets (m.pl) dangereux *Fr*
Sondermüll (m) *De*

Darlehen (nt) *De*
loan *En*
emprunt (m) *Fr*

data analysis *En*
analyse (f) des données *Fr*
Datenanalyse (f) *De*

data bank/base *En*
banque (f) de données *Fr*
Datenbank (f), -bestand (m) *De*

data collection *En*
rassemblement (m) de données *Fr*
Datenerfassung (f) *De*

data management *En*
gestion (f) de l'informatique *Fr*
Datenverwaltung (f) *De*

data processing *En*
traitement (m) d'informatique *Fr*
Datenverarbeitung (f) *De*

data protection *En*
protection (f) des données *Fr*
Datenschutz (m) *De*

data retrieval *En*
recherche (f) d'informations *Fr*
Datenabruf (m) *De*

data transmission *En*
transmission (f) des données *Fr*
Datenübertragung (f) *De*

database management *En*
gestion (f) de la base de données *Fr*
Datenbankverwaltung (f) *De*

date (f) de livraison *Fr*
Liefertermin (m) *De*
delivery date *En*

date (f) limite *Fr*
Verfallstermin (m) *De*
deadline *En*

date stamp *En*
dateur (m) *Fr*
Tagesstempel (m) *De*

Datenabruf (m) *De*
data retrieval *En*
recherche (f) d'informations *Fr*

Datenanalyse (f) *De*
data analysis *En*
analyse (f) des données *Fr*

Datenbank (f), -bestand (m) *De*
data bank/base *En*
banque (f) de données *Fr*

Datenbankverwaltung (f) *De*
database management *En*
gestion (f) de la base de données *Fr*

Datenerfassung (f) *De*
data collection *En*
rassemblement (m) de données *Fr*

Datenschutz (m) *De*
data protection *En*
protection (f) des données *Fr*

Datenspeichersystem (nt) *De*
file management system *En*
système (m) de gestion de fichiers *Fr*

Datenübertragung (f) *De*
data transmission *En*
transmission (f) des données *Fr*

Datenverarbeitung (f) *De*
data processing *En*
traitement (m) d'informatique *Fr*

Datenverwaltung (f) *De*
data management *En*
gestion (f) de l'informatique *Fr*

dateur (m) *Fr*
Tagesstempel (m) *De*
date stamp *En*

Dauerkarte (f) *De*
season ticket *En*
carte (f) d'abonnement *Fr*

day nursery *En*
crèche (f) collective *Fr*
Kindertagesheim (nt), Kindertagesstätte (f) *De*

day release *En*
jour (m) de permission accordé pour la formation professionnelle *Fr*
tageweise Freistellung (f) (zur Fortbildung) *De*

daywork *En*
travail (m) à la journée *Fr*
Tagesarbeit (f) *De*

deadline *En*
date (f) limite *Fr*
Verfallstermin (m) *De*

death certificate *En*
acte (m) de décès *Fr*
Todesschein (m) *De*

*** see/siehe/voir: Introduction page IX**

death rate *En*
taux (m) de la mortalité *Fr*
Sterblichkeitsziffer (f), Sterberate (f) *De*

débat (m) *Fr*
Debatte (f) *De*
debate (noun) *En*

debate (noun) *En*
débat (m) *Fr*
Debatte (f) *De*

debate (vb) *En*
débattre (vb) *Fr*
debattieren (vb) *De*

Debatte (f) *De*
debate (noun) *En*
débat (m) *Fr*

(Debatte usw) beschließen (vb) *De*
wind up (vb) (debate etc) *En*
résumer (vb) (un débat etc) *Fr*

debattieren (vb) *De*
debate (vb) *En*
débattre (vb) *Fr*

débattre (vb) *Fr*
debattieren (vb) *De*
debate (vb) *En*

débilité (f) mentale *Fr*
geistige Behinderung (f) *De*
mental handicap *En*

débit (m) direct *Fr*
direkte Belastung (f) *De*
direct debit *En*

débiter (vb) des foutaises *Fr*
Müll/Schutt abladen (vb) *De*
tip (vb) *En*

débiteur (m) (-trice f.) *Fr*
Schuldner/-in (m/f) *De*
debtor *En*

débours (m) injustifié porté à la charge du responsable *Fr*
Zuschlag (m) *De*
surcharge *En*

debt *En*
dette (f) *Fr*
Schuld (f) *De*

debt financing *En*
règlement (m) de la dette *Fr*
Fremdfinanzierung (f) *De*

debtor *En*
débiteur (m) (-trice f.) *Fr*
Schuldner/-in (m/f) *De*

décentralisateur (m) (-trice f.) (adj) *Fr*
dezentralisierend (adj) *De*
decentralizing (adj) *En*

decentralization *En*
décentralisation(f) *Fr*
Dezentralisierung (f) *De*

décentralisation(f) *Fr*
Dezentralisierung (f) *De*
decentralization *En*

décentralisé (adj) *Fr*
dezentralisiert (adj) *De*
decentralized (adj) *En*

decentralized (adj) *En*
décentralisé (adj) *Fr*
dezentralisiert (adj) *De*

décentraliser (vb) *Fr*
dezentralisieren (vb) *De*
decentralize (vb) *En*

decentralizing (adj) *En*
décentralisateur (m) (-trice f.) (adj) *Fr*
dezentralisierend (adj) *De*

decentralize (vb) *En*
décentraliser (vb) *Fr*
dezentralisieren (vb) *De*

décharge (f) d'impôt *Fr*
Ermäßigung (f) der Gemeindeabgaben *De*
rate rebate *En*

décharge (f) (d'ordures etc) *Fr*
Schuttabladen (nt) *De*
tipping *En*

décharge (f) des ordures *Fr*
Abfallbeseitigung (f) *De*
refuse disposal *En*

décharge (f) illégale *Fr*
illegales Müllabladen (nt) *De*
fly tipping *En*

décharge (f) publique *Fr*
Müllabladeplatz (m) *De*
refuse tip *En*

décharge (f) publique *Fr*
Müllhalde (f) *De*
rubbish dump *En*

déchéance (f) *Fr*
Verlust (m) *De*
forfeiture *En*

déchets (m.pl) *Fr*
Abfall (m), Müll (m) *De*
waste *En*

déchets (m.pl) *Fr*
Müll (m) *De*
refuse (noun) *En*

déchets (m.pl) agricoles *Fr*
landwirtschaftlicher Abfall (m) *De*
agricultural waste *En*

déchets (m.pl) agricoles *Fr*
landwirtschaftlicher Abfall (m) *De*
farm waste *En*

déchets (m.pl) chimiques *Fr*
chemische Abfälle (m.pl) *De*
chemical waste *En*

déchets (m.pl) d'hôpital *Fr*
Krankenhausabfall (m) *De*
hospital waste *En*

déchets (m.pl) dangereux *Fr*
Sondermüll (m) *De*
dangerous waste *En*

déchets (m.pl) dangereux *Fr*
Sondermüll (m) *De*
hazardous waste *En*

déchets (m.pl) industriels *Fr*
Industriemüll (m) *De*
industrial waste *En*

déchets (m.pl) liquides *Fr*
Abwasser (nt) *De*
liquid waste *En*

déchets (m.pl) nucléaires *Fr*
Atommüll (m) *De*
nuclear waste *En*

déchêts (m.pl) organiques *Fr*
organischer Abfall (m) *De*
organic waste *En*

déchets (m.pl) solides *Fr*
feste Abfälle (m.pl) *De*
solid waste *En*

déchêts (m.pl) toxiques *Fr*
giftige Abfälle (m.pl) *De*
poisonous waste *En*

déchets (m.pl) toxiques *Fr*
Giftmüll (m) *De*
toxic waste *En*

decision *En*
décision (f) *Fr*
Entscheidung (f) *De*

décision (f) *Fr*
Entscheidung (f) *De*
decision *En*

decision-making body *En*
conseil (m) qui a le droit de prendre des décisions *Fr*
Entscheidungsträger (m) *De*

*** see/siehe/voir: Introduction page IX**

decision-making *En*
prise (f) de décision *Fr*
Beschlußfassung (f) *De*

déclaration (f) des droits des citoyens *Fr*
Bill of Rights (f) *De*
bill of rights *En*

déclarer (vb) (une naissance etc) *Fr*
eine Geburt eintragen lassen (vb) *De*
register (vb) (a birth etc) *En*

déclin (m) de l'activité industrielle *Fr*
industrieller Rückgang (m) *De*
industrial decline *En*

déclin (m) économique *Fr*
Konjunkturrückgang (m) *De*
economic decline *En*

decontamination *En*
désinfection *Fr*
Dekontamination (f) *De*

dédouanement (m) *Fr*
Zollabfertigung (f) *De*
customs clearance *En*

déductible des impôts (adj) *Fr*
(steuerlich) absetzbar (adj) *De*
tax deductible (adj) *En*

déductions (f.pl) fiscales *Fr*
Steuerguthaben (nt) *De*
tax credits *En*

déductions (f.pl) fiscales sur les investissements *Fr*
Vermögenszuteilung (f) *De*
capital allowance *En*

deeds *En*
acte (m) *Fr*
Urkunde (f) *De*

deemed consent *En*
autorisation (f) quasi-effective *Fr*
durchdachte Zustimmung (f) *De*

default (vb) *En*
faire (vb) défaut *Fr*
versagen (vb) *De*

défaut (m); faire (vb) —. *Fr*
versagen (vb) *De*
default (vb) *En*

défaut (m) de paiement *Fr*
Nichtzahlung (f) *De*
non-payment *En*

défavorisé (adj) *Fr*
unterprivilegiert (adj) *De*
underprivileged (adj) *En*

defect (in building) *En*
vice (m) de construction *Fr*
Defekt (m) *De*

defective (adj) *En*
en mauvais état *Fr*
defekt (adj) *De*

defekt (adj) *De*
defective (adj) *En*
en mauvais état *Fr*

Defekt (m) *De*
defect (in building) *En*
vice (m) de construction *Fr*

defendant *En*
défendeur (m) (-eresse f.) *Fr*
Angeklagte(-r) (m/f) *De*

défendeur (m) (-eresse f.) *Fr*
Angeklagte(-r) (m/f) *De*
defendant *En*

deferred taxation *En*
imposition (f) différée *Fr*
latente Steuerpflicht (f) *De*

deficit *En*
déficit (m) *Fr*
Defizit (nt) *De*

déficit (m) *Fr*
Defizit (nt) *De*
deficit *En*

déficit (m) du commerce extérieur *Fr*
Handelsbilanzdefizit (m) *De*
trade gap *En*

définir (vb) (une politique etc) *Fr*
(Grundsatz usw) formulieren (vb) *De*
formulate (vb) (policy etc) *En*

définition (f) d'un emploi *Fr*
Arbeitsbedingungen (f.pl) *De*
conditions of employment *En*

définition (f) d'un programme *Fr*
Entwurfsanweisungen (f.pl) *De*
design brief *En*

Defizit (nt) *De*
deficit *En*
déficit (m) *Fr*

dégats (m.pl) à l'environnement *Fr*
Umweltschäden (m.pl) *De*
environmental damage *En*

dégradation (f) *Fr*
Verfall (m) *De*
dilapidation *En*

Dekontamination (f) *De*
decontamination *En*
désinfection *Fr*

délabrement (m) progressif *Fr*
fortschreitender Zusammenbruch (m) *De*
progressive collapse *En*

délabrement (m) urbain *Fr*
Verslumung (f) *De*
urban decay/decline *En*

délai (m) de paiement *Fr*
Frist (f) *De*
time limit (for payment) *En*

délai (m) de rigueur *Fr*
Endabrechnung (f) *De*
final account *En*

delegated authority/powers *En*
pouvoirs (m. pl) délégués *Fr*
delegierte Autorität (f) *De*

delegation *En*
délégation (f) *Fr*
Delegation (f) *De*

Delegation (f) *De*
delegation *En*
délégation (f) *Fr*

délégation (f) *Fr*
Delegation (f) *De*
delegation *En*

délégation (f) de pouvoir *Fr*
Dezentralisierung (f) *De*
devolution *En*

delegierte Autorität (f) *De*
delegated authority/powers *En*
pouvoirs (m. pl) délégués *Fr*

délégué (m) syndical *Fr*
Vertrauensmann (m) *De*
shop steward *En*

déléguer (vb) des pouvoirs (à) *Fr*
(Verantwortung usw) übertragen (vb) *De*
devolve (vb) powers (to) *En*

*** see/siehe/voir: Introduction page IX**

Delikt (nt) *De*
offence *En*
infraction (f) à la loi *Fr*

Delikt (nt) *De*
tort *En*
délit (m) civil *Fr*

délinquance (f) *Fr*
Jugendkriminalität (f) *De*
juvenile crime *En*

délinquant (m) *Fr*
Straffällige (-r) (m/f) *De*
offender *En*

délit (m) civil *Fr*
Delikt (nt) *De*
tort *En*

délit (m) *Fr*
strafbare Handlung (f), Delikt (nt) *De*
indictable offence *En*

delivery date *En*
date (f) de livraison *Fr*
Liefertermin (m) *De*

delivery note *En*
bordereau (m) de livraison *Fr*
Lieferschein (m) *De*

delivery of a writ *En*
signification (f) d'un acte *Fr*
Zustellung (f) einer Verfügung *De*

dem Vorstand angehöriger Arbeitnehmer (m) *De*
worker director *En*
gérant-ouvrier (m) *Fr*

demand analysis *En*
analyse (f) de la demande *Fr*
Nachfrageanalyse (f) *De*

demand assessment *En*
évaluation (f) de la demande *Fr*
Nachfrageschätzung (f) *De*

demand elasticity *En*
élasticité (f) de la demande *Fr*
Nachfrageelastizität (f) *De*

demand forecast *En*
prévision (f) de la demande *Fr*
Nachfrageprognose (f) *De*

demande (f) *Fr*
Anforderung (f) *De*
requisition *En*

demande (f) d'allocation *Fr*
Antrag (m) auf Zuschuß *De*
grant application *En*

demande (f) d'autorisation de construire *Fr*
Antrag (m) auf Bauerlaubnis *De*
planning application *En*

demande (f) d'emprunts du secteur public *Fr*
Kreditbedarf (m) der öffentlichen Hand *De*
public sector borrowing requirement *En*

demande (f) d'énergie *Fr*
Energiebedarf (m) *De*
energy demand *En*

demande (f) de l'électricité *Fr*
Strombedarf (m) *De*
electricity demand *En*

demande (f) de logement *Fr*
Wohnantrag (m) *De*
housing application *En*

demande (f) de main-d'oeuvre *Fr*
Arbeitskräftenachfrage (f) *De*
labour demand *En*

demande (f) en logement *Fr*
Wohnraumbedarf (m) *De*
housing demand *En*

démarches (f.pl) recommandées *Fr*
empfohlene Vorgehensweise (f) *De*
recommended course of action *En*

démission (f) *Fr*
Rücktritt (m) *De*
resignation *En*

démissionner (vb) *Fr*
zurücktreten (vb) *De*
resign (vb) *En*

democracy *En*
démocratie (f) *Fr*
Demokratie (f) *De*

democratic (adj) *En*
démocratique (adj) *Fr*
demokratisch (adj) *De*

democratic accountability *En*
responsabilité (f) démocratique *Fr*
demokratische Verantwortlichkeit (f) *De*

démocratie (f) *Fr*
Demokratie (f) *De*
democracy *En*

démocratie (f) industrielle *Fr*
Demokratie (f) im Betrieb *De*
industrial democracy *En*

démocratie (f) locale *Fr*
örtliche Demokratie (f) *De*
local democracy *En*

démocratique (adj) *Fr*
demokratisch (adj) *De*
democratic (adj) *En*

demographic analysis *En*
analyse (f) démographique *Fr*
demographische Analyse (f) *De*

demographic change *En*
variations (f.pl) démographiques *Fr*
demographische Veränderung (f) *De*

demographic projection(s) *En*
prévision (f) démographique *Fr*
demographische Voraussagen (f.pl) *De*

demographic trend *En*
mouvement (m) démographique *Fr*
Bevölkerungstrend (m) *De*

Demographie (f) *De*
demography *En*
démographie (f) *Fr*

démographie (f) *Fr*
Demographie (f) *De*
demography *En*

demographische Analyse (f) *De*
demographic analysis *En*
analyse (f) démographique *Fr*

demographische Veränderung (f) *De*
demographic change *En*
variations (f.pl) démographiques *Fr*

demographische Voraussagen (f.pl) *De*
demographic projection(s) *En*
prévision (f) démographique *Fr*

demography *En*
démographie (f) *Fr*
Demographie (f) *De*

Demokratie (f) *De*
democracy *En*
démocratie (f) *Fr*

Demokratie (f) im Betrieb *De*
industrial democracy *En*
démocratie (f) industrielle *Fr*

*** see/siehe/voir: Introduction page IX**

demokratisch (adj) *De*
democratic (adj) *En*
démocratique (adj) *Fr*

demokratische Verantwortlichkeit (f) *De*
democratic accountability *En*
responsabilité (f) démocratique *Fr*

demolieren, abreißen (vb) *De*
demolish (vb) *En*
démolir (vb) *Fr*

Demolierung (f), Abriß (m) *De*
demolition *En*
démolition (f) *Fr*

démolir (vb) *Fr*
demolieren, abreißen (vb) *De*
demolish (vb) *En*

demolish (vb) *En*
démolir (vb) *Fr*
demolieren, abreißen (vb) *De*

demolition *En*
démolition (f) *Fr*
Demolierung (f), Abriß (m) *De*

démolition (f) *Fr*
Demolierung (f), Abriß (m) *De*
demolition *En*

Demonstration (f) *De*
demonstration (protest) *En*
manifestation (f) *Fr*

demonstration (protest) *En*
manifestation (f) *Fr*
Demonstration (f) *De*

deniers (m.pl) publics *Fr*
öffentliche Mittel (nt.pl) *De*
public funds *En*

Denkmalschutz (m) *De*
rescue archaeology *En*
archéologie (f) de sauvegarde *Fr*

densité (f) de la population *Fr*
Bevölkerungsdichte (f) *De*
density of population *En*

densité (f) de la population *Fr*
Bevölkerungsdichte (f) *De*
population density *En*

densité (f) du logement *Fr*
Wohndichte (f) *De*
housing density *En*

density of population *En*
densité (f) de la population *Fr*
Bevölkerungsdichte (f) *De*

dental care *En*
soins (m.pl) dentaires *Fr*
Zahnpflege (f) *De*

dentist *En*
dentiste (m/f) *Fr*
Zahnarzt/-ärztin (m/f) *De*

dentiste (m/f) *Fr*
Zahnarzt/-ärztin (m/f) *De*
dentist *En*

dentisterie (f) *Fr*
Zahnmedizin (f) *De*
dentistry *En*

dentistry *En*
dentisterie (f) *Fr*
Zahnmedizin (f) *De*

déontologie (f) *Fr*
berufliches Verhalten (nt) *De*
professional conduct *En*

déontologie (f) professionnelle *Fr*
Berufsethos (nt) *De*
professional ethics *En*

department *En*
service (m) *Fr*
Abteilung (f) *De*

dependants *En*
charges (f.pl) de famille *Fr*
abhängige Angehörige (pl) *De*

dependent children *En*
enfants (m/f. pl) à charge *Fr*
abhängige Kinder (nt.pl) *De*

dépense (f) *Fr*
Ausgaben (f.pl) *De*
expenditure *En*

dépense(s) (f) *Fr*
Ausgaben (f.pl) *De*
spending *En*

dépense (f) déductible *Fr*
abziehbare Unkosten (pl) *De*
allowable expense *En*

dépenser (vb) *Fr*
ausgeben (vb) *De*
spend (vb) *En*

dépenser (vb) au delà des moyens *Fr*
zuviel ausgeben (vb) *De*
overspend (vb) *En*

dépenses (f.pl) *Fr*
Auszahlungen (f.pl) *De*
disbursements *En*

dépenses (f.pl) courantes *Fr*
Steuerabgaben (f.pl) *De*
revenue expenditure *En*

dépenses (f.pl) d'investissement *Fr*
Kapitalaufwand (m) *De*
capital spending *En*

dépenses (f.pl) de fonctionnement *Fr*
laufende Ausgaben (f.pl) *De*
current expenditure *En*

dépenses (f.pl) de l'Etat *Fr*
Staatsausgaben (f.pl) *De*
government expenditure *En*

dépenses (f.pl) des collectivités territoriales *Fr*
Kommunalabgaben (f.pl) *De*
local authority expenditure *En*

dépenses (f.pl) discrétionnaires (par le conseil municipal) *Fr*
nach eigenem Ermessen verfügbare/Ausgaben (f.pl) *De*
discretionary spending *En*

dépenses (f.pl) du gouvernement local *Fr*
Kommunalabgaben (f.pl) *De*
local government expenditure *En*

dépenses (f.pl) en dessous des chiffres prévus dans le budget *Fr*
Budgetunterschreitung (f) *De*
underspending *En*

dépenses (f.pl) publiques *Fr*
öffentliche Ausgaben (f.pl) *De*
public expenditure *En*

dépot (m) de marchandises *Fr*
Güterbahnhof (m) *De*
goods yard *En*

dépotoir (m) *Fr*
Müllgrube (f) *De*
landfill site *En*

dépotoir (m) (d'ordures etc) *Fr*
Müllkippe (f) *De*
tip (noun) *En*

depreciate (vb) *En*
déprécier (vb) *Fr*
entwerten (vb) *De*

*** see/siehe/voir: Introduction page IX**

depreciation *En*
dépréciation (f) *Fr*
Entwertung (f) *De*

dépréciation (f) *Fr*
Entwertung (f) *De*
depreciation *En*

déprécier (vb) *Fr*
entwerten (vb) *De*
depreciate (vb) *En*

depressed area *En*
région (f) touchée par la crise *Fr*
unter Depression leidendes Gebiet (nt) *De*

depression *En*
crise (f) économique *Fr*
Wirtschaftskrise (f) *De*

Depression (f) *De*
depression (economic) *En*
dépression (f) économique *Fr*

Depression (f) *De*
slump *En*
crise (f) économique *Fr*

depression (economic) *En*
dépression (f) économique *Fr*
Depression (f) *De*

dépression (f) économique *Fr*
Depression (f) *De*
depression (economic) *En*

Deprivation (f); Aberkennung (f) *De*
deprivation *En*
privation (f) *Fr*

deprivation *En*
privation (f) *Fr*
Aberkennung (f), Deprivation (f) *De*

deprived (adj) *En*
privé (adj) *Fr*
benachteiligt, depriviert (adj) *De*

depriviert, benachteiligt (adj) *De*
deprived (adj) *En*
privé (adj) *Fr*

député (m) *Fr*
Abgeordnete(r) (m/f) *De*
Member of Parliament *En*

deregulation *En*
marché (m) libre *Fr*
Wettbewerbsfreiheit (f) *De*

derelict building *En*
bâtiment (m) en état d'abandon *Fr*
verfallenes Gebäude (nt) *De*

derelict land *En*
terrain (m) vague *Fr*
nicht bewirtschaftetes Land (nt) *De*

dernier (m) rappel *Fr*
letzte Mahnung (f) *De*
final demand *En*

dernier versement (m) *Fr*
letzte Rate (f) *De*
final instalment *En*

désavantagé (adj) *Fr*
gesellschaftlich/sozial benachteiligt (adj) *De*
socially deprived (adj) *En*

désavantage (m) social *Fr*
gesellschaftliche Benachteiligung (f) *De*
social disadvantage *En*

descriptif (m) *Fr*
Angaben (f.pl); Beschreibung (f) *De*
specification *En*

description (f) de la fonction *Fr*
Tätigkeitsbeschreibung (f) *De*
job description *En*

design (noun) *En*
dessein (m) *Fr*
Entwurf (m) *De*

design brief *En*
définition (f) d'un programme *Fr*
Entwurfsanweisungen (f.pl) *De*

design guide *En*
objectif (m) d'un projet *Fr*
Entwurfsvorlage (f), -richtlinien (f.pl) *De*

design office *En*
bureau (m) d'études *Fr*
Entwurfsbüro (nt) *De*

désinfection (f) *Fr*
Ausräucherung (f) *De*
fumigation *En*

désinfection (f) *Fr*
Dekontamination (f) *De*
decontamination *En*

désinsectisation (f); dératisation (f) *Fr*
Schädlingsbekämpfung (f) *De*
pest control *En*

desk *En*
bureau (m) *Fr*
Schreibtisch (m) *De*

desk top publishing *En*
publication (f) assistée par ordinateur (PAO) *Fr*
Desktop-Publishing (nt) *De*

Desktop-Publishing (nt) *De*
desk top publishing *En*
publication (f) assistée par ordinateur (PAO) *Fr*

Desktop-Publishing (nt) *De*
electronic publishing *En*
édition (f) électronique *Fr*

déssèchement (m) du terrain *Fr*
Landgewinnung (f) *De*
land reclamation *En*

dessein (m) *Fr*
Entwurf (m) *De*
design (noun) *En*

dessein (m) assisté par ordinateur (DAO) *Fr*
computergestützter Entwurf (m) *De*
computer aided design *En*

dessein (m) de construction *Fr*
Bauentwurf (m), Bauplan (m) *De*
building design *En*

dessin (m) de construction *Fr*
Konstruktionszeichnung (f) *De*
working drawing *En*

dessin (m) de mécanique *Fr*
technische Zeichnung (f) *De*
engineering drawing *En*

dessin (m) en perspective *Fr*
perspektivische Zeichnung (f) *De*
perspective drawing *En*

dessinateur (m) (en architecture) *Fr*
Zeichner/-in (m/f) *De*
draughtsman *En*

dessins (m.pl) *Fr*
Zeichnungen (f.pl) *De*
drawings *En*

destitution (f) illégale *Fr*
gesetzwidrige Entlassung (f) *De*
unlawful dismissal *En*

destitution (f) sans cause *Fr*
ungerechtfertigte Entlassung (f) *De*
unfair dismissal *En*

detached house *En*
maison (f) separée *Fr*
Einzelhaus (nt) *De*

*** see/siehe/voir: Introduction page IX**

détachement (m) *Fr*
vorübergehende Versetzung (f) *De*
secondment *En*

detention centre *En*
maison (f) de rééducation *Fr*
Jugendstrafanstalt (f) *De*

détention (f) préventive *Fr*
Untersuchungshaft (f) *De*
remand (noun) *En*

détritus (m) *Fr*
Abfälle (m.pl) *De*
litter *En*

dette (f) *Fr*
Schuld (f) *De*
debt *En*

devaluation *En*
dévaluation (f) *Fr*
(Währungs)abwertung (f) *De*

dévaluation (f) *Fr*
(Währungs)abwertung (f) *De*
devaluation *En*

developer *En*
lotisseur (m) *Fr*
Bauunternehmer (m) *De*

development area *En*
zone (f) d'exploitation *Fr*
Entwicklungsgebiet (nt) *De*

development company *En*
société (f) d'exploitation *Fr*
Wohnungsbaugesellschaft (f) *De*

development control *En*
contrôle (m) de l'aménagement *Fr*
Erschließungskontrolle (f) der Entwicklung *De*

development grant *En*
aide (f) financiaire à l'aménagement *Fr*
Entwicklungshilfe (f) *De*

development land *En*
terrains (m.pl) bâtissables *Fr*
Erschließungsgebiet (nt) *De*

development plan *En*
plan (m) d'aménagement *Fr*
Entwicklungsplan (m) *De*

development site *En*
zone (f) de développement *Fr*
Erschließungsgelände (nt) *De*

development value *En*
coût (m) foncier *Fr*
Erschließungswert (m) *De*

développement (m) commercial *Fr*
Geschäftsentwicklung (f) *De*
business development *En*

développement (m) commercial *Fr*
wirtschaftliche Entwicklung (f) *De*
commercial development *En*

développement (m) communautaire *Fr*
Gemeindeentwicklung (f) *De*
community development *En*

développement (m) de la carrière *Fr*
berufliche Entwicklung (f) *De*
career development *En*

développement (m) des villes *Fr*
städtebauliche Erschließung (f) *De*
urban development *En*

développement (m) du marché *Fr*
Marktlage (f), -entwicklung (f) *De*
market development *En*

développement (m) du personnel *Fr*
Personalentwicklung (f) *De*
staff development *En*

développement (m) du plan d'études *Fr* *
Lehrplangestaltung (f) *De*
curriculum development *En*

développement (m) économique *Fr*
Konjunkturentwicklung (f) *De*
economic development *En*

développement (m) tertiaire *Fr*
Büroerweiterung (f) *De*
office development *En*

déversement (m) de population *Fr*
Bevölkerungsüberschuß (m) *De*
overspill *En*

déviation (f) *Fr*
Umleitung (f) *De*
diversion *En*

déviation (f) *Fr*
Umleitung (f) *De*
traffic diversion *En*

déviation (f) normale *Fr*
Standardabweichung (f) *De*
standard deviation *En*

devis (m) *Fr*
Kostenvorschläge (m.pl) *De*
bills of quantities *En*

devis (m) *Fr*
Voranschlag (m) *De*
estimate *En*

devise (f) forte *Fr*
harte Währung (f) *De*
hard currency *En*

Devisenkontrolle (f) *De*
currency control *En*
contrôle (m) des changes *Fr*

Devisenkontrolle (f) *De*
exchange control *En*
contrôle (m) des changes *Fr*

devoir (m) *Fr*
Aufgabe (f); Pflicht (f) *De*
duty *En*

devoirs (m.pl) civiques *Fr*
staatsbürgerliche Pflichten (f.pl) *De*
civic duties *En*

devoirs (m.pl) *Fr*
Hausaufgaben (f.pl) *De*
homework *En*

devolution *En*
délégation (f) de pouvoir *Fr*
Dezentralisierung (f) *De*

devolve (vb) powers (to) *En*
déléguer (vb) des pouvoirs (à) *Fr*
(Verantwortung usw) übertragen (vb) *De*

dévoué (adj) au bien public *Fr*
von Gemeinsinn zeugend (adj) *De*
public spirited (adj) *En*

dezentralisieren (vb) *De*
decentralize (vb) *En*
décentraliser (vb) *Fr*

dezentralisierend (adj) *De*
decentralizing (adj) *En*
décentralisateur (m) (-trice f.) (adj) *Fr*

dezentralisiert (adj) *De*
decentralized (adj) *En*
décentralisé (adj) *Fr*

Dezentralisierung (f) *De*
decentralization *En*
décentralisation(f) *Fr*

*** see/siehe/voir: Introduction page IX**

Dezentralisierung (f) *De*
devolution *En*
délégation (f) de pouvoir *Fr*

diary *En*
agenda (m) *Fr*
Terminkalender (m) *De*

dichter Wohnungsbau (m) *De*
high density housing *En*
logement (m) à forte densité *Fr*

dictaphoniste (f) *Fr*
Audiotypistin (f) *De*
audio-typist *En*

dictating machine *En*
machine (f) à dictée *Fr*
Diktaphon (nt) *De*

Dienstgrad (m) *De*
grade *En*
grade (m) *Fr*

Dienstleistungen (f.pl) *De*
service delivery/provision *En*
assurance (f) d'un service *Fr*

Dienstleistungsbetrieb (m) *De*
direct service organization *En*
service (m) exploité en régie directe *Fr*

Dienstleistungsniveau (nt) *De*
service level *En*
niveau (m) de service *Fr*

Dienstleistungssektor (m) *De*
service sector *En*
secteur (m) tertiaire *Fr*

Dienstleistungsversorgung (f) *De*
provision of services *En*
offre (f) de services *Fr*

Dienstleistungsvertrag (m) *De*
service (level) agreement *En*
contrat (m) de service *Fr*

diffamation (f) *Fr*
Verleumdung (f) (schriftliche) *De*
libel *En*

diffusion (f) d'informations *Fr*
Informationsverbreitung (f) *De*
dissemination of information *En*

diffusion (f) des informations *Fr*
Informationsvermittlung (f) *De*
information dissemination *En*

Diktaphon (nt) *De*
dictating machine *En*
machine (f) à dictée *Fr*

dilapidation *En*
dégradation (f) *Fr*
Verfall (m) *De*

diminué (-ée f.) physique *Fr*
körperbehindert (adj) *De*
physically disabled/handicapped *En*

diminution (f) du loyer *Fr*
Mietbeihilfe (f) *De*
rent allowance *En*

diminution (f) visuelle *Fr*
Sehbehinderung (f) *De*
visual handicap *En*

direct debit *En*
débit (m) direct *Fr*
direkte Belastung (f) *De*

direct labour organization *En*
service (m) exploité en régie directe *Fr*
Regiebetrieb (m) *De*

direct service organization *En*
service (m) exploité en régie directe *Fr*
Dienstleistungsbetrieb (m) *De*

direct tax *En*
impôt (m) direct *Fr*
direkte Steuer (f) *De*

direct taxation *En*
contributions (f.pl) directes *Fr*
direkte Steuern (f.pl) *De*

directeur (m) commercial *Fr*
Betriebsführer (m), kaufmännischer Direktor (m) *De*
business manager *En*

directeur (m) de l'architecture *Fr*
leitender Architekt (m) *De*
chief architect *En*

directeur (m) de projet *Fr*
Projektleiter/-in (m/f) *De*
project manager *En*

directeur (m) (-trice f.) des études (d'un groupe d'étudiants) *Fr*
(Privat)lehrer/-in (m/f) *De*
tutor *En*

directeur (m) (-trice f.) du scrutin *Fr*
Wahlleiter/-in (m/f) *De*
returning officer (in election) *En*

directeur (m) (-trice f.) *Fr*
Manager/-in (m/f) *De*
manager *En*

directeur (m) (-trice f.) /principal (m) *Fr*
Schulleiter/-in (m/f) *De*
head teacher (primary/secondary) *En*

directeur-général (m) (région, département) *Fr*
Hauptverwaltungsbeamte(-r)/(-in) (m/f) *De*
chief executive (county) *En*

direction (f) (d'une entreprise) *Fr*
Aufsicht (f) *De*
supervision *En*

direction (f) des affaires sociales *Fr*
Sozialamt (nt) *De*
social services department *En*

direction (f) des bâtiments *Fr*
Liegenschaftsamt (nt) *De*
estates department *En*

direction (f) des bâtiments *Fr*
Schätzungsabteilung (f) *De*
valuer's department *En*

direction (f) des normes de conformité *Fr*
Gewerbeordnungsabteilung (f) *De*
trading standards department *En*

direction (f) du personnel *Fr*
Personalleitung (f) *De*
personnel management *En*

direction (f) par objectifs *Fr*
zielorientiertes Management (nt) *De*
management by objectives *En*

directive *En*
directive (f) *Fr*
Direktive (f) *De*

directive (f) *Fr*
Direktive (f) *De*
directive *En*

direkte Belastung (f) *De*
direct debit *En*
débit (m) direct *Fr*

*** see/siehe/voir: Introduction page IX**

direkte Steuer (f) *De*
direct tax *En*
impôt (m) direct *Fr*

direkte Steuern (f.pl) *De*
direct taxation *En*
contributions (f.pl) directes *Fr*

Direktive (f) *De*
directive *En*
directive (f) *Fr*

dirigeant (m) *Fr*
leitende(r) Angestellte(r) (m/f) *De*
executive (business) *En*

diriger (vb) (une entreprise) *Fr*
beaufsichtigen (vb) *De*
supervise (vb) *En*

disability *En*
incapacité (f) *Fr*
Behinderung (f) *De*

disabled person *En*
personne (f) handicappée *Fr*
Behinderte(-r) (m/f) *De*

disablement benefit *En*
allocation (f) d'adulte handicappé *Fr*
Erwerbsunfähigkeits-, Invalidenrente (f) *De*

disadvantaged group *En*
groupe (m) désavantagé *Fr*
Benachteiligte (pl) *De*

disaster planning *En*
plan (m) de protection civile *Fr*
Katastrophenschutz (m) *De*

disbursements account *En*
compte (m) des dépenses *Fr*
Auszahlungskonto (nt) *De*

disbursements *En*
dépenses (f.pl) *Fr*
Auszahlungen (f.pl) *De*

disciplinary procedure *En*
procédures (f.pl) disciplinaires *Fr*
Disziplinarverfahren (nt) *De*

disclosure of information *En*
divulgation (f) d'informations *Fr*
Offenlegung (f) von Information *De*

discours (m) (faire/prononcer un-) *Fr*
eine Rede halten *De*
speech (to make a) *En*

discretion *En*
discrétion (f) *Fr*
Ermessen (nt) *De*

discrétion (f) *Fr*
Ermessen (nt) *De*
discretion *En*

discretionary power *En*
pouvoir (m) discrétionnaire (du maire) *Fr*
Entscheidungsgewalt (f) *De*

discretionary spending *En*
dépenses (f.pl) discrétionnaires (par le conseil municipal) *Fr*
nach eigenem Ermessen verfügbare Ausgaben (f.pl) *De*

discriminate (vb) *En*
faire (vb) des distinctions (f.pl) contre quelqu'un *Fr*
diskriminieren (vb) *De*

discrimination *En*
discrimination (f) *Fr*
Diskriminierung (f) *De*

discrimination (f) *Fr*
Diskriminierung (f) *De*
discrimination *En*

discrimination (f) positive *Fr*
positive Diskriminierung (f) *De*
positive discrimination *En*

discrimination (f) raciale *Fr*
Rassendiskriminierung (f) *De*
racial discrimination *En*

discrimination (f) sexuelle *Fr*
sexuelle Diskriminierung (f) *De*
sex discrimination *En*

discussion (f) officieuse/informelle *Fr*
informelles Gespräch (nt) *De*
informal discussion *En*

Diskontsatz (m) *De*
bank rate *En*
taux (m) officiel de l'escompte *Fr*

diskriminieren (vb) *De*
discriminate (vb) *En*
faire (vb) des distinctions (f.pl) contre quelqu'un *Fr*

Diskriminierung (f) *De*
discrimination *En*
discrimination (f) *Fr*

dismiss (vb) *En*
congédier (vb) *Fr*
entlassen (vb) *De*

dismissal *En*
renvoi (m) *Fr*
Entlassung (f) *De*

dispensaire (m) *Fr*
Klinik (f) *De*
clinic *En*

disponibilité (f) de terrain *Fr*
Bodenangebot (nt) *De*
land availability *En*

disponibilité (f) de terrain *Fr*
(gesamte) bebaubare Fläche (f) *De*
land supply *En*

disposable income *En*
revenu (m) disponible *Fr*
verfügbares Einkommen (nt) *De*

dispositif (m) d'évacuation des eaux usées *Fr*
Abwasserbeseitigung (f) *De*
effluent disposal *En*

dispositions (f.pl) d'un contrat *Fr*
Vertragsvorschriften (f.pl) *De*
contract regulations *En*

dissemination of information *En*
diffusion (f) d'informations *Fr*
Informationsverbreitung (f) *De*

distance learning *En*
enseignement (m) à distance *Fr*
Fernstudium (nt) *De*

distinctions (f.pl); faire (vb) des — contre quelqu'un *Fr*
diskriminieren (vb) *De*
discriminate (vb) *En*

distribuer (vb) les papiers etc *Fr*
(Akten usw) zirkulieren lassen (vb) *De*
circulate (vb) papers etc *En*

distributeur (m) d'argent comptant *Fr*
Bargeldauszahlungsautomat (m) *De*
cash dispenser *En*

distribution (f) par âge *Fr*
Altersverteilung (f) *De*
age distribution *En*

distributor *En*
concessionnaire (m) *Fr*
Konzessionär (m) *De*

district *En*
district (m) *Fr*
Bezirk (m) *De*

district (m) *Fr*
Bezirk (m) *De*
district *En*

district auditor *En*
conseiller (m) à la chambre régionale des comptes *Fr*
Rechnungsprüfer (m) *De*

district council *En* *
conseil (m) municipal *Fr*
Kreisausschuß (m), Kreisrat (m) *De*

district plan *En*
plan (m) d'aménagement urbain *Fr*
Bezirksverwaltungsplan (m) *De*

district valuer *En*
inspecteur (m) des domaines *Fr*
Bezirksschätzer (m), Taxator (m) *De*

Disziplinarverfahren (nt) *De*
disciplinary procedure *En*
procédures (f.pl) disciplinaires *Fr*

diversion *En*
déviation (f) *Fr*
Umleitung (f) *De*

dividend *En*
dividende (m) *Fr*
Dividende (f) *De*

Dividende (f) *De*
dividend *En*
dividende (m) *Fr*

dividende (m) *Fr*
Dividende (f) *De*
dividend *En*

divulgation (f) d'informations *Fr*
Offenlegung (f) von Information *De*
disclosure of information *En*

docklands *En*
quartiers (m.pl) des docks (m.pl) *Fr*
Hafenviertel (nt) *De*

dockyard *En*
chantier (m) de construction des navires *Fr*
Werft (f) *De*

doctor *En*
médecin (m) (f = femme médecin) *Fr*
Arzt/Ärztin (m/f) *De*

document (m) de base *Fr*
Quellenmaterial (nt) *De*
source document *En*

document (m) de travail *Fr*
Bericht (m) *De*
working paper *En*

documentaliste(m/f) *Fr*
Archivkraft (f) *De*
filing clerk *En*

documentation *En*
documentation (f) *Fr*
Dokumentation (f) *De*

documentation (f) *Fr*
Dokumentation (f) *De*
documentation *En*

dogme (m) politique *Fr*
politisches Dogma (nt) *De*
political dogma *En*

Dokumentation (f) *De*
documentation *En*
documentation (f) *Fr*

dole *En*
indemnité (f) de chômage *Fr*
Stempelgeld (nt) *De*

Dolmetscher/-in (m/f) *De*
interpreter *En*
interprète (m/f) *Fr*

domestic architecture *En*
architecture (f) domestique *Fr*
inländische Architektur (f) *De*

domestic rate *En*
impôt (m) mobilier *Fr*
Gebühren (f.pl) für Privathaushalte *De*

domestic refuse/waste *En*
ordures (f.pl) ménagères *Fr*
Hausmüll (m) *De*

domiciliary care *En*
assistance (f) à domicile *Fr*
Hauspflege (f) *De*

dommages-intérêts (m.pl) fixés en argent *Fr*
Folgeschäden (m.pl) *De*
liquidated damages *En*

dommages-intérêts (m.pl) *Fr*
Schadenersatz (m) *De*
damages *En*

domotique (f) *Fr*
Hauspflege (f) *De*
home care *En*

données (f.pl) d'exécution *Fr*
Arbeitsbeschreibung (f) *De*
job specification *En*

données (f.pl) de base *Fr*
Hintergrundinformation (f) *De*
background information *En*

donner (vb) des instructions (à un architecte etc) *Fr*
Anweisungen geben, unterweisen (vb) (Architekt usw.) *De*
brief (vb) (an architect etc) *En*

donner (vb) un avis *Fr*
beschließen, zu empfehlen (vb) *De*
resolve (vb) to recommend *En*

donner (vb) une vocation aux terrains *Fr*
Grund-und-Bodenverteilung (f) *De*
land allocation *En*

Doppelhaushälfte (f) *De*
semi-detached house *En*
maison (f) jumelle *Fr*

dossier (m) (documents) *Fr*
Akte (f) *De*
file (noun) *En*

dossier (m) médical *Fr*
medizinische Unterlagen (f.pl) *De*
medical record *En*

dossier (m) personnel *Fr*
Personalakte (f) *De*
personal file *En*

dotations (f.pl) de l'Etat aux collectivités *Fr*
Einnahmenbeihilfe (f) *De*
revenue support grant *En*

douane (f) *Fr*
Zoll (m) *De*
customs *En*

Down's syndrome *En*
maladie (f) de Down *Fr*
Down-Syndrom (nt) *De*

Down-Syndrom (nt) *De*
Down's syndrome *En*
maladie (f) de Down *Fr*

Dozent/-in (m/f) *De*
lecturer *En*
maître (m) de conférences *Fr*

draft (noun) *En*
projet (m) *Fr*
Entwurf (m) *De*

draft (vb) *En*
rédiger (vb) *Fr*
entwerfen (vb) *De*

draft report *En*
projet (m) d'un rapport *Fr*
Entwurf (m) eines Berichts *De*

*** see/siehe/voir: Introduction page IX**

drafting ***En***
rédaction (f) *Fr*
Entwurf (m) *De*

drainage ***En***
système (m) d'égouts *Fr*
Kanalisation (f) *De*

draughtsman ***En***
dessinateur (m) (en architecture) *Fr*
Zeichner/-in (m/f) *De*

draw up (vb) (contract etc) ***En***
préparer (vb) le projet d'un contract *Fr*
(Vertrag usw) aufsetzen (vb) *De*

drawing office ***En***
bureau (m) d'études *Fr*
Konstruktionsbüro (nt) *De*

drawings ***En***
dessins (m.pl) *Fr*
Zeichnungen (f.pl) *De*

dresser (vb) le procès-verbal ***Fr***
protokollieren (vb) *De*
minute (vb) *En*

dresser (vb) un acte de naissance etc ***Fr***
Geburtsurkunde (f) usw ausstellen lassen (vb) *De*
issue (vb) birth certificate etc *En*

drink driving ***En***
conduite (f) en état d'ivresse *Fr*
Alkohol (m) am Steuer *De*

drinking water ***En***
eau (f) potable *Fr*
Trinkwasser (nt) *De*

Dritte(r) (m/f) ***De***
third party *En*
tierce personne (f) *Fr*

dritte Welt (f) ***De***
third world *En*
tiers monde (m) *Fr*

Drogen (f.pl), Rauschgift (nt) ***De***
drugs *En*
narcotiques (m.pl) *Fr*

Drogenabhängigkeit (f) ***De***
drug dependence *En*
toxicomanie (f) *Fr*

Drogenmißbrauch (m) ***De***
drug abuse *En*
abus (m) des narcotiques *Fr*

Drogensüchtige(-r) (m/f) ***De***
drug addict *En*
toxicomane (m) *Fr*

droit (m) ***Fr***
Anwaltschaft (f) *De*
legal profession *En*

droit; à qui de — ; ***Fr***
an alle, die es angeht *De*
to whom it may concern *En*

droit (m) à l'information ***Fr***
Zugang (m) zu Informationen *De*
access to information *En*

droit (m) civil ***Fr***
Zivilrecht (nt) *De*
civil law *En*

droit (m) commercial ***Fr***
Gesellschaftsrecht (nt) *De*
company law *En*

droit (m) constitutionnel ***Fr***
Verfassungsrecht (nt) *De*
constitutional law *En*

droit (m) coutumier ***Fr***
Gewohnheitsrecht (nt) *De*
common law *En*

droit (m) criminel ***Fr***
Strafrecht (nt) *De*
criminal law *En*

droit (m) d'accès aux documents administratifs ***Fr***
Informationsfreiheit (f) *De*
freedom of information *En*

droit (m) d'accès ***Fr***
Besuchsrecht (nt); Wegerecht (nt) *De*
right of access *En*

droit (m) d'achat ***Fr***
Kaufrecht (nt) *De*
right to buy *En*

droit (m) d'appel ***Fr***
Berufungsrecht (nt) *De*
right of appeal *En*

droit (m) d'entrée ***Fr***
Wegerecht (nt) (zu einem Haus) *De*
right of entry *En*

droit (m) de logement ***Fr***
Wohnungsbaugesetz (nt) *De*
housing law *En*

droit (m) de passage ***Fr***
Durchgangsrecht (nt) *De*
right of way *En*

droit (m) de passage ***Fr***
Straßengebühr (f) *De*
toll *En*

droit (m) de timbre ***Fr***
Stempelsteuer (f) *De*
stamp duty *En*

droit (m) de vote ***Fr***
Wahlrecht (nt) *De*
franchise (political) *En*

droit (m) des obligations ***Fr***
Vertragsrecht (nt) *De*
contract law *En*

droit (m) des obligations ***Fr***
Vertragsrecht (nt) *De*
law of contract *En*

droit (m) du consommateur ***Fr*** *****
Konsumgesetz (nt) *De*
consumer law *En*

droit (m) électoral ***Fr***
Wahlrecht (nt) *De*
electoral law *En*

droit (m) international ***Fr***
Völkerrecht (nt) *De*
international law *En*

droit (m) sur la consommation ***Fr***
Verbrauchsabgabe (f) *De*
excise duty *En*

droit(s) (m/m.pl) de douane ***Fr***
Zoll (m) *De*
duties (customs) *En*

droite (f) ***Fr***
Rechte (f) *De*
right wing *En*

droite; de droite (adj) ***Fr***
rechte (-r,-s) (adj) *De*
right wing (adj) *En*

droits (m.pl) civils ***Fr***
Rechte (nt.pl) *De*
legal rights *En*

droits (m.pl) civiques ***Fr***
Bürgerrechte (nt.pl) *De*
civil rights *En*

droits (m.pl) de l'homme ***Fr***
Menschenrechte (nt.pl) *De*
human rights *En*

*** see/siehe/voir: Introduction page IX**

droits (m.pl) de la femme *Fr*
Frauenrechte (nt.pl) *De*
women's rights *En*

droits (m.pl) de la main-d'oeuvre *Fr*
Arbeiterrechte (nt.pl) *De*
workers' rights *En*

droits (m.pl) de régie *Fr*
Verbrauch(s)steuer (f) *De*
excise duties *En*

droits (m.pl) des parents *Fr*
Elternrechte (nt.pl) *De*
parental rights *En*

droits (m.pl) du locataire *Fr*
Mieterschutz (m) *De*
protected tenancy *En*

droits (m.pl) du logement *Fr*
Wohnrechte (nt.pl) *De*
housing rights *En*

droits (m.pl) du tenancier *Fr*
Mieterrechte (nt.pl) *De*
tenants' rights *En*

droits (m.pl) égaux *Fr*
Gleichberechtigung (f) *De*
equal rights *En*

drop-in centre *En*
centre (m) social *Fr*
Gemeindezentrum (nt) *De*

drug abuse *En*
abus (m) des narcotiques *Fr*
Drogenmißbrauch (m) *De*

drug addict *En*
toxicomane (m) *Fr*
Drogensüchtige(-r) (m/f) *De*

drug dependence *En*
toxicomanie (f) *Fr*
Drogenabhängigkeit (f) *De*

drugs *En*
narcotiques (m.pl) *Fr*
Drogen (f.pl), Rauschgift (nt) *De*

dual carriageway *En*
route (f) jumelée *Fr*
zweispurige Straße (f) *De*

dual use building *En*
bâtiment (m) partagé *Fr*
Zweizweckgebäude (nt) *De*

dump (noun) (refuse) *En*
terrain (m) de décharge *Fr*
Müllkippe (f) *De*

dumping (computer) *En*
vidange (m) (ordinateur) *Fr*
Dumping (nt) *De*

Dumping (nt) *De*
dumping (computer) *En*
vidange (m) (ordinateur) *Fr*

durchdachte Zustimmung (f) *De*
deemed consent *En*
autorisation (f) quasi-effective *Fr*

durchführbares Projekt (nt) *De*
viable proposition *En*
proposition (f) praticable *Fr*

Durchführung (f) (des Gesetzes) *De*
law enforcement *En*
application (f) de la loi *Fr*

Durchgangslager (nt) *De*
reception centre *En*
centre (m) d'accueil *Fr*

Durchgangsrecht (nt) *De*
right of way *En*
droit (m) de passage *Fr*

Durchgangsverkehr (m) *De*
through traffic *En*
circulation (f) directe *Fr*

Durchsuchungsbefehl (m) *De*
search warrant *En*
mandat (m) de perquisition *Fr*

dustbin *En*
poubelle (f) *Fr*
Mülltonne (f) *De*

dustcart *En*
voiture (f) des boueurs *Fr*
Müllwagen (m) *De*

dustman *En*
boueur (m) *Fr*
Müllwerker (m), -mann (m) *De*

duties (customs) *En*
droit(s) (m/m.pl) de douane *Fr*
Zoll (m) *De*

duties (professional) *En*
fonctions (f.pl) *Fr*
Aufgaben (f.pl) *De*

duty *En*
devoir (m) *Fr*
Aufgabe (f); Pflicht (f) *De*

dwelling *En*
habitation (f) *Fr*
Wohnung (f) *De*

dynamisch (adj) *De*
index-linked (adj) *En*
indexé (adj) *Fr*

E

early retirement *En*
retraite (f) prématurée *Fr*
vorzeitiger Ruhestand (m) *De*

earnings *En*
revenu(s) (m/m.pl) *Fr*
Verdienst (m) *De*

earth-moving equipment *En*
engins (m.pl) de chantier *Fr*
Baumaschinen (f.pl) für Erdarbeiten *De*

earthworks *En*
travaux (m.pl) en terre *Fr*
Erdarbeiten (f.pl) *De*

eau (f) douce *Fr*
Süßwasser (nt) *De*
fresh water *En*

eau (f) du robinet *Fr*
Leitungswasser (nt) *De*
tap water *En*

eau (f) potable *Fr*
Trinkwasser (nt) *De*
drinking water *En*

eau (f) superficielle *Fr*
Oberflächenwasser (nt) *De*
surface water *En*

ébouage (m) des rues *Fr*
Straßenreinigung (f), -fegen (nt) *De*
street sweeping *En*

échafaudage (m) *Fr*
Gerüst (nt) *De*
scaffolding *En*

échange (m) de l'information *Fr*
Informationsaustausch (m) *De*
information exchange *En*

échantillonnage (m) au hasard *Fr*
Stichprobe (f) *De*
random sampling *En*

échelle (f) indicière *Fr*
Gehaltsskala (f) *De*
salary scale *En*

échelle (f) mobile *Fr*
gleitende Skala (f) *De*
sliding scale *En*

échelon (m) *Fr*
Erhöhung (f) *De*
increment *En*

échevin (m) (Belg.) *Fr* *
Alderman (m), Stadtrat (m) *De*
alderman *En*

écho (m) *Fr*
Feedback (nt) *De*
feedback *En*

éclairage (m) de securité *Fr*
Notbeleuchtung (f) *De*
emergency lighting *En*

éclairage (m) de sécurité *Fr*
Sicherheitsbeleuchtung (f) *De*
security lighting *En*

éclairage (m) des routes *Fr*
Straßenbeleuchtung (f) *De*
road lighting *En*

éclairage (m) des rues *Fr*
Straßenbeleuchtung (f) *De*
street lighting *En*

école (f) *Fr*
Schule (f) *De*
school *En*

école (f) confessionnelle *Fr* *
Konfessionsschule (f) *De*
voluntary aided school *En*

école (f) de redressement pour jeunes gens *Fr*
Jugendstrafanstalt (f) *De*
borstal *En*

école (f) laïque *Fr*
maintained school *En*
staatliche Schule (f) *De*

école (f) libre *Fr*
Privatschule (f) *De*
independent school *En*

école (f) maternelle *Fr*
Kindergarten (m) *De*
nursery school *En*

école (f) normale *Fr*
Pädagogische Hochschule (f) *De*
college of education *En*

école (f) pour enfants de 8/9 à 12/13 ans *Fr*
Schule (f) für 8/ 9- bis 12/13-jährige *De*
middle school *En*

école (f) pour les enfants de 5 à 8 ans *Fr*
Grundschule(f) für die ersten zwei Jahrgänge *De*
infant school *En*

école (f) pour les enfants de 8 à 11 ans *Fr*
Grundschule (f) für 8- bis 11-jährige Kinder *De*
junior school *En*

école (f) primaire *Fr*
Grundschule (f) *De*
primary school *En*

école (f.) professionnelle d'enseignement supérieur *Fr* *
Hochschule (f.) *De*
college of higher education *En*

écolier (m) *Fr*
Schuljunge (m), Schüler (m) *De*
schoolboy *En*

écolière (f) *Fr*
Schulmädchen (nt), Schülerin (f) *De*
schoolgirl *En*

*** see/siehe/voir: Introduction page IX**

écoliers (m) ***Fr***
Schulkinder (nt.pl), Schüler (m.pl) *De*
school children *En*

ecological (adj) ***En***
écologique (adj) *Fr*
ökologisch (adj) *De*

ecological park ***En***
parc (m) écologique *Fr*
ökologischer Park (m) *De*

écologie (f) ***Fr***
Ökologie (f) *De*
ecology *En*

écologique (adj) ***Fr***
ökologisch (adj) *De*
ecological (adj) *En*

ecologist ***En***
écologiste (m/f) *Fr*
ökologe/-gin (m/f) *De*

écologiste (m/f) ***Fr***
ökologe/-gin (m/f) *De*
ecologist *En*

écologiste (m/f) ***Fr***
Umweltschützer/-in (m/f) *De*
environmentalist *En*

ecology ***En***
écologie (f) *Fr*
Ökologie (f) *De*

econometric model ***En***
modèle (m) économétrique *Fr*
ökonometrisches Modell (nt) *De*

economic analysis ***En***
analyse (f) économique *Fr*
Wirtschaftsanalyse (f) *De*

economic area ***En***
secteur (m) économique *Fr*
Wirtschaftsgebiet (nt) *De*

economic change ***En***
changement (m) économique *Fr*
Strukturwandlung (f) *De*

economic climate ***En***
état (m) économique *Fr*
Wirtschaftslage (f) *De*

economic decline ***En***
déclin (m) économique *Fr*
Konjunkturrückgang (m) *De*

economic development ***En***
développement (m) économique *Fr*
Konjunkturentwicklung (f) *De*

economic development officer ***En***
responsable (m) du développement économique *Fr*
Wirtschaftsförderer (m) *De*

economic development strategy ***En***
stratégie (f) de développement économique *Fr*
Konjunkturentwicklungsplan (m) *De*

economic forecasting ***En***
pronostication (f) économique *Fr*
Konjunkturvorhersage (f) *De*

economic growth ***En***
croissance (f) économique *Fr*
Wirtschaftswachstum (nt) *De*

economic initiatives ***En***
initiatives (f.pl) économiques *Fr*
Wirtschaftsinitiativen (f.pl) *De*

economic model ***En***
modèle (m) économique *Fr*
Wirtschaftsmodell (nt) *De*

economic planning ***En***
programme (m) de développement économique *Fr*
Wirtschaftsplanung (f) *De*

economic policy ***En***
politique (f) économique *Fr*
Wirtschaftspolitik (f) *De*

economic recession ***En***
récession (f) économique *Fr*
Konjunkturrückgang (m) *De*

economic recovery ***En***
reprise (f) économique *Fr*
Konjunkturaufschwung (m) *De*

economic strategy ***En***
stratégie (f) économique *Fr*
langfristige Konjunkturpolitik (f) *De*

economic structure ***En***
structure (f) économique *Fr*
Wirtschaftsstruktur (f) *De*

economics ***En***
sciences (f.pl) économiques *Fr*
Wirtschaftswissenschaften (f.pl) *De*

économie (f) de marché ***Fr***
Marktwirtschaft (f) *De*
market economy *En*

économie (f) domestique ***Fr***
Hauswirtschaft(slehre) (f) *De*
home economics *En*

économie (f) ***Fr***
Wirtschaft (f) *De*
economy *En*

économie (f) locale ***Fr***
Kommunalwirtschaft (f) *De*
local economy *En*

économie (f) mixte ***Fr***
Mischwirtschaft (f) *De*
mixed economy *En*

économie (f) rurale ***Fr***
Landwirtschaft (f) *De*
rural economy *En*

économie(s) (f/f.pl) d'énergie ***Fr***
Energieeinsparung (f) *De*
energy conservation/saving *En*

économies (f.pl) de grande échelle ***Fr***
System (nt) der degressiven Kosten *De*
economies of scale *En*

economies of scale ***En***
économies (f.pl) de grande échelle *Fr*
System (nt) der degressiven Kosten *De*

economist ***En***
économiste (m) *Fr*
Wirtschaftswissenschaftler/-in (m/f) *De*

économiste (m) ***Fr***
Wirtschaftswissenschaftler/-in (m/f) *De*
economist *En*

economy ***En***
économie (f) *Fr*
Wirtschaft (f) *De*

ecosystem ***En***
écosystème (m) *Fr*
Ökosystem (nt) *De*

écosystème (m) ***Fr***
Ökosystem (nt) *De*
ecosystem *En*

écoulement (m) de la circulation ***Fr***
Verkehrsfluß (m) *De*
traffic flow *En*

écrire (vb) à la machine ***Fr***
(auf der) Schreibmaschine schreiben (vb) *De*
type (vb) *En*

*** see/siehe/voir: Introduction page IX**

écriture (f) *Fr*
Schreibarbeit (f) *De*
paperwork *En*

édifice (m) social *Fr*
Sozialstruktur (f) *De*
social structure *En*

édition (f) électronique *Fr*
Desktop-Publishing (nt) *De*
electronic publishing *En*

éducateur-formateur (m) auprès des jeunes *Fr*
Jugendfürsorger/-in (m/f) *De*
youth worker *En*

education *En*
éducation (f) *Fr*
Erziehung (f), Ausbildung (f) *De*

éducation (f) *Fr*
Erziehung (f), Ausbildung (f) *De*
education *En*

education authority/ department/service *En* *
service (m) de l'éducation *Fr*
Erziehungs- und Ausbildungsbehörde (f)/ Schulbehörde (f), /-amt (nt) *De*

éducation (f) à l'environnement *Fr*
Umwelterziehung (f) *De*
environmental education *En*

éducation (f) à l'hygiène/de la santé *Fr*
Gesundheitslehre (f) *De*
health education *En*

éducation (f) civique *Fr* *
Gemeinschaftskunde (f) *De*
community education *En*

éducation (f) permanente *Fr*
Fortbildung (f) *De*
continuing education *En*

éducation (f) physique *Fr*
Leibeserziehung (f); Sport(unterricht) (m) *De*
physical education *En*

éducation (f) professionnelle de l'enseignement *Fr*
Lehrerausbildung (f) *De*
teacher education/training *En*

éducation (f) professionnelle *Fr*
Berufserziehung (f), /-ausbildung (f) *De*
vocational education/training *En*

éducation (f) professionnelle *Fr*
Berufserziehung (f) *De*
occupational training *En*

éducation (f) spécialisée *Fr*
Ausbildung (f) für Behinderte u. Schwererziehbare *De*
special education *En*

éducation- formation (f) des jeunes *Fr*
Ausbildungsprogramm (nt) für Jugendliche *De*
youth training scheme *En*

education management *En*
gestion (f) de l'éducation *Fr*
Erziehungs- und Ausbildungsleitung (f) *De*

education policy *En*
politique (f) de l'éducation *Fr*
Schulpolitik (f) *De*

éducation-formation (f) des jeunes *Fr*
Jugendarbeit (f) *De*
youth work *En*

educational psychology *En*
psychologie (f) scolaire *Fr*
Schulpsychologie (f) *De*

educational reform *En*
réforme (f) pédagogique *Fr*
Schulreform (f) *De*

educational research *En*
recherche (f) pédagogique *Fr*
pädagogische Forschung (f) *De*

efficace (adj) *Fr*
leistungsfähig, rationell (adj) *De*
efficient (adj) *En*

efficient (adj) *En*
efficace (adj) *Fr*
leistungsfähig, rationell (adj) *De*

effluent *En*
effluent (m) *Fr*
Abwasser (nt) *De*

effluent (m) *Fr*
Abwasser (nt) *De*
effluent *En*

effluent (m) *Fr*
Abwasser (nt) *De*
sewage *En*

effluent disposal *En*
dispositif (m) d'évacuation des eaux usées *Fr*
Abwasserbeseitigung (f) *De*

effluent (m) industriel *Fr*
Industrieabwasser (nt) *De*
industrial effluent *En*

égalité (f) *Fr*
Gleichheit (f) *De*
equality *En*

égalité (f) des chances *Fr*
Chancengleichheit (f) *De*
equality of opportunity *En*

égalité (f) raciale *Fr*
Rassengleichheit (f) *De*
race equality *En*

égalite (f) sexuelle *Fr*
Gleichheit (f) von Mann und Frau *De*
sex equality *En*

égout (m) *Fr*
Abwasserkanal (m) *De*
sewer *En*

égout (m) entretenu par la municipalité *Fr*
öffentlicher Abwasserkanal (m) *De*
adopted sewer *En*

Eigenbesitz (m) (von Häusern/Wohnungen) *De*
home ownership *En*
possession (f) de propriété *Fr*

Eigenheimbesitzer (m) *De*
owner occupier *En*
propriétaire-occupant (m) *Fr*

Eigentums- *De*
freehold (adj) *En*
tenu en propriété perpétuelle et libre (adj) *Fr*

(Eigentums)übertragung (f) *De*
conveyancing *En*
rédaction (f) des actes translatifs de propriété *Fr*

Eigentumsrecht (nt) *De*
property law *En*
code (m) de construction et d'urbanisme *Fr*

Eilzustellung (f) *De*
express delivery *En*
envoi (m) par exprès *Fr*

ein-, anstellen (vb) *De*
employ (vb) *En*
employer (vb) *Fr*

(eine) Eingabe machen, petitionieren (vb) *De*
petition (vb) *En*
requérir (vb) *Fr*

*** see/siehe/voir: Introduction page IX**

(eine) Entscheidung anfechten (vb) *De*
challenge (vb) a decision *En*
porter (vb) une réclamation contre une decision *Fr*

(eine) Geburt eintragen lassen (vb) *De*
register (vb) (a birth etc) *En*
déclarer (vb) (une naissance etc) *Fr*

Einelternfamilie (f) *De*
one parent family *En*
famille (f) monoparentale *Fr*

Eingabe (f), Petition (f) *De*
petition (noun) *En*
requête (f) *Fr*

eingeben (vb) *De*
input (vb) (computer) *En*
introduire (vb) des données *Fr*

eingeschoßiges Gebäude (nt) *De*
single storey building *En*
bâtiment (m) sans étage *Fr*

(eingetragenes) Warenzeichen (nt) *De*
trade mark (registered) *En*
marque (f) déposée *Fr*

einheitliche Geschäftsgebühr (f) *De*
unified business rate *En*
taxe (f) professionnelle *Fr*

Einheitssatz (m) *De*
flat rate *En*
tarif (m) uniforme *Fr*

Einkaufspassage (f) *De*
shopping arcade *En*
galerie (f) marchande *Fr*

Einkaufszentrum (nt) *De*
shopping area/centre/mall *En*
centre (m) commercial *Fr*

Einkommen (nt) *De*
income *En*
revenu (m) *Fr*

Einkommen (nt); (Familie usw) mit mittlerem —. *De*
middle income (adj) *En*
à revenus moyens *Fr*

einkommensschwache Familie (f) *De*
low income family *En*
famille (f) à revenu faible *Fr*

Einkommensteuer (f) *De*
income tax *En*
impôt (m) sur le revenu *Fr*

einlegen (vb) (Berufung usw) *De*
lodge (vb) an appeal *En*
interjeter (vb) appel *Fr*

Einleitung (f) *De*
preamble *En*
préliminaires (m.pl) (d'un traité etc) *Fr*

Einnahmebuch (nt) *De*
receipts account *En*
compte (m) de provisions *Fr*

Einnahmeerwartungen (f.pl) *De*
revenue estimates *En*
prévisions (f.pl) budgétaires *Fr*

Einnahmen (f.pl) *De*
receipts *En*
recettes (f.pl) *Fr*

Einnahmen (f.pl) *De*
revenue account *En*
trésor (m) public *Fr*

Einnahmen (f.pl); öffentliche —. *De*
revenue *En*
fisc (m) *Fr*

Einnahmenbeihilfe (f) *De*
revenue support grant *En*
dotations (f.pl) de l'Etat aux collectivités *Fr*

einreichen (vb); ein Angebot für einen Vertrag —. *De*
tender (vb) for a contract *En*
soumissioner (vb) à une adjudication *Fr*

Einrichtungsgegenstände (m.pl) *De*
furnishings *En*
ameublement (m) *Fr*

Einsatzbesprechung (f) *De*
briefing meeting (with chairman) *En*
réunion (f) préparatoire (avec le président) *Fr*

einschränken (vb) (Entwicklung usw) *De*
restrict (vb) (development etc) *En*
limiter (vb) *Fr*

einschränkender Vertrag (m) *De*
restrictive covenant *En*
accord (m) restrictif *Fr*

Einschränkung (f) der Ausgaben *De*
restriction of expenditure *En*
réduction (f) des dépenses *Fr*

Einschreibebrief (m) *De*
registered letter *En*
lettre (f) recommendée *Fr*

Einschreibung (f) *De*
enrolment *En*
immatriculation (f) (d'étudiant) *Fr*

Einspruch (m) *De*
appeal (noun, legal) *En*
appel (m) *Fr*

Einspruch gegen eine Entscheidung einlegen (vb) *De*
appeal (vb) against a decision *En*
porter (vb) une réclamation contre une décision *Fr*

Einspruchsverfahren (nt) *De*
appeals procedure *En*
procédure (f) d'appel *Fr*

einstufen (vb) *De*
band (vb) *En*
répartir (vb) les élèves en sections de force homogène *Fr*

eintragen lassen (vb); eine Geburt — — usw. *De*
register (vb) (a birth etc) *En*
déclarer (vb) (une naissance etc) *Fr*

Einwanderer/-in (m/f) *De*
immigrant *En*
immigrant (m) (-ante f.) *Fr*

Einwanderung (f) *De*
immigration *En*
immigration (f) *Fr*

Einwanderungskontrolle (f) *De*
immigration control *En*
contrôle (m) de l'immigration *Fr*

Einwanderungspolitik (f) *De*
immigration policy *En*
politique (f) de l'immigration *Fr*

Einzelhandel (m) *De*
retail industry *En*
commerce (m) au détail *Fr*

*** see/siehe/voir: Introduction page IX**

Einzelhändler (m) *De*
retailer *En*
commerçant (m) (-ante f.) au détail *Fr*

Einzelhaus (nt) *De*
detached house *En*
maison (f) separée *Fr*

Einzelunterkunft (f) *De*
single person housing *En*
logement (m) pour célibataires *Fr*

Einzugsgebiet (nt) *De*
catchment area *En*
secteur (m)/réseau (m) de ramassage (des écoliers) *Fr*

Eisenbahn (f) *De*
railway *En*
chemin (m) de fer *Fr*

Eisenbahnbeförderung (f) *De*
rail transport *En*
transport (m) par chemin de fer *Fr*

Eisenbahnnetz (nt) *De*
rail network *En*
réseau (m) ferroviaire *Fr*

élaboration (f) des politiques *Fr*
Zielformulierung (f) *De*
policy formulation/making *En*

élasticité (f) de la demande *Fr*
Nachfrageelastizität (f) *De*
demand elasticity *En*

élasticité-prix (m) *Fr*
Preiselastizität (f) *De*
price elasticity *En*

elastischer Etat (m) *De*
flexible budget *En*
budget (m) adaptable *Fr*

elderly people *En*
personnes (f.pl) agées *Fr*
ältere Menschen (m.pl) *De*

elected mayor *En*
maire (m) élu *Fr*
gewählter Bürgermeister (m) *De*

elected member *En*
membre (m) élu *Fr*
gewähltes Mitglied (nt) *De*

électeur (m) (-trice f.) *Fr*
Wähler/-in (m/f) *De*
constituent *En*

électeur (m) (-trice f.) *Fr*
Wähler/-in (m/f) *De*
elector *En*

électeur (m) (-trice f.) *Fr*
Wähler/-in (m/f) *De*
voter *En*

election *En*
élection (f) *Fr*
Wahl (f) *De*

election expenses *En*
frais (m.pl) de l'élection *Fr*
Wahlkosten (pl) *De*

élection (f) *Fr*
Wahl (f) *De*
election *En*

élection (f) municipale/départemental e/régionale *Fr*
Kommunalwahl (f) *De*
local election *En*

élection (f) partielle *Fr*
Nachwahl (f) *De*
by-election *En*

electioneering *En*
manoeuvres (f.pl) électorales *Fr*
Wahlkampf (m); Agitation (f) *De*

élections (f.pl) *Fr*
Stimmabgabe (f) *De*
polling *En*

élections (f.pl) législatives *Fr*
allgemeine Wahlen (f.pl) *De*
general election *En*

elector *En*
électeur (m) (-trice f.) *Fr*
Wähler/-in (m/f) *De*

electoral (adj) *En*
électoral (adj) *Fr*
Wahl- *De*

électoral (adj) *Fr*
Wahl- *De*
electoral (adj) *En*

electoral law *En*
droit (m) électoral *Fr*
Wahlrecht (nt) *De*

electoral reform *En*
réforme (f) électorale *Fr*
Wahlreform (f) *De*

electoral register/roll *En*
liste (f) électorale *Fr*
Wählerverzeichnis (nt) *De*

electoral system *En*
système (m) électoral *Fr*
Wahlsystem (nt) *De*

electoral ward *En*
circonscription (f) électorale *Fr*
Wahlbezirk (m) *De*

electorate *En*
corps (m) électoral *Fr*
Wähler (m.pl), Wählerschaft (f) *De*

electric power *En*
énergie (f) électrique *Fr*
elektrische Energie (f) *De*

electrical engineering *En*
électromécanique (f) *Fr*
Elektrotechnik (f) *De*

electrical power station *En*
centrale (f) électrique *Fr*
Elektrizitätswerk (nt) *De*

electrical safety *En*
sécurite (f) électrique *Fr*
Sicherheit (f) der Stromversorgung *De*

electrical supply *En*
service (m) de courant *Fr*
Elektrizitätsversorgung (f) *De*

électricité (f) *Fr*
Elektrizität (f), Strom (m) *De*
electricity *En*

electricity *En*
électricité (f) *Fr*
Elektrizität (f), Strom (m) *De*

electricity consumption *En*
consommation (f) de l'électricité *Fr*
Stromverbrauch (m) *De*

electricity demand *En*
demande (f) de l'électricité *Fr*
Strombedarf (m) *De*

electricity generation *En*
alimentation (f) électrique *Fr*
Elektrizitäts-, Stromerzeugung (f) *De*

électromécanique (f) *Fr*
Elektrotechnik (f) *De*
electrical engineering *En*

electronic mail *En*
courrier (m) électronique *Fr*
elektronische Post (f) *De*

electronic office *En*
bureau (m) électronique *Fr*
elektronisches Büro (nt) *De*

electronic publishing *En*
édition (f) électronique *Fr*
Desktop-Publishing (nt) *De*

electronics industry *En*
industrie (f) électronique *Fr*
Elektronenindustrie (f) *De*

elektrische Energie (f) *De*
electric power *En*
énergie (f) électrique *Fr*

Elektrizität (f), Strom (m) *De*
electricity *En*
électricité (f) *Fr*

Elektrizitäts-, Stromerzeugung (f) *De*
electricity generation *En*
alimentation (f) électrique *Fr*

Elektrizitätsversorgung (f) *De*
electrical supply *En*
service (m) de courant *Fr*

Elektrizitätswerk (nt) *De*
electrical power station *En*
centrale (f) électrique *Fr*

Elektronenindustrie (f) *De*
electronics industry *En*
industrie (f) électronique *Fr*

elektronische Post (f) *De*
electronic mail *En*
courrier (m) électronique *Fr*

elektronisches Büro (nt) *De*
electronic office *En*
bureau (m) électronique *Fr*

Elektrotechnik (f) *De*
electrical engineering *En*
électromécanique (f) *Fr*

élément (m) d'un tableau statistique *Fr*
statistische Tatsache (f) *De*
statistic *En*

elevated road *En*
route (f) surélevée *Fr*
aufgeschüttete Straße (f) *De*

élévation (f) *Fr*
Aufriß (m) *De*
elevations *En*

elevations *En*
élévation (f) *Fr*
Aufriß (m) *De*

élever (vb) (un enfant) *Fr*
in Pflege haben (vb) *De*
foster (vb) *En*

éligibilité (f) *Fr*
Berechtigung (f) *De*
eligibility *En*

eligibility *En*
éligibilité (f) *Fr*
Berechtigung (f) *De*

élimination (f) des déchets *Fr*
Abfallbeseitigung (f) *De*
waste disposal *En*

elterliche Rolle (f) *De*
parental involvement *En*
rôle (m) des parents *Fr*

Eltern-Lehrerbeziehungen (f.pl) *De*
home-school relations *En*
rapports (m.pl) école-famille *Fr*

Elternbeirat (m) *De*
parent teacher association (PTA) *En*
association (f) de parents d'élèves *Fr*

Elternpflicht (f) *De*
parental responsibility *En*
responsabilité (f) des parents *Fr*

Elternrechte (nt.pl) *De*
parental rights *En*
droits (m.pl) des parents *Fr*

emancipation *En*
affranchisement (m) *Fr*
Emanzipation (f) *De*

Emanzipation (f) *De*
emancipation *En*
affranchisement (m) *Fr*

embassy *En*
ambassade (f) *Fr*
Botschaft (f) *De*

emergency lighting *En*
éclairage (m) de securité *Fr*
Notbeleuchtung (f) *De*

emergency planning *En*
programmation (f) des secours *Fr*
Notstandsplanung (f) *De*

emergency repair *En*
réparations (f.pl) d'urgence *Fr*
Schnellreparatur (f) *De*

emergency service *En*
service (m) de secours *Fr*
Not-, Hilfsdienst (m) *De*

emergency vehicle *En*
voiture (f) de secours *Fr*
Hilfsfahrzeug (nt) *De*

émigrant (m) (-te f.) *Fr*
Auswanderer/-rin (m/f) *De*
emigrant *En*

emigrant *En*
émigrant (m) *Fr*
Auswanderer/-in (m/f) *De*

emission control *En*
contrôle (m) d'émission *Fr*
Abgaskontrolle (f) *De*

emmagasinage (m) *Fr*
Lagerung (f) *De*
storage *En*

Empfang bestätigen (vb) *De*
acknowledge (vb) receipt (of) *En*
accuser (vb) réception (de) *Fr*

Empfangsbestätigung (f) *De*
acknowledgment of receipt *En*
accusé (m) de réception *Fr*

Empfangschef (m) -dame (f) *De*
receptionist *En*
réceptionniste (m/f) *Fr*

Empfehlung (f) *De*
recommendation *En*
recommendation (f) *Fr*

empfohlene Vorgehensweise (f) *De*
recommended course of action *En*
démarches (f.pl) recommandées *Fr*

emploi (m) *Fr*
Arbeit (f), Beschäftigung (f) *De*
employment *En*

emploi (m) *Fr*
Stelle (f) *De*
job *En*

emploi (m) (à titre) provisoire *Fr*
vorübergehende Anstellung (f) *De*
temporary employment/work *En*

emploi (m) du temps (école) *Fr*
Stundenplan (m) (Schule) *De*
timetable (school) *En*

emplois (m.pl) réservés *Fr*
Beschäftigung (f) in beschützenden Werkstätten *De*
sheltered employment *En*

employ (vb) *En*
employer (vb) *Fr*
ein-, anstellen (vb) *De*

employé (m) (-ée f.) *Fr*
Angestellte(-r) (m/f), Arbeitnehmer/-in (m/f) *De*
employee *En*

*** see/siehe/voir: Introduction page IX**

employé (m) (-ée f.) de bureau *Fr*
Büroangestellte(r) (m/f) *De*
office worker *En*

employé (m) d'un service public *Fr*
Inhaber/-in (m/f) eines öffentlichen Amtes *De*
public servant *En*

employee *En*
employé (m) (-ée f.) *Fr*
Angestellte(-r) (m/f), Arbeitnehmer/-in (m/f) *De*

employer *En*
patron (m) (-onne f.) *Fr*
Arbeitgeber/-in (m/f) *De*

employer (vb) *Fr*
ein-, anstellen (vb) *De*
employ (vb) *En*

employment *En*
emploi (m) *Fr*
Arbeit (f), Beschäftigung (f) *De*

employment agency/office *En*
bureau (m) de placement *Fr*
Stellenvermittlung (f) *De*

employment conditions *En*
conditions (f.pl) d'emploi *Fr*
Arbeitsbedingungen (f.pl) *De*

employment creation *En*
création (f) d'emploi *Fr*
Arbeitsbeschaffung (f) *De*

employment initiative *En*
programme (m) de création d'emploi *Fr*
Arbeitsbeschaffungsprogramm (nt) *De*

employment law *En*
statut (m) de la fonction publique territoriale; code (m) du travail (secteur privé) *Fr*
Arbeitsrecht (nt) *De*

employment planning *En*
programmation (f) de l'emploi *Fr*
Arbeitsplanung (f) *De*

employment policy *En*
politique (f) de l'emploi *Fr*
Arbeitsmarktpolitik (f) *De*

employment protection *En*
sécurité (f) de l'emploi *Fr*
Arbeitsschutz (m) *De*

emprisonnement (m) *Fr*
Haft (f), Gefangenschaft (f) *De*
imprisonment *En*

emprunt (m) *Fr*
Darlehen (nt) *De*
loan *En*

emprunt (m) *Fr*
Hypothek (f) *De*
mortgage *En*

emprunt (m) garanti *Fr*
Kreditbürgschaft (f) *De*
loan guarantee *En*

emprunts (m.pl) du secteur public *Fr*
Kreditaufnahme (f) der öffentlichen Hand *De*
public sector borrowing *En*

enable (vb) *En*
habiliter (vb) (quelqu'un à faire qch) *Fr*
ermöglichen (vb) *De*

enabling role *En*
concession (f) de services publics *Fr*
Ermöglichung (f) *De*

encadrement (m) des loyers *Fr*
Mietpreisbindung (f) *De*
rent control *En*

encadrement (m) supérieur *Fr*
Geschäftsleitung (f) *De*
senior management *En*

encombrement (m) de circulation *Fr*
(Verkehrs)stau (m) *De*
traffic congestion *En*

Endabrechnung (f) *De*
final account *En*
délai (m) de rigueur *Fr*

Endstation (f) *De*
rail terminus *En*
terminus (m) *Fr*

énergie (f) atomique *Fr*
Atomenergie (f) *De*
atomic energy *En*

énergie (f) électrique *Fr*
elektrische Energie (f) *De*
electric power *En*

énergie (f) hydraulique *Fr*
hydroelektrische Energie (f) *De*
hydro-electric power *En*

énergie (f) nucléaire/atomique *Fr*
Kern-, Atomenergie (f) *De*
nuclear energy *En*

énergie (f) thermique *Fr*
thermische Energie (f) *De*
thermal energy *En*

Energiebedarf (m) *De*
energy demand *En*
demande (f) d'énergie *Fr*

Energieeinsparung (f) *De*
energy conservation/saving *En*
économie(s) (f/f.pl) d'énergie *Fr*

Energieleistungsfähigkeit (f) *De*
energy efficiency *En*
rendement (m) énergétique *Fr*

Energiepolitik (f) *De*
energy policy *En*
politique (f) d'énergie *Fr*

energiesparende Bauweise (f) *De*
low energy building *En*
bâtiment (m) isolé thermiquement *Fr*

Energieverbrauch (m) *De*
power consumption *En*
consommation (f) d'énergie *Fr*

Energieversorgung (f) *De*
energy supply *En*
alimentation (f) en énergie *Fr*

Energieversorgung (f) *De*
power supply *En*
sources (f.pl) d'énergie *Fr*

Energiewirtschaft (f) *De*
energy management *En*
gestion (f) d'énergie *Fr*

energy conservation/saving *En*
économie(s) (f/f.pl) d'énergie *Fr*
Energieeinsparung (f) *De*

energy demand *En*
demande (f) d'énergie *Fr*
Energiebedarf (m) *De*

energy efficiency *En*
rendement (m) énergétique *Fr*
Energieleistungsfähigkeit (f) *De*

energy management *En*
gestion (f) d'énergie *Fr*
Energiewirtschaft (f) *De*

energy policy *En*
politique (f) d'énergie *Fr*
Energiepolitik (f) *De*

energy supply *En*
alimentation (f) en énergie *Fr*
Energieversorgung (f) *De*

enfance (f) en danger *Fr*
gefährdete Kinder (nt.pl) *De*
children at risk *En*

enfant (m/f) à problème *Fr*
verhaltensgestörtes Kind (nt) *De*
maladjusted child *En*

enfant (m/f) martyr(e) *Fr*
Opfer (nt) der Kindesmißhandlung *De*
victim of child abuse *En*

enfants (m/f. pl) à charge *Fr*
abhängige Kinder (nt.pl) *De*
dependent children *En*

enfants (m/f pl) au-dessous de cinq ans *Fr*
Kinder (nt.pl) unter fünf Jahren *De*
under fives *En*

enfants (m/f.pl) doués *Fr*
hochbegabte Kinder (nt.pl) *De*
gifted children *En*

enfants (m/f.pl) handicapés *Fr*
behinderte Kinder (nt.pl) *De*
handicapped children *En*

enfants (m/f.pl) placés *Fr*
Kinder (nt.pl) in Pflege *De*
children in care *En*

enfoncer (vb) des pieux dans le sol *Fr*
rammen (vb) *De*
pile drive (vb) *En*

enforcement notice *En*
avis (m) d'application (d'une loi etc) *Fr*
Vollstreckungsbenachrichtigung (f) *De*

engineer *En*
ingénieur (m) *Fr*
Ingenieur/-in (m/f) *De*

engineering drawing *En*
dessin (m) de mécanique *Fr*
technische Zeichnung (f) *De*

engineering *En*
ingénierie (f) *Fr*
Technik (f) *De*

engins (m.pl) de chantier *Fr*
Baumaschinen (f.pl) für Erdarbeiten *De*
earth-moving equipment *En*

enhance (vb) (environment etc) *En*
améliorer (vb) (l'environnement etc) *Fr*
(Umgebung usw) verschönern (vb) *De*

enquête (f) *Fr*
Anfrage (f) *De*
enquiry *En*

enquête (f) *Fr*
gerichtliche Untersuchung (f) *De*
inquest *En*

enquête (f) *Fr*
Untersuchung (f) *De*
inquiry *En*

enquête (f) commodo-incommodo *Fr*
lokale Untersuchung (f) *De*
local inquiry *En*

enquête (f) d'aménagement *Fr*
Planungsanhörung (f) *De*
planning inquiry *En*

enquête (f) de commodo et incommodo *Fr*
öffentliche Untersuchung (f) *De*
public inquiry *En*

enquête (f) de commodo *Fr*
öffentliche Untersuchung (f) *De*
inquiry in public *En*

enquête (f) judiciaire *Fr*
gerichtliche Untersuchung (f) *De*
judicial inquiry *En*

enquête (f) par sondage *Fr*
Stichprobenerhebung (f) *De*
sample survey *En*

enquête (f) publique *Fr*
öffentliche Prüfung (f) *De*
examination in public (E.I.P.) *En*

enquête (f) sociale *Fr*
Sozialerhebung (f) *De*
social survey *En*

enquête (f) sur les ressources familiales *Fr*
Überprüfung (f) der Bedürftigkeit *De*
means test *En*

enquiry *En*
enquête (f) *Fr*
Anfrage (f) *De*

enregistreur (m) de temps *Fr*
Stechuhr (f) *De*
time clock *En*

enrolment *En*
immatriculation (f) (d'étudiant) *Fr*
Einschreibung (f) *De*

enseignement (m) *Fr*
Lehrberuf (m) *De*
teaching *En*

enseignant (m) stagiaire (en première année d'enseignement) *Fr*
Referendar/-in (m/f) *De*
probationary teacher *En*

enseignement (m) à distance *Fr*
Fernstudium (nt) *De*
distance learning *En*

enseignement (m) de la langue maternelle *Fr*
Unterricht (m) (in) der Muttersprache *De*
mother tongue teaching *En*

enseignement (m) des adultes *Fr*
Erwachsenenbildung (f) *De*
adult education *En*

enseignement (m) des langues *Fr*
Fremdsprachenunterricht (m) *De*
language tuition *En*

enseignement (m) libre *Fr*
Privatschulausbildung (f) *De*
private education *En*

enseignement (m) postscolaire *Fr*
Weiterbildung (f) *De*
further education *En*

enseignement (m) préélémentaire *Fr*
Vorschulerziehung (f) *De*
nursery education *En*

enseignement (m) primaire *Fr*
Grundschulerziehung (f) *De*
primary education *En*

enseignement (m) public *Fr*
staatliches Erziehungswesen (nt) *De*
state education *En*

enseignement (m) scientifique *Fr*
Unterricht (m) in den Naturwissenschaften *De*
science education *En*

*** see/siehe/voir: Introduction page IX**

enseignement (m) secondaire *Fr*
höhere Schulbildung (f) *De*
secondary education *En*

enseignement (m) technologique *Fr*
tertiärer Bildungsbereich (m) *De*
tertiary education *En*

enseigner (vb) *Fr*
unterrichten (vb) *De*
teach (vb) *En*

ensemble (m) des activités économiques *Fr*
Gesamtwirtschaft (f) *De*
aggregate economic activity *En*

Enteignung (f) *De*
compulsory purchase *En*
expropriation (f) *Fr*

Enteignungsbeschluß (m) *De*
compulsory purchase order (CPO) *En*
contrat (m) d'expropriation *Fr*

entériner (vb) (loi,décret) *Fr*
ratifizieren (vb) *De*
ratify (vb) *En*

enterprise agency *En*
agence (f) de promotion de l'entreprise *Fr*
Unternehmerorganisation (f) *De*

enterprise *En*
entreprise (f) *Fr*
Unternehmen (nt) *De*

enterprise initiative *En*
initiative (f) d'entreprise *Fr*
Unternehmungs-, Unternehmerinitiative (f) *De*

enterprise zone *En*
zone (f) d'entreprise *Fr*
wirtschaftliches Fördergebiet (nt) *De*

entfernen (vb); (einen Mieter —.) De
evict (vb) (a tenant) En
expulser (vb) un locataire Fr

enthalten (vb); sich der Stimme — . *De*
abstain (vb) *En*
s'abstenir (vb) *Fr*

entitlement *En*
allocation (f) à laquelle on a droit *Fr*
Anspruch (m) *De*

entlassen (vb) *De*
dismiss (vb) *En*
congédier (vb) *Fr*

entlassenes/überzähliges Personal (nt) De
redundant staff *En*
personnel (m) en surnombre *Fr*

Entlassung (f) De
dismissal *En*
renvoi (m) *Fr*

Entlastungsstraße (f) *De*
relief road *En*
chemin (m) de desserte *Fr*

entre régions (adj) *Fr*
interregional (adj) *De*
interregional (adj) *En*

entreposage (m) (de marchandises) *Fr*
Lagerung (f) *De*
warehousing (customs) *En*

entrepôt (m) *Fr*
Lager (nt) *De*
warehouse *En*

entrepreneur *En*
entrepreneur (m) *Fr*
Unternehmer/-in (m/f) *De*

entrepreneur (m) *Fr*
Unternehmer/-in (m/f) *De*
entrepreneur *En*

entrepreneurial (adj) *En*
qui a l'esprit d'entreprise *Fr*
unternehmerisch (adj) *De*

entreprise (f) *Fr*
Unternehmen (nt) *De*
enterprise *En*

entreprise (f); qui a l'esprit d' — . *Fr*
unternehmerisch (adj) *De*
entrepreneurial *En*

entreprise (f) de bâtiments *Fr*
Wohnungsbau (m) *De*
house building *En*

entreprise (f) de moyenne importance *Fr*
mittelgroße Firma (f) *De*
medium sized business *En*

entreprise (f) en participation *Fr*
Joint-Venture (nt) *De*
joint venture *En*

entreprise (f) locale *Fr*
örtliches Unternehmen (nt) *De*
local enterprise *En*

entreprise (f) municipale *Fr*
Gemeindeunternehmen (nt) *De*
municipal enterprise *En*

entreprise (f) privée *Fr*
Privatunternehmen (nt) *De*
private enterprise *En*

entreprise (f) publique *Fr*
öffentliches Unternehmen (nt) *De*
public enterprise *En*

entretenir (vb) *Fr*
unterhalten, instandhalten, warten (vb) *De*
maintain (vb) *En*

entretien (m) *Fr*
Instandhaltungsbeihilfe (f) *De*
maintenance *En*

entretien (m) des ponts et chaussées *Fr*
Straßeninstandhaltung (f) *De*
highway maintenance *En*

entretien (m) des routes *Fr*
Straßeninstandhaltung (f), -wartung (f) *De*
road maintenance *En*

entretien (m) des terrains de jeu *Fr*
Sportplatzunterhaltung (f) *De*
grounds maintenance *En*

entretien (m) du logement *Fr*
Wohnungsinstandhaltung (f) *De*
housing maintenance *En*

entretien (m) préventif *Fr*
Präventivinstandhaltung (f) *De*
preventive maintenance *En*

entretien (m) prévu *Fr*
geplante Instandhaltung (f) *De*
planned maintenance *En*

Entschädigung (f) *De*
indemnity *En*
indemnité (f) *Fr*

Entscheidung (f) *De*
decision *En*
décision (f) *Fr*

Entscheidungsgewalt (f) *De*
discretionary power *En*
pouvoir (m) discrétionnaire (du maire) *Fr*

*** see/siehe/voir: Introduction page IX**

Entscheidungsträger (m) ***De***
decision-making body *En*
conseil (m) qui a le droit de prendre des décisions *Fr*

entwerfen (vb) ***De***
draft (vb) *En*
rédiger (vb) *Fr*

entwerten (vb) ***De***
depreciate (vb) *En*
déprécier (vb) *Fr*

Entwertung (f) ***De***
depreciation *En*
dépréciation (f) *Fr*

Entwicklungsgebiet (nt) ***De***
development area *En*
zone (f) d'exploitation *Fr*

Entwicklungsgebiet (nt) ***De***
growth area *En*
secteur (m) de croissance *Fr*

Entwicklungshilfe (f) ***De***
development grant *En*
aide (f) financiaire à l'aménagement *Fr*

Entwicklungsplan (m) ***De***
development plan *En*
plan (m) d'aménagement *Fr*

Entwurf (m) ***De***
design (noun) *En*
dessein (m) *Fr*

Entwurf (m) ***De***
draft (noun) *En*
projet (m) *Fr*

Entwurf (m) ***De***
drafting *En*
rédaction (f) *Fr*

Entwurf (m) eines Berichts ***De***
draft report *En*
projet (m) d'un rapport *Fr*

Entwürfe überprüfen (vb) ***De***
check (vb) draft minutes/report *En*
vérifier (vb) un projet de procès-verbal/rapport *Fr*

Entwurfsanweisungen (f.pl) ***De***
design brief *En*
définition (f) d'un programme *Fr*

Entwurfsbüro (nt) ***De***
design office *En*
bureau (m) d'études *Fr*

Entwurfsvorlage (f), -richtlinien (f.pl) ***De***
design guide *En*
objectif (m) d'un projet *Fr*

enumeration district ***En***
secteur (m) de recensement *Fr*
Zählungsbezirk (m) *De*

enveloppe (f) à fenêtre ***Fr***
Fensterbriefumschlag (m) *De*
window envelope *En*

environment ***En***
environnement (m) *Fr*
Umwelt (f) *De*

environmental conservation/policy ***En***
protection (f) de l'environnement *Fr*
Umweltschutz (m)/-politik (f) *De*

environmental control ***En***
contrôle (m) de l'environnement *Fr*
Umweltkontrolle (f) *De*

environmental damage ***En***
dégats (m.pl) à l'environnement *Fr*
Umweltschäden (m.pl) *De*

environmental education ***En***
éducation (f) à l'environnement *Fr*
Umwelterziehung (f) *De*

environmental group ***En***
groupe (m) écologiste *Fr*
Umweltschutzgruppe (f) *De*

environmental health ***En***
salubrité (f) publique *Fr*
(Umwelt)gesundheitsdienst (m) *De*

environmental health officer ***En***
inspecteur (m) (-trice f.) de la salubrité publique *Fr*
Beamte(-r)/-in (m/f) im Umweltamt *De*

environmental improvement ***En***
amélioration (f) en matière d'environnement *Fr*
Umweltverbesserung (f) *De*

environmental management ***En***
gestion (f) de l'environnement *Fr*
Umweltschutzleitung (f) *De*

environmental planning ***En***
programmation (f) de l'environnement *Fr*
Umweltplanung (f) *De*

environmental pollution ***En***
pollution (f) de l'environnement *Fr*
Umweltverschmutzung (f) *De*

environmental services ***En***
services (m.pl) de l'environnement *Fr*
Umweltschutzorganisation (f) *De*

environmentalist ***En***
écologiste (m/f) *Fr*
Umweltschützer/-in (m/f) *De*

environmentally friendly ***En***
qui ne nuit pas à l'environnement *Fr*
umweltfreundlich (adj) *De*

environmentally sensitive area ***En***
région (f) d'importance écologique *Fr*
umweltbewußtes Gebiet (nt) *De*

environnement (m) ***Fr***
Umwelt (f) *De*
environment *En*

environnement (m); qui ne nuit pas à l' — . ***Fr***
umweltfreundlich (adj) *De*
environmentally friendly *En*

envoi (m) par exprès ***Fr***
Eilzustellung (f) *De*
express delivery *En*

épuration (f) de l'eau ***Fr***
Wasserreinigung (f) *De*
water purification *En*

épuration (f) des eaux usées ***Fr***
Abwasserklärung (f) *De*
sewage treatment *En*

equal opportunities ***En***
chances (f.pl) égales *Fr*
Chancengleichheit (f) *De*

equal opportunities policy ***En***
politique (f) d'égalité des chances *Fr*
Politik (f) der Chancengleichheit *De*

equal pay ***En***
salaire (m) égal *Fr*
gleicher Lohn (m) (für gleiche Arbeit) *De*

equal rights ***En***
droits (m.pl) égaux *Fr*
Gleichberechtigung (f) *De*

*** see/siehe/voir: Introduction page IX**

equality *En*
égalité (f) *Fr*
Gleichheit (f) *De*

equality of opportunity *En*
égalité (f) des chances *Fr*
Chancengleichheit (f) *De*

équilibrer (vb) le budget *Fr*
bilanzieren (vb) *De*
balance (vb) the budget *En*

équipe (f) de dactylos *Fr*
Schreibkräfte (f.pl) *De*
typing pool (staff) *En*

équipe (f) de nuit *Fr*
Nachtschicht (f) *De*
night shift *En*

équipe (f) régionale *Fr*
Regionalgruppe (f) *De*
area team *En*

équipement (m) de loisirs *Fr*
Freizeiteinrichtungen (f.pl) *De*
leisure facilities *En*

équipement (m) de récréation *Fr*
Spielmöglichkeiten (f.pl) *De*
play facilities *En*

équipements (m.pl) de loisirs *Fr*
Möglichkeiten (f.pl) zur Freizeitgestaltung *De*
recreation facilities *En*

Erdarbeiten (f.pl) *De*
earthworks *En*
travaux (m.pl) en terre *Fr*

Erdgas (nt) *De*
natural gas *En*
gaz (m) naturel *Fr*

Ergebnisanalyse (f) *De*
performance analysis *En*
tableau (m) comparatif de performances *Fr*

Erhaltung (f) *De*
preservation *En*
conservation (f) *Fr*

erheben (vb); Steuer usw — . *De*
levy (vb) (a tax etc) *En*
lever (un impôt) (vb) *Fr*

Erhöhung (f) *De*
increment *En*
échelon (m) *Fr*

Erlaß (m) *De*
remission (of tax) *En*
remise (f) d'un impôt *Fr*

Erlaubnis (f), Genehmigung (f) *De*
warrant (travel) *En*
feuille (f) de route *Fr*

ermäßigter Tarif (m) *De*
concessionary fare *En*
tarif (m) réduit *Fr*

Ermäßigung (f) der Gemeindeabgaben *De*
rate rebate *En*
décharge (f) d'impôt *Fr*

Ermäßigung (f) der Gemeindeabgaben *De*
rate relief *En*
allégement (m) des impôts *Fr*

Ermessen (nt) *De*
discretion *En*
discrétion (f) *Fr*

ermöglichen (vb) *De*
enable (vb) *En*
habiliter (vb) (quelqu'un à faire qch) *Fr*

ermöglichen (vb) *De*
facilitate (vb) *En*
faciliter (vb) *Fr*

Ermöglichung (f) *De*
enabling role *En*
concession (f) de services publics *Fr*

ernennen (vb) *De*
appoint (vb) *En*
nommer (vb) *Fr*

Ernennung (f) (Stelle) *De*
appointment (job) *En*
nomination (f) (emploi) *Fr*

erneuern (vb); den Belag einer Straße — . *De*
resurface (vb) a road *(En)*
refaire (vb) le revêtement d'une route *Fr*

Erneuerung (f) *De*
regeneration *En*
régéneration (f) *Fr*

Erschließungsgebiet (nt) *De*
development land *En*
terrains (m.pl) bâtissables *Fr*

Erschließungsgebiet (nt) *De*
improvement area *En*
zone (f) d'amélioration *Fr*

Erschließungsgelände (nt) *De*
development site *En*
zone (f) de développement *Fr*

Erschließungskontrolle (f) der Entwicklung *De*
development control *En*
contrôle (m) de l'aménagement *Fr*

Erschließungsprogramm (nt) *De*
improvement scheme *En*
programme (m) de modernisation *Fr*

Erschließungswert (m) *De*
development value *En*
coût (m) foncier *Fr*

erschwingliche Miete (f) *De*
affordable rent *En*
loyer (m) de faible montant *Fr*

erschwingliche Wohnungen (f.pl) *De*
affordable housing *En*
logement (m) à loyer modéré *Fr*

erstatten (vb); Kosten — . *De*
award (vb) costs *En*
accorder (vb) les frais et depens (m.pl) *Fr*

erteilen (vb); (die) Lizenz — . *De*
franchise (vb) *En*
octroyer (vb) une concession Fr

Erwachsenenbildung (f) *De*
adult training *En*
formation (f) pour adultes *Fr*

Erwachsenenbildung (f) *De*
adult education *En*
enseignement (m) des adultes *Fr*

Erwachsenenbildungs-programm (nt) *De*
adult training strategy *En*
programme (m) de formation pour adultes *Fr*

Erwerbsunfähigkeits-, Invalidenrente (f) *De*
disablement benefit *En*
allocation (f) d'adulte handicappé *Fr*

Erwerbsunfähigkeitsrente (f), Krankenunterstützung (f) *De*
invalidity benefit/pension *En*
pension (f) d'invalidité *Fr*

*** see/siehe/voir: Introduction page IX**

Erziehung (f), Ausbildung (f) De
education *En*
éducation (f) *Fr*

Erziehungs- und Ausbildungsbehörde (f)/ Schulbehörde (f),/-amt (nt) De *
education authority/department/service *En*
service (m) de l'éducation *Fr*

Erziehungs- und Ausbildungsleitung (f) De
education management *En*
gestion (f) de l'éducation *Fr*

escalier (m)/échelle (f) de secours Fr
Feuertreppe (f) *De*
fire escape *En*

escape route En
itinéraire (m) de sortie de secours *Fr*
Fluchtweg (m) *De*

espace (m) naturel sensible Fr
wissenschaftliche Sehenswürdigkeit (f) *De*
Site of Special Scientific Interest (SSI) *En*

espace (m) public Fr
öffentliche Anlagen (f.pl) *De*
public open space *En*

Essen (nt) auf Rädern De
meals-on-wheels *En*
repas (m.pl) à domicile *Fr*

estate agency En
agence (f) immobilière *Fr*
Immobilienmakler/-in (m/f) *De*

estate (housing) En
lotissement (m) *Fr*
Siedlung (f) *De*

estate management En
gestion (f) de logement *Fr*
Immobilienverwaltung (f) *De*

estates department En
direction (f) des bâtiments *Fr*
Liegenschaftsamt (nt) *De*

esthétique (f) industrielle Fr
industrielle Formgebung (f) *De*
industrial design *En*

estimate En
devis (m) *Fr*
Voranschlag (m) *De*

estimate (vb) En
prévoir (vb) *Fr*
schätzen (vb) *De*

estimation En
estimation (f) *Fr*
Schätzung (f) *De*

estimation (f) Fr
Schätzung (f) *De*
estimation *En*

établi par la loi (adj) Fr
gesetzlich (adj) *De*
statutory (adj) *En*

établir (vb) le budget Fr
(Budget usw) festlegen (vb) *De*
fix (vb) the budget *En*

établissement (m) du plan d'occupation des sols Fr
Strukturprogramm (nt) *De*
structure planning *En*

établissement (m) spécialisé Fr
Sonderschule (f) *De*
special school *En*

état; en mauvais — (adj) Fr
defekt (adj) *De*
defective (adj) *En*

état (m) civil Fr
Standesamt (nt) *De*
registry office *En*

état (m) de finances Fr
Wirtschaftserklärung (f) *De*
financial statement *En*

état (m) économique Fr
Wirtschaftslage (f) *De*
economic climate *En*

état (m) providence Fr
Wohlfahrtsstaat (m) *De*
welfare state *En*

états-membres (m.pl) Fr
Mitglied(s)staaten (m.pl) *De*
member states *En*

étayer (vb) Fr
(ab)stützen (vb) *De*
underpin (vb) *En*

ethnic group En
groupe (m) ethnique *Fr*
ethnische Gruppe (f) *De*

ethnic minority En
minorité (f) ethnique *Fr*
ethnische Minderheit (f) *De*

ethnic origin En
origine (f) ethnique *Fr*
ethnische Herkunft (f) *De*

ethnische Gruppe (f) De
ethnic group *En*
groupe (m) ethnique *Fr*

ethnische Herkunft (f) De
ethnic origin *En*
origine (f) ethnique *Fr*

ethnische Minderheit (f) De
ethnic minority *En*
minorité (f) ethnique *Fr*

étiquetage (m) de la nourriture Fr
Lebensmitteletikettierung (f) *De*
food labelling *En*

étude (f) d'une route Fr
Straßenplanung (f) *De*
road design *En*

étude (f) de faisabilité Fr
Tauglichkeits-, Eignungsstudie (f) *De*
feasibility study *En*

étude (f) de marché Fr
Marktforschung (f) *De*
market research *En*

étude (f) du travail Fr
Arbeitsstudie (f) *De*
work study *En*

étude (f) individuelle Fr
Fallstudie (f) *De*
case study *En*

études (f.pl) supérieures Fr
Hochschulausbildung (f) *De*
higher education *En*

études (f) préalables à l'opération de construction Fr
Geländekontrolle (f) *De*
site investigation *En*

étudiant (m) (-ante f.) Fr
Student/-in (m/f) *De*
student *En*

étudiant (m) (-ante f.) qui prépare la licence Fr
Student/-in (m/f) *De*
undergraduate *En*

*** see/siehe/voir: Introduction page IX**

étudier (vb) *Fr*
studieren (vb) *De*
study (vb) *En*

etwas außer Haus machen lassen (vb) *De*
put out (vb) to contract *En*
mettre (vb) en adjudication *Fr*

europäisch (adj) *De*
European (adj) *En*
européen (-enne f.) (adj) *Fr*

Europäische Investitionsbank (f) *De*
European Investment Bank *En*
Banque (f) Européenne d'Investissement *Fr*

Europäische Kommission (f) *De*
European Commission *En*
Commission (f) des Communautés Européennes *Fr*

Europäische Wirtschafts-gemeinschaft (f) *De*
European Economic Community *En*
Communauté (f) Economique Européenne *Fr*

europäischer Binnenmarkt (m) *De*
Single European Market *En*
marché (m) européen unique *Fr*

Europäischer Kohesionsfond (m) *De*
European Cohesion Fund *En*
Fonds (m) Européen de Cohésion *Fr*

Europäischer Regionalfond (m) *De*
European Regional Fund *En*
Fonds (m) Européen Régional *Fr*

Europäischer Sozialfond (m) *De*
European Social Fund *En*
Fonds (m) Européen Social *Fr*

Europäischer Strukturfond (m) *De*
European Structural Funds *En*
Fonds (m.pl) Européens Structurels *Fr*

Europäisches Währungssystem (nt) *De*
European Monetary System *En*
Système (m) Européen Monétaire *Fr*

European (adj) *En*
européen (-enne f.) (adj) *Fr*
europäisch (adj) *De*

European Cohesion Fund *En*
Fonds (m) Européen de Cohésion *Fr*
Europäischer Kohesionsfond (m) *De*

European Commission *En*
Commission (f) des Communautés Européennes *Fr*
Europäische Kommission (f) *De*

European Economic Community *En*
Communauté (f) Economique Européenne *Fr*
Europäische Wirtschaftsgemeinschaft (f) *De*

European Investment Bank *En*
Banque (f) Européenne d'Investissement *Fr*
Europäische Investitionsbank (f) *De*

European Monetary System *En*
Système (m) Européen Monétaire *Fr*
Europäisches Währungssystem (nt) *De*

European Regional Fund *En*
Fonds (m) Européen Régional *Fr*
Europäischer Regionalfond (m) *De*

European Social Fund *En*
Fonds (m) Européen Social *Fr*
Europäischer Sozialfond (m) *De*

European Structural Funds *En*
Fonds (m.pl) Européens Structurels *Fr*
Europäischer Strukturfond (m) *De*

européen (-enne f.) (adj) *Fr*
europäisch (adj) *De*
European (adj) *En*

evaluation *En*
évaluation (f) *Fr*
Schätzung (f) *De*

évaluation (f) *Fr*
Beurteilung (f) *De*
appraisal *En*

évaluation (f) *Fr*
Schätzung (f) *De*
evaluation *En*

évaluation (f) *Fr*
Schätzung (f) *De*
valuation *En*

évaluation (f) de la demande *Fr*
Nachfrageschätzung (f) *De*
demand assessment *En*

évaluation (f) de politique *Fr*
Grundsatzanalyse (f) *De*
policy analysis *En*

évaluation (f) de progrès *Fr*
Ziele (nt.pl) *De*
attainment target *En*

évaluation (f) de propriété *Fr*
Grundvermögensbewertung (f) *De*
assessment of property *En*

évaluation (f) des politiques *Fr*
Überprüfung (f) der Politik *De*
policy review *En*

évaluation (f) du coût *Fr*
Kostenberechnung (f) *De*
costing *En*

évaluation (f) du personnel *Fr*
Personalbewertung (f) *De*
personnel appraisal *En*

évaluation (f) du potentiel (personnel) *Fr*
Potentialbeurteilung (f) (Personal) *De*
assessment of potential (staff) *En*

évaluation (f) du programme *Fr*
Programmbewertung (f) *De*
programme evaluation *En*

évaluation (f) du projet *Fr*
Unternehmensbewertung (f) *De*
project appraisal/evaluation *En*

évaluation (f) du quotient familial *Fr*
Beurteilung (f) sozialer Bedürftigkeit *De*
needs assessment *En*

évaluation (f) prudente *Fr*
vorsichtige Schätzung (f) *De*
conservative estimate *En*

evasion of taxes *En*
fraude (f) fiscale *Fr*
Steuerhinterziehung (f) *De*

evict (vb) (a tenant) *En*
expulser (vb) (un locataire) *Fr*
(einen Mieter) entfernen (vb) *De*

évolution (f) démographique *Fr*
Bevölkerungswandel (m) *De*
population change *En*

évolution (f) des ménages *Fr*
Haushaltsplan (m) *De*
household projection *En*

ex-officio member *En*
membre (m) à titre d'office *Fr*
Mitglied (nt) von Amts wegen *De*

examen (m) *Fr*
Prüfung (f) *De*
examination *En*

examen (m) médical *Fr*
ärztliche Untersuchung (f) *De*
medical examination *En*

examen (m) oral *Fr*
mündliche Prüfung (f) *De*
oral examination *En*

examination *En*
examen (m) *Fr*
Prüfung (f) *De*

examination in public (E.I.P.) *En*
enquête (f) publique *Fr*
öffentliche Prüfung (f) *De*

examination result *En*
résultat (m) d'examen *Fr*
Prüfungsergebnis (nt) *De*

excavation *En*
excavation (f) *Fr*
Ausgrabung (f) *De*

excavation (f) *Fr*
Ausgrabung (f) *De*
excavation *En*

exchange control *En*
contrôle (m) des changes *Fr*
Devisenkontrolle (f) *De*

exchange rate *En*
cours (m) du change *Fr*
Wechselkurs (m) *De*

excise duties *En*
droits (m.pl) de régie *Fr*
Verbrauch(s)steuer (f) *De*

excise duty *En*
droit (m) sur la consommation *Fr*
Verbrauchsabgabe (f) *De*

exécution (f) de contrat *Fr*
Vertragseinhaltung (f) *De*
contract compliance *En*

exécution (f) des politiques *Fr*
programmatische Umsetzung (f) *De*
policy implementation *En*

executive (business) *En*
dirigeant (m) *Fr*
leitende(r) Angestellte(r) (m/f) *De*

executive officer (public sector) *En*
rédacteur (m) *Fr*
Beamte(r)/-in (m/f) *De*

exempt (vb) *En*
exempter (vb) *Fr*
befreien (vb) *De*

exempter (vb) *Fr*
befreien (vb) *De*
exempt (vb) *En*

exemption *En*
exemption (f) *Fr*
Befreiung (f) *De*

exemption (f) *Fr*
Befreiung (f) *De*
exemption *En*

exercice (m) de sauvetage en cas d'incendie *Fr*
Probealarm (m) *De*
fire drill *En*

exhibition centre *En*
salon (m) d'exposition *Fr*
Ausstellungsgelände (nt) *De*

éxonération (f) d'impôt *Fr*
Steuerfreiheit (f) *De*
tax exemption *En*

exonéré (adj) d'impôts *Fr*
steuerfrei (adj) *De*
tax free (adj) *En*

exonéré (adj) d'impôts *Fr*
steuerfrei (adj) *De*
free of tax (adj) *En*

expandierende Stadt (f) *De*
expanding town *En*
ville (f) en plein développement *Fr*

expanding town *En*
ville (f) en plein développement *Fr*
expandierende Stadt (f) *De*

expédition (f) *Fr*
Versendung (f) *De*
consignment *En*

expenditure cut *En*
réduction de la dépense *Fr*
Ausgabenkürzung (f) *De*

expenditure *En*
dépense (f) *Fr*
Ausgaben (f.pl) *De*

expenses *En*
frais (m.pl) *Fr*
Spesen (pl) *De*

expert-conseil (m) *Fr*
Berater/-in (m/f) *De*
consultant *En*

exploitation (f) de la houille *Fr*
Kohlenbergbau (m) *De*
coal mining *En*

exploitation (f) des renseignements *Fr*
Informationsverarbeitung (f) *De*
information processing *En*

exploitation (f) industrielle *Fr*
industrielle Erschließung (f) *De*
industrial development *En*

Export (m) *De*
exportations (f.pl) *Fr*
exports *En*

export manager *En*
chef (m) du service exportation *Fr*
Exportabteilungsleiter (m) *De*

export (vb) *En*
exporter (vb) *Fr*
exportieren (vb) *De*

Exportabteilungsleiter (m) *De*
export manager *En*
chef (m) du service exportation *Fr*

exportateur (m) (-trice f.) *Fr*
Exporteur (m) *De*
exporter *En*

exportations (f.pl) *Fr*
Export (m) *De*
exports *En*

exporter *En*
exportateur (m) (-trice f.) *Fr*
Exporteur (m) *De*

exporter (vb) *Fr*
exportieren (vb) *De*
export (vb) *En*

Exporteur (m) *De*
exporter *En*
exportateur (m) (-trice f.) *Fr*

exportieren (vb) *De*
export (vb) *En*
exporter (vb) *Fr*

*** see/siehe/voir: Introduction page IX**

exports *En*
exportations (f.pl) *Fr*
Export (m) *De*

express delivery *En*
envoi (m) par exprès *Fr*
Eilzustellung (f) *De*

expressway *En*
voie (f) rapide *Fr*
Schnellstrasse (f) *De*

expropriation (f) *Fr*
Enteignung (f) *De*
compulsory purchase *En*

expulser (vb) (un locataire) *Fr*
(einen Mieter) entfernen (vb) *De*
evict (vb) (a tenant) *En*

extension *En*
extension (f) *Fr*
Verlängerung (f) *De*

extension (f) *Fr*
Verlängerung (f) *De*
extension *En*

extension (f) d'une maison *Fr*
Anbau (m) *De*
house extension *En*

extension (f) urbaine en bordure de route *Fr*
Zeilenbauweise (f) *De*
ribbon development *En*

extension of credit *En*
prolongation (f) d'un crédit *Fr*
Verlängerung (f) einer Zahlungsfrist *De*

external audit *En*
contrôle (m) externe *Fr*
externe Rechnungsprüfung (f) *De*

external works *En*
travaux (m.pl) extérieurs *Fr*
Außenarbeiten (f.pl) *De*

externe Rechnungsprüfung (f) *De*
external audit *En*
contrôle (m) externe *Fr*

extincteur (m) d'incendie *Fr*
Feuerlöscher (m) *De*
fire extinguisher *En*

extra charge *En*
supplément (m) *Fr*
Zuschlagsgebühr (f) *De*

extraordinary general meeting *En*
assemblée (f) générale extraordinaire *Fr*
außerordentliche Generalversammlung (f) *De*

*** see/siehe/voir: Introduction page IX**

F

fabricant (m) *Fr*
Hersteller (m) *De*
manufacturer *En*

fabrication (f) *Fr*
Herstellung (f) *De*
manufacture *En*

Fabrik (f) *De*
factory *En*
usine (f) *Fr*

facade *En*
façade (f) *Fr*
Fassade (f) *De*

façade (f) *Fr*
Fassade (f) *De*
facade *En*

Facharbeit (f) *De*
skilled labour *En*
main-d'oeuvre (f) spécialisée *Fr*

Facharbeiter (m); Fachkraft (f) *De*
skilled worker *En*
ouvrier (m) (-ière f.) qualifié(e) *Fr*

Fachhochschule (f) *De*
technical college *En*
collège (m) technique; lycée (m) technique *Fr*

(fachliche) Qualifikation (f) *De*
professional qualification *En*
aptitude (f) professionnelle *Fr*

Fachpersonalmangel (m) *De*
skill shortage *En*
manque (m) de personnel qualifié *Fr*

Fachverband (m) *De*
trade association *En*
syndicat (m) professionnel *Fr*

Fachzentrum (nt) *De*
skill centre *En*
centre (m) de formation *Fr*

facilitate (vb) *En*
faciliter (vb) *Fr*
ermöglichen (vb) *De*

faciliter (vb) *Fr*
ermöglichen (vb) *De*
facilitate (vb) *En*

facsimile transmission (fax) *En*
téléfax (m); télécopie (f) *Fr*
Faksimileübertragung (f), Fax (nt) *De*

factor analysis *En*
analyse (f) des facteurs *Fr*
Faktorenanalyse (f) *De*

factory *En*
usine (f) *Fr*
Fabrik (f) *De*

facture (f) *Fr*
Rechnung (f) *De*
invoice *En*

facturer (vb) *Fr*
fakturieren (vb) *De*
invoice (vb) *En*

Fahrbahn (f) *De*
carriageway *En*
chaussée (f) *Fr*

Fahrbücherei (f) *De*
mobile library *En*
bibliobus (m) *Fr*

fahrendes Volk (nt) *De*
travelling people *En*
nomades (m.pl) *Fr*

Fahrpreisgefüge (nt) *De*
fare structure *En*
structure (f) des prix du voyage *Fr*

Fahrradspur (f); Radweg (m) De
cycle lane/path En
piste (f) cyclable Fr

Fahrtschreiber (m) *De*
tachograph *En*
tachygraphe (m) *Fr*

failli (m) *Fr*
Gemeinschuldner (m) *De*
bankrupt *En*

faillite (f) *Fr*
Bankrott (m) *De*
bankruptcy *En*

faillite (f) *Fr*
Insolvenz (f), Zahlungsunfähigkeit (f) *De*
insolvency *En*

faillite (f); faire — . *Fr*
Pleite machen (vb) *De*
bankrupt (to go) (vb) *En*

fair rent *En*
loyer (m) raisonnable *Fr*
angemessene Miete (f) *De*

faire supporter (vb) (au responsable) une erreur de paiement *Fr*
Zuschlag erheben (vb) *De*
surcharge (vb) *En*

Faksimileübertragung (f), Fax (nt) *De*
facsimile transmission (fax) *En*
téléfax (m); télécopie (f) *Fr*

Faktorenanalyse (f) *De*
factor analysis *En*
analyse (f) des facteurs *Fr*

fakturieren (vb) *De*
invoice (vb) *En*
facturer (vb) *Fr*

Fallbesprechung (f) *De*
case conference *En*
réunion (f) de concertation *Fr*

fallout shelter *En*
abri (m) anti-atomique *Fr*
Atombunker (m) *De*

Fallrecht (nt) *De*
case law *En*
jurisprudence (f) *Fr*

*** see/siehe/voir: Introduction page IX**

Fallstudie (f) *De*
case study *En*
étude (f) individuelle *Fr*

Familienberatungsstelle (f) *De*
family planning clinic *En*
clinique (f) du planning familial *Fr*

Familienpflege (f) *De*
family care/support/welfare *En*
aide (f) sociale *Fr*

Familienplanung (f) *De*
family planning *En*
planning (m) familial *Fr*

Familienzulage (f) *De*
family income supplement/support *En*
allocations (f.pl) familiales *Fr*

famille (f) à revenu faible *Fr*
einkommensschwache Familie (f) *De*
low income family *En*

famille (f) monoparentale *Fr*
Einelternfamilie (f) *De*
one parent family *En*

famille (f) sans asile *Fr*
obdachlose Familie (f) *De*
homeless family *En*

family allowance *En*
allocation (f) familiale *Fr*
Kindergeld (nt) *De*

family care/support/welfare *En*
aide (f) sociale *Fr*
Familienpflege (f) *De*

family income supplement/support *En*
allocations (f.pl) familiales *Fr*
Familienzulage (f) *De*

family planning clinic *En*
clinique (f) du planning familial *Fr*
Familienberatungsstelle (f) *De*

family planning *En*
planning (m) familial *Fr*
Familienplanung (f) *De*

family practitioner *En*
médecin (m) de famille *Fr*
Hausarzt (m)/Hausärztin (f) *De*

Farbige (pl) *De*
coloured people *En*
gens (m.pl) de couleur *Fr*

fare structure *En*
structure (f) des prix du voyage *Fr*
Fahrpreisgefüge (nt) *De*

fares policy *En*
politique (f) des prix du voyage *Fr*
Tarifpolitik (f) *De*

farm waste *En*
déchets (m.pl) agricoles *Fr*
landwirtschaftlicher Abfall (m) *De*

farming *En*
agriculture (f) *Fr*
Landwirtschaft (f) *De*

farmland *En*
terre (f) agricole *Fr*
Ackerland (nt) *De*

Fassade (f) *De*
facade *En*
façade (f) *Fr*

fausse déclaration (f) *Fr*
Verdrehung (f) *De*
misrepresentation *En*

faute (f) de frappe *Fr*
Tippfehler (m) *De*
typing error *En*

fauteuil (m) roulant *Fr*
Rollstuhl (m) *De*
wheelchair *En*

faux frais (m.pl) *Fr*
Nebenkosten (pl) *De*
incidental expenses *En*

feasibility study *En*
étude (f) de faisabilité *Fr*
Tauglichkeits-, Eignungsstudie (f) *De*

federal (adj) *En*
fédéral (adj) *Fr*
Bundes- *De*

fédéral (adj) *Fr*
Bundes- *De*
federal (adj) *En*

federal government *En*
gouvernement (m) fédéral *Fr*
Bundesregierung (f) *De*

federalism *En*
fédéralisme (m) *Fr*
Föderalismus (m) *De*

fédéralisme (m) *Fr*
Föderalismus (m) *De*
federalism *En*

feedback *En*
écho (m) *Fr*
Feedback (nt) *De*

Feedback (nt) *De*
feedback *En*
écho (m) *Fr*

fees *En*
frais (m.pl) *Fr*
Gebühren (f.pl) *De*

Feldforschung (f) *De*
fieldwork *En*
recherches (f.pl) sur le terrain *Fr*

femme (f) professionnelle *Fr*
berufstätige Frau (f) *De*
working woman *En*

femme-agent (f) de police *Fr*
Polizistin (f) *De*
policewoman *En*

Fensterbriefumschlag (m) *De*
window envelope *En*
enveloppe (f) à fenêtre *Fr*

Fernmeldeamt (nt) *De*
telephone exchange *En*
central (m) téléphonique *Fr*

Fernmeldewesen (nt) *De*
telecommunication *En*
télécommunication (f) *Fr*

Fernsprechbuch (nt) *De*
telephone directory; phone book *En*
annuaire (m) des téléphones *Fr*

Fernstraße (f) *De*
trunk road *En*
grande route (f) *Fr*

Fernstudium (nt) *De*
distance learning *En*
enseignement (m) à distance *Fr*

Fertigbau (m) *De*
prefabricated building *En*
bâtiment (m) préfabriqué *Fr*

Fertigbeton (m) *De*
ready-mixed concrete *En*
béton (m) malaxé *Fr*

Fertighäuser (nt.pl) *De*
prefabricated housing *En*
habitation (f) préfabriquée *Fr*

fertility rate *En*
taux (m) de fertilité *Fr*
Fruchtbarkeitsziffer (f) *De*

feste Abfälle (m.pl) *De*
solid waste *En*
déchets (m.pl) solides *Fr*

Feststoffentsorgungsanlage (f) *De*
solid waste transfer station *En*
usine (f) d'incinération des déchets *Fr*

Feststoffentsorgungsbetrieb (m) *De*
solid waste management *En*
gestion (f) des déchets solides *Fr*

fête (f) légale *Fr*
gesetzlicher Feiertag (m) *De*
bank holiday *En*

fête (f) légale *Fr*
gesetzlicher Feiertag (m) *De*
public holiday *En*

Feuergefahr (f) *De*
fire hazard *En*
risque (m) d'incendie *Fr*

feuergefährliches Material (nt) *De*
flammable material *En*
matière (f) inflammable *Fr*

Feuergefährlichkeit (f) *De*
flammability *En*
inflammabilité (f) *Fr*

feuerhemmend (adj) *De*
flame retardant (adj) *En*
ignifuge (adj) *Fr*

Feuerlöschanlagen (f.pl) *De*
fire fighting equipment *En*
matériel (m) d'incendie *Fr*

Feuerlöscher (m) *De*
fire extinguisher *En*
extincteur (m) d'incendie *Fr*

Feuermelder (m) *De*
fire alarm *En*
sirène (f) d'incendie *Fr*

feuerpolizeiliches Zeugnis (nt) *De*
fire certificate *En*
certificat (m) de tenue au feu *Fr*

Feuerschutz (m) *De*
fire precautions *En*
précautions (f.pl) contre l'incendie *Fr*

Feuerschutzbestimmung (f) *De*
fire regulations *En*
restrictions (f.pl) relatives à l'incendie *Fr*

Feuerschutztür (f) *De*
fire door *En*
porte (f) coupe-feu *Fr*

Feuersicherheit (f) *De*
fire safety *En*
securité (f) contre l'incendie *Fr*

Feuertreppe (f) *De*
fire escape *En*
escalier (m)/échelle (f) de secours *Fr*

Feuerwache (f) *De*
fire station *En*
poste (m) d'incendie *Fr*

Feuerwehr (f) *De*
fire brigade/service *En*
corps (m) de sapeurs-pompiers *Fr*

Feuerwehrmann (m) *De*
fireman *En*
pompier (m) *Fr*

feuille (f) de présence *Fr*
Stechkarte (f) *De*
time sheet *En*

feuille (f) de route *Fr*
Erlaubnis (f), Genehmigung (f) *De*
warrant (travel) *En*

feux (m.pl) de circulation *Fr*
(Verkehrs)ampel (f) *De*
traffic lights *En*

Öffentlichkeitsreferent/-in (m/f) *De*
public relations officer *En*
responsable (m) des relations publiques *Fr*

Öffnungszeiten (f.pl) *De*
opening hours *En*
heures (f.pl) d'ouverture *Fr*

fidéicommis (m) *Fr*
Treuhandgesellschaft (f); Treuhänderschaft (f) *De*
trust; trusteeship *En*

field survey *En*
levé (m) du terrain *Fr*
Absatzforschung (f) *De*

fieldwork *En*
recherches (f.pl) sur le terrain *Fr*
Feldforschung (f) *De*

file (noun) *En*
dossier (m) (documents) *Fr*
Akte (f) *De*

file (vb) *En*
classer (vb) *Fr*
ablegen (vb) *De*

file management system *En*
système (m) de gestion de fichiers *Fr*
Datenspeichersystem (nt) *De*

filing *En*
classement (m) (de documents) *Fr*
Ablage (f) *De*

filing cabinet *En*
classeur (m) *Fr*
Aktenschrank (m) *De*

filing clerk *En*
documentaliste(m/f) *Fr*
Archivkraft (f) *De*

final account *En*
délai (m) de rigueur *Fr*
Endabrechnung (f) *De*

final demand *En*
dernier (m) rappel *Fr*
letzte Mahnung (f) *De*

final instalment *En*
dernier versement (m) *Fr*
letzte Rate (f) *De*

finance *En*
finance(s) (f/f.pl) *Fr*
Finanzen (pl) *De*

finance company *En*
société (f) de financement *Fr*
Finanzierungsgesellschaft (f) *De*

finance department *En*
service (m) financier *Fr*
Finanzabteilung (f) *De*

finance officer *En*
administrateur (m) des finances *Fr*
Finanzbeamte(r)/-in (m/f) *De*

finance(s) (f/f.pl) *Fr*
Finanzen (pl) *De*
finance *En*

financement (m) d'investissement *Fr*
Kapitalanlage (f) *De*
capital funding *En*

financement (m) *Fr*
Finanzierung (f) *De*
financing *En*

*** see/siehe/voir: Introduction page IX**

financement (m) *Fr*
Finanzierung (f) *De*
resourcing *En*

finances (f.pl) communales/départementales/régionales *Fr*
Gesamtfinanzen (pl) *De*
aggregate finance *En*

finances (f.pl) des collectivités territoriales *Fr*
Kommunalfinanzen (pl) *De*
local authority finance *En*

finances (f.pl) du gouvernement local *Fr*
Kommunalfinanzen (pl) *De*
local government finance *En*

finances (f.pl) publiques *Fr*
öffentliche Finanzen (pl) *De*
public finance *En*

financial advice *En*
conseil (m) financier *Fr*
Finanzberatung (f) *De*

financial assistance *En*
aide (f) financière *Fr*
Finanzhilfe (f) *De*

financial control *En*
contrôle (m) des finances *Fr*
Finanzkontrolle (f) *De*

financial information system *En*
système (m) d'informations financières *Fr*
Finanzinformationssystem (nt) *De*

financial limits *En*
limites (f.pl) financières *Fr*
finanzielle Grenzen (f.pl) *De*

financial management *En*
responsabilité (f) des finances *Fr*
Finanzplanung (f) *De*

financial market *En*
marché (m) financier *Fr*
Finanzmarkt (m) *De*

financial planning *En*
programmation (f) financière *Fr*
Finanzplanung (f) *De*

financial policy *En*
politique (f) financière *Fr*
Finanzpolitik (f) *De*

financial resources *En*
ressources (f.pl) fiscales *Fr*
Finanzierungsmittel (nt.pl) *De*

financial restraint *En*
restrictions (f.pl) financières *Fr*
finanzielle Einschränkung (f) *De*

financial services *En*
services (m.pl) financiers *Fr*
Finanzverwaltung (f) *De*

financial statement *En*
état (m) de finances *Fr*
Wirtschaftserklärung (f) *De*

financial year *En*
annuité (f) *Fr*
Rechnungsjahr (nt) *De*

financing *En*
financement (m) *Fr*
Finanzierung (f) *De*

Finanzabteilung (f) *De*
finance department *En*
service (m) financier *Fr*

Finanzamt (nt) *De*
tax office *En*
bureau (m) des contributions *Fr*

Finanzbeamte(r)/-in (m/f) *De*
finance officer *En*
administrateur (m) des finances *Fr*

Finanzberatung (f) *De*
financial advice *En*
conseil (m) financier *Fr*

Finanzen (pl) *De*
finance *En*
finance(s) (f/f.pl) *Fr*

Finanzhilfe (f) *De*
financial assistance *En*
aide (f) financière *Fr*

finanzielle Einschränkung (f) *De*
financial restraint *En*
restrictions (f.pl) financières *Fr*

finanzielle Grenzen (f.pl) *De*
financial limits *En*
limites (f.pl) financières *Fr*

finanzieller Anteil (m) *De*
monetary interest *En*
intérêt (m) pécuniaire *Fr*

finanzieren (vb) *De*
fund (vb) *En*
consolider (vb) *Fr*

Finanzierung (f) *De*
financing *En*
financement (m) *Fr*

Finanzierung (f) *De*
resourcing *En*
financement (m) *Fr*

Finanzierung (f) nach Formel *De*
formula funding *En*
montage (m) financier *Fr*

Finanzierungsgesellschaft (f) *De*
finance company *En*
société (f) de financement *Fr*

Finanzierungsmittel (nt.pl) *De*
financial resources *En*
ressources (f.pl) fiscales *Fr*

Finanzinformationssystem (nt) *De*
financial information system *En*
système (m) d'informations financières *Fr*

Finanzkontrolle (f) *De*
financial control *En*
contrôle (m) des finances *Fr*

Finanzmarkt (m) *De*
financial market *En*
marché (m) financier *Fr*

Finanzplanung (f) *De*
financial management *En*
responsabilité (f) des finances *Fr*

Finanzplanung (f) *De*
financial planning *En*
programmation (f) financière *Fr*

Finanzpolitik (f) *De*
financial policy *En*
politique (f) financière *Fr*

Finanzpolitik (f) *De*
fiscal policy *En*
politique (f) budgétaire *Fr*

Finanzverwaltung (f) *De*
financial services *En*
services (m.pl) financiers *Fr*

fine *En*
amende (f) *Fr*
Geldstrafe (f) *De*

fine (vb) *En*
frapper (vb) quelqu'un d'une amende *Fr*
mit einer Geldstrafe belegen (vb) *De*

fire *En*
incendie (m) *Fr*
Brand (m) *De*

fire alarm *En*
sirène (f) d'incendie *Fr*
Feuermelder (m) *De*

fire brigade/service *En*
corps (m) de sapeurs-pompiers *Fr*
Feuerwehr (f) *De*

fire certificate *En*
certificat (m) de tenue au feu *Fr*
feuerpolizeiliches Zeugnis (nt) *De*

fire door *En*
porte (f) coupe-feu *Fr*
Feuerschutztür (f) *De*

fire drill *En*
exercice (m) de sauvetage en cas d'incendie *Fr*
Probealarm (m) *De*

fire engine *En*
voiture (f) de pompiers *Fr*
Löschfahrzeug (nt) *De*

fire escape *En*
escalier (m)/échelle (f) de secours *Fr*
Feuertreppe (f) *De*

fire extinguisher *En*
extincteur (m) d'incendie *Fr*
Feuerlöscher (m) *De*

fire fighting equipment *En*
matériel (m) d'incendie *Fr*
Feuerlöschanlagen (f.pl) *De*

fire hazard *En*
risque (m) d'incendie *Fr*
Feuergefahr (f) *De*

fire precautions *En*
précautions (f.pl) contre l'incendie *Fr*
Feuerschutz (m) *De*

fire regulations *En*
restrictions (f.pl) relatives à l'incendie *Fr*
Feuerschutzbestimmung (f) *De*

fire risk *En*
risque (m) d'incendie *Fr*
Brandgefahr (f) *De*

fire safety *En*
securité (f) contre l'incendie *Fr*
Feuersicherheit (f) *De*

fire station *En*
poste (m) d'incendie *Fr*
Feuerwache (f) *De*

fireman *En*
pompier (m) *Fr*
Feuerwehrmann (m) *De*

firm *En*
firme (f) *Fr*
Firma (f) *De*

Firma (f) *De*
firm *En*
firme (f) *Fr*

firme (f) *Fr*
Firma (f) *De*
firm *En*

Firmenimage (nt) *De*
corporate image *En*
image (f) de marque de la firme/de l'organisation *Fr*

Firmenleitung (f) *De*
corporate management *En*
management (m) *Fr*

fisc (m) *Fr*
(öffentliche) Einnahmen (f.pl) *De*
revenue *En*

fiscal (adj) *En*
fiscal (adj) *Fr*
fiskalisch, finanzpolitisch (adj) *De*

fiscal (adj) *Fr*
fiskalisch, finanzpolitisch (adj) *De*
fiscal (adj) *En*

fiscal policy *En*
politique (f) budgétaire *Fr*
Finanzpolitik (f) *De*

fiscal year *En*
année (f) budgétaire *Fr*
Rechnungsjahr (nt) *De*

fiscalité (f) locale *Fr*
Kommunalsteuerwesen (nt) *De*
rating system *En*

fiskalisch, finanzpolitisch (adj) *De*
fiscal (adj) *En*
fiscal (adj) *Fr*

fix (vb) the budget *En*
établir (vb) le budget *Fr*
(Budget usw) festlegen (vb) *De*

fixation (f) de loyer *Fr*
Mietschätzung (f) *De*
rent assessment *En*

fixed assets *En*
Anlagevermögen (nt) *De*
immobilisations (f.pl) *Fr*

fixed term contract *En*
contrat (m) à durée déterminée *Fr*
Fixvertrag (m) *De*

Fixvertrag (m) *De*
fixed term contract *En*
contrat (m) à durée déterminée *Fr*

Fläche (f); (gesamte) bebaubare — *De*
land supply *En*
disponibilité (f) de terrain *Fr*

flame retardant (adj) *En*
ignifuge (adj) *Fr*
feuerhemmend (adj) *De*

flammability *En*
inflammabilité (f) *Fr*
Feuergefährlichkeit (f) *De*

flammable material *En*
matière (f) inflammable *Fr*
feuergefährliches Material (nt) *De*

flat *En*
appartement (m) *Fr*
Wohnung (f) *De*

flat rate *En*
tarif (m) uniforme *Fr*
Einheitssatz (m) *De*

flexible Anstellung (f) *De*
flexible tenure *En*
tenure (f) flexible *Fr*

flexible budget *En*
budget (m) adaptable *Fr*
elastischer Etat (m) *De*

flexible tenure *En*
tenure (f) flexible *Fr*
flexible Anstellung (f) *De*

flexible working *En*
mobilité (f) horaire *Fr*
anpassungsfähige Arbeitsweise (f) *De*

flexibler Wechselkurs (m) *De*
floating exchange rate *En*
taux (m) de change flottant *Fr*

flexitime *En*
horaire (f) personnalisée *Fr*
Gleitzeit (f) *De*

floating exchange rate *En*
taux (m) de change flottant *Fr*
flexibler Wechselkurs (m) *De*

flood barrier *En*
barrage (m) contre les inondations *Fr*
Hochwasserbarriere (f) *De*

flood prevention/protection *En*
protection (f) contre les inondations *Fr*
Hochwasserschutz (m) *De*

flood warning system *En*
alerte (f) aux crues *Fr*
Flutwarnung (f) *De*

floor area *En*
superficie (f) *Fr*
Grund-. Bodenfläche (f) *De*

floor slab *En*
pavage (m) *Fr*
Pflasterstein (m) *De*

flotation (of company etc) *En*
lancement (m) (d'une compagnie etc) *Fr*
Lancierung (f) *De*

flow chart *En*
ordinogramme (m) *Fr*
Flußdiagramm (nt) *De*

flow chart (vb) *En*
faire (vb) l'ordinogramme *Fr*
ein Flußdiagramm aufstellen (vb) *De*

Flüchtling (m) *De*
refugee *En*
réfugié (-ée f.) *Fr*

Fluchtmöglichkeit (f) *De*
means of escape *En*
moyen (m) de fuite *Fr*

Fluchtweg (m) *De*
escape route *En*
itinéraire (m) de sortie de secours *Fr*

fluctuate (vb) *En*
fluctuer (vb) *Fr*
schwanken (vb) *De*

fluctuating rate *En*
taux (m) variable *Fr*
schwankender Kurs (m) *De*

fluctuation *En*
fluctuation (f) *Fr*
Schwankung (f) *De*

fluctuation (f) *Fr*
Schwankung (f) *De*
fluctuation *En*

fluctuations (f.pl) de personnel *Fr*
Personalwechsel (m) *De*
labour turnover *En*

fluctuer (vb) *Fr*
schwanken (vb) *De*
fluctuate (vb) *En*

Flughafenkapazität (f) *De*
airport capacity *En*
capacité (f) d'accueil d'un aéroport *Fr*

Flußdiagramm (nt) *De*
flow chart *En*
ordinogramme (m) *Fr*

(ein) Flußdiagram (m) (nt) aufstellen (vb) *De*
flowchart (vb) *En*
faire l'ordinogramme (vb) *Fr*

flüssige Mittel (nt.pl) *De*
liquid assets *En*
valeurs (f.pl) disponibles *Fr*

Flußtransport (m) *De*
river freight/transport *En*
transport (m) par voie d'eau *Fr*

Flußverschmutzung (f) *De*
river pollution *En*
pollution (f) des cours d'eau *Fr*

Flutwarnung (f) *De*
flood warning system *En*
alerte (f) aux crues *Fr*

fly tipping *En*
décharge (f) illégale *Fr*
illegales Müllabladen (nt) *De*

flyover *En*
passage (m) supérieur *Fr*
Überführung (f) *De*

Föderalismus (m) *De*
federalism *En*
fédéralisme (m) *Fr*

foire (f) commerciale *Fr*
Messe (f) *De*
trade fair *En*

Folgeschaden (m) *De*
consequential loss *En*
perte (f) indirecte *Fr*

Folgeschäden (m.pl) *De*
liquidated damages *En*
dommages-intérêts (m.pl) fixés en argent *Fr*

fonctionnaire (m) chargé de la dératisation *Fr*
Rattenfänger (m) *De*
rodent officer *En*

fonctionnaire (m) territorial *Fr*
Kommunalbeamte(-r)/-in (m/f) *De*
local government officer *En*

fonctionnaire (m/f) *Fr*
(Staats)beamte(-r)/-beamtin (m/f) *De*
civil servant *En*

fonctionnel (m) *Fr*
persönliche(-r) Referent/-in (m/f) *De*
personal assistant *En*

fonctions (f.pl) *Fr*
Aufgaben (f.pl) *De*
duties (professional) *En*

fondation (f) (d'un édifice) *Fr*
Fundament (nt) *De*
foundation (of building) *En*

fondation (f) sur pilotis *Fr*
Pfahlgründung (f) *De*
pile foundation *En*

fonds (m) *Fr*
Mittel (nt.pl) *De*
fund(s) *En*

fonds (m) d'amortissement *Fr*
Tilgungsfonds (m) *De*
sinking fund *En*

fonds (m) de concours *Fr*
Planungsgewinn (m) *De*
planning gain *En*

fonds (m) de dépôts *Fr*
Treuhandvermögen (nt) *De*
trust fund *En*

Fonds (m) Européen de Cohésion *Fr*
Europäischer Kohesionsfond (m) *De*
European Cohesion Fund *En*

Fonds (m) Européen Régional *Fr*
Europäischer Regionalfond (m) *De*
European Regional Fund *En*

Fonds (m) Européen Social *Fr*
Europäischer Sozialfond (m) *De*
European Social Fund *En*

Fonds (m) Monétaire International (F.M.I.) *Fr*
internationaler Währungsfonds (m) *De*
International Monetary Fund (I.M.F.) *En*

fonds (m.pl) de roulement *Fr*
Betriebskapital (nt) *De*
working capital *En*

Fonds (m.pl) Européens Structurels *Fr*
Europäischer Strukturfond (m) *De*
European Structural Funds *En*

fonds (m) social *Fr*
Sozialfonds (m) *De*
Social Fund *En*

food contamination *En*
contamination (f) de la nourriture *Fr*
Lebensmittelverseuchung (f) *De*

food hygiene *En*
hygiène (f) alimentaire *Fr*
Lebensmittelhygiene (f) *De*

food industry *En*
industrie (f) d'alimentation *Fr*
Lebensmittelindustrie (f) *De*

food labelling *En*
étiquetage (m) de la nourriture *Fr*
Lebensmitteletikettierung (f) *De*

footbridge *En*
pont (m) pour piétons *Fr*
Fußgängerbrücke (f) *De*

footing *En*
base (f) (en béton) *Fr*
Bankett (nt) *De*

footwear industry *En*
manufacture (f) des chaussures *Fr*
Schuhindustrie (f) *De*

force (f) tactique *Fr*
Sonderkommando (nt) *De*
task force *En*

Förderaufgaben (f.pl) *De*
remedial work *En*
réparations (f.pl) *Fr*

Förderunterricht (m) *De*
remedial education *En*
action (f) pour combler le retard scolaire *Fr*

forecast (vb) *En*
prévoir (vb) *Fr*
vorhersagen (vb) *De*

forecasting *En*
pronostication (f) *Fr*
Voraussage (f), Prognose (f) *De*

forefront (in the) *En*
au premier plan *Fr*
in vorderster Linie *De*

foreign investment *En*
investissement (m) extérieur *Fr*
Auslandsinvestition (f) *De*

foreign trade *En*
commerce (m) extérieur *Fr*
Auslandsgeschäft (nt) *De*

foreman *En*
contremaître (m) *Fr*
Vorarbeiter (m) *De*

forestry *En*
sylviculture (f) *Fr*
Forstwirtschaft (f) *De*

forfeiture *En*
déchéance (f) *Fr*
Verlust (m) *De*

form *En*
formule (f) *Fr*
Formular (nt) *De*

form of contract *En*
modèle (m) de contrat *Fr*
Vertragsform (f) *De*

form of tender *En*
modèle (m) de soumission *Fr*
Angebot (nt) *De*

formation (f) *Fr*
Ausbildung (f) *De*
training *En*

formation (f) continue *Fr*
Berufschulerziehung (f) *De*
non advanced further education *En*

formation (f) du personnel *Fr*
Personalausbildung (f) *De*
staff training *En*

formation (f) industrielle *Fr*
Arbeitsunterricht (m) *De*
industrial training *En*

formation (f) pour adultes *Fr*
Erwachsenenbildung (f) *De*
adult training *En*

former (vb) *Fr*
ausbilden (vb) *De*
train (vb) *En*

formula funding *En*
montage (m) financier *Fr*
Finanzierung (f) nach Formel *De*

formulaire (m) de demande *Fr*
Antragsformular (nt) *De*
application form *En*

Formular (nt) *De*
form *En*
formule (f) *Fr*

formulate (vb) (policy etc) *En*
définir (vb) (une politique etc) *Fr*
(Grundsatz usw) formulieren (vb) *De*

formule (f) *Fr*
Formular (nt) *De*
form *En*

formuler (vb) un projet *Fr*
planen (vb) *De*
plan (vb) *En*

Forschungsprogramm (nt) *De*
research project *En*
projet (m) de recherche *Fr*

Forstwirtschaft (f) *De*
forestry *En*
sylviculture (f) *Fr*

Fortbildung (f) *De*
continuing education *En*
éducation (f) permanente *Fr*

fortschreitender Zusammenbruch (m) *De*
progressive collapse *En*
délabrement (m) progressif *Fr*

forward planning *En*
planification (f) stratégique *Fr*
Zukunftsplanung (f) *De*

fossé (m) d'évacuation *Fr*
Abflußgraben (m) *De*
storm drain *En*

foster (vb) *En*
élever (vb) (un enfant) *Fr*
in Pflege haben (vb) *De*

foster care *En*
placement (m) familial *Fr*
Pflege (f) *De*

foster home *En*
foyer (m) des parents nourriciers *Fr*
Pflegestelle (f), -heim (nt) *De*

foster parents *En*
parents (m.pl) nourriciers *Fr*
Pflegeeltern (pl) *De*

fostering *En*
prise (f) d'un enfant en nourrice *Fr*
Pflege (f) *De*

*** see/siehe/voir: Introduction page IX**

Fotokopie (f) *De*
photocopy (noun) *En*
photocopie (f) *Fr*

fotokopieren (vb) *De*
photocopy (vb) *En*
photocopier (vb) *Fr*

Fotokopiergerät (nt) *De*
photocopier *En*
photocopieur (m) *Fr*

foundation (of building) *En*
fondation (f) (d'un édifice) *Fr*
Fundament (nt) *De*

fournir (vb) (qn de qch) *Fr*
liefern (vb) *De*
supply (vb) *En*

fournisseur (m) *Fr*
Lieferant (m) *De*
supplier *En*

foyer (m) *Fr*
Wohnheim (nt) *De*
hostel *En*

foyer (m) des jeunes *Fr*
Jugendzentrum (nt) *De*
youth centre *En*

foyer (m) des parents nourriciers *Fr*
Pflegestelle (f), -heim (nt) *De*
foster home *En*

Fracht (f) De
commercial transport *En*
transport (m) routier *Fr*

Fracht (f) De
freight *En*
transport (m) (de marchandises) *Fr*

frachtfrei (adj) De
carriage free (adj) *En*
franco (adj) *Fr*

Frachtpolitik (f) De
freight policy *En*
politique (f) du transport de marchandises *Fr*

Fragebogen (m) *De*
questionnaire *En*
questionnaire (m) *Fr*

frais (m.pl) *Fr*
Gebühren (f.pl) *De*
fees *En*

frais (m.pl) *Fr*
Spesen (pl) *De*
expenses *En*

frais (m.pl) bancaires *Fr*
Bankspesen (pl) *De*
bank charges *En*

frais (m.pl) d'exploitation *Fr*
Betriebskosten (pl) *De*
operating cost *En*

frais (m.pl) d'exploitation *Fr*
Betriebskosten (pl) *De*
running cost *En*

frais (m.pl) de déplacement *Fr*
Pflegegeld (nt) *De*
attendance allowance *En*

frais (m.pl) de l'élection *Fr*
Wahlkosten (pl) *De*
election expenses *En*

frais (m.pl) de magasinage *Fr*
Lagerkosten (pl) *De*
storage costs *En*

frais (m.pl) de transport *Fr*
Beförderungs-, Transportkosten (pl) *De*
transport costs *En*

frais (m.pl) de voyage *Fr*
Reisekosten (pl) *De*
travelling expenses *En*

frais (m.pl) divers *Fr*
verschiedene Ausgaben (f.pl) *De*
sundry expenses *En*

frais (m.pl) fonciers *Fr*
Grundlasten (f.pl) *De*
land charges *En*

frais (m.pl) généraux *Fr*
Gemeinkosten (pl) *De*
overheads *En*

framed construction *En*
bâtiment à (m) structure discontinue *Fr*
Tragkonstruktion (f) *De*

franchise (business) *En*
concession (f) *Fr*
Lizenz (f) *De*

franchise (political) *En*
droit (m) de vote *Fr*
Wahlrecht (nt) *De*

franchise (vb) *En*
octroyer une concession (vb) *Fr*
(die) Lizenz erteilen (vb) *De*

franco (adj) *Fr*
frachtfrei (adj) *De*
carriage free (adj) *En*

franco de port (adj) *Fr*
portofrei (adj) *De*
post free (adj) *En*

Frankiermaschine (f) De
franking machine *En*
machine (f) à affranchir *Fr*

franking machine *En*
machine (f) à affranchir *Fr*
Frankiermaschine (f) *De*

frapper (vb) quelqu'un d'une amende *Fr*
mit einer Geldstrafe belegen (vb) *De*
fine (vb) *En*

fraud *En*
fraude (f) *Fr*
Betrug (m) *De*

fraude (f) *Fr*
Betrug (m) *De*
fraud *En*

fraude (f) fiscale *Fr*
Steuerhinterziehung (f) *De*
evasion of taxes *En*

fraudulent (adj) *En*
frauduleux (-euse f.) (adj) *Fr*
betrügerisch (adj) *De*

frauduleux (-euse f.) (adj) *Fr*
betrügerisch (adj) *De*
fraudulent (adj) *En*

Frauenemanzipation (f); Frauenbewegung (f) De
women's liberation *En*
mouvement (m) pour la libération de la femme (MLF) *Fr*

Frauengruppe (f) De
women's group *En*
groupe (m) qui est partisan du MLF *Fr*

Frauenhaus (nt) De
women's refuge *En*
asile (m) pour femmes *Fr*

Frauenklinik (f) De
well woman clinic *En*
centre (m) de soins gynécologiques *Fr*

Frauenrechte (nt.pl) De
women's rights *En*
droits (m.pl) de la femme *Fr*

free enterprise *En*
libre entreprise (f) *Fr*
freie Wirtschaft (f) *De*

*** see/siehe/voir: Introduction page IX**

free market *En*
marché (m) libre *Fr*
freier Markt (m) *De*

free of tax (adj) *En*
exonéré d'impôts (adj) *Fr*
steuerfrei (adj) *De*

free port *En*
port (m) franc *Fr*
Freihafen (m) *De*

free public transport *En*
transports (m.pl) en commun gratuits *Fr*
kostenloser öffentlicher Personenverkehr (m) *De*

free speech *En*
libre parole (f) *Fr*
Redefreiheit (f) *De*

free trade *En*
libre-échange (m) *Fr*
Freihandel (m) *De*

free trade zone *En*
zone (f) franche (de commerce) *Fr*
Freihandelszone (f) *De*

freedom *En*
liberté (f) *Fr*
Freiheit (f) *De*

freedom of choice *En*
liberté (f) de choix arbitraire *Fr*
Wahlfreiheit (f) *De*

freedom of expression *En*
liberté (f) d'expression *Fr*
Meinungsfreiheit (f) *De*

freedom of information *En*
droit (m) d'accès aux documents administratifs *Fr*
Informationsfreiheit (f) *De*

freehold (adj) *En*
tenu en propriété perpétuelle et libre (adj) *Fr*
Eigentums- *De*

freehold *En*
propriété (f) foncière perpétuelle et libre *Fr*
freier Grundbesitz (m) *De*

freier Grundbesitz (m) *De*
freehold *En*
propriété (f) foncière perpétuelle et libre *Fr*

freie Regierungsform (f) *De*
open government *En*
transparence (f) *Fr*

freie Stelle (f) *De*
job vacancy *En*
poste (m) vacant *Fr*

freie Stelle (f) *De*
vacancy (staff) *En*
poste (m) vacant *Fr*

freie Wirtschaft (f) *De*
free enterprise *En*
libre entreprise (f) *Fr*

freier Markt (m) *De*
free market *En*
marché (m) libre *Fr*

freight *En*
transport (m) (de marchandises) *Fr*
Fracht (f) *De*

freight policy *En*
politique (f) du transport de marchandises *Fr*
Frachtpolitik (f) *De*

Freihafen (m) *De*
free port *En*
port (m) franc *Fr*

Freihandel (m) *De*
free trade *En*
libre-échange (m) *Fr*

Freihandelszone (f) *De*
free trade zone *En*
zone (f) franche (de commerce) *Fr*

Freiheit (f) *De*
freedom *En*
liberté (f) *Fr*

Freiheit (f) *De*
liberty *En*
liberté (f) *Fr*

Freiheit (f) des Einzelnen, individuelle Freiheit *De*
individual liberty *En*
liberté (f) civile *Fr*

freiwillige Arbeit (f) *De*
voluntary work *En*
travail (m) volontaire *Fr*

freiwillige(r) Helfer/-in (m/f); Freiwillige(r) (m/f) *De*
voluntary worker/volunteer *En*
volontaire (m) *Fr*

Freiwilligenverband (m) *De*
voluntary agency/organisation *En*
organisation (f) bénévole *Fr*

freiwilliger Dienst (m) *De*
voluntary service *En*
service (m) volontaire *Fr*

freiwilliger Sektor (m) *De*
voluntary sector *En*
secteur (m) non-gouvernemental *Fr*

Freizeit (f) *De*
leisure *En*
loisir (m) *Fr*

Freizeitamt (nt) *De*
leisure department *En*
service (m) de la culture/des sports *Fr*

Freizeitbeschäftigungen (f.pl) im Freien *De*
outdoor recreation *En*
jeux (m.pl) de plein-air *Fr*

Freizeiteinrichtungen (f.pl) *De*
leisure facilities *En*
équipement (m) de loisirs *Fr*

Freizeitgelände (nt) *De*
recreation area *En*
cour (f) de récréation *Fr*

Freizeitpolitik (f) *De*
leisure policy *En*
politique (f) des loisirs *Fr*

Freizeitzentrum (nt) *De*
amenity centre *En*
centre (m) de récréations *Fr*

Freizeitzentrum (nt) *De*
leisure centre *En*
centre (m) social *Fr*

Freizeitzentrum (nt) *De*
recreation centre *En*
centre (m) de loisirs *Fr*

Fremdenverkehrsamt (nt) *De*
tourist board *En*
service (m) de tourisme *Fr*

Fremdfinanzierung (f) *De*
debt financing *En*
règlement (m) de la dette *Fr*

Fremdsprachenunterricht (m) *De*
language tuition *En*
enseignement (m) des langues *Fr*

fresh water *En*
eau (f) douce *Fr*
Süßwasser (nt) *De*

Friedensrichter/-in (m/f) *De*
magistrate *En*
magistrat (m) *Fr*

*** see/siehe/voir: Introduction page IX**

fringe benefits *En*
compléments (m.pl) de salaire en nature *Fr*
zusätzliche Leistungen (f.pl) *De*

Frist (f) *De*
time limit (for payment) *En*
délai (m) de paiement *Fr*

frontier *En*
frontière (f) *Fr*
Grenze (f) *De*

frontière (f) *Fr*
Grenze (f) *De*
boundary *En*

frontière (f) *Fr*
Grenze (f) *De*
frontier *En*

Fruchtbarkeitsziffer (f) *De*
fertility rate *En*
taux (m) de fertilité *Fr*

Frühstückspension (f) *De*
bed and breakfast establishment *En*
hôtel (m) garni *Fr*

fuel *En*
combustible (m) *Fr*
Brenn-, Kraftstoff (m) *De*

fuel consumption *En*
consommation (f) de combustible *Fr*
Brennstoffverbrauch (m) *De*

fuel cost/price *En*
prix (m) du combustible *Fr*
Brennstoffkosten (pl) *De*

fuel efficiency *En*
rendement (m) énergétique *Fr*
Brennstoffleistung (f) *De*

fuel tax *En*
impôt (m) sur le combustible *Fr*
Brennstoffsteuer (f) *De*

Führer/-in (m/f) *De*
leader *En*
chef (m) *Fr*

Führung (f) *De*
leadership *En*
qualités (f.pl) de chef *Fr*

Führungsinformation (f) *De*
management information *En*
informatique (f) de gestion *Fr*

full-time (adj) *En*
à plein temps *Fr*
Ganztags- *De*

fumigation *En*
désinfection (f) *Fr*
Ausräucherung (f) *De*

fund raising scheme *En*
projet (m) pour se procurer des fonds *Fr*
Spendenaktion (f) *De*

fund(s) *En*
fonds (m) *Fr*
Mittel (nt.pl) *De*

fund (vb) *En*
consolider (vb) *Fr*
finanzieren (vb) *De*

Fundament (nt) *De*
foundation (of building) *En*
fondation (f) (d'un édifice) *Fr*

Fundierung (f) *De*
funding *En*
consolidation (f) *Fr*

funding *En*
consolidation (f) *Fr*
Fundierung (f) *De*

für *De*
on behalf of *En*
de la part de *Fr*

furnished accommodation *En*
meublé (m) *Fr*
möblierte Wohnung (f) *De*

furnishings *En*
ameublement (m) *Fr*
Einrichtungsgegenstände (m.pl) *De*

Fürsorge (f) *De*
caring services *En*
service (m) des soins *Fr*

Fürsorgeerziehungsverfahren (nt) *De*
care proceedings *En*
procédure (f) d'ordonnance de placement *Fr*

further details *En*
plus amples renseignements (m.pl) *Fr*
nähere Umstände (m.pl) *De*

further education college *En*
lycée (m) professionnel *Fr*
weiterbildende Schule (f) *De*

further education *En*
enseignement (m) postscolaire *Fr*
Weiterbildung (f) *De*

further information *En*
renseignements (m.pl) complémentaires *Fr*
weitere Auskunft (f) *De*

Fußgängerbrücke (f) *De*
footbridge *En*
pont (m) pour piétons *Fr*

Fußgängerüberweg (m) *De*
pedestrian crossing *En*
passage (m) pour piétons *Fr*

Fußgängerzone (f) *De*
pedestrian area/precinct/zone *En*
zone (f) piétonne *Fr*

Fusion (f) *De*
merger *En*
fusion (f) *Fr*

fusion (f) *Fr*
Fusion (f) *De*
merger *En*

*** see/siehe/voir: Introduction page IX**

G

galerie (f) marchande *Fr*
Einkaufspassage (f) *De*
shopping arcade *En*

Ganztags- *De*
full-time (adj) *En*
à plein temps *Fr*

garage (m) à étages *Fr*
Parkhaus (nt) *De*
multi-storey car park *En*

garantie (f) d'une échéance *Fr*
Sicherheit (f) *De*
security for a debt *En*

Garantie (f) *De*
guarantee *En*
garantie (f) *Fr*

garantie (f) *Fr*
Garantie (f) *De*
guarantee *En*

garantir (vb) *Fr*
gewährleisten (vb) *De*
guarantee (vb) *En*

garde (f) à vue (pour les mineurs) *Fr*
Jugendstrafe (f) *De*
youth custody *En*

garden city *En*
cité-jardin (f) *Fr*
Gartenstadt (f) *De*

gardien (m) *Fr*
Vormund (m) *De*
guardian *En*

gardien (m) *Fr*
Wächter (m) *De*
security guard *En*

gardiennage (m) *Fr*
Betreuung (f) *De*
caretaking *En*

gare (f) des marchandises *Fr*
Güterbahnhof (m) *De*
rail depot *En*

gare (f) routière *Fr*
Busbahnhof (m) *De*
coach station *En*

Gartenbau (m) *De*
horticulture *En*
horticulture (f) *Fr*

Gartenstadt (f) *De*
garden city *En*
cité-jardin (f) *Fr*

gas *En*
gaz (m) *Fr*
Gas (nt) *De*

Gas (nt) *De*
gas *En*
gaz (m) *Fr*

gas cooled reactor *En*
réacteur (m) refroidi au gaz *Fr*
gasgekühlter Kernreaktor (m) *De*

gas industry *En*
industrie (f) du gaz *Fr*
Gasindustrie (f) *De*

gas meter *En*
compteur (m) à gaz *Fr*
Gaszähler (m) *De*

gas supply *En*
service (m) de gaz *Fr*
Gasversorgung (f) *De*

gas works *En*
usine (f) à gaz *Fr*
Gaswerk (nt) *De*

gasgekühlter Kernreaktor (m) *De*
gas cooled reactor *En*
réacteur (m) refroidi au gaz *Fr*

Gasindustrie (f) *De*
gas industry *En*
industrie (f) du gaz *Fr*

Gasversorgung (f) *De*
gas supply *En*
service (m) de gaz *Fr*

Gaswerk (nt) *De*
gas works *En*
usine (f) à gaz *Fr*

Gaszähler (m) *De*
gas meter *En*
compteur (m) à gaz *Fr*

gauche (f) *Fr*
linker Flügel (m) *De*
left wing *En*

gauche; de — (adj) *Fr*
linke(-r,-s) (adj) *De*
left wing (adj) *En*

gaz (m) *Fr*
Gas (nt) *De*
gas *En*

gaz (m) de ville *Fr*
Stadtgas (nt) *De*
town gas *En*

gaz (m) naturel *Fr*
Erdgas (nt) *De*
natural gas *En*

Gebäude (nt) *De*
building *En*
bâtiment (m) *Fr*

Gebäude (nt) *De*
premises *En*
locaux (m.pl) *Fr*

Gebäude (nt) mit wenigen Stockwerken *De*
low rise building *En*
bâtiment (m) bas *Fr*

Gebäude (nt) unter Denkmalschutz *De*
listed building *En*
bâtiment (m) classé d'intérêt historique ou architectural *Fr*

Gebäudebestand (m) *De*
building stock *En*
parc (m) de bâtiments *Fr*

*** see/siehe/voir: Introduction page IX**

Gebiet (nt), Region (f) ***De***
region *En*
région (f) *Fr*

Gebietshilfe (f) ***De***
regional aid *En*
aides (f.pl) régionales *Fr*

Gebrauchsänderung (f) ***De***
change of use *En*
changement (m) d'usage *Fr*

Gebühren (f.pl) ***De***
fees *En*
frais (m.pl) *Fr*

Gebühren (f.pl) für Privathaushalte ***De***
domestic rate *En*
impôt (m) mobilier *Fr*

gebührenpflichtige Brücke (f) ***De***
toll bridge *En*
pont (m) à péage *Fr*

gebührenpflichtige Straße (f) ***De***
toll road *En*
route (f) à péage *Fr*

Geburtsurkunde (f) ***De***
birth certificate *En*
acte (m) de naissance *Fr*

Geburtsurkunde (f) usw ausstellen lassen (vb) ***De***
issue (vb) birth certificate etc *En*
dresser (vb) un acte de naissance etc *Fr*

gefährdete Kinder (nt.pl) ***De***
children at risk *En*
enfance (f) en danger *Fr*

gefährliche Konstruktion (f) ***De***
dangerous structure *En*
construction (f) dangereuse *Fr*

gefährlicher Stoff (m) ***De***
dangerous substance *En*
matière (f) dangereuse *Fr*

gefesselt (adj); ans Haus — . ***De***
housebound (adj) *En*
immobilisé à la maison *Fr*

Gegend (f) ***De***
neighbourhood *En*
voisinage (m) *Fr*

gegenseitiges Einvernehmen (nt) ***De***
mutual agreement *En*
accord (m) mutuel *Fr*

gegnerische Splittergruppen (f.pl) ***De***
opposing factions *En*
groupes (m.pl) d'opposition *Fr*

Gehalt (nt) ***De***
salary *En*
traitement (m) *Fr*

Gehaltsskala (f) ***De***
salary scale *En*
échelle (f) indicière *Fr*

geheime Wahl (f) ***De***
secret ballot *En*
scrutin (m) secret *Fr*

geisteskrank (adj) ***De***
mentally ill (adj) *En*
aliéné(e) (adj) *Fr*

Geisteskrankenpflege (f) ***De***
mental health care *En*
soins (m.pl) psychiatriques *Fr*

Geisteskrankheit (f) ***De***
mental illness *En*
maladie (f) mentale *Fr*

geistig Behinderte (pl) ***De***
mentally handicapped people *En*
handicapés (m.pl) (-ées f.pl) mentaux (m.pl) (-ales f.pl) *Fr*

geistige Behinderung (f) ***De***
mental handicap *En*
débilité (f) mentale *Fr*

Geländearbeiten (f.pl) ***De***
site works *En*
travaux (m.pl) préparatoires sur un terrain *Fr*

Geländeentwässerung (f) ***De***
land drainage *En*
assainissement (m) du terrain *Fr*

Geländeerschließung (f) ***De***
site development *En*
construction (f) du terrain *Fr*

Geländekontrolle (f) ***De***
site investigation *En*
études (f) préalables à l'opération de construction *Fr*

Geldmarkt (m) ***De***
money market *En*
marché (m) monétaire *Fr*

Geldpolitik (f) ***De***
money management *En*
politique (f) monétaire *Fr*

Geldstrafe (f) ***De***
fine *En*
amende (f) *Fr*

Geldumlauf (m) ***De***
money supply *En*
masse (f) monétaire *Fr*

Geldzuwendung (f) ***De***
resource allocation *En*
répartition (f) des moyens *Fr*

Gelenkfahrzeug (nt) ***De***
articulated vehicle *En*
semi-remorque (f) (pl. semi-remorques) *Fr*

Gemeinde (f) ***De***
local community *En*
gens (m/f.pl) du pays *Fr*

Gemeinde (f) ***De***
municipality *En*
municipalité (f) *Fr*

Gemeinde (f) ***De***
parish *En*
paroisse (f) *Fr*

(Gemeinde)schriftführer (m) ***De*** *
clerk to the council *En*
secrétaire-général (m) *Fr*

Gemeindeamt (nt) ***De***
regional authority *En*
service (m) administratif régional *Fr*

Gemeindeentwicklung (f) ***De***
community development *En*
développement (m) communautaire *Fr*

Gemeindefürsorge (f) ***De***
community care *En*
action (f) sociale *Fr*

Gemeindehalle (f) ***De***
community hall *En*
centre (m) social *Fr*

Gemeindeland (nt) ***De***
common land *En*
champs (m.pl) communs *Fr*

Gemeinderat (m) ***De***
local councillor *En*
conseiller (m) (-ère f.) municipal(e) *Fr*

*** see/siehe/voir: Introduction page IX**

Gemeinderat (m) *De*
parish council *En*
conseil (m) municipal (d'une petite commune) *Fr*

Gemeinderat/-rätin (m/f) *De*
local council *En*
conseil (m) municipal *Fr*

Gemeinderats-, Stadtratsmitglied (nt) *De*
council member *En*
membre (m) du conseil *Fr*

Gemeindereform (f) *De*
local government reform *En*
réforme (f) du gouvernement local *Fr*

Gemeindesteuer (f) *De*
community charge *En*
impôts (m.pl) locaux *Fr*

Gemeindesteuer (f) *De*
council tax *En*
impôt (m) local *Fr*

Gemeindesteuer (f) *De*
local tax *En*
impôt (m) local *Fr*

Gemeindesteuerverzeichnis (nt) *De*
community charge register *En*
liste (f) des contribuables *Fr*

Gemeindeumorganisation (f) *De*
local government reorganisation *En*
réorganisation (f) du gouvernement local *Fr*

Gemeindeunternehmen (nt) *De*
municipal enterprise *En*
entreprise (f) municipale *Fr*

Gemeindezentrum (nt) *De*
drop-in centre *En*
centre (m) social *Fr*

Gemeinkosten (pl) *De*
overheads *En*
frais (m.pl) généraux *Fr*

gemeinnützige Institution (f) *De*
non profit organisation *En*
organisation (f) à but non lucratif *Fr*

gemeinsame Agrarpolitik (f) *De*
common agricultural policy *En*
politique (f) agricole commune *Fr*

gemeinsame Bereitstellung (f) *De*
joint provision *En*
prévision (f) collective *Fr*

Gemeinsamer Markt (m) *De*
common market *En*
marché (m) commun *Fr*

Gemeinschaft (f) *De*
community *En*
communauté (f) *Fr*

Gemeinschaftsaktion (f) *De*
community action *En*
action (f) communautaire *Fr*

Gemeinschaftsfinanzierung (f) *De*
joint finance/funding *En*
montage (m) financier *Fr*

Gemeinschaftskunde (f) *De*
community education *En*
éducation (f) civique *Fr*

Gemeinschaftsplanung (f) *De*
joint planning *En*
programmation (f) collective *Fr*

Gemeinschaftspraxis (f) *De*
group practice *En*
groupement (m) médical *Fr*

Gemeinschaftszentrum (nt) *De*
community centre *En*
centre (m) social *Fr*

Gemeinschuldner (m) *De*
bankrupt *En*
failli (m) *Fr*

Gemeinsinn (m) *De*
public spirit *En*
amour (m) du bien public *Fr*

Gemeinsinn (m); von — zeugend (adj) *De*
public spirited (adj) *En*
dévoué (adj) au bien public *Fr*

gemischtrassig, mehrrassig (adj) *De*
multi-racial (adj) *En*
multiracial (adj) *Fr*

genehmigter Wohnbau (m) *De*
permitted development *En*
aménagement (m) autorisé *Fr*

general certificate of secondary education *En*
certificat (m) de fin d'études du premier cycle *Fr*
Abschluß (m) der Sekundarstufe *De*

general election *En*
élections (f.pl) législatives *Fr*
allgemeine Wahlen (f.pl) *De*

general improvement area *En*
zone (f) d'embellissement général *Fr*
Verschönerungsgebiet (nt) *De*

general practice *En*
médecine (f) générale *Fr*
Allgemeinmedizin (f) *De*

general practitioner *En*
médecin (m) généraliste *Fr*
praktischer Arzt (m)/praktische Ärztin (f) *De*

gens (m.pl) de couleur *Fr*
Farbige (pl) *De*
coloured people *En*

gens (m/f.pl) du pays *Fr*
Gemeinde (f) *De*
local community *En*

gepachtet, gemietet (adj) *De*
leasehold *En*
tenure (f) à bail *Fr*

geplante Instandhaltung (f) *De*
planned maintenance *En*
entretien (m) prévu *Fr*

geprüfte Geschäftsbücher (nt.pl) *De*
audited accounts *En*
comptes (m.pl) vérifiés et certifiés *Fr*

gérant-ouvrier (m) *Fr*
dem Vorstand angehöriger Arbeitnehmer (m) *De*
worker director *En*

Gerechtigkeit (f) *De*
justice *En*
justice (f) *Fr*

gérer (vb) le changement *Fr*
Veränderungsmanagement (nt) *De*
managing change *En*

geriatric (adj) *En*
gériatrique (adj) *Fr*
geriatrisch (adj) *De*

*** see/siehe/voir: Introduction page IX**

géríatrique (adj) *Fr*
geriatrisch (adj) *De*
geriatric (adj) *En*

geriatrisch (adj) *De*
geriatric (adj) *En*
gériatrique (adj) *Fr*

Gericht (nt) *De*
court *En*
tribunal (m) *Fr*

Gericht (nt) *De*
tribunal *En*
tribunal (m) *Fr*

gerichtlich (adj) *De*
judicial (adj) *En*
judiciaire (adj) *Fr*

(gerichtlich) vorladen (vb) *De*
summons (vb) (to appear in court) *En*
citer (vb) (quelqu'un à comparaître) *Fr*

gerichtliche Untersuchung (f) *De*
inquest *En*
enquête (f) *Fr*

gerichtliche Untersuchung (f) *De*
judicial inquiry *En*
enquête (f) judiciaire *Fr*

gerichtliche Verfügung (f) *De*
court order *En*
autorité (f) de justice *Fr*

Gerichtsbarkeit (f) *De*
jurisdiction *En*
juridiction (f) *Fr*

Gerichtsgebäude (nt) *De*
law court *En*
cour (f) de justice *Fr*

Gerichtsverfahren (nt) *De*
legal action *En*
poursuites (f.pl) judiciaires *Fr*

Gerichtsvollzieher (m) *De*
bailiff *En*
agent (m) de poursuites *Fr*

Gerüst (nt) *De*
scaffolding *En*
échafaudage (m) *Fr*

Gesamtfinanzen (pl) *De*
aggregate finance *En*
finances (f.pl) communales/départementales/ régionales *Fr*

Gesamtschule (f) *De*
comprehensive school *En*
collège (m) *Fr*

Gesamtverantwortung (f) *De*
corporate responsibility *En*
responsabilité (f) corporative *Fr*

Gesamtverwaltung (f) *De*
overall control *En*
majorité (f) absolue *Fr*

Gesamtwirtschaft (f) *De*
aggregate economic activity *En*
ensemble (m) des activités économiques *Fr*

Geschäft (nt), Betrieb (m), Unternehmen (nt) *De*
business *En*
affaires (f.pl) *Fr*

geschäftlicher Ratschlag (m) *De*
business advice *En*
conseil (m) commercial *Fr*

Geschäftsbilanz (f) *De*
management accounts *En*
comptes (m.pl) de gestion *Fr*

Geschäftsentwicklung (f) *De*
business development *En*
développement (m) commercial *Fr*

Geschäftsführer/-in (m/f) *De*
managing director *En*
administrateur (m) délégué *Fr*

Geschäftsgeheimnis (nt) *De*
trade secret *En*
secret (m) de fabrique *Fr*

Geschäftskreise (m.pl), Geschäftswelt (f) *De*
business community *En*
monde (m) des affaires *Fr*

Geschäftsleitung (f) *De*
senior management *En*
encadrement (m) supérieur *Fr*

Geschäftsordnung (f) *De*
standing orders *En*
ordres (m.pl) permanents *Fr*

Geschäftsplan (m) *De*
business plan *En*
plan (m) d'aménagement *Fr*

Geschäftspolitik (f) *De*
corporate policy *En*
politique (f) de la firme *Fr*

Geschäftsräume (m.pl) *De*
commercial premises *En*
locaux (m.pl) commerciaux *Fr*

Geschäftsrechnungsprüfung (f) *De*
management audit *En*
contrôle (m) de gestion *Fr*

Geschäftsstraße (f) *De*
shopping street *En*
rue (f) commerçante *Fr*

Geschäftszentrum (nt) *De*
central business district *En*
zone (f) centrale de commerce *Fr*

geschlossene Ortschaft (f) *De*
built up area *En*
agglomération (f) *Fr*

Geschwindigkeitsbeschränkung (f) *De*
speed limit *En*
limite (f) de vitesse autorisée *Fr*

Gesellschaft (f) *De*
company *En*
société (f) *Fr*

Gesellschaft (f) mit beschränkter Haftung (GmbH)
limited company (Co.Ltd) *En*
société (f) à responsabilité limitée (SARL) *Fr*

gesellschaftlich/sozial benachteiligt (adj) *De*
socially deprived (adj) *En*
désavantagé (adj) *Fr*

gesellschaftliche Benachteiligung (f) *De*
social disadvantage *En*
désavantage (m) social *Fr*

gesellschaftliche Minderheit (f) *De*
social minority *En*
minorité (f) sociale *Fr*

Gesellschaftsrecht (nt) *De*
company law *En*
droit (m) commercial *Fr*

Gesetz (nt) *De*
statute *En*
loi (f) *Fr*

Gesetz (nt), Recht (nt) *De*
law *En*
loi (f) *Fr*

(einen) Gesetzentwurf (m) verabschieden (vb) *De*
pass (vb) (a law) *En*
voter (vb) (une loi) *Fr*

*** see/siehe/voir: Introduction page IX**

gesetzgebend (adj) *De*
legislative (adj) *En*
législatif (adj) *Fr*

gesetzgebende Körperschaft (f) *De*
statutory authority/body *En*
autorité (f) publique *Fr*

gesetzgeberische Gewalt (f) *De*
legislative power *En*
pouvoir (m) législatif *Fr*

Gesetzgebung (f) *De*
legislation *En*
législation (f) *Fr*

gesetzlich (adj) *De*
statutory (adj) *En*
établi par la loi (adj) *Fr*

gesetzliche Dienstleistungen (f.pl) *De*
statutory services *En*
services (m.pl) publics *Fr*

gesetzliche Kraft (f) *De*
statutory power *En*
pouvoir (m) législatif *Fr*

gesetzliche Urkunde (f) *De*
statutory instrument *En*
règlement (m) statutaire *Fr*

gesetzlicher Feiertag (m) *De*
bank holiday *En*
fête (f) légale *Fr*

gesetzlicher Feiertag (m) *De*
public holiday *En*
fête (f) légale *Fr*

gesetzliches Krankengeld (nt) *De*
statutory sick pay *En*
prestations (f.pl) en cas de maladie *Fr*

gesetzwidrige Entlassung (f) *De*
unlawful dismissal *En*
destitution (f) illégale *Fr*

gesichertes Mietverhältnis (nt) *De*
regulated tenancy *En*
aide (f) personalisée au logement (A.P.L.) *Fr*

Gesindehaus (nt); Dienstwohnung (f) *De*
tied accommodation/housing *En*
logement (m) de fonction *Fr*

gestaffelte Arbeitszeiten (f.pl) *De*
staggered work hours *En*
heures (f.pl) de travail échelonnées *Fr*

Gestehungskosten (pl) *De*
actual cost *En*
prix (m) de revient effectif *Fr*

gestion (f); direction (f) *Fr*
Management (nt) *De*
management *En*

gestion (f) d'énergie *Fr*
Energiewirtschaft (f) *De*
energy management *En*

gestion (f) de contrat *Fr*
Projektmanagement (nt) *De*
contract management *En*

gestion (f) de l'éducation *Fr*
Erziehungs- und Ausbildungsleitung (f) *De*
education management *En*

gestion (f) de l'environnement *Fr*
Umweltschutzleitung (f) *De*
environmental management *En*

gestion (f) de l'information *Fr*
Informationsmanagement (nt) *De*
information management *En*

gestion (f) de l'informatique *Fr*
Datenverwaltung (f) *De*
data management *En*

gestion (f) de la base de données *Fr*
Datenbankverwaltung (f) *De*
database management *En*

gestion (f) de la circulation *Fr*
Verkehrsregelung (f) *De*
traffic management *En*

gestion (f) de logement *Fr*
Immobilienverwaltung (f) *De*
estate management *En*

gestion (f) de projet *Fr*
Projektmanagement (nt) *De*
project management *En*

gestion (f) de transport *Fr*
Transportleitung (f) *De*
transport management *En*

gestion (f) des archives *Fr*
Aufzeichnung (f) *De*
records management *En*

gestion (f) des déchets solides *Fr*
Feststoffentsorgungsbetrieb (m) *De*
solid waste management *En*

gestion (f) des ressources humaines *Fr*
Personalleitung (f) *De*
human resource management *En*

gestion (f) des ressources humaines *Fr*
Personalplanung (f) *De*
manpower planning *En*

gestion (f) des risques *Fr*
Absicherung (f) von Risiken *De*
risk management *En*

gestion (f) du logement *Fr*
Wohnungsverwaltung (f) *De*
housing management *En*

gestion (f) financiaire *Fr*
Ressourcemanagement (nt) *De*
resource management *En*

gestion (f) immobilière *Fr*
Immobilienverwaltung (f) *De*
property management *En*

gestion (f) par ordinateur *Fr*
Computersteuerung (f) *De*
computer control *En*

Gesundheit (f) *De*
health *En*
santé (f) *Fr*

Gesundheitsbehörde (f), -dienst (m) *De*
health authority/service *En*
services (m.pl) d'hygiène *Fr*

Gesundheitsdienst (m) *De*
medical service *En*
services (m.pl) médicaux *Fr*

Gesundheitsfürsorge (f) *De*
health care *En*
soins (m.pl) médicaux *Fr*

Gesundheitsgefährdung (f) *De*
health hazard *En*
qui peut nuire à la santé *Fr*

Gesundheitslehre (f) *De*
health education *En*
éducation (f) à l'hygiène/de la santé *Fr*

gewählter Bürgermeister (m) *De*
elected mayor *En*
maire (m) élu *Fr*

*** see/siehe/voir: Introduction page IX**

gewähltes Mitglied (nt) *De*
elected member *En*
membre (m) élu *Fr*

gewährleisten (vb) *De*
guarantee (vb) *En*
garantir (vb) *Fr*

gewalzter Asphalt (m) *De*
rolled asphalt *En*
asphalte (m) damé *Fr*

Gewerbeordnung (f) *De*
trading standards *En*
règlement (m) du commerce *Fr*

Gewerbeordnungsabteilung (f) *De*
trading standards department *En*
direction (f) des normes de conformité *Fr*

Gewerbesteuer (f) *De*
business rate *En*
taxe (f) professionnelle *Fr*

Gewerbesteuer (f) *De*
industrial rate *En*
impôts (m.pl) industriels *Fr*

Gewerbesteuer (f) *De*
non domestic rate *En*
taxe (f) professionnelle *Fr*

gewerbliche Genossenschaft (f) *De*
industrial co-operative *En*
coopérative (f) industrielle *Fr*

Gewerkschaft (f) *De*
trade union *En*
syndicat (m) ouvrier *Fr*

Gewerkschaftler/-in (m/f) *De*
trade unionist *En*
syndicaliste (m/f) *Fr*

Gewerkschaftsbeitrag (m) *De*
trade union rate *En*
taux (m) syndical *Fr*

Gewichtbeschränkung (f) *De*
weight limit/restriction *En*
limite (f) de poids *Fr*

Gewinn (m), Profit (m) *De*
profit *En*
profit (m) *Fr*

Gewinnbeteiligung (f) *De*
profit sharing *En*
partage (m) des bénéfices *Fr*

Gewinnbeteiligung (f) *De*
profit-sharing *En*
participation (f) aux bénéfices *Fr*

Gewinnbringung (f), Rentabilität (f) *De*
profit making *En*
réalisation (f) de bénéfices *Fr*

Gewinnsatz (m) *De*
rate of return *En*
taux (m) de rendement *Fr*

Gewinnspanne (f) *De*
marginal profit *En*
bénéfice (m) marginal *Fr*

Gewohnheitsrecht (nt) *De*
common law *En*
droit (m) coutumier *Fr*

gifted children *En*
enfants (m/f.pl) doués *Fr*
hochbegabte Kinder (nt.pl) *De*

giftige Abfälle (m.pl) *De*
poisonous waste *En*
déchêts (m.pl) toxiques *Fr*

Giftmüll (m) *De*
toxic waste *En*
déchets (m.pl) toxiques *Fr*

Giftstoff (m) *De*
toxic material *En*
matière (f) toxique *Fr*

gipsy site *En*
aire (f) de stationnement pour nomades *Fr*
Zigeunerlager (nt) *De*

giro *En*
chèque (m) postal *Fr*
Giro (nt), Postscheck (m) *De*

Giro (nt), Postscheck (m) *De*
giro *En*
chèque (m) postal *Fr*

Girobank (f) *De*
clearing bank *En*
banque (f) de virement *Fr*

give (vb) evidence *En*
porter (vb) témoignage *Fr*
aussagen (vb) *De*

Gläubiger/-in (m/f) *De*
creditor *En*
créancier (m) *Fr*

Gleichberechtigung (f) *De*
equal rights *En*
droits (m.pl) égaux *Fr*

gleicher Lohn (m) (für gleiche Arbeit) *De*
equal pay *En*
salaire (m) égal *Fr*

Gleichheit (f) *De*
equality *En*
égalité (f) *Fr*

Gleichheit (f) von Mann und Frau *De*
sex equality *En*
égalite (f) sexuelle *Fr*

gleitende Skala (f) *De*
sliding scale *En*
échelle (f) mobile *Fr*

Gleitzeit (f) *De*
flexitime *En*
horaire (f) personnalisée *Fr*

glissière (f) *Fr*
Leitplanke (f) *De*
crash barrier *En*

glissière (f) *Fr*
Leitplanke (f) *De*
safety barrier *En*

glossaire (m) *Fr*
Glossar (nt) *De*
glossary *En*

Glossar (nt) *De*
glossary *En*
glossaire (m) *Fr*

glossary *En*
glossaire (m) *Fr*
Glossar (nt) *De*

goods traffic/transport *En*
transport (m) de marchandises *Fr*
Güterverkehr (m), -transport (m) *De*

goods vehicle *En*
véhicule (m) industriel *Fr*
Nutzfahrzeug (nt) *De*

goods yard *En*
dépot (m) de marchandises *Fr*
Güterbahnhof (m) *De*

gouvernement (m) *Fr*
Regierung (f) *De*
government *En*

gouvernement (m) central *Fr*
Zentralregierung (f) *De*
central government *En*

gouvernement (m) fédéral *Fr*
Bundesregierung (f) *De*
federal government *En*

gouvernement (m) local *Fr*
Kommunalverwaltung (f) *De*
local government *En*

*** see/siehe/voir: Introduction page IX**

gouvernement (m) régional *Fr*
Regionalregierung (f) *De*
regional government *En*

governing board/body *En*
conseil (m) d'administration *Fr*
Vorstand (m) *De*

government *En*
gouvernement (m) *Fr*
Regierung (f) *De*

government agency *En*
service (m) gouvernemental *Fr*
Regierungsamt (nt) *De*

government contract *En*
contrat (m) gouvernemental *Fr*
Regierungsauftrag (m) *De*

government department *En*
ministère (m) *Fr*
Regierungsstelle (f), -behörde (f) *De*

government expenditure *En*
dépenses (f.pl) de l'Etat *Fr*
Staatsausgaben (f.pl) *De*

government policy *En*
politique (f) gouvernementale *Fr*
Regierungspolitik (f) *De*

grade *En*
grade (m) *Fr*
Dienstgrad (m) *De*

grade (m) *Fr*
Dienstgrad (m) *De*
grade *En*

graduate *En*
licencié (m) (-iée f.) *Fr*
(Hochschul)absolvent/-in (m/f) *De*

graduated pension scheme *En*
retraite (f) des cadres *Fr*
abgestuftes Sozialrentensystem (nt) *De*

Graduierten- *De*
post-graduate (adj) *En*
post-universitaire (adj) *Fr*

graffiti *En*
graffiti (m.pl) *Fr*
Graffiti (pl) *De*

graffiti (m.pl) *Fr*
Graffiti (pl) *De*
graffiti *En*

Graffiti (pl) *De*
graffiti *En*
graffiti (m.pl) *Fr*

Grafschaft (f) (in GB) *De* *
county (GB) *En*
comté (m) (en GB) *Fr*

Grafschaftsgericht (nt) *De* *
county court *En*
tribunaux (m.pl) de première instance *Fr*

Grafschaftshauptstadt (f) *De*
county town *En*
chef-lieu de comté/département *Fr*

Grafschaftsrat (m) *De*
county council *En*
conseil (m) départemental/général *Fr*

Grafschaftsverordnete(r) (m/f) *De* *
county councillor *En*
conseiller (m) général *Fr*

grammar school *En*
lycée (m) *Fr*
Gymnasium (nt) *De*

(grande) route (f) à stationnement interdit *Fr*
Straße (f) mit Halteverbot *De*
clearway *En*

grande route (f) *Fr*
Fernstraße (f) *De*
trunk road *En*

grande route (f) *Fr*
Hauptstraße (f) *De*
main road *En*

grande route (f) *Fr*
Hauptverkehrsstraße (f) *De*
major road *En*

grande route (f) *Fr*
(öffentliche) Straße (f) *De*
highway *En*

grande rue (f) *Fr*
Hauptstraße (f) *De*
high street *En*

(grande) ville (f) *Fr*
(Groß)stadt (f) *De*
city *En*

grande voie (f) de communication *Fr*
Hauptverkehrsstraße (f) *De*
arterial road *En*

grant (noun) *En*
bourse (f) *Fr*
(Studien)beihilfe (f); Zuschuß (m); Subvention (f) *De*

grant aid *En*
subvention (f) *Fr*
Subvention (f) *De*

grant aid (vb) *En*
subventionner (vb) *Fr*
bewilligen (vb) *De*

grant application *En*
demande (f) d'allocation *Fr*
Antrag (m) auf Zuschuß *De*

grant maintained school (GB) *En* *
collège (m) subventionné par l'Etat (en GB) *Fr*
subventionierte Schule (f) (in GB) *De*

granulats (m.pl) *Fr*
Zuschlagstoffe (m.pl) *De*
aggregates (civil eng.) *En*

graph *En*
graphe (m) *Fr*
Kurvendiagramm (nt) *De*

graph paper *En*
papier (m) millimétré *Fr*
Millimeterpapier (nt) *De*

graphe (m) *Fr*
Kurvendiagramm (nt) *De*
graph *En*

graphic design/graphics *En*
graphique (f) *Fr*
Graphik (f) *De*

graphical (adj) *En*
graphique (adj) *Fr*
graphisch (adj) *De*

Graphik (f) *De*
graphic design/graphics *En*
graphique (f) *Fr*

graphique (adj) *Fr*
graphisch (adj) *De*
graphical (adj) *En*

graphique (f) *Fr*
Computergraphik (f) *De*
computer graphics *En*

graphique (f) *Fr*
Graphik (f) *De*
graphic design/graphics *En*

*** see/siehe/voir: Introduction page IX**

graphisch (adj) *De*
graphical (adj) *En*
graphique (adj) *Fr*

grassroots democracy *En*
populisme (m) *Fr*
Basisdemokratie (f) *De*

gratte-ciel (m) (pl. grattes-ciel) *Fr*
Wolkenkratzer (m) *De*
sky-scraper *En*

gratte-ciel (m) (pl. les grattes-ciel) *Fr*
Hochhaus (nt) *De*
high rise block *En*

gravel *En*
gravier (m) *Fr*
Kies (m) *De*

gravel pit *En*
gravière (f) *Fr*
Kiesgrube (f) *De*

gravier (m) *Fr*
Kies (m) *De*
gravel *En*

gravière (f) *Fr*
Kiesgrube (f) *De*
gravel pit *En*

green belt *En*
zone (f) verte *Fr*
Grüngürtel (m) *De*

green field site *En*
terrain (m) vièrge *Fr*
Bauplatz (m) im Grünen *De*

green initiative *En*
initiative (f) écologique *Fr*
grüne Initiative (f) *De*

green issues *En*
questions (f.pl) écologiques *Fr*
grüne Fragen (f.pl) *De*

Grenzänderung (f) *De*
boundary change *En*
modification (f) des circonscriptions électorales *Fr*

Grenze (f) *De*
boundary *En*
frontière (f) *Fr*

Grenze (f) *De*
frontier *En*
frontière (f) *Fr*

Grenzkosten (pl) *De*
marginal cost *En*
coût (m) marginal *Fr*

grève (f) *Fr*
Streik (m) *De*
strike *En*

grief (m) *Fr*
Beschwerde (f) *De*
grievance *En*

grievance *En*
grief (m) *Fr*
Beschwerde (f) *De*

Großhandel (m) *De*
wholesale trade *En*
commerce (m) en gros *Fr*

Großmarkt (m) *De*
hypermarket *En*
hypermarché (m) *Fr*

Großraumbüro (nt) *De*
open plan office *En*
bureau (m) sans cloisons *Fr*

Großrechner (m) *De*
mainframe computer *En*
unité (f) centrale de traitement *Fr*

gross domestic product *En*
produit (m) national brut *Fr*
Bruttoinlandsprodukt (nt) *De*

gross profit *En*
bénéfice (m) brut *Fr*
Bruttogewinn (m) *De*

(Groß)stadt (f) *De*
city *En*
(grande) ville (f) *Fr*

ground rent *En*
rente (f) foncière *Fr*
Grundrente (f) *De*

grounds maintenance *En*
entretien (m) des terrains de jeu *Fr*
Sportplatzunterhaltung (f) *De*

group heating *En*
chauffage (m) urbain *Fr*
Sammelheizung (f) *De*

group practice *En*
groupement (m) médical *Fr*
Gemeinschaftspraxis (f) *De*

groupe (m) consommateur *Fr*
Abnehmerverein (m) *De*
consumer group *En*

groupe (m) d'action *Fr*
Initiative (f) *De*
action group *En*

groupe (m) de HLM *Fr*
Wohnsiedlung (f) *De*
housing estate (council) *En*

groupe (m) de HLM *Fr*
Wohnviertel (nt) mit Sozialwohnungen *De*
council estate *En*

groupe (m) de pression *Fr*
Pressure-group (f) *De*
pressure group *En*

groupe (m) de travail *Fr*
Arbeitsgruppe (f) *De*
working party *En*

groupe (m) désavantagé *Fr*
Benachteiligte (pl) *De*
disadvantaged group *En*

groupe (m) écologiste *Fr*
Umweltschutzgruppe (f) *De*
environmental group *En*

groupe (m) ethnique *Fr*
ethnische Gruppe (f) *De*
ethnic group *En*

groupe (m) politique *Fr*
politische Einheit (f) *De*
political group *En*

groupe (m) qui est partisan du MLF *Fr*
Frauengruppe (f) *De*
women's group *En*

groupe (m) qui représente une minorité *Fr*
Minderheit (f) *De*
minority group *En*

groupe (m) socio-économique *Fr*
sozioökonomische Gruppe (f) *De*
socio-economic group *En*

groupement (m) d'intérêt *Fr*
Interessengruppe (f) *De*
interest group *En*

groupement (m) médical *Fr*
Gemeinschaftspraxis (f) *De*
group practice *En*

groupes (m.pl) d'opposition *Fr*
gegnerische Splittergruppen (f.pl) *De*
opposing factions *En*

growth area *En*
secteur (m) de croissance *Fr*
Entwicklungsgebiet (nt) *De*

Grund-Bodenfläche (f) *De*
floor area *En*
superficie (f) *Fr*

Grund-und-Bodenerschließung (f) *De*
land development *En*
aménagement (m) du terrain *Fr*

Grund-und-Bodenverteilung (f) *De*
land allocation *En*
donner (vb) une vocation aux terrains *Fr*

Grundbesitzer (m) *De*
landowner *En*
propriétaire (m) foncier *Fr*

Grundbuch (nt) *De*
land register *En*
registre (m) du cadastre *Fr*

Grundbuchamt (nt) *De*
land registry *En*
bureau (m) du cadastre *Fr*

Grundbucheintragung (f) *De*
land registration *En*
inscription (f) au cadastre *Fr*

Grundlasten (f.pl) *De*
land charges *En*
frais (m.pl) fonciers *Fr*

Grundrente (f) *De*
ground rent *En*
rente (f) foncière *Fr*

Grundsatz (m), Prinzip (nt) *De*
principle *En*
principe (m) *Fr*

(Grundsatz usw) formulieren (vb) *De*
formulate (vb) (policy etc) *En*
définir (vb) (une politique etc) *Fr*

Grundsatz-und-Ressourcenausschuß (m) *De*
policy & resources committee *En*
commission des finances *Fr*

Grundsatzanalyse (f) *De*
policy analysis *En*
évaluation (f) de politique *Fr*

Grundschule (f) *De*
primary school *En*
école (f) primaire *Fr*

Grundschule (f) für 8- bis 11-jährige Kinder *De*
junior school *En*
école (f) pour les enfants de 8 à 11 ans *Fr*

Grundschule(f) für die ersten zwei Jahrgänge *De*
infant school *En*
école (f) pour les enfants de 5 à 8 ans *Fr*

Grundschulerziehung (f) *De*
primary education *En*
enseignement (m) primaire *Fr*

Grundsteuer (f) *De*
land tax *En*
contributions (f.pl) foncières *Fr*

Grundstücksbeschaffung (f) *De*
land supply *En*
disponibilité (f) de terrain *Fr*

Grundstückserschließung (f) *De*
property development *En*
opération (f) immobilière *Fr*

Grundstücksverkauf (m) *De*
land disposal *En*
vente (f) du terrain *Fr*

Grundstücksverwaltung (f) *De*
land management *En*
urbanisme (m) *Fr*

Grundvermögensbewertung (f) *De*
assessment of property *En*
évaluation (f) de propriété *Fr*

grüne Fragen (f.pl) *De*
green issues *En*
questions (f.pl) écologiques *Fr*

grüne Initiative (f) *De*
green initiative *En*
initiative (f) écologique *Fr*

Grüngürtel (m) *De*
green belt *En*
zone (f) verte *Fr*

guarantee *En*
garantie (f) *Fr*
Garantie (f) *De*

guarantee (vb) *En*
garantir (vb) *Fr*
gewährleisten (vb) *De*

guardian *En*
gardien (m) *Fr*
Vormund (m) *De*

guidance note *En*
circulaire (m) d'application *Fr*
Anleitung (f) *De*

Gully (m) *De*
surface drain *En*
tranchée (f) à ciel ouvert *Fr*

Gutachter (m) *De*
surveyor (of property) *En*
architecte (m.) expert *Fr*

Güterbahnhof (m) *De*
goods yard *En*
dépot (m) de marchandises *Fr*

Güterbahnhof (m) *De*
rail depot *En*
gare (f) des marchandises *Fr*

Gütertransport (m) *De*
rail freight *En*
transport (m) de marchandises par chemin de fer *Fr*

Güterverkehr (m), -transport (m) *De*
goods traffic/transport *En*
transport (m) de marchandises *Fr*

Gutschriftanzeige (f) *De*
credit note *En*
avis (m) de crédit *Fr*

Gymnasium (nt) *De*
grammar school *En*
lycée (m) *Fr*

gyratory system *En*
système (m) de circulation giratoire *Fr*
Kreisverkehr (m) *De*

*** see/siehe/voir: Introduction page IX**

habeas corpus ***En***
habeas corpus (m) *Fr*
Habeaskorpusakte (f) *De*

habeas corpus (m) ***Fr***
Habeaskorpusakte (f) *De*
habeas corpus *En*

Habeaskorpusakte (f) ***De***
habeas corpus *En*
habeas corpus (m) *Fr*

habiliter (vb) (quelqu'un à faire qch) ***Fr***
ermöglichen (vb) *De*
enable (vb) *En*

habitant (m) (-ante f.) ***Fr***
Bewohner/-in (m/f) *De*
resident *En*

habitation (f) ***Fr***
Wohnung (f) *De*
dwelling *En*

habitation (f) à loyer modéré (H.L.M.) ***Fr***
Sozialwohnung (f) *De*
council dwelling/flat/house *En*

habitation (f) à loyer modéré (H.L.M.) ***Fr***
Sozialwohnungen (f.pl) *De*
local authority housing *En*

habitation (f) préfabriquée ***Fr***
Fertighäuser (nt.pl) *De*
prefabricated housing *En*

Hafen (m) ***De***
harbour *En*
port (m) *Fr*

Hafenviertel (nt) ***De***
docklands *En*
quartiers (m.pl) des docks (m.pl) *Fr*

Haft (f), Gefangenschaft (f) ***De***
imprisonment *En*
emprisonnement (m) *Fr*

Haftbefehl (m) ***De***
warrant (arrest) *En*
mandat (m) d'arrêt *Fr*

Haftpflichtversicherung (f) ***De***
third party insurance *En*
assurance (f) au tiers *Fr*

Haftung (f) ***De***
liability *En*
responsabilité (f) *Fr*

haltbare Entwicklung (f) ***De***
sustainable development *En*
réalisation (f) possible *Fr*

Hand-, Schwerarbeiter (m) ***De***
manual worker *En*
travailleur (m) manuel *Fr*

Handel (m) ***De***
commerce *En*
commerce (m) *Fr*

Handel (m); Gewerbe (nt) ***De***
trade *En*
commerce (m) *Fr*

Handel treiben (vb) ***De***
trade (vb) *En*
faire (vb) le commerce (de/en qch, avec qn) *Fr*

Handelsbank (f) ***De***
merchant bank *En*
banque (f) commerciale *Fr*

Handelsbevollmächtigte(r) (m) ***De***
accredited agent *En*
agent (m) accrédité *Fr*

Handelsbilanz (f) ***De***
trade balance *En*
balance (f) commerciale *Fr*

Handelsbilanzdefizit (m) ***De***
trade gap *En*
déficit (m) du commerce extérieur *Fr*

Handelskammer (f) ***De***
chamber of commerce/trade *En*
chambre (f) de commerce *Fr*

Handelsmarke (f) ***De***
trade mark *En*
marque (f) de commerce *Fr*

Handelsrate (f) ***De***
commercial rate *En*
taxe (f) professionnelle *Fr*

Handelsschranke (f) ***De***
trade barrier *En*
barrière (f) commerciale *Fr*

Handelsvertreter (m) ***De***
appointed agent *En*
agent (m) attitré *Fr*

Handelszentrum (nt) ***De***
commercial centre *En*
centre (m) commercial *Fr*

handicap ***En***
handicap (m) *Fr*
Behinderung (f) *De*

handicap (m) ***Fr***
Behinderung (f) *De*
handicap *En*

handicapé (adj) moteur ou mental ***Fr***
lernbehindert (adj) *De*
learning disabilities (with) *En*

handicapé (adj) moteur ou mental ***Fr***
lernbehindert (adj) *De*
learning difficulties (with) *En*

handicapés (m.pl) (-ées f.pl) mentaux (m.pl) (-ales f.pl) ***Fr***
geistig Behinderte (pl) *De*
mentally handicapped people *En*

handicapped children ***En***
enfants (m/f.pl) handicapés *Fr*
behinderte Kinder (nt.pl) *De*

*** see/siehe/voir: Introduction page IX**

handicapped people *En*
personnes (f.pl) handicapées *Fr*
Behinderte (m/f.pl) *De*

(Handlungs)berechtigung (f) *De*
power (i.e. to act) *En*
pouvoir (m) *Fr*

handlungsfähige Mehrheit (f) *De*
working majority *En*
majorité (f) suffisante *Fr*

Handlungsforschung (f) *De*
action research *En*
recherche (f) appliquée *Fr*

Handwerker (m) *De*
craftsman *En*
artisan (m) *Fr*

harbour *En*
port (m) *Fr*
Hafen (m) *De*

harcèlement (m) sexuel *Fr*
(sexuelle) Belästigung (f) *De*
sexual harrassment *En*

hard currency *En*
devise (f) forte *Fr*
harte Währung (f) *De*

hard shoulder *En*
accotement (m) *Fr*
Randstreifen (m) *De*

hardship *En*
privation (f) *Fr*
Not (f) *De*

harte Währung (f) *De*
hard currency *En*
devise (f) forte *Fr*

Hauptausschuß (m) *De*
management committee *En*
comité (m) de direction *Fr*

Hauptbetrieb (m) *De*
central service *En*
service (m) central *Fr*

Haupteinkaufsabteilung (f) *De*
central purchasing office *En*
centrale (f) d'achats *Fr*

Hauptstraße (f) *De*
high street *En*
grande rue (f) *Fr*

Hauptstraße (f) *De*
main road *En*
grande route (f) *Fr*

Hauptverkehrsstraße (f) *De*
arterial road *En*
grande voie (f) de communication *Fr*

Hauptverkehrsstraße (f) *De*
major road *En*
grande route (f) *Fr*

Hauptverkehrsstraße (f) *De*
primary/principal road *En*
route (f) à grande circulation *Fr*

Hauptverkehrszeit (f), Stoßzeit (f) *De*
rush hour *En*
heures (f.pl) d'affluence *Fr*

Hauptverwaltungsbeamte (-r)/(-in) (m/f) *De*
chief executive (county) *En*
directeur-général (m) (région, département) *Fr*

Hauptverwaltungsbeamte (-r)/(-in) (m/f) Stadtdirektor/-in (m/f) *De*
chief executive (city/borough/town) *En*
secrétaire -général (m) (commune)/secrétaire-communal (m) (Belg.) *Fr*

Hauptwasserleitung (f) *De*
water main *En*
conduite (f) d'eau *Fr*

Haus-, Wohnungseigentümer/-in (m/f) *De*
home owner *En*
proprietaire (m/f) *Fr*

Hausarzt (m)/Hausärztin (f) *De*
family practitioner *En*
médecin (m) de famille *Fr*

Hausaufgaben (f.pl) *De*
homework *En*
devoirs (m.pl) *Fr*

Hausbesetzer/-in (m/f) *De*
squatter *En*
squatter (m) *Fr*

Hausbesetzung (f) *De*
squatting *En*
occupation (f) d'une maison etc en qualité de squatter *Fr*

Hausbesitzer (m); Vermieter (m) *De*
landlord *En*
propriétaire (m) *Fr*

Hausfrau (f) *De*
housewife *En*
ménagère (f) *Fr*

Haushalt (m) *De*
household *En*
ménage (m) *Fr*

Haushaltseinkommen (nt) *De*
household income *En*
revenu (m) de la famille *Fr*

Haushaltsfreibetrag (m) für Alleinerziehende *De*
one parent family benefit *En*
allocation (f) parent isolé (API) *Fr*

Haushaltskreislauf (m) *De*
annual budget cycle *En*
cycle (m) budgétaire annuel *Fr*

Haushaltsplan (m) *De*
household projection *En*
évolution (f) des ménages *Fr*

Haushaltspolitik (f) *De*
budget policy *En*
politique (f) budgétaire *Fr*

Haushaltsstruktur (f) *De*
household composition/structure *En*
composition (f) de la famille *Fr*

Hauskauf (m) *De*
house purchase *En*
achat (m) du logement *Fr*

(häuslicher) Müll (m), Abfall (m) *De*
household waste *En*
ordures (f.pl) ménagères *Fr*

Hausmeister (m) *De*
caretaker *En*
concièrge (m/f) *Fr*

Hausmüll (m) *De*
domestic refuse/waste *En*
ordures (f.pl) ménagères *Fr*

Hauspflege (f) *De*
domiciliary care *En*
assistance (f) à domicile *Fr*

Hauspflege (f) *De*
home care *En*
domotique (f) *Fr*

Hausreparatur (f) *De*
housing repair *En*
réparations (f.pl) du logement *Fr*

Hausunterricht (m) *De*
home tuition *En*
instruction (f) à domicile *Fr*

*** see/siehe/voir: Introduction page IX**

Hauswirtschaft(slehre) (f) *De*
home economics *En*
économie (f) domestique *Fr*

Haute Cour (f) de Justice *Fr*
oberster Gerichtshof (m) *De*
high court *En*

haute technologie (f) *Fr*
Hoch-, Spitzentechnologie (f) *De*
high tech/technology *En*

hazardous waste *En*
déchets (m.pl) dangereux *Fr*
Sondermüll (m) *De*

head of department *En*
chef (m) de service *Fr*
Abteilungsleiter/-in (m/f) *De*

head office *En*
siège (m) *Fr*
Zentrale (f) *De*

head teacher (primary/secondary) *En*
directeur (m) (-trice f.) /principal (m) *Fr*
Schulleiter/-in (m/f) *De*

health *En*
santé (f) *Fr*
Gesundheit (f) *De*

health authority/service *En* *
services (m.pl) d'hygiène *Fr*
Gesundheitsbehörde (f), -dienst (m) *De*

health care *En*
soins (m.pl) médicaux *Fr*
Gesundheitsfürsorge (f) *De*

health centre *En*
centre (m) médical *Fr*
Poliklinik (f) *De*

health education *En*
éducation (f) à l'hygiène/de la santé *Fr*
Gesundheitslehre (f) *De*

health hazard *En*
qui peut nuire à la santé *Fr*
Gesundheitsgefährdung (f) *De*

health visitor *En*
infirmière (f) à domicile *Fr*
Krankenschwester (f) im Sozialdienst *De*

hearing (court) *En*
audience (f) *Fr*
Verhandlung (f) *De*

hearing impaired (adj) *En*
oreille (f) dure (qui a l') *Fr*
schwerhörig (adj) *De*

heat treatment *En*
traitement (m) thermique *Fr*
Wärmebehandlung (f) *De*

heating system *En*
installation (f) de chauffage *Fr*
Heizanlage (f) *De*

heavy goods vehicle *En*
véhicule (m) industriel *Fr*
Last(kraft)wagen (m) *De*

heavy lorry *En*
camion (m) lourd *Fr*
Schwerlastwagen (m) *De*

heavy traffic *En*
circulation (f) intense *Fr*
starker Verkehr (m) *De*

hébergement (m) *Fr*
Unterkunft (f) *De*
lodging *En*

heikles Thema (nt) *De*
sensitive issue *En*
question (f) délicate *Fr*

Heilbehandlung (f) *De*
remedial treatment *En*
traitement (m) curatif *Fr*

Heimarbeit (f) *De*
outwork *En*
travail (m) fait à domicile *Fr*

Heizanlage (f) *De*
heating system *En*
installation (f) de chauffage *Fr*

herewith (adv) *En*
ci-joint (adv) *Fr*
hiermit (adv) *De*

Hersteller (m) *De*
manufacturer *En*
fabricant (m) *Fr*

Herstellung (f) *De*
manufacture *En*
fabrication (f) *Fr*

heures (f.pl) d'affluence *Fr*
Hauptverkehrszeit (f), Stoßzeit (f) *De*
rush hour *En*

heures (f.pl) d'ouverture *Fr*
Öffnungszeiten (f.pl) *De*
opening hours *En*

heures (f.pl) de bureau *Fr*
Bürostunden (f.pl) *De*
office hours *En*

heures (f.pl) de présence *Fr*
Arbeitsstunden (f.pl) *De*
hours of work *En*

heures (f.pl) de travail échelonnées *Fr*
gestaffelte Arbeitszeiten (f.pl) *De*
staggered work hours *En*

heures (f.pl) de travail *Fr*
Arbeitszeit (f) *De*
working hours *En*

heures (f.pl) indues *Fr*
ausserhalb der normalen Arbeitszeiten (f.pl) *De*
unsocial hours *En*

heures (f.pl) supplémentaires *Fr*
Überstunden (f.pl) *De*
overtime *En*

heurt (m) d'intérêts *Fr*
Interessenkonflikt (m) *De*
conflict of interest *En*

Hierarchie (f) *De*
hierarchy *En*
hiérarchie (f) *Fr*

hiérarchie (f) *Fr*
Hierarchie (f) *De*
hierarchy *En*

hierarchy *En*
hiérarchie (f) *Fr*
Hierarchie (f) *De*

hiermit (adv) *De*
herewith (adv) *En*
ci-joint (adv) *Fr*

high court *En*
Haute Cour (f) de Justice *Fr*
oberster Gerichtshof (m) *De*

high density housing *En*
logement (m) à forte densité *Fr*
dichter Wohnungsbau (m) *De*

high rise block *En*
gratte-ciel (m) (pl. les grattes-ciel) *Fr*
Hochhaus (nt) *De*

high risk strategy *En*
stratégie (f) hasardeuse *Fr*
risikoreiche Strategie (f), Risikostrategie (f) *De*

high school *En*
collège (m) *Fr*
Oberschule (f) *De*

*** see/siehe/voir: Introduction page IX**

high speed train *En*
train (m) à grande vitesse (TGV) *Fr*
Hochgeschwindigkeitszug (m) *De*

high street *En*
grande rue (f) *Fr*
Hauptstraße (f) *De*

high tech/technology *En*
haute technologie (f) *Fr*
Hoch-, Spitzentechnologie (f) *De*

higher education *En*
études (f.pl) supérieures *Fr*
Hochschulausbildung (f) *De*

highway *En*
grande route (f) *Fr*
(öffentliche) Straße (f) *De*

highway authority/department *En*
service (m) de la voirie *Fr*
Straßenbauamt (nt) *De*

highway capacity *En*
capacité (f) des grandes routes *Fr*
Straßenauslastung (f) *De*

highway construction *En*
construction (f) des grandes routes *Fr*
Straßenbau (m) *De*

highway design *En*
conception (f) des grandes routes *Fr*
Straßenplanung (f) *De*

highway engineer *En*
ingénieur (m) des ponts et chaussées *Fr*
Straßenbauingenieur (m) *De*

highway improvement *En*
amélioration (f) des grandes routes *Fr*
Straßenausbau (m) *De*

highway maintenance *En*
entretien (m) des ponts et chaussées *Fr*
Straßeninstandhaltung (f) *De*

highway network *En*
réseau (m) des artères *Fr*
Straßennetz (nt) *De*

highway planning *En*
programmation (f) des ponts et chaussées *Fr*
Verkehrsplanung (f) *De*

Hilfsarbeit (f) *De*
unskilled labour *En*
main-d'oeuvre (f) non qualifiée *Fr*

Hilfsfahrzeug (nt) *De*
emergency vehicle *En*
voiture (f) de secours *Fr*

Hilfspersonal (nt) *De*
ancillary stafF *En*
personnel (m) auxiliaire *Fr*

Hilfspersonal (nt) *De*
auxiliary staff *En*
personnel (m) auxiliaire *Fr*

Hilfspolizist/-in (m/f); Politesse (f) *De*
traffic warden *En*
contractuel (m) (-elle f.) *Fr*

Hintergrundinformation (f) *De*
background information *En*
données (f.pl) de base *Fr*

hire purchase *En*
achat (m) à crédit *Fr*
Ratenkauf (m) *De*

historic building *En*
monument (m) historique *Fr*
Baudenkmal (nt) *De*

historisches Denkmal (nt) *De*
ancient monument *En*
monument (m) historique *Fr*

hoarding *En*
palissade (f) *Fr*
Reklamewand (f) *De*

Hoch-, Spitzentechnologie (f) *De*
high tech/technology *En*
haute technologie (f) *Fr*

Hoch- und Tiefbau (m) *De*
civil engineering *En*
travaux (m.pl) publics *Fr*

Hochbauingenieur/-in (m/f) *De*
structural engineer *En*
ingénieur (m) constructeur *Fr*

hochbegabte Kinder (nt.pl) *De*
gifted children *En*
enfants (m/f.pl) doués *Fr*

Hochgeschwindigkeitszug (m) *De*
high speed train *En*
train (m) à grande vitesse (TGV) *Fr*

Hochhaus (nt) *De*
high rise block *En*
gratte-ciel (m) (pl. les grattes-ciel) *Fr*

Hochhaus (nt) *De*
tower block *En*
immeuble-tour (m) (pl. immeubles-tours) *Fr*

hochqualifizierte Facharbeiter (m.pl) *De*
key workers *En*
personnel (m) de base *Fr*

(Hochschul)absolvent/-in (m/f) *De*
graduate *En*
licencié (m) (-iée f.) *Fr*

Hochschulausbildung (f) *De*
higher education *En*
études (f.pl) supérieures *Fr*

Hochschule (f.) *De* *
college of higher education *En*
école (f.) professionnelle d'enseignement supérieur *Fr*

Höchstgrenze (f) für Kommunalabgaben *De* *
charge capping *En*
limitation (f) des impôts locaux par le gouvernement central *Fr*

Hochwasserbarriere (f) *De*
flood barrier *En*
barrage (m) contre les inondations *Fr*

Hochwasserschutz (m) *De*
flood prevention/protection *En*
protection (f) contre les inondations *Fr*

Höhenmarke (f) *De*
benchmark *En*
repère (m) *Fr*

höhere Schulbildung (f) *De*
secondary education *En*
enseignement (m) secondaire *Fr*

höhere Schule (f) *De*
secondary school *En*
collège (m) (classique/moderne/technique) *Fr*

höherer Beamter/höhere Beamtin (m/f) *De*
senior officer *En*
cadre (m) supérieur *Fr*

hold the line, please (telephone) *En*
ne quittez pas (téléphone) *Fr*
am Apparat bleiben, bitte (Telefon) *De*

*** see/siehe/voir: Introduction page IX**

holiday entitlement *En*
congé (m) statutaire *Fr*
Urlaubanspruch (m) *De*

holiday with pay *En*
congé (m) payé *Fr*
bezahlter Urlaub (m) *De*

home care *En*
domotique (f) *Fr*
Hauspflege (f) *De*

home economics *En*
économie (f) domestique *Fr*
Hauswirtschaft(slehre) (f) *De*

home improvement grant *En*
subvention (f) destinée à la modernisation *Fr*
Modernisierungsbeihilfe (f) *De*

home (m) d'enfants *Fr*
Kinderheim (nt) *De*
children's home *En*

Home Office *En*
Ministère (m) de l'Intérieur *Fr*
Innenministerium (nt) *De*

home owner *En*
proprietaire (m/f) *Fr*
Haus-, Wohnungseigentümer/-in (m/f) *De*

home ownership *En*
possession (f) de propriété *Fr*
Eigenbesitz (m) (von Häusern/Wohnungen) *De*

home tuition *En*
instruction (f) à domicile *Fr*
Hausunterricht (m) *De*

home-school relations *En*
rapports (m.pl) école-famille *Fr*
Eltern-Lehrerbeziehungen (f.pl) *De*

homeless *En*
sans-gîte (m.pl) *Fr*
Obdachlose (-n) (pl) *De*

homeless family *En*
famille (f) sans asile *Fr*
obdachlose Familie (f) *De*

homelessness *En*
problème (m) des sans-gîte *Fr*
Obdachlosigkeit (f) *De*

homework *En*
devoirs (m.pl) *Fr*
Hausaufgaben (f.pl) *De*

hooligan *En*
voyou (m) *Fr*
Hooligan (m), Rowdy (m) *De*

Hooligan (m), Rowdy (m) *De*
hooligan *En*
voyou (m) *Fr*

hooliganism *En*
voyouterie (f) *Fr*
Hooliganismus (m), Rowdytum (nt) *De*

Hooliganismus (m), Rowdytum (nt) *De*
hooliganism *En*
voyouterie (f) *Fr*

hôpital (m) *Fr*
Krankenhaus (nt) *De*
hospital *En*

hôpital (m) privé *Fr*
Privatkrankenhaus (nt) *De*
private hospital *En*

hôpital (m) psychiatrique *Fr*
psychiatrische Klinik (f) *De*
mental hospital *En*

hôpital (m) psychiatrique *Fr*
psychiatrische Klinik (f) *De*
psychiatric hospital *En*

horaire (f) personnalisée *Fr*
Gleitzeit (f) *De*
flexitime *En*

horaire (m) minute *Fr*
sehr knapper Zeitplan (m) *De*
tight schedule *En*

hors cadre (être mis hors cadre) *Fr*
vorübergehend versetzt sein *De*
seconded (to be seconded) *En*

Hörsaal (m) *De*
lecture theatre *En*
salle (f) de conférences *Fr*

horticulture *En*
horticulture (f) *Fr*
Gartenbau (m) *De*

horticulture (f) *Fr*
Gartenbau (m) *De*
horticulture *En*

hospice *En*
hospice (m) *Fr*
Sterbeklinik (f) *De*

hospice (m) *Fr*
Sterbeklinik (f) *De*
hospice *En*

hospital *En*
hôpital (m) *Fr*
Krankenhaus (nt) *De*

hospital service *En*
service (m) des hôpitaux *Fr*
Krankenhausdienst (m) *De*

hospital trust (in GB) *En* *
conseil (m) d'administration d'un hôpital (en GB) *Fr*
Krankenhaustreuhandgesellschaft (f) (in GB) *De*

hospital waste *En*
déchets (m.pl) d'hôpital *Fr*
Krankenhausabfall (m) *De*

hostel *En*
foyer (m) *Fr*
Wohnheim (nt) *De*

hot water supply *En*
arrivée (f) d'eau chaude *Fr*
Warmwasserversorgung (f) *De*

hot water system *En*
installation (f) d'eau chaude *Fr*
Warmwasseranlage (f) *De*

hotel industry *En*
hôtellerie (f) *Fr*
Hotelgewerbe (nt) *De*

hôtel (m) de ville *Fr*
Rathaus (nt) *De*
City Hall *En*

hôtel (m) de ville; mairie (f) *Fr*
Rathaus (nt) *De*
town hall *En*

hôtel (m) du département *Fr*
Kreishaus (nt) *De*
county hall *En*

hôtel (m) garni *Fr*
Frühstückspension (f) *De*
bed and breakfast establishment *En*

hôtel (m) garni *Fr*
Pension (f) *De*
lodging house *En*

Hotelgewerbe (nt) *De*
hotel industry *En*
hôtellerie (f) *Fr*

hôtellerie (f) *Fr*
Hotelgewerbe (nt) *De*
hotel industry *En*

hours of work *En*
heures (f.pl) de présence *Fr*
Arbeitsstunden (f.pl) *De*

house (vb) *En*
loger (vb) *Fr*
unterbringen (vb) *De*

*** see/siehe/voir: Introduction page IX**

house building *En*
entreprise (f) de bâtiments *Fr*
Wohnungsbau (m) *De*

house conversion *En*
aménagement (m) d'une maison *Fr*
Umbau (m) *De*

house extension *En*
extension (f) d'une maison *Fr*
Anbau (m) *De*

house purchase *En*
achat (m) du logement *Fr*
Hauskauf (m) *De*

house renovation *En*
rénovation (f) de maison *Fr*
Renovierung (f) *De*

house repair *En*
réparations (f.pl) de maison *Fr*
Instandsetzungsarbeit (f) *De*

housebound (adj) *En*
immobilisé à la maison (adj) *Fr*
(ans) Haus gefesselt (adj) *De*

household *En*
ménage (m) *Fr*
Haushalt (m) *De*

household composition/structure *En*
composition (f) de la famille *Fr*
Haushaltsstruktur (f) *De*

household income *En*
revenu (m) de la famille *Fr*
Haushaltseinkommen (nt) *De*

household projection *En*
évolution (f) des ménages *Fr*
Haushaltsplan (m) *De*

household waste *En*
ordures (f.pl) ménagères *Fr*
(häuslicher) Müll (m), Abfall (m) *De*

housewife *En*
ménagère (f) *Fr*
Hausfrau (f) *De*

housing *En*
logement (m) *Fr*
Wohnungen (f.pl) *De*

housing adaptation *En*
adaptation (f) des maisons *Fr*
Wohnungsanpassung (f) *De*

housing advice centre *En*
centre (m) de conseil résidentiel *Fr*
Wohnberatungsbüro (nt) *De*

housing agency *En*
agence (f) immobilière *Fr*
Wohnungsamt (nt) *De*

housing application *En*
demande (f) de logement *Fr*
Wohnantrag (m) *De*

housing authority/department *En*
service (m) du logement *Fr*
Wohnungsamt (nt) *De*

housing benefit *En*
aide (f) personnalisée au logement *Fr*
Wohngeld (nt) *De*

housing co-operative *En*
société (f) coopérative de logement *Fr*
Wohnkollektiv (nt) *De*

housing condition *En*
condition (f) des maisons *Fr*
Wohnbedingungen (f.pl) *De*

housing demand *En*
demande (f) en logement *Fr*
Wohnraumbedarf (m) *De*

housing density *En*
densité (f) du logement *Fr*
Wohndichte (f) *De*

housing estate (council) *En*
groupe (m) de HLM *Fr*
Wohnsiedlung (f) *De*

housing grant *En*
aide (f) au logement *Fr*
Wohnungbauzuschuß (m) *De*

housing improvement *En*
amélioration (f) du logement *Fr*
Verbesserung (f) der Wohnverhältnisse *De*

housing investment *En*
investissement (m) immobilier *Fr*
Wohnungsbauinvestition (f) *De*

housing land *En*
terrain (m) affecté au logement *Fr*
Wohngebiet (nt) *De*

housing law *En*
droit (m) de logement *Fr*
Wohnungsbaugesetz (nt) *De*

housing maintenance *En*
entretien (m) du logement *Fr*
Wohnungsinstandhaltung (f) *De*

housing management *En*
gestion (f) du logement *Fr*
Wohnungsverwaltung (f) *De*

housing market *En*
marché (m) immobilier *Fr*
Wohnungsmarkt (m) *De*

housing need *En*
besoin (m) en logement *Fr*
Wohnungsnot (f) *De*

housing policy *En*
politique (f) du logement *Fr*
Wohnungspolitik (f) *De*

housing programme *En*
programme (m) de logement *Fr*
Wohnungsbauprogramm (nt) *De*

housing renewal *En*
rénovation (f) du logement *Fr*
Sanierung (f) (von Häusern/Wohnungen) *De*

housing repair *En*
réparations (f.pl) du logement *Fr*
Hausreparatur (f) *De*

housing rights *En*
droits (m.pl) du logement *Fr*
Wohnrechte (nt.pl) *De*

housing shortage *En*
crise (f) du logement *Fr*
Mangel (m) an Häusern/Wohnungen *De*

housing stock/supply *En*
parc (m) de logements *Fr*
Wohnungsbestand (m) *De*

housing strategy *En*
stratégie (f) de l'habitat *Fr*
Wohnstrategie (f) *De*

housing trust *En*
syndicat (m) de logement/copropriétaires *Fr*
Wohnstiftung (f) *De*

human resource management *En*
gestion (f) des ressources humaines *Fr*
Personalleitung (f) *De*

human resources *En*
ressources (f.pl) humaines *Fr*
Humanvermögen (nt) *De*

human rights *En*
droits (m.pl) de l'homme *Fr*
Menschenrechte (nt.pl) *De*

Humanvermögen (nt) *De*
human resources *En*
ressources (f.pl) humaines *Fr*

humidité (f) qui monte du sol *Fr*
aufsteigende Feuchtigkeit (f) *De*
rising damp *En*

hung council *En*
conseil (m) où aucun parti n'a la majorité absolue *Fr*
Rat (m), in dem keine Partei die absolute Mehrheit hat *De*

hydro-electric power *En*
énergie (f) hydraulique *Fr*
hydroelektrische Energie (f) *De*

hydroelektrische Energie (f) *De*
hydro-electric power *En*
énergie (f) hydraulique *Fr*

hygiène (f) alimentaire *Fr*
Lebensmittelhygiene (f) *De*
food hygiene *En*

hygiène (f) du travail *Fr*
Arbeitshygiene (f) *De*
occupational health/hygiene *En*

hygiène (f) publique *Fr*
Kanalisation (f) und Abfallbeseitigung (f) *De*
sanitation *En*

hypermarché (m) *Fr*
Großmarkt (m) *De*
hypermarket *En*

hypermarket *En*
hypermarché (m) *Fr*
Großmarkt (m) *De*

Hypothek (f) *De*
mortgage *En*
emprunt (m) *Fr*

Hypothekenschulden (f.pl) *De*
mortgage arrears *En*
arriéré (m) d'emprunt *Fr*

Hypothekenzahlung (f) *De*
mortgage repayment *En*
remboursement (m) de l'emprunt *Fr*

Hypothekenzins (m) *De*
mortgage interest *En*
intérêt (m) de l'emprunt *Fr*

hypothermia *En*
hypothermie (f) *Fr*
Hypothermie (f) *De*

Hypothermie (f) *De*
hypothermia *En*
hypothermie (f) *Fr*

hypothermie (f) *Fr*
Hypothermie (f) *De*
hypothermia *En*

I

identity card *En*
carte (f) d'identité *Fr*
Personalausweis (m) *De*

Ideologie (f) *De*
ideology *En*
idéologie (f) *Fr*

idéologie (f) *Fr*
Ideologie (f) *De*
ideology *En*

ideology *En*
idéologie (f) *Fr*
Ideologie (f) *De*

ignifuge (adj) *Fr*
feuerhemmend (adj) *De*
flame retardant (adj) *En*

ill health *En*
mauvaise santé (f) *Fr*
schwache Gesundheit (f), Kränklichkeit (f) *De*

illegal (adj) *De*
illegal (adj) *En*
illégal (adj) *Fr*

illegal (adj) *En*
illégal (adj) *Fr*
illegal (adj) *De*

illégal (adj) *Fr*
illegal (adj) *De*
illegal (adj) *En*

illégal (adj) *Fr*
ungesetzlich (adj) *De*
unlawful (adj) *En*

illegal immigrant *En*
immigrant (m) (-ante f.) illégal(le) *Fr*
illegale(-r) Einwanderer/-in (m/f) *De*

illegale(-r) Einwanderer/-in (m/f) *De*
illegal immigrant *En*
immigrant (m) (-ante f.) illégal(le) *Fr*

illegales Müllabladen (nt) *De*
fly tipping *En*
décharge (f) illégale *Fr*

illiteracy *En*
analphabétisme (m) *Fr*
Analphabetentum (nt) *De*

illness *En*
maladie (f) *Fr*
Krankheit (f) *De*

îlotage (m) *Fr*
Bürgerwehr (f) *De*
neighbourhood policing *En*

image (f) de marque de la firme/de l'organisation *Fr*
Firmenimage (nt) *De*
corporate image *En*

immatriculation (f) (d'étudiant) *Fr*
Einschreibung (f) *De*
enrolment *En*

immeuble (m) à plusieurs étages *Fr*
mehrstöckige Wohnungen (f.pl) *De*
multi-storey dwellings *En*

immeuble (m) *Fr*
Wohnblock (m) *De*
block of flats *En*

immeuble-tour (m) (pl. immeubles-tours) *Fr*
Hochhaus (nt) *De*
tower block *En*

immigrant (m) (-ante f.) *Fr*
Einwanderer/-in (m/f) *De*
immigrant *En*

immigrant (m) (-ante f.) illégal(le) *Fr*
illegale(-r) Einwanderer/-in (m/f) *De*
illegal immigrant *En*

immigrant *En*
immigrant (m) (-ante f.) *Fr*
Einwanderer/-in (m/f) *De*

immigration *En*
immigration (f) *Fr*
Einwanderung (f) *De*

immigration (f) *Fr*
Einwanderung (f) *De*
immigration *En*

immigration control *En*
contrôle (m) de l'immigration *Fr*
Einwanderungskontrolle (f) *De*

immigration policy *En*
politique (f) de l'immigration *Fr*
Einwanderungspolitik (f) *De*

Immobilie (f), Besitz (m) *De*
property *En*
propriété (f) *Fr*

Immobiliengesellschaft (f), Bauunternehmer (m) *De*
property company/developer *En*
société (f) d'exploitation *Fr*

Immobilieninvestition (f) *De*
property investment *En*
investissements (m.pl) immobiliers *Fr*

Immobilienmakler/-in (m/f) *De*
estate agency *En*
agence (f) immobilière *Fr*

Immobilienmarkt (m) *De*
property market *En*
marché (m) immobilier *Fr*

Immobilienverwaltung (f) *De*
estate management *En*
gestion (f) de logement *Fr*

Immobilienverwaltung (f) *De*
property management *En*
gestion (f) immobilière *Fr*

Immobilienwert (m) *De*
property value *En*
valeur (f) immobilière *Fr*

*** see/siehe/voir: Introduction page IX**

immobilisations (f.pl) ***Fr***
fixed assets *En*
Anlagevermögen (nt) *De*

immobilisations (f.pl) ***Fr***
Kapitalauslagen (f.pl) *De*
capital expenditure *En*

immobilisé à la maison (adj) ***Fr***
(ans) Haus gefesselt (adj) *De*
housebound (adj) *En*

immunisation ***En***
immunisation (f) *Fr*
Immunisierung (f) *De*

immunisation (f) ***Fr***
Immunisierung (f) *De*
immunisation *En*

Immunisierung (f) ***De***
immunisation *En*
immunisation (f) *Fr*

impact analysis ***En***
analyse (f) des résultats (d'une politique/action etc) *Fr*
Wirkungsanalyse (f) *De*

implantation (f) d'une société étrangère ***Fr***
ausländische Direktinvestition (f) *De*
inward investment *En*

import (vb) ***En***
importer (vb) *Fr*
importieren, einführen (vb) *De*

importations (f.pl) ***Fr***
Importe (m.pl), Importgüter (nt.pl) *De*
imports *En*

Importe (m.pl), Importgüter (nt.pl) ***De***
imports *En*
importations (f.pl) *Fr*

importer (vb) ***Fr***
importieren, einführen (vb) *De*
import (vb) *En*

importieren, einführen (vb) ***De***
import (vb) *En*
importer (vb) *Fr*

imports ***En***
importations (f.pl) *Fr*
Importe (m.pl), Importgüter (nt.pl) *De*

imposer (vb) ***Fr***
besteuern (vb) *De*
tax (vb) *En*

imposition (f) ***Fr***
Besteuerung (f) *De*
taxation *En*

imposition (f) différée ***Fr***
latente Steuerpflicht (f) *De*
deferred taxation *En*

imposition (f) nulle ***Fr***
Befreiung (f) von der Mehrwertsteuer *De*
zero rating *En*

impôt (m); taxe (f) ***Fr***
Steuer (f) *De*
tax *En*

impôt (m) direct ***Fr***
direkte Steuer (f) *De*
direct tax *En*

impôt (m) foncier ***Fr***
Vermögenssteuer (f) *De*
property tax *En*

impôt (m) local ***Fr*** *
Gemeindesteuer (f) *De*
council tax *En*

impôt (m) local ***Fr***
Gemeindesteuer (f) *De*
local tax *En*

impôt (m) local ***Fr***
Kommunalsteuern (f.pl), Gemeindeabgaben (f.pl) *De*
rates *En*

impôt (m) local supplémentaire (en GB) ***Fr*** *
zusätzliche Gemeindesteuern (f.pl) *De*
supplementary rate *En*

impôt (m) local sur le revenu ***Fr***
regionale Einkommensteuer (f) *De*
local income tax *En*

impôt (m) mobilier ***Fr***
Gebühren (f.pl) für Privathaushalte *De*
domestic rate *En*

impôt (m) sur la plus-value ***Fr***
Steuer (f) auf Kapitalgewinn *De*
capital gains tax *En*

impôt (m) sur le combustible ***Fr***
Brennstoffsteuer (f) *De*
fuel tax *En*

impôt (m) sur le revenu des sociétés ***Fr***
Körperschaftssteuer (f) *De*
corporation tax *En*

impôt (m) sur le revenu ***Fr***
Einkommensteuer (f) *De*
income tax *En*

impôt (m) sur le revenu prélevé sur le salaire/traitement ***Fr***
Lohnsteuerabzugsverfahren (nt) *De*
pay as you earn (PAYE) *En*

impôt (m) sur les plus-values ***Fr***
Wertzuwachsabgabe (f) *De*
betterment levy *En*

impôts (m.pl) industriels ***Fr***
Gewerbesteuer (f) *De*
industrial rate *En*

impôts (m.pl) locaux ***Fr***
Gemeindesteuer (f) *De*
community charge *En*

imprisonment ***En***
emprisonnement (m) *Fr*
Haft (f), Gefangenschaft (f) *De*

improvement ***En***
amélioration (f) *Fr*
Verbesserung (f) *De*

improvement area ***En***
zone (f) d'amélioration *Fr*
Erschließungsgebiet (nt) *De*

improvement grant ***En***
subvention (f) destinée à la réhabilitation *Fr*
Renovierungszuschuß (m) *De*

improvement scheme ***En***
programme (m) de modernisation *Fr*
Erschließungsprogramm (nt) *De*

in-patient ***En***
malade (m/f) hospitalisé(e) *Fr*
(stationär behandelter) Krankenhauspatient (m) *De*

in-service training/INSET ***En***
cours (m) de perfectionnement (à l'établissement où on travaille) *Fr*
innerbetriebliche Fortbildung (f) *De*

incapacité (f) ***Fr***
Behinderung (f) *De*
disability *En*

*** see/siehe/voir: Introduction page IX**

incapacité (f) physique *Fr*
Körperbehinderung (f) *De*
physical handicap *En*

incapacité (f) professionnelle *Fr*
Ineffizienz (f) *De*
inefficiency *En*

incendie (m) *Fr*
Brand (m) *De*
fire *En*

incentive allowance *En*
primes (f.pl) de rendement *Fr*
Leistungszuschlag (m) *De*

incentive scheme *En*
système (m) d'incitations monétaires *Fr*
Anreizsystem (nt) *De*

incidental expenses *En*
faux frais (m.pl) *Fr*
Nebenkosten (pl) *De*

incinérateur (m) *Fr*
Verbrennungsanlage (f) *De*
incinerator *En*

incineration *En*
incinération (f) *Fr*
Verbrennung (f) *De*

incinération (f) *Fr*
Verbrennung (f) *De*
incineration *En*

incinerator *En*
incinérateur (m) *Fr*
Verbrennungsanlage (f) *De*

incitation (f) fiscale *Fr*
Steueranreiz (m) *De*
tax incentive *En*

income *En*
revenu (m) *Fr*
Einkommen (nt) *De*

income support *En*
complément (f) de revenu *Fr*
zusätzliche Hilfe (f) zum Lebensunterhalt *De*

income tax *En*
impôt (m) sur le revenu *Fr*
Einkommensteuer (f) *De*

incompetence *En*
incompétence (f) *Fr*
Unfähigkeit (f) *De*

incompétence (f) *Fr*
Unfähigkeit (f) *De*
incompetence *En*

incontinence *En*
incontinence (f) *Fr*
Inkontinenz (f) *De*

incontinence (f) *Fr*
Inkontinenz (f) *De*
incontinence *En*

increment *En*
échelon (m) *Fr*
Erhöhung (f) *De*

indemnité (f) *Fr*
Entschädigung (f) *De*
indemnity *En*

indemnité (f) *Fr*
Sozialhilfe (f) *De*
benefit *En*

indemnité (f) allouée après enquête sur les ressources familiales *Fr*
nach Bedürftigkeit gestaffelte Unterstützung (f) *De*
means tested benefit *En*

indemnité (f) de chômage *Fr*
Arbeitslosengeld (nt) *De*
unemployment benefit *En*

indemnité (f) de chômage *Fr*
Stempelgeld (nt) *De*
dole *En*

indemnité (f) de déplacement *Fr*
Kilometergeld (nt) *De*
mileage allowance *En*

indemnité (f) de déplacement *Fr*
staatliche Geldleistung (f) für Gehbehinderte *De*
mobility allowance *En*

indemnité (f) de licenciement *Fr*
Abfindung (f) *De*
redundancy payment *En*

indemnité (f) journalière (d'un membre élu) *Fr*
Mitgliedsbeilage *De*
member's allowance *En*

indemnité (f) journalière *Fr*
Aussendienstzulage (f) *De*
subsistence allowance *En*

indemnité (f) pour accidents du travail *Fr*
Berufsunfallversorgung (f) *De*
industrial injuries benefit *En*

indemnity *En*
indemnité (f) *Fr*
Entschädigung (f) *De*

independent school *En*
école (f) libre *Fr*
Privatschule (f) *De*

Index; cost of living — . *En*
indice (m) du coût de la vie *Fr*
Lebenshaltungsindex (m) *De*

index-linked (adj) *En*
indexé (adj) *Fr*
dynamisch (adj) *De*

indexage (m) *Fr*
Indexierung (f) *De*
indexation *En*

indexation *En*
indexage (m) *Fr*
Indexierung (f) *De*

indexé (adj) *Fr*
dynamisch (adj) *De*
index-linked (adj) *En*

Indexierung (f) *De*
indexation *En*
indexage (m) *Fr*

indicateur (m) de performance *Fr*
Leistungsindikator (m) *De*
performance indicator *En*

indice (m) des prix de détail *Fr*
Preisindex (m) des Einzelhandels *De*
retail price index *En*

indice (m) du coût de la vie *Fr*
Lebenshaltungsindex (m) *De*
index; cost of living — . *En*

indictable offence *En*
délit (m) *Fr*
strafbare Handlung (f), Delikt (nt) *De*

indirect taxation *En*
contributions (f.pl) indirectes *Fr*
indirekte Steuern (f.pl) *De*

indirekte Steuern (f.pl) *De*
indirect taxation *En*
contributions (f.pl) indirectes *Fr*

individual liberty *En*
liberté (f) civile *Fr*
Freiheit (f) des Einzelnen, individuelle Freiheit *De*

*** see/siehe/voir: Introduction page IX**

indoor sports centre *En*
salle (f) des sports *Fr*
Sporthalle (f) *De*

industrial accident *En*
accident (m) du travail *Fr*
Arbeitsunfall (m) *De*

industrial area/estate *En*
zone (f) industrielle *Fr*
Industriegelände (nt) *De*

industrial building allowance *En*
subvention (f) de bâtiment industriel *Fr*
Steuerfreibetrag (m) für gewerbliche Gebäude *De*

industrial co-operative *En*
coopérative (f) industrielle *Fr*
gewerbliche Genossenschaft (f) *De*

industrial decline *En*
déclin (m) de l'activité industrielle *Fr*
industrieller Rückgang (m) *De*

industrial democracy *En*
démocratie (f) industrielle *Fr*
Demokratie (f) im Betrieb *De*

industrial design *En*
esthétique (f) industrielle *Fr*
industrielle Formgebung (f) *De*

industrial development *En*
exploitation (f) industrielle *Fr*
industrielle Erschließung (f) *De*

industrial dispute *En*
conflit (m) du travail *Fr*
Arbeitskonflikt (m) *De*

industrial effluent *En*
effluent (m) industriel *Fr*
Industrieabwasser (nt) *De*

industrial improvement area *En*
zone (f) d'expansion industrielle *Fr*
Industrieverbesserungsgebiet (nt) *De*

industrial injuries benefit *En*
indemnité (f) pour accidents du travail *Fr*
Berufsunfallversorgung (f) *De*

industrial injury *En*
accidents (m.pl) du travail *Fr*
Arbeitsverletzung (f) *De*

industrial investment *En*
investissement (m) industriel *Fr*
Vermögensanlage (f) in Industriewerten *De*

industrial land *En*
terrain (m) industriel *Fr*
Industrielandschaft (f) *De*

industrial performance *En*
production (f) industrielle *Fr*
Arbeitsleistung (f) *De*

industrial policy *En*
politique (f) industrielle *Fr*
Industriepolitik (f) *De*

industrial pollution *En*
pollution (f) industrielle *Fr*
Verschmutzung (f) durch die Industrie *De*

industrial premises *En*
locaux (m.pl) industriels *Fr*
Industriegebäude (nt) *De*

industrial production *En*
production (f) industrielle *Fr*
Industrieproduktion (f) *De*

industrial promotion *En*
promotion (f) de l'industrie *Fr*
Industrieförderung (f) *De*

industrial rate *En*
impôts (m.pl) industriels *Fr*
Gewerbesteuer (f) *De*

industrial regeneration/renewal *En*
reprise (f) de l'activité industrielle *Fr*
industrielle Reform (f) *De*

industrial relations *En*
relations (f.pl) humaines dans l'entreprise *Fr*
Beziehungen (f.pl) zwischen Arbeitgebern und Gewerkschaften *De*

industrial relocation *En*
changement (m) d'implantation *Fr*
Industrieverlegung (f) *De*

industrial safety *En*
sécurité (f) industrielle *Fr*
Betriebssicherheit (f) *De*

industrial strategy *En*
stratégie (f) industrielle *Fr*
industrielle Strategie (f) *De*

industrial training *En*
formation (f) industrielle *Fr*
Arbeitsunterricht (m) *De*

industrial tribunal *En*
tribunal (m) industriel *Fr*
Arbeitsgericht (nt) *De*

industrial unit *En*
atelier (m) *Fr*
Industrieanlage (f) *De*

industrial waste *En*
déchets (m.pl) industriels *Fr*
Industriemüll (m) *De*

industrialist *En*
industriel (m) *Fr*
Industrielle(r) (m/f) *De*

Industrie (f) *De*
industry *En*
industrie (f) *Fr*

industrie (f) *Fr*
Industrie (f) *De*
industry *En*

industrie (f) automobile *Fr*
Kraftfahrzeugindustrie (f) *De*
motor industry *En*

industrie (f) d'alimentation *Fr*
Lebensmittelindustrie (f) *De*
food industry *En*

industrie (f) de fabrication *Fr*
verarbeitende Industrie (f) *De*
manufacturing industry *En*

industrie (f) du gaz *Fr*
Gasindustrie (f) *De*
gas industry *En*

industrie (f) électronique *Fr*
Elektronenindustrie (f) *De*
electronics industry *En*

industrie (f) houillère *Fr*
Kohle(n)industrie (f) *De*
coal industry *En*

industrie (f) informatique *Fr*
Computerindustrie (f) *De*
computer industry *En*

industrie (f) nationalisée *Fr*
verstaatlichter Wirtschaftszweig (m)/verstaatlichte Industrie (f) *De*
nationalised industry *En*

industrie (f) sidérurgique *Fr*
Stahlindustrie (f) *De*
steel industry *En*

Industrieabwasser (nt) *De*
industrial effluent *En*
effluent (m) industriel *Fr*

Industrieanlage (f) De
industrial unit *En*
atelier (m) *Fr*

Industrieförderung (f) De
industrial promotion *En*
promotion (f) de l'industrie *Fr*

Industriegelände (nt) De
industrial area/estate *En*
zone (f) industrielle *Fr*

Industriegelände (nt) De
industrial area/estate *En*
locaux (m.pl) industriels *Fr*

industriel (m) Fr
Industrielle(r) (m/f) *De*
industrialist *En*

Industrielandschaft (f) De
industrial land *En*
terrain (m) industriel *Fr*

industrielle Erschließung (f) De
industrial development *En*
exploitation (f) industrielle *Fr*

industrielle Formgebung (f) De
industrial design *En*
esthétique (f) industrielle *Fr*

industrielle Forschung (f) De
research and development *En*
recherche (f) industrielle *Fr*

Industrielle(r) (m/f) De
industrialist *En*
industriel (m) *Fr*

industrielle Reform (f) De
industrial regeneration/renewal *En*
reprise (f) de l'activité industrielle *Fr*

industrielle Strategie (f) De
industrial strategy *En*
stratégie (f) industrielle *Fr*

industrieller Rückgang (m) De
industrial decline *En*
déclin (m) de l'activité industrielle *Fr*

Industriemüll (m) De
industrial waste *En*
déchets (m.pl) industriels *Fr*

Industriepolitik (f) De
industrial policy *En*
politique (f) industrielle *Fr*

Industrieproduktion (f) De
industrial production *En*
production (f) industrielle *Fr*

Industrieverbesserungsgebiet (nt) De
industrial improvement area *En*
zone (f) d'expansion industrielle *Fr*

Industrieverlegung (f) De
industrial relocation *En*
changement (m) d'implantation *Fr*

industry En
industrie (f) *Fr*
Industrie (f) *De*

inefficiency En
incapacité (f) professionnelle *Fr*
Ineffizienz (f) *De*

Ineffizienz (f) De
inefficiency *En*
incapacité (f) professionnelle *Fr*

inégalité (f) raciale Fr
Ungleichheit (f) zwischen den Rassen *De*
racial inequality *En*

inexperimenté (adj) Fr
ungelernt (adj) *De*
unskilled (adj) *En*

infant mortality En
mortalité (f) infantile *Fr*
Säuglingssterblichkeit (f) *De*

infant school En
école (f) pour les enfants de 5 à 8 ans *Fr*
Grundschule(f) für die ersten zwei Jahrgänge *De*

infectious disease En
maladie (f) contagieuse *Fr*
ansteckende Krankheit (f) *De*

infill; infilling En
urbanisation (f) contrôlée *Fr*
Baulückenschließung (f) *De*

infirmière (f) à domicile Fr
Krankenschwester (f) im Sozialdienst *De*
health visitor *En*

inflammabilité (f) Fr
Feuergefährlichkeit (f) *De*
flammability *En*

inflation En
inflation (f) *Fr*
Inflation (f) *De*

Inflation (f) De
inflation *En*
inflation (f) *Fr*

inflation (f) Fr
Inflation (f) *De*
inflation *En*

inflation rate En
taux (m) d'inflation *Fr*
Inflationsrate (f) *De*

Inflationsrate (f) De
inflation rate *En*
taux (m) d'inflation *Fr*

informal discussion En
discussion (f) officieuse/informelle *Fr*
informelles Gespräch (nt) *De*

informaticien (m) (-ienne f.) Fr
Auskunftsbeamte(r)/-beamtin (m/f) *De*
information officer *En*

information En
renseignements (m.pl) *Fr*
Auskunft (f) *De*

Informatik (f) De
Information Technology (IT) *En*
informatique (f) *Fr*

information centre En
bureau (m) de renseignements *Fr*
Auskunftsbüro (nt) *De*

information dissemination En
diffusion (f) des informations *Fr*
Informationsvermittlung (f) *De*

information exchange En
échange (m) de l'information *Fr*
Informationsaustausch (m) *De*

information handling En
manipulation (f) de l'information *Fr*
Informationsverarbeitung (f) *De*

information management En
gestion (f) de l'information *Fr*
Informationsmanagement (nt) *De*

information network En
réseau (m) informatique *Fr*
Informationsnetz (nt) *De*

information officer En
informaticien (m) (-ienne f.) *Fr*
Auskunftsbeamte(r)/-beamtin (m/f) *De*

*** see/siehe/voir: Introduction page IX**

information processing *En*
exploitation (f) des renseignements *Fr*
Informationsverarbeitung (f) *De*

information retrieval *En*
recherche (f) d'informations *Fr*
Informationswiedergewinnung (f) *De*

information service *En*
service (m) (de l') informatique *Fr*
Auskunftsdienst (m) *De*

information system *En*
système (m) informatique *Fr*
Informationssystem (nt) *De*

Information Technology (IT) *En*
informatique (f) *Fr*
Informatik (f) *De*

information technology centre *En*
centre (m) de traitement de l'information *Fr*
Zentrum (nt) für Informationstechnik *De*

Informationsaustausch (m) *De*
information exchange *En*
échange (m) de l'information *Fr*

Informationsfreiheit (f) *De*
freedom of information *En*
droit (m) d'accès aux documents administratifs *Fr*

Informationsmanagement (nt) *De*
information management *En*
gestion (f) de l'information *Fr*

Informationsnetz (nt) *De*
information network *En*
réseau (m) informatique *Fr*

Informationssystem (nt) *De*
information system *En*
système (m) informatique *Fr*

Informationstechnik (f) *De*
information technology (IT) *En*
informatique (f) *Fr*

Informationsverarbeitung (f) *De*
information handling *En*
manipulation (f) de l'information *Fr*

Informationsverarbeitung (f) *De*
information processing *En*
exploitation (f) des renseignements *Fr*

Informationsverbreitung (f) *De*
dissemination of information *En*
diffusion (f) d'informations *Fr*

Informationsvermittlung (f) *De*
information dissemination *En*
diffusion (f) des informations *Fr*

Informationswiedergewinnung (f) *De*
information retrieval *En*
recherche (f) d'informations *Fr*

informatique (f) *Fr*
Informatik (f) *De*
Information Technology (IT) *En*

informatique (f) de gestion *Fr*
Führungsinformation (f) *De*
management information *En*

informatisation (f) *Fr*
Computerisierung (f) *De*
computerization *En*

informelles Gespräch (nt) *De*
informal discussion *En*
discussion (f) officieuse/informelle *Fr*

infraction (f) à la loi *Fr*
Delikt (nt) *De*
offence *En*

infrastructure *En*
infrastructure (f) *Fr*
Infrastruktur (f) *De*

infrastructure (f) *Fr*
Infrastruktur (f) *De*
infrastructure *En*

Infrastruktur (f) *De*
infrastructure *En*
infrastructure (f) *Fr*

ingénierie (f) *Fr*
Technik (f) *De*
engineering *En*

ingénieur (m) constructeur *Fr*
Bauingenieur/-in (m/f) *De*
civil engineer *En*

ingénieur (m) constructeur *Fr*
Hochbauingenieur/-in (m/f) *De*
structural engineer *En*

ingénieur (m) des ponts et chaussées *Fr*
Straßenbauingenieur (m) *De*
highway engineer *En*

ingénieur (m) *Fr*
Ingenieur/-in (m/f) *De*
engineer *En*

ingénieur (m) système *Fr*
Softwaretechniker/-in (m/f) *De*
software engineer *En*

Ingenieur/-in (m/f) *De*
engineer *En*
ingénieur (m) *Fr*

Inhaber/-in (m/f) eines öffentlichen Amtes *De*
public servant *En*
employé (m) d'un service public *Fr*

Initiative (f) *De*
action group *En*
groupe (m) d'action *Fr*

initiative (f) communautaire *Fr*
Kommunalinitiative (f) *De*
community initiative *En*

initiative (f) d'entreprise *Fr*
Unternehmungs-, Unternehmerinitiative (f) *De*
enterprise initiative *En*

initiative (f) écologique *Fr*
grüne Initiative (f) *De*
green initiative *En*

initiative (f) locale pour la création de l'emploi *Fr*
kommunales Arbeitsbeschaffungs programm (nt) *De*
local employment initiative *En*

initiatives (f.pl) économiques *Fr*
Wirtschaftsinitiativen (f.pl) *De*
economic initiatives *En*

injonction (f) (à qn de s'abstenir de faire qch) *Fr*
Verfügung (f) *De*
injunction *En*

injunction *En*
injonction (f) (à qn de s'abstenir de faire qch) *Fr*
Verfügung (f) *De*

Inkontinenz (f) *De*
incontinence *En*
incontinence (f) *Fr*

inländische Architektur (f) De
domestic architecture *En*
architecture (f) domestique *Fr*

Innenministerium (nt) De
Home Office *En*
Ministère (m) de l'Intérieur *Fr*

Innenstadt (f) De
city centre *En*
centre (m) de la ville *Fr*

Innenstadt (f), -bezirk (m) De
inner city *En*
centre (m) ville *Fr*

inner city En
centre (m) ville *Fr*
Innenstadt (f), -bezirk (m) *De*

inner city policy En
politique (f) de revitalisation de centre ville *Fr*
innerstädtische Politik (f) *De*

inner city regeneration En
revitalisation (f) du centre ville *Fr*
Neubelebung (f) der Innenstadt *De*

inner ring road En
périphérique (m) intérieur *Fr*
innere Ringstraße (f) *De*

innerbetriebliche Fortbildung (f) De
in-service training/INSET *En*
cours (m) de perfectionnement (à l'établissement où on travaille) *Fr*

innerbetriebliche Rechnungsprüfung (f) De
internal audit *En*
contrôle (m) interne *Fr*

innere Ringstraße (f) De
inner ring road *En*
périphérique (m) intérieur *Fr*

innerstädtische Politik (f) De
inner city policy *En*
politique (f) de revitalisation de centre ville *Fr*

innovation (f) technologique Fr
technische Innovation (f) *De*
technological innovation *En*

inoffiziell (adj) De
unofficial (adj) *En*
non officel (adj) *Fr*

input (vb) (computer) En
introduire (vb) des données *Fr*
eingeben (vb) *De*

inquest En
enquête (f) *Fr*
gerichtliche Untersuchung (f) *De*

inquiry En
enquête (f) *Fr*
Untersuchung (f) *De*

inquiry in public En
enquête (f) de commodo *Fr*
öffentliche Untersuchung (f) *De*

inscription (f) au cadastre Fr
Grundbucheintragung (f) *De*
land registration *En*

insolvency En
faillite (f) *Fr*
Insolvenz (f), Zahlungsunfähigkeit (f) *De*

Insolvenz (f), Zahlungsunfähigkeit (f) De
insolvency *En*
faillite (f) *Fr*

inspecteur (m) de la construction Fr
Bauinspektor (m) *De*
building inspector *En*

inspecteur (m) des domaines Fr
Bezirksschätzer (m), Taxator (m) *De*
district valuer *En*

inspecteur (m) (-trice f.)(d'Académie/de l'Education Nationale) Fr *
Aufsichtsbeamte(-r)/-in (m/f) *De*
inspector *En*

inspecteur (m) (-trice f.) de la salubrité publique Fr
Beamte(-r)/-in (m/f) im Umweltamt *De*
environmental health officer *En*

inspecteur (m) (-trice f.) de salubrité Fr
Beamte(-r)/-in (m/f) der Gesundheitsbehörde *De*
public health officer *En*

inspection (f) aérienne Fr
Luftbildmessung (f) *De*
aerial survey *En*

inspector En *
inspecteur (m) (-trice f.) (d'Académie/de l'Education Nationale) *Fr*
Aufsichtsbeamte(-r)/-in (m/f) *De*

inspector of taxes En
contrôleur (m) des contributions directes *Fr*
Steuerinspektor/-in (m/f) *De*

inspectorate En
corps (m) d'inspecteurs *Fr*
Inspektion (f) *De*

Inspektion (f) De
inspectorate *En*
corps (m) d'inspecteurs *Fr*

inspizieren (vb) De
survey (vb) *En*
faire (vb) le levé (d'une ville, d'un édifice etc) *Fr*

installation (f) d'eau chaude Fr
Warmwasseranlage (f) *De*
hot water system *En*

installation (f) de chauffage Fr
Heizanlage (f) *De*
heating system *En*

installations (f.pl) sportives Fr
Sportanlagen (f.pl) *De*
sports facilities *En*

Installationsarbeiten (f.pl) De
plumbing *En*
plomberie (f) *Fr*

Instandhaltungsbeihilfe (f) De
maintenance *En*
entretien (m) *Fr*

Instandsetzungsarbeit (f) De
house repair *En*
réparations (f.pl) de maison *Fr*

institut (m) Fr
Institut (nt) *De*
institute *En*

Institut (nt) De
institute *En*
institut (m) *Fr*

institute En
institut (m) *Fr*
Institut (nt) *De*

instituteur (m) (-trice f.) Fr
Lehrer/-in (m/f) *De*
teacher (primary) *En*

*** see/siehe/voir: Introduction page IX**

instruction (f) à domicile *Fr*
Hausunterricht (m) *De*
home tuition *En*

insurance *En*
assurance (f) *Fr*
Versicherung (f) *De*

insurance certificate *En*
certificat (m) d'assurance *Fr*
Versicherungsschein (m) *De*

insurance company *En*
société (f) d'assurance(s) *Fr*
Versicherungsgesellschaft (f) *De*

insurance policy *En*
police (f) d'assurance *Fr*
Versicherungspolice (f) *De*

insurance premium *En*
prime (f) d'assurance *Fr*
Versicherungsprämie (f) *De*

intégration (f) des races *Fr*
Rassenintegration (f) *De*
racial integration *En*

intégration (f) sociale *Fr*
soziale Integration (f) *De*
social integration *En*

intégration (f) sociale locale *Fr*
Verhältnis (nt) zwischen Bevölkerungsgruppen *De*
community relations *En*

Intensivkrankenpflege (f) *De*
acute health care *En*
service (m) de soins intensifs *Fr*

interaction *En*
action (f) réciproque *Fr*
Interaktion (f) *De*

Interaktion (f) *De*
interaction *En*
action (f) réciproque *Fr*

interdiction (f) aux poids-lourds *Fr*
Lastkraftwagenverbot (nt) *De*
lorry ban *En*

interdire (vb) *Fr*
verbieten (vb) *De*
ban (vb) *En*

Interessengemeinschaft (f) von Benachbarten *De*
residents' association *En*
association (f) de propriétaires/locataires *Fr*

Interessengruppe (f) *De*
interest group *En*
groupement (m) d'intérêt *Fr*

Interessenkonflikt (m) *De*
conflict of interest *En*
heurt (m) d'intérêts *Fr*

interest group *En*
groupement (m) d'intérêt *Fr*
Interessengruppe (f) *De*

interest rate *En*
taux (m) d'intérêts *Fr*
Zinssatz (m) *De*

interest relief *En*
allégement (m) des intérêts *Fr*
Zinsfreibetrag (m) *De*

intérêt (m) de l'emprunt *Fr*
Hypothekenzins (m) *De*
mortgage interest *En*

intérêt (m) pécuniaire *Fr*
finanzieller Anteil (m) *De*
monetary interest *En*

intérêt (m) public *Fr*
öffentliches Interesse (nt) *De*
public interest *En*

interface *En*
interface (f) *Fr*
Schnittstelle (f) *De*

interface (f) *Fr*
Schnittstelle (f) *De*
interface *En*

interjeter (vb) appel *Fr*
einlegen (vb) (Berufung usw) *De*
lodge (vb) an appeal *En*

intermediate treatment *En*
traitement (m) intermédiaire *Fr*
Zwischenbehandlung (f) *De*

internal audit *En*
contrôle (m) interne *Fr*
innerbetriebliche Rechnungsprüfung (f) *De*

internal market *En*
marché (m) intérieur *Fr*
Binnenmarkt (m) *De*

international law *En*
droit (m) international *Fr*
Völkerrecht (nt) *De*

International Monetary Fund (IMF) *En*
Fonds (m) Monétaire International (FMI) *Fr*
internationaler Währungsfonds (m) *De*

internationaler Währungsfonds (m) *De*
International Monetary Fund (IMF) *En*
Fonds (m) Monétaire International (FMI) *Fr*

interpretation *En*
interprétation (f) *Fr*
Interpretation (f) *De*

Interpretation (f) *De*
interpretation *En*
interprétation (f) *Fr*

interprétation (f) *Fr*
Interpretation (f) *De*
interpretation *En*

interprète (m/f) *Fr*
Dolmetscher/-in (m/f) *De*
interpreter *En*

interpreter *En*
interprète (m/f) *Fr*
Dolmetscher/-in (m/f) *De*

interregional (adj) *De*
interregional (adj) *En*
entre régions (adj) *Fr*

interregional (adj) *En*
entre régions (adj) *Fr*
interregional (adj) *De*

interruption (f) dans la carrière *Fr*
Unterbrechung (f) der Berufstätigkeit *De*
career break *En*

intersection *En*
carrefour (m) *Fr*
Kreuzung (f) *De*

intervention (f) *Fr*
Vermittlung (f) *De*
mediation *En*

interview *En*
interview (f) *Fr*
Vorstellungsgespräch (nt), Interview (nt) *De*

interview (f) *Fr*
Vorstellungsgespräch (nt), Interview (nt) *De*
interview *En*

interviewé (m) (-wée f.) *Fr*
(Stellen)bewerber/-in (m/f) *De*
interviewee *En*

interviewee *En*
interviewé (m) (-wée f.) *Fr*
(Stellen)bewerber/-in (m/f) *De*

interviewer *En*
intervieweur (m) *Fr*
Vorstellungsgesprächsleiter (m), Interviewer (m) *De*

intervieweur (m) *Fr*
Vorstellungsgesprächsleiter (m), Interviewer (m) *De*
interviewer *En*

introduire (vb) des données *Fr*
eingeben (vb) *De*
input (vb) (computer) *En*

invalid care allowance *En*
aide (f) d'adulte handicappé *Fr*
Pflegegeld (nt) für Erwerbsunfähige *De*

invalidity benefit/pension *En*
pension (f) d'invalidité *Fr*
Erwerbsunfähigkeitsrente (f), Krankenunterstützung *De*

investissement (m) extérieur *Fr*
Auslandsinvestition (f) *De*
foreign investment *En*

investissement (m) *Fr*
Investition (f) *De*
investment *En*

investissement (m) *Fr*
Vermögensfinanzierung (f) *De*
capital finance *En*

investissement (m) immobilier *Fr*
Wohnungsbauinvestition (f) *De*
housing investment *En*

investissement (m) industriel *Fr*
Vermögensanlage (f) in Industriewerten *De*
industrial investment *En*

investissement (m) privé *Fr*
Privatinvestition (f) *De*
private investment *En*

investissement (m) public *Fr*
öffentliche Geldanlage (f) *De*
public investment *En*

investissements (m.pl) immobiliers *Fr*
Immobilieninvestition (f) *De*
property investment *En*

investisseur (m) *Fr*
Investor/-in (m/f) *De*
investor *En*

Investition (f) *De*
investment *En*
investissement (m) *Fr*

Investitionspolitik (f) *De*
investment policy *En*
politique (f) d'investissement *Fr*

Investitionsprogramm (nt) *De*
capital programme *En*
programme (m) d'investissement *Fr*

Investitionsabschätzung (f) *De*
investment appraisal *En*
appréciation (f) des investissements *Fr*

Investitionszuschuß (m) *De*
investment grant *En*
subvention (f) d'investissement *Fr*

Investitionszuschüße (m.pl) *De*
capital grants *En*
subventions (f.pl) spécifiques *Fr*

investment *En*
investissement (m) *Fr*
Investition (f) *De*

investment appraisal *En*
appréciation (f) des investissements *Fr*
Investitionsabschätzung (f) *De*

investment grant *En*
subvention (f) d'investissement *Fr*
Investitionszuschuß (m) *De*

investment policy *En*
politique (f) d'investissement *Fr*
Investitionspolitik (f) *De*

investor *En*
investisseur (m) *Fr*
Investor/-in (m/f) *De*

Investor/-in (m/f) *De*
investor *En*
investisseur (m) *Fr*

invitation to tender *En*
mise (f) d'un travail en adjudication *Fr*
Angebotsaufforderung (f) *De*

invoice *En*
facture (f) *Fr*
Rechnung (f) *De*

invoice (vb) *En*
facturer (vb) *Fr*
fakturieren (vb) *De*

inward investment *En*
implantation (f) d'une société étrangère *Fr*
ausländische Direktinvestition (f) *De*

isolation (f) acoustique *Fr*
Schallisolierung (f) *De*
sound insulation; soundproofing *En*

isolation (f) thermique *Fr*
Wärmeisolierung (f) *De*
thermal insulation *En*

isoloir (m) *Fr*
Wahlkabine (f) *De*
polling booth *En*

issue (vb) birth certificate etc *En*
dresser (vb) un acte de naissance etc *Fr*
Geburtsurkunde (f) usw ausstellen lassen (vb) *De*

itinéraire (m) de sortie de secours *Fr*
Fluchtweg (m) *De*
escape route *En*

itinéraire (m) poids-lourds *Fr*
Lastkraftwagenstrecke (f) *De*
lorry route *En*

*** see/siehe/voir: Introduction page IX**

J

Jahresabschluß (m) *De*
annual accounts *En*
bilan (m) annuel *Fr*

Jahresbasis (f) *De*
annual basis *En*
annuellement (adv) *Fr*

Jahresbericht (m) *De*
annual report *En*
rapport (m) annuel (de gestion) *Fr*

Jahreshauptversammlung (f) *De*
annual general meeting (shareholders) *En*
assemblée (f) d'actionnaires annuelle *Fr*

jardin (m) d'enfants *Fr*
Kindergarten (m) *De*
play group *En*

jardin (m) d'enfants *Fr*
Kindergarten (m) *De*
pre-school playgroup *En*

jargon *En*
jargon (m) *Fr*
Jargon (m) *De*

Jargon (m) *De*
jargon *En*
jargon (m) *Fr*

jargon (m) *Fr*
Jargon (m) *De*
jargon *En*

jeune délinquant (m) (-ante f.) en liberté surveillée *Fr*
auf Bewährung Freigelassene(-r) (m/f) *De*
probationer *En*

jeune personne (f) qui a terminé ses études scolaires *Fr*
Schulabgänger/-in (m/f) *De*
school leaver *En*

jeux (m.pl) de plein-air *Fr*
Freizeitbeschäftigungen (f.pl) im Freien *De*
outdoor recreation *En*

job *En*
emploi (m) *Fr*
Stelle (f) *De*

job analysis/evaluation *En*
analyse (f) de la fonction *Fr*
Arbeitsplatzstudie (f)/-bewertung (f) *De*

job centre *En*
bureau (m) de placement *Fr*
Arbeitsamt (nt) *De*

job creation programme *En*
programme (m) de création de l'emploi *Fr*
Arbeitsbeschaffungsmaßnahmen (f.pl) *De*

job description *En*
description (f) de la fonction *Fr*
Tätigkeitsbeschreibung (f) *De*

job loss *En*
perte (f) de l'emploi *Fr*
Arbeitsplatzverlust (m) *De*

job market *En*
marché (m) du travail *Fr*
Arbeitsmarkt (m) *De*

job mobility *En*
mobilité (f) de l'emploi *Fr*
Arbeitsplatzflexibilität (f) *De*

job specifications *En*
données (f.pl) d'exécution *Fr*
Arbeitsbeschreibung (f) *De*

job vacancy *En*
poste (m) vacant *Fr*
freie Stelle (f) *De*

Job-sharing (nt) *De*
work sharing *En*
partage (m) du travail *Fr*

joint finance/funding *En*
montage (m) financier *Fr*
Gemeinschaftsfinanzierung (f) *De*

joint planning *En*
programmation (f) collective *Fr*
Gemeinschaftsplanung (f) *De*

joint provision *En*
prévision (f) collective *Fr*
gemeinsame Bereitstellung (f) *De*

joint venture *En*
entreprise (f) en participation *Fr*
Joint-Venture (nt) *De*

joint venture project *En*
association (f) projetée *Fr*
Joint-Venture-Projekt (nt) *De*

Joint-Venture (nt) *De*
joint venture *En*
entreprise (f) en participation *Fr*

Joint-Venture-Projekt (nt) *De*
joint venture project *En*
association (f) projetée *Fr*

jour (m) de liquidation *Fr*
Abrechnungstag (m) *De*
account day *En*

jour (m) de permission accordé pour la formation professionnelle *Fr*
tageweise Freistellung (f) (zur Fortbildung) *De*
day release *En*

judge *En*
juge (m) *Fr*
Richter/-in (m/f) *De*

judgement *En*
jugement (m) *Fr*
Urteil (nt) *De*

judiciaire (adj) *Fr*
gerichtlich (adj) *De*
judicial (adj) *En*

*** see/siehe/voir: Introduction page IX**

judicial (adj) *En*
judiciaire (adj) *Fr*
gerichtlich (adj) *De*

judicial inquiry *En*
enquête (f) judiciaire *Fr*
gerichtliche Untersuchung (f) *De*

judiciary *En*
magistrature (f) *Fr*
Richterschaft (f) *De*

juge (m) *Fr*
Richter/-in (m/f) *De*
judge *En*

jugement (m) *Fr*
Urteil (nt) *De*
judgement *En*

jugement (m) par jury *Fr*
Schwurgerichtsverfahren (nt) *De*
trial by jury *En*

Jugendamt (nt) *De*
juvenile bureau *En*
bureau (m) pour la prévention de la délinquance *Fr*

Jugendarbeit (f) *De*
youth service *En*
service (m) de la jeunesse *Fr*

Jugendarbeit (f) *De*
youth work *En*
éducation-formation (f) des jeunes *Fr*

Jugendarbeitslosigkeit (f) *De*
youth unemployment *En*
chômage (m) des jeunes *Fr*

Jugendfürsorgeanordnung (f) *De*
care order *En*
ordonnance (f) de placement en maison d'enfants *Fr*

Jugendfürsorger/-in (m/f) *De*
youth worker *En*
éducateur-formateur (m) auprès des jeunes *Fr*

Jugendgericht (nt) *De*
juvenile court *En*
tribunal (m) pour enfants et adolescents *Fr*

Jugendkriminalität (f) *De*
juvenile crime *En*
délinquance (f) *Fr*

jugendliche(r) Straftäter/-in (m/f) *De*
juvenile offender *En*
accusé (m) mineur *Fr*

Jugendorganisation (f) *De*
youth organisation *En*
organisme (m) de jeunesse *Fr*

Jugendstrafanstalt (f) *De*
borstal *En*
école (f) de redressement pour jeunes gens *Fr*

Jugendstrafanstalt (f) *De*
detention centre *En*
maison (f) de rééducation *Fr*

Jugendstrafe (f) *De*
youth custody *En*
garde (f) à vue (pour les mineurs) *Fr*

Jugendzentrum (nt) *De*
youth centre *En*
foyer (m) des jeunes *Fr*

juggernaut *En*
mastodonte (m) de la route *Fr*
Riesenlaster (m) *De*

jumelage (m) *Fr*
Zwillingsverbindung (f) *De*
twinning *En*

junction *En*
carrefour (m) *Fr*
Kreuzung (f) *De*

junior school *En*
école (f) pour les enfants de 8 à 11 ans *Fr*
Grundschule (f) für 8- bis 11-jährige Kinder *De*

juridiction (f) *Fr*
Gerichtsbarkeit (f) *De*
jurisdiction *En*

jurisdiction *En*
juridiction (f) *Fr*
Gerichtsbarkeit (f) *De*

jurisprudence (f) *Fr*
Fallrecht (nt) *De*
case law *En*

jurisprudence (f) *Fr*
kodifiziertes Recht (nt) *De*
statute law *En*

juristischer Rat (m) *De*
legal advice *En*
conseil (m) judiciaire *Fr*

justice *En*
justice (f) *Fr*
Gerechtigkeit (f) *De*

justice (f) *Fr*
Gerechtigkeit (f) *De*
justice *En*

juvenile bureau *En*
bureau (m) pour la prévention de la délinquance *Fr*
Jugendamt (nt) *De*

juvenile court *En*
tribunal (m) pour enfants et adolescents *Fr*
Jugendgericht (nt) *De*

juvenile crime *En*
délinquance (f) *Fr*
Jugendkriminalität (f) *De*

juvenile offender *En*
accusé (m) mineur *Fr*
jugendliche(r) Straftäter/-in (m/f) *De*

Kabinett (nt) *De*
cabinet *En*
cabinet (m) *Fr*

Kai (m) *De*
quay/wharf *En*
quai (m) *Fr*

Kampagne (f) gegen das Analphabetentum *De*
adult literacy campaign *En*
campagne (f) contre l'analphabétisme *Fr*

Kanalisation (f) *De*
drainage *En*
système (m) d'égouts *Fr*

Kanalisation (f) und Abfallbeseitigung (f) *De*
sanitation *En*
hygiène (f) publique *Fr*

Kanaltunnel (m) *De*
channel link/tunnel *En*
tunnel (m) trans-Manche *Fr*

Kandidat/-in (m/f) *De*
candidate *En*
candidat (m) *Fr*

Kapitalanlage (f) *De*
capital funding *En*
financement (m) d'investissement *Fr*

Kapitalaufwand (m) *De*
capital spending *En*
dépenses (f.pl) d'investissement *Fr*

Kapitalaufwendungen (f.pl) *De*
capital expenditure *En*
charges (f.pl) d'investissement *Fr*

Kapitalauslagen (f.pl) *De*
capital expenditure *En*
immobilisations (f.pl) *Fr*

Kapitaleinkommen (nt) *De*
unearned income *En*
rente (f) *Fr*

Kapitalertrag (m) *De*
return on capital *En*
rémunération (f) du capital *Fr*

Kapitalkontrolle (f) *De*
capital accounting/budget *En*
section (f) d'investissement dans le budget *Fr*

Kapitalkosten (pl) *De*
capital cost *En*
coût (m) d'investissement *Fr*

Katastrophenschutz (m) *De*
disaster planning *En*
plan (m) de protection civile *Fr*

Käufer/-in (m/f) *De*
shopper *En*
acheteur (m) (-euse f.) *Fr*

Kaufrecht (nt) *De*
right to buy *En*
droit (m) d'achat *Fr*

Kern-, Atomenergie (f) *De*
nuclear energy *En*
énergie (f) nucléaire/atomique *Fr*

Kern-. Atomkraftwerk (nt) *De*
nuclear power station *En*
centrale (f) atomique *Fr*

Kernreaktor (m) *De*
nuclear reactor *En*
réacteur (m) nucléaire *Fr*

Kernstrahlung (f) *De*
nuclear radiation *En*
rayonnement (m) nucléaire *Fr*

key issue *En*
question (f) vitale *Fr*
Schlüsselfrage (f) *De*

key workers *En*
personnel (m) de base *Fr*
hochqualifizierte Facharbeiter (m.pl) *De*

keyboard (computer) *En*
clavier (m) *Fr*
Tastatur (f) *De*

Kies (m) *De*
gravel *En*
gravier (m) *Fr*

Kiesgrube (f) *De*
gravel pit *En*
gravière (f) *Fr*

Kilometergeld (nt) *De*
mileage allowance *En*
indemnité (f) de déplacement *Fr*

Kinder (nt.pl) in Pflege *De*
children in care *En*
enfants (m/f.pl) placés *Fr*

Kinder (nt.pl) unter fünf Jahren *De*
under fives *En*
enfants (m/f pl) au-dessous de cinq ans *Fr*

Kinderabteilung (f) im Gesundheitsamt *De*
child welfare centre *En*
centre (m) de protection maternelle et enfantile *Fr*

Kinderfürsorge (f) *De*
child care *En*
soin (m) des enfants *Fr*

Kinderfürsorge (f) *De*
child welfare *En*
protection (f) de l'enfance *Fr*

Kindergarten (m) *De*
nursery school *En*
école (f) maternelle *Fr*

Kindergarten (m) *De*
play group *En*
jardin (m) d'enfants *Fr*

Kindergarten (m) *De*
pre-school playgroup *En*
jardin (m) d'enfants *Fr*

*** see/siehe/voir: Introduction page IX**

Kindergeld (nt) *De*
child benefit *En*
allocation (f) familiale *Fr*

Kindergeld (nt) *De*
family allowance *En*
allocation (f) familiale *Fr*

Kinderheim (nt) *De*
children's home *En*
home (m) d'enfants *Fr*

Kinderkrippe (f) *De*
creche *En*
crèche (f) *Fr*

Kindertagesheim (nt), Kindertagesstätte (f) *De*
day nursery *En*
crèche (f) collective *Fr*

Kindesmißhandlung (f) *De*
child abuse *En*
violence (f) contre les enfants *Fr*

Kläranlage (f) *De*
sewage works *En*
station (f) d'épuration *Fr*

Klassenzimmer (nt) *De*
classroom *En*
salle (f) de classe *Fr*

Klein- und Mittelbetriebe (m.pl) *De*
Small & Medium-Sized Enterprises (SMEs) *En*
petites et moyennes entreprises (PMEs)(f.pl) *Fr*

Kleinbetrieb (m) *De*
small enterprise/firm *En*
petite entreprise (f) *Fr*

kleiner Kreisverkehr (m) *De*
mini roundabout *En*
(petit) giratoire (m); rond-point (m) (pl. ronds-points) *Fr*

Klinik (f) *De*
clinic *En*
dispensaire (m) *Fr*

klinisch (adj) *De*
clinical (adj) *En*
clinique (adj) *Fr*

Klumpen-, Sammelanalyse (f) *De*
cluster analysis *En*
analyse (f) d'un fichier *Fr*

know-how *En*
technique (f) opérationnelle *Fr*
Know-how (nt) *De*

Know-how (nt) *De*
know-how *En*
technique (f) opérationnelle *Fr*

Koalition (f) *De*
coalition *En*
coalition (f) *Fr*

(eine) Koalition bilden (vb) *De*
coalition (to form a) (vb) *En*
se coaliser (vb) *Fr*

kodifiziertes Recht (nt) *De*
statute law *En*
jurisprudence (f) *Fr*

Kohle(n)industrie (f) *De*
coal industry *En*
industrie (f) houillère *Fr*

Kohlenbergbau (m) *De*
coal mining *En*
exploitation (f) de la houille *Fr*

Kohlenbergwerk (nt) *De*
coal mine *En*
mine (f) de charbon *Fr*

Kohlenrevier (nt) *De*
coalfield *En*
région (f) carbonifère *Fr*

kommunal (adj) *De*
communal (adj) *En*
communal (adj) *Fr*

kommunal, städtisch (adj); Gemeinde- *De*
municipal (adj) *En*
municipal (adj) *Fr*

Kommunalabgaben (f.pl) *De*
local authority expenditure *En*
dépenses (f.pl) des collectivités territoriales *Fr*

Kommunalabgaben (f.pl) *De*
local government expenditure *En*
dépenses (f.pl) du gouvernement local *Fr*

Kommunalautonomie (f) *De*
local autonomy *En*
autonomie (f) locale *Fr*

Kommunalbeamte(r)/-in (m/f) *De*
local government officer *En*
fonctionnaire (m) territorial *Fr*

Kommunalbehörde (f) *De*
local authority *En*
collectivité (f) territoriale *Fr*

Kommunalbehörden-ausschuß (m) *De*
local authority association *En*
association (f) des collectivités territoriales *Fr*

kommunales Arbeitsbeschaffungs-programm (nt) *De*
local employment initiative *En*
initiative (f) locale pour la création de l'emploi *Fr*

Kommunalfinanzen (pl) *De*
local authority finance *En*
finances (f.pl) des collectivités territoriales *Fr*

Kommunalfinanzen (pl) *De*
local government finance *En*
finances (f.pl) du gouvernement local *Fr*

Kommunalgrundstück (nt) *De*
community land *En*
champs (m.pl) communs *Fr*

Kommunalinitiative (f) *De*
community initiative *En*
initiative (f) communautaire *Fr*

Kommunalprogramm (nt) *De*
regional plan *En*
plan (m) de développement régional *Fr*

Kommunalsteueraufstellung (f) *De*
schedule of rates *En*
cédule (f) d'impôts locaux *Fr*

Kommunalsteuerbescheid (m) *De*
rate bill/demand *En*
avis (m) d'imposition *Fr*

Kommunalsteuereinziehung (f) *De*
rate collection *En*
perception (f) des impôts locaux *Fr*

Kommunalsteuern (f.pl), Gemeindeabgaben (f.pl) *De*
rates *En*
impôt (m) local *Fr*

Kommunalsteuerschulden (f.pl) *De*
rate arrears *En*
arriéré (m) d'impôts locaux *Fr*

*** see/siehe/voir: Introduction page IX**

Kommunalsteuersubvention (f) (in GB) *De* *
rate support grant (GB) *En*
subvention (f) des impôts locaux (en GB) par l'Etat *Fr*

Kommunalsteuerwesen (nt) *De*
rating system *En*
fiscalité (f) locale *Fr*

Kommunalsteuerzahler/-in (m/f) *De*
ratepayer *En*
contribuable (m/f) à l'impôt local *Fr*

Kommunalüberwachung (f) *De*
community policing *En*
maintien (m) de l'ordre locale *Fr*

Kommunalunternehmen (nt) *De*
community enterprise *En*
société (f) d'économie mixte *Fr*

Kommunalverband (m) *De*
community association *En*
association (f) communautaire *Fr*

Kommunalverwaltung (f) *De*
local government *En*
gouvernement (m) local *Fr*

Kommunalverwaltungs-personal (nt) *De*
local government staff *En*
personnel (m) du gouvernement local *Fr*

Kommunalverwaltungsrefor-men durchsetzen (vb) *De*
reform (vb) local government *En*
apporter (vb) des réformes au gouvernement local *Fr*

Kommunalwahl (f) *De*
local election *En*
élection (f) municipale/départementale/régionale *Fr*

Kommunalwirtschaft (f) *De*
local economy *En*
économie (f) locale *Fr*

Kommune (f) *De*
commune *En*
commune (f) *Fr*

Kommunikation (f) *De*
communication *En*
communication (f) *Fr*

Kommunismus (m) *De*
communism *En*
communisme (m) *Fr*

Konferenz (f) *De*
conference *En*
congrès (m) *Fr*

Konferenzzentrum (nt) *De*
conference centre *En*
centre (m) de conférences *Fr*

Konfessionsschule (f) *De* *
voluntary aided school *En*
école (f) confessionnelle *Fr*

Konfrontation (f) *De*
confrontation *En*
confrontation (f) *Fr*

Konjunkturaufschwung (m) *De*
economic recovery *En*
reprise (f) économique *Fr*

Konjunkturentwicklung (f) *De*
economic development *En*
développement (m) économique *Fr*

Konjunkturentwicklungsplan (m) *De*
economic development strategy *En*
stratégie (f) de développement économique *Fr*

Konjunkturrückgang (m) *De*
economic decline *En*
déclin (m) économique *Fr*

Konjunkturrückgang (m) *De*
economic recession *En*
récession (f) économique *Fr*

Konjunkturvorhersage (f) *De*
economic forecasting *En*
pronostication (f) économique *Fr*

konkurrenzfähiges Angebot (nt) *De*
competitive tender *En*
soumission (f) compétitive *Fr*

Konkursverwalter/-in (m/f) *De*
receiver *En*
syndic (m) de faillite *Fr*

Konservative(r) (m/f) *De*
conservative *En*
conservateur (m) (-trice f.) *Fr*

konsolidierter Kontenabschluß (m) *De*
consolidated accounts *En*
comptes (m.pl) consolidés *Fr*

Konsortium (nt) *De*
consortium *En*
consortium (m) *Fr*

Konstruktionsbüro (nt) *De*
drawing office *En*
bureau (m) d'études *Fr*

Konstruktionszeichnung (f) *De*
working drawing *En*
dessin (M) de construction *Fr*

Konsulat (nt) *De*
consulate *En*
consulat (m) *Fr*

Konsumgenossenschaft (f) *De*
consumer council *En*
comité (m) consultatif de consommateurs *Fr*

Konsumgesetz (nt) *De*
consumer law *En*
droit (m) du consommateur *Fr*

Konsumgüter (nt.pl) *De*
consumer goods *En*
biens (m.pl) de consommation *Fr*

Kontaktgruppenleiter (m) *De*
account executive *En*
chef (m) de comptes client *Fr*

kontinental (adj) *De*
continental (adj) *En*
continental (adj) *Fr*

Konto (nt); Rechnung (f) *De*
account *En*
compte (m) *Fr*

Konto (nt) überzogen *De*
account overdrawn *En*
compte (m) découvert *Fr*

Kontoauszug (m) *De*
bank statement *En*
relevé (m) de compte *Fr*

kontrollieren (vb) *De*
monitor (vb) (performance etc) *En*
surveiller (vb) *Fr*

Konurbation (f) *De*
conurbation *En*
conurbation (f) *Fr*

Konzessionär (m) *De*
distributor *En*
concessionnaire (m) *Fr*

* see/siehe/voir: Introduction page IX

Kooptation (f) De
co-option *En*
cooptation (f) *Fr*

Koordinator/-in (m/f) De
co-ordinator *En*
coordonnateur (m) (-trice f.) *Fr*

Kopfsteuer (f) De *
poll tax *En*
capitation (f) *Fr*

Kopie (f) zur Information De
copy for information *En*
copie (f) pour information *Fr*

körperbehindert (adj) De
physically disabled/handicapped *En*
diminué (-ée f.) physique *Fr*

Körperbehinderung (f) De
physical handicap *En*
incapacité (f) physique *Fr*

Körperschaftssteuer (f) De
corporation tax *En*
impôt (m) sur le revenu des sociétés *Fr*

Korporationsplan (m) De
corporate plan *En*
plan (m) d'ensemble *Fr*

Korrespondenz (f) De
correspondence *En*
correspondance(f) *Fr*

Kosten (pl) De
costs *En*
prix (m.pl) de revient *Fr*

Kosten (pl) erstatten (vb) De
award (vb) costs *En*
accorder (vb) les frais et dépens *Fr*

Kosten (pl) pro Einheit De
unit cost *En*
coût (m) de l'unité *Fr*

Kosten-Nutzen-Analyse (f) De
cost benefit analysis *En*
analyse (f) des coûts et rendements *Fr*

Kostenanalyse (f) De
cost analysis *En*
analyse (f) des coûts *Fr*

Kostenberechnung (f) De
costing *En*
évaluation (f) du coût *Fr*

Kostenkontrolle (f) De
cost control *En*
contrôle (m) des coûts *Fr*

kostenloser öffentlicher Personenverkehr (m) De
free public transport *En*
transports (m.pl) en commun gratuits *Fr*

Kostenplanung (f) De
cost planning *En*
programmation (f) des dépenses *Fr*

Kostenstelle (f) De
cost centre *En*
centre (m) de responsabilité *Fr*

Kostenverringerung (f) De
cost cutting *En*
réduction (f) des coûts *Fr*

Kostenvoranschlag (m) De
quotation *En*
prix (m) *Fr*

Kostenvorschläge (m.pl) De
bills of quantities *En*
devis (m) *Fr*

Kräfte (f.pl) des freien Markts De
market forces *En*
conjoncture (f) du marché *Fr*

Kraftfahrzeugindustrie (f) De
motor industry *En*
industrie (f) automobile *Fr*

Kraftfahrzeugsteuer (f) De
road tax *En*
vignette (f) *Fr*

Kraftwerk (nt) De
power station *En*
centrale (f) électrique *Fr*

Krankengeld (nt) De
medical benefit *En*
aide (f) médicale gratuite *Fr*

Krankengeld (nt) De
sick pay; sickness benefit *En*
allocation/indemnité (f) de maladie *Fr*

Krankenhaus (nt) De
hospital *En*
hôpital (m) *Fr*

Krankenhausabfall (m) De
hospital waste *En*
déchets (m.pl) d'hôpital *Fr*

Krankenhausdienst (m) De
hospital service *En*
service (m) des hôpitaux *Fr*

Krankenhauspatient (m) De
in-patient *En*
malade (m/f) hospitalisé(e) *Fr*

Krankenhaustreuhandgesellschaft (f) (in GB) De *
hospital trust (in GB) *En*
conseil (m) d'administration d'un hôpital (en GB) *Fr*

Krankenpflege (f) De
nursing *En*
soins (m.pl) des malades *Fr*

Krankenpflege (f) De
patient care *En*
soins (m.pl) des malades *Fr*

Krankenschwester (f) im Sozialdienst De
health visitor *En*
infirmière (f) à domicile *Fr*

Krankenurlaub (m); Krankengeld (nt) De
sick leave/sickness benefit *En*
congé (m) de maladie *Fr*

Krankenversicherung (f) De
medical insurance *En*
assurance (f) médicale *Fr*

Krankheit (f) De
illness *En*
maladie (f) *Fr*

Kredit (m) De
credit *En*
crédit (m) *Fr*

Kreditaufnahme (f) der öffentlichen Hand De
public sector borrowing *En*
emprunts (m.pl) du secteur public *Fr*

Kreditbedarf (m) De
borrowing requirement *En*
besoin (m) d'emprunt *Fr*

Kreditbedarf (m) der öffentlichen Hand De
public sector borrowing requirement *En*
demande (f) d'emprunts du secteur public *Fr*

Kreditbegrenzung (f) De
cash limit *En*
plafond (m) du budget *Fr*

Kreditbürgschaft (f) De
loan guarantee *En*
emprunt (m) garanti *Fr*

*** see/siehe/voir: Introduction page IX**

Kreditbürgschaftsprogramm (nt) *De*
loan guarantee scheme *En*
système (m) de garanti d'emprunt *Fr*

Kreditkarte (f) *De*
credit card *En*
carte (f) de crédit *Fr*

Kreisausschuß (m), Kreisrat (m) *De* *
district council *En*
conseil (m) municipal *Fr*

Kreisdiagramm (nt) *De*
pie chart *En*
camembert (m) *Fr*

Kreishaus (nt) *De*
county hall *En*
hôtel (m) du département *Fr*

Kreisverkehr (m) *De*
gyratory system *En*
système (m) de circulation giratoire *Fr*

Kreisverkehr (m) *De*
roundabout *En*
rond-point (m) (pl. ronds-points) *Fr*

Kreuzung (f) *De*
intersection *En*
carrefour (m) *Fr*

Kreuzung (f) *De*
junction *En*
carrefour (m) *Fr*

Kriminalitätsrate (f) *De*
crime rate *En*
taux (m) du crime *Fr*

kritische Pfadanalyse (f) *De*
critical path analysis *En*
analyse (f) de chemin critique *Fr*

Kulturpolitik (f) *De*
arts policy *En*
politique (f) culturelle *Fr*

Kulturpolitik (f) *De*
cultural policy *En*
politique (f) culturelle *Fr*

Kulturzentrum (nt) *De*
arts centre *En*
maison (f) de culture *Fr*

Kunde (m) *De*
client *En*
client (m) *Fr*

Kunde/Kundin (m/f) *De*
client; customer *En*
client (m) *Fr*

Kundenbetreuung (f) *De*
customer care *En*
soins (m.pl) du client *Fr*

Kundenbeziehungen (f.pl) *De*
customer relations *En*
relations (f.pl) avec la clientèle *Fr*

Kundendienst (m) *De*
customer service *En*
service (m) de la clientèle *Fr*

Kündigung (f) *De*
notice to quit *En*
congé (m) *Fr*

Kündigungsschutz (m) *De*
security of tenure *En*
sécurité (f) de l'emploi *Fr*

Kundschaft (f) *De*
client group *En*
clientèle (f) *Fr*

Kurator/-in (m/f); Verwalter/-in (m/f) *De*
trustee *En*
membre (m) du conseil d'administration (d'une fondation) *Fr*

Kurvendiagramm (nt) *De*
graph *En*
graphe (m) *Fr*

Kurzarbeit (f) *De*
short time working *En*
chômage (m) partiel *Fr*

kurzfristig (adj) *De*
short term (adj) *En*
à court terme (adj) *Fr*

Kurzschrift (f) *De*
shorthand *En*
sténographie (f) *Fr*

Kürzung (f) *De*
cutback *En*
réduction (f) *Fr*

Kürzung (f) der Kommunalabgaben durch die Zentralregierung *De* *
rate capping *En*
limitation (f) des impôts locaux (en GB) par l'Etat *Fr*

kurzzeitiges Mietverhältnis (nt) *De*
short hold tenancy *En*
location (f) temporaire *Fr*

*** see/siehe/voir: Introduction page IX**

L

labour ***En***
travail (m) *Fr*
Arbeit (f) *De*

labour costs ***En***
prix (m) de la main-d'oeuvre *Fr*
Arbeitskosten (pl) *De*

labour demand ***En***
demande (f) de main-d'oeuvre *Fr*
Arbeitskräftenachfrage (f) *De*

labour force ***En***
main-d'oeuvre (f) *Fr*
Arbeiterschaft (f) *De*

labour law ***En***
législation (f) du travail *Fr*
Arbeitsrecht (nt) *De*

labour market ***En***
marché (m) du travail *Fr*
Arbeitsmarkt (m) *De*

labour mobility ***En***
mobilité (f) de la main-d'oeuvre *Fr*
Arbeitermobilität (f) *De*

Labour Party ***En***
parti (m) travailliste *Fr*
Labour Party (f) *De*

Labour Party (f) ***De***
Labour Party *En*
parti (m) travailliste *Fr*

labour relations ***En***
rapports (m.pl) du travail *Fr*
Beziehungen zwischen Arbeitgebern und -nehmern *De*

labour supply ***En***
offre (f) de main-d'oeuvre *Fr*
Angebot (nt) an Arbeitskräften *De*

labour turnover ***En***
fluctuations (f.pl) de personnel *Fr*
Personalwechsel (m) *De*

Laden (m), Geschäft (nt) ***De***
shop *En*
magasin (m) *Fr*

Ladenbesitzer/-in (m/f) ***De***
shopkeeper *En*
commerçant (m) (-ante f.) *Fr*

Ladendiebstahl (m) ***De***
shoplifting *En*
vol (m) à l'étalage *Fr*

Ladenmiete (f) ***De***
shop rent *En*
bail (m) commercial (pl. baux commerciaux) *Fr*

Lagebericht (m) ***De***
position statement *En*
analyse (f) de l'existant *Fr*

Lagebericht (m) ***De***
update (noun) *En*
rapport (m) périodique *Fr*

Lager (nt) ***De***
warehouse *En*
entrepôt (m) *Fr*

Lagerkosten (pl) ***De***
storage costs *En*
frais (m.pl) de magasinage *Fr*

Lagerung (f) ***De***
storage *En*
emmagasinage (m) *Fr*

Lagerung (f) ***De***
warehousing (customs) *En*
entreposage (m) (de marchandises) *Fr*

lancement (m) (d'une compagnie etc) ***Fr***
Lancierung (f) *De*
flotation (of company etc) *En*

lancer (vb) une assignation ***Fr***
eine Vorladung beantragen (vb) *De*
summons (vb) (to issue a) *En*

Lancierung (f) ***De***
flotation (of company etc) *En*
lancement (m) (d'une compagnie etc) *Fr*

land allocation ***En***
donner (vb) une vocation aux terrains *Fr*
Grund-und-Bodenverteilung (f) *De*

land availability ***En***
disponibilité (f) de terrain *Fr*
Bodenangebot (nt) *De*

land charges ***En***
frais (m.pl) fonciers *Fr*
Grundlasten (f.pl) *De*

land development ***En***
aménagement (m) du terrain *Fr*
Grund-und-Bodenerschließung (f) *De*

land disposal ***En***
vente (f) du terrain *Fr*
Grundstücksverkauf (m) *De*

land drainage ***En***
assainissement (m) du terrain *Fr*
Geländeentwässerung (f) *De*

land management ***En***
urbanisme (m) *Fr*
Grundstücksverwaltung (f) *De*

land policy ***En***
politique (f) foncière *Fr*
Bodenpolitik (f) *De*

land price ***En***
prix (m) du terrain *Fr*
Bodenpreis (m) *De*

land reclamation ***En***
déssèchement (m) du terrain *Fr*
Landgewinnung (f) *De*

land register ***En***
registre (m) du cadastre *Fr*
Grundbuch (nt) *De*

land registration ***En***
inscription (f) au cadastre *Fr*
Grundbucheintragung (f) *De*

land registry ***En***
bureau (m) du cadastre *Fr*
Grundbuchamt (nt) *De*

*** see/siehe/voir: Introduction page IX**

land rent ***En***
loyer (m) foncier *Fr*
Pacht (f) *De*

Land-, Stadtstreicher/-in (m/f) ***De***
vagrant *En*
vagabond (m) *Fr*

Land-, Stadtstreicherei (f) ***De***
vagrancy *En*
vagabondage (m) *Fr*

land supply ***En***
disponibilité (f) de terrain *Fr*
(gesamte) bebaubare Fläche (f) *De*

land survey ***En***
levé (m) du terrain *Fr*
Landvermessung (f) *De*

land tax ***En***
contributions (f.pl) foncières *Fr*
Grundsteuer (f) *De*

land use ***En***
utilisation (f) des terrains *Fr*
Bodennutzung (f) *De*

Landesplanung (f) ***De***
country planning *En*
aménagement (m) des campagnes *Fr*

landfill site ***En***
dépotoir (m) *Fr*
Müllgrube (f) *De*

Landgemeinde (f) ***De***
rural community *En*
communauté (f) rurale *Fr*

Landgewinnung (f) ***De***
land reclamation *En*
déssèchement (m) du terrain *Fr*

ländliche Entwicklung (f) ***De***
rural development *En*
aménagement (m) rural *Fr*

ländliche Planung (f) ***De***
rural planning *En*
aménagement (m) des campagnes *Fr*

ländliche Politik (f) ***De***
rural policy *En*
politique (f) rurale *Fr*

ländliches Gebiet (nt), Landgebiet (nt) ***De***
rural area/district *En*
région (f) rurale *Fr*

landlord ***En***
propriétaire (m) *Fr*
Vermieter (m), Hausbesitzer (m) *De*

landowner ***En***
propriétaire (m) foncier *Fr*
Grundbesitzer (m) *De*

landscape architect ***En***
architecte (m/f) paysagiste *Fr*
Landschaftsarchitekt/-in (m/f) *De*

landscape architecture ***En***
architecture (f) de paysage *Fr*
Landschaftsgestaltung (f) *De*

landscape planning; landscaping ***En***
aménagement (m) du paysage *Fr*
Landschaftsplanung (f)/ Landschaftsgestaltung (f) *De*

Landschaftsarchitekt/-in (m/f) ***De***
landscape architect *En*
architecte (m/f) paysagiste *Fr*

Landschaftsgestaltung (f) ***De***
landscape architecture *En*
architecture (f) de paysage *Fr*

Landschaftsplanung (f)/ Landschaftsgestaltung (f) ***De***
landscape planning; landscaping *En*
aménagement (m) du paysage *Fr*

Landschaftsschutzgebiet (nt) ***De***
Area Of Outstanding Natural Beauty *En*
région (f) naturelle remarquable *Fr*

Landvermessung (f) ***De***
land survey *En*
levé (m) du terrain *Fr*

Landwirtschaft (f) ***De***
agriculture/farming/rural/economy *En*
agriculture (f) *Fr*

Landwirtschaft (f) ***De***
farming *En*
agriculture (f) *Fr*

landwirtschaftlicher Abfall (m) ***De***
agricultural waste *En*
déchets (m.pl) agricoles *Fr*

landwirtschaftlicher Abfall (m) ***De***
farm waste *En*
déchets (m.pl) agricoles *Fr*

langage (m) de programmation ***Fr***
Programmiersprache (f) *De*
programming language *En*

langage (m) machine ***Fr***
Programmiersprache (f) *De*
computer programming language *En*

langage (m) synthétique ***Fr***
synthetische Sprache (f) *De*
synthetic language (computer) *En*

langfristige Konjunkturpolitik (f) ***De***
economic strategy *En*
stratégie (f) économique *Fr*

langfristiger Mietvertrag (m) ***De***
long lease *En*
bail (m) à long terme *Fr*

langlebige Konsumgüter (nt.pl) ***De***
consumer durables *En*
biens (m.pl) de consommation durables *Fr*

language tuition ***En***
enseignement (m) des langues *Fr*
Fremdsprachenunterricht (m) *De*

Langzeitarbeitslosigkeit (f) ***De***
long term unemployment *En*
chômage (m) de longue durée *Fr*

Langzeitplanung (f) ***De***
long term planning *En*
planification (f) à long terme *Fr*

Lärmbekämpfung (f) ***De***
noise abatement *En*
réduction (f) du bruit *Fr*

Lärmwall (m) ***De***
noise barrier *En*
mur (m) anti-bruit *Fr*

Last(kraft)wagen (m) ***De***
heavy goods vehicle *En*
véhicule (m) industriel *Fr*

Lastkraftwagenkontrolle (f) ***De***
lorry control *En*
contrôle (m) des poids-lourds *Fr*

Lastkraftwagenstrecke (f) *De*
lorry route *En*
itinéraire (m) poids-lourds *Fr*

Lastkraftwagenverbot (nt) *De*
lorry ban *En*
interdiction (f) aux poids-lourds *Fr*

latente Steuerpflicht (f) *De*
deferred taxation *En*
imposition (f) différée *Fr*

laufende Ausgaben (f.pl) *De*
current expenditure *En*
dépenses (f.pl) de fonctionnement *Fr*

laufende Betriebskostenrechnung (f) *De*
current cost accounting *En*
comptabilité (f) en monnaie constante *Fr*

law *En*
loi (f) *Fr*
Gesetz (nt), Recht (nt) *De*

law and order *En*
ordre (m) public *Fr*
Ruhe und Ordnung (f) *De*

law court *En*
cour (f) de justice *Fr*
Gerichtsgebäude (nt) *De*

law enforcement *En*
application (f) de la loi *Fr*
Durchführung (f) (des Gesetzes) *De*

law of contract *En*
droit (m) des obligations *Fr*
Vertragsrecht (nt) *De*

law officer *En*
conseiller (m) (-ère f.) juridique *Fr*
Rechtsberater/-in (m/f) *De*

law reform *En*
réforme (f) juridique *Fr*
Rechtsreform (f) *De*

law report *En*
rapport (m) juridique *Fr*
Urteils- und Entscheidungssammlung (f) *De*

lawful (adj) *En*
légal (adj) *Fr*
rechtmäßig (adj) *De*

lawyer *En*
notaire (m) *Fr*
Rechtsanwalt/-anwältin (m/f) *De*

leader *En*
chef (m) *Fr*
Führer/-in (m/f) *De*

leadership *En*
qualités (f.pl) de chef *Fr*
Führung (f) *De*

learning difficulties (with) *En*
handicapé (adj) moteur ou mental *Fr*
lernbehindert (adj) *De*

learning disabilities (with) *En*
handicapé (adj) moteur ou mental *Fr*
lernbehindert (adj) *De*

lease *En*
bail (m) *Fr*
Pacht-, Mietvertrag (m) *De*

leasehold *En*
tenure (f) à bail *Fr*
gepachtet, gemietet (adj) *De*

leaseholder *En*
locataire (m/f) à bail *Fr*
Pächter/-in, Mieter/-in (m/f) *De*

leasing *En*
crédit-bail (m) *Fr*
Leasing (nt) *De*

Leasing (nt) *De*
leasing *En*
crédit-bail (m) *Fr*

Lebendgeburt (f) *De*
live birth *En*
naissance (f) *Fr*

Lebenshaltungsindex (m) *De*
index; cost of living *En*
indice (m) du coût de la vie *Fr*

Lebenshaltungskosten (pl) *De*
cost of living *En*
coût (m) de la vie *Fr*

Lebensmitteletikettierung (f) *De*
food labelling *En*
étiquetage (m) de la nourriture *Fr*

Lebensmittelhygiene (f) *De*
food hygiene *En*
hygiène (f) alimentaire *Fr*

Lebensmittelindustrie (f) *De*
food industry *En*
industrie (f) d'alimentation *Fr*

Lebensmittelverseuchung (f) *De*
food contamination *En*
contamination (f) de la nourriture *Fr*

Lebensstandard (m) *De*
standard of living *En*
niveau (m) de vie *Fr*

lecture *En*
conférence (f) *Fr*
Vorlesung (f) *De*

lecture (vb) *En*
faire (vb) une conférence *Fr*
eine Vorlesung halten (vb) *De*

lecture theatre *En*
salle (f) de conférences *Fr*
Hörsaal (m) *De*

lecturer *En*
maître (m) de conférences *Fr*
Dozent/-in (m/f) *De*

leerstehende Wohnung (f) *De*
vacant accommodation/dwelling *En*
logement (m) inoccupé *Fr*

left wing (adj) *En*
de gauche (adj) *Fr*
linke(-r,-s) (adj) *De*

left wing *En*
gauche (f) *Fr*
linker Flügel (m) *De*

legal (adj) *De*
legal (adj) *En*
légal (adj) *Fr*

legal (adj) *En*
légal (adj) *Fr*
legal (adj) *De*

légal (adj) *Fr*
legal (adj) *De*
legal (adj) *En*

légal (adj) *Fr*
rechtmäßig (adj) *De*
lawful (adj) *En*

legal action *En*
poursuites (f.pl) judiciaires *Fr*
Gerichtsverfahren (nt) *De*

legal advice *En*
conseil (m) judiciaire *Fr*
juristischer Rat (m) *De*

legal aid *En*
aide (f) judiciaire *Fr*
Prozeßkostenhilfe (f) *De*

*** see/siehe/voir: Introduction page IX**

legal opinion *En*
pensée (f) légale *Fr*
Rechtsgutachten (nt) *De*

legal profession *En*
droit (m) *Fr*
Anwaltschaft (f) *De*

legal rights *En*
droits (m.pl) civils *Fr*
Rechte (nt.pl) *De*

legal service *En*
service (m) du cotentieux *Fr*
Rechtsberatung (f) *De*

législatif (adj) *Fr*
gesetzgebend (adj) *De*
legislative (adj) *En*

legislation *En*
législation (f) *Fr*
Gesetzgebung (f) *De*

législation (f) *Fr*
Gesetzgebung (f) *De*
legislation *En*

législation (f) du travail *Fr*
Arbeitsrecht (nt) *De*
labour law *En*

legislative (adj) *En*
législatif (adj) *Fr*
gesetzgebend (adj) *De*

legislative power *En*
pouvoir (m) législatif *Fr*
gesetzgeberische Gewalt (f) *De*

Lehr-/Unterrichtsmethode (f) *De*
teaching method *En*
méthode (f) d'enseignement *Fr*

Lehrberuf (m) *De*
teaching *En*
enseignement (m) *Fr*

Lehrberuf (m) *De*
teaching profession *En*
corps (m) enseignant *Fr*

Lehre (f) *De*
apprenticeship *En*
apprentissage (m) *Fr*

Lehrer/-in (m/f) *De*
teacher (primary) *En*
instituteur (m) (-trice f.) *Fr*

Lehrer/-in (m/f) *De*
teacher (secondary) *En*
professeur (m) *Fr*

Lehrerausbildung (f) *De*
teacher education/training *En*
éducation (f) professionnelle de l'enseignement *Fr*

Lehrling (m) *De*
apprentice *En*
apprenti (m) *Fr*

Lehrmittel (nt) *De*
teaching aid/material *En*
matériel (m) pédagogique *Fr*

Lehrplan (m) *De*
curriculum *En*
programme (m) d'études *Fr*

Lehrplan (m) *De*
school curriculum *En*
programme (m) d'études *Fr*

Lehrplan (m) *De*
syllabus *En*
programme (m) (d'un cours) *Fr*

Lehrplangestaltung (f) *De*
curriculum development *En*
développement (m) du plan d'études *Fr*

Leibeserziehung (f); Sport(unterricht) (m) *De*
physical education *En*
éducation (f) physique *Fr*

Leistungsbeurteilung (f) *De*
performance appraisal/evaluation *En*
analyse (f) des performances *Fr*

leistungsbezogene Bezahlung (f) *De*
performance related pay *En*
salaire (m) au mérite (secteur privé) *Fr*

leistungsfähig, rationell (adj) *De*
efficient (adj) *En*
efficace (adj) *Fr*

Leistungsindikator (m) *De*
performance indicator *En*
indicateur (m) de performance *Fr*

Leistungszuschlag (m) *De*
incentive allowance *En*
primes (f.pl) de rendement *Fr*

leisure *En*
loisir (m) *Fr*
Freizeit (f) *De*

leisure centre *En*
centre (m) social *Fr*
Freizeitzentrum (nt) *De*

leisure department *En*
service (m) de la culture/des sports *Fr*
Freizeitamt (nt) *De*

leisure facilities *En*
équipement (m) de loisirs *Fr*
Freizeiteinrichtungen (f.pl) *De*

leisure policy *En*
politique (f) des loisirs *Fr*
Freizeitpolitik (f) *De*

leitende(r) Angestellte(r) (m/f) *De*
executive (business) *En*
dirigeant (m) *Fr*

leitender Architekt (m) *De*
chief architect *En*
directeur (m) de l'architecture *Fr*

leitender Auftragnehmer (m) *De*
managing contractor *En*
maître (m) d'oeuvre *Fr*

Leiter/-in (m/f) der Finanzverwaltung *De*
treasurer *En*
trésorier (m) *Fr*

Leitplanke (f) *De*
crash barrier *En*
glissière (f) *Fr*

Leitplanke (f) *De*
safety barrier *En*
glissière (f) *Fr*

Leitungswasser (nt) *De*
tap water *En*
eau (f) du robinet *Fr*

Lenkungsausschuß (m) *De*
steering committee *En*
comité (m) de direction *Fr*

lernbehindert (adj) *De*
learning disabilities (with) *En*
handicapé (adj) moteur ou mental *Fr*

lernbehindert (adj) *De*
learning difficulties (with) *En*
handicapé (adj) moteur ou mental *Fr*

Lese- und Schreibfertigkeit (f) *De*
literacy *En*
aptitude (f) à lire et écrire *Fr*

lessee *En*
locataire (m/f) *Fr*
Pächter/-in (m/f) *De*

*** see/siehe/voir: Introduction page IX**

lessor *En*
bailleur (m) bailleresse (f) *Fr*
Verpächter/-in (m/f) *De*

letting *En*
location (f) *Fr*
Verpachtung (f), Vermietung (f) *De*

lettre (f) circulaire *Fr*
Rundbrief (m) *De*
circular *En*

lettre (f) d'avis *Fr*
Anzeige (f) *De*
advice note *En*

lettre (f) de change *Fr*
Wechsel (m) *De*
bill of exchange *En*

lettre (f) recommendée *Fr*
Einschreibebrief (m) *De*
registered letter *En*

letzte Mahnung (f) *De*
final demand *En*
dernier (m) rappel *Fr*

letzte Rate (f) *De*
final instalment *En*
dernier versement (m) *Fr*

levé (m) *Fr*
(Bau)inspektion (f) *De*
survey (noun) (construction) *En*

levé (m); faire (vb) le — (d'une ville, d'un edifice etc) *Fr*
inspizieren (vb) *De*
survey (vb) *En*

levé (m) du terrain *Fr*
Absatzforschung (f) *De*
field survey *En*

levé (m) du terrain *Fr*
Landvermessung (f) *De*
land survey *En*

levée (f) *Fr*
(Steuer)erhebung (f) *De*
levy *En*

lever (vb) (un impôt) *Fr*
erheben (vb); Steuer usw — . *De*
levy (vb) (a tax etc) *En*

levy *En*
levée (f) *Fr*
(Steuer)erhebung (f) *De*

levy (vb) (a tax etc) *En*
lever (un impôt) (vb) *Fr*
erheben (vb); Steuer usw — . *De*

liabilities *En*
obligations (f.pl) *Fr*
Verbindlichkeiten (f.pl) *De*

liability *En*
responsabilité (f) *Fr*
Haftung (f) *De*

liaise (vb) *En*
faire (vb) la liaison *Fr*
zusammenarbeiten (vb) *De*

liaison (f); faire la — (vb) *Fr*
liaise (vb) *En*
zusammenarbeiten (vb) *De*

libel *En*
diffamation (f) *Fr*
Verleumdung (schriftliche) (f) *De*

Liberal Democrat *En*
libéral(e)-démocrate (m/f) (pl. libéraux-démocrates) *Fr*
Liberal-Demokrat/-in (m/f) *De*

libéral(e)-démocrate (m/f) (pl. libéraux-démocrates) *Fr*
Liberal-Demokrat/-in (m/f) *De*
Liberal Democrat *En*

Liberal-Demokrat/-in (m/f) *De*
Liberal Democrat *En*
libéral(e)-démocrate (m/f) (pl. libéraux-démocrates) *Fr*

liberté (f) civile *Fr*
bürgerliche Freiheit (f) *De*
civil liberty *En*

liberté; en — surveillé *Fr*
auf Bewährung (f) *De*
on probation *En*

liberté (f) *Fr*
Freiheit (f) *De*
freedom *En*

liberté (f) *Fr*
Freiheit (f) *De*
liberty *En*

liberté (f) civile *Fr*
Freiheit (f) des Einzelnen, individuelle Freiheit *De*
individual liberty *En*

liberté (f) d'expression *Fr*
Meinungsfreiheit (f) *De*
freedom of expression *En*

liberté (f) de choix arbitraire *Fr*
Wahlfreiheit (f) *De*
freedom of choice *En*

liberty *En*
liberté (f) *Fr*
Freiheit (f) *De*

librarian *En*
bibliothécaire (m/f) *Fr*
Bibliothekar/-in (m/f) *De*

libraries department *En*
bibliothèque (f) *Fr*
Bibliotheksamt (nt) *De*

library *En*
bibliothèque (f) *Fr*
Bibliothek (f) *De*

libre entreprise (f) *Fr*
freie Wirtschaft (f) *De*
free enterprise *En*

libre parole (f) *Fr*
Redefreiheit (f) *De*
free speech *En*

libre possession (f) *Fr*
(with) vacant possession *En*
bezugsfertig (adj) *De*

libre-échange (m) *Fr*
Freihandel (m) *De*
free trade *En*

licence *En*
permis (m) *Fr*
Lizenz (f) *De*

licencié (m) (-iée f.) *Fr*
(Hochschul)absolvent/-in (m/f) *De*
graduate *En*

licenciement (m) *Fr*
Beschäftigungslosigkeit (f) *De*
redundancy *En*

license (vb) *En*
accorder (vb) un permis *Fr*
lizensieren (vb) *De*

licensing authority *En*
police (f) municipale administrative *Fr*
Lizenzbehörde (f) *De*

Lieferant (m) *De*
supplier *En*
fournisseur (m) *Fr*

liefern (vb) *De*
supply (vb) *En*
fournir (vb) (qn de qch) *Fr*

Lieferschein (m) *De*
delivery note *En*
bordereau (m) de livraison *Fr*

*** see/siehe/voir: Introduction page IX**

Liefertermin (m) *De*
delivery date *En*
date (f) de livraison *Fr*

Liegenschaftsamt (nt) *De*
estates department *En*
direction (f) des bâtiments *Fr*

light rail transit *En*
chemin de fer (m) à voie étroite *Fr*
Personenverkehr (m) *De*

limit (vb) expenditure *En*
limiter (vb) les dépenses *Fr*
Ausgaben kürzen (vb) *De*

limitation (f) de largeur *Fr*
Breitenbeschränkung (f) *De*
width restriction *En*

limitation (f) de vitesse *Fr*
Verkehrsberuhigung (f) *De*
traffic calming *En*

limitation (f) des dépenses publiques *Fr*
Begrenzung (f) öffentlicher Ausgaben *De*
capping of public expenditure *En*

limitation (f) des impôts locaux (en GB) par l'Etat *Fr* *
Kürzung (f) der Kommunalabgaben durch die Zentralregierung *De*
rate capping *En*

limitation (f) des impôts locaux par le gouvernement central *Fr* *
Höchstgrenze (f) für Kommunalabgaben *De*
charge capping *En*

limite (f) de poids *Fr*
Gewichtbeschränkung (f) *De*
weight limit/restriction *En*

limite (f) de vitesse autorisée *Fr*
Geschwindigkeitsbeschränkung (f) *De*
speed limit *En*

limited company (Co.Ltd) *En*
société (f) à responsabilité limitée (SARL) *Fr*
Gesellschaft (f) mit beschränkter Haftung (GmbH) *De*

limiter (vb) *Fr*
einschränken (vb) (Entwicklung usw) *De*
restrict (vb) (development etc) *En*

limiter (vb) l'urbanisation *Fr*
Baubeschränkung (f) *De*
planning restraint *En*

limiter (vb) les dépenses *Fr*
Ausgaben kürzen (vb) *De*
limit (vb) expenditure *En*

limites (f.pl) financières *Fr*
finanzielle Grenzen (f.pl) *De*
financial limits *En*

linear programming *En*
programmation (f) linéaire *Fr*
Linearplanung (f) *De*

Linearplanung (f) *De*
linear programming *En*
programmation (f) linéaire *Fr*

linguistic minority *En*
minorité (f) linguistique *Fr*
Sprachminderheit (f) *De*

linke(-r,-s) (adj) *De*
left wing (adj) *En*
de gauche (adj) *Fr*

link road *En*
route (f) d'accès *Fr*
Verbindungsstraße (f) *De*

linker Flügel (m) *De*
left wing *En*
gauche (f) *Fr*

Linie (f); in vorderster —. *De*
forefront (in the) *En*
au premier plan *Fr*

liquid assets *En*
valeurs (f.pl) disponibles *Fr*
flüssige Mittel (nt.pl) *De*

liquid waste *En*
déchets (m.pl) liquides *Fr*
Abwasser (nt) *De*

liquidated damages *En*
dommages-intérêts (m.pl) fixés en argent *Fr*
Folgeschäden (m.pl) *De*

liquidation *En*
liquidation (f) *Fr*
Auflösung (f) *De*

liquidation (f) *Fr*
Auflösung (f) *De*
liquidation *En*

Liquidität (f) *De*
liquidity *En*
liquidité (f) *Fr*

liquidité (f) *Fr*
Liquidität (f) *De*
liquidity *En*

liquidity *En*
liquidité (f) *Fr*
Liquidität (f) *De*

liste (f) d'attente *Fr*
Warteliste (f) *De*
waiting list *En*

liste (f) de diffusion *Fr*
Adressenkartei (f) *De*
mailing list *En*

liste (f) des contribuables *Fr*
Gemeindesteuerverzeichnis (nt) *De*
community charge register *En*

liste (f) des élèves *Fr*
Schülerzahl (f) *De*
school roll *En*

liste (f) électorale *Fr*
Wählerverzeichnis (nt) *De*
electoral register/roll *En*

listed building *En*
bâtiment (m) classé d'intérêt historique ou architectural *Fr*
Gebäude (nt) unter Denkmalschutz *De*

literacy *En*
aptitude (f) à lire et écrire *Fr*
Lese- und Schreibfertigkeit (f) *De*

litigation *En*
litige (m) *Fr*
Rechtsstreit (m) *De*

litige (m) *Fr*
Rechtsstreit (m) *De*
litigation *En*

litter *En*
détritus (m) *Fr*
Abfälle (m.pl) *De*

litter bin *En*
boîte (f) à ordures *Fr*
Abfalleimer (m) *De*

live birth *En*
naissance (f) *Fr*
Lebendgeburt (f) *De*

livret (m) scolaire *Fr*
Register der Leistungen (f.pl) *De*
record of achievement *En*

livret (m) scolaire *Fr*
Schulzeugnis (nt) *De*
school report *En*

*** see/siehe/voir: Introduction page IX**

lizensieren (vb) *De*
license (vb) *En*
accorder (vb) un permis *Fr*

Lizenz (f) *De*
franchise (business) *En*
concession (f) *Fr*

Lizenz (f) *De*
licence *En*
permis (m) *Fr*

Lizenz; (die) — erteilen *De*
franchise (vb) *En*
octroyer (vb) une concession *Fr*

Lizenzbehörde (f) *De*
licensing authority *En*
police (f) municipale administrative *Fr*

loan *En*
emprunt (m) *Fr*
Darlehen (nt) *De*

loan guarantee *En*
emprunt (m) garanti *Fr*
Kreditbürgschaft (f) *De*

loan guarantee scheme *En*
système (m) de garanti d'emprunt *Fr*
Kreditbürgschaftsprogramm (nt) *De*

local accountability *En*
responsabilité (f) locale *Fr*
Ortsverantwortung (f) *De*

local authority association *En*
association (f) des collectivités territoriales *Fr*
Kommunalbehördenausschuß (m) *De*

local authority *En*
collectivité (f) territoriale *Fr*
Kommunalbehörde (f) *De*

local authority expenditure *En*
dépenses (f.pl) des collectivités territoriales *Fr*
Kommunalabgaben (f.pl) *De*

local authority finance *En*
finances (f.pl) des collectivités territoriales *Fr*
Kommunalfinanzen (pl) *De*

local authority housing *En*
habitation (f) à loyer modéré (HLM) *Fr*
Sozialwohnungen (f.pl) *De*

local autonomy *En*
autonomie (f) locale *Fr*
Kommunalautonomie (f) *De*

local broadcasting *En*
radiodiffusion (f) locale *Fr*
Lokalsendung (f) *De*

local business *En*
affaires (f.pl) de la place *Fr*
örtliches Gewerbe (nt) *De*

local community *En*
gens (m/f.pl) du pays *Fr*
Gemeinde (f) *De*

local council *En*
conseil (m) municipal *Fr*
Gemeinderat (m) *De*

local councillor *En*
conseiller (m) (-ère f.) municipal(e) *Fr*
Gemeinderat/-rätin (m/f) *De*

local democracy *En*
démocratie (f) locale *Fr*
örtliche Demokratie (f) *De*

local development agency *En*
agence (f) d'aménagement territorial *Fr*
örtliche Planungsorganisation (f) *De*

local development *En*
aménagement (m) territorial *Fr*
örtliche Entwicklung (f) *De*

local economy *En*
économie (f) locale *Fr*
Kommunalwirtschaft (f) *De*

local education authority *En* *
service (m) municipal/régional de l'enseignement *Fr*
Schulamt (nt) *De*

local election *En*
élection (f) municipale/départementale/régionale *Fr*
Kommunalwahl (f) *De*

local employment initiative *En*
initiative (f) locale pour la création de l'emploi *Fr*
kommunales Arbeitsbeschaffungs-programm (nt) *De*

local enterprise agency *En*
agence (f) pour la promotion de l'entreprise locale *Fr*
örtlicher Unternehmerverband (m) *De*

local enterprise *En*
entreprise (f) locale *Fr*
örtliches Unternehmen (nt) *De*

local government *En*
gouvernement (m) local *Fr*
Kommunalverwaltung (f) *De*

local government expenditure *En*
dépenses (f.pl) du gouvernement local *Fr*
Kommunalabgaben (f.pl) *De*

local government finance *En*
finances (f.pl) du gouvernement local *Fr*
Kommunalfinanzen (pl) *De*

local government officer *En*
fonctionnaire (m) territorial *Fr*
Kommunalbeamte(r)/-in (m/f) *De*

local government reform *En*
réforme (f) du gouvernement local *Fr*
Gemeindereform (f) *De*

local government reorganization *En*
réorganisation (f) du gouvernement local *Fr*
Gemeindeumorganisation (f) *De*

local government staff *En*
personnel (m) du gouvernement local *Fr*
Kommunalverwaltungspersonal (nt) *De*

local income tax *En*
impôt (m) local sur le revenu *Fr*
regionale Einkommensteuer (f) *De*

local inquiry *En*
enquête (f) commodo-incommodo *Fr*
lokale Untersuchung (f) *De*

local labour market *En*
marché (m) local du travail *Fr*
örtlicher Arbeitsmarkt (m) *De*

local plan *En*
plan (m) d'aménagement local *Fr*
örtliche Bauplanung (f) *De*

local sales tax *En*
taxe (f) de consommation locale *Fr*
örtliche Umsatzsteuer (f) *De*

local tax *En*
impôt (m) local *Fr*
Gemeindesteuer (f) *De*

*** see/siehe/voir: Introduction page IX**

locataire (m/f) *Fr*
Mieter/-in (m/f) *De*
tenant *En*

locataire (m/f) *Fr*
Pächter/-in (m/f) *De*
lessee *En*

locataire (m/f) à bail *Fr*
Pächter/-in, Mieter/-in (m/f) *De*
leaseholder *En*

location (f) *Fr*
Mietverhältnis (nt) *De*
tenancy *En*

location (f) *Fr*
Verpachtung (f), Vermietung (f) *De*
letting *En*

location (f) temporaire *Fr*
kurzzeitiges Mietverhältnis (nt) *De*
short hold tenancy *En*

locaux (m.pl) commerciaux *Fr*
Geschäftsräume (m.pl) *De*
commercial premises *En*

locaux (m.pl) *Fr*
Gebäude (nt) *De*
premises *En*

locaux (m.pl) industriels *Fr*
Industriegebäude (nt) *De*
industrial premises *En*

locaux (m.pl) pour bureaux *Fr*
Büroräume (m.pl) *De*
office accommodation *En*

locaux (m.pl) scolaires *Fr*
Schulgebäude (nt), -gelände (nt) *De*
school premises *En*

lodge (vb) an appeal *En*
interjeter (vb) appel *Fr*
einlegen (vb) (Berufung usw) *De*

lodging *En*
hébergement (m) *Fr*
Unterkunft (f) *De*

lodging house *En*
hôtel (m) garni *Fr*
Pension (f) *De*

logement (m) *Fr*
Unterkunft (f) *De*
accommodation *En*

logement (m) *Fr*
Unterkunft (f) *De*
residential accommodation *En*

logement (m) *Fr*
Wohnungen (f.pl) *De*
housing *En*

logement (m) à forte densité *Fr*
dichter Wohnungsbau (m) *De*
high density housing *En*

logement (m) à loyer modéré *Fr*
erschwingliche Wohnungen (f.pl) *De*
affordable housing *En*

logement (m) à prix modéré *Fr*
preisgünstige Wohnungen (f.pl) *De*
low cost housing *En*

logement (m) de fonction *Fr*
Gesindehaus (nt); Dienstwohnung (f) *De*
tied accommodation/housing *En*

logement (m) des étudiants *Fr*
Studentenwohnungen (f.pl) *De*
student accommodation *En*

logement (m) inhabitable *Fr*
unbewohnbare Unterkunft (f) *De*
unfit dwelling/housing *En*

logement (m) inoccupé *Fr*
leerstehende Wohnung (f) *De*
vacant accommodation/dwelling *En*

logement (m) loué *Fr*
Mietwohnungen (f.pl) *De*
rented accommodation/housing *En*

logement (m) non meublé *Fr*
unmöblierte Wohnung (f) *De*
unfurnished accommodation *En*

logement (m) pour célibataires *Fr*
Einzelunterkunft (f) *De*
single person housing *En*

logement (m) pour personnes à revenus modestes *Fr*
Wohnungsbau (m) für Kleinverdiener *De*
low income housing *En*

logement (m) pour personnes handicapées *Fr*
Wohnungen (f.pl) für Behinderte/Senioren *De*
sheltered accommodation *En*

logement (m) privé locatif *Fr*
private Mietwohnung (f) *De*
private rented accommodation *En*

logement (m) provisoire *Fr*
provisorische Unterkunft (f) *De*
temporary accommodation *En*

logement (m) public *Fr*
Sozialwohnungen (f.pl) *De*
public sector housing *En*

loger (vb) *Fr*
unterbringen (vb) *De*
accommodate (vb) *En*

loger (vb) *Fr*
unterbringen (vb) *De*
house (vb) *En*

logiciel (m) *Fr*
Software (f) *De*
computer software *En*

logiciel (m) *Fr*
Software (f) *De*
software *En*

Lohn (m) *De*
pay *En*
salaire (m) (secteur privé)/traitement (de fonctionnaire) *Fr*

Lohn (m) *De*
wage *En*
salaire (m) *Fr*

(Lohn)abzüge (m.pl) *De*
stoppages (from pay) *En*
retenues (f.pl) sur les appointements *Fr*

(eine) Lohnerhöhung gewähren (vb) De
award (vb) a wage increase En
accorder (vb) une augmentation de salaires Fr

Lohnsatz (m) *De*
pay rate *En*
taux (m) de salaire *Fr*

Lohnsatz (m) *De*
wage rate *En*
taux (m) des salaires *Fr*

Lohnsteuerabzugsverfahren (nt) *De*
pay as you earn (PAYE) *En*
impôt (m) sur le revenu prélevé sur le salaire/traitement *Fr*

Lohnstopp (m) *De*
wage freeze *En*
blocage (m) des salaires *Fr*

Lohntarifverhandlung (f) *De*
wage bargaining *En*
négotiation (f) salariale *Fr*

*** see/siehe/voir: Introduction page IX**

loi (f) de l'administration *Fr*
Verwaltungsrecht (nt) *De*
administrative law *En*

loi (f) *Fr*
Gesetz (nt) *De*
statute *En*

loi (f) *Fr*
Gesetz (nt), Recht (nt) *De*
law *En*

loi (f) *Fr*
Parlamentsakte (f) *De*
Act of Parliament *En*

loisir (m) *Fr*
Freizeit (f) *De*
leisure *En*

Lokalarchitektur (f) *De*
community architecture *En*
architecture (f) intégrée *Fr*

lokale Untersuchung (f) *De*
local inquiry *En*
enquête (f) commodo-incommodo *Fr*

Lokalsendung (f) *De*
local broadcasting *En*
radiodiffusion (f) locale *Fr*

long lease *En*
bail (m) à long terme *Fr*
langfristiger Mietvertrag (m) *De*

long term planning *En*
planification (f) à long terme *Fr*
Langzeitplanung (f) *De*

long term unemployment *En*
chômage (m) de longue durée *Fr*
Langzeitarbeitslosigkeit (f) *De*

lorry ban *En*
interdiction (f) aux poids-lourds *Fr*
Lastkraftwagenverbot (nt) *De*

lorry control *En*
contrôle (m) des poids-lourds *Fr*
Lastkraftwagenkontrolle (f) *De*

lorry route *En*
itinéraire (m) poids-lourds *Fr*
Lastkraftwagenstrecke (f) *De*

Löschfahrzeug (nt) *De*
fire engine *En*
voiture (f) de pompiers *Fr*

Lösungsmittelmißbrauch (m) *De*
solvent abuse *En*
abus (m) de dissolvants *Fr*

loterie (f) *Fr*
Lotterie (f) *De*
lottery *En*

lotissement (m) *Fr*
Siedlung (f) *De*
estate (housing) *En*

lotisseur (m) *Fr*
Bauunternehmer (m) *De*
developer *En*

Lotterie (f) *De*
lottery *En*
loterie (f) *Fr*

lottery *En*
loterie (f) *Fr*
Lotterie (f) *De*

low cost housing *En*
logement (m) à prix modéré *Fr*
preisgünstige Wohnungen (f.pl) *De*

low energy building *En*
bâtiment (m) isolé thermiquement *Fr*
energiesparende Bauweise (f) *De*

low income family *En*
famille (f) à revenu faible *Fr*
einkommensschwache Familie (f) *De*

low income housing *En*
logement (m) pour personnes à revenus modestes *Fr*
Wohnungsbau (m) für Kleinverdiener *De*

low paid (adj) *En*
personnes (f.pl) économiquement faibles *Fr*
schlecht bezahlt (adj) *De*

low pay *En*
revenu (m) modeste *Fr*
schlechte Bezahlung (f) *De*

low rent *En*
loyer (m) modéré *Fr*
niedrige Miete (f) *De*

low rise building *En*
bâtiment (m) bas *Fr*
Gebäude (nt) mit wenigen Stockwerken *De*

loyer (m) *Fr*
Miete (f) *De*
rent *En*

loyer (m) commercial *Fr*
Büromiete (f) *De*
office rent *En*

loyer (m) de faible montant *Fr*
erschwingliche Miete (f) *De*
affordable rent *En*

loyer (m) du marché *Fr*
Marktmiete (f) *De*
market rent *En*

loyer (m) foncier *Fr*
Pacht (f) *De*
land rent *En*

loyer (m) modéré *Fr*
niedrige Miete (f) *De*
low rent *En*

loyer (m) raisonnable *Fr*
angemessene Miete (f) *De*
fair rent *En*

loyers (m.pl) soumis à réglementation HLM *Fr*
Mietpreisüberwachnung (f) *De*
controlled tenancy *En*

Luft(fracht)verkehr (m) *De*
air transport *En*
transport (m) aérien *Fr*

Luftbildmessung (f) *De*
aerial survey *En*
inspection (f) aérienne *Fr*

Luftqualität (f) *De*
air quality *En*
qualité (f) de l'air *Fr*

Luftqualitätskontrolle (f) *De*
air monitoring *En*
contrôle (m) de l'air *Fr*

Luftschadstoff (m) *De*
air pollutant *En*
agent (m) de pollution de l'air *Fr*

Luftverschmutzung (f) *De*
air pollution *En*
pollution (f) de l'air *Fr*

lycée (m) *Fr*
Gymnasium (nt) *De*
grammar school *En*

lycée (m) *Fr*
Oberstufenzentrum (nt) *De*
sixth form college *En*

lycée (m) *Fr*
Schule (f) für den tertiären Bildungsbereich *De*
tertiary college *En*

lycée (m) professionnel *Fr*
weiterbildende Schule (f) *De*
further education college *En*

*** see/siehe/voir: Introduction page IX**

macadamiser (vb) ***Fr***
makadamisieren (vb) *De*
tarmacadam (vb) *En*

machine (f) à affranchir ***Fr***
Frankiermaschine (f) *De*
franking machine *En*

machine (f) à calculer ***Fr***
Rechenmaschine (f) *De*
calculator *En*

machine (f) à dictée ***Fr***
Diktaphon (nt) *De*
dictating machine *En*

machine (f) à écrire ***Fr***
Schreibmaschine (f) *De*
typewriter *En*

machine (f) à imprimer les adresses ***Fr***
Adressiermaschine (f) *De*
addressing machine *En*

machine (f) de traitement de textes ***Fr***
Textverarbeitungssystem (nt) *De*
word processor *En*

macro economic (adj) ***En***
macro-économique (adj) *Fr*
makroökonomisch (adj) *De*

macro economics ***En***
macro-économie (f) *Fr*
Makroökonomie (f) *De*

macro-économique (adj) ***Fr***
makroökonomisch (adj) *De*
macro economic (adj) *En*

macro-économie (f) ***Fr***
Makroökonomie (f) *De*
macro economics *En*

magasin (m) ***Fr***
Laden (m), Geschäft (nt) *De*
shop *En*

magistrat (m) ***Fr***
Friedensrichter/-in (m/f) *De*
magistrate *En*

magistrate ***En***
magistrat (m) *Fr*
Friedensrichter/-in (m/f) *De*

magistrates' court ***En***
tribunal (m) d'instance *Fr*
Schiedsgericht (nt) *De*

magistrature (f) ***Fr***
Richterschaft (f) *De*
judiciary *En*

mail ***En***
courrier (m) *Fr*
Post (f) *De*

mail order ***En***
commande (f) par correspondance *Fr*
Mail-order (f), Versandhandel (m) *De*

Mail-order (f), Versandhandel (m) ***De***
mail order *En*
commande (f) par correspondance *Fr*

mailing list ***En***
liste (f) de diffusion *Fr*
Adressenkartei (f) *De*

main road ***En***
grande route (f) *Fr*
Hauptstraße (f) *De*

main-d'oeuvre (f) ***Fr***
Arbeiterschaft (f), Belegschaft (f) *De*
work force *En*

main-d'oeuvre (f) ***Fr***
Arbeiterschaft (f) *De*
labour force *En*

main-d'oeuvre (f) ***Fr***
Arbeitskräfte (f.pl) *De*
manpower *En*

main-d'oeuvre (f) non qualifiée ***Fr***
Hilfsarbeit (f) *De*
unskilled labour *En*

main-d'oeuvre (f) spécialisée ***Fr***
Facharbeit (f) *De*
skilled labour *En*

mainframe computer ***En***
unité (f) centrale de traitement *Fr*
Großrechner (m) *De*

maintain (vb) ***En***
entretenir (vb) *Fr*
unterhalten, instandhalten, warten (vb) *De*

maintained school ***En***
école (f) laïque *Fr*
staatliche Schule (f) *De*

maintenance ***En***
entretien (m) *Fr*
Instandhaltungsbeihilfe (f) *De*

maintenance grant ***En***
bourse (f) d'entretien *Fr*
Unterhaltsbeihilfe (f) *De*

maintien (m) de l'ordre ***Fr***
polizeiliche Überwachung (f) *De*
policing *En*

maintien (m) de l'ordre locale ***Fr***
Kommunalüberwachung (f) *De*
community policing *En*

maintien (m) du pouvoir d'achat ***Fr***
Zuschuß (m) zu den Lebenshaltungskosten *De*
cost of living allowance *En*

maire (m)/bourgmestre (m) (Belg.) ***Fr*** *
Bürgermeister (m) *De*
mayor *En*

maire (m) élu ***Fr***
gewählter Bürgermeister (m) *De*
elected mayor *En*

maison (f) de culture ***Fr***
Kulturzentrum (nt) *De*
arts centre *En*

*** see/siehe/voir: Introduction page IX**

maison (f) de détention provisoire *Fr*
Untersuchungsgefängnis (nt) *De*
remand centre *En*

maison (f) de rapport divisée en appartements *Fr*
Wohnblock (m) *De*
tenement block *En*

maison (f) de rééducation *Fr*
Jugendstrafanstalt (f) *De*
detention centre *En*

maison (f) de retraite *Fr*
Alten-, Altersheim (nt) *De*
old people's home *En*

maison (f) de santé *Fr*
Nervenklinik (f) *De*
mental home *En*

maison (f) inoccupée *Fr*
Leere (f.pl) *De*
void *En*

maison (f) jumelle *Fr*
Doppelhaushälfte (f) *De*
semi-detached house *En*

maison (f) particulière *Fr*
Privathaus (nt) *De*
private house *En*

maison (f) separée *Fr*
Einzelhaus (nt) *De*
detached house *En*

Maison(n)ette (f), zweistöckige Wohnung (f) *De*
maisonette *En*
appartement (m) duplex *Fr*

maisonette *En*
appartement (m) duplex *Fr*
Maison(n)ette (f), zweistöckige Wohnung (f) *De*

maisons (f.pl) particulières *Fr*
privatwirtschaftlicher Wohnungsbau (m) *De*
private sector housing *En*

maître (m) de conférences *Fr*
Dozent/-in (m/f) *De*
lecturer *En*

maître (m) d'oeuvre *Fr*
leitender Auftragnehmer (m) *De*
managing contractor *En*

major road *En*
grande route (f) *Fr*
Hauptverkehrsstraße (f) *De*

majorité (f) absolue *Fr*
Gesamtverwaltung (f) *De*
overall control *En*

majorité (f) suffisante *Fr*
handlungsfähige Mehrheit (f) *De*
working majority *En*

majority party *En*
parti (m) majoritaire *Fr*
Mehrheitspartei (f) *De*

Makadam (m) *De*
tarmacadam *En*
tarmacadam (m) *Fr*

makadamisieren (vb) *De*
tarmacadam (vb) *En*
macadamiser (vb) *Fr*

Makroökonomie (f) *De*
macro economics *En*
macro-économie (f) *Fr*

makroökonomisch (adj) *De*
macro economic (adj) *En*
macro-économique (adj) *Fr*

malade (m/f) *Fr*
Patient/-in (m/f) *De*
patient *En*

malade (m/f) hospitalisé(e) *Fr*
(stationär behandelter) Krankenhauspatient (m) *De*
in-patient *En*

maladie (f) *Fr*
Krankheit (f) *De*
illness *En*

maladie (f) contagieuse *Fr*
ansteckende Krankheit (f) *De*
infectious disease *En*

maladie (f) de Down *Fr*
Down-Syndrom (nt) *De*
Down's syndrome *En*

maladie (f) mentale *Fr*
Geisteskrankheit (f) *De*
mental illness *En*

maladie (f) professionnelle *Fr*
Berufskrankheit (f) *De*
occupational disease *En*

maladie (f) psychiatrique *Fr*
psychiatrische Krankheit (f) *De*
psychiatric illness *En*

maladjusted child *En*
enfant (m/f) à problème *Fr*
verhaltensgestörtes Kind (nt) *De*

maladministration *En*
mauvaise administration (f) *Fr*
Mißwirtschaft (f) *De*

malpractice *En*
négligence (f) *Fr*
Amtsvergehen (nt) *De*

malvoyant (adj) *Fr*
sehbehindert (adj) *De*
visually handicapped (adj) *En*

malvoyant (-ante f.) (adj) *Fr*
sehbehindert (adj) *De*
partially sighted (adj) *En*

management *En*
gestion (f); direction (f) *Fr*
Management (nt) *De*

management (m) *Fr*
Firmenleitung (f) *De*
corporate management *En*

Management (nt) *De*
management *En*
gestion (f); direction (f) *Fr*

management accounts *En*
comptes (m.pl) de gestion *Fr*
Geschäftsbilanz (f) *De*

management audit *En*
contrôle (m) de gestion *Fr*
Geschäftsrechnungsprüfung (f) *De*

management by objectives *En*
direction (f) par objectifs *Fr*
zielorientiertes Management (nt) *De*

management committee *En*
comité (m) de direction *Fr*
Hauptausschuß (m) *De*

management consultant *En*
conseil (m) en gestion *Fr*
Unternehmensberater (m) *De*

management information *En*
informatique (f) de gestion *Fr*
Führungsinformation (f) *De*

management information system *En*
système (m) d'informatique de gestion *Fr*
Management-Informationssystem (nt) *De*

Management (nt) für Freizeitgestaltung *De*
recreation management *En*
service (m) de la culture et des loisirs *Fr*

*** see/siehe/voir: Introduction page IX**

management team *En*
conseil (m) d'administration *Fr*
Managementteam (nt) *De*

Management-Informationssystem (nt) *De*
management information system *En*
système (m) d'informatique de gestion *Fr*

Managementteam (nt) *De*
management team *En*
conseil (m) d'administration *Fr*

manager *En*
directeur (m) (-trice f.) *Fr*
Manager/-in (m/f) *De*

Manager/-in (m/f) *De*
manager (m) *En*
directeur (m) (-trice f.) *Fr*

managing change *En*
gérer (vb) le changement *Fr*
Veränderungsmanagement (nt) *De*

managing contractor *En*
maître (m) d'oeuvre *Fr*
leitender Auftragnehmer (m) *De*

managing director *En*
administrateur (m) délégué *Fr*
Geschäftsführer/-in (m/f) *De*

mandat (m) *Fr*
Anweisungen (f.pl) *De*
terms of reference *En*

mandat (m) d'arrêt *Fr*
Haftbefehl (m) *De*
warrant (arrest) *En*

mandat (m) de perquisition *Fr*
Durchsuchungsbefehl (m) *De*
search warrant *En*

mandat (m) de surveillance *Fr*
Aufsichtspflicht (f) *De*
supervision order *En*

Mangel (m) an Häusern/Wohnungen *De*
housing shortage *En*
crise (f) du logement *Fr*

Manifest (nt) *De*
manifesto *En*
manifeste (m) *Fr*

manifestation (f) *Fr*
Demonstration (f) *De*
demonstration (protest) *En*

manifeste (m) *Fr*
Manifest (nt) *De*
manifesto *En*

manifesto *En*
manifeste (m) *Fr*
Manifest (nt) *De*

manipulation (f) de l'information *Fr*
Informationsverarbeitung (f) *De*
information handling *En*

manoeuvres (f.pl) électorales *Fr*
Wahlkampf (m); Agitation (f) *De*
electioneering *En*

manpower *En*
main-d'oeuvre (f) *Fr*
Arbeitskräfte (f.pl) *De*

manpower planning *En*
gestion (f) des ressources humaines *Fr*
Personalplanung (f) *De*

manpower policy *En*
politique (f) d'emploi *Fr*
Beschäftigungspolitik (f) *De*

manque (m) de personnel *Fr*
Personalmangel (m) *De*
staff shortage *En*

manque (m) de personnel qualifié *Fr*
Fachpersonalmangel (m) *De*
skill shortage *En*

manquer (vb) de personnel *Fr*
(an) Personalmangel leiden *De*
understaffed (to be) *En*

manual labour *En*
travail (m) manuel *Fr*
manuelle Tätigkeit (f) *De*

manual worker *En*
travailleur (m) manuel *Fr*
Hand-, Schwerarbeiter (m) *De*

manuelle Tätigkeit (f) *De*
manual labour *En*
travail (m) manuel *Fr*

manufacture *En*
fabrication (f) *Fr*
Herstellung (f) *De*

manufacture (f) des chaussures *Fr*
Schuhindustrie (f) *De*
footwear industry *En*

manufacturer *En*
fabricant (m) *Fr*
Hersteller (m) *De*

manufacturing industry *En*
industrie (f) de fabrication *Fr*
verarbeitende Industrie (f) *De*

marché (m) commun *Fr*
Gemeinsamer Markt (m) *De*
common market *En*

marché (m) du travail *Fr*
Arbeitsmarkt (m) *De*
job market *En*

marché (m) du travail *Fr*
Arbeitsmarkt (m) *De*
labour market *En*

marché (m) européen unique *Fr*
europäischer Binnenmarkt (m) *De*
Single European Market *En*

marché (m) financier *Fr*
Finanzmarkt (m) *De*
financial market *En*

marché (m) immobilier *Fr*
Immobilienmarkt (m) *De*
property market *En*

marché (m) immobilier *Fr*
Wohnungsmarkt (m) *De*
housing market *En*

marché (m) intérieur *Fr*
Binnenmarkt (m) *De*
internal market *En*

marché (m) libre *Fr*
freier Markt (m) *De*
free market *En*

marché (m) libre *Fr*
Wettbewerbsfreiheit (f) *De*
deregulation *En*

marché (m) local du travail *Fr*
örtlicher Arbeitsmarkt (m) *De*
local labour market *En*

marché (m) monétaire *Fr*
Geldmarkt (m) *De*
money market *En*

marginal cost *En*
coût (m) marginal *Fr*
Grenzkosten (pl) *De*

*** see/siehe/voir: Introduction page IX**

marginal profit *En*
bénéfice (m) marginal *Fr*
Gewinnspanne (f) *De*

marine (f) maritime *Fr*
Schiffsverkehr (m) *De*
shipping *En*

market analysis *En*
analyse (f) de marché *Fr*
Marktanalyse (f) *De*

market development *En*
développement (m) du marché *Fr*
Marktlage (f), -entwicklung (f) *De*

market economy *En*
économie (f) de marché *Fr*
Marktwirtschaft (f) *De*

market forces *En*
conjoncture (f) du marché *Fr*
Kräfte (f.pl) des freien Markts *De*

market rent *En*
loyer (m) du marché *Fr*
Marktmiete (f) *De*

market research *En*
étude (f) de marché *Fr*
Marktforschung (f) *De*

market value *En*
valeur (f) marchande *Fr*
Marktwert (m) *De*

marketing agreement *En*
accord (m) de commercialisation *Fr*
Absatzübereinkommen (nt) *De*

marketing campaign *En*
campagne (f) de commercialisation *Fr*
Werbekampagne (f) *De*

marketing *En*
commercialisation (f)/techniques (f.pl) commerciales *Fr*
Marketing (nt) *De*

Marketing (nt) *De*
marketing *En*
commercialisation (f)/techniques (f.pl) commerciales *Fr*

Marktanalyse (f) *De*
market analysis *En*
analyse (f) de marché *Fr*

Marktforschung (f) *De*
market research *En*
étude (f) de marché *Fr*

Marktlage (f), -entwicklung (f) *De*
market development *En*
développement (m) du marché *Fr*

Marktmiete (f) *De*
market rent *En*
loyer (m) du marché *Fr*

Marktwert (m) *De*
market value *En*
valeur (f) marchande *Fr*

Marktwirtschaft (f) *De*
market economy *En*
économie (f) de marché *Fr*

marquage (m) routier *Fr*
Straßenmarkierung (f) *De*
road marking *En*

marquages (m.pl) en zigzag *Fr*
Zickzackmarkierung (f) *De*
zig zag marking *En*

marque (f) de commerce *Fr*
Handelsmarke (f) *De*
trade mark *En*

marque (f) déposée *Fr*
(eingetragenes) Warenzeichen (nt) *De*
trade mark (registered) *En*

marriage certificate *En*
acte (m) de mariage *Fr*
Trauschein (m) *De*

Maschinen (f.pl) *De*
plant *En*
matériel (m) *Fr*

Maschinenbau (m) *De*
mechanical engineering *En*
constructions (f.pl) mécaniques *Fr*

Maschineschreiben (nt) *De*
typing *En*
dactylographie (f) *Fr*

masse (f) monétaire *Fr*
Geldumlauf (m) *De*
money supply *En*

Masse und Gewichte (pl) *De*
weights and measures *En*
poids (m.pl) et mesures (f.pl) *Fr*

mastodonte (m) de la route *Fr*
Riesenlaster (m) *De*
juggernaut *En*

matériel (m) *Fr*
Maschinen (f.pl) *De*
plant *En*

matériel (m) d'incendie *Fr*
Feuerlöschanlagen (f.pl) *De*
fire fighting equipment *En*

matériel (m) de bureau *Fr*
Bürobedarf (m), -maschinen (f.pl) *De*
office equipment/machinery *En*

matériel (m) de sécurité *Fr*
Sicherheitsausrüstung (f) *De*
safety equipment *En*

matériel (m) pédagogique *Fr*
Lehrmittel (nt) *De*
teaching aid/material *En*

maternity allowance/benefit *En*
primes (f.pl) de maternité *Fr*
Mutterschaftshilfe (f) *De*

maternity care *En*
soins (m.pl) de maternité *Fr*
Wochenpflege (f) *De*

maternity leave *En*
congé (m) de maternité *Fr*
Mutterschaftsurlaub (m) *De*

matière (f) dangereuse *Fr*
gefährlicher Stoff (m) *De*
dangerous substance *En*

matière (f) inflammable *Fr*
feuergefährliches Material (nt) *De*
flammable material *En*

matière (f) toxique *Fr*
Giftstoff (m) *De*
toxic material *En*

matières (f.pl) premières *Fr*
Rohstoff (m) *De*
raw material *En*

matter of judgment *En*
question (f) de jugement *Fr*
Urteilssache (f) *De*

matter of trust *En*
question (f) de confiance *Fr*
Vertrauenssache (f) *De*

mauvaise administration (f) *Fr*
Mißwirtschaft (f) *De*
maladministration *En*

mauvaise gestion (f) *Fr*
Mißwirtschaft (f) *De*
mismanagement *En*

*** see/siehe/voir: Introduction page IX**

mauvaise santé (f) *Fr*
schwache Gesundheit (f), Kränklichkeit (f) *De*
ill health *En*

mauvaises dettes (f.pl) *Fr*
uneinbringliche Schulden (f.pl) *De*
bad debts *En*

mayor *En* *
maire (m)/bourgmestre (m) (Belg.) *Fr*
Bürgermeister (m) *De*

meals-on-wheels *En*
repas (m.pl) à domicile *Fr*
Essen (nt) auf Rädern *De*

means of escape *En*
moyen (m) de fuite *Fr*
Fluchtmöglichkeit (f) *De*

means test *En*
enquête (f) sur les ressources familiales *Fr*
Überprüfung (f) der Bedürftigkeit *De*

means tested benefit *En*
indemnité (f) allouée après enquête sur les ressources familiales *Fr*
nach Bedürftigkeit gestaffelte Unterstützung (f) *De*

mechanical engineering *En*
constructions (f.pl) mécaniques *Fr*
Maschinenbau (m) *De*

médecin (m) (f = femme médecin) *Fr*
Arzt/Ärztin (m/f) *De*
doctor *En*

médecin (m) de famille *Fr*
Hausarzt (m)/Hausärztin (f) *De*
family practitioner *En*

médecin (m) généraliste *Fr*
praktischer Arzt (m)/praktische Ärztin (f) *De*
general practitioner *En*

médecin-directeur (m) *Fr*
Amtsarzt (m) *De*
Medical Officer *En*

médecine (f) *Fr*
Medizin (f) *De*
medicine (faculty) *En*

médecine (f) générale *Fr*
Allgemeinmedizin (f) *De*
general practice *En*

médecine (f) préventive *Fr*
Präventivmedizin (f) *De*
preventive medicine *En*

médecine (f) privée *Fr*
private Gesundheitspflege (f) *De*
private health care *En*

media *En*
moyens (m.pl) de communication et d'information de masse *Fr*
Medien (nt.pl) *De*

médiateur (m) de la République/ commissaire (m) du parlement (Belg.) *Fr*
Ombudsmann (m) *De*
ombudsman *En*

mediation *En*
intervention (f) *Fr*
Vermittlung (f) *De*

medical benefit *En*
aide (f) médicale gratuite *Fr*
Krankengeld (nt) *De*

medical examination *En*
examen (m) médical *Fr*
ärztliche Untersuchung (f) *De*

medical insurance *En*
assurance (f) médicale *Fr*
Krankenversicherung (f) *De*

Medical Officer *En*
médecin-directeur (m) *Fr*
Amtsarzt (m) *De*

medical record *En*
dossier (m) médical *Fr*
medizinische Unterlagen (f.pl) *De*

medical service *En*
services (m.pl) médicaux *Fr*
Gesundheitsdienst (m) *De*

medical treatment *En*
traitement (m) médical *Fr*
ärztliche Behandlung (f) *De*

medicine (faculty) *En*
médecine (f) *Fr*
Medizin (f) *De*

Medien (nt.pl) *De*
media *En*
moyens (m.pl) de communication et d'information de masse *Fr*

medium sized business *En*
entreprise (f) de moyenne importance *Fr*
mittelgroße Firma (f) *De*

medium term (adj) *En*
à moyen terme (adj) *Fr*
mittelfristig (adj) *De*

medium term plan *En*
plan (m) à moyen terme *Fr*
mittelfristiger Plan (m) *De*

Medizin (f) *De*
medicine (faculty) *En*
médecine (f) *Fr*

medizinische Unterlagen (f.pl) *De*
medical record *En*
dossier (m) médical *Fr*

meeting *En*
réunion (f) *Fr*
Versammlung (f); Besprechung (f) *De*

Mehrheitspartei (f) *De*
majority party *En*
parti (m) majoritaire *Fr*

mehrstöckige Wohnungen (f.pl) *De*
multi-storey dwellings *En*
immeuble (m) à plusieurs étages *Fr*

Mehrwert (f) *De*
added value *En*
valeur (f) ajoutée *Fr*

Mehrwertsteuer (MWSt) (f) *De*
value added tax (VAT) *En*
taxe (f) à la valeur ajoutée (TVA) *Fr*

Meinungsfreiheit (f) *De*
freedom of expression *En*
liberté (f) d'expression *Fr*

Meinungsumfrage (f) *De*
opinion poll/survey *En*
sondage (m) d'opinion publique *Fr*

Member of Parliament *En*
député (m) *Fr*
Abgeordnete(-r) (m/f) *De*

member states *En*
états-membres (m.pl) *Fr*
Mitglied(s)staaten (m.pl) *De*

member's allowance *En*
indemnité (f) journalière (d'un membre élu) *Fr*
Mitgliedsbeilage (f) *De*

membre (m) à titre d'office *Fr*
Mitglied (nt) von Amts wegen *De*
ex-officio member *En*

*** see/siehe/voir: Introduction page IX**

membre (m) coopté du conseil *Fr*
berufene(r) Sachkundige(r) (m/f) *De*
co-opted member (of council) *En*

membre (m) du conseil d'administration (d'une fondation) *Fr*
Kurator/-in (m/f); Verwalter/-in (m/f) *De*
trustee *En*

membre (m) du conseil d'administration *Fr*
Mitglied (nt) des Schulbeirats *De*
school governor *En*

membre (m) du conseil *Fr*
Gemeinderats-, Stadtratsmitglied (nt) *De*
council member *En*

membre (m) du service du personnel *Fr*
Personalsachbearbeiter/-in (m/f) *De*
personnel officer *En*

membre (m) élu *Fr*
gewähltes Mitglied (nt) *De*
elected member *En*

ménage (m) *Fr*
Haushalt (m) *De*
household *En*

ménagère (f) *Fr*
Hausfrau (f) *De*
housewife *En*

Menschenrechte (nt.pl) *De*
human rights *En*
droits (m.pl) de l'homme *Fr*

mental handicap *En*
débilité (f) mentale *Fr*
geistige Behinderung (f) *De*

mental health care *En*
soins (m.pl) psychiatriques *Fr*
Geisteskrankenpflege (f) *De*

mental health *En*
santé (f) mentale *Fr*
seelische Gesundheit (f) *De*

mental home *En*
maison (f) de santé *Fr*
Nervenklinik (f) *De*

mental hospital *En*
hôpital (m) psychiatrique *Fr*
psychiatrische Klinik (f) *De*

mental illness *En*
maladie (f) mentale *Fr*
Geisteskrankheit (f) *De*

mentally handicapped people *En*
handicapés (-ées f.pl) mentaux (-ales f.pl) *Fr*
geistig Behinderte (pl) *De*

mentally ill (adj) *En*
aliéné(e) (adj) *Fr*
geisteskrank (adj) *De*

merchant bank *En*
banque (f) commerciale *Fr*
Handelsbank (f) *De*

merger *En*
fusion (f) *Fr*
Fusion (f) *De*

Messe (f) *De*
trade fair *En*
foire (f) commerciale *Fr*

mesures (f.pl) provisoires *Fr*
provisorische Maßnahmen (f.pl) *De*
temporary measures *En*

méthode (f) d'enseignement *Fr*
Lehr-/Unterrichtsmethode (f) *De*
teaching method *En*

méthode (f) statistique *Fr*
statistisches Verfahren (nt) *De*
statistical methods *En*

métier (m) *Fr*
Beruf (m), Tätigkeit (f) *De*
occupation *En*

métrage (m) *Fr*
Baukostenkalkulation (f) *De*
quantity surveying *En*

métreur (m) vérificateur *Fr*
Baukostenkalkulator/-in (m/f) *De*
quantity surveyor *En*

mettre (vb) en valeur *Fr*
sanieren (vb) *De*
redevelop (vb) *En*

mettre (vb) en adjudication *Fr*
etwas außer Haus machen lassen (vb) *De*
put out (vb) to contract *En*

meublé (m) *Fr*
möblierte Wohnung (f) *De*
furnished accommodation *En*

microcomputer *En*
"PC" (m) *Fr*
Mikrocomputer (m), -prozessor (m) *De*

microfiche *En*
microfiche (f) *Fr*
Mikrofiche (nt) *De*

microfiche (f) *Fr*
Mikrofiche (nt) *De*
microfiche *En*

middle income (adj) *En*
à revenus moyens *Fr*
Einkommen (nt); (Familie usw) mit mittlerem —. *De*

middle management (public sector) *En*
cadres (m.pl) moyens *Fr*
Middlemanagement (nt) *De*

middle school *En*
école (f) pour enfants de 8/9 à 12/13 ans *Fr*
Schule (f) für 8/9- bis 12/13-jährige *De*

Middlemanagement (nt) *De*
middle management (public sector) *En*
cadres (m.pl) moyens *Fr*

Mietbeihilfe (f) *De*
rent allowance *En*
diminution (f) du loyer *Fr*

Miete (f) *De*
rent *En*
loyer (m) *Fr*

Mieteintreibung (f) *De*
rent collection *En*
perception (f) de loyers *Fr*

Mieter/-in (m/f) *De*
sitting tenant *En*
occupant (m) (-ante f.) *Fr*

Mieter/-in (m/f) *De*
tenant *En*
locataire (m/f) *Fr*

Mieterausschuß (m) *De*
tenants' association *En*
association (f) de locataires *Fr*

Mieterhöhung (f) *De*
rent increase *En*
augmentation (f) de loyer *Fr*

Mietermäßigung (f) *De*
rent rebate *En*
réduction (f) de loyer *Fr*

*** see/siehe/voir: Introduction page IX**

Mieterrechte (nt.pl) *De*
tenants' rights *En*
droits (m.pl) du tenancier *Fr*

Mieterschutz (m) *De*
protected tenancy *En*
droits (m.pl) du locataire *Fr*

Mietpreisbindung (f) *De*
rent control *En*
encadrement (m) des loyers *Fr*

Mietpreisüberwachung (f) *De*
controlled tenancy *En*
loyers (m.pl) soumis à réglementation HLM *Fr*

Mietquittung (f) *De*
rent book *En*
quittance (f) de loyer *Fr*

Mietregulierung (f) *De*
rent regulation *En*
règlement (m) de loyer *Fr*

Mietschätzung (f) *De*
rent assessment *En*
fixation (f) de loyer *Fr*

Mietschulden (f.pl) *De*
rent arrears *En*
arriérés (m.pl) de loyer *Fr*

Mietshaus (nt) *De*
tenement *En*
appartement (m) *Fr*

Mietverhältnis (nt) *De*
tenancy *En*
location (f) *Fr*

Mietvertrag (m) *De*
tenancy agreement *En*
contrat (m) de location *Fr*

Mietwohngrundstück (nt) *De*
rented property *En*
propriété (f) louée *Fr*

Mietwohnungen (f.pl) *De*
rented accommodation/housing *En*
logement (m) loué *Fr*

migrant worker *En*
travailleur (m) saisonnier *Fr*
Wander-, Gastarbeiter (m) *De*

Mikrocomputer (m), -prozessor (m) *De*
microcomputer *En*
"PC" (m) *Fr*

Mikrofiche (nt) *De*
microfiche *En*
microfiche (f) *Fr*

mileage allowance *En*
indemnité (f) de déplacement *Fr*
Kilometergeld (nt) *De*

Millimeterpapier (nt) *De*
graph paper *En*
papier (m) millimétré *Fr*

Minderheit (f) *De*
minority group *En*
groupe (m) qui représente une minorité *Fr*

Minderheiten (f.pl) *De*
minorities *En*
minorités (f.pl) *Fr*

Mindestlohn (m) *De*
minimum wage *En*
salaire (m) minimum interprofessionnel de croissance (SMIC) *Fr*

mine (f) de charbon *Fr*
Kohlenbergwerk (nt) *De*
coal mine *En*

mini computer *En*
miniordinateur (m) *Fr*
Minicomputer (m) *De*

mini roundabout *En*
(petit) giratoire (m); rond-point (m) (pl. ronds-points) *Fr*
kleiner Kreisverkehr (m) *De*

Minicomputer (m) *De*
mini computer *En*
miniordinateur (m) *Fr*

minimum wage *En*
salaire (m) minimum interprofessionnel de croissance (SMIC) *Fr*
Mindestlohn (m) *De*

miniordinateur (m) *Fr*
Minicomputer (m) *De*
mini computer *En*

Minister/-in (m/f) *De*
Secretary of State *En*
ministre (m) *Fr*

Ministère (m) de l'Intérieur *Fr*
Innenministerium (nt) *De*
Home Office *En*

ministère (m) *Fr*
Regierungsstelle (f), -behörde (f) *De*
government department *En*

ministre (m) *Fr*
Minister/-in (m/f) *De*
Secretary of State *En*

minor road *En*
route (f) secondaire *Fr*
Nebenstraße (f) *De*

minor works *En*
petits travaux (m.pl) *Fr*
nebensächliche Arbeiten (f.pl) *De*

minorité (f) de religion *Fr*
religiöse Minderheit (f) *De*
religious minority *En*

minorité (f) ethnique *Fr*
ethnische Minderheit (f) *De*
ethnic minority *En*

minorité (f) linguistique *Fr*
Sprachminderheit (f) *De*
linguistic minority *En*

minorité (f) sociale *Fr*
gesellschaftliche Minderheit (f) *De*
social minority *En*

minorités (f.pl) *Fr*
Minderheiten (f.pl) *De*
minorities *En*

minorities *En*
minorités (f.pl) *Fr*
Minderheiten (f.pl) *De*

minority group *En*
groupe (m) qui représente une minorité *Fr*
Minderheit (f) *De*

minute (vb) *En*
dresser (vb) le procès-verbal *Fr*
protokollieren (vb) *De*

minutes (of meeting) *En*
procès-verbal (m) *Fr*
Protokoll (nt *De*

Mischform (f) *De*
mixed development *En*
aménagement (m) mixte *Fr*

Mischwirtschaft (f) *De*
mixed economy *En*
économie (f) mixte *Fr*

mise (f) à l'épreuve *Fr*
Strafaussetzung (f) zur Bewährung *De*
probation order *En*

mise (f) d'un travail en adjudication *Fr*
Angebotsaufforderung (f) *De*
invitation to tender *En*

*** see/siehe/voir: Introduction page IX**

mise (f) d'un travail en adjudication *Fr*
Ausschreibung (f) *De*
competitive tendering *En*

mise (f) d'un travail en adjudication obligatoire *Fr*
Pflichtausschreibung (f) *De*
compulsory competitive tendering *En*

mise (f) en valeur *Fr*
Wiedergewinnung (f) *De*
reclamation *En*

mismanagement *En*
mauvaise gestion (f) *Fr*
Mißwirtschaft (f) *De*

misrepresentation *En*
fausse déclaration (f) *Fr*
Verdrehung (f) *De*

Mißwirtschaft (f) *De*
maladministration *En*
mauvaise administration (f) *Fr*

Mißwirtschaft (f) *De*
mismanagement *En*
mauvaise gestion (f) *Fr*

mit einer Geldstrafe belegen (vb) *De*
fine (vb) *En*
frapper (vb) quelqu'un d'une amende *Fr*

Mitglied (nt) des Schulbeirats *De*
school governor *En*
membre (m) du conseil d'administration *Fr*

Mitglied (nt) von Amts wegen *De*
ex-officio member *En*
membre (m) à titre d'office *Fr*

Mitglied(s)staaten (m.pl) *De*
member states *En*
états-membres (m.pl) *Fr*

Mitgliedsbeilage (f) *De*
member's allowance *En*
indemnité (f) journalière (d'un membre élu) *Fr*

Mitteilung (f) *De*
notification *En*
avis (m) *Fr*

Mittel (nt.pl) *De*
fund(s) *En*
fonds (m) *Fr*

mittelfristig (adj) *De*
medium term (adj) *En*
à moyen terme (adj) *Fr*

mittelfristiger Plan (m) *De*
medium term plan *En*
plan (m) à moyen terme *Fr*

mittelgroße Firma (f) *De*
medium sized business *En*
entreprise (f) de moyenne importance *Fr*

mixed development *En*
aménagement (m) mixte *Fr*
Mischform (f) *De*

mixed economy *En*
économie (f) mixte *Fr*
Mischwirtschaft (f) *De*

mobile library *En*
bibliobus (m) *Fr*
Fahrbücherei (f) *De*

mobilité (f) de l'emploi *Fr*
Arbeitsplatzflexibilität (f) *De*
job mobility *En*

mobilité (f) de la main-d'oeuvre *Fr*
Arbeitermobilität (f) *De*
labour mobility *En*

mobilité (f) horaire *Fr*
anpassungsfähige Arbeitsweise (f) *De*
flexible working *En*

mobility allowance *En*
indemnité (f) de déplacement *Fr*
staatliche Geldleistung (f) für Gehbehinderte *De*

möblierte Wohnung (f) *De*
furnished accommodation *En*
meublé (m) *Fr*

modèle (m) de contrat de construction *Fr*
Vordruck (m) eines Bauvertrages *De*
standard form of building contract *En*

modèle (m) de contrat *Fr*
Vertragsform (f) *De*
form of contract *En*

modèle (m) de préliminaires de contrat *Fr*
Vertragsvorbemerkungsvordruck (m) *De*
standard contract preamble *En*

modèle (m) de soumission *Fr*
Angebot (nt) *De*
form of tender *En*

modèle (m) économétrique *Fr*
ökonometrisches Modell (nt) *De*
econometric model *En*

modèle (m) économique *Fr*
Wirtschaftsmodell (nt) *De*
economic model *En*

Modernisierungsbeihilfe (f) *De*
home improvement grant *En*
subvention (f) destinée à la modernisation *Fr*

modification (f) des circonscriptions électorales *Fr*
Grenzänderung (f) *De*
boundary change *En*

Möglichkeiten (f.pl) zur Freizeitgestaltung *De*
recreation facilities *En*
équipements (m.pl) de loisirs *Fr*

monde (m) des affaires *Fr*
Geschäftskreise (m.pl), Geschäftswelt (f) *De*
business community *En*

monetary interest *En*
intérêt (m) pécuniaire *Fr*
finanzieller Anteil (m) *De*

money management *En*
politique (f) monétaire *Fr*
Geldpolitik (f) *De*

money market *En*
marché (m) monétaire *Fr*
Geldmarkt (m) *De*

money supply *En*
masse (f) monétaire *Fr*
Geldumlauf (m) *De*

monitor (vb) (performance etc) *En*
surveiller (vb) *Fr*
kontrollieren (vb) *De*

Monopol (nt) *De*
monopoly *En*
monopole (m) *Fr*

monopole (m) *Fr*
Monopol (nt) *De*
monopoly *En*

*** see/siehe/voir: Introduction page IX**

monopoly ***En***
monopole (m) *Fr*
Monopol (nt) *De*

montage (m) financier ***Fr***
Finanzierung (f) nach Formel *De*
formula funding *En*

montage (m) financier ***Fr***
Gemeinschaftsfinanzierung (f) *De*
joint finance/funding *En*

monument (m) historique ***Fr***
Baudenkmal (nt) *De*
historic building *En*

monument (m) historique ***Fr***
historisches Denkmal (nt) *De*
ancient monument *En*

moratoire (m) ***Fr***
Moratorium (nt) *De*
moratorium *En*

moratorium ***En***
moratoire (m) *Fr*
Moratorium (nt) *De*

Moratorium (nt) ***De***
moratorium *En*
moratoire (m) *Fr*

mort (f) périnatale ***Fr***
perinatale Mortalität (f) *De*
perinatal death *En*

Mortalität (f) ***De***
mortality rate *En*
taux (m) de mortalité *Fr*

mortalité (f) infantile ***Fr***
Säuglingssterblichkeit (f) *De*
infant mortality *En*

mortality rate ***En***
taux (m) de mortalité *Fr*
Mortalität (f) *De*

mortgage arrears ***En***
arriéré (m) d'emprunt *Fr*
Hypothekenschulden (f.pl) *De*

mortgage ***En***
emprunt (m) *Fr*
Hypothek (f) *De*

mortgage interest ***En***
intérêt (m) de l'emprunt *Fr*
Hypothekenzins (m) *De*

mortgage repayment ***En***
remboursement (m) de l'emprunt *Fr*
Hypothekenzahlung (f) *De*

mortinaissance (f) ***Fr***
Totgeburt (f) *De*
stillbirth *En*

mortinatalité (f) ***Fr***
Totgeburtenzahl (f) *De*
stillbirths rate *En*

mother tongue teaching ***En***
enseignement (m) de la langue maternelle *Fr*
Unterricht (m) (in) der Muttersprache *De*

motivation ***En***
motivation (f) *Fr*
Motivation (f) *De*

Motivation (f) ***De***
motivation *En*
motivation (f) *Fr*

motivation (f) ***Fr***
Motivation (f) *De*
motivation *En*

motor industry ***En***
industrie (f) automobile *Fr*
Kraftfahrzeugindustrie (f) *De*

motorway ***En***
autoroute (f) *Fr*
Autobahn (f) *De*

motorway planning ***En***
programmation (f) des autoroutes *Fr*
Autobahnplanung (f) *De*

motorway service area ***En***
aire (f) de services (au bord d'une autoroute) *Fr*
Autobahnraststätte (f) *De*

mouvement (m) démographique ***Fr***
Bevölkerungstrend (m) *De*
demographic trend *En*

mouvement (m) pour la libération de la femme (MLF) ***Fr***
Frauenemanzipation (f); Frauenbewegung (f) *De*
womens' liberation *En*

moyen (m) de fuite ***Fr***
Fluchtmöglichkeit (f) *De*
means of escape *En*

moyen terme; à — — (adj) ***Fr***
mittelfristig (adj) *De*
medium term (adj) *En*

moyens (m.pl) de communication et d'information de masse ***Fr***
Medien (nt.pl) *De*
media *En*

Müll (m) ***De***
refuse (noun) *En*
déchets (m.pl) *Fr*

Müll (m), Abfall (m) ***De***
rubbish *En*
ordures (f.pl) *Fr*

Müll/Schutt abladen (vb) ***De***
tip (vb) *En*
débiter (vb) des foutaises *Fr*

Müllabfuhr (f) ***De***
refuse collection *En*
ramassage (m) des ordures *Fr*

Müllabfuhr (f) ***De***
waste collection *En*
ramassage (m) des ordures *Fr*

Müllabladeplatz (m) ***De***
refuse tip *En*
décharge (f) publique *Fr*

Müllgrube (f) ***De***
landfill site *En*
dépotoir (m) *Fr*

Müllhalde (f) ***De***
refuse transfer station *En*
usine (f) d'incinération *Fr*

Müllhalde (f) ***De***
rubbish dump *En*
décharge (f) publique *Fr*

Müllkippe (f) ***De***
dump (noun) (refuse) *En*
terrain (m) de décharge *Fr*

Müllkippe (f) ***De***
tip (noun) *En*
dépotoir (m) (d'ordures etc) *Fr*

Mülltonne (f) auf Rädern ***De***
wheeled bin *En*
poubelle (f) roulante *Fr*

Mülltonne (f) ***De***
dustbin *En*
poubelle (f) *Fr*

Mülltonne (f) ***De***
refuse bin *En*
boîte (f) à ordures *Fr*

Müllwagen (m) ***De***
dustcart *En*
voiture (f) des boueurs *Fr*

*** see/siehe/voir: Introduction page IX**

Müllwerker (m), -mann (m) *De*
dustman *En*
boueur (m) *Fr*

multi-ethnic (adj) *En*
multiethnique (adj) *Fr*
multiethnisch (adj) *De*

multi-racial (adj) *En*
multiracial (adj) *Fr*
gemischtraßig, mehrraßig (adj) *De*

multi-storey car park *En*
garage (m) à étages *Fr*
Parkhaus (nt) *De*

multi-storey dwellings *En*
immeuble (m) à plusieurs étages *Fr*
mehrstöckige Wohnungen (f.pl) *De*

multiethnique (adj) *Fr*
multiethnisch (adj) *De*
multi-ethnic (adj) *En*

multiethnisch (adj) *De*
multi-ethnic (adj) *En*
multiethnique (adj) *Fr*

multinational company *En*
société (f) multinationale *Fr*
multinationaler Konzern (m) *De*

multinationaler Konzern (m) *De*
multinational company *En*
société (f) multinationale *Fr*

multiracial (adj) *Fr*
gemischtraßig, mehrraßig (adj) *De*
multi-racial (adj) *En*

Mündel (m) (unter Amtsvormundschaft) *De*
ward of court *En*
pupille (m/f) sous tutelle judiciaire *Fr*

mündliche Prüfung (f) *De*
oral examination *En*
examen (m) oral *Fr*

municipal (adj) *En*
municipal (adj) *Fr*
kommunal, städtisch (adj); Gemeinde- *De*

municipal (adj) *Fr*
kommunal, städtisch (adj); Gemeinde- *De*
municipal (adj) *En*

municipal building *En*
bâtiment (m) municipal *Fr*
Bürgerbau (m) *De*

municipal enterprise *En*
entreprise (f) municipale *Fr*
Gemeindeunternehmen (nt) *De*

municipal refuse/waste *En*
ordures (f.pl) de ville *Fr*
städtischer Müll (m)/Abfall (m) *De*

municipalité (f) *Fr*
Gemeinde (f) *De*
municipality *En*

municipality *En*
municipalité (f) *Fr*
Gemeinde (f) *De*

mur (m) anti-bruit *Fr*
Lärmwall (m) *De*
noise barrier *En*

musée (m) *Fr*
Museum (nt) *De*
museum *En*

museum *En*
musée (m) *Fr*
Museum (nt) *De*

Museum (nt) *De*
museum *En*
musée (m) *Fr*

Mutterboden (m) *De*
topsoil *En*
terre (f) végétale *Fr*

Mutterschaftshilfe (f) *De*
maternity allowance/benefit *En*
primes (f.pl) de maternité *Fr*

Mutterschaftsurlaub (m) *De*
maternity leave *En*
congé (m) de maternité *Fr*

mutual agreement *En*
accord (m) mutuel *Fr*
gegenseitiges Einvernehmen (nt) *De*

*** see/siehe/voir: Introduction page IX**

N

nach Abzug der Steuern; netto (adj) *De*
tax paid (adj) *En*
net d'impôt (adj) *Fr*

nach Bedürftigkeit gestaffelte Unterstützung (f) *De*
means tested benefit *En*
indemnité (f) allouée après enquête sur les ressources familiales *Fr*

nach eigenem Ermessen verfügbare Ausgaben (f.pl) *De*
discretionary spending *En*
dépenses (f.pl) discrétionnaires (par le conseil municipal) *Fr*

Nachbar/-in (m/f) *De*
neighbour *En*
voisin (m) (-ine f.) *Fr*

Nachfrageanalyse (f) *De*
demand analysis *En*
analyse (f) de la demande *Fr*

Nachfrageelastizität (f) *De*
demand elasticity *En*
élasticité (f) de la demande *Fr*

Nachfrageprognose (f) *De*
demand forecast *En*
prévision (f) de la demande *Fr*

Nachfrageschätzung (f) *De*
demand assessment *En*
évaluation (f) de la demande *Fr*

Nachlässigkeit (f) *De*
neglect *En*
négligence (f) *Fr*

Nachtarbeit (f) *De*
night work *En*
travail (m) de nuit *Fr*

Nachtasyl (nt) *De*
night shelter *En*
asile (m) de nuit *Fr*

Nachtschicht (f) *De*
night shift *En*
équipe (f) de nuit *Fr*

Nachwahl (f) *De*
by-election *En*
élection (f) partielle *Fr*

Nagetier (nt) *De*
rodent *En*
rongeur (m) *Fr*

nähere Umstände (m.pl) *De*
further details *En*
plus amples renseignements (m.pl) *Fr*

naissance (f) *Fr*
Lebendgeburt (f) *De*
live birth *En*

narcotiques (m.pl) *Fr*
Drogen (f.pl), Rauschgift (nt) *De*
drugs *En*

national curriculum *En* *
programme (m) d'études national *Fr*
staatlicher Lehrplan (m) *De*

national grid *En*
réseau (m) électrique national *Fr*
nationales Verbundnetz (nt) *De*

national insurance *En*
assurance (f) d'état *Fr*
staatliche Versicherung (f) *De*

national insurance *En*
assurances (f.pl) sociales *Fr*
Sozialversicherung (f) *De*

national park *En*
parc (m) national *Fr*
Nationalpark (m) *De*

National Vocational Qualification (GB) *En* *
qualification (f) nationale professionnelle (en GB) *Fr*
staatliche Berufsausbildung (f) (in GB) *De*

nationales Verbundnetz (nt) *De*
national grid *En*
réseau (m) électrique national *Fr*

nationalised industry *En*
industrie (f) nationalisée *Fr*
verstaatlichter Wirtschaftszweig (m); verstaatlichte Industrie (f) *De*

nationalité (f) *Fr*
Staatsangehörigkeit (f) *De*
nationality *En*

nationality *En*
nationalité (f) *Fr*
Staatsangehörigkeit (f) *De*

Nationalpark (m) *De*
national park *En*
parc (m) national *Fr*

natural gas *En*
gaz (m) naturel *Fr*
Erdgas (nt) *De*

nature conservation *En*
conservation (f) de la nature *Fr*
Naturschutz (m) *De*

nature reserve *En*
réserve (f) naturelle *Fr*
Naturschutzgebiet (nt) *De*

natürliche Abnutzung (f) *De*
wear and tear *En*
usure (f) normale *Fr*

Naturschutz-, Landschaftsschutzgebiet (nt) *De*
conservation area *En*
zone (f) protégée *Fr*

Naturschutz (m) *De*
nature conservation *En*
conservation (f) de la nature *Fr*

Naturschutzgebiet (nt) *De*
nature reserve *En*
réserve (f) naturelle *Fr*

ne quittez pas (téléphone) *Fr*
am Apparat bleiben, bitte (Telefon) *De*
hold the line, please (telephone) *En*

*** see/siehe/voir: Introduction page IX**

Nebenkosten (pl) *De*
incidental expenses *En*
faux frais (m.pl) *Fr*

nebensächliche Arbeiten (f.pl) *De*
minor works *En*
petits travaux (m.pl) *Fr*

Nebenstraße (f) *De*
minor road *En*
route (f) secondaire *Fr*

Nebenstraße (f) *De*
secondary road *En*
route (f) secondaire *Fr*

needs assessment *En*
évaluation (f) du quotient familial *Fr*
Beurteilung (f) sozialer Bedürftigkeit *De*

neglect *En*
négligence (f) *Fr*
Nachlässigkeit (f) *De*

négligence (f) *Fr*
Amtsvergehen (nt) *De*
malpractice *En*

négligence (f) *Fr*
Nachlässigkeit (f) *De*
neglect *En*

négligence (f) professionnelle *Fr*
Vernachlässigung (f) der Berufspflichten *De*
professional negligence *En*

négociateur (m) (-trice f.) *Fr*
Unterhändler (m) *De*
negotiator *En*

négociation (f) *Fr*
Verhandlung (f) *De*
negotiation *En*

négocier (vb) *Fr*
verhandeln (vb) *De*
negotiate (vb) *En*

negotiate (vb) *En*
négocier (vb) *Fr*
verhandeln (vb) *De*

negotiation *En*
négociation (f) *Fr*
Verhandlung (f) *De*

négotiation (f) salariale *Fr*
Lohntarifverhandlung (f) *De*
wage bargaining *En*

négotiation (f) salariale *Fr*
Tarifverhandlung (f) *De*
pay bargaining/negotiation *En*

negotiator *En*
négociateur (m) (-trice f.) *Fr*
Unterhändler (m) *De*

neighbour *En*
voisin (m) (-ine f.) *Fr*
Nachbar/-in (m/f) *De*

neighbourhood *En*
voisinage (m) *Fr*
Gegend (f) *De*

neighbourhood development *En*
aménagement (m) d'un quartier *Fr*
Stadtteilentwicklung (f) *De*

neighbourhood policing *En*
îlotage (m) *Fr*
Bürgerwehr (f) *De*

Nervenklinik (f) *De*
mental home *En*
maison (f) de santé *Fr*

net budget *En*
budget (m) prévisionnel avec décisions modificatives *Fr*
Nettobudget (nt) *De*

net d'impôt (adj) *Fr*
nach Abzug der Steuern; netto (adj) *De*
tax paid (adj) *En*

netto (adj); nach Abzug der Steuern *De*
tax paid (adj) *En*
net d'impôt (adj) *Fr*

Nettobudget (nt) *De*
net budget *En*
budget (m) prévisionnel avec décisions modificatives *Fr*

Nettolohn (m) *De*
take-home pay *En*
salaire (m) net *Fr*

nettoyage (m) au contrat *Fr*
Auftragsreinigung (f) *De*
contract cleaning *En*

nettoyage (m) de bureau *Fr*
Bürosäuberung (f) *De*
office cleaning *En*

nettoyage (m) des rues *Fr*
Straßenreinigung (f) *De*
street cleaning/cleansing *En*

nettoyage (m) *Fr*
Reinigung (f), Putzen (nt) *De*
cleaning *En*

nettoyeur (m)/ nettoyeuse (f) *Fr*
Raumpfleger/-in (m/f) *De*
cleaner *En*

network analysis *En*
analyse (f) du réseau *Fr*
Netzanalyse (f) *De*

Netzanalyse (f) *De*
network analysis *En*
analyse (f) du réseau *Fr*

neu einstellen (vb) *De*
recruit (vb) *En*
recruter (vb) *Fr*

Neubelebung (f) der Innenstadt *De*
inner city regeneration *En*
revitalisation (f) du centre ville *Fr*

neue Stadt (f) *De*
new town *En*
ville (f) nouvelle *Fr*

neue Technologie (f) *De*
new technology *En*
technologie (f) nouvelle *Fr*

Neueinstellung (f) *De*
recruitment *En*
recrutement (m) *Fr*

Neufestsetzung (f) der Miete *De*
rent review *En*
révision (f) de loyer *Fr*

new technology *En*
technologie (f) nouvelle *Fr*
neue Technologie (f) *De*

new town *En*
ville (f) nouvelle *Fr*
neue Stadt (f) *De*

newsletter *En*
bulletin (m) (d'informations) *Fr*
Rundschreiben (nt) *De*

nicht beitreten (vb) *De*
contract out (vb) *En*
renoncer (vb) par contrat *Fr*

nicht bewirtschaftetes Land (nt) *De*
derelict land *En*
terrain (m) vague *Fr*

nicht übertragbar (adj) *De*
not negotiable (adj) *En*
non négociable (adj) *Fr*

Nichtzahlung (f) *De*
non-payment *En*
défaut (m) de paiement *Fr*

*** see/siehe/voir: Introduction page IX**

niedrige Miete (f) De
low rent *En*
loyer (m) modéré *Fr*

night shelter En
asile (m) de nuit *Fr*
Nachtasyl (nt) *De*

night shift En
équipe (f) de nuit *Fr*
Nachtschicht (f) *De*

night work En
travail (m) de nuit *Fr*
Nachtarbeit (f) *De*

niveau (m) (de gouvernement etc) Fr
Rang (m) (Regierung usw) *De*
tier (of government etc) *En*

niveau (m) de service Fr
Dienstleistungsniveau (nt) *De*
service level *En*

niveau (m) de vie Fr
Lebensstandard (m) *De*
standard of living *En*

noise abatement En
réduction (f) du bruit *Fr*
Lärmbekämpfung (f) *De*

noise barrier En
mur (m) anti-bruit *Fr*
Lärmwall (m) *De*

noise insulation regulations En
règlements (m.pl) de l'isolation contre le bruit *Fr*
Schallisolierungsvorschriften (f.pl) *De*

nomades (m.pl) Fr
fahrendes Volk (nt) *De*
travelling people *En*

nomination (f) (emploi) Fr
Ernennung (f) (Stelle) *De*
appointment (job) *En*

nomination (f) politique Fr
politische Ernennung (f) *De*
political appointment *En*

nommer (vb) Fr
ernennen (vb) *De*
appoint (vb) *En*

non advanced further education En
formation (f) continue *Fr*
Berufschulerziehung (f) *De*

non domestic rate En
taxe (f) professionnelle *Fr*
Gewerbesteuer (f) *De*

non meublé (adj) Fr
unmöbliert (adj) *De*
unfurnished (adj) *En*

non négociable (adj) Fr
nicht übertragbar (adj) *De*
not negotiable (adj) *En*

non officel (adj) Fr
inoffiziell (adj) *De*
unofficial (adj) *En*

non profit organisation En
organisation (f) à but non lucratif *Fr*
gemeinnützige Institution (f) *De*

non-payment En
défaut (m) de paiement *Fr*
Nichtzahlung (f) *De*

Not (f) De
hardship *En*
privation (f) *Fr*

Not-, Hilfsdienst (m) De
emergency service *En*
service (m) de secours *Fr*

not negotiable (adj) En
non négociable (adj) *Fr*
nicht übertragbar (adj) *De*

notaire (m) Fr
Rechtsanwalt/-anwältin (m/f) *De*
lawyer *En*

notaire (m) Fr
Rechtsanwalt/-anwältin (m/f) *De*
solicitor *En*

Notbehelf (m) De
stop-gap *En*
bouche-trou (m) *Fr*

Notbeleuchtung (f) De
emergency lighting *En*
éclairage (m) de securité *Fr*

notice to quit En
congé (m) *Fr*
Kündigung (f) *De*

notification En
avis (m) *Fr*
Mitteilung (f) *De*

Notstandsplanung (f) De
emergency planning *En*
programmation (f) des secours *Fr*

nouveau placement (m) Fr
Reinvestition (f) *De*
reinvestment *En*

nuclear energy En
énergie (f) nucléaire/atomique *Fr*
Kern-, Atomenergie (f) *De*

nuclear free zone En
zone (f) non nucléaire *Fr*
atomwaffenfreie Zone (f) *De*

nuclear power station En
centrale (f) atomique *Fr*
Kern-. Atomkraftwerk (nt) *De*

nuclear radiation En
rayonnement (m) nucléaire *Fr*
Kernstrahlung (f) *De*

nuclear reactor En
réacteur (m) nucléaire *Fr*
Kernreaktor (m) *De*

nuclear safety En
sécurité (f) nucléaire *Fr*
nukleare Sicherheit (f) *De*

nuclear waste En
déchets (m.pl) nucléaires *Fr*
Atommüll (m) *De*

nukleare Sicherheit (f) De
nuclear safety *En*
sécurité (f) nucléaire *Fr*

Null (m or nt); auf — basierender Haushalt (m) De
zero based budgeting *En*
budgétisation (f) à base zero *Fr*

numéro (m) d'immatriculation Fr
amtliches Kennzeichen (nt) *De*
registration number (vehicle) *En*

numéro (m) de téléphone Fr
Telefonnummer (f) *De*
telephone number *En*

nursery education En
enseignement (m) préélémentaire *Fr*
Vorschulerziehung (f) *De*

nursery school En
école (f) maternelle *Fr*
Kindergarten (m) *De*

nursing En
soins (m.pl) des malades *Fr*
Krankenpflege (f) *De*

Nutzfahrzeug (nt) De
goods vehicle *En*
véhicule (m) industriel *Fr*

*** see/siehe/voir: Introduction page IX**

obdachlose Familie (f) *De*
homeless family *En*
famille (f) sans asile *Fr*

Obdachlose (-n) (pl) *De*
homeless *En*
sans-gîte (m.pl) *Fr*

Obdachlosigkeit (f) *De*
homelessness *En*
problème (m) des sans-gîte *Fr*

obenerwähnt (adj) *De*
above-mentioned (adj) *En*
susmentionné (adj) *Fr*

Oberflächenwasser (nt) *De*
surface water *En*
eau (f) superficielle *Fr*

Oberschule (f) *De*
high school *En*
collège (m) *Fr*

oberster Gerichtshof (m) *De*
high court *En*
Haute Cour (f) de Justice *Fr*

Oberstufenzentrum (nt) *De*
sixth form college *En*
lycée (m) *Fr*

objectif (m) d'un projet *Fr*
Entwurfsvorlage (f), -richtlinien (f.pl) *De*
design guide *En*

objectives *En*
buts (m.pl) *Fr*
Ziele (nt.pl) *De*

obligations (f.pl) *Fr*
Verbindlichkeiten (f.pl) *De*
liabilities *En*

occasions (f.pl) civiques *Fr*
(offizielle) Stadtanlässe (m.pl) *De*
civic occasions *En*

occupancy *En*
occupation (f) *Fr*
Bewohnung (f) *De*

occupant (m) (-ante f.) *Fr*
Mieter/-in (m/f) *De*
sitting tenant *En*

occupation *En*
métier (m) *Fr*
Beruf (m), Tätigkeit (f) *De*

occupation (f) *Fr*
Bewohnung (f) *De*
occupancy *En*

occupation (f) d'une maison etc en qualité de squatter *Fr*
Hausbesetzung (f) *De*
squatting *En*

occupational disease *En*
maladie (f) professionnelle *Fr*
Berufskrankheit (f) *De*

occupational hazards *En*
risques (m.pl) du travail *Fr*
Berufsrisiken (nt.pl) *De*

occupational health/hygiene *En*
hygiène (f) du travail *Fr*
Arbeitshygiene (f) *De*

occupational pension scheme *En*
retraite (f) des cadres *Fr*
Betriebsaltersversorgung (f) *De*

occupational safety *En*
sécurité (f) au travail *Fr*
Arbeitsschutz (m) *De*

occupational training *En*
éducation (f) professionnelle *Fr*
Berufserziehung (f) *De*

octroyer une concession (vb) *Fr*
(die) Lizenz erteilen (vb) *De*
franchise (vb) *En*

oeuvres (f.pl) sociales *Fr*
Sozialarbeit (f) *De*
community work *En*

oeuvres (f.pl) sociales *Fr*
Sozialarbeit (f) *De*
social work *En*

off street parking *En*
parcage (m) (en retrait de la rue) *Fr*
Stellplätze (m.pl) *De*

offence *En*
infraction (f) à la loi *Fr*
Delikt (nt) *De*

offender *En*
délinquant (m) *Fr*
Straffällige (-r) (m/f) *De*

Offenlegung (f) von Information *De*
disclosure of information *En*
divulgation (f) d'informations *Fr*

öffentliche Anlagen (f.pl) *De*
public open space *En*
espace (m) public *Fr*

öffentliche Anlagen/Einrichtungen (f.pl) *De*
amenities of a region/town *En*
agréments (m.pl) d'une région/ville *Fr*

öffentliche Ausgaben (f.pl) *De*
public expenditure *En*
dépenses (f.pl) publiques *Fr*

öffentliche Beschaffung (f) *De*
public procurement *En*
acquisition (f) (par la personne) publique *Fr*

öffentliche Bücherei (f) *De*
public library *En*
bibliothèque (f) municipale *Fr*

(öffentliche) Einnahmen (f.pl) *De*
revenue *En*
fisc (m) *Fr*

*** see/siehe/voir: Introduction page IX**

öffentliche Einsparungen (f.pl) *De*
public expenditure cuts *En*
réductions (f.pl) des dépenses publiques *Fr*

öffentliche Finanzen (pl) *De*
public finance *En*
finances (f.pl) publiques *Fr*

öffentliche Geldanlage (f) *De*
public investment *En*
investissement (m) public *Fr*

öffentliche Mittel (nt.pl) *De*
public funds *En*
deniers (m.pl) publics *Fr*

(öffentliche) Ämter (nt.pl) *De*
public authorities *En*
pouvoirs (m.pl) publics *Fr*

öffentliche Ordnung (f) *De*
public order *En*
ordre (m) public *Fr*

öffentliche Prüfung (f) *De*
examination in public (E.I.P.) *En*
enquête (f) publique *Fr*

öffentliche Sitzung (f) *De*
public meeting *En*
séance (f) publique *Fr*

öffentliche Straße (f) *De*
adopted road *En*
rue/route (f) entretenue par la municipalité *Fr*

(öffentliche) Straße (f) *De*
highway *En*
grande route (f) *Fr*

öffentliche Untersuchung (f) *De*
inquiry in public *En*
enquête (f) de commodo *Fr*

öffentliche Untersuchung (f) *De*
public inquiry *En*
enquête (f) de commodo et incommodo *Fr*

öffentliche Verantwortlichkeit (f) *De*
public accountability *En*
responsabilité (f) personnelle *Fr*

öffentliche Verkehrsmittel (nt.pl) *De*
public transport *En*
transports (m.pl) en commun *Fr*

öffentliche Versorgungsbetriebe (m.pl) *De*
public utilities *En*
services (m.pl) publics *Fr*

(öffentliche) Versorgungsbetriebe (m.pl) *De*
utilities *En*
services (m.pl) publics *Fr*

öffentliche Verwaltung (f) *De*
public administration *En*
administration (f) publique *Fr*

öffentliche (adj); das — Wohl (nt) *De*
public good *En*
bien (m) public *Fr*

öffentlicher Abwasserkanal (m) *De*
adopted sewer *En*
égout (m) entretenu par la municipalité *Fr*

öffentlicher Sektor (m) *De*
public sector *En*
secteur (m) public *Fr*

öffentliches Gebäude (nt) *De*
public building *En*
bâtiment (m) public *Fr*

öffentliches Interesse (nt) *De*
public interest *En*
intérêt (m) public *Fr*

öffentliches Unternehmen (nt) *De*
public enterprise *En*
entreprise (f) publique *Fr*

office *En*
bureau (m) *Fr*
Büro (nt) *De*

office accommodation *En*
locaux (m.pl) pour bureaux *Fr*
Büroräume (m.pl) *De*

office block/building *En*
bâtiment (m) administratif *Fr*
Bürohaus (nt), -gebäude (nt) *De*

office cleaning *En*
nettoyage (m) de bureau *Fr*
Bürosäuberung (f) *De*

office development *En*
développement (m) tertiaire *Fr*
Büroerweiterung (f) *De*

office equipment/machinery *En*
matériel (m) de bureau *Fr*
Bürobedarf (m), -maschinen (f.pl) *De*

office hours *En*
heures (f.pl) de bureau *Fr*
Bürostunden (f.pl) *De*

office management *En*
administration (f) du bureau *Fr*
Büroleitung (f) *De*

office rent *En*
loyer (m) commercial *Fr*
Büromiete (f) *De*

office staff *En*
personnel (m) de bureau *Fr*
Büropersonal (nt) *De*

office worker *En*
employé (m) (-ée f.) de bureau *Fr*
Büroangestellte(-r) (m/f) *De*

official (adj) *En*
officiel (adj) *Fr*
amtlich (adj) *De*

officiel (adj) *Fr*
amtlich (adj) *De*
official (adj) *En*

(offizielle) Stadtanlässe (m.pl) *De*
civic occasions *En*
occasions (f.pl) civiques *Fr*

offre (f) de main-d'oeuvre *Fr*
Angebot (nt) an Arbeitskräften *De*
labour supply *En*

offre (f) de services *Fr*
Dienstleistungsversorgung (f) *De*
provision of services *En*

offre (f) et la demande *Fr*
Angebot (nt) und Nachfrage (f) *De*
supply and demand *En*

offre (m) de rachat *Fr*
Übernahmeangebot (nt) *De*
take-over bid *En*

offset printing *En*
tirage (m) par offset *Fr*
Offsetdruck (m) *De*

Offsetdruck (m) *De*
offset printing *En*
tirage (m) par offset *Fr*

ohne Verbindlichkeit (f) *De*
without prejudice *En*
sous toutes réserves (f.pl) *Fr*

*** see/siehe/voir: Introduction page IX**

ökologe /-gin (m/f) *De*
ecologist *En*
écologiste (m/f) *Fr*

Ökologie (f) *De*
ecology *En*
écologie (f) *Fr*

ökologisch (adj) *De*
ecological (adj) *En*
écologique (adj) *Fr*

ökologischer Park (m) *De*
ecological park *En*
parc (m) écologique *Fr*

ökonometrisches Modell (nt) *De*
econometric model *En*
modèle (m) économétrique *Fr*

Ökosystem (nt) *De*
ecosystem *En*
écosystème (m) *Fr*

old age pension *En*
pension (f) de retraite *Fr*
Altersrente (f) *De*

(old age) pensioner *En*
retraité (m) (-ée f.) *Fr*
Rentner/-in (m/f) *De*

old people's home *En*
maison (f) de retraite *Fr*
Alten-, Altersheim (nt) *De*

ombudsman *En*
médiateur (m) de la République/ commissaire (m) du parlement (Belg.) *Fr*
Ombudsmann (m) *De*

Ombudsmann (m) *De*
ombudsman *En*
médiateur (m) de la République/ commissaire (m) du parlement (Belg.) *Fr*

on behalf of *En*
de la part de *Fr*
für *De*

one parent family benefit *En*
allocation (f) parent isolé (API) *Fr*
Haushaltsfreibetrag (m) für Alleinerziehende *De*

one parent family *En*
famille (f) monoparentale *Fr*
Eineltemfamilie (f) *De*

open government *En*
transparence (f) *Fr*
freie Regierungsform (f) *De*

open plan office *En*
bureau (m) sans cloisons *Fr*
Großraumbüro (nt) *De*

opening hours *En*
heures (f.pl) d'ouverture *Fr*
Öffnungszeiten (f.pl) *De*

opérateur (m) (-trice f.) *Fr*
Vermittlung (f) *De*
operator *En*

operating cost *En*
frais (m.pl) d'exploitation *Fr*
Betriebskosten (pl) *De*

opération (f) immobilière *Fr*
Grundstückserschließung (f) *De*
property development *En*

operational research *En*
recherche (f) opérationnelle *Fr*
Unternehmensforschung (f) *De*

operator *En*
opérateur (m) (-trice f.) *Fr*
Vermittlung (f) *De*

Opfer (nt) der Kindesmißhandlung *De*
victim of child abuse *En*
enfant (m/f) martyr(e) *Fr*

Opferhilfe (f) *De*
victim support *En*
soutien (m) des victimes du crime *Fr*

opinion poll/survey *En*
sondage (m) d'opinion publique *Fr*
Meinungsumfrage (f) *De*

opposing factions *En*
groupes (m.pl) d'opposition *Fr*
gegnerische Splittergruppen (f.pl) *De*

opposition *En*
opposition (f) *Fr*
Opposition (f) *De*

Opposition (f) *De*
opposition *En*
opposition (f) *Fr*

opposition (f) *Fr*
Opposition (f) *De*
opposition *En*

opposition party *En*
parti (m) de l'opposition *Fr*
Oppositionspartei (f) *De*

Oppositionspartei (f) *De*
opposition party *En*
parti (m) de l'opposition *Fr*

opt out (vb) *En*
se retirer (vb) *Fr*
austreten (vb) *De*

option to purchase *En*
possibilité (f) d'achat *Fr*
Vorkaufsrecht (nt) *De*

oral examination *En*
examen (m) oral *Fr*
mündliche Prüfung (f) *De*

orbital motorway *En*
autoroute (f) périphérique *Fr*
Autobahn (f) um eine Stadt *De*

order (noun) *En*
commande (f) *Fr*
Bestellung (f) *De*

order (vb) *En*
commander (vb) *Fr*
bestellen (vb) *De*

ordinateur (m) *Fr*
Computer (m) *De*
computer *En*

ordinogramme (m) *Fr*
Flußdiagramm (nt) *De*
flow chart *En*

(faire (vb) l') ordinogramme *Fr*
ein Flußdiagramm aufstellen (vb) *De*
flow chart (vb) *En*

ordonnance (f) de placement en maison d'enfants *Fr*
Jugendfürsorgeanordnung (f) *De*
care order *En*

ordre (m) bancaire *Fr*
Bankauftrag (m) *De*
banker's order *En*

ordre (m) du jour *Fr*
Tagesordnung (f) *De*
agenda *En*

ordre (m) public *Fr*
öffentliche Ordnung (f) *De*
public order *En*

ordre (m) public *Fr*
Ruhe und Ordnung (f) *De*
law and order *En*

ordres (m.pl) permanents *Fr*
Geschäftsordnung (f) *De*
standing orders *En*

ordures (f.pl) de ville *Fr*
städtischer Müll (m)/Abfall (m) *De*
municipal refuse/waste *En*

*** see/siehe/voir: Introduction page IX**

ordures (f.pl) ***Fr***
Müll (m), Abfall (m) *De*
rubbish *En*

ordures (f.pl) ménagères ***Fr***
(häuslicher) Müll (m), Abfall (m) *De*
household waste *En*

ordures (f.pl) ménagères ***Fr***
Hausmüll (m) *De*
domestic refuse/waste *En*

oreille (f) dure (qui a l') ***Fr***
schwerhörig (adj) *De*
hearing impaired (adj) *En*

organic waste ***En***
déchêts (m.pl) organiques *Fr*
organischer Abfall (m) *De*

organisation (f) ***Fr***
Organisation (f) *De*
organization *En*

organisation (f) à but non lucratif ***Fr***
gemeinnützige Institution (f) *De*
non profit organization *En*

organisation (f) bénévole ***Fr***
Freiwilligenverband (m) *De*
voluntary agency/organization *En*

Organisation (f) ***De***
organization *En*
organisation (f) *Fr*

organisation (f) du temps ***Fr***
Zeitplanung (f) *De*
time management *En*

organischer Abfall (m) ***De***
organic waste *En*
déchêts (m.pl) organiques *Fr*

organisme (m) charicatif ***Fr***
Stiftung (f) *De*
charitable trust *En*

organisme (m) de jeunesse ***Fr***
Jugendorganisation (f) *De*
youth organization *En*

organization ***En***
organisation (f) *Fr*
Organisation (f) *De*

orientation (f) professionnelle ***Fr***
Berufsberatung (f) *De*
vocational guidance *En*

origine (f) ethnique ***Fr***
ethnische Herkunft (f) *De*
ethnic origin *En*

örtliche Bauplanung (f) ***De***
local plan *En*
plan (m) d'aménagement local *Fr*

örtliche Demokratie (f) ***De***
local democracy *En*
démocratie (f) locale *Fr*

örtliche Entwicklung (f) ***De***
local development *En*
aménagement (m) territorial *Fr*

örtliche Planungs-organisation (f) ***De***
local development agency *En*
agence (f) d'aménagement territorial *Fr*

örtliche Umsatzsteuer (f) ***De***
local sales tax *En*
taxe (f) de consommation locale *Fr*

örtlicher Arbeitsmarkt (m) ***De***
local labour market *En*
marché (m) local du travail *Fr*

örtlicher Unternehmerverband (m) ***De***
local enterprise agency *En*
agence (f) pour la promotion de l'entreprise locale *Fr*

örtliches Gewerbe (nt) ***De***
local business *En*
affaires (f.pl) de la place *Fr*

örtliches Unternehmen (nt) ***De***
local enterprise *En*
entreprise (f) locale *Fr*

Ortsverantwortung (f) ***De***
local accountability *En*
responsabilité (f) locale *Fr*

outdoor recreation ***En***
jeux (m.pl) de plein-air *Fr*
Freizeitbeschäftigungen (f.pl) im Freien *De*

outpatients' department ***En***
service (m) des consultations externes *Fr*
Poliklinik (f) *De*

output ***En***
rendement (m) *Fr*
Output (m) *De*

Output (m) ***De***
output *En*
rendement (m) *Fr*

Output (m) ***De***
outturn *En*
résultat (m) *Fr*

outrage (m) au tribunal ***Fr***
Ungebühr (f) vor Gericht *De*
contempt of court *En*

outturn ***En***
résultat (m) *Fr*
Output (m) *De*

outwork ***En***
travail (m) fait à domicile *Fr*
Heimarbeit (f) *De*

ouvrier (m) (-ière f.) ***Fr***
Arbeiter/-in (m/f) *De*
blue collar worker *En*

ouvrier (m) (-ière f.) ***Fr***
Arbeiter/-in (m/f) *De*
Worker *En*

ouvrier (m) (-ière f.) non qualifié(e) ***Fr***
ungelernte(-r) Arbeiter/-in (m/f), Hilfsarbeiter/-in (m/f) *De*
unskilled worker *En*

ouvrier (m) (-ière f.) qualifié(e) ***Fr***
Facharbeiter (m); Fachkraft (f) *De*
skilled worker *En*

over-representation ***En***
surreprésentation (f) *Fr*
Überrepräsentation (f) *De*

overall control ***En***
majorité (f) absolue *Fr*
Gesamtverwaltung (f) *De*

overheads ***En***
frais (m.pl) généraux *Fr*
Gemeinkosten (pl) *De*

overmanning ***En***
avoir un personnel trop nombreux *Fr*
Überbesetzung (f) *De*

overspend (vb) ***En***
dépenser (vb) au delà des moyens *Fr*
zuviel ausgeben (vb) *De*

overspill ***En***
déversement (m) de population *Fr*
Bevölkerungsüberschuß (m) *De*

overtime ***En***
heures (f.pl) supplémentaires *Fr*
Überstunden (f.pl) *De*

owner occupier ***En***
propriétaire-occupant (m) *Fr*
Eigenheimbesitzer (m) *De*

*** see/siehe/voir: Introduction page IX**

P

"PC" (m) *Fr*
Mikrocomputer (m), -prozessor (m) *De*
microcomputer *En*

Pacht (f) *De*
land rent *En*
loyer (m) foncier *Fr*

Pacht-, Mietvertrag (m) *De*
lease *En*
bail (m) *Fr*

Pächter/-in (m/f) *De*
lessee *En*
locataire (m/f) *Fr*

Pächter/-in, Mieter/-in (m/f) *De*
leaseholder *En*
locataire (m/f) à bail *Fr*

pädagogische Forschung (f) *De*
educational research *En*
recherche (f) pédagogique *Fr*

Pädagogische Hochschule (f) *De*
college of education *En*
école (f) normale *Fr*

paid holidays *En*
congés (m.pl) payés *Fr*
bezahlter Urlaub (m) *De*

paiement (m) par anticipation *Fr*
Vorauszahlung (f) *De*
advance payment *En*

palissade (f) *Fr*
Reklamewand (f) *De*
hoarding *En*

paperwork *En*
écriture (f) *Fr*
Schreibarbeit (f) *De*

papier (m) de rebut *Fr*
Papierabfall (m) *De*
waste paper *En*

papier (m) millimétré *Fr*
Millimeterpapier (nt) *De*
graph paper *En*

Papierabfall (m) *De*
waste paper *En*
papier (m) de rebut *Fr*

Papierkorb (m) *De*
waste paper basket *En*
corbeille (f) à papiers *Fr*

par tête (adj) *Fr*
pro Kopf (adj) *De*
per capita (adj) *En*

parc (m) de bâtiments *Fr*
Gebäudebestand (m) *De*
building stock *En*

parc (m) de logements *Fr*
Wohnungsbestand (m) *De*
housing stock/supply *En*

parc (m) écologique *Fr*
ökologischer Park (m) *De*
ecological park *En*

parc (m) national *Fr*
Nationalpark (m) *De*
national park *En*

parcage (m) (en retrait de la rue) *Fr*
Stellplätze (m.pl) *De*
off street parking *En*

parcomètre (m) *Fr*
Parkuhr (f) *De*
parking meter *En*

parent teacher association (PTA) *En*
association (f) de parents d'élèves *Fr*
Elternbeirat (m) *De*

parental involvement *En*
rôle (m) des parents *Fr*
elterliche Rolle (f) *De*

parental responsibility *En*
responsabilité (f) des parents *Fr*
Elternpflicht (f) *De*

parental rights *En*
droits (m.pl) des parents *Fr*
Elternrechte (nt.pl) *De*

parents (m.pl) nourriciers *Fr*
Pflegeeltern (pl) *De*
foster parents *En*

parish *En*
paroisse (f) *Fr*
Gemeinde (f) *De*

parish council *En*
conseil (m) municipal (d'une petite commune) *Fr*
Gemeinderat (m) *De*

Park-, Rastplatz m *De*
parking area; layby *En*
aire (f) de stationnement *Fr*

Parkausweis (m) *De*
parking permit *En*
permis (m) de stationnement *Fr*

Parkgebühr (f) *De*
parking charge *En*
tarif (m) de stationnement *Fr*

Parkhaus (nt) *De*
multi-storey car park *En*
garage (m) à étages *Fr*

parking area; layby *En*
aire (f) de stationnement *Fr*
Park-, Rastplatz m *De*

parking charge *En*
tarif (m) de stationnement *Fr*
Parkgebühr (f) *De*

parking meter *En*
parcomètre (m) *Fr*
Parkuhr (f) *De*

parking permit *En*
permis (m) de stationnement *Fr*
Parkausweis (m) *De*

parking policy *En*
politique (f) de stationnement *Fr*
Parkpolitik (f) *De*

Parkkralle (f) *De*
wheel clamp *En*
sabot (m) de Denver; pince (f) d'immobilisation *Fr*

Parkpolitik (f) *De*
parking policy *En*
politique (f) de stationnement *Fr*

Parkuhr (f) *De*
parking meter *En*
parcomètre (m) *Fr*

parlamentarischer Wahlkreis (m) *De*
parliamentary constituency *En*
circonscription (f) électorale *Fr*

Parlamentsakte (f) *De*
Act of Parliament *En*
loi (f) *Fr*

parliamentary constituency *En*
circonscription (f) électorale *Fr*
parlamentarischer Wahlkreis (m) *De*

paroisse (f) *Fr*
Gemeinde (f) *De*
parish *En*

part ; de la — de *Fr*
für *De*
on behalf of *En*

part-time work *En*
travail (m) à temps partiel *Fr*
Teilzeitarbeit (f) *De*

partage (m) *Fr*
Zuteilung (f) *De*
apportionment *En*

partage (m) des bénéfices *Fr*
Gewinnbeteiligung (f) *De*
profit sharing *En*

partage (m) du travail *Fr*
Job-sharing (nt) *De*
work sharing *En*

Partei (f) *De*
party *En*
parti (m) *Fr*

Parteipolitik (f) *De*
party politics *En*
politique (f) de parti *Fr*

parti (m) de l'opposition *Fr*
Oppositionspartei (f) *De*
opposition party *En*

parti (m) *Fr*
Partei (f) *De*
party *En*

parti (m) majoritaire *Fr*
Mehrheitspartei (f) *De*
majority party *En*

parti (m) politique *Fr*
politische Partei (f) *De*
political party *En*

parti (m) travailliste *Fr*
Labour Party (f) *De*
Labour Party *En*

partially sighted (adj) *En*
malvoyant (m) (-ante f.) (adj) *Fr*
sehbehindert (adj) *De*

participation (f) à la maintenance d'un bâtiment historique *Fr*
Beihilfe (f) für unter Denkmalschutz stehendes Gebäude *De*
conservation grant *En*

participation (f) aux bénéfices *Fr*
Gewinnbeteiligung (f) *De*
profit-sharing *En*

partisan (m) (-ane f.) de la conservation *Fr*
Umweltschützer/-in (m/f) *De*
conservationist *En*

partner *En*
associé (m) *Fr*
Partner/-in (m/f) *De*

Partner/-in (m/f) *De*
partner *En*
associé (m) *Fr*

Partnerschaft (f) *De*
partnership *En*
association (f) *Fr*

partnership *En*
association (f) *Fr*
Partnerschaft (f) *De*

Partnerstadt (f) *De*
twin town *En*
ville (f) jumelle *Fr*

party *En*
parti (m) *Fr*
Partei (f) *De*

party politics *En*
politique (f) de parti *Fr*
Parteipolitik (f) *De*

Paß (m) (Reisepaß) *De*
passport *En*
passeport (m) *Fr*

pass (vb) a law *En*
voter (vb) une loi *Fr*
(einen Gesetzentwurf) verabschieden (vb) *De*

pass (vb) the budget *En*
voter (vb) le budget *Fr*
(das Budget) bewilligen (vb) *De*

passage (m) pour piétons *Fr*
Fußgängerüberweg (m) *De*
pedestrian crossing *En*

passage (m) pour piétons *Fr*
Zebrastreifen (m) *De*
zebra crossing *En*

passage (m) souterrain *Fr*
Unterführung (f) *De*
subway *En*

passage (m) souterrain *Fr*
Unterführung (f) *De*
underpass *En*

passage (m) supérieur *Fr*
Überführung (f) *De*
flyover *En*

passenger traffic *En*
trafic (m) voyageurs *Fr*
Personenverkehr (m) *De*

passenger transport *En*
transports (m.pl) en commun *Fr*
Personenbeförderung (f) *De*

passeport (m) *Fr*
(Reise)paß (m) *De*
passport *En*

passport *En*
passeport (m) *Fr*
(Reise)paß (m) *De*

paternity leave *En*
congé (m) de paternité *Fr*
Vaterschaftsurlaub (m) *De*

patient *En*
malade (m/f) *Fr*
Patient/-in (m/f) *De*

Patient/-in (m/f) *De*
patient *En*
malade (m/f) *Fr*

patient care *En*
soins (m.pl) des malades *Fr*
Krankenpflege (f) *De*

patron (m) (-onne f.) *Fr*
Arbeitgeber/-in (m/f) *De*
employer *En*

Pauschalsubvention (f) *De*
block grant *En*
subvention (f) de l'Etat *Fr*

pauvreté (f) ***Fr***
Armut (f) *De*
poverty *En*

pavage (m) ***Fr***
Pflaster (nt) *De*
paving *En*

pavage (m) ***Fr***
Pflasterstein (m) *De*
floor slab *En*

pavement ***En***
trottoir (m) *Fr*
Bürgersteig (m) *De*

paving ***En***
pavage (m) *Fr*
Pflaster (nt) *De*

paving block ***En***
pierre (f) à paver *Fr*
Pflasterstein (m) *De*

pay ***En***
salaire (m) (secteur privé)/traitement (de fonctionnaire) *Fr*
Lohn (m) *De*

pay as you earn (PAYE) ***En***
impôt (m) sur le revenu prélevé sur le salaire/traitement *Fr*
Lohnsteuerabzugsverfahren (nt) *De*

pay bargaining/negotiation ***En***
négotiation (f) salariale *Fr*
Tarifverhandlung (f) *De*

pay out (vb) benefits ***En***
verser (vb) les prestations *Fr*
(Beihilfe) auszahlen (vb) *De*

pay rate ***En***
taux (m) de salaire *Fr*
Lohnsatz (m) *De*

"PC" (m) ***Fr***
Personalcomputer (m) *De*
personal computer *En*

pedestrian area/precinct/zone ***En***
zone (f) piétonne *Fr*
Fußgängerzone (f) *De*

pedestrian crossing ***En***
passage (m) pour piétons *Fr*
Fußgängerüberweg (m) *De*

penalty ***En***
sanction (f) *Fr*
Strafe (f) *De*

penalty clause ***En***
clause (f) pénale (de dommages-intérêts) *Fr*
Strafklausel (f) *De*

Pendler/-in (m/f) ***De***
commuter *En*
personne (f) qui fait un long trajet journalier entre résidence et travail *Fr*

pensée (f) légale ***Fr***
Rechtsgutachten (nt) *De*
legal opinion *En*

penalty ***En***
sanction (f) *Fr*
Strafe (f) *De*

pension ***En***
pension (f) de retraite *Fr*
Rente (f), Pension (f) *De*

Pension (f), Rente (f) ***De***
pension *En*
pension (f) de retraite *Fr*

Pension (f) ***De***
lodging house *En*
hôtel (m) garni *Fr*

pension age ***En***
âge (m) de retraite *Fr*
Renten-, Pensionsalter (nt) *De*

pension (f) d'invalidité ***Fr***
Erwerbsunfähigkeitsrente (f), Krankenunterstützung *De*
invalidity benefit/pension *En*

pension (f) de retraite ***Fr***
(Alters)rente (f), Pension (f) *De*
retirement pension *En*

pension (f) de retraite ***Fr***
Altersrente (f) *De*
old age pension *En*

pension (f) de retraite ***Fr***
Rente (f), Pension (f) *De*
pension *En*

pension (f) de retraite ***Fr***
Rentengeld (nt) *De*
superannuation benefit *En*

pension (f) de retraite ***Fr***
staatliche Rente/Pension (f) *De*
state pension *En*

pension fund ***En***
caisse (f) de retraite *Fr*
Pensionsfonds (m) *De*

pension scheme ***En***
retraite (f) des cadres *Fr*
Rentenversicherung (f) *De*

pensioner; old age —. ***En***
retraité (m) (-ée f.) *Fr*
Rentner/-in (m/f) *De*

Pensionierte(-n) (pl) ***De***
retired people *En*
retraités (m.pl) *Fr*

Pensions —, Rentenalter (nt) ***De***
retirement age *En*
âge (m) dela retraite *Fr*

Pensionsfonds (m) ***De***
pension fund *En*
caisse (f) de retraite *Fr*

per capita (adj) ***En***
par tête (adj) *Fr*
pro Kopf (adj) *De*

perception (f) de loyers ***Fr***
Mieteintreibung (f) *De*
rent collection *En*

perception (f) des impôts locaux ***Fr***
Kommunalsteuereinziehung (f) *De*
rate collection *En*

performance analysis ***En***
tableau (m) comparatif de performances *Fr*
Ergebnisanalyse (f) *De*

performance appraisal/evaluation ***En***
analyse (f) des performances *Fr*
Leistungsbeurteilung (f) *De*

performance indicator ***En***
indicateur (m) de performance *Fr*
Leistungsindikator (m) *De*

performance related pay ***En***
salaire (m) au mérite (secteur privé) *Fr*
leistungsbezogene Bezahlung (f) *De*

perinatal death ***En***
mort (f) périnatale *Fr*
perinatale Mortalität (f) *De*

perinatale Mortalität (f) ***De***
perinatal death *En*
mort (f) périnatale *Fr*

(période de) jouissance (f) ***Fr***
Besitz (m); Amtszeit (f) *De*
tenure *En*

période (f) de session ***Fr***
Sitzungsturnus (m) *De*
committee cycle *En*

*** see/siehe/voir: Introduction page IX**

périphérique (m) intérieur *Fr*
innere Ringstraße (f) *De*
inner ring road *En*

permis (m) *Fr*
Lizenz (f) *De*
licence *En*

permis (m) de stationnement *Fr*
Parkausweis (m) *De*
parking permit *En*

permitted development *En*
aménagement (m) autorisé *Fr*
genehmigter Wohnbau (m) *De*

Personal (nt) *De*
personnel *En*
personnel (m) *Fr*

Personal (nt) *De*
staff *En*
personnel (m) *Fr*

personal allowance *En*
abatement (m) personnel (sur l'impôt) *Fr*
Steuerfreibetrag (m) *De*

personal assistant *En*
fonctionnel (m) *Fr*
persönliche(-r) Referent/-in (m/f) *De*

personal computer *En*
"PC" (m) *Fr*
Personalcomputer (m) *De*

(Personal)einstellung (f); Personalwahl (f) *De*
staff recruitment/selection *En*
recrutement (m) du personnel *Fr*

personal file *En*
dossier (m) personnel *Fr*
Personalakte (f) *De*

personal income *En*
revenu (m) des personnes physiques *Fr*
persönliches Einkommen (nt) *De*

Personalabteilung (f) *De*
personnel department *En*
service (m) du personnel *Fr*

Personalakte (f) *De*
personal file *En*
dossier (m) personnel *Fr*

Personalausbildung (f) *De*
staff training *En*
formation (f) du personnel *Fr*

Personalausweis (m) *De*
identity card *En*
carte (f) d'identité *Fr*

Personalbeurteilung (f) *De*
staff appraisal/assessment *En*
appréciation (f) de valeur professionnelle *Fr*

Personalbewertung (f) *De*
personnel appraisal *En*
évaluation (f) du personnel *Fr*

Personalcomputer (m) *De*
personal computer *En*
"PC" (m) *Fr*

Personalentwicklung (f) *De*
staff development *En*
développement (m) du personnel *Fr*

Personalleiter/-in (m/f) *De*
personnel manager *En*
chef (m) du personnel *Fr*

Personalleitung (f) *De*
human resource management *En*
gestion (f) des ressources humaines *Fr*

Personalleitung (f) *De*
personnel management *En*
direction (f) du personnel *Fr*

Personalmangel (m) *De*
staff shortage *En*
manque (m) de personnel *Fr*

Personalmangel (m); an — leiden (vb) *De*
understaffed (to be) *En*
manquer (vb) de personnel *Fr*

Personalplanung (f) *De*
manpower planning *En*
gestion (f) des ressources humaines *Fr*

Personalsachbearbeiter/-in (m/f) *De*
personnel officer *En*
membre (m) du service du personnel *Fr*

Personalwechsel (m) *De*
labour turnover *En*
fluctuations (f.pl) de personnel *Fr*

Personenbeförderung (f) *De*
passenger transport *En*
transports (m.pl) en commun *Fr*

Personenverkehr (m) *De*
light rail transit *En*
chemin de fer (m) à voie étroite *Fr*

Personenverkehr (m) *De*
passenger traffic *En*
trafic (m) voyageurs *Fr*

persönliche(-r) Referent/-in (m/f) *De*
personal assistant *En*
fonctionnel (m) *Fr*

persönliches Einkommen (nt) *De*
personal income *En*
revenu (m) des personnes physiques *Fr*

personne (f) âgée *Fr*
Senior/-in (m/f) *De*
senior citizen *En*

personne (f) handicappée *Fr*
Behinderte(-r) (m/f) *De*
disabled person *En*

personne (f) qui fait un long trajet journalier entre résidence et travail *Fr*
Pendler/-in (m/f) *De*
commuter *En*

personnel *En*
personnel (m) *Fr*
Personal (nt) *De*

personnel (m) *Fr*
Personal (nt) *De*
personnel *En*

personnel (m) *Fr*
Personal (nt) *De*
staff *En*

personnel appraisal *En*
évaluation (f) du personnel *Fr*
Personalbewertung (f) *De*

personnel department *En*
service (m) du personnel *Fr*
Personalabteilung (f) *De*

personnel (m) (à titre) provisoire *Fr*
Aushilfe (f), Aushilfskräfte (f.pl) *De*
temporary staff *En*

personnel (m) auxiliaire *Fr*
Hilfspersonal (nt) *De*
ancillary staff *En*

personnel (m) auxiliaire *Fr*
Hilfspersonal (nt) *De*
auxiliary staff *En*

personnel (m) d'exécution *Fr*
Büropersonal (nt) *De*
clerical staff *En*

personnel (m) de base *Fr*
hochqualifizierte Facharbeiter (m.pl) *De*
key workers *En*

*** see/siehe/voir: Introduction page IX**

personnel (m) de bureau *Fr*
Büropersonal (nt) *De*
office staff *En*

personnel (m) du gouvernement local *Fr*
Kommunalverwaltungspersonal (nt) *De*
local government staff *En*

personnel (m) en surnombre *Fr*
entlassenes/überzähliges Personal (nt) *De*
redundant staff *En*

personnel management *En*
direction (f) du personnel *Fr*
Personalleitung (f) *De*

personnel manager *En*
chef (m) du personnel *Fr*
Personalleiter/-in (m/f) *De*

personnel officer *En*
membre (m) du service du personnel *Fr*
Personalsachbearbeiter/-in (m/f) *De*

personnes (f.pl) agées *Fr*
ältere Menschen (m.pl) *De*
elderly people *En*

personnes (f.pl) économiquement faibles *Fr*
schlecht bezahlt (adj) *De*
low paid (adj) *En*

personnes (f.pl) handicapées *Fr*
Behinderte (m/f.pl) *De*
handicapped people *En*

perspective drawing *En*
dessin (m) en perspective *Fr*
perspektivische Zeichnung (f) *De*

perspektivische Zeichnung (f) *De*
perspective drawing *En*
dessin (m) en perspective *Fr*

perte (f) de l'emploi *Fr*
Arbeitsplatzverlust (m) *De*
job loss *En*

perte (f) indirecte *Fr*
Folgeschaden (m) *De*
consequential loss *En*

pest control *En*
désinsectisation (f); dératisation (f) *Fr*
Schädlingsbekämpfung (f) *De*

(petit) giratoire (m); rond-point (m) (pl. ronds-points) *Fr*
kleiner Kreisverkehr (m) *De*
mini roundabout *En*

petite entreprise (f) *Fr*
Kleinbetrieb (m) *De*
small enterprise/firm *En*

petites et moyennes entreprises (PMEs)(f.pl) *Fr*
Klein- und Mittelbetriebe (m.pl) *De*
Small & Medium-Sized Enterprises (SMEs) *En*

Petition (f), Eingabe (f) *De*
petition (noun) *En*
requête (f) *Fr*

petition (noun) *En*
requête (f) *Fr*
Petition (f), Eingabe (f) *De*

petition (vb) *En*
requérir (vb) *Fr*
eine Eingabe machen, petitionieren (vb) *De*

petits travaux (m.pl) *Fr*
nebensächliche Arbeiten (f.pl) *De*
minor works *En*

Pfahl (m) *De*
pile *En*
pieu (m) *Fr*

Pfahlgründung (f) *De*
pile foundation *En*
fondation (f) sur pilotis *Fr*

Pflanzen (nt) *De*
planting *En*
plantage (m) *Fr*

Pflaster (nt) *De*
paving *En*
pavage (m) *Fr*

Pflasterstein (m) *De*
floor slab *En*
pavage (m) *Fr*

Pflasterstein (m) *De*
paving block *En*
pierre (f) à paver *Fr*

Pflege (f) *De*
foster care *En*
placement (m) familial *Fr*

Pflege (f) *De*
fostering *En*
prise (f) d'un enfant en nourrice *Fr*

Pflege (f); in — haben (vb) *De*
foster (vb) *En*
élèver (vb) (un enfant) *Fr*

Pflege (f) für unheilbar Kranke *De*
terminal care *En*
soins (m.pl) terminaux *Fr*

Pflegeeltern (pl) *De*
foster parents *En*
parents (m.pl) nourriciers *Fr*

Pflegegeld (nt) *De*
attendance allowance *En*
frais (m.pl) de déplacement *Fr*

Pflegegeld (nt) für Erwerbsunfähige *De*
invalid care allowance *En*
aide (f) d'adulte handicappé *Fr*

Pflegeleitung (f) *De*
care management *En*
action (f) sociale *Fr*

Pflegestelle (f), -heim (nt) *De*
foster home *En*
foyer (m) des parents nourriciers *Fr*

Pflichtausschreibung (f) *De*
compulsory competitive tendering *En*
mise (f) d'un travail en adjudication obligatoire *Fr*

phone book/telephone directory *En*
annuaire (m) des téléphones *Fr*
Fernsprechbuch *De*

photocopie (f) *Fr*
Fotokopie (f) *De*
photocopy (noun) *En*

photocopier *En*
photocopieur (m) *Fr*
Fotokopiergerät (nt) *De*

photocopier (vb) *Fr*
fotokopieren (vb) *De*
photocopy (vb) *En*

photocopieur (m) *Fr*
Fotokopiergerät (nt) *De*
photocopier *En*

photocopy (noun) *En*
photocopie (f) *Fr*
Fotokopie (f) *De*

photocopy (vb) *En*
photocopier (vb) *Fr*
fotokopieren (vb) *De*

physical education *En*
éducation (f) physique *Fr*
Leibeserziehung (f); Sport(unterricht) (m) *De*

*** see/siehe/voir: Introduction page IX**

physical handicap *En*
incapacité (f) physique *Fr*
Körperbehinderung (f) *De*

physically disabled/handicapped *En*
diminué (-ée f.) physique *Fr*
körperbehindert (adj) *De*

pie chart *En*
camembert (m) *Fr*
Kreisdiagramm (nt) *De*

pierre (f) à paver *Fr*
Pflasterstein (m) *De*
paving block *En*

pieu (m) *Fr*
Pfahl (m) *De*
pile *En*

pile *En*
pieu (m) *Fr*
Pfahl (m) *De*

pile drive (vb) *En*
enfoncer (vb) des pieux dans le sol *Fr*
rammen (vb) *De*

pile driver *En*
sonnette (f) *Fr*
Ramme (f) *De*

pile foundation *En*
fondation (f) sur pilotis *Fr*
Pfahlgründung (f) *De*

pipe *En*
tuyau (m) *Fr*
Rohr (nt) *De*

piste (f) cyclable *Fr*
Radweg (m), Fahrradspur (f) *De*
cycle lane/path *En*

pistes (f.pl) cyclables *Fr*
Verkehrseinrichtungen (f.pl) für Radfahrer *De*
cycle facilities *En*

placement *En*
placement (m) *Fr*
Plazierung (f) *De*

placement (m) *Fr*
Plazierung (f) *De*
placement *En*

placement (m) familial *Fr*
Pflege (f) *De*
foster care *En*

plafond (m) du budget *Fr*
Kreditbegrenzung (f) *De*
cash limit *En*

plan *En*
plan (m) *Fr*
Plan (m) *De*

Plan (m) *De*
plan *En*
plan (m) *Fr*

plan (m) *Fr*
Plan (m) *De*
plan *En*

plan (vb) *En*
formuler (vb) un projet *Fr*
planen (vb) *De*

plan (m); au premier — . *Fr*
in vorderster Linie *De*
forefront (in the) *En*

plan (m) à moyen terme *Fr*
mittelfristiger Plan (m) *De*
medium term plan *En*

plan (m) d'action *Fr*
Aktionsprogramm (nt) *De*
action plan *En*

plan (m) d'aménagement *Fr*
Entwicklungsplan (m) *De*
development plan *En*

plan (m) d'aménagement *Fr*
Geschäftsplan (m) *De*
business plan *En*

plan (m) d'aménagement local *Fr*
örtliche Bauplanung (f) *De*
local plan *En*

plan (m) d'aménagement urbain *Fr*
Bezirksverwaltungsplan (m) *De*
district plan *En*

plan (m) d'ensemble du comté/département *Fr*
Bezirksstrukturplan (m) *De*
county structure plan *En*

plan (m) d'ensemble *Fr*
Korporationsplan (m) *De*
corporate plan *En*

plan (m) d'occupation des sols *Fr*
Strukturplan (m) *De*
structure plan *En*

plan (m) de développement de la municipalité *Fr*
Bezirks/-Stadtteilentwicklungsplan (m) *De*
borough (development) plan *En*

plan (m) de développement de la ville *Fr*
Stadtplan (m) *De*
town plan *En*

plan (m) de développement *Fr*
strategischer Plan (m) *De*
strategic plan *En*

plan (m) de développement régional *Fr*
Kommunalprogramm (nt) *De*
regional plan *En*

plan (m) de mise en exécution (commerce) *Fr*
Zeitplan (m) *De*
timetable (commerce) *En*

plan (m) de protection civile *Fr*
Katastrophenschutz (m) *De*
disaster planning *En*

planen (vb) *De*
plan (vb) *En*
formuler (vb) un projet *Fr*

Planer/-in (m/f) *De*
planner *En*
urbaniste (m/f) *Fr*

planification (f) à long terme *Fr*
Langzeitplanung (f) *De*
long term planning *En*

planification (f) des politiques *Fr*
Zielplanung (f) *De*
policy planning *En*

planification (f) stratégique *Fr*
Zukunftsplanung (f) *De*
forward planning *En*

planned maintenance *En*
entretien (m) prévu *Fr*
geplante Instandhaltung (f) *De* *

planner *En*
urbaniste (m/f) *Fr*
Planer/-in (m/f) *De*

planning *En*
urbanisme (m) *Fr*
Planung (f) *De*

planning appeal *En*
recours (m) contre un acte d'urbanisme *Fr*
Bauplanungseinspruch (m) *De*

planning application *En*
demande (f) d'autorisation de construire *Fr*
Antrag (m) auf Bauerlaubnis *De*

*** see/siehe/voir: Introduction page IX**

planning consent/permission *En*
autorisation (f)/permis (m) de construire *Fr*
Baugenehmigung (f) *De*

planning control *En*
service (m) d'autorisation et droit des sols *Fr*
Bauaufsicht (f) *De*

planning department *En*
service (m) d'urbanisme *Fr*
Bauabteilung (f) *De*

planning & development committee *En*
commission (f) d'urbanisme *Fr*
(Bau)planungsausschuß (m) *De*

planning gain *En*
fonds (m) de concours *Fr*
Planungsgewinn (m) *De*

planning inquiry *En*
enquête (f) d'aménagement *Fr*
Planungsanhörung (f) *De*

planning (m) familial *Fr*
Familienplanung (f) *De*
family planning *En*

planning policy *En*
politique (f) d'urbanisme *Fr*
Baupolitik (f) *De*

planning powers *En*
pouvoirs (m.pl) en ce qui concerne l'urbanisme *Fr*
Planungsbefugnis (f) *De*

planning procedure/process/system *En*
procédures (f.pl) d'urbanisme *Fr*
Planungsverfahren (nt) *De*

planning regulation *En*
règlements (m.pl) d'urbanisme *Fr*
Bauvorschrift (f) *De*

planning restraint *En*
limiter (vb) l'urbanisation *Fr*
Baubeschränkung (f) *De*

plant *En*
matériel (m) *Fr*
Maschinen (f.pl) *De*

plantage (m) *Fr*
Pflanzen (nt) *De*
planting *En*

plantage (m) (des arbres) *Fr*
Baumpflanzung (f) *De*
tree planting *En*

planting *En*
plantage (m) *Fr*
Pflanzen (nt) *De*

Planung (f) *De*
planning *En*
urbanisme (m) *Fr*

Planung (f) für Freizeitgestaltung *De*
recreation planning *En*
programmation (f) culturelle et des loisirs *Fr*

Planungsanhörung (f) *De*
planning inquiry *En*
enquête (f) d'aménagement *Fr*

Planungsbefugnis (f) *De*
planning powers *En*
pouvoirs (m.pl) en ce qui concerne l'urbanisme *Fr*

Planungsgewinn (m) *De*
planning gain *En*
fonds (m) de concours *Fr*

Planungsverfahren (nt) *De*
planning procedure/process/system *En*
procédures (f.pl) d'urbanisme *Fr*

Plastikbelag (m) *De*
synthetic surface *En*
surface (f) synthétique *Fr*

play area/ground *En*
cour (f) de récréation *Fr*
Spielplatz (m) *De*

play facilities *En*
équipement (m) de récréation *Fr*
Spielmöglichkeiten (f.pl) *De*

play group *En*
jardin (m) d'enfants *Fr*
Kindergarten (m) *De*

playing field *En*
terrain (m) de jeux/sports *Fr*
Sportplatz (m) *De*

Plazierung (f) *De*
placement *En*
placement (m) *Fr*

plein temps; à — —. *Fr*
Ganztags- *De*
full-time (adj) *En*

Pleite machen (vb) *De*
bankrupt (to go) (vb) *En*
faire (vb) faillite *Fr*

plomberie (f) *Fr*
Installationsarbeiten (f.pl) *De*
plumbing *En*

plumbing *En*
plomberie (f) *Fr*
Installationsarbeiten (f.pl) *De*

plus amples renseignements (m.pl) *Fr*
nähere Umstände (m.pl) *De*
further details *En*

poids (m.pl) et mesures (f.pl) *Fr*
Masse und Gewichte (pl) *De*
weights and measures *En*

point (m) de seuil *Fr*
Rentabilitätsgrenze (f) *De*
break-even point *En*

poisonous waste *En*
déchêts (m.pl) toxiques *Fr*
giftige Abfälle (m.pl) *De*

polarisation *En*
polarisation (f) *Fr*
Polarisation (f) *De*

Polarisation (f) *De*
polarisation *En*
polarisation (f) *Fr*

polarisation (f) *Fr*
Polarisation (f) *De*
polarisation *En*

police (f) *Fr*
Polizei (f) *De*
police (force) *En*

police (f) d'assurance *Fr*
Versicherungspolice (f) *De*
insurance policy *En*

police (f) municipale administrative *Fr*
Lizenzbehörde (f) *De*
licensing authority *En*

police (force) *En*
police (f) *Fr*
Polizei (f) *De*

police officer *En*
agent (m) de police *Fr*
Polizeibeamte(r)/-in (m/f) *De*

police powers *En*
pouvoirs (m.pl) de police *Fr*
Polizeikräfte (f.pl) *De*

police record *En*
casier (m) judiciaire *Fr*
Vorstrafen (f.pl) *De*

police station *En*
poste (m) de police *Fr*
Polizeiwache (f) *De*

*** see/siehe/voir: Introduction page IX**

policewoman *En*
femme-agent (f) de police *Fr*
Polizistin (f) *De*

policing *En*
maintien (m) de l'ordre *Fr*
polizeiliche Überwachung (f) *De*

policy *En*
politique (f) *Fr*
Politik (f) *De*

policy analysis *En*
évaluation (f) de politique *Fr*
Grundsatzanalyse (f) *De*

policy and resources committee *En*
commission (f) des finances *Fr*
Grundsatz-und-Ressourcenausschuß (m) *De*

policy change *En*
changement (m) de politique *Fr*
Richtungswechsel (m) *De*

policy formulation/making *En*
élaboration (f) des politiques *Fr*
Zielformulierung (f) *De*

policy implementation *En*
exécution (f) des politiques *Fr*
programmatische Umsetzung (f) *De*

policy planning *En*
planification (f) des politiques *Fr*
Zielplanung (f) *De*

policy review *En*
évaluation (f) des politiques *Fr*
Überprüfung (f) der Politik *De*

Poliklinik (f) *De*
health centre *En*
centre (m) médical *Fr*

Poliklinik (f) *De*
outpatients' department *En*
service (m) des consultations externes *Fr*

political (adj) *En*
politique (adj) *Fr*
politisch (adj) *De*

political appointment *En*
nomination (f) politique *Fr*
politische Ernennung (f) *De*

political control *En*
contrôle (m) politique *Fr*
politische Kontrolle (f) *De*

political dogma *En*
dogme (m) politique *Fr*
politisches Dogma (nt) *De*

political group *En*
groupe (m) politique *Fr*
politische Einheit (f) *De*

political party *En*
parti (m) politique *Fr*
politische Partei (f) *De*

political theory *En*
théorie (f) politique *Fr*
politische Theorie (f) *De*

politician *En*
politique (m) *Fr*
Politiker/-in (m/f) *De*

politicization *En*
politisation (f) *Fr*
Politisierung (f) *De*

politics *En*
politique (f) *Fr*
Politik (f) *De*

Politik (f) *De*
policy *En*
politique (f) *Fr*

Politik (f) *De*
politics *En*
politique (f) *Fr*

Politik (f) der Chancengleichheit *De*
equal opportunities policy *En*
politique (f) d'égalité des chances *Fr*

Politiker/-in (m/f) *De*
politician *En*
politique (m) *Fr*

politique (f) *Fr*
Politik (f) *De*
policy *En*

politique (f) *Fr*
Politik (f) *De*
politics *En*

politique (m) *Fr*
Politiker/-in (m/f) *De*
politician *En*

politique (adj) *Fr*
politisch (adj) *De*
political (adj) *En*

politique (f) agricole commune *Fr*
gemeinsame Agrarpolitik (f) *De*
common agricultural policy *En*

politique (f) agricole *Fr*
Agrarpolitik (f) *De*
agricultural policy *En*

politique (f) budgétaire *Fr*
Finanzpolitik (f) *De*
fiscal policy *En*

politique (f) budgétaire *Fr*
Haushaltspolitik (f) *De*
budget policy *En*

politique (f) culturelle *Fr*
Kulturpolitik (f) *De*
arts policy *En*

politique (f) culturelle *Fr*
Kulturpolitik (f) *De*
cultural policy *En*

politique (f) d'égalité des chances *Fr*
Politik (f) der Chancengleichheit *De*
equal opportunities policy *En*

politique (f) d'emploi *Fr*
Beschäftigungspolitik (f) *De*
manpower policy *En*

politique (f) d'énergie *Fr*
Energiepolitik (f) *De*
energy policy *En*

politique (f) d'investissement *Fr*
Investitionspolitik (f) *De*
investment policy *En*

politique (f) d'urbanisme *Fr*
Baupolitik (f) *De*
planning policy *En*

politique (f) de formation *Fr*
Ausbildungspolitik (f) *De*
training policy *En*

politique (f) de l'éducation *Fr*
Schulpolitik (f) *De*
education policy *En*

politique (f) de l'emploi *Fr*
Arbeitsmarktpolitik (f) *De*
employment policy *En*

politique (f) de l'immigration *Fr*
Einwanderungspolitik (f) *De*
immigration policy *En*

politique (f) de la firme *Fr*
Geschäftspolitik (f) *De*
corporate policy *En*

politique (f) de parti *Fr*
Parteipolitik (f) *De*
party politics *En*

politique (f) de revitalisation de centre ville *Fr*
innerstädtische Politik (f) *De*
inner city policy *En*

*** see/siehe/voir: Introduction page IX**

politique (f) de stationnement *Fr*
Parkpolitik (f) *De*
parking policy *En*

politique (f) de transport *Fr*
Beförderungspolitik (f) *De*
transport policy *En*

politique (f) des loisirs *Fr*
Freizeitpolitik (f) *De*
leisure policy *En*

politique (f) des prix du voyage *Fr*
Tarifpolitik (f) *De*
fares policy *En*

politique (f) du logement *Fr*
Wohnungspolitik (f) *De*
housing policy *En*

politique (f) du transport de marchandises *Fr*
Frachtpolitik (f) *De*
freight policy *En*

politique (f) économique alternative *Fr*
Alternativwirtschaftsprogramm (nt) *De*
alternative economic strategy *En*

politique (f) économique *Fr*
Wirtschaftspolitik (f) *De*
economic policy *En*

politique (f) financière *Fr*
Finanzpolitik (f) *De*
financial policy *En*

politique (f) foncière *Fr*
Bodenpolitik (f) *De*
land policy *En*

politique (f) gouvernementale *Fr*
Regierungspolitik (f) *De*
government policy *En*

politique (f) industrielle *Fr*
Industriepolitik (f) *De*
industrial policy *En*

politique (f) monétaire *Fr*
Geldpolitik (f) *De*
money management *En*

politique (f) régionale *Fr*
Regionalpolitik (f) *De*
regional policy *En*

politique (f) routière *Fr*
Straßenbaupolitik (f) *De*
road policy *En*

politique (f) rurale *Fr*
ländliche Politik (f) *De*
rural policy *En*

politique (f) sociale *Fr*
Sozialpolitik (f) *De*
social policy *En*

politique (f) sociale *Fr*
Wohlfahrtspolitik (f) *De*
welfare policy *En*

politique (f) urbaine *Fr*
Städtepolitik (f) *De*
urban policy *En*

politisation (f) *Fr*
Politisierung (f) *De*
politicization *En*

politisch (adj) *De*
political (adj) *En*
politique (adj) *Fr*

politische Einheit (f) *De*
political group *En*
groupe (m) politique *Fr*

politische Ernennung (f) *De*
political appointment *En*
nomination (f) politique *Fr*

politische Kontrolle (f) *De*
political control *En*
contrôle (m) politique *Fr*

politische Partei (f) *De*
political party *En*
parti (m) politique *Fr*

politische Theorie (f) *De*
political theory *En*
théorie (f) politique *Fr*

politisches Dogma (nt) *De*
political dogma *En*
dogme (m) politique *Fr*

Politisierung (f) *De*
politicization *En*
politisation (f) *Fr*

Polizei (f) *De*
police (force) *En*
police (f) *Fr*

Polizeibeamte(r)/-in (m/f) *De*
police officer *En*
agent (m) de police *Fr*

Polizeikräfte (f.pl) *De*
police powers *En*
pouvoirs (m.pl) de police *Fr*

polizeiliche Überwachung (f) *De*
policing *En*
maintien (m) de l'ordre *Fr*

Polizeipräsident (m) *De* *
chief constable *En*
commissaire (m) de police *Fr*

Polizeiwache (f) *De*
police station *En*
poste (m) de police *Fr*

Polizist/-in (m/f) *De*
constable *En*
agent (m) de police *Fr*

Polizistin (f) *De*
policewoman *En*
femme-agent (f) de police *Fr*

poll *En*
scrutin (m) *Fr*
Abstimmung (f), Wahl (f) *De*

poll clerk *En*
secrétaire (m/f) du scrutin *Fr*
Angestellte(-r) (m/f) eines Wahlvorstands *De*

poll tax *En* *
capitation (f) *Fr*
Kopfsteuer (f) *De*

Poller (m) *De*
bollard *En*
borne (f) *Fr*

polling *En*
élections (f.pl) *Fr*
Stimmabgabe (f) *De*

polling booth *En*
isoloir (m) *Fr*
Wahlkabine (f) *De*

polling station *En*
bureau (m) de vote *Fr*
Wahllokal (nt) *De*

pollution *En*
pollution (f) *Fr*
(Umwelt)verschmutzung (f) *De*

pollution (f) *Fr*
(Umwelt)verschmutzung (f) *De*
pollution *En*

pollution (f) atmosphérique *Fr*
atmosphärische Verschmutzung (f) *De*
atmospheric pollution *En*

pollution control/monitoring *En*
contrôle (m) de la pollution *Fr*
Verschmutzungskontrolle (f) *De*

pollution (f) de l'air *Fr*
Luftverschmutzung (f) *De*
air pollution *En*

*** see/siehe/voir: Introduction page IX**

pollution (f) de l'eau *Fr*
Wasserverschmutzung (f) *De*
water pollution *En*

pollution (f) de l'environnement *Fr*
Umweltverschmutzung (f) *De*
environmental pollution *En*

pollution (f) des cours d'eau *Fr*
Flußverschmutzung (f) *De*
river pollution *En*

pollution (f) industrielle *Fr*
Verschmutzung (f) durch die Industrie *De*
industrial pollution *En*

pompier (m) *Fr*
Feuerwehrmann (m) *De*
fireman *En*

pont (m) à péage *Fr*
gebührenpflichtige Brücke (f) *De*
toll bridge *En*

pont (m) pour piétons *Fr*
Fußgängerbrücke (f) *De*
footbridge *En*

pont (m) routier *Fr*
Straßenbrücke (f) *De*
road bridge *En*

pont-bascule (m) (pl.ponts-bascules) *Fr*
Brückenwaage (f) *De*
weighbridge *En*

population *En*
population (f) *Fr*
Bevölkerung (f) *De*

population (f) *Fr*
Bevölkerung (f) *De*
population *En*

population change *En*
évolution (f) démographique *Fr*
Bevölkerungswandel (m) *De*

population decline *En*
baisse (f) démographique *Fr*
Bevölkerungsschwund (m) *De*

population density *En*
densité (f) de la population *Fr*
Bevölkerungsdichte (f) *De*

population distribution *En*
répartition (f) de la population *Fr*
Bevölkerungsverteilung (f) *De*

population estimate *En*
population (f) estimative *Fr*
Bevölkerungsschätzung (f) *De*

population (f) estimative *Fr*
Bevölkerungsschätzung (f) *De*
population estimate *En*

population forecast/projection *En*
prévision (f) démographique *Fr*
Bevölkerungsprognose (f) *De*

population growth *En*
accroissement (m) démographique *Fr*
Bevölkerungszuwachs (m) *De*

population statistics *En*
statistiques (f.pl) démographiques *Fr*
Bevölkerungsstatistik (f) *De*

populisme (m) *Fr*
Basisdemokratie (f) *De*
grassroots democracy *En*

port (m) *Fr*
Hafen (m) *De*
harbour *En*

port (m) franc *Fr*
Freihafen (m) *De*
free port *En*

port (m) payé *Fr*
portofrei (adj) *De*
postage paid (adj) *En*

port (m) pour conteneurs *Fr*
Containerterminal (nt) *De*
container terminal *En*

porte (f) coupe-feu *Fr*
Feuerschutztür (f) *De*
fire door *En*

portée; à la — de l'utilisateur/"facilement utilisable" *Fr*
benutzerfreundlich (adj) *De*
user friendly (adj) *En*

porte-parole (m/f) *Fr*
Sprecher/-in (m/f) *De*
spokesman/spokesperson *En*

porter (vb) témoignage *Fr*
aussagen (vb) *De*
give (vb) evidence *En*

porter (vb) une réclamation contre une decision *Fr*
eine Entscheidung anfechten (vb) *De*
challenge (vb) a decision *En*

porter (vb) une réclamation contre une décision *Fr*
Einspruch gegen eine Entscheidung einlegen (vb) *De*
appeal (vb) against a decision *En*

portofrei (adj) *De*
post free (adj) *En*
franco de port (adj) *Fr*

portofrei (adj) *De*
postage paid (adj) *En*
port (m) payé *Fr*

position statement *En*
analyse (f) de l'existant *Fr*
Lagebericht (m) *De*

positive discrimination *En*
discrimination (f) positive *Fr*
positive Diskriminierung (f) *De*

positive Diskriminierung (f) *De*
positive discrimination *En*
discrimination (f) positive *Fr*

possession (f) d'actions *Fr*
Aktienbesitz (m) *De*
shareholding *En*

possession (f) de propriété *Fr*
Eigenbesitz (m) (von Häusern/Wohnungen) *De*
home ownership *En*

possibilité (f) d'achat *Fr*
Vorkaufsrecht (nt) *De*
option to purchase *En*

Post (f) *De*
mail *En*
courrier (m) *Fr*

Post (f) *De*
post office *En*
bureau (m) de poste *Fr*

post free (adj) *En*
franco de port (adj) *Fr*
portofrei (adj) *De*

post office *En*
bureau (m) de poste *Fr*
Post (f) *De*

post room *En*
salle (f) du courrier *Fr*
Poststelle (f) *De*

Post-, Zustellbezirk (m) *De*
postal district *En*
secteur (m) postal *Fr*

post-graduate (adj) *En*
post-universitaire (adj) *Fr*
Graduierten- *De*

post-universitaire (adj) ***Fr***
Graduierten- *De*
post-graduate (adj) *En*

postage paid (adj) ***En***
port (m) payé *Fr*
portofrei (adj) *De*

postal district ***En***
secteur (m) postal *Fr*
Post-, Zustellbezirk (m) *De*

postal service ***En***
services (m.pl) postaux *Fr*
Postdienst (m) *De*

postal survey ***En***
recherche (f) de l'information par questionnaire *Fr*
postalische Umfrage (f) *De*

postalische Umfrage (f) ***De***
postal survey *En*
recherche (f) de l'information par questionnaire *Fr*

postcode ***En***
code (m) postal *Fr*
Postleitzahl (f) *De*

Postdienst (m) ***De***
postal service *En*
services (m.pl) postaux *Fr*

poste (m) d'incendie ***Fr***
Feuerwache (f) *De*
fire station *En*

poste (m) de police ***Fr***
Polizeiwache (f) *De*
police station *En*

poste (m) vacant ***Fr***
freie Stelle (f) *De*
job vacancy *En*

poste (m) vacant ***Fr***
freie Stelle (f) *De*
vacancy (staff) *En*

Postleitzahl (f) ***De***
postcode *En*
code (m) postal *Fr*

Poststelle (f) ***De***
post room *En*
salle (f) du courrier *Fr*

poteau (m) indicateur ***Fr***
Wegweiser (m) *De*
signpost *En*

Potentialbeurteilung (f) (Personal) ***De***
assessment of potential (staff) *En*
évaluation (f) du potentiel (personnel) *Fr*

poubelle (f) ***Fr***
Mülltonne (f) *De*
dustbin *En*

poubelle (f) roulante ***Fr***
Mülltonne (f) auf Rädern *De*
wheeled bin *En*

poursuites (f.pl) judiciaires ***Fr***
Gerichtsverfahren (nt) *De*
legal action *En*

poursuites (f.pl) judiciaires ***Fr***
(strafrechtliche) Verfolgung (f) *De*
prosecution *En*

poursuivre (vb) quelqu'un en justice répressive ***Fr***
(strafrechtlich) verfolgen (vb) *De*
prosecute (vb) *En*

pouvoir (m) discrétionnaire (du maire) ***Fr***
Entscheidungsgewalt (f) *De*
discretionary power *En*

pouvoir (m) ***Fr***
(Handlungs)berechtigung (f) *De*
power (i.e. to act) *En*

pouvoir (m) législatif ***Fr***
gesetzgeberische Gewalt (f) *De*
legislative power *En*

pouvoir (m) législatif ***Fr***
gesetzliche Kraft (f) *De*
statutory power *En*

pouvoirs (m.pl) de police ***Fr***
Polizeikräfte (f.pl) *De*
police powers *En*

pouvoirs (m. pl) délégués ***Fr***
delegierte Autorität (f) *De*
delegated authority/powers *En*

pouvoirs (m.pl) en ce qui concerne l'urbanisme ***Fr***
Planungsbefugnis (f) *De*
planning powers *En*

pouvoirs (m.pl) publics ***Fr***
(öffentliche) Ämter (nt.pl) *De*
public authorities *En*

poverty ***En***
pauvreté (f) *Fr*
Armut (f) *De*

power (i.e. to act) ***En***
pouvoir (m) *Fr*
(Handlungs)berechtigung (f) *De*

power consumption ***En***
consommation (f) d'énergie *Fr*
Energieverbrauch (m) *De*

power station ***En***
centrale (f) électrique *Fr*
Kraftwerk (nt) *De*

power supply ***En***
sources (f.pl) d'énergie *Fr*
Energieversorgung (f) *De*

pragmatic (adj) ***En***
pragmatique (adj) *Fr*
pragmatisch (adj) *De*

pragmatique (adj) ***Fr***
pragmatisch (adj) *De*
pragmatic (adj) *En*

pragmatisch (adj) ***De***
pragmatic (adj) *En*
pragmatique (adj) *Fr*

praktischer Arzt (m)/ praktische Ärztin (f) ***De***
general practitioner *En*
médecin (m) généraliste *Fr*

Prämiensystem (nt) ***De***
bonus scheme *En*
prime (f) *Fr*

Präsenzbibliothek (f) ***De***
reference library *En*
bibliothèque (f) d'ouvrages de référence *Fr*

Präsident/-in (m/f) ***De***
president *En*
président (m) (-ente f.) *Fr*

Präventivinstandhaltung (f) ***De***
preventive maintenance *En*
entretien (m) préventif *Fr*

Präventivmedizin (f) ***De***
preventive medicine *En*
médecine (f) préventive *Fr*

pre-meeting ***En***
réunion (f) préparatoire *Fr*
Vorbesprechung (f) *De*

pre-school playgroup ***En***
jardin (m) d'enfants *Fr*
Kindergarten (m) *De*

preamble ***En***
préliminaires (m.pl) (d'un traité etc) *Fr*
Einleitung (f) *De*

precast concrete ***En***
béton (m) prémoulé *Fr*
vorgefertigter Beton (m) *De*

précautions (f.pl) contre l'incendie ***Fr***
Feuerschutz (m) *De*
fire precautions *En*

*** see/siehe/voir: Introduction page IX**

prefabricated building *En*
bâtiment (m) préfabriqué *Fr*
Fertigbau (m) *De*

prefabricated housing *En*
habitation (f) préfabriquée *Fr*
Fertighäuser (nt.pl) *De*

préfabrication (f) *Fr*
Systembauweise (f) *De*
system building *En*

préfabriqué (adj) *Fr*
vorgefertigt (adj) *De*
system built (adj) *En*

Preiselastizität (f) *De*
price elasticity *En*
élasticité-prix (m) *Fr*

preisgünstige Wohnungen (f.pl) *De*
low cost housing *En*
logement (m) à prix modéré *Fr*

Preisindex (m) des Einzelhandels *De*
retail price index *En*
indice (m) des prix de détail *Fr*

prejudice *En*
préjugés (m.pl) *Fr*
Vorurteil (nt) *De*

préjugés (m.pl) *Fr*
Vorurteil (nt) *De*
prejudice *En*

préliminaires (m.pl) (d'un traité etc) *Fr*
Einleitung (f) *De*
preamble *En*

premises *En*
locaux (m.pl) *Fr*
Gebäude (nt) *De*

prendre (vb) sa retraite *Fr*
in den Ruhestand treten (vb) *De*
retire (vb) *En*

préparer (vb) le projet d'un contrat *Fr*
(Vertrag usw) aufsetzen (vb) *De*
draw up (vb) (contract etc) *En*

présenter (vb) un rapport en commission *Fr*
(einem Ausschuß) Bericht erstatten (vb) *De*
report (vb) to committee *En*

preservation *En*
conservation (f) *Fr*
Erhaltung (f) *De*

présidence (f) *Fr*
Vorsitz (m) *De*
chairmanship *En*

president *En*
président (m) (-ente f.) *Fr*
Präsident/-in (m/f) *De*

président (m) (-ente f.) d'un comité *Fr*
Ausschußvorsitzende(-r) (m/f) *De*
committee chair(man) *En*

président (m) (-ente f.) *Fr*
Präsident/-in (m/f) *De*
president *En*

président (m) (-ente f.) *Fr*
Vorsitzende(r) (m/f) *De*
chair/chairman/chairperson *En*

press *En*
presse (f) *Fr*
Presse (f) *De*

press conference *En*
conférence (f) de presse *Fr*
Pressekonferenz (f) *De*

press cutting *En*
coupure (f) de journal *Fr*
Zeitungsausschnitt (m) *De*

press release *En*
communiqué (m) de presse *Fr*
Presseinformation (f) *De*

Presse (f) *De*
press *En*
presse (f) *Fr*

presse (f) *Fr*
Presse (f) *De*
press *En*

Presseinformation (f) *De*
press release *En*
communiqué (m) de presse *Fr*

Pressekonferenz (f) *De*
press conference *En*
conférence (f) de presse *Fr*

pressure group *En*
groupe (m) de pression *Fr*
Pressure-group (f) *De*

Pressure-group (f) *De*
pressure group *En*
groupe (m) de pression *Fr*

prestations (f.pl) en cas de maladie *Fr*
gesetzliches Krankengeld (nt) *De*
statutory sick pay *En*

prestations (f.pl) sociales *Fr*
Sozialhilfe (f) *De*
social benefits *En*

prestressed concrete *En*
béton (m) précontraint *Fr*
Spannbeton (m) *De*

prêt (m) bancaire *Fr*
Bankdarlehen (nt) *De*
bank loan *En*

prévention (f) routière *Fr*
Verkehrssicherheit (f) *De*
road safety *En*

preventive maintenance *En*
entretien (m) préventif *Fr*
Präventivinstandhaltung (f) *De*

preventive medicine *En*
médecine (f) préventive *Fr*
Präventivmedizin (f) *De*

prévision (f) *Fr*
(Voraus)planung (f) *De*
projection *En*

prévision (f) collective *Fr*
gemeinsame Bereitstellung (f) *De*
joint provision *En*

prévision (f) de la demande *Fr*
Nachfrageprognose (f) *De*
demand forecast *En*

prévision (f) démographique *Fr*
Bevölkerungsprognose (f) *De*
population forecast/projection *En*

prévision (f) démographique *Fr*
demographische Voraussagen (f.pl) *De*
demographic projection(s) *En*

prévision (f) financiaire *Fr*
Ressourceplanung (f) *De*
resource planning *En*

prévisions (f.pl) budgétaires *Fr*
Einnahmeerwartungen (f.pl) *De*
revenue estimates *En*

prévoir (vb) *Fr*
schätzen (vb) *De*
estimate (vb) *En*

prévoir (vb) *Fr*
vorhersagen (vb) *De*
forecast (vb) *En*

price elasticity *En*
élasticité-prix (m) *Fr*
Preiselastizität (f) *De*

primäre Pflege (f) *De*
primary care *En*
soins (m.pl) primaires *Fr*

Primärversorgung (f) *De*
primary health care *En*
soins (m.pl) primaires de la santé *Fr*

primary care *En*
soins (m.pl) primaires *Fr*
primäre Pflege (f) *De*

primary education *En*
enseignement (m) primaire *Fr*
Grundschulerziehung (f) *De*

primary health care *En*
soins (m.pl) primaires de la santé *Fr*
Primärversorgung (f) *De*

primary school *En*
école (f) primaire *Fr*
Grundschule (f) *De*

primary/principal road *En*
route (f) à grande circulation *Fr*
Hauptverkehrsstraße (f) *De*

prime (f) *Fr*
Prämiensystem (nt) *De*
bonus scheme *En*

prime (f) d'assurance *Fr*
Versicherungsprämie (f) *De*
insurance premium *En*

primes (f.pl) de maternité *Fr*
Mutterschaftshilfe (f) *De*
maternity allowance/benefit *En*

primes (f.pl) de rendement *Fr*
Leistungszuschlag (m) *De*
incentive allowance *En*

principal (college) *En*
proviseur (m) (lycée) *Fr*
Rektor (m) *De*

principe (m) *Fr*
Prinzip (nt), Grundsatz (m) *De*
principle *En*

principle *En*
principe (m) *Fr*
Prinzip (nt), Grundsatz (m) *De*

Prinzip (nt), Grundsatz (m) *De*
principle *En*
principe (m) *Fr*

Prinzip (nt) der Gemeindeabgaben *De*
rate precept *En*
avis (m) d'imposition *Fr*

Priorität (f), Vorrang (m) *De*
priority *En*
priorité (f) *Fr*

Prioritätserschließungsgebiet (nt) *De*
special development area *En*
zone (f) d'aménagement concerté (ZAC) *Fr*

Prioritätszone (f) *De*
priority area *En*
zone (f) prioritaire *Fr*

priorité (f) *Fr*
Priorität (f), Vorrang (m) *De*
priority *En*

priority *En*
priorité (f) *Fr*
Priorität (f), Vorrang (m) *De*

priority area *En*
zone (f) prioritaire *Fr*
Prioritätszone (f) *De*

prise (f) d'un enfant en nourrice *Fr*
Pflege (f) *De*
fostering *En*

prise (f) de décision *Fr*
Beschlußfassung (f) *De*
decision-making *En*

prise (f) en charge d'une rue par la municipalité *Fr*
Übernahme (f) *De*
adoption (of road by council) *En*

(Privat)lehrer/-in (m/f) *De*
tutor *En*
directeur (m) (-trice f.) des études (d'un groupe d'étudiants) *Fr*

private and confidential (adj) *En*
secret et confidentiel (adj) *Fr*
streng vertraulich (adj) *De*

private citizen *En*
simple citoyen (m) (-enne f.) *Fr*
Privatperson (f) *De*

private contractor *En*
contractant (m) privé *Fr*
privater Auftragnehmer (m) *De*

private education *En*
enseignement (m) libre *Fr*
Privatschulausbildung (f) *De*

private enterprise *En*
entreprise (f) privée *Fr*
Privatunternehmen (nt) *De*

private Gesundheitspflege (f) *De*
private health care *En*
médecine (f) privée *Fr*

private health care *En*
médecine (f) privée *Fr*
private Gesundheitspflege (f) *De*

private health insurance *En*
assurance (f) maladie privée *Fr*
private Krankenkasse (f) *De*

private home *En*
clinique (f) privée *Fr*
privates Pflegeheim (nt) *De*

private hospital *En*
hôpital (m) privé *Fr*
Privatkrankenhaus (nt) *De*

private house *En*
maison (f) particulière *Fr*
Privathaus (nt) *De*

private investment *En*
investissement (m) privé *Fr*
Privatinvestition (f) *De*

private Krankenkasse (f) *De*
private health insurance *En*
assurance (f) maladie privée *Fr*

private Mietwohnung (f) *De*
private rented accommodation *En*
logement (m) privé locatif *Fr*

private office *En*
cabinet (m) particulier *Fr*
privates Büro (nt) *De*

private property *En*
propriété (f) privée *Fr*
Privateigentum (nt) *De*

private rented accommodation *En*
logement (m) privé locatif *Fr*
private Mietwohnung (f) *De*

private road *En*
chemin (m) privé *Fr*
Privatstraße (f) *De*

private sector *En*
secteur (m) privé *Fr*
Privatwirtschaft (f), privater Sektor (m) *De*

private sector housing *En*
maisons (f.pl) particulières *Fr*
privatwirtschaftlicher Wohnungsbau (m) *De*

Privateigentum (nt) *De*
private property *En*
propriété (f) privée *Fr*

*** see/siehe/voir: Introduction page IX**

privater Auftragnehmer (m) *De*
private contractor *En*
contractant (m) privé *Fr*

privates Büro (nt) *De*
private office *En*
cabinet (m) particulier *Fr*

privates Pflegeheim (nt) *De*
private home *En*
clinique (f) privée *Fr*

Privathaus (nt) *De*
private house *En*
maison (f) particulière *Fr*

Privatinvestition (f) *De*
private investment *En*
investissement (m) privé *Fr*

privation (f) *Fr*
Aberkennung (f), Deprivation (f) *De*
deprivation *En*

privation (f) *Fr*
Not (f) *De*
hardship *En*

privatisation (f) *Fr*
Privatisierung (f) *De*
privatization *En*

Privatisierung (f) *De*
privatization *En*
privatisation (f) *Fr*

privatization *En*
privatisation (f) *Fr*
Privatisierung (f) *De*

Privatkrankenhaus (nt) *De*
private hospital *En*
hôpital (m) privé *Fr*

Privatperson (f) *De*
private citizen *En*
simple citoyen (m) (-enne f.) *Fr*

Privatschulausbildung (f) *De*
private education *En*
enseignement (m) libre *Fr*

Privatschule (f) *De*
independent school *En*
école (f) libre *Fr*

Privatschule (f) *De*
public school *En*
collège (m) privé *Fr*

Privatstraße (f) *De*
private road *En*
chemin (m) privé *Fr*

Privatunternehmen (nt) *De*
private enterprise *En*
entreprise (f) privée *Fr*

Privatweg (m), -straße (f) *De*
unadopted road *En*
chemin (m) privé *Fr*

Privatwirtschaft (f), privater Sektor (m) *De*
private sector *En*
secteur (m) privé *Fr*

privatwirtschaftlicher Wohnungsbau (m) *De*
private sector housing *En*
maisons (f.pl) particulières *Fr*

privé (adj) *Fr*
benachteiligt, depriviert (adj) *De*
deprived (adj) *En*

prix (m) *Fr*
Kostenvoranschlag (m) *De*
quotation *En*

prix (m) de la main-d'oeuvre *Fr*
Arbeitskosten (pl) *De*
labour costs *En*

prix (m) de revient comptable *Fr*
Buchwert (m) der Einkäufe (f) *De*
book cost *En*

prix (m) de revient effectif *Fr*
Gestehungskosten (pl) *De*
actual cost *En*

prix (m) du combustible *Fr*
Brennstoffkosten (pl) *De*
fuel cost/price *En*

prix (m) du terrain *Fr*
Bodenpreis (m) *De*
land price *En*

prix (m.pl) de revient *Fr*
Kosten (pl) *De*
costs *En*

prix (m) réduit du voyage *Fr*
Reisekonzession (f) *De*
travel concession *En*

pro Kopf (adj) *De*
per capita (adj) *En*
par tête (adj) *Fr*

proactif (adj) *Fr*
proaktiv (adj) *De*
proactive (adj) *En*

proactive (adj) *En*
proactif (adj) *Fr*
proaktiv (adj) *De*

proaktiv (adj) *De*
proactive (adj) *En*
proactif (adj) *Fr*

probation *En*
probation (f) *Fr*
Bewährung (f) *De*

probation (f) *Fr*
Bewährung (f) *De*
probation *En*

probation; on — *En*
en liberté surveillée (adj) *Fr*
auf Bewährung *De*

probation officer *En*
agent (m) de probation *Fr*
Bewährungshelfer/-in (m/f) *De*

probation order *En*
mise (f) à l'épreuve *Fr*
Strafaussetzung (f) zur Bewährung *De*

probation service *En*
comité (m) de probation *Fr*
Bewährungsdienst (m) *De*

probationary teacher *En*
enseignant (m) stagiaire (en première année d'enseignement) *Fr*
Referendar/-in (m/f) *De*

probationer *En*
jeune délinquant (m) (-ante f.) en liberté surveillée *Fr*
auf Bewährung Freigelassene(-r) (m/f) *De*

Probealarm (m) *De*
fire drill *En*
exercice (m) de sauvetage en cas d'incendie *Fr*

problème (m) des sans-gîte *Fr*
Obdachlosigkeit (f) *De*
homelessness *En*

problème (m) social *Fr*
soziales Problem (nt) *De*
social problem *En*

procedural matter *En*
question (f) de procédure *Fr*
verfahrensmäßige Angelegenheit (f) *De*

procédure (f) d'appel *Fr*
Einspruchsverfahren (nt) *De*
appeals procedure *En*

procédure (f) d'ordonnance de placement *Fr*
Fürsorgeerziehungsverfahren (nt) *De*
care proceedings *En*

procédure (f) pour porter plainte *Fr*
Beschwerdeverfahren (nt) *De*
complaints procedure *En*

procédures (f.pl) d'urbanisme *Fr*
Planungsverfahren (nt) *De*
planning procedure/process/system *En*

procédures (f.pl) disciplinaires *Fr*
Disziplinarverfahren (nt) *De*
disciplinary procedure *En*

procès-verbal (m) *Fr*
Protokoll (nt) *De*
minutes (of meeting) *En*

Procurator Fiscal (Scotland) *En*
Commissaire (m) de la République *Fr*
Staatsanwalt (m) *De*

production (f) industrielle *Fr*
Arbeitsleistung (f) *De*
industrial performance *En*

production (f) industrielle *Fr*
Industrieproduktion (f) *De*
industrial production *En*

productivité (f) *Fr*
Produktivität (f) *De*
productivity *En*

productivity *En*
productivité (f) *Fr*
Produktivität (f) *De*

produit (m) national brut *Fr*
Bruttoinlandsprodukt (nt) *De*
gross domestic product *En*

Produktivgenossenschaft (f) *De*
worker co-operative *En*
coopérative (f) ouvrière de production (COOP) *Fr*

Produktivität (f) *De*
productivity *En*
productivité (f) *Fr*

professeur (m) *Fr*
Lehrer/-in (m/f) *De*
teacher (secondary) *En*

professional association *En*
association (f) professionnelle *Fr*
Berufsorganisation (f) *De*

professional conduct *En*
déontologie (f) *Fr*
berufliches Verhalten (nt) *De*

professional ethics *En*
déontologie (f) professionnelle *Fr*
Berufsethos (nt) *De*

professional indemnity *En*
assurance (f) professionnelle *Fr*
Berufsabsicherung (f) *De*

professional negligence *En*
négligence (f) professionnelle *Fr*
Vernachlässigung (f) der Berufspflichten *De*

professional qualification *En*
aptitude (f) professionnelle *Fr*
(fachliche) Qualifikation (f) *De*

profit *En*
profit (m) *Fr*
Gewinn (m), Profit (m) *De*

profit (m) *Fr*
Gewinn (m), Profit (m) *De*
profit *En*

profit making *En*
réalisation (f) de bénéfices *Fr*
Gewinnbringung (f), Rentabilität (f) *De*

profit sharing *En*
partage (m) des bénéfices *Fr*
Gewinnbeteiligung (f) *De*

profit-sharing *En*
participation (f) aux bénéfices *Fr*
Gewinnbeteiligung (f) *De*

profitability *En*
rentabilité (f) *Fr*
Rentabilität (f) *De*

progiciel (m) *Fr*
Softwarepaket (nt) *De*
software package *En*

Prognose (f), Voraussage (f) *De*
pronostication (f) *Fr*
forecasting *En*

program (noun) *En*
programme (m) *Fr*
Programm (nt) *De*

program (vb) *En*
programmer (vb) *Fr*
programmieren (vb) *De*

Programm (nt) *De*
program (noun) *En*
programme (m) *Fr*

Programmanalyse (f) *De*
programme analysis *En*
analyse (f) *Fr*

programmation (f) *Fr*
Programmplanung (f) *De*
programme planning *En*

programmation (f) collective *Fr*
Gemeinschaftsplanung (f) *De*
joint planning *En*

programmation (f) culturelle et des loisirs *Fr*
Planung (f) für Freizeitgestaltung *De*
recreation planning *En*

programmation (f) de l'emploi *Fr*
Arbeitsplanung (f) *De*
employment planning *En*

programmation (f) de l'environnement *Fr*
Umweltplanung (f) *De*
environmental planning *En*

programmation (f) de projet(s) *Fr*
Projektplanung (f) *De*
project planning *En*

programmation (f) de transport *Fr*
Transportplanung (f) *De*
transport planning *En*

programmation (f) des autoroutes *Fr*
Autobahnplanung (f) *De*
motorway planning *En*

programmation (f) des dépenses *Fr*
Kostenplanung (f) *De*
cost planning *En*

programmation (f) des ponts et chaussées *Fr*
Verkehrsplanung (f) *De*
highway planning *En*

programmation (f) des routes *Fr*
Straßenplanung (f) *De*
road planning *En*

programmation (f) des secours *Fr*
Notstandsplanung (f) *De*
emergency planning *En*

*** see/siehe/voir: Introduction page IX**

programmation (f) financière *Fr*
Finanzplanung (f) *De*
financial planning *En*

programmation (f) linéaire *Fr*
Linearplanung (f) *De*
linear programming *En*

programmation (f) régionale *Fr*
Regionalplanung (f) *De*
regional planning *En*

programmation (f) scolaire *Fr*
Schulbauprogramm (nt) *De*
school building programme *En*

programmatische Umsetzung (f) *De*
policy implementation *En*
exécution (f) des politiques *Fr*

Programmbewertung (f) *De*
programme evaluation *En*
évaluation (f) du programme *Fr*

Programmbudget (nt) *De*
programme budget *En*
budget (m) de programme *Fr*

programme (m) *Fr*
Programm (nt) *De*
program (noun) *En*

programme (m); à travers le — d'études *Fr*
quer durch das Pensum (nt) *De*
cross-curricular (adj) *En*

programme analysis *En*
analyse (f) *Fr*
Programmanalyse (f) *De*

programme budget *En*
budget (m) de programme *Fr*
Programmbudget (nt) *De*

programme evaluation *En*
évaluation (f) du programme *Fr*
Programmbewertung (f) *De*

programme (m) d'études *Fr*
Lehrplan (m) *De*
curriculum *En*

programme (m) d'études *Fr*
Lehrplan (m) *De*
school curriculum *En*

programme (m) d'études national *Fr* *
staatlicher Lehrplan (m) *De*
national curriculum *En*

programme (m) d'expansion commerciale *Fr*
Betriebsförderungsprogramm (nt) *De*
business expansion scheme *En*

programme (m) d'investissement *Fr*
Investitionsprogramm (nt) *De*
capital programme *En*

programme (m) (d'un cours) *Fr*
Lehrplan (m) *De*
syllabus *En*

programme (m) de création d'emploi *Fr*
Arbeitsbeschaffungsprogramm (nt) *De*
employment initiative *En*

programme (m) de création de l'emploi *Fr*
Arbeitsbeschaffungsmaßnahmen (f.pl) *De*
job creation programme *En*

programme (m) de développement économique *Fr*
Wirtschaftsplanung (f) *De*
economic planning *En*

programme (m) de formation *Fr*
Ausbildungsprogramm (nt) *De*
training scheme *En*

programme (m) de formation pour adultes *Fr*
Erwachsenenbildungsprogramm (nt) *De*
adult training strategy *En*

programme (m) de logement *Fr*
Wohnungsbauprogramm (nt) *De*
housing programme *En*

programme (m) de modernisation *Fr*
Erschließungsprogramm (nt) *De*
improvement scheme *En*

programme (m) de travail *Fr*
Arbeitslast (f) *De*
workload *En*

programme (m) machine *Fr*
(Computer)programm (nt) *De*
computer program *En*

programme (m) pour l'imprévu *Fr*
Alternativplan (m) *De*
contingency plan *En*

programme planning *En*
programmation (f) *Fr*
Programmplanung (f) *De*

programmer (vb) *Fr*
programmieren (vb) *De*
program (vb) *En*

programmeur (m) *Fr*
Programmierer (m) *De*
computer programmer *En*

programmieren (vb) *De*
program (vb) *En*
programmer (vb) *Fr*

Programmierer (m) *De*
computer programmer *En*
programmeur (m) *Fr*

Programmiersprache (f) *De*
computer programming language *En*
langage (m) machine *Fr*

Programmiersprache (f) *De*
programming language *En*
langage (m) de programmation *Fr*

programming language *En*
langage (m) de programmation *Fr*
Programmiersprache (f) *De*

Programmplanung (f) *De*
programme planning *En*
programmation (f) *Fr*

progress report *En*
rapport (m) périodique *Fr*
Tätigkeitsbericht (m) *De*

progressive collapse *En*
délabrement (m) progressif *Fr*
fortschreitender Zusammenbruch (m) *De*

prohibition order *En*
arrêté (m) d'interdiction *Fr*
Verbotsbestimmung (f) *De*

project appraisal/evaluation *En*
évaluation (f) du projet *Fr*
Unternehmensbewertung (f) *De*

project control *En*
contrôle (m) du projet *Fr*
Projektaufsicht (f) *De*

project co-ordination *En*
coordination (f) des projets *Fr*
Unternehmensbewertung (f) *De*

*** see/siehe/voir: Introduction page IX**

project management *En*
gestion (f) de projet *Fr*
Projektmanagement (nt) *De*

project manager *En*
directeur (m) de projet *Fr*
Projektleiter/-in (m/f) *De*

project planning *En*
programmation (f) de projet(s) *Fr*
Projektplanung (f) *De*

projection *En*
prévision (f) *Fr*
(Voraus)planung (f) *De*

Projektaufsicht (f) *De*
project control *En*
contrôle (m) du projet *Fr*

Projektleiter/-in (m/f) *De*
project manager *En*
directeur (m) de projet *Fr*

Projektmanagement (nt) *De*
contract management *En*
gestion (f) de contrat *Fr*

Projektmanagement (nt) *De*
project management *En*
gestion (f) de projet *Fr*

Projektplanung (f) *De*
project planning *En*
programmation (f) de projet(s) *Fr*

projet (m) *Fr*
Entwurf (m) *De*
draft (noun) *En*

projet (m) d'un rapport *Fr*
Entwurf (m) eines Berichts *De*
draft report *En*

projet (m) de recherche *Fr*
Forschungsprogramm (nt) *De*
research project *En*

projet (m) pour se procurer des fonds *Fr*
Spendenaktion (f) *De*
fund raising scheme *En*

prolongation (f) d'un crédit *Fr*
Verlängerung (f) einer Zahlungsfrist *De*
extension of credit *En*

promotion (staff) *En*
avancement (m) (personnel) *Fr*
Beförderung (f) *De*

promotion (commerce) *En*
promotion (f) (commerce) *Fr*
Werbung (f) *De*

promotion (f) (commerce) *Fr*
Werbung (f) *De*
promotion (commerce) *En*

promotion (f) de l'industrie *Fr*
Industrieförderung (f) *De*
industrial promotion *En*

prononcer (vb) une condamnation (contre quelqu'un) *Fr*
verurteilen (vb) *De*
sentence (vb) *En*

pronostication (f) économique *Fr*
Konjunkturvorhersage (f) *De*
economic forecasting *En*

pronostication (f) *Fr*
Voraussage (f), Prognose (f) *De*
forecasting *En*

propaganda *En*
propagande (f) *Fr*
Propaganda (f) *De*

Propaganda (f) *De*
propaganda *En*
propagande (f) *Fr*

propagande (f) *Fr*
Propaganda (f) *De*
propaganda *En*

property *En*
propriété (f) *Fr*
Besitz (m), Immobilie (f) *De*

property company/developer *En*
société (f) d'exploitation *Fr*
Immobiliengesellschaft (f), Bauunternehmer (m) *De*

property development *En*
opération (f) immobilière *Fr*
Grundstückserschließung (f) *De*

property investment *En*
investissements (m.pl) immobiliers *Fr*
Immobilieninvestition (f) *De*

property law *En*
code (m) de construction et d'urbanisme *Fr*
Eigentumsrecht (nt) *De*

property management *En*
gestion (f) immobilière *Fr*
Immobilienverwaltung (f) *De*

property market *En*
marché (m) immobilier *Fr*
Immobilienmarkt (m) *De*

property tax *En*
impôt (m) foncier *Fr*
Vermögenssteuer (f) *De*

property value *En*
valeur (f) immobilière *Fr*
Immobilienwert (m) *De*

proportional representation *En*
représentation (f) proportionnelle *Fr*
Verhältniswahlsystem (nt) *De*

proposal *En*
proposition (f) *Fr*
Vorschlag (m) *De*

proposition (f) *Fr*
Vorschlag (m) *De*
proposal *En*

proposition (f) praticable *Fr*
durchführbares Projekt (nt) *De*
viable proposition *En*

propriétaire (m) foncier *Fr*
Grundbesitzer (m) *De*
landowner *En*

propriétaire (m) *Fr*
Vermieter (m), Hausbesitzer (m) *De*
landlord *En*

propriétaire (m/f) *Fr*
Haus-, Wohnungseigentümer/-in (m/f) *De*
home owner *En*

propriétaire-occupant (m) *Fr*
Eigenheimbesitzer (m) *De*
owner occupier *En*

propriété (f) *Fr*
Besitz (m), Immobilie (f) *De*
property *En*

propriété (f) foncière perpétuelle et libre *Fr*
freier Grundbesitz (m) *De*
freehold *En*

propriété (f) louée *Fr*
Mietwohngrundstück (nt) *De*
rented property *En*

propriété (f) privée *Fr*
Privateigentum (nt) *De*
private property *En*

propriété (f) résidentielle *Fr*
Wohnhaus (nt) *De*
residential property *En*

proscription (f) *Fr*
Verbot (nt) *De*
ban (noun) *En*

prosecute (vb) *En*
poursuivre (vb) quelqu'un en justice repressive *Fr*
(strafrechtlich) verfolgen (vb) *De*

prosecution *En*
poursuites (f.pl) judiciaires *Fr*
(strafrechtliche) Verfolgung (f) *De*

prospectus *En*
prospectus (m) *Fr*
Prospekt (m) *De*

prospectus (m) *Fr*
Prospekt (m) *De*
prospectus *En*

Prospekt (m) *De*
prospectus *En*
prospectus (m) *Fr*

prosperité (f) *Fr*
Wohlstand (m) *De*
prosperity *En*

prosperity *En*
prosperité (f) *Fr*
Wohlstand (m) *De*

protected tenancy *En*
droits (m.pl) du locataire *Fr*
Mieterschutz (m) *De*

protection (f) civile *Fr*
Zivilschutz (m) *De*
civil defence *En*

protection (f) contre les inondations *Fr*
Hochwasserschutz (m) *De*
flood prevention/protection *En*

protection (f) de l'enfance *Fr*
Kinderfürsorge (f) *De*
child welfare *En*

protection (f) de l'environnement *Fr*
Umweltschutz (m)/-politik (f) *De*
environmental conservation/policy *En*

protection (f) des données *Fr*
Datenschutz (m) *De*
data protection *En*

protection (f) réglementaire (d'un arbre) *Fr*
Baumschutzanweisung (f) *De*
tree preservation order *En*

protective clothing *En*
vêtements (m.pl) protecteurs *Fr*
Schutz(be)kleidung (f) *De*

protocol *En*
protocole (m) *Fr*
Protokoll (nt) *De*

protocole (m) *Fr*
Protokoll (nt) *De*
protocol *En*

Protokoll (nt *De*
minutes (of meeting) *En*
procès-verbal (m) *Fr*

Protokoll (nt) *De*
protocol *En*
protocole (m) *Fr*

protokollieren (vb) *De*
minute (vb) *En*
dresser (vb) le procès-verbal *Fr*

provincial (adj) *En*
provincial (adj) *Fr*
Provinz- *De*

provincial (adj) *Fr*
Provinz- *De*
provincial (adj) *En*

Provinz- *De*
provincial (adj) *En*
provincial (adj) *Fr*

proviseur (m) (lycée) *Fr*
Rektor (m) *De*
principal (college) *En*

provision (f) *Fr*
Sonderrücklage (f) *De*
contingency reserve *En*

provision of services *En*
offre (f) de services *Fr*
Dienstleistungsversorgung (f) *De*

provisoirement (adv) *Fr*
provisorisch (adv) *De*
temporary basis (on a) (adv) *En*

provisorisch (adv) *De*
temporary basis (on a) (adv) *En*
provisoirement (adv) *Fr*

provisorische Maßnahmen (f.pl) *De*
temporary measures *En*
mesures (f.pl) provisoires *Fr*

provisorische Unterkunft (f) *De*
temporary accommodation *En*
logement (m) provisoire *Fr*

Prozeßkostenhilfe (f) *De*
legal aid *En*
aide (f) judiciaire *Fr*

prüfen (vb) *De*
audit (vb) *En*
vérifier et certifier (vb) *Fr*

Prüfung (f) *De*
examination *En*
examen (m) *Fr*

Prüfungsergebnis (nt) *De*
examination result *En*
résultat (m) d'examen *Fr*

psychiatric care *En*
soins (m.pl) psychiatriques *Fr*
psychiatrische Behandlung (f) *De*

psychiatric hospital *En*
hôpital (m) psychiatrique *Fr*
psychiatrische Klinik (f) *De*

psychiatric illness *En*
maladie (f) psychiatrique *Fr*
psychiatrische Krankheit (f) *De*

psychiatrische Behandlung (f) *De*
psychiatric care *En*
soins (m.pl) psychiatriques *Fr*

psychiatrische Klinik (f) *De*
mental hospital *En*
hôpital (m) psychiatrique *Fr*

psychiatrische Klinik (f) *De*
psychiatric hospital *En*
hôpital (m) psychiatrique *Fr*

psychiatrische Krankheit (f) *De*
psychiatric illness *En*
maladie (f) psychiatrique *Fr*

psychologie (f) scolaire *Fr*
Schulpsychologie (f) *De*
educational psychology *En*

public accountability *En*
responsabilité (f) personnelle *Fr*
öffentliche Verantwortlichkeit (f) *De*

public administration *En*
administration (f) publique *Fr*
öffentliche Verwaltung (f) *De*

public authorities *En*
pouvoirs (m.pl) publics *Fr*
(öffentliche) Ämter (nt.pl) *De*

public building *En*
bâtiment (m) public *Fr*
öffentliches Gebäude (nt) *De*

public confidence *En*
confiance (f) publique *Fr*
Vertrauen (nt) der Öffentlichkeit *De*

public enterprise *En*
entreprise (f) publique *Fr*
öffentliches Unternehmen (nt) *De*

*** see/siehe/voir: Introduction page IX**

public expenditure cuts *En*
réductions (f.pl) des dépenses publiques *Fr*
öffentliche Einsparungen (f.pl) *De*

public expenditure *En*
dépenses (f.pl) publiques *Fr*
öffentliche Ausgaben (f.pl) *De*

public finance *En*
finances (f.pl) publiques *Fr*
öffentliche Finanzen (pl) *De*

public funds *En*
deniers (m.pl) publics *Fr*
öffentliche Mittel (nt.pl) *De*

public good *En*
bien (m) public *Fr*
das öffentliche Wohl (nt) *De*

public health officer *En*
inspecteur (m) (-trice f.) de salubrité *Fr*
Beamte(-r)/-in (m/f) der Gesundheitsbehörde *De*

public holiday *En*
fête (f) légale *Fr*
gesetzlicher Feiertag (m) *De*

public inquiry *En*
enquête (f) de commodo et incommodo *Fr*
öffentliche Untersuchung (f) *De*

public interest *En*
intérêt (m) public *Fr*
öffentliches Interesse (nt) *De*

public investment *En*
investissement (m) public *Fr*
öffentliche Geldanlage (f) *De*

public library *En*
bibliothèque (f) municipale *Fr*
öffentliche Bücherei (f) *De*

public limited company (plc) *En*
Société (f) anonyme (SA) *Fr*
Aktiengesellschaft (AG) (f) *De*

public meeting *En*
séance (f) publique *Fr*
öffentliche Sitzung (f) *De*

public open space *En*
espace (m) public *Fr*
öffentliche Anlagen (f.pl) *De*

public order *En*
ordre (m) public *Fr*
öffentliche Ordnung (f) *De*

public procurement *En*
acquisition (f) (par la personne) publique *Fr*
öffentliche Beschaffung (f) *De*

public relations officer *En*
responsable (m) des relations publiques *Fr*
Öffentlichkeitsreferent/-in (m/f) *De*

public school *En*
collège (m) privé *Fr*
Privatschule (f) *De*

public sector borrowing *En*
emprunts (m.pl) du secteur public *Fr*
Kreditaufnahme (f) der öffentlichen Hand *De*

public sector borrowing requirement *En*
demande (f) d'emprunts du secteur public *Fr*
Kreditbedarf (m) der öffentlichen Hand *De*

public sector *En*
secteur (m) public *Fr*
öffentlicher Sektor (m) *De*

public sector housing *En*
logement (m) public *Fr*
Sozialwohnungen (f.pl) *De*

public servant *En*
employé (m) d'un service public *Fr*
Inhaber/-in (m/f) eines öffentlichen Amtes *De*

public spirit *En*
amour (m) du bien public *Fr*
Gemeinsinn (m) *De*

public spirited (adj) *En*
dévoué (adj) au bien public *Fr*
von Gemeinsinn zeugend (adj) *De*

public transport *En*
transports (m.pl) en commun *Fr*
öffentliche Verkehrsmittel (nt.pl) *De*

public utilities *En*
services (m.pl) publics *Fr*
öffentliche Versorgungsbetriebe (m.pl) *De*

publication (f) assistée par ordinateur (PAO) *Fr*
Desktop Publishing (nt) *De*
desk top publishing *En*

publicité (f) *Fr*
Publicity (f) *De*
publicity *En*

publicité (f) *Fr*
Werbung (f) *De*
advertising *En*

publicity *En*
publicité (f) *Fr*
Publicity (f) *De*

Publicity (f) *De*
publicity *En*
publicité (f) *Fr*

puce (f) informatique *Fr*
Siliziumchip (m) *De*
silicon chip *En*

pump-priming *En*
aide (f) initiale financiaire *Fr*
Anstoßfinanzierung (f) *De*

Punkt (m) auf der Tagesordnung *De*
agenda item *En*
question (f) à l'ordre du jour *Fr*

pupille (m/f) sous tutelle judiciaire *Fr*
Mündel (m) (unter Amtsvormundschaft) *De*
ward of court *En*

purpose-built (adj) *En*
construit en vue d'un usage déterminé (adj) *Fr*
speziell gebaut; Zweck- *De*

put out (vb) to contract *En*
mettre (vb) en adjudication *Fr*
etwas außer Haus machen lassen (vb) *De*

Putzen (nt); Reinigung (f) *De*
cleaning *En*
nettoyage (m) *Fr*

*** see/siehe/voir: Introduction page IX**

Q

quai (m) *Fr*
Kai (m) *De*
quay/wharf *En*

qualification (diploma etc) *En*
qualification (f) (diplôme etc) *Fr*
Qualifikation (f) (Diplom usw) *De*

qualification (f) (diplôme etc) *Fr*
Qualifikation (f) (Diplom usw) *De*
qualification (diploma etc) *En*

qualification (f) nationale professionnelle (en GB) *Fr* *
staatliche Berufsausbildung (f) (in GB) *De*
National Vocational Qualification (GB) *En*

Qualifikation (f) (Diplom usw) *De*
qualification (diploma etc) *En*
qualification (f) (diplôme etc) *Fr*

Qualitätsgarantie (f), -kontrolle (f) *De*
quality assurance/control *En*
contrôle (m) de qualité *Fr*

qualité (f) de l'air *Fr*
Luftqualität (f) *De*
air quality *En*

qualité; de — inférieure (adj) *Fr*
unzulänglich (adj) *De*
sub-standard (adj) *En*

qualités (f.pl) de chef *Fr*
Führung (f) *De*
leadership *En*

quality assurance/control *En*
contrôle (m) de qualité *Fr*
Qualitätsgarantie (f), -kontrolle (f) *De*

quantity surveying *En*
métrage (m) *Fr*
Baukostenkalkulation (f) *De*

quantity surveyor *En*
métreur (m) vérificateur *Fr*
Baukostenkalkulator/-in (m/f) *De*

quartier (m) residentiel *Fr*
Wohngebiet (nt), -gegend (f) *De*
residential area *En*

quartiers (m.pl) des docks (m.pl) *Fr*
Hafenviertel (nt) *De*
docklands *En*

quay/wharf *En*
quai (m) *Fr*
Kai (m) *De*

Quellenmaterial (nt) *De*
source document *En*
document (m) de base *Fr*

quer durch das Pensum (nt) *De*
cross-curricular *En*
à travers le programme d'études *Fr*

question (f) à l'ordre du jour *Fr*
Punkt (m) auf der Tagesordnung *De*
agenda item *En*

question (f) de confiance *Fr*
Vertrauenssache (f) *De*
matter of trust *En*

question (f) de jugement *Fr*
Urteilssache (f) *De*
matter of judgment *En*

question (f) de procédure *Fr*
verfahrensmäßige Angelegenheit (f) *De*
procedural matter *En*

question (f) délicate *Fr*
heikles Thema (nt) *De*
sensitive issue *En*

question (f) vitale *Fr*
Schlüsselfrage (f) *De*
key issue *En*

questionnaire *En*
questionnaire (m) *Fr*
Fragebogen (m) *De*

questionnaire (m) *Fr*
Fragebogen (m) *De*
questionnaire *En*

questions (f.pl) controversables *Fr*
strittige Fragen (f.pl) *De*
controversial issues *En*

questions (f.pl) écologiques *Fr*
grüne Fragen (f.pl) *De*
green issues *En*

qui a l'esprit d'entreprise *Fr*
unternehmerisch (adj) *De*
entrepreneurial (adj) *En*

qui ne nuit pas à l'environnement *Fr*
umweltfreundlich (adj) *De*
environmentally friendly *En*

qui peut nuire à la santé *Fr*
Gesundheitsgefährdung (f) *De*
health hazard *En*

quittance (f) d'eau *Fr*
Wasserrechnung (f) *De*
water bill *En*

quittance (f) de loyer *Fr*
Mietquittung (f) *De*
rent book *En*

Quittung (f) *De*
receipt *En*
reçu (m) *Fr*

quorum *En*
quorum (m) *Fr*
beschlußfähige Anzahl (f) *De*

quorum (m) *Fr*
beschlußfähige Anzahl (f) *De*
quorum *En*

quotation *En*
prix (m) *Fr*
Kostenvoranschlag (m) *De*

*** see/siehe/voir: Introduction page IX**

R

rabais (m) *Fr*
Rückzahlung (f) *De*
rebate *En*

raccourci (m) *Fr*
Schleichweg (m) *De*
rat run *En*

race equality *En*
égalité (f) raciale *Fr*
Rassengleichheit (f) *De*

race (f) minoritaire *Fr*
rassische Minderheit (f) *De*
racial minority *En*

race relations *En*
rapports (m.pl) entre les races différentes *Fr*
Beziehungen (f.pl) zwischen den Rassen *De*

racial discrimination *En*
discrimination (f) raciale *Fr*
Rassendiskriminierung (f) *De*

racial inequality *En*
inégalité (f) raciale *Fr*
Ungleichheit (f) zwischen den Rassen *De*

racial integration *En*
intégration (f) des races *Fr*
Rassenintegration (f) *De*

racial minority *En*
race (f) minoritaire *Fr*
rassische Minderheit (f) *De*

racial prejudice/racism *En*
racisme (m) *Fr*
Rassenvorurteil (nt), Rassismus (m) *De*

racisme (m) *Fr*
Rassenvorurteil (nt), Rassismus (m) *De*
racial prejudice/racism *En*

Radfahrer/-in (m/f) *De*
cyclist *En*
cycliste (m/f) *Fr*

radical (adj) *En*
radical (adj) *Fr*
radikal (adj) *De*

radical (adj) *Fr*
radikal (adj) *De*
radical (adj) *En*

radikal (adj) *De*
radical (adj) *En*
radical (adj) *Fr*

radiodiffusion (f) locale *Fr*
Lokalsendung (f) *De*
local broadcasting *En*

Radweg (m), Fahrradspur (f) *De*
cycle lane/path *En*
piste (f) cyclable *Fr*

rail depot *En*
gare (f) des marchandises *Fr*
Güterbahnhof (m) *De*

rail freight *En*
transport (m) de marchandises par chemin de fer *Fr*
Gütertransport (m) *De*

rail network *En*
réseau (m) ferroviaire *Fr*
Eisenbahnnetz (nt) *De*

rail terminus *En*
terminus (m) *Fr*
Endstation (f) *De*

rail transport *En*
transport (m) par chemin de fer *Fr*
Eisenbahnbeförderung (f) *De*

railway *En*
chemin (m) de fer *Fr*
Eisenbahn (f) *De*

ralentisseur (m); "gendarme (m) couché" *Fr*
Bodenschwelle (f) *De*
sleeping policeman *En*

ramassage (m) des ordures *Fr*
Müllabfuhr (f) *De*
refuse collection *En*

ramassage (m) des ordures *Fr*
Müllabfuhr (f) *De*
waste collection *En*

Ramme (f) *De*
pile driver *En*
sonnette (f) *Fr*

rammen (vb) *De*
pile drive (vb) *En*
enfoncer (vb) des pieux dans le sol *Fr*

random sampling *En*
échantillonnage (m) au hasard *Fr*
Stichprobe (f) *De*

Randstreifen (m) *De*
hard shoulder *En*
accotement (m) *Fr*

Rang (m) (Regierung usw) *De*
tier (of government etc) *En*
niveau (m) (de gouvernement etc) *Fr*

rangée (f) de maisons de style uniforme *Fr*
Reihenhäuser (nt.pl) *De*
terraced houses *En*

rapport (m) annuel (de gestion) *Fr*
Jahresbericht (m) *De*
annual report *En*

rapport (m) au comité *Fr*
Ausschußbericht (m) *De*
committee report *En*

rapport (m) des vérificateurs des comptes *Fr*
Bericht (m) des Abschlußprüfers *De*
auditor's report *En*

*** see/siehe/voir: Introduction page IX**

rapport (m) juridique *Fr*
Urteils- und Entscheidungssammlung (f) *De*
law report *En*

rapport (m) périodique *Fr*
Lagebericht (m) *De*
update (noun) *En*

rapport (m) périodique *Fr*
Tätigkeitsbericht (m) *De*
progress report *En*

rapport (m) qualité-prix *Fr*
Rentabilität (f) *De*
cost effectiveness *En*

rapports (m.pl) du travail *Fr*
Beziehungen zwischen Arbeitgebern und -nehmern *De*
labour relations *En*

rapports (m.pl) école-famille *Fr*
Eltern-Lehrerbeziehungen (f.pl) *De*
home-school relations *En*

rapports (m.pl) entre les races différentes *Fr*
Beziehungen (f.pl) zwischen den Rassen *De*
race relations *En*

rassemblement (m) de données *Fr*
Datenerfassung (f) *De*
data collection *En*

Rassendiskriminierung (f) *De*
racial discrimination *En*
discrimination (f) raciale *Fr*

Rassengleichheit (f) *De*
race equality *En*
égalité (f) raciale *Fr*

Rassenintegration (f) *De*
racial integration *En*
intégration (f) des races *Fr*

Rassenvorurteil (nt), Rassismus (m) *De*
racial prejudice/racism *En*
racisme (m) *Fr*

rassische Minderheit (f) *De*
racial minority *En*
race (f) minoritaire *Fr*

Rassismus (m); Rassenvorurteil (nt) *De*
racial prejudice/racism *En*
racisme (m) *Fr*

Rat (m), in dem keine Partei die absolute Mehrheit hat *De*
hung council *En*
conseil (m) où aucun parti n'a la majorité absolue *Fr*

Rat (m) mit Kräftegleichgewicht *De*
balanced council *En*
conseil (m) où aucun parti n'a la majorité absolue *Fr*

rat run *En*
raccourci (m) *Fr*
Schleichweg (m) *De*

rate arrears *En*
arriéré (m) d'impôts locaux *Fr*
Kommunalsteuerschulden (f.pl) *De*

rate bill/demand *En*
avis (m) d'imposition *Fr*
Kommunalsteuerbescheid (m) *De*

rate capping *En* *
limitation (f) des impôts locaux (en GB) par l'Etat *Fr*
Kürzung (f) der Kommunalabgaben durch die Zentralregierung *De*

rate collection *En*
perception (f) des impôts locaux *Fr*
Kommunalsteuereinziehung (f) *De*

rate of interest *En*
taux (m) d'intérêt *Fr*
Zinssatz (m) *De*

rate of return *En*
taux (m) de rendement *Fr*
Gewinnsatz (m) *De*

rate precept *En*
avis (m) d'imposition *Fr*
Prinzip (nt) der Gemeindeabgaben *De*

rate rebate *En*
décharge (f) d'impôt *Fr*
Ermäßigung (f) der Gemeindeabgaben *De*

rate relief *En*
allégement (m) des impôts *Fr*
Ermäßigung (f) der Gemeindeabgaben *De*

rate support grant (GB) *En* *
subvention (f) des impôts locaux (en GB) par l'Etat *Fr*
Kommunalsteuersubvention (f) (in GB) *De*

rateable value *En*
valeur (f) locative imposable *Fr*
steuerbarer Wert (m) *De*

Ratenkauf (m) *De*
hire purchase *En*
achat (m) à crédit *Fr*

ratepayer *En*
contribuable (m/f) à l'impôt local *Fr*
Kommunalsteuerzahler/-in (m/f) *De*

rates *En*
impôt (m) local *Fr*
Kommunalsteuern (f.pl), Gemeindeabgaben (f.pl) *De*

Rathaus (nt) *De*
City Hall *En*
hôtel (m) de ville *Fr*

Rathaus (nt) *De*
town hall *En*
hôtel (m) de ville; mairie (f) *Fr*

ratifizieren (vb) *De*
ratify (vb) *En*
entériner (vb) (loi,décret) *Fr*

ratify (vb) *En*
entériner (vb) (loi,décret) *Fr*
ratifizieren (vb) *De*

rating system *En*
fiscalité (f) locale *Fr*
Kommunalsteuerwesen (nt) *De*

Ratssitzung (f) *De*
council meeting *En*
réunion (f) du conseil *Fr*

Rattenfänger (m) *De*
rodent officer *En*
fonctionnaire (m) chargé de la dératisation *Fr*

Raub (m) *De*
robbery *En*
vol (m) *Fr*

Raumpfleger/-in (m/f) *De*
cleaner *En*
nettoyeur (m)/ nettoyeuse (f) *Fr*

raw material *En*
matières (f.pl) premières *Fr*
Rohstoff (m) *De*

rayonnement (m) nucléaire *Fr*
Kernstrahlung (f) *De*
nuclear radiation *En*

reçu (m) *Fr*
Quittung (f) *De*
receipt *En*

*** see/siehe/voir: Introduction page IX**

réacteur (m) nucléaire *Fr*
Kernreaktor (m) *De*
nuclear reactor *En*

réacteur (m) refroidi au gaz *Fr*
gasgekühlter Kernreaktor (m) *De*
gas cooled reactor *En*

ready-mixed concrete *En*
béton (m) malaxé *Fr*
Fertigbeton (m) *De*

réalisation (f) de bénéfices *Fr*
Gewinnbringung (f), Rentabilität (f) *De*
profit making *En*

réalisation (f) possible *Fr*
haltbare Entwicklung (f) *De*
sustainable development *En*

rebate *En*
rabais (m) *Fr*
Rückzahlung (f) *De*

rebuilding *En*
reconstruction (f) *Fr*
Umbau (m) *De*

receipt *En*
reçu (m) *Fr*
Quittung (f) *De*

receipts account *En*
compte (m) de provisions *Fr*
Einnahmebuch (nt) *De*

receipts *En*
recettes (f.pl) *Fr*
Einnahmen (f.pl) *De*

receiver *En*
syndic (m) de faillite *Fr*
Konkursverwalter/-in (m/f) *De*

recensement (m) de la circulation *Fr*
Verkehrszählung (f) *De*
traffic census/count *En*

recensement (m) de la population *Fr*
Volkszählung (f) *De*
census of population *En*

recensement (m) *Fr*
Volkszählung (f), Zensus (m) *De*
census *En*

reception area *En*
accueil (m) *Fr*
Rezeption (f) *De*

reception centre *En*
centre (m) d'accueil *Fr*
Durchgangslager (nt) *De*

receptionist *En*
réceptionniste (m/f) *Fr*
Empfangschef (m) -dame (f) *De*

réceptionniste (m/f) *Fr*
Empfangschef (m) -dame (f) *De*
receptionist *En*

recession *En*
récession (f) *Fr*
Rezession (f), Konjunkturrückgang (m) *De*

récession (f) économique *Fr*
Konjunkturrückgang (m) *De*
economic recession *En*

récession (f) *Fr*
Rezession (f), Konjunkturrückgang (m) *De*
recession *En*

recettes (f.pl) *Fr*
Einnahmen (f.pl) *De*
receipts *En*

Rechenmaschine (f) *De*
calculator *En*
machine (f) à calculer *Fr*

recherche (f) appliquée *Fr*
Handlungsforschung (f) *De*
action research *En*

recherche (f) d'informations *Fr*
Datenabruf (m) *De*
data retrieval *En*

recherche (f) d'informations *Fr*
Informationswiedergewinnung (f) *De*
information retrieval *En*

recherche (f) de l'information par questionnaire *Fr*
postalische Umfrage (f) *De*
postal survey *En*

recherche (f) industrielle *Fr*
industrielle Forschung (f) *De*
research and development *En*

recherche (f) opérationnelle *Fr*
Unternehmensforschung (f) *De*
operational research *En*

recherche (f) pédagogique *Fr*
pädagogische Forschung (f) *De*
educational research *En*

recherches (f.pl) sur le terrain *Fr*
Feldforschung (f) *De*
fieldwork *En*

Rechnung (f) *De*
invoice *En*
facture (f) *Fr*

Rechnungsjahr (nt) *De*
financial year *En*
annuité (f) *Fr*

Rechnungsjahr (nt) *De*
fiscal year *En*
année (f) budgétaire *Fr*

Rechnungsprüfer (m) *De*
district auditor *En*
conseiller (m) à la chambre régionale des comptes *Fr*

Rechnungsprüfer/-in (m/f) *De*
auditor *En*
commissaire (m) de comptes *Fr*

Rechnungsprüfung (f) *De*
audit *En*
vérification (f) de comptes *Fr*

Rechte (f) *De*
right wing *En*
droite (f) *Fr*

Rechte (nt.pl) *De*
legal rights *En*
droits (m.pl) civils *Fr*

rechte(-r,-s) (adj) *De*
right wing (adj) *En*
de droite (adj) *Fr*

(rechtliche) Vereinbarung (f) *De*
agreement (legal) *En*
convention (f) *Fr*

rechtmäßig (adj) *De*
lawful (adj) *En*
légal (adj) *Fr*

Rechtsanwalt/-anwältin (m/f) *De*
barrister *En*
avocat (m) *Fr*

Rechtsanwalt/-anwältin (m/f) *De*
lawyer *En*
notaire (m) *Fr*

Rechtsanwalt/-anwältin (m/f) *De*
solicitor *En*
notaire (m) *Fr*

*** see/siehe/voir: Introduction page IX**

Rechtsberater/-in (m/f) *De*
law officer *En*
conseiller (m) (-ère f.) juridique *Fr*

Rechtsberatung (f) *De*
legal service *En*
service (m) du cotentieux *Fr*

Rechtsgutachten (nt) *De*
legal opinion *En*
pensée (f) légale *Fr*

Rechtsreform (f) *De*
law reform *En*
réforme (f) juridique *Fr*

Rechtsstreit (m) *De*
litigation *En*
litige (m) *Fr*

réclamant (m) *Fr*
Antragssteller/-in (m/f) *De*
claimant *En*

reclamation *En*
mise (f) en valeur *Fr*
Wiedergewinnung (f) *De*

réclamer (vb) *Fr*
beantragen (vb) *De*
claim (vb) *En*

recommendation *En*
recommendation (f) *Fr*
Empfehlung (f) *De*

recommendation (f) *Fr*
Empfehlung (f) *De*
recommendation *En*

recommended course of action *En*
démarches (f.pl) recommandées *Fr*
empfohlene Vorgehensweise (f) *De*

reconnaissance (f) du terrain *Fr*
Bauinspektion (f) *De*
site inspection *En*

reconstruction (f) *Fr*
Umbau (m) *De*
rebuilding *En*

reconversion (f) *Fr*
Umverlegung (f) *De*
redeployment *En*

record keeping *En*
archivage (m) *Fr*
Aufzeichnung (f) *De*

record of achievement *En*
livret (m) scolaire *Fr*
Register der Leistungen (f.pl) *De*

records management *En*
gestion (f) des archives *Fr*
Aufzeichnung (f) *De*

recours (m) contre un acte d'urbanisme *Fr*
Bauplanungseinspruch (m) *De*
planning appeal *En*

recreation area *En*
cour (f) de récréation *Fr*
Freizeitgelände (nt) *De*

recreation centre *En*
centre (m) de loisirs *Fr*
Freizeitzentrum (nt) *De*

recreation facilities *En*
équipements (m.pl) de loisirs *Fr*
Möglichkeiten (f.pl) zur Freizeitgestaltung *De*

recreation management *En*
service (m) de la culture et des loisirs *Fr*
Management (nt) für Freizeitgestaltung *De*

recreation planning *En*
programmation (f) culturelle et des loisirs *Fr*
Planung (f) für Freizeitgestaltung *De*

recruit (vb) *En*
recruter (vb) *Fr*
neu einstellen (vb) *De*

recruitment *En*
recrutement (m) *Fr*
Neueinstellung (f) *De*

recrutement (m) du personnel *Fr*
(Personal)einstellung (f); Personalwahl (f) *De*
staff recruitment/selection *En*

recrutement (m) *Fr*
Neueinstellung (f) *De*
recruitment *En*

recruter (vb) *Fr*
neu einstellen (vb) *De*
recruit (vb) *En*

récuperation (f) des déchets *Fr*
Abfallrückgewinnung (f) *De*
waste recovery *En*

recyclage (m) des déchets *Fr*
(Abfall)wiederaufbereitung (f); Recycling (nt) *De*
waste recycling *En*

recyclage (m) *Fr*
Recycling (nt) *De*
recycling *En*

recyclage (m) *Fr*
Umschulung (f) *De*
retraining *En*

recyclage (m) *Fr*
Wiederaufbereitung (f) *De*
reprocessing *En*

recycle (vb) *En*
recycler (vb) *Fr*
wiederverwerten (vb) *De*

recycler (vb) *Fr*
wiederverwerten (vb) *De*
recycle (vb) *En*

recycler (vb) (personnel) *Fr*
umschulen (vb) *De*
retrain (vb) (staff) *En*

recycling *En*
recyclage (m) *Fr*
Recycling (nt) *De*

Recycling (nt) *De*
recycling *En*
recyclage (m) *Fr*

rédacteur (m) *Fr*
Beamte(-r)/-in (m/f) *De*
executive officer (public sector) *En*

rédaction (f) *Fr*
Entwurf (m) *De*
drafting *En*

rédaction (f) de rapports *Fr*
Berichterstattung (f) *De*
report writing *En*

rédaction (f) des actes translatifs de propriété *Fr*
(Eigentums)übertragung (f) *De*
conveyancing *En*

(eine) Rede halten (vb) *De*
speech (to make a) (vb) *En*
discours (m) (faire/prononcer un —) *Fr*

Redefreiheit (f) *De*
free speech *En*
libre parole (f) *Fr*

redéploiement (m) du personnel *Fr*
Versetzung (f) *De*
relocation (staff) *En*

redeployment *En*
reconversion (f) *Fr*
Umverlegung (f) *De*

redesign (vb) *En*
redessiner (vb) *Fr*
umgestalten (vb) *De*

redessiner (vb) *Fr*
umgestalten (vb) *De*
redesign (vb) *En*

redevance (f) de l'eau *Fr*
Wassergebühren (f.pl) *De*
water charge *En*

redevelop (vb) *En*
mettre (vb) en valeur *Fr*
sanieren (vb) *De*

redevelopment area *En*
zone (f) de réhabilitation *Fr*
Sanierungsgebiet (nt) *De*

rédiger (vb) *Fr*
entwerfen (vb) *De*
draft (vb) *En*

réduction (f) *Fr*
Kürzung (f) *De*
cutback *En*

réduction de la dépense *Fr*
Ausgabenkürzung (f) *De*
expenditure cut *En*

réduction (f) d'impôt *Fr*
Steuersenkung (f) *De*
tax cut *En*

réduction (f) de loyer *Fr*
Mietermäßigung (f) *De*
rent rebate *En*

réduction (f) des coûts *Fr*
Kostenverringerung (f) *De*
cost cutting *En*

réduction (f) des dépenses *Fr*
Einschränkung (f) der Ausgaben *De*
restriction of expenditure *En*

réduction (f) du bruit *Fr*
Lärmbekämpfung (f) *De*
noise abatement *En*

réductions (f.pl) des dépenses publiques *Fr*
öffentliche Einsparungen (f.pl) *De*
public expenditure cuts *En*

redundancy *En*
licenciement (m) *Fr*
Beschäftigungslosigkeit (f) *De*

redundancy payment *En*
indemnité (f) de licenciement *Fr*
Abfindung (f) *De*

redundant building *En*
bâtiment (m) en surnombre *Fr*
unbenutztes Gebäude (nt) *De*

redundant staff *En*
personnel (m) en surnombre *Fr*
entlassenes/überzähliges Personal (nt) *De*

refaire (vb) le revêtement d'une route *Fr*
(den Belag einer Straße) erneuern (vb) *De*
resurface (vb) a road *En*

référence (f) de banquier *Fr*
Bankzeugnis (nt) *De*
banker's reference *En*

reference library *En*
bibliothèque (f) d'ouvrages de référence *Fr*
Präsenzbibliothek (f) *De*

Referendar/-in (m/f) *De*
probationary teacher *En*
enseignant (m) stagiaire (en première année d'enseignement) *Fr*

referendum *En*
référendum (m) *Fr*
Volksabstimmung (f), Referendum (nt) *De*

référendum (m) *Fr*
Volksabstimmung (f), Referendum (nt) *De*
referendum *En*

reform (vb) local government *En*
apporter (vb) des réformes au gouvernement local *Fr*
Kommunalverwaltungsreformen durchsetzen (vb) *De*

réforme (f) constitutionnelle *Fr*
Verfassungsreform (f) *De*
constitutional reform *En*

réforme (f) du gouvernement local *Fr*
Gemeindereform (f) *De*
local government reform *En*

réforme (f) électorale *Fr*
Wahlreform (f) *De*
electoral reform *En*

réforme (f) fiscale *Fr*
Steuerreform (f) *De*
tax reform *En*

réforme (f) juridique *Fr*
Rechtsreform (f) *De*
law reform *En*

réforme (f) pédagogique *Fr*
Schulreform (f) *De*
educational reform *En*

refuge (m) (pour piétons) *Fr*
Verkehrsinsel (f) *De*
traffic island *En*

refugee *En*
réfugié (m) (-ée f.) *Fr*
Flüchtling (m) *De*

réfugié (m) (-ée f.) *Fr*
Flüchtling (m) *De*
refugee *En*

refurbish (vb) *En*
remettre (vb) à neuf *Fr*
renovieren (vb) *De*

refus (m) *Fr*
Ablehnung (f); Verweigerung (f) *De*
refusal *En*

refusal *En*
refus (m) *Fr*
Ablehnung (f); Verweigerung (f) *De*

refuse (noun) *En*
déchets (m.pl) *Fr*
Müll (m) *De*

refuse bin *En*
boîte (f) à ordures *Fr*
Mülltonne (f) *De*

refuse collection *En*
ramassage (m) des ordures *Fr*
Müllabfuhr (f) *De*

refuse disposal *En*
décharge (f) des ordures *Fr*
Abfallbeseitigung (f) *De*

refuse tip *En*
décharge (f) publique *Fr*
Müllabladeplatz (m) *De*

refuse transfer station *En*
usine (f) d'incinération *Fr*
Müllhalde (f) *De*

Regelung (f); Vorschrift (f) *De*
regulation *En*
règlement (m) *Fr*

Regelveranlagung (f) (in GB) *De* *
Standard Spending Assessment (SSA) *En*
système (m) de limitation de dépenses (en GB) *Fr*

regeneration *En*
régéneration (f) *Fr*
Erneuerung (f) *De*

régéneration (f) *Fr*
Erneuerung (f) *De*
regeneration *En*

Regiebetrieb (m) *De*
direct labour organization *En*
service (m) exploité en régie directe *Fr*

Regierung (f) *De*
government *En*
gouvernement (m) *Fr*

Regierungsamt (nt) *De*
government agency *En*
service (m) gouvernemental *Fr*

Regierungsauftrag (m) *De*
government contract *En*
contrat (m) gouvernemental *Fr*

Regierungspolitik (f) *De*
government policy *En*
politique (f) gouvernementale *Fr*

Regierungsstelle (f), -behörde (f) *De*
government department *En*
ministère (m) *Fr*

region *En*
région (f) *Fr*
Gebiet (nt), Region (f) *De*

région (f) *Fr*
Gebiet (nt), Region (f) *De*
region *En*

région (f) carbonifère *Fr*
Kohlenrevier (nt) *De*
coalfield *En*

région (f) d'importance écologique *Fr*
umweltbewußtes Gebiet (nt) *De*
environmentally sensitive area *En*

région (f) naturelle remarquable *Fr*
Landschaftsschutzgebiet (nt) *De*
Area Of Outstanding Natural Beauty *En*

région (f) rurale *Fr*
ländliches Gebiet (nt), Landgebiet (nt) *De*
rural area/district *En*

région (f) touchée par la crise *Fr*
unter Depression leidendes Gebiet (nt) *De*
depressed area *En*

région (f) touristique *Fr*
Touristengebiet (nt) *De*
tourism area *En*

regional (adj) *De*
regional (adj) *En*
régional (adj) *Fr*

regional (adj) *En*
régional (adj) *Fr*
regional (adj) *De*

régional (adj) *Fr*
regional (adj) *De*
regional (adj) *En*

regional aid *En*
aides (f.pl) régionales *Fr*
Gebietshilfe (f) *De*

regional assembly/council *En*
conseil (m) régional *Fr*
Regionalausschuß (m), Gemeinderat (m) *De*

regional authority *En*
service (m) administratif régional *Fr*
Gemeindeamt (nt) *De*

regional development *En*
aménagement (m) régional *Fr*
Regionalplanung (f) *De*

regional government *En*
gouvernement (m) régional *Fr*
Regionalregierung (f) *De*

regional health authority *En*
service (m) régional de la santé *Fr*
regionale Gesundheitsbehörde (f) *De*

regional plan *En*
plan (m) de développement régional *Fr*
Kommunalprogramm (nt) *De*

regional planning *En*
programmation (f) régionale *Fr*
Regionalplanung (f) *De*

regional policy *En*
politique (f) régionale *Fr*
Regionalpolitik (f) *De*

regional strategy *En*
stratégie (f) régionale *Fr*
Regionalstrategie (f) *De*

regional transport authority *En*
syndicat (m) régional des transports en commun *Fr*
regionales Amt (nt) für Verkehr *De*

Regionalausschuß (m) *De*
Committee of the Regions *En*
Comité (m) des Régions *Fr*

Regionalausschuß (m), Gemeinderat (m) *De*
regional assembly/council *En*
conseil (m) régional *Fr*

regionale Einkommensteuer (f) *De*
local income tax *En*
impôt (m) local sur le revenu *Fr*

regionale Gesundheitsbehörde (f) *De*
regional health authority *En*
service (m) régional de la santé *Fr*

regionales Amt (nt) für Verkehr *De*
regional transport authority *En*
syndicat (m) régional des transports en commun *Fr*

Regionalgruppe (f) *De*
area team *En*
équipe (f) régionale *Fr*

Regionalplanung (f) *De*
regional development *En*
aménagement (m) régional *Fr*

Regionalplanung (f) *De*
regional planning *En*
programmation (f) régionale *Fr*

Regionalpolitik (f) *De*
regional policy *En*
politique (f) régionale *Fr*

Regionalregierung (f) *De*
regional government *En*
gouvernement (m) régional *Fr*

Regionalstrategie (f) *De*
regional strategy *En*
stratégie (f) régionale *Fr*

Register der Leistungen (f.pl) *De*
record of achievement *En*
livret (m) scolaire *Fr*

*** see/siehe/voir: Introduction page IX**

register (vb) (a birth etc) *En*
déclarer (vb) (une naissance etc) *Fr*
eine Geburt eintragen lassen (vb) *De*

registered letter *En*
lettre (f) recommendée *Fr*
Einschreibebrief (m) *De*

registration number (vehicle) *En*
numéro (m) d'immatriculation *Fr*
amtliches Kennzeichen (nt) *De*

registre (m) du cadastre *Fr*
Grundbuch (nt) *De*
land register *En*

registry office *En*
état (m) civil *Fr*
Standesamt (nt) *De*

règlement (m) *Fr*
Regelung (f); Vorschrift (f) *De*
regulation *En*

règlement (m) de la dette *Fr*
Fremdfinanzierung (f) *De*
debt financing *En*

règlement (m) de loyer *Fr*
Mietregulierung (f) *De*
rent regulation *En*

règlement (m) du commerce *Fr*
Gewerbeordnung (f) *De*
trading standards *En*

règlement (m) statutaire *Fr*
gesetzliche Urkunde (f) *De*
statutory instrument *En*

règlements (m.pl) d'urbanisme *Fr*
Bauvorschrift (f) *De*
planning regulation *En*

règlements (m.pl) de construction *Fr*
Bauordnung (f) *De*
building regulations *En*

règlements (m.pl) de l'isolation contre le bruit *Fr*
Schallisolierungsvorschriften (f.pl) *De*
noise insulation regulations *En*

règlements (m.pl) sur la circulation *Fr*
Straßenverkehrsordnung (f) *De*
traffic regulations *En*

regulated tenancy *En*
aide (f) personalisée au logement (A.P.L.) *Fr*
gesichertes Mietverhältnis (nt) *De*

regulation *En*
règlement (m) *Fr*
Regelung (f); Vorschrift (f) *De*

rehabilitate (vb) *En*
rénover (vb) *Fr*
renovieren (vb) *De*

réhabilitation (f) urbaine *Fr*
Stadterneuerung (f) *De*
urban renewal *En*

rehouse (vb) *En*
reloger (vb) *Fr*
umquartieren (vb) *De*

rehousing *En*
relogement (m) *Fr*
Umquartierung (f) *De*

Reihenhäuser (nt.pl) *De*
terraced houses *En*
rangée (f) de maisons de style uniforme *Fr*

reimbursement *En*
remboursement (m) *Fr*
Rückzahlung (f) *De*

reinforced concrete *En*
béton (m) armé *Fr*
Stahlbeton (m) *De*

Reinigung (f), Putzen (nt) *De*
cleaning *En*
nettoyage (m) *Fr*

Reinigungsdienst (m) *De*
cleansing service *En*
service (m) d'assainissement *Fr*

reinstatement *En*
réintégration (f) *Fr*
Wiederherstellung (f) *De*

réintégration (f) *Fr*
Wiederherstellung (f) *De*
reinstatement *En*

Reinvestition (f) *De*
reinvestment *En*
nouveau placement (m) *Fr*

reinvestment *En*
nouveau placement (m) *Fr*
Reinvestition (f) *De*

(Reise)paß (m) *De*
passport *En*
passeport (m) *Fr*

Reisekonzession (f) *De*
travel concession *En*
prix (m) réduit du voyage *Fr*

Reisekosten (pl) *De*
travelling expenses *En*
frais (m.pl) de voyage *Fr*

Reisescheck (m) *De*
traveller's cheque *En*
chèque (m) de voyage *Fr*

Reitweg (m) *De*
bridle Path/bridleway *En*
sentier (m) pour cavaliers *Fr*

Reklamewand (f) *De*
hoarding *En*
palissade (f) *Fr*

Rektor (m) *De*
principal (college) *En*
proviseur (m) (lycée) *Fr*

relations (f.pl) avec la clientèle *Fr*
Kundenbeziehungen (f.pl) *De*
customer relations *En*

relations (f.pl) humaines dans l'entreprise *Fr*
Beziehungen (f.pl) zwischen Arbeitgebern und Gewerkschaften *De*
industrial relations *En*

relevant development *En*
aménagement (m) cohérent *Fr*
relevante Entwicklung (f) *De*

relevante Entwicklung (f) *De*
relevant development *En*
aménagement (m) cohérent *Fr*

relevé (m) de compte *Fr*
Kontoauszug (m) *De*
bank statement *En*

relief road *En*
chemin (m) de desserte *Fr*
Entlastungsstraße (f) *De*

religiöse Gruppe (f) *De*
religious group *En*
secte (f) religieuse *Fr*

religiöse Minderheit (f) *De*
religious minority *En*
minorité (f) de religion *Fr*

religious group *En*
secte (f) religieuse *Fr*
religiöse Gruppe (f) *De*

*** see/siehe/voir: Introduction page IX**

religious minority *En*
minorité (f) de religion *Fr*
religiöse Minderheit (f) *De*

relocation (staff) *En*
redéploiement (m) du personnel *Fr*
Versetzung (f) *De*

relogement (m) *Fr*
Umquartierung (f) *De*
rehousing *En*

reloger (vb) *Fr*
umquartieren (vb) *De*
rehouse (vb) *En*

remand (noun) *En*
détention (f) préventive *Fr*
Untersuchungshaft (f) *De*

remand centre *En*
maison (f) de détention provisoire *Fr*
Untersuchungsgefängnis (nt) *De*

remboursement (m) de l'emprunt *Fr*
Hypothekenzahlung (f) *De*
mortgage repayment *En*

remboursement (m) *Fr*
Rückzahlung (f) *De*
reimbursement *En*

remedial education *En*
action (f) pour combler le retard scolaire *Fr*
Förderunterricht (m) *De*

remedial treatment *En*
traitement (m) curatif *Fr*
Heilbehandlung (f) *De*

remedial work *En*
réparations (f.pl) *Fr*
Förderaufgaben (f.pl) *De*

remettre (vb) à neuf *Fr*
renovieren (vb) *De*
refurbish (vb) *En*

remise (f) d'un impôt *Fr*
Erlaß (m) *De*
remission (of tax) *En*

remission (of sentence) *En*
sursis (m) *Fr*
Straferlaß (m) *De*

remission (of tax) *En*
remise (f) d'un impôt *Fr*
Erlaß (m) *De*

remuneration *En*
rémunération (f) *Fr*
Bezahlung (f) *De*

rémunération (f) *Fr*
Bezahlung (f) *De*
remuneration *En*

rémunération (f) du capital *Fr*
Kapitalertrag (m) *De*
return on capital *En*

rémunération (f) insuffisante *Fr*
Unterbezahlung (f) *De*
underpayment *En*

rendement (m) *Fr*
Output (m) *De*
output *En*

rendement (m) énergétique *Fr*
Brennstoffleistung (f) *De*
fuel efficiency *En*

rendement (m) énergétique *Fr*
Energieleistungsfähigkeit (f) *De*
energy efficiency *En*

rendez-vous (m) *Fr*
Termin (m) *De*
appointment (meeting) *En*

renoncer (vb) par contrat *Fr*
nicht beitreten (vb) *De*
contract out (vb) *En*

renovation *En*
rénovation (f) *Fr*
Renovierung (f) *De*

rénovation (f) *Fr*
Renovierung (f) *De*
renovation *En*

rénovation (f) de maison *Fr*
Renovierung (f) *De*
house renovation *En*

rénovation (f) du logement *Fr*
Sanierung (f) (von Häusern/Wohnungen) *De*
housing renewal *En*

rénover (vb) *Fr*
renovieren (vb) *De*
rehabilitate (vb) *En*

renovieren (vb) *De*
refurbish (vb) *En*
remettre (vb) à neuf *Fr*

renovieren (vb) *De*
rehabilitate (vb) *En*
rénover (vb) *Fr*

Renovierung (f) *De*
house renovation *En*
rénovation (f) de maison *Fr*

Renovierung (f) *De*
renovation *En*
rénovation (f) *Fr*

Renovierungszuschuß (m) *De*
improvement grant *En*
subvention (f) destinée à la réhabilitation *Fr*

reseignements; plus amples —. (m.pl) *Fr*
nähere Umstände (m.pl) *De*
further details *En*

renseignements (m.pl) complémentaires *Fr*
weitere Auskunft (f) *De*
further information *En*

renseignements (m.pl) *Fr*
Auskunft (f) *De*
information *En*

rent *En*
loyer (m) *Fr*
Miete (f) *De*

rent allowance *En*
diminution (f) du loyer *Fr*
Mietbeihilfe (f) *De*

rent arrears *En*
arriérés (m.pl) de loyer *Fr*
Mietschulden (f.pl) *De*

rent assessment *En*
fixation (f) de loyer *Fr*
Mietschätzung (f) *De*

rent book *En*
quittance (f) de loyer *Fr*
Mietquittung (f) *De*

rent collection *En*
perception (f) de loyers *Fr*
Mieteintreibung (f) *De*

rent control *En*
encadrement (m) des loyers *Fr*
Mietpreisbindung (f) *De*

rent increase *En*
augmentation (f) de loyer *Fr*
Mieterhöhung (f) *De*

rent rebate *En*
réduction (f) de loyer *Fr*
Mietermäßigung (f) *De*

rent regulation *En*
règlement (m) de loyer *Fr*
Mietregulierung (f) *De*

rent review *En*
révision (f) de loyer *Fr*
Neufestsetzung (f) der Miete *De*

Rentabilität (f) *De*
cost effectiveness *En*
rapport (m) qualité-prix *Fr*

Rentabilität (f) *De*
profitability *En*
rentabilité (f) *Fr*

Rentabilität (f), Gewinnbringung (f) *De*
profit making *En*
réalisation (f) de bénéfices *Fr*

Rentabilitätsgrenze (f) *De*
break-even point *En*
point (m) de seuil *Fr*

rentabilité (f) *Fr*
Rentabilität (f) *De*
profitability *En*

Rente (f) *De*
superannuation *En*
retraite (f) par limite d'âge *Fr*

rente (f) foncière *Fr*
Grundrente (f) *De*
ground rent *En*

rente (f) *Fr*
Kapitaleinkommen (nt) *De*
unearned income *En*

Rente (f), Pension (f) *De*
pension *En*
pension (f) de retraite *Fr*

rented accommodation/housing *En*
logement (m) loué *Fr*
Mietwohnungen (f.pl) *De*

rented property *En*
propriété (f) louée *Fr*
Mietwohngrundstück (nt) *De*

Renten-, Pensionsalter (nt) *De*
pension age *En*
âge (m) de retraite *Fr*

Renten-, Pensionsalter (nt) *De*
retirement age *En*
âge (m) de la retraite *Fr*

Rentenfonds (m) *De*
superannuation fund *En*
caisse (f) des retraités *Fr*

Rentengeld (nt) *De*
superannuation benefit *En*
pension (f) de retraite *Fr*

Rentenversicherung (f) *De*
pension scheme *En*
retraite (f) des cadres *Fr*

Rentner/-in (m/f) *De*
old age pensioner *En*
retraité (m) (-ée f.) *Fr*

rentrée (f) en possession *Fr*
Wiederinbesitznahme (f) *De*
repossession *En*

renvoi (m) *Fr*
Entlassung (f) *De*
dismissal *En*

reorganization *En*
réorganisation (f) *Fr*
Umorganisation (f) *De*

réorganisation (f) du gouvernement local *Fr*
Gemeindeumorganisation (f) *De*
local government reorganization *En*

réorganisation (f) *Fr*
Umorganisation (f) *De*
reorganization *En*

réorganisation (f) *Fr*
Umstrukturierung (f) *De*
restructuring *En*

reorganize (vb) *En*
réorganiser (vb) *Fr*
umorganisieren (vb) *De*

réorganiser (vb) *Fr*
umorganisieren (vb) *De*
reorganize (vb) *En*

réorganiser (vb) *Fr*
umstrukturieren (vb) *De*
restructure (vb) *En*

repair grant *En*
subvention (f) de réhabilitation *Fr*
Ausbesserungszuschuß (m) *De*

réparations (f.pl) *Fr*
Förderaufgaben (f.pl) *De*
remedial work *En*

réparations (f.pl) d'urgence *Fr*
Schnellreparatur (f) *De*
emergency repair *En*

réparations (f.pl) de maison *Fr*
Instandsetzungsarbeit (f) *De*
house repair *En*

réparations (f.pl) du logement *Fr*
Hausreparatur (f) *De*
housing repair *En*

répartir (vb) les élèves en sections de force homogène *Fr*
einstufen (vb) *De*
band (vb) *En*

répartition (f) de la population *Fr*
Bevölkerungsverteilung (f) *De*
population distribution *En*

répartition (f) des moyens *Fr*
Geldzuwendung (f) *De*
resource allocation *En*

répartition (f) des moyens *Fr*
Zuweisung (f) der Mittel *De*
allocation of resources *En*

repas (m.pl) à domicile *Fr*
Essen (nt) auf Rädern *De*
meals-on-wheels *En*

repère (m) *Fr*
Höhenmarke (f) *De*
benchmark *En*

report (vb) to committee *En*
présenter (vb) un rapport en commission *Fr*
(einem Ausschuß) Bericht erstatten (vb) *De*

report writing *En*
rédaction (f) de rapports *Fr*
Berichterstattung (f) *De*

repossession *En*
rentrée (f) en possession *Fr*
Wiederinbesitznahme (f) *De*

représentation (f) proportionnelle *Fr*
Verhältniswahlsystem (nt) *De*
proportional representation *En*

reprise (f) de l'activité industrielle *Fr*
industrielle Reform (f) *De*
industrial regeneration/renewal *En*

reprise (f) économique *Fr*
Konjunkturaufschwung (m) *De*
economic recovery *En*

reprocessing *En*
recyclage (m) *Fr*
Wiederaufbereitung (f) *De*

*** see/siehe/voir: Introduction page IX**

reprographics *En*
réprographie (f) *Fr*
Reprographie (f) *De*

Reprographie (f) *De*
reprographics *En*
réprographie (f) *Fr*

réprographie (f) *Fr*
Reprographie (f) *De*
reprographics *En*

requérir (vb) *Fr*
eine Eingabe machen, petitionieren (vb) *De*
petition (vb) *En*

requête (f) *Fr*
Petition (f), Eingabe (f) *De*
petition (noun) *En*

requisition *En*
demande (f) *Fr*
Anforderung (f) *De*

rescue archaeology *En*
archéologie (f) de sauvegarde *Fr*
Denkmalschutz (m) *De*

research and development *En*
recherche (f) industrielle *Fr*
industrielle Forschung (f) *De*

research project *En*
projet (m) de recherche *Fr*
Forschungsprogramm (nt) *De*

réseau (m) des artères *Fr*
Straßennetz (nt) *De*
highway network *En*

réseau (m) électrique national *Fr*
nationales Verbundnetz (nt) *De*
national grid *En*

réseau (m) ferroviaire *Fr*
Eisenbahnnetz (nt) *De*
rail network *En*

réseau (m) informatique *Fr*
Informationsnetz (nt) *De*
information network *En*

réseau (m) routier *Fr*
Straßennetz (nt) *De*
road network *En*

réserve (f) naturelle *Fr*
Naturschutzgebiet (nt) *De*
nature reserve *En*

reserves *En*
réserves (f.pl) (bancaires) *Fr*
Rücklagen (f.pl) *De*

réserves (f.pl) (bancaires) *Fr*
Rücklagen (f.pl) *De*
reserves *En*

résidence (f) pour personnes âgées *Fr*
Alten- Altersheim (nt) *De*
community home *En*

resident *En*
habitant (m) (-ante f.) *Fr*
Bewohner/-in (m/f) *De*

residential accommodation *En*
logement (m) *Fr*
Unterkunft (f) *De*

residential area *En*
quartier (m) residentiel *Fr*
Wohngebiet (nt), -gegend (f) *De*

residential care *En*
soins (m.pl) à domicile *Fr*
stationäre Pflege (f) *De*

residential development *En*
aménagement (m) urbain *Fr*
Wohnsiedlung (f) *De*

residential land *En*
terrain (m) constructible résidentiel *Fr*
Wohnbebauungsland (nt) *De*

residential property *En*
propriété (f) résidentielle *Fr*
Wohnhaus (nt) *De*

residential road *En*
rue (f) résidentielle *Fr*
Wohnstraße (f) *De*

residents' association *En*
association (f) de propriétaires/locataires *Fr*
Interessengemeinschaft (f) von Benachbarten *De*

resign (vb) *En*
démissionner (vb) *Fr*
zurücktreten (vb) *De*

resignation *En*
démission (f) *Fr*
Rücktritt (m) *De*

resolve (vb) to recommend *En*
donner (vb) un avis *Fr*
beschließen, zu empfehlen (vb) *De*

resource allocation *En*
répartition (f) des moyens *Fr*
Geldzuwendung (f) *De*

resource management *En*
gestion (f) financiaire *Fr*
Ressourcemanagement (nt) *De*

resource planning *En*
prévision (f) financiaire *Fr*
Ressourceplanung (f) *De*

resourcing *En*
financement (m) *Fr*
Finanzierung (f) *De*

responsabilité (f) corporative *Fr*
Gesamtverantwortung (f) *De*
corporate responsibility *En*

responsabilité (f) démocratique *Fr*
demokratische Verantwortlichkeit (f) *De*
democratic accountability *En*

responsabilité (f) des finances *Fr*
Finanzplanung (f) *De*
financial management *En*

responsabilité (f) des parents *Fr*
Elternpflicht (f) *De*
parental responsibility *En*

responsabilité (f) *Fr*
Haftung (f) *De*
liability *En*

responsabilité (f) *Fr*
Verantwortlichkeit (f) *De*
accountability *En*

responsabilité (f) locale *Fr*
Ortsverantwortung (f) *De*
local accountability *En*

responsabilité (f) personnelle *Fr*
öffentliche Verantwortlichkeit (f) *De*
public accountability *En*

responsable (adj) *Fr*
verantwortlich (adj) *De*
accountable (adj) *En*

responsable (m) des relations publiques *Fr*
Öffentlichkeitsreferent/-in (m/f) *De*
public relations officer *En*

responsable (m) du développement économique *Fr*
Wirtschaftsförderer (m) *De*
economic development officer *En*

*** see/siehe/voir: Introduction page IX**

responsable (m/f) de l'éducation ***Fr*** *
Stadtschulrat (m) *De*
chief education officer *En*

responsable (m/f) de la formation ***Fr***
Ausbildungsoffizier (m) *De*
training officer *En*

response rate ***En***
taux (m) de réponse *Fr*
Antwortsrate (f) *De*

responsive (adj) ***En***
sensible (adj) *Fr*
aufgeschloßen (adj) *De*

Ressourcemanagement (nt) ***De***
resource management *En*
gestion (f) financiaire *Fr*

Ressourceplanung (f) ***De***
resource planning *En*
prévision (f) financiaire *Fr*

ressources (f.pl) fiscales ***Fr***
Finanzierungsmittel (nt.pl) *De*
financial resources *En*

ressources (f.pl) humaines ***Fr***
Humanvermögen (nt) *De*
human resources *En*

restrict (vb) (development etc) ***En***
limiter (vb) *Fr*
einschränken (vb) (Entwicklung usw) *De*

restriction of expenditure ***En***
réduction (f) des dépenses *Fr*
Einschränkung (f) der Ausgaben *De*

restrictions (f.pl) financières ***Fr***
finanzielle Einschränkung (f) *De*
financial restraint *En*

restrictions (f.pl) relatives à l'incendie ***Fr***
Feuerschutzbestimmung (f) *De*
fire regulations *En*

restrictive covenant ***En***
accord (m) restrictif *Fr*
einschränkender Vertrag (m) *De*

restructure (vb) ***En***
réorganiser (vb) *Fr*
umstrukturieren (vb) *De*

restructuring ***En***
réorganisation (f) *Fr*
Umstrukturierung (f) *De*

résultat (m) d'examen ***Fr***
Prüfungsergebnis (nt) *De*
examination result *En*

résultat (m) ***Fr***
Output (m) *De*
outturn *En*

résultats (m.pl) du recensement ***Fr***
Zensusdaten (nt.pl) *De*
census data *En*

résumé (m) ***Fr***
Abriß (m) *De*
abstract *En*

résumer (vb) (un débat etc) ***Fr***
(Debatte usw) beschließen (vb) *De*
wind up (vb) (debate etc) *En*

resurface (vb) a road ***En***
refaire (vb) le revêtement d'une route *Fr*
(den Belag einer Straße) erneuern (vb) *De*

retail industry ***En***
commerce (m) au détail *Fr*
Einzelhandel (m) *De*

retail price index ***En***
indice (m) des prix de détail *Fr*
Preisindex (m) des Einzelhandels *De*

retailer ***En***
commerçant (m) (-ante f.) au détail *Fr*
Einzelhändler (m) *De*

retenue (f) pour la retraite ***Fr***
Beitrag (m) zur Rentenversicherung *De*
superannuation contribution *En*

retenues (f.pl) sur les appointements ***Fr***
(Lohn)abzüge (m.pl) *De*
stoppages (from pay) *En*

retire (vb) ***En***
prendre (vb) sa retraite *Fr*
in den Ruhestand treten (vb) *De*

retired (adj) ***En***
en retraite (adj) *Fr*
im Ruhestand; pensioniert (adj) *De*

retired people ***En***
retraités (m.pl) *Fr*
Pensionierte(-n) (pl) *De*

retirement age ***En***
âge (m) de la retraite *Fr*
Renten-, Pensionsalter (nt) *De*

retirement ***En***
retraite (f) *Fr*
Ruhestand (m) *De*

retirement pension ***En***
pension (f) de retraite *Fr*
(Alters)rente (f), Pension (f) *De*

retrain (vb) (staff) ***En***
recycler (vb) (personnel) *Fr*
umschulen (vb) *De*

retraining ***En***
recyclage (m) *Fr*
Umschulung (f) *De*

retraite (f) ***Fr***
Ruhestand (m) *De*
retirement *En*

retraite; en — (adj) ***Fr***
im Ruhestand; pensioniert (adj) *De*
retired (adj) *En*

retraité (m) (-ée f.) ***Fr***
Rentner/-in (m/f) *De*
old age pensioner *En*

retraite (f) des cadres ***Fr***
abgestuftes Sozialrentensystem (nt) *De*
graduated pension scheme *En*

retraite (f) des cadres ***Fr***
Betriebsaltersversorgung (f) *De*
occupational pension scheme *En*

retraite (f) des cadres ***Fr***
Rentenversicherung (f) *De*
pension scheme *En*

retraite (f) par limite d'âge ***Fr***
Rente (f) *De*
superannuation *En*

retraite (f) prématurée ***Fr***
vorzeitiger Ruhestand (m) *De*
early retirement *En*

retraités (m.pl) ***Fr***
Pensionierte(-n) (pl) *De*
retired people *En*

retrospective (adj) ***En***
avec effet rétrospectif (adj) *Fr*
rückwirkend (adj) *De*

return on capital ***En***
rémunération (f) du capital *Fr*
Kapitalertrag (m) *De*

*** see/siehe/voir: Introduction page IX**

returning officer (in election) *En*
directeur (m) (-trice f.) du scrutin *Fr*
Wahlleiter/-in (m/f) *De*

réunion (f) *Fr*
Versammlung (f); Besprechung (f) *De*
meeting *En*

réunion (f) d'un comité *Fr*
Ausschußsitzung (f) *De*
committee meeting *En*

réunion (f) de concertation *Fr*
Fallbesprechung (f) *De*
case conference *En*

réunion (f) du conseil *Fr*
Ratssitzung (f) *De*
council meeting *En*

réunion (f) du conseil *Fr*
Vorstandssitzung (f) *De*
board meeting *En*

réunion (f) préparatoire (avec le président) *Fr*
Einsatzbesprechung (f) *De*
briefing meeting (with chairman) *En*

réunion (f) préparatoire *Fr*
Vorbesprechung (f) *De*
pre-meeting *En*

révalorisation (f) *Fr*
Aufwertung (f) *De*
revaluation *En*

revaluation *En*
révalorisation (f) *Fr*
Aufwertung (f) *De*

revenu (m) *Fr*
Einkommen (nt) *De*
income *En*

revenu (m) de la famille *Fr*
Haushaltseinkommen (nt) *De*
household income *En*

revenu (m) des personnes physiques *Fr*
persönliches Einkommen (nt) *De*
personal income *En*

revenu (m) disponible *Fr*
verfügbares Einkommen (nt) *De*
disposable income *En*

revenu (m) imposable *Fr*
steuerpflichtiges Einkommen (nt) *De*
taxable income *En*

revenu (m) modeste *Fr*
schlechte Bezahlung (f) *De*
low pay *En*

revenu(s) (m/m.pl) *Fr*
Verdienst (m) *De*
earnings *En*

revenue *En*
fisc (m) *Fr*
(öffentliche) Einnahmen (f.pl) *De*

revenue account *En*
trésor (m) public *Fr*
Einnahmen (f.pl) *De*

revenue estimates *En*
prévisions (f.pl) budgétaires *Fr*
Einnahmeerwartungen (f.pl) *De*

revenue expenditure *En*
dépenses (f.pl) courantes *Fr*
Steuerabgaben (f,pl) *De*

revenue support grant *En*
dotations (f.pl) de l'Etat aux collectivités *Fr*
Einnahmenbeihilfe (f) *De*

revenus moyens; à — —. *Fr*
Einkommen (nt); Familie mit mittlerem —. *De*
middle income (adj) *En*

révision (f) de loyer *Fr*
Neufestsetzung (f) der Miete *De*
rent review *En*

revitalisation (f) du centre ville *Fr*
Neubelebung (f) der Innenstadt *De*
inner city regeneration *En*

Rezeption (f) *De*
reception area *En*
accueil (m) *Fr*

Rezession (f), Konjunkturrückgang (m) *De*
recession *En*
récession (f) *Fr*

ribbon development *En*
extension (f) urbaine en bordure de route *Fr*
Zeilenbauweise (f) *De*

Richter/-in (m/f) *De*
judge *En*
juge (m) *Fr*

Richterschaft (f) *De*
judiciary *En*
magistrature (f) *Fr*

Richtungswechsel (m) *De*
policy change *En*
changement (m) de politique *Fr*

Riesenlaster (m) *De*
juggernaut *En*
mastodonte (m) de la route *Fr*

right of access *En*
droit (m) d'accès *Fr*
Besuchsrecht (nt); Wegerecht (nt) *De*

right of appeal *En*
droit (m) d'appel *Fr*
Berufungsrecht (nt) *De*

right of entry *En*
droit (m) d'entrée *Fr*
Wegerecht (nt) (zu einem Haus) *De*

right of way *En*
droit (m) de passage *Fr*
Durchgangsrecht (nt) *De*

right to buy *En*
droit (m) d'achat *Fr*
Kaufrecht (nt) *De*

right wing (adj) *En*
de droite (adj) *Fr*
rechte(-r,-s) (adj) *De*

right wing *En*
droite (f) *Fr*
Rechte (f) *De*

ring road *En*
boulevard (m) périphérique *Fr*
Umgehungsstraße (f) *De*

Risikoanalyse (f) *De*
risk analysis *En*
analyse (f) des risques *Fr*

Risikoeinschätzung (f) *De*
risk assessment *En*
appréciation (f) des risques *Fr*

Risikokapital (nt) *De*
risk capital *En*
capitaux (m.pl) spéculatifs *Fr*

risikoreiche Strategie (f), Risikostrategie (f) *De*
high risk strategy *En*
stratégie (f) hasardeuse *Fr*

rising damp *En*
humidité (f) qui monte du sol *Fr*
aufsteigende Feuchtigkeit (f) *De*

risk analysis *En*
analyse (f) des risques *Fr*
Risikoanalyse (f) *De*

*** see/siehe/voir: Introduction page IX**

risk assessment *En*
appréciation (f) des risques *Fr*
Risikoeinschätzung (f) *De*

risk capital *En*
capitaux (m.pl) spéculatifs *Fr*
Risikokapital (nt) *De*

risk management *En*
gestion (f) des risques *Fr*
Absicherung (f) von Risiken *De*

risque (m) d'incendie *Fr*
Brandgefahr (f) *De*
fire risk *En*

risque (m) d'incendie *Fr*
Feuergefahr (f) *De*
fire hazard *En*

risques (m.pl) du travail *Fr*
Berufsrisiken (nt.pl) *De*
occupational hazards *En*

river freight/transport *En*
transport (m) par voie d'eau *Fr*
Flußtransport (m) *De*

river pollution *En*
pollution (f) des cours d'eau *Fr*
Flußverschmutzung (f) *De*

road accident *En*
accident (m) de la route *Fr*
Verkehrsunfall (m) *De*

road alignment *En*
alignement (m) de la route *Fr*
Straßenausrichtung (f) *De*

road bridge *En*
pont (m) routier *Fr*
Straßenbrücke (f) *De*

road building/construction *En*
construction (f) routière *Fr*
Straßenbau (m) *De*

road capacity *En*
capacité (m) de trafic de la route *Fr*
Straßenauslastung (f) *De*

road closure *En*
barrage (m) de la route *Fr*
Straßensperrung (f) *De*

road design *En*
étude (f) d'une route *Fr*
Straßenplanung (f) *De*

road haulage *En*
transports (m.pl) routiers *Fr*
Spedition (f) *De*

road improvement *En*
amélioration (f) de la route *Fr*
Straßenerneuerung (f) *De*

road junction *En*
carrefour (m) *Fr*
Straßenkreuzung (f) *De*

road lighting *En*
éclairage (m) des routes *Fr*
Straßenbeleuchtung (f) *De*

road maintenance *En*
entretien (m) des routes *Fr*
Straßeninstandhaltung (f), -wartung (f) *De*

road marking *En*
marquage (m) routier *Fr*
Straßenmarkierung (f) *De*

road network *En*
réseau (m) routier *Fr*
Straßennetz (nt) *De*

road planning *En*
programmation (f) des routes *Fr*
Straßenplanung (f) *De*

road policy *En*
politique (f) routière *Fr*
Straßenbaupolitik (f) *De*

road safety *En*
prévention (f) routière *Fr*
Verkehrssicherheit (f) *De*

road sign *En*
signal (m) routier *Fr*
Straßenschild (nt), Verkehrszeichen (nt) *De*

road signing *En*
signalisation (f) routière *Fr*
Straßenbeschilderung (f) *De*

road tax *En*
vignette (f) *Fr*
Kraftfahrzeugsteuer (f) *De*

road traffic *En*
circulation (f) routière *Fr*
Straßenverkehr (m) *De*

road transport *En*
transports (m.pl) routiers *Fr*
Straßengüterverkehr (m) *De*

road works *En*
travaux (m.pl) de voirie *Fr*
Straßenarbeiten (f.pl) *De*

roadway *En*
chaussée (f) *Fr*
Straße (f); Fahrbahn (f) *De*

robbery *En*
vol (m) *Fr*
Raub (m) *De*

rodent *En*
rongeur (m) *Fr*
Nagetier (nt) *De*

rodent officer *En*
fonctionnaire (m) chargé de la dératisation *Fr*
Rattenfänger (m) *De*

Rohr (nt) *De*
pipe *En*
tuyau (m) *Fr*

Rohstoff (m) *De*
raw material *En*
matières (f.pl) premières *Fr*

rôle (m) des parents *Fr*
elterliche Rolle (f) *De*
parental involvement *En*

rolled asphalt *En*
asphalte (m) damé *Fr*
gewalzter Asphalt (m) *De*

Rollstuhl (m) *De*
wheelchair *En*
fauteuil (m) roulant *Fr*

rond-point (m) (pl. ronds-points) *Fr*
Kreisverkehr (m) *De*
roundabout *En*

rongeur (m) *Fr*
Nagetier (nt) *De*
rodent *En*

roundabout *En*
rond-point (m) (pl. ronds-points) *Fr*
Kreisverkehr (m) *De*

route (f) à grande circulation *Fr*
Hauptverkehrsstraße (f) *De*
primary/principal road *En*

route (f) à péage *Fr*
gebührenpflichtige Straße (f) *De*
toll road *En*

route (f) d'accès *Fr*
Verbindungsstraße (f) *De*
link road *En*

route (f) d'accès *Fr*
Zufahrtsstraße (f) *De*
access road *En*

*** see/siehe/voir: Introduction page IX**

route (f) d'accès *Fr*
Zufahrtsstraße (f) *De*
approach road *En*

route (f) d'évitement *Fr*
Umgehungsstraße (f) *De*
by-pass *En*

route (f) jumelée *Fr*
zweispurige Straße (f) *De*
dual carriageway *En*

route (f) secondaire *Fr*
Nebenstraße (f) *De*
minor road *En*

route (f) secondaire *Fr*
Nebenstraße (f) *De*
secondary road *En*

route (f) surélevée *Fr*
aufgeschüttete Straße (f) *De*
elevated road *En*

Rowdy (m) *De*
vandal *En*
vandale (m/f) *Fr*

rubbish *En*
ordures (f.pl) *Fr*
Müll (m), Abfall (m) *De*

rubbish dump *En*
décharge (f) publique *Fr*
Müllhalde (f) *De*

Rücklagen (f.pl) *De*
reserves *En*
réserves (f.pl) (bancaires) *Fr*

Rücktritt (m) *De*
resignation *En*
démission (f) *Fr*

rückwirkend (adj) *De*
retrospective (adj) *En*
avec effet rétrospectif (adj) *Fr*

Rückzahlung (f) *De*
rebate *En*
rabais (m) *Fr*

Rückzahlung (f) *De*
reimbursement *En*
remboursement (m) *Fr*

rue (f) commerçante *Fr*
Geschäftsstraße (f) *De*
shopping street *En*

rue (f) résidentielle *Fr*
Wohnstraße (f) *De*
residential road *En*

rue/route (f) entretenue par la municipalité *Fr*
öffentliche Straße (f) *De*
adopted road *En*

Ruhe und Ordnung (f) *De*
law and order *En*
ordre (m) public *Fr*

Ruhestand (m) *De*
retirement *En*
retraite (f) *Fr*

Ruhestand; in den — treten (vb) *De*
retire (vb) *En*
prendre (vb) sa retraite *Fr*

Ruhestand; im — ; pensioniert (adj) *De*
retired (adj) *En*
en retraite (adj) *Fr*

Rundbrief (m) *De*
circular *En*
lettre (f) circulaire *Fr*

Rundschreiben (nt) *De*
newsletter *En*
bulletin (m) (d'informations) *Fr*

running cost *En*
frais (m.pl) d'exploitation *Fr*
Betriebskosten (pl) *De*

rupture (f) de contrat *Fr*
Vertragsbruch (m) *De*
breach of contract *En*

rural area/district *En*
région (f) rurale *Fr*
ländliches Gebiet (nt), Landgebiet (nt) *De*

rural community *En*
communauté (f) rurale *Fr*
Landgemeinde (f) *De*

rural development *En*
aménagement (m) rural *Fr*
ländliche Entwicklung (f) *De*

rural economy *En*
économie (f) rurale *Fr*
Landwirtschaft (f) *De*

rural planning *En*
aménagement (m) des campagnes *Fr*
ländliche Planung (f) *De*

rural policy *En*
politique (f) rurale *Fr*
ländliche Politik (f) *De*

rush hour *En*
heures (f.pl) d'affluence *Fr*
Hauptverkehrszeit (f), Stoßzeit (f) *De*

S

s'abstenir (vb) ***Fr***
sich der Stimme enthalten (vb) *De*
abstain (vb) *En*

s'établir (vb) comme squatter dans une maison inoccupée (sans titre) ***Fr***
ein Haus besetzen (vb) *De*
squat (vb) *En*

sabot (m) de Denver; pince (f) d'immobilisation ***Fr***
Parkkralle (f) *De*
wheel clamp *En*

safeguard (vb) ***En***
sauvegarder (vb) *Fr*
schützen (vb) *De*

safety barrier ***En***
glissière (f) *Fr*
Leitplanke (f) *De*

safety equipment ***En***
matériel (m) de sécurité *Fr*
Sicherheitsausrüstung (f) *De*

saisonabhängige Arbeitslosigkeit (f) ***De***
seasonal unemployment *En*
chômage (m) saisonnier *Fr*

Saisonarbeit (f) ***De***
seasonal work *En*
travail (m) saisonnier *Fr*

salaire (m) ***Fr***
Lohn (m) *De*
wage *En*

salaire (m) au mérite (secteur privé)_ ***Fr***
leistungsbezogene Bezahlung (f) *De*
performance related pay *En*

salaire (m) égal ***Fr***
gleicher Lohn (m) (für gleiche Arbeit) *De*
equal pay *En*

salaire (m) minimum interprofessionnel de croissance (SMIC) ***Fr***
Mindestlohn (m) *De*
minimum wage *En*

salaire (m) net ***Fr***
Nettolohn (m) *De*
take-home pay *En*

salaire (m) (secteur privé)/traitement (de fonctionnaire) ***Fr***
Lohn (m) *De*
pay *En*

salary ***En***
traitement (m) *Fr*
Gehalt (nt) *De*

salary scale ***En***
échelle (f) indicière *Fr*
Gehaltsskala (f) *De*

sales tax ***En***
taxe (f) de vente *Fr*
Verkaufssteuer (f) *De*

salle (f) d'hôpital ***Fr***
Station (f) *De*
ward (hospital) *En*

salle (f) de classe ***Fr***
Klassenzimmer (nt) *De*
classroom *En*

salle (f) de conférences ***Fr***
Hörsaal (m) *De*
lecture theatre *En*

salle (f) des dactylos ***Fr***
Schreibbüro (nt) *De*
typing pool (room) *En*

salle (f) des sports ***Fr***
Sporthalle (f) *De*
indoor sports centre *En*

salle (f) du conseil ***Fr***
Sitzungssaal (m) des Rats *De*
council chamber *En*

salle (f) du courrier ***Fr***
Poststelle (f) *De*
post room *En*

salle (f) informatique ***Fr***
Computerbüro (nt) *De*
computer suite *En*

salon (m) d'exposition ***Fr***
Ausstellungsgelände (nt) *De*
exhibition centre *En*

salubrité (f) publique ***Fr***
(Umwelt)gesundheitsdienst (m) *De*
environmental health *En*

Sammelheizung (f) ***De***
group heating *En*
chauffage (m) urbain *Fr*

sample survey ***En***
enquête (f) par sondage *Fr*
Stichprobenerhebung (f) *De*

sanction (f) ***Fr***
Strafe (f) *De*
penalty *En*

sanieren (vb) ***De***
redevelop (vb) *En*
mettre (vb) en valeur *Fr*

Sanierung (f) (von Häusern/Wohnungen) ***De***
housing renewal *En*
rénovation (f) du logement *Fr*

Sanierungsgebiet (nt) ***De***
redevelopment area *En*
zone (f) de réhabilitation *Fr*

sanitation ***En***
hygiène (f) publique *Fr*
Kanalisation (f) und Abfallbeseitigung (f) *De*

sans profit (adj) ***Fr***
unvorteilhaft (adj) *De*
unprofitable (adj) *En*

sans-gîte (m.pl) ***Fr***
Obdachlose(-n) *De*
homeless *En*

santé (f) *Fr*
Gesundheit (f) *De*
health *En*

santé (f); qui peut nuire à la — . *Fr*
Gesundheitsgefährdung (f) *De*
health hazard *En*

santé (f) mentale *Fr*
seelische Gesundheit (f) *De*
mental health *En*

Säuglingssterblichkeit (f) *De*
infant mortality *En*
mortalité (f) infantile *Fr*

sauvegarde (f) d'un quartier *Fr*
Städteerhaltung (f) *De*
urban conservation *En*

sauvegarder (vb) *Fr*
schützen (vb) *De*
safeguard (vb) *En*

savings bank *En*
caisse (f) d'épargne *Fr*
Sparkasse (f) *De*

scaffolding *En*
échafaudage (m) *Fr*
Gerüst (nt) *De*

Schadenersatz (m) *De*
damages *En*
dommages-intérêts (m.pl) *Fr*

Schadenersatz zugestehen (vb) *De*
award (vb) damages *En*
adjuger (vb) des dommages-intérêts *Fr*

Schädlingsbekämpfung (f) *De*
pest control *En*
désinsectisation (f); dératisation (f) *Fr*

Schallisolierung (f) *De*
sound insulation; soundproofing *En*
isolation (f) acoustique *Fr*

Schallisolierungsvorschriften (f.pl) *De*
noise insulation regulations *En*
règlements (m.pl) de l'isolation contre le bruit *Fr*

Schalung (f) *De*
shuttering *En*
coffrage (m) (du béton) *Fr*

schätzen (vb) *De*
estimate (vb) *En*
prévoir (vb) *Fr*

Schätzung (f) *De*
estimation *En*
estimation (f) *Fr*

Schätzung (f) *De*
evaluation *En*
évaluation (f) *Fr*

Schätzung (f) *De*
valuation *En*
évaluation (f) *Fr*

Schätzungsabteilung (f) *De*
valuer's department *En*
direction (f) des bâtiments *Fr*

schedule of rates *En*
cédule (f) d'impôts locaux *Fr*
Kommunalsteueraufstellung (f) *De*

Schichtarbeit (f) *De*
shift work *En*
travail (m) par équipes *Fr*

Schiedsgericht (nt) *De*
magistrates' court *En*
tribunal (m) d'instance *Fr*

Schiffbau (m) *De*
shipbuilding *En*
construction (f) navale *Fr*

Schiffsverkehr (m) *De*
shipping *En*
marine (f) maritime *Fr*

schlafen (vb); im Freien — . *De*
sleep (vb) rough *En*
coucher (vb) sur la dure *Fr*

schlecht bezahlt (adj) *De*
low paid (adj) *En*
personnes (f.pl) économiquement faibles *Fr*

schlechte Bezahlung (f) *De*
low pay *En*
revenu (m) modeste *Fr*

Schleichweg (m) *De*
rat run *En*
raccourci (m) *Fr*

Schlichtung (f) *De*
arbitration *En*
arbitrage (m) *Fr*

Schlichtung (f) *De*
conciliation *En*
conciliation (f) *Fr*

Schlüsselfrage (f) *De*
key issue *En*
question (f) vitale *Fr*

Schnellreparatur (f) *De*
emergency repair *En*
réparations (f.pl) d'urgence *Fr*

Schnellstrasse (f) *De*
expressway *En*
voie (f) rapide *Fr*

Schnittstelle (f) *De*
interface *En*
interface (f) *Fr*

school *En*
école (f) *Fr*
Schule (f) *De*

school age *En*
âge (m) scolaire *Fr*
Schulalter (nt) *De*

school building programme *En*
programmation (f) scolaire *Fr*
Schulbauprogramm (nt) *De*

school bus *En*
car (m) scolaire *Fr*
Schulbus (m) *De*

school children *En*
écoliers (m) *Fr*
Schulkinder (nt.pl), Schüler (m.pl) *De*

school curriculum *En*
programme (m) d'études *Fr*
Lehrplan (m) *De*

school governor *En*
membre (m) du conseil d'administration *Fr*
Mitglied (nt) des Schulbeirats *De*

school grounds *En*
terrain (m) scolaire *Fr*
Schulgelände (nt) *De*

school leaver *En*
jeune personne (f) qui a terminé ses études scolaires *Fr*
Schulabgänger/-in (m/f) *De*

school leaving age *En*
âge (m) de fin de scolarité *Fr*
Schulabgangsalter (nt) *De*

school management *En*
administration (f) de l'école *Fr*
Schulleitung (f) *De*

school premises *En*
locaux (m.pl) scolaires *Fr*
Schulgebäude (nt), -gelände (nt) *De*

school report *En*
livret (m) scolaire *Fr*
Schulzeugnis (nt) *De*

school roll *En*
liste (f) des élèves *Fr*
Schülerzahl (f) *De*

school transport *En*
transport (m) d'enfants *Fr*
Schultransport (m) *De*

schoolboy *En*
écolier (m) *Fr*
Schuljunge (m), Schüler (m) *De*

schoolgirl *En*
écolière (f) *Fr*
Schulmädchen (nt), Schülerin (f) *De*

Schreibarbeit (f) *De*
paperwork *En*
écriture (f) *Fr*

Schreibbüro (nt) *De*
typing pool (room) *En*
salle (f) des dactylos *Fr*

Schreibkraft (f) *De*
typist *En*
dactylo(graphe) (m/f) *Fr*

Schreibkräfte (f.pl) *De*
typing pool (staff) *En*
équipe (f) de dactylos *Fr*

Schreibmaschine (f) *De*
typewriter *En*
machine (f) à écrire *Fr*

Schreibmaschine (f); auf der — schreiben (vb) *De*
type (vb) *En*
écrire (vb) à la machine *Fr*

Schreibtisch (m) *De*
desk *En*
bureau (m) *Fr*

Schuhindustrie (f) *De*
footwear industry *En*
manufacture (f) des chaussures *Fr*

Schulabgänger/-in (m/f) *De*
school leaver *En*
jeune personne (f) qui a terminé ses études scolaires *Fr*

Schulabgangsalter (nt) *De*
school leaving age *En*
âge (m) de fin de scolarité *Fr*

Schulalter (nt) *De*
school age *En*
âge (m) scolaire *Fr*

Schulamt (nt) *De* *
local education authority *En*
service (m) municipal/régional de l'enseignement *Fr*

Schulbauprogramm (nt) *De*
school building programme *En*
programmation (f) scolaire *Fr*

Schulbus (m) *De*
school bus *En*
car (m) scolaire *Fr*

Schuld (f) *De*
debt *En*
dette (f) *Fr*

(Schulden, Verlust) abschreiben (vb) *De*
write off (vb) (a debt, a loss) *En*
amortir (vb) (une dette, une perte) *Fr*

Schuldner/-in (m/f) *De*
debtor *En*
débiteur (m) (-trice f.) *Fr*

Schule (f) *De*
school *En*
école (f) *Fr*

Schule (f) für 8/9- bis 12/13-jährige *De*
middle school *En*
école (f) pour enfants de 8/9 à 12/13 ans *Fr*

Schule (f) für den tertiären Bildungsbereich *De*
tertiary college *En*
lycée (m) *Fr*

Schülerzahl (f) *De*
school roll *En*
liste (f) des élèves *Fr*

Schulgebäude (nt), -gelände (nt) *De*
school premises *En*
locaux (m.pl) scolaires *Fr*

Schulgelände (nt) *De*
school grounds *En*
terrain (m) scolaire *Fr*

Schuljunge (m), Schüler (m) *De*
schoolboy *En*
écolier (m) *Fr*

Schulkinder (nt.pl), Schüler (m.pl) *De*
school children *En*
écoliers (m) *Fr*

Schulleiter/-in (m/f) *De*
head teacher (primary/secondary) *En*
directeur (m) (-trice f.) /principal (m) *Fr*

Schulleitung (f) *De*
school management *En*
administration (f) de l'école *Fr*

Schulmädchen (nt), Schülerin (f) *De*
schoolgirl *En*
écolière (f) *Fr*

Schulpolitik (f) *De*
education policy *En*
politique (f) de l'éducation *Fr*

Schulpsychologie (f) *De*
educational psychology *En*
psychologie (f) scolaire *Fr*

Schulreform (f) *De*
educational reform *En*
réforme (f) pédagogique *Fr*

Schultransport (m) *De*
school transport *En*
transport (m) d'enfants *Fr*

Schulzeugnis (nt) *De*
school report *En*
livret (m) scolaire *Fr*

Schuttabladen (nt) *De*
tipping *En*
décharge (f) (d'ordures etc) *Fr*

Schutz(be)kleidung (f) *De*
protective clothing *En*
vêtements (m.pl) protecteurs *Fr*

schützen (vb) *De*
safeguard (vb) *En*
sauvegarder (vb) *Fr*

schwache Gesundheit (f), Kränklichkeit (f) *De*
ill health *En*
mauvaise santé (f) *Fr*

schwanken (vb) *De*
fluctuate (vb) *En*
fluctuer (vb) *Fr*

schwankender Kurs (m) *De*
fluctuating rate *En*
taux (m) variable *Fr*

Schwankung (f) *De*
fluctuation *En*
fluctuation (f) *Fr*

schwerhörig (adj) *De*
hearing impaired (adj) *En*
oreille (f) dure (qui a l') *Fr*

Schwerlastwagen (m) *De*
heavy lorry *En*
camion (m) lourd *Fr*

*** see/siehe/voir: Introduction page IX**

Schwertransport (m) mit Überbreite *De*
abnormal load *En*
convoi (m) exceptionnel *Fr*

Schwurgerichtsverfahren (nt) *De*
trial by jury *En*
jugement (m) par jury *Fr*

science education *En*
enseignement (m) scientifique *Fr*
Unterricht (m) in den Naturwissenschaften *De*

science park *En*
campus (m) scientifique *Fr*
Technologiepark (m) *De*

sciences (f.pl) économiques *Fr*
Wirtschaftswissenschaften (f.pl) *De*
economics *En*

scrutateur (m); recenseur (m) *Fr*
Stimmenzähler/-in (m/f) *De*
teller (at election) *En*

scrutin (m) *Fr*
Abstimmung (f) *De*
ballot *En*

scrutin (m) *Fr*
Abstimmung (f), Wahl (f) *De*
poll *En*

scrutin (m) secret *Fr*
geheime Wahl (f) *De*
secret ballot *En*

se coaliser (vb) *Fr*
eine Koalition bilden (vb) *De*
coalition (to form a) (vb) *En*

se retirer (vb) *Fr*
austreten (vb) *De*
opt out (vb) *En*

séance (f) (d'un comité etc) *Fr*
Sitzung (f) *De*
sitting (of committee) *En*

séance (f) publique *Fr*
öffentliche Sitzung (f) *De*
public meeting *En*

search warrant *En*
mandat (m) de perquisition *Fr*
Durchsuchungsbefehl (m) *De*

season ticket *En*
carte (f) d'abonnement *Fr*
Dauerkarte (f) *De*

seasonal unemployment *En*
chômage (m) saisonnier *Fr*
saisonabhängige Arbeitslosigkeit (f) *De*

seasonal work *En*
travail (m) saisonnier *Fr*
Saisonarbeit (f) *De*

second (vb) (a motion) *En*
appuyer (vb) (une proposition) *Fr*
(einen Antrag) unterstützen (vb) *De*

secondary education *En*
enseignement (m) secondaire *Fr*
höhere Schulbildung (f) *De*

secondary road *En*
route (f) secondaire *Fr*
Nebenstraße (f) *De*

secondary school *En*
collège (m) (classique/moderne/technique) *Fr*
höhere Schule (f) *De*

seconded (to be seconded) *En*
hors cadre (être mis hors cadre) *Fr*
vorübergehend versetzt sein *De*

secondment *En*
détachement (m) *Fr*
vorübergehende Versetzung (f) *De*

secret ballot *En*
scrutin (m) secret *Fr*
geheime Wahl (f) *De*

secret et confidentiel (adj) *Fr*
streng vertraulich (adj) *De*
private and confidential (adj) *En*

secret (m) de fabrique *Fr*
Geschäftsgeheimnis (nt) *De*
trade secret *En*

secrétaire; de —. (adj) *Fr*
Sekretariats- *De*
secretarial (adj) *En*

secrétaire -général(m) (commune)/secrétaire-communal (m) (Belg.) *Fr* *
Hauptverwaltungsbeamte(-r)/-in(m/f); Stadtdirektor/-n (m/f) *De*
chief executive (city/borough/town) *En*

secrétaire (m/f)/agent (m) administratif (public sector) *Fr*
Sekretär/-in (m/f) *De*
secretary *En*

secrétaire (m/f) de la municipalité *Fr* *
Stadtdirektor (m) *De*
town clerk *En*

secrétaire (m/f) de séance *Fr*
Ausschußsekretär/-in (m/f) *De*
committee clerk *En*

secrétaire (m/f) du scrutin *Fr*
Angestellte(-r) (m/f) eines Wahlvorstands *De*
poll clerk *En*

secrétaire-général (m) *Fr* *
(Gemeinde)schriftführer (m) *De*
clerk to the council *En*

secretarial (adj) *En*
de secrétaire (adj) *Fr*
Sekretariats- *De*

secretariat *En*
secrétariat (m) *Fr*
Sekretariat (nt) *De*

secrétariat (m) *Fr*
Sekretariat (nt) *De*
secretariat *En*

secretary *En*
secrétaire (m/f)/agent (m) administratif (public sector) *Fr*
Sekretär/-in (m/f) *De*

Secretary of State *En*
ministre (m) *Fr*
Minister/-in (m/f) *De*

secte (f) religieuse *Fr*
religiöse Gruppe (f) *De*
religious group *En*

secteur (m) de croissance *Fr*
Entwicklungsgebiet (nt) *De*
growth area *En*

secteur (m) de recensement *Fr*
Zählungsbezirk (m) *De*
enumeration district *En*

secteur (m) économique *Fr*
Wirtschaftsgebiet (nt) *De*
economic area *En*

secteur (m) non-gouvernemental *Fr*
freiwilliger Sektor (m) *De*
voluntary sector *En*

*** see/siehe/voir: Introduction page IX**

secteur (m) postal *Fr*
Post-, Zustellbezirk (m) *De*
postal district *En*

secteur (m) privé *Fr*
Privatwirtschaft (f), privater Sektor (m) *De*
private sector *En*

secteur (m) public *Fr*
öffentlicher Sektor (m) *De*
public sector *En*

secteur (m)/réseau (m) de ramassage (des écoliers) *Fr*
Einzugsgebiet (nt) *De*
catchment area *En*

secteur (m) tertiaire *Fr*
Dienstleistungssektor (m) *De*
service sector *En*

secteur (m) urbain *Fr*
Stadtbezirk (m) *De*
urban area *En*

section *En*
section (f) *Fr*
Abteilung (f) *De*

section (f) *Fr*
Abteilung (f) *De*
section *En*

section (f) d'investissement dans le budget *Fr*
Kapitalkontrolle (f) *De*
capital accounting/budget *En*

section head *En*
chef (m) de section *Fr*
Abteilungsleiter/-in (m/f) *De*

sectorisation (f) *Fr*
bezirksgebundene/stadtteilgebundene Einteilung (f) *De*
zoning (school catchment areas) *En*

secure accommodation *En*
asile (m) assuré *Fr*
sichere Unterrkunft (f) *De*

sécurité (f) au travail *Fr*
Arbeitsschutz (m) *De*
occupational safety *En*

securité (f) contre l'incendie *Fr*
Feuersicherheit (f) *De*
fire safety *En*

sécurité (f) de l'emploi *Fr*
Arbeitsschutz (m) *De*
employment protection *En*

sécurité (f) de l'emploi *Fr*
Kündigungsschutz (m) *De*
security of tenure *En*

sécurite (f) électrique *Fr*
Sicherheit (f) der Stromversorgung *De*
electrical safety *En*

sécurité (f) industrielle *Fr*
Betriebssicherheit (f) *De*
industrial safety *En*

sécurité (f) nucléaire *Fr*
nukleare Sicherheit (f) *De*
nuclear safety *En*

sécurité (f) sociale *Fr*
Sozialhilfe (f); soziales Wohl (nt) *De*
social security/welfare *En*

securities *En*
titres (m.pl) *Fr*
Wertpapiere (nt.pl) *De*

security for a debt *En*
garantie (f) d'une échéance *Fr*
Sicherheit (f) *De*

security guard *En*
gardien (m) *Fr*
Wächter (m) *De*

security lighting *En*
éclairage (m) de sécurité *Fr*
Sicherheitsbeleuchtung (f) *De*

security of tenure *En*
sécurité (f) de l'emploi *Fr*
Kündigungsschutz (m) *De*

seelische Gesundheit (f) *De*
mental health *En*
santé (f) mentale *Fr*

sehbehindert (adj) *De*
partially sighted (adj) *En*
malvoyant (-ante f.) (adj) *Fr*

sehbehindert (adj) *De*
visually handicapped (adj) *En*
malvoyant (adj) *Fr*

Sehbehinderung (f) *De*
visual handicap *En*
diminution (f) visuelle *Fr*

sehr knapper Zeitplan (m) *De*
tight schedule *En*
horaire (m) minute *Fr*

Sekretär/-in (m/f) *De*
secretary *En*
secrétaire (m/f)/agent (m) administratif (public sector) *Fr*

Sekretariat (nt) *De*
secretariat *En*
secrétariat (m) *Fr*

Sekretariats- *De*
secretarial (adj) *En*
de secrétaire (adj) *Fr*

Selbständige(-r) (m/f) *De*
self-employed person *En*
travailleur (m) indépendant *Fr*

Selbstbeurteilung (f) *De*
self appraisal *En*
autocritique (f) *Fr*

self appraisal *En*
autocritique (f) *Fr*
Selbstbeurteilung (f) *De*

self-employed person *En*
travailleur (m) indépendant *Fr*
Selbständige(-r) (m/f) *De*

semaine (f) de travail *Fr*
Arbeitswoche (f) *De*
working week *En*

semi skilled *En*
semi-qualifié (-ée f.) *Fr*
angelernt (adj) *De*

semi-detached house *En*
maison (f) jumelle *Fr*
Doppelhaushälfte (f) *De*

semi-qualifié (-ée f.) *Fr*
angelernt (adj) *De*
semi skilled *En*

semi-remorque (f) (pl. semi-remorques) *Fr*
Gelenkfahrzeug (nt) *De*
articulated vehicle *En*

Senior/-in (m/f) *De*
senior citizen *En*
personne (f) âgée *Fr*

senior citizen *En*
personne (f) âgée *Fr*
Senior/-in (m/f) *De*

senior management *En*
encadrement (m) supérieur *Fr*
Geschäftsleitung (f) *De*

senior officer *En*
cadre (m) supérieur *Fr*
höherer Beamter/höhere Beamtin (m/f) *De*

Senkung (f) *De*
subsidence *En*
abaissement (m) (du terrain) *Fr*

*** see/siehe/voir: Introduction page IX**

sensible (adj) *Fr*
aufgeschloßen (adj) *De*
responsive (adj) *En*

sensitive issue *En*
question (f) délicate *Fr*
heikles Thema (nt) *De*

sentence (vb) *En*
prononcer (vb) une condamnation (contre quelqu'un) *Fr*
verurteilen (vb) *De*

sentier (m) pour cavaliers *Fr*
Reitweg (m) *De*
bridle Path/bridleway *En*

service (m) *Fr*
Abteilung (f) *De*
department *En*

service delivery/provision *En*
assurance (f) d'un service *Fr*
Dienstleistungen (f.pl) *De*

service (level) agreement *En*
contrat (m) de service *Fr*
Dienstleistungsvertrag (m) *De*

service level *En*
niveau (m) de service *Fr*
Dienstleistungsniveau (nt) *De*

service (m) administratif régional *Fr*
Gemeindeamt (nt) *De*
regional authority *En*

service (m) central *Fr*
Hauptbetrieb (m) *De*
central service *En*

service (m) conseil *Fr*
Beratungsdienst (m) *De*
counselling service *En*

service (m) conseil *Fr*
Beratungsstelle (f) *De*
advice centre *En*

service (m) consultatif *Fr*
Beratungsdienst (m) *De*
advisory service *En*

service (m) d'architecture *Fr*
Bauaufsichtsamt (nt) *De*
architect's department *En*

service (m) d'assainissement *Fr*
Reinigungsdienst (m) *De*
cleansing service *En*

service (m) d'autorisation et droit des sols *Fr*
Bauaufsicht (f) *De*
planning control *En*

service (m) d'orientation professionnelle *Fr*
Berufsbeamtentum (nt) *De*
careers service *En*

service (m) d'urbanisme *Fr*
Bauabteilung (f) *De*
planning department *En*

service (m) de courant *Fr*
Elektrizitätsversorgung (f) *De*
electrical supply *En*

service (m) de gaz *Fr*
Gasversorgung (f) *De*
gas supply *En*

service (m) (de l') informatique *Fr*
Auskunftsdienst (m) *De*
information service *En*

service (m) de l'éducation *Fr**
Erziehungs- und Ausbildungsbehörde (f)/ Schulbehörde (f), -amt (nt) *De*
education authority/ department/service *En*

service (m) de la clientèle *Fr*
Kundendienst (m) *De*
customer service *En*

service (m) de la culture et des loisirs *Fr*
Management (nt) für Freizeitgestaltung *De*
recreation management *En*

service (m) de la culture/des sports *Fr*
Freizeitamt (nt) *De*
leisure department *En*

service (m) de la jeunesse *Fr*
Jugendarbeit (f) *De*
youth service *En*

service (m) de la voirie *Fr*
Straßenbauamt (nt) *De*
highway authority/department *En*

service (m) de santé communautaire *Fr*
Bezirksgesundheitsamt (nt) *De*
community health service *En*

service (m) de santé *Fr*
Bezirksgesundheitspflege (f) *De*
community health care /medecine *En*

service (m) de secours *Fr*
Not-, Hilfsdienst (m) *De*
emergency service *En*

service (m) de soins intensifs *Fr*
Intensivkrankenpflege (f) *De*
acute health care *En*

service (m) de tourisme *Fr*
Fremdenverkehrsamt (nt) *De*
tourist board *En*

service (m) des consultations externes *Fr*
Poliklinik (f) *De*
outpatients' department *En*

service (m) des eaux *Fr*
Wasserversorgung (f) *De*
water supply *En*

service (m) des eaux *Fr*
Wasserversorgungsamt (nt) *De*
water authority *En*

service (m) des hôpitaux *Fr*
Krankenhausdienst (m) *De*
hospital service *En*

service (m) des soins *Fr*
Fürsorge (f) *De*
caring services *En*

service (m) du cotentieux *Fr*
Rechtsberatung (f) *De*
legal service *En*

service (m) du logement *Fr*
Wohnungsamt (nt) *De*
housing authority/department *En*

service (m) du personnel *Fr*
Personalabteilung (f) *De*
personnel department *En*

service (m) exploité en régie directe *Fr*
Dienstleistungsbetrieb (m) *De*
direct service organization *En*

service (m) exploité en régie directe *Fr*
Regiebetrieb (m) *De*
direct labour organization *En*

service (m) financier *Fr*
Finanzabteilung (f) *De*
finance department *En*

service (m) gouvernemental *Fr*
Regierungsamt (nt) *De*
government agency *En*

service (m) informatique *Fr*
Computerdienst (m) *De*
computer service *En*

*** see/siehe/voir: Introduction page IX**

service (m) municipal/régional de l'enseignement *Fr* *
Schulamt (nt) *De*
local education authority *En*

service (m) régional de la santé *Fr*
regionale Gesundheitsbehörde (f) *De*
regional health authority *En*

service (m) volontaire *Fr*
freiwilliger Dienst (m) *De*
voluntary service *En*

service sector *En*
secteur (m) tertiaire *Fr*
Dienstleistungssektor (m) *De*

services (m.pl) d'hygiène *Fr* *
Gesundheitsbehörde (f), -dienst (m) *De*
health authority/service *En*

services (m.pl) de l'environnement *Fr*
Umweltschutzorganisation (f) *De*
environmental services *En*

services (m.pl) financiers *Fr*
Finanzverwaltung (f) *De*
financial services *En*

services (m.pl) médicaux *Fr*
Gesundheitsdienst (m) *De*
medical service *En*

services (m.pl) postaux *Fr*
Postdienst (m) *De*
postal service *En*

services (m.pl) publics *Fr*
gesetzliche Dienstleistungen (f.pl) *De*
statutory services *En*

services (m.pl) publics *Fr*
öffentliche Versorgungsbetriebe (m.pl) *De*
public utilities *En*

services (m.pl) publics *Fr*
(öffentliche) Versorgungsbetriebe (m.pl) *De*
utilities *En*

services (m.pl) sociaux *Fr*
Sozialverwaltung (f) *De*
social administration *En*

services (m.pl) techniques *Fr*
technischer Dienst (m) *De*
technical services *En*

seuil (m) d'imposition *Fr*
Steuergrenze (f) *De*
tax threshold *En*

severance pay *En*
compensation (f) pour perte d'emploi *Fr*
Abfindung (f) *De*

sewage *En*
effluent (m) *Fr*
Abwasser (nt) *De*

sewage treatment *En*
épuration (f) des eaux usées *Fr*
Abwasserklärung (f) *De*

sewage works *En*
station (f) d'épuration *Fr*
Kläranlage (f) *De*

sewer *En*
égout (m) *Fr*
Abwasserkanal (m) *De*

sex discrimination *En*
discrimination (f) sexuelle *Fr*
sexuelle Diskriminierung (f) *De*

sex equality *En*
égalite (f) sexuelle *Fr*
Gleichheit (f) von Mann und Frau *De*

sexual harrassment *En*
harcèlement (m) sexuel *Fr*
sexuelle Belästigung (f) *De*

sexuelle Belästigung (f) *De*
sexual harrassment *En*
harcèlement (m) sexuel *Fr*

sexuelle Diskriminierung (f) *De*
sex discrimination *En*
discrimination (f) sexuelle *Fr*

share *En*
action (f) *Fr*
Aktie (f) *De*

shareholder *En*
actionnaire (m/f) *Fr*
Aktionär/-in (m/f) *De*

shareholding *En*
possession (f) d'actions *Fr*
Aktienbesitz (m) *De*

sheltered accommodation *En*
logement (m) pour personnes handicapées *Fr*
Wohnungen (f.pl) für Behinderte/Senioren *De*

sheltered employment *En*
emplois (m.pl) réservés *Fr*
Beschäftigung (f) in beschützenden Werkstätten *De*

sheltered workshop *En*
atelier (m) pour les handicapés *Fr*
beschützende Werkstätte (f) *De*

shift work *En*
travail (m) par équipes *Fr*
Schichtarbeit (f) *De*

shipbuilding *En*
construction (f) navale *Fr*
Schiffbau (m) *De*

shipping *En*
marine (f) maritime *Fr*
Schiffsverkehr (m) *De*

shipyard *En*
chantier (m) naval (pl. chantiers navals) *Fr*
Werft (f) *De*

shop *En*
magasin (m) *Fr*
Laden (m), Geschäft (nt) *De*

shop rent *En*
bail (m) commercial (pl. baux commerciaux) *Fr*
Ladenmiete (f) *De*

shop steward *En*
délégué (m) syndical *Fr*
Vertrauensmann (m) *De*

shopkeeper *En*
commerçant (m) (-ante f.) *Fr*
Ladenbesitzer/-in (m/f) *De*

shoplifting *En*
vol (m) à l'étalage *Fr*
Ladendiebstahl (m) *De*

shopper *En*
acheteur (m) (-euse f.) *Fr*
Käufer/-in (m/f) *De*

shopping arcade *En*
galerie (f) marchande *Fr*
Einkaufspassage (f) *De*

shopping area/centre/mall *En*
centre (m) commercial *Fr*
Einkaufszentrum (nt) *De*

shopping street *En*
rue (f) commerçante *Fr*
Geschäftsstraße (f) *De*

shopworker *En*
vendeur (m) (-euse f.) *Fr*
Verkäufer/-in (m/f) *De*

* see/siehe/voir: Introduction page IX

short hold tenancy *En*
location (f) temporaire *Fr*
kurzzeitiges Mietverhältnis (nt) *De*

short term (adj) *En*
à court terme (adj) *Fr*
kurzfristig (adj) *De*

short time working *En*
chômage (m) partiel *Fr*
Kurzarbeit (f) *De*

shorthand *En*
sténographie (f) *Fr*
Kurzschrift (f) *De*

shuttering *En*
coffrage (m) (du béton) *Fr*
Schalung (f) *De*

sich beraten, konsultieren (vb) *De*
consult (vb) *En*
consulter (vb) *Fr*

sich der Stimme enthalten (vb) *De*
abstain (vb) *En*
s'abstenir (vb) *Fr*

sichere Unterrkunft (f) *De*
secure accommodation *En*
asile (m) assuré *Fr*

Sicherheit (f) *De*
security for a debt *En*
garantie (f) d'une échéance *Fr*

Sicherheit (f) der Stromversorgung *De*
electrical safety *En*
sécurite (f) électrique *Fr*

Sicherheitsausrüstung (f) *De*
safety equipment *En*
matériel (m) de sécurité *Fr*

Sicherheitsbeleuchtung (f) *De*
security lighting *En*
éclairage (m) de sécurité *Fr*

sick leave *En*
congé (m) de maladie *Fr*
Krankenurlaub (m) *De*

sick pay; sickness benefit *En*
allocation/indeminité (f) de maladie *Fr*
Krankengeld (nt) *De*

Siedlung (f) *De*
estate (housing) *En*
lotissement (m) *Fr*

siège (m) *Fr*
Zentrale (f) *De*
head office *En*

sigle (m) *Fr*
Akronym (nt) *De*
Acronym *En*

signal (m) routier *Fr*
Straßenschild (nt), Verkehrszeichen (nt) *De*
road sign *En*

signalisation (f) routière *Fr*
Straßenbeschilderung (f) *De*
road signing *En*

signification (f) d'un acte *Fr*
Zustellung (f) einer Verfügung *De*
delivery of a writ *En*

signpost *En*
poteau (m) indicateur *Fr*
Wegweiser (m) *De*

silicon chip *En*
puce (f) informatique *Fr*
Siliziumchip (m) *De*

Siliziumchip (m) *De*
silicon chip *En*
puce (f) informatique *Fr*

simple citoyen (m) (-enne f.) *Fr*
Privatperson (f) *De*
private citizen *En*

simplified planning zone *En*
zone (f) d'aménagement concerté (ZAC) *Fr*
Bebauungsplangebiet (nt) *De*

Single European Market *En*
marché (m) européen unique *Fr*
europäischer Binnenmarkt (m) *De*

single person housing *En*
logement (m) pour célibataires *Fr*
Einzelunterkunft (f) *De*

single storey building *En*
bâtiment (m) sans étage *Fr*
eingeschoßiges Gebäude (nt) *De*

sinking fund *En*
fonds (m) d'amortissement *Fr*
Tilgungsfonds (m) *De*

sirène (f) d'incendie *Fr*
Feuermelder (m) *De*
fire alarm *En*

site development *En*
construction (f) du terrain *Fr*
Geländeerschließung (f) *De*

site inspection *En*
reconnaissance (f) du terrain *Fr*
Bauinspektion (f) *De*

site investigation *En*
études (f) préalables à l'opération de construction *Fr*
Geländekontrolle (f) *De*

Site of Special Scientific Interest (SSI) *En*
espace (m) naturel sensible *Fr*
wissenschaftliche Sehenswürdigkeit (f) *De*

site works *En*
travaux (m.pl) préparatoires sur un terrain *Fr*
Geländearbeiten (f.pl) *De*

sitting (of committee) *En*
séance (f) (d'un comité etc) *Fr*
Sitzung (f) *De*

sitting tenant *En*
occupant (m) (-ante f.) *Fr*
Mieter/-in (m/f) *De*

Sitzung (f) *De*
sitting (of committee) *En*
séance (f) (d'un comité etc) *Fr*

Sitzungssaal (m) des Rats *De*
council chamber *En*
salle (f) du conseil *Fr*

Sitzungsturnus (m) *De*
committee cycle *En*
période (f) de session *Fr*

sixth form college *En*
lycée (m) *Fr*
Oberstufenzentrum (nt) *De*

sixth form *En*
classes (f.pl) terminales *Fr*
Abschlußklasse (f) *De*

skill centre *En*
centre (m) de formation *Fr*
Fachzentrum (nt) *De*

skill shortage *En*
manque (m) de personnel qualifié *Fr*
Fachpersonalmangel (m) *De*

skilled labour *En*
main-d'oeuvre (f) spécialisée *Fr*
Facharbeit (f) *De*

skilled worker *En*
ouvrier (m) (-ière f.) qualifié(e) *Fr*
Facharbeiter (m); Fachkraft (f) *De*

sky-scraper *En*
gratte-ciel (m) (pl. grattes-ciel) *Fr*
Wolkenkratzer (m) *De*

sleep (vb) rough *En*
coucher (vb) sur la dure *Fr*
(im Freien) schlafen (vb) *De*

sleeping policeman *En*
ralentisseur (m); "gendarme (m) couché" *Fr*
Bodenschwelle (f) *De*

sliding scale *En*
échelle (f) mobile *Fr*
gleitende Skala (f) *De*

slum *En*
taudis (m) *Fr*
Slum (m) *De*

Slum (m) *De*
slum *En*
taudis (m) *Fr*

slum clearance *En*
suppression (f) des taudis *Fr*
Slumsanierung (f) *De*

slump *En*
crise (f) économique *Fr*
Depression (f) *De*

Slumsanierung (f) *De*
slum clearance *En*
suppression (f) des taudis *Fr*

small enterprise/firm *En*
petite entreprise (f) *Fr*
Kleinbetrieb (m) *De*

Small & Medium-Sized Enterprises (SMEs) *En*
petites et moyennes entreprises (PMEs)(f.pl) *Fr*
Klein- und Mittelbetriebe (m.pl) *De*

social administration *En*
services (m.pl) sociaux *Fr*
Sozialverwaltung (f) *De*

social benefits *En*
prestations (f.pl) sociales *Fr*
Sozialhilfe (f) *De*

social democracy *En*
sociale-démocratie (f) *Fr*
Sozialdemokratie (f) *De*

social disadvantage *En*
désavantage (m) social *Fr*
gesellschaftliche Benachteiligung (f) *De*

Social Fund *En*
fonds (m) social *Fr*
Sozialfonds (m) *De*

social integration *En*
intégration (f) sociale *Fr*
soziale Integration (f) *De*

social minority *En*
minorité (f) sociale *Fr*
gesellschaftliche Minderheit (f) *De*

social policy *En*
politique (f) sociale *Fr*
Sozialpolitik (f) *De*

social problem *En*
problème (m) social *Fr*
soziales Problem (nt) *De*

social security/welfare *En*
sécurité (f) sociale *Fr*
Sozialhilfe (f); soziales Wohl (nt) *De*

social services department *En*
direction (f) des affaires sociales *Fr*
Sozialamt (nt) *De*

social structure *En*
édifice (m) social *Fr*
Sozialstruktur (f) *De*

social survey *En*
enquête (f) sociale *Fr*
Sozialerhebung (f) *De*

social work *En*
oeuvres (f.pl) sociales *Fr*
Sozialarbeit (f) *De*

social worker *En*
assistant (m) (-ante f.) social(e) *Fr*
Sozialarbeiter/-in (m/f) *De*

sociale-démocratie (f) *Fr*
Sozialdemokratie (f) *De*
social democracy *En*

socialism *En*
socialisme (m) *Fr*
Sozialismus (m) *De*

socialisme (m) *Fr*
Sozialismus (m) *De*
socialism *En*

socialist *En*
socialiste (m/f) *Fr*
Sozialist/-in (m/f) *De*

socialiste (m/f) *Fr*
Sozialist/-in (m/f) *De*
socialist *En*

socially deprived (adj) *En*
désavantagé (adj) *Fr*
gesellschaftlich/sozial benachteiligt (adj) *De*

société (f) *Fr*
Gesellschaft (f) *De*
company *En*

société (f) à responsabilité limitée (SARL) *Fr*
Gesellschaft (f) mit beschränkter Haftung (GmbH) *De*
limited company (Co.Ltd) *En*

Société (f) anonyme (SA) *Fr*
Aktiengesellschaft (AG) (f) *De*
public limited company (plc) *En*

société (f) coopérative de logement *Fr*
Wohnkollektiv (nt) *De*
housing co-operative *En*

société (f) d'assurance(s) *Fr*
Versicherungsgesellschaft (f) *De*
insurance company *En*

société (f) d'économie mixte *Fr*
Kommunalunternehmen (nt) *De*
community enterprise *En*

société (f) d'exploitation *Fr*
Immobiliengesellschaft (f), Bauunternehmer (m) *De*
property company/developer *En*

société (f) d'exploitation *Fr*
Wohnungsbaugesellschaft (f) *De*
development company *En*

société (f) de financement *Fr*
Finanzierungsgesellschaft (f) *De*
finance company *En*

société (f) immobilière *Fr*
Bausparkasse (f) *De*
building society *En*

société (f) multinationale *Fr*
multinationaler Konzern (m) *De*
multinational company *En*

socio-economic group *En*
groupe (m) socio-économique *Fr*
sozioökonomische Gruppe (f) *De*

sociological (adj) *En*
sociologique (adj) *Fr*
soziologisch (adj) *De*

sociologie (f) *Fr*
Soziologie (f) *De*
sociology *En*

sociologique (adj) *Fr*
soziologisch (adj) *De*
sociological (adj) *En*

*** see/siehe/voir: Introduction page IX**

sociologist *En*
sociologue (m/f) *Fr*
Soziologe/-gin (m/f) *De*

sociologue (m/f) *Fr*
Soziologe/-gin (m/f) *De*
sociologist *En*

sociology *En*
sociologie (f) *Fr*
Soziologie (f) *De*

software *En*
logiciel (m) *Fr*
Software (f) *De*

Software (f) *De*
computer software *En*
logiciel (m) *Fr*

Software (f) *De*
software *En*
logiciel (m) *Fr*

software engineer *En*
ingénieur (m) système *Fr*
Softwaretechniker/-in (m/f) *De*

software package *En*
progiciel (m) *Fr*
Softwarepaket (nt) *De*

Softwarepaket (nt) *De*
software package *En*
progiciel (m) *Fr*

Softwaretechniker/-in (m/f) *De*
software engineer *En*
ingénieur (m) système *Fr*

soil pipe *En*
conduit (m) d'effluent *Fr*
Abflußrohr (nt) *De*

soil testing *En*
analyse (f) des sols *Fr*
Bodenanalyse (f) *De*

soin (m) des enfants *Fr*
Kinderfürsorge (f) *De*
child care *En*

soins (m.pl) à domicile *Fr*
stationäre Pflege (f) *De*
residential care *En*

soins (m.pl) de maternité *Fr*
Wochenpflege (f) *De*
maternity care *En*

soins (m.pl) dentaires *Fr*
Zahnpflege (f) *De*
dental care *En*

soins (m.pl) des malades *Fr*
Krankenpflege (f) *De*
nursing *En*

soins (m.pl) des malades *Fr*
Krankenpflege (f) *De*
patient care *En*

soins (m.pl) des personnes âgées *Fr*
Altenpflege (f) *De*
care of the aged *En*

soins (m.pl) du client *Fr*
Kundenbetreuung (f) *De*
customer care *En*

soins (m.pl) médicaux *Fr*
Gesundheitsfürsorge (f) *De*
health care *En*

soins (m.pl) primaires de la santé *Fr*
Primärversorgung (f) *De*
primary health care *En*

soins (m.pl) primaires *Fr*
primäre Pflege (f) *De*
primary care *En*

soins (m.pl) psychiatriques *Fr*
Geisteskrankenpflege (f) *De*
mental health care *En*

soins (m.pl) psychiatriques *Fr*
psychiatrische Behandlung (f) *De*
psychiatric care *En*

soins (m.pl) terminaux *Fr*
Pflege (f) für unheilbar Kranke *De*
terminal care *En*

solar heating *En*
chauffage (m) solaire *Fr*
Sonnenheizung (f) *De*

solde (m) en banque *Fr*
Bankguthaben (nt) *De*
bank balance *En*

solicitor *En*
notaire (m) *Fr*
Rechtsanwalt/-anwältin (m/f) *De*

solid waste *En*
déchets (m.pl) solides *Fr*
feste Abfälle (m.pl) *De*

solid waste management *En*
gestion (f) des déchets solides *Fr*
Feststoffentsorgungsbetrieb (m) *De*

solid waste transfer station *En*
usine (f) d'incinération des déchets *Fr*
Feststoffentsorgungsanlage (f) *De*

solliciter (vb) (la voix etc) *Fr*
werben (vb) *De*
canvass (vb) (vote etc) *En*

solvent abuse *En*
abus (m) de dissolvants *Fr*
Lösungsmittelmißbrauch (m) *De*

sondage (m) d'opinion publique *Fr*
Meinungsumfrage (f) *De*
opinion poll/survey *En*

Sonderkommando (nt) *De*
task force *En*
force (f) tactique *Fr*

Sonderlernanspruch (m) *De*
special educational need *En*
besoin (m) en éducation spécialisée *Fr*

Sondermüll (m) *De*
dangerous waste *En*
déchets (m.pl) dangereux *Fr*

Sondermüll (m) *De*
hazardous waste *En*
déchets (m.pl) dangereux *Fr*

Sonderrücklage (f) *De*
contingency reserve *En*
provision (f) *Fr*

Sonderschule (f) *De*
special school *En*
établissement (m) spécialisé *Fr*

Sondersubvention (m) *De*
specific grant *En*
subvention (f) de l'Etat *Fr*

Sonnenheizung (f) *De*
solar heating *En*
chauffage (m) solaire *Fr*

sonnette (f) *Fr*
Ramme (f) *De*
pile driver *En*

sortie (f) sur imprimante *Fr*
Computerausdruck (m) *De*
computer printout *En*

soumission (f) compétitive *Fr*
konkurrenzfähiges Angebot (nt) *De*
competitive tender *En*

soumissionner (vb) à une adjudication *Fr*
ein Angebot für einen Vertrag einreichen (vb) *De*
tender (vb) for a contract *En*

sound insulation; soundproofing *En*
isolation (f) acoustique *Fr*
Schallisolierung (f) *De*

source document *En*
document (m) de base *Fr*
Quellenmaterial (nt) *De*

sources (f.pl) d'énergie *Fr*
Energieversorgung (f) *De*
power supply *En*

sous toutes réserves *Fr*
ohne Verbindlichkeit (f) *De*
without prejudice *En*

sous-comité (m) *Fr*
Unterausschuß (m) *De*
sub-committee *En*

sous-location (f) *Fr*
Untervermietung (f) *De*
sub-letting *En*

sous-louer (vb) *Fr*
untervermieten (vb) *De*
sub-let (vb) *En*

sous-sol (m) *Fr*
Untergrund (m) *De*
subsoil *En*

sous-traité (m) *Fr*
Untervertrag (m) *De*
sub-contract (noun) *En*

sous-traiter (vb) *Fr*
(an) Subunternehmer vergeben (vb) *De*
sub-contract (vb) *En*

sousfinancement (m) *Fr*
Unterfinanzierung (f) *De*
underfunding *En*

soutien (m) *Fr*
Unterhalt (m) *De*
support *En*

soutien (m) des victimes du crime *Fr*
Opferhilfe (f) *De*
victim support *En*

Sozialamt (nt) *De*
social services department *En*
direction (f) des affaires sociales *Fr*

Sozialarbeit (f) *De*
casework *En*
assistance (f) individuelle *Fr*

Sozialarbeit (f) *De*
community work *En*
oeuvres (f.pl) sociales *Fr*

Sozialarbeit (f) *De*
social work *En*
oeuvres (f.pl) sociales *Fr*

Sozialarbeit (f) *De*
welfare work *En*
assistance (f) sociale *Fr*

Sozialarbeiter/-in (m/f) *De*
social worker *En*
assistant (m) (-ante f.) social(-e) *Fr*

Sozialarbeiter/-in (m/f) *De*
welfare worker *En*
assistant (m) (-ante f.) social(-e) *Fr*

Sozialberufler/-in (m/f) *De*
community worker *En*
assistant (m) (-ante f.) social(-e) *Fr*

Sozialdemokratie (f) *De*
social democracy *En*
sociale-démocratie (f) *Fr*

Sozialdienst (m) *De*
community service *En*
Travaux (m.pl) d'Intérêt Général (TIG) *Fr*

soziale Integration (f) *De*
social integration *En*
intégration (f) sociale *Fr*

Sozialerhebung (f) *De*
social survey *En*
enquête (f) sociale *Fr*

soziales Problem (nt) *De*
social problem *En*
problème (m) social *Fr*

Sozialfonds (m) *De*
Social Fund *En*
fonds (m) social *Fr*

Sozialhilfe (f) *De*
benefit *En*
indemnité (f) *Fr*

Sozialhilfe (f) *De*
social benefits *En*
prestations (f.pl) sociales *Fr*

Sozialhilfe (f); soziales Wohl (nt) *De*
social security/welfare *En*
sécurité (f) sociale *Fr*

Sozialismus (m) *De*
socialism *En*
socialisme (m) *Fr*

Sozialist/-in (m/f) *De*
socialist *En*
socialiste (m/f) *Fr*

Sozialpolitik (f) *De*
social policy *En*
politique (f) sociale *Fr*

Sozialstruktur (f) *De*
social structure *En*
édifice (m) social *Fr*

Sozialversicherung (f) *De*
national insurance *En*
assurances (f.pl) sociales *Fr*

Sozialverwaltung (f) *De*
social administration *En*
services (m.pl) sociaux *Fr*

Sozialwohnung (f) *De*
council dwelling/flat/house *En*
habitation (f) à loyer modéré (H.L.M.) *Fr*

Sozialwohnungen (f.pl) *De*
local authority housing *En*
habitation (f) à loyer modéré (H.L.M.) *Fr*

Sozialwohnungen (f.pl) *De*
public sector housing *En*
logement (m) public *Fr*

Soziologe/-gin (m/f) *De*
sociologist *En*
sociologue (m/f) *Fr*

Soziologie (f) *De*
sociology *En*
sociologie (f) *Fr*

soziologisch (adj) *De*
sociological (adj) *En*
sociologique (adj) *Fr*

sozioökonomische Gruppe (f) *De*
socio-economic group *En*
groupe (m) socio-économique *Fr*

Spannbeton (m) *De*
prestressed concrete *En*
béton (m) précontraint *Fr*

Sparkasse (f) *De*
savings bank *En*
caisse (f) d'épargne *Fr*

special development area *En*
zone (f) d'aménagement concerté (ZAC) *Fr*
Prioritätserschließungsgebiet (nt) *De*

special education *En*
éducation (f) spécialisée *Fr*
Ausbildung (f) für Behinderte u. Schwererziehbare *De*

*** see/siehe/voir: Introduction page IX**

special educational need *En*
besoin (m) en éducation spécialisée *Fr*
Sonderlernanspruch (m) *De*

special school *En*
établissement (m) spécialisé *Fr*
Sonderschule (f) *De*

specific grant *En*
subvention (f) de l'Etat *Fr*
Sondersubvention (m) *De*

specification *En*
descriptif (m) *Fr*
Angaben (f.pl); Beschreibung (f) *De*

speculate (vb) *En*
spéculer (vb) *Fr*
spekulieren (vb) *De*

spéculer (vb) *Fr*
spekulieren (vb) *De*
speculate (vb) *En*

Spedition (f) *De*
road haulage *En*
transports (m.pl) routiers *Fr*

speech (to make a) *En*
discours (m) (faire/prononcer un- *Fr*
eine Rede halten *De*

speed limit *En*
limite (f) de vitesse autorisée *Fr*
Geschwindigkeitsbeschränkung (f) *De*

spekulieren (vb) *De*
speculate (vb) *En*
spéculer (vb) *Fr*

spend (vb) *En*
dépenser (vb) *Fr*
ausgeben (vb) *De*

Spendenaktion (f) *De*
fund raising scheme *En*
projet (m) pour se procurer des fonds *Fr*

spending *En*
dépense(s) (f) *Fr*
Ausgaben (f.pl) *De*

Spesen (pl) *De*
expenses *En*
frais (m.pl) *Fr*

speziell gebaut; Zweck- *De*
purpose-built (adj) *En*
construit en vue d'un usage déterminé (adj) *Fr*

Spielmöglichkeiten (f.pl) *De*
play facilities *En*
équipement (m) de récréation *Fr*

Spielplatz (m) *De*
play area/ground *En*
cour (f) de récréation *Fr*

spokesman/spokesperson *En*
porte-parole (m/f) *Fr*
Sprecher/-in (m/f) *De*

Sponsorschaft (f) *De*
sponsorship *En*
subvention (f) *Fr*

sponsorship *En*
subvention (f) *Fr*
Sponsorschaft (f) *De*

Sportanlagen (f.pl) *De*
sports facilities *En*
installations (f.pl) sportives *Fr*

Sporthalle (f) *De*
indoor sports centre *En*
salle (f) des sports *Fr*

Sportplatz (m) *De*
playing field *En*
terrain (m) de jeux/sports *Fr*

Sportplatzunterhaltung (f) *De*
grounds maintenance *En*
entretien (m) des terrains de jeu *Fr*

sports centre *En*
complex (m) sportif *Fr*
Sportzentrum (nt) *De*

sports facilities *En*
installations (f.pl) sportives *Fr*
Sportanlagen (f.pl) *De*

Sportzentrum (nt) *De*
sports centre *En*
complex (m) sportif *Fr*

Sprachminderheit (f) *De*
linguistic minority *En*
minorité (f) linguistique *Fr*

spreadsheet *En*
tableur (m) *Fr*
Arbeitsblatt (nt), Tabellenkalkulation (f) *De*

Sprecher/-in (m/f) *De*
spokesman/spokesperson *En*
porte-parole (m/f) *Fr*

squat (vb) *En*
s'établir (vb) comme squatter dans une maison inoccupée (sans titre) *Fr*
ein Haus besetzen (vb) *De*

squatter *En*
squatter (m) *Fr*
Hausbesetzer/-in (m/f) *De*

squatter (m) *Fr*
Hausbesetzer/-in (m/f) *De*
squatter *En*

squatting *En*
occupation (f) d'une maison etc en qualité de squatter *Fr*
Hausbesetzung (f) *De*

staatliche Berufsausbildung (f) (in GB) *De* *
National Vocational Qualification (GB) *En*
qualification (f) nationale professionnelle (en GB) *Fr*

staatliche Geldleistung (f) für Gehbehinderte *De*
mobility allowance *En*
indemnité (f) de déplacement *Fr*

staatliche Rente/Pension (f) *De*
state pension *En*
pension (f) de retraite *Fr*

staatliche Schule (f) *De*
école (f) laïque *Fr*
maintained school *En*

staatliche Versicherung (f) *De*
national insurance *En*
assurance (f) d'état *Fr*

staatlicher Lehrplan (m) *De* *
national curriculum *En*
programme (m) d'études national *Fr*

staatliches Erziehungswesen (nt) *De*
state education *En*
enseignement (m) public *Fr*

(Staats)beamte(-r)/-beamtin (m/f) *De*
civil servant *En*
fonctionnaire (m/f) *Fr*

Staatsangehörigkeit (f) *De*
nationality *En*
nationalité (f) *Fr*

Staatsanwalt (m) *De*
Procurator Fiscal (Scotland) *En*
Commissaire (m) de la République *Fr*

Staatsausgaben (f.pl) *De*
government expenditure *En*
dépenses (f.pl) de l'Etat *Fr*

*** see/siehe/voir: Introduction page IX**

staatsbürgerliche Pflichten (f.pl) *De*
civic duties *En*
devoirs (m.pl) civiques *Fr*

Stadt (f) *De*
town *En*
ville (f) *Fr*

(Stadt)gemeinde (f), Bezirk (m) *De*
borough *En*
ville; municipalité (f) *Fr*

Stadt- Landschafts- planung (f) *De*
town and country planning *En*
aménagement (m) urbain et rural *Fr*

Stadtbeihilfe (f) *De*
urban aid *En*
subvention (f) pour le réaménagement du centre ville *Fr*

Stadtbezirk (m) *De*
urban area *En*
secteur (m) urbain *Fr*

Stadtdirektor (m) *De* *
town clerk *En*
secrétaire (m/f) de la municipalité *Fr*

Städtebau (m) *De*
urban design *En*
architecture (f) urbaine *Fr*

städtebauliche Erschließung (f) *De*
urban development *En*
développement (m) des villes *Fr*

Städteerhaltung (f) *De*
urban conservation *En*
sauvegarde (f) d'un quartier *Fr*

Städtepolitik (f) *De*
urban policy *En*
politique (f) urbaine *Fr*

Stadterneuerung (f) *De*
urban renewal *En*
réhabilitation (f) urbaine *Fr*

Stadtgas (nt) *De*
town gas *En*
gaz (m) de ville *Fr*

städtisch (adj); Stadt- *De*
urban (adj) *En*
urbain (adj) *Fr*

städtischer Müll (m)/Abfall (m) *De*
municipal refuse/waste *En*
ordures (f.pl) de ville *Fr*

(städtisches) Freizeitzentrum (nt) *De*
civic amenity centre *En*
centre (m) de récréations *Fr*

Stadtmitte (f) *De*
town centre *En*
centre (m) ville *Fr*

Stadtmitte (f) *De*
urban centre *En*
centre (m) urbain *Fr*

Stadtplan (m) *De*
town plan *En*
plan (m) de développement de la ville *Fr*

Stadtplaner/-in (m/f) *De*
town planner *En*
urbaniste (m/f) *Fr*

Stadtplanung (f) *De*
town planning *En*
urbanisme (m) *Fr*

Stadtplanung (f) *De*
urban planning *En*
urbanisme (m) *Fr*

Stadtrat (m) *De*
City Council *En*
conseil (m) municipal *Fr*

Stadtrat (m) *De*
town council *En*
conseil (m) municipal *Fr*

Stadtschulrat (m) *De* *
chief education officer *En*
responsable (m/f) de l'éducation *Fr*

Stadtteilentwicklung (f) *De*
neighbourhood development *En*
aménagement (m) d'un quartier *Fr*

Stadtverordnete(-r) (m/f) *De*
councillor *En*
conseiller (m) (-ère f.)/membre (m) du conseil *Fr*

Stadtverwaltung (f), Gemeinderat (m) *De* *
borough council *En*
conseil (m) municipal *Fr*

staff *En*
personnel (m) *Fr*
Personal (nt) *De*

staff appraisal/assessment *En*
appréciation (f) de valeur professionnelle *Fr*
Personalbeurteilung (f) *De*

staff development *En*
développement (m) du personnel *Fr*
Personalentwicklung (f) *De*

staff recruitment/selection *En*
recrutement (m) du personnel *Fr*
(Personal)einstellung (f); Personalwahl (f) *De*

staff shortage *En*
manque (m) de personnel *Fr*
Personalmangel (m) *De*

staff training *En*
formation (f) du personnel *Fr*
Personalausbildung (f) *De*

stage (m) de pratique professionnelle *Fr*
Arbeitserfahrung (f) *De*
work experience *En*

staggered work hours *En*
heures (f.pl) de travail échelonnées *Fr*
gestaffelte Arbeitszeiten (f.pl) *De*

stagiaire (m/f) *Fr*
Trainee (m/f) *De*
trainee *En*

Stahlbeton (m) *De*
reinforced concrete *En*
béton (m) armé *Fr*

Stahlindustrie (f) *De*
steel industry *En*
industrie (f) sidérurgique *Fr*

Stahlwerk (nt) *De*
steelworks *En*
aciérie (f) *Fr*

stamp duty *En*
droit (m) de timbre *Fr*
Stempelsteuer (f) *De*

standard assessment tasks *En* *
tâches (f.pl) évaluées (à l'école en GB) *Fr*
Beurteilungsaufgaben (f.pl) *De*

standard contract preamble *En*
modèle (m) de préliminaires de contrat *Fr*
Vertragsvorbemerkungsvordruck (m) *De*

*** see/siehe/voir: Introduction page IX**

standard deviation *En*
déviation (f) normale *Fr*
Standardabweichung (f) *De*

standard form of building contract *En*
modèle (m) de contrat de construction *Fr*
Vordruck (m) eines Bauvertrages *De*

standard of living *En*
niveau (m) de vie *Fr*
Lebensstandard (m) *De*

Standard Spending Assessment (SSA) *En*
système (m) de limitation de dépenses (en GB) *Fr*
Regelveranlagung (f) (in GB) *De*

Standardabweichung (f) *De*
standard deviation *En*
déviation (f) normale *Fr*

Standesamt (nt) *De*
registry office *En*
état (m) civil *Fr*

standing orders *En*
ordres (m.pl) permanents *Fr*
Geschäftsordnung (f) *De*

starker Verkehr (m) *De*
heavy traffic *En*
circulation (f) intense *Fr*

state education *En*
enseignement (m) public *Fr*
staatliches Erziehungswesen (nt) *De*

state pension *En*
pension (f) de retraite *Fr*
staatliche Rente/Pension (f) *De*

Station (f) *De*
ward (hospital) *En*
salle (f) d'hôpital *Fr*

station (f) d'épuration *Fr*
Kläranlage (f) *De*
sewage works *En*

station (f) de travail *Fr*
Arbeitsplatz (m) *De*
work station *En*

stationäre Pflege (f) *De*
residential care *En*
soins (m.pl) à domicile *Fr*

statistic *En*
élément (m) d'un tableau statistique *Fr*
statistische Tatsache (f) *De*

statistical (adj) *En*
statistique (adj) *Fr*
statistisch (adj) *De*

statistical analysis *En*
analyse (f) statistique *Fr*
statistische Analyse (f) *De*

statistical methods *En*
méthode (f) statistique *Fr*
statistisches Verfahren (nt) *De*

statistics *En*
statistique(s) (f.sing. or pl) *Fr*
Statistik (f) *De*

Statistik (f) *De*
statistics *En*
statistique(s) (f.sing. or pl) *Fr*

statistique (adj) *Fr*
statistisch (adj) *De*
statistical (adj) *En*

statistique(s) (f.sing. or pl) *Fr*
Statistik (f) *De*
statistics *En*

statistiques (f.pl) démographiques *Fr*
Bevölkerungsstatistik (f) *De*
population statistics *En*

statistisch (adj) *De*
statistical (adj) *En*
statistique (adj) *Fr*

statistische Analyse (f) *De*
statistical analysis *En*
analyse (f) statistique *Fr*

statistische Tatsache (f) *De*
statistic *En*
élément (m) d'un tableau statistique *Fr*

statistisches Verfahren (nt) *De*
statistical methods *En*
méthode (f) statistique *Fr*

statu quo (m.inv) *Fr*
Status quo (m) *De*
status quo *En*

status *En*
statut (m) légal *Fr*
Status (m) *De*

Status (m) *De*
status *En*
statut (m) légal *Fr*

status quo *En*
statu quo (m) *Fr*
Status quo (m) *De*

Status quo (m) *De*
status quo *En*
statu quo (m) *Fr*

statut (m) de la fonction publique territoriale; code (m) du travail (secteur privé) *Fr*
Arbeitsrecht (nt) *De*
employment law *En*

statut (m) légal *Fr*
Status (m) *De*
status *En*

statute *En*
loi (f) *Fr*
Gesetz (nt) *De*

statute law *En*
jurisprudence (f) *Fr*
kodifiziertes Recht (nt) *De*

statutory (adj) *En*
établi par la loi (adj) *Fr*
gesetzlich (adj) *De*

statutory authority/body *En*
autorité (f) publique *Fr*
gesetzgebende Körperschaft (f) *De*

statutory instrument *En*
règlement (m) statutaire *Fr*
gesetzliche Urkunde (f) *De*

statutory power *En*
pouvoir (m) législatif *Fr*
gesetzliche Kraft (f) *De*

statutory services *En*
services (m.pl) publics *Fr*
gesetzliche Dienstleistungen (f.pl) *De*

statutory sick pay *En*
prestations (f.pl) en cas de maladie *Fr*
gesetzliches Krankengeld (nt) *De*

Staustufe (f) *De*
barrage *En*
barrage (m) *Fr*

Stechkarte (f) *De*
time sheet *En*
feuille (f) de présence *Fr*

Stechuhr (f) *De*
time clock *En*
enregistreur (m) de temps *Fr*

steel industry *En*
industrie (f) sidérurgique *Fr*
Stahlindustrie (f) *De*

steelworks *En*
aciérie (f) *Fr*
Stahlwerk (nt) *De*

*** see/siehe/voir: Introduction page IX**

steering committee *En*
comité (m) de direction *Fr*
Lenkungsausschuß (m) *De*

Stelle (f) *De*
job *En*
emploi (m) *Fr*

(Stellen)bewerber/-in (m/f) *De*
interviewee *En*
interviewé (m) (-wée f.) *Fr*

Stellenvermittlung (f) *De*
employment agency/office *En*
bureau (m) de placement *Fr*

Stellplätze (m.pl) *De*
off street parking *En*
parcage (m) (en retrait de la rue) *Fr*

stellvertretende(-r) Vorsitzende(-r) (m/f) *De*
vice-chair/chairman/chairperson *En*
vice-président (m) (-ente f.) *Fr*

Stempelgeld (nt) *De*
dole *En*
indemnité (f) de chômage *Fr*

Stempelsteuer (f) *De*
stamp duty *En*
droit (m) de timbre *Fr*

sténographie (f) *Fr*
Kurzschrift (f) *De*
shorthand *En*

Sterbeklinik (f) *De*
hospice *En*
hospice (m) *Fr*

Sterblichkeitsziffer (f), Sterberate (f) *De*
death rate *En*
taux (m) de la mortalité *Fr*

Steuer (f) *De*
tax *En*
impôt (m); taxe (f) *Fr*

Steuer (f) auf Kapitalgewinn *De*
capital gains tax *En*
impôt (m) sur la plus-value *Fr*

(Steuer)erhebung (f) *De*
levy *En*
levée (f) *Fr*

Steuerabgaben (f,pl) *De*
revenue expenditure *En*
dépenses (f.pl) courantes *Fr*

Steueranreiz (m) *De*
tax incentive *En*
incitation (f) fiscale *Fr*

steuerbarer Wert (m) *De*
rateable value *En*
valeur (f) locative imposable *Fr*

steuerfrei (adj) *De*
free of tax (adj) *En*
exonéré d'impôts (adj) *Fr*

steuerfrei (adj) *De*
tax free (adj) *En*
exonéré (adj) d'impôts *Fr*

Steuerfreibetrag (m) *De*
personal allowance *En*
abatement (m) personnel (sur l'impôt) *Fr*

Steuerfreibetrag (m) *De*
tax allowance *En*
abattement (m) personnel (sur l'impôt) *Fr*

Steuerfreibetrag (m) für gewerbliche Gebäude *De*
industrial building allowance *En*
subvention (f) de bâtiment industriel *Fr*

Steuerfreiheit (f) *De*
tax exemption *En*
éxonération (f) d'impôt *Fr*

Steuergrenze (f) *De*
tax threshold *En*
seuil (m) d'imposition *Fr*

Steuerguthaben (nt) *De*
tax credits *En*
déductions (f.pl) fiscales *Fr*

Steuerhinterziehung (f) *De*
evasion of taxes *En*
fraude (f) fiscale *Fr*

Steuerinspektor/-in (m/f) *De*
inspector of taxes *En*
contrôleur (m) des contributions directes *Fr*

(steuerlich) absetzbar (adj) *De*
tax deductible (adj) *En*
déductible des impôts (adj) *Fr*

steuerliche Vergünstigung (f) *De*
tax benefit/concession/relief *En*
abattement (m) d'impôt *Fr*

steuerpflichtiges Einkommen (nt) *De*
taxable income *En*
revenu (m) imposable *Fr*

Steuerreform (f) *De*
tax reform *En*
réforme (f) fiscale *Fr*

Steuersatz (m) *De*
tax rate *En*
taux (m) de l'impôt *Fr*

Steuersenkung (f) *De*
tax cut *En*
réduction (f) d'impôt *Fr*

Steuerzahler/-in (m/f) *De*
taxpayer *En*
contribuable (m/f) *Fr*

Stichprobe (f) *De*
random sampling *En*
échantillonnage (m) au hasard *Fr*

Stichprobenerhebung (f) *De*
sample survey *En*
enquête (f) par sondage *Fr*

Stiftung (f) *De*
charitable trust *En*
organisme (m) charicatif *Fr*

stillbirth *En*
mortinaissance (f) *Fr*
Totgeburt (f) *De*

stillbirths rate *En*
mortinatalité (f) *Fr*
Totgeburtenzahl (f) *De*

Stimmabgabe (f) *De*
polling *En*
élections (f.pl) *Fr*

Stimme (f) (m/f) *De*
vote (noun) *En*
vote (m) *Fr*

Stimmenzähler/-in (m/f) *De*
teller (at election) *En*
scrutateur (m); recenseur (m) *Fr*

Stipendium (nt) *De*
bursary *En*
bourse (f) *Fr*

stock control *En*
contrôle (m) des stocks *Fr*
Warenbestandkontrolle (f) *De*

stock exchange *En*
bourse (f) *Fr*
Börse (f) *De*

stockbroker *En*
courtier (m) en bourse *Fr*
Börsenmakler (m) *De*

stop-gap *En*
bouche-trou (m) *Fr*
Notbehelf (m) *De*

*** see/siehe/voir: Introduction page IX**

stoppages (from pay) ***En***
retenues (f.pl) sur les appointements *Fr*
(Lohn)abzüge (m.pl) *De*

storage ***En***
emmagasinage (m) *Fr*
Lagerung (f) *De*

storage costs ***En***
frais (m.pl) de magasinage *Fr*
Lagerkosten (pl) *De*

storm drain ***En***
fossé (m) d'évacuation *Fr*
Abflußgraben (m) *De*

Strafaussetzung (f) zur Bewährung ***De***
probation order *En*
mise (f) à l'épreuve *Fr*

strafbare Handlung (f), Delikt (nt) ***De***
indictable offence *En*
délit (m) *Fr*

Strafe (f) ***De***
penalty *En*
sanction (f) *Fr*

Strafe (f) mit Bewährung ***De***
suspended sentence *En*
condamnation (f) avec sursis *Fr*

Straferlaß (m) ***De***
remission (of sentence) *En*
sursis (m) *Fr*

Straffällige (-r) (m/f) ***De***
offender *En*
délinquant (m) *Fr*

Strafgericht (nt) ***De***
criminal court *En*
tribunal (m) criminel *Fr*

Strafklausel (f) ***De***
penalty clause *En*
clause (f) pénale (de dommages-intérêts) *Fr*

Strafrecht (nt) ***De***
criminal law *En*
droit (m) criminel *Fr*

(strafrechtlich) verfolgen (vb) ***De***
prosecute (vb) *En*
poursuivre (vb) quelqu'un en justice repressive *Fr*

(strafrechtliche) Verfolgung (f) ***De***
prosecution *En*
poursuites (f.pl) judiciaires *Fr*

Straße (f); Fahrbahn (f) ***De***
roadway *En*
chaussée (f) *Fr*

Straße (f) mit Halteverbot ***De***
clearway *En*
(grande) route (f) à stationnement interdit *Fr*

Straßengebühr (f) ***De***
toll *En*
droit (m) de passage *Fr*

Straßenarbeiten (f.pl) ***De***
road works *En*
travaux (m.pl) de voirie *Fr*

Straßenausbau (m) ***De***
highway improvement *En*
amélioration (f) des grandes routes *Fr*

Straßenauslastung (f) ***De***
highway capacity *En*
capacité (f) des grandes routes *Fr*

Straßenauslastung (f) ***De***
road capacity *En*
capacité (m) de trafic de la route *Fr*

Straßenausrichtung (f) ***De***
road alignment *En*
alignement (m) de la route *Fr*

Straßenbau (m) ***De***
highway construction *En*
construction (f) des grandes routes *Fr*

Straßenbau (m) ***De***
road building/construction *En*
construction (f) routière *Fr*

Straßenbauamt (nt) ***De***
highway authority/department *En*
service (m) de la voirie *Fr*

Straßenbauingenieur (m) ***De***
highway engineer *En*
ingénieur (m) des ponts et chaussées *Fr*

Straßenbaupolitik (f) ***De***
road policy *En*
politique (f) routière *Fr*

Straßenbeleuchtung (f) ***De***
road lighting *En*
éclairage (m) des routes *Fr*

Straßenbeleuchtung (f) ***De***
street lighting *En*
éclairage (m) des rues *Fr*

Straßenbeschilderung (f) ***De***
road signing *En*
signalisation (f) routière *Fr*

Straßenbrücke (f) ***De***
road bridge *En*
pont (m) routier *Fr*

Straßenerneuerung (f) ***De***
road improvement *En*
amélioration (f) de la route *Fr*

Straßenfeger (m) ***De***
street sweeper (person) *En*
balayeur (m) de rues (personne) *Fr*

Straßengüterverkehr (m) ***De***
road transport *En*
transports (m.pl) routiers *Fr*

Straßeninstandhaltung (f) ***De***
highway maintenance *En*
entretien (m) des ponts et chaussées *Fr*

Straßeninstandhaltung (f), -wartung (f) ***De***
road maintenance *En*
entretien (m) des routes *Fr*

Straßenkehrmaschine (f) ***De***
street sweeper (machine) *En*
balayeuse (f) de rues (machine) *Fr*

Straßenkreuzung (f) ***De***
road junction *En*
carrefour (m) *Fr*

Straßenmarkierung (f) ***De***
road marking *En*
marquage (m) routier *Fr*

Straßennetz (nt) ***De***
highway network *En*
réseau (m) des artères *Fr*

Straßennetz (nt) ***De***
road network *En*
réseau (m) routier *Fr*

Straßenplanung (f) ***De***
highway design *En*
conception (f) des grandes routes *Fr*

Straßenplanung (f) ***De***
road design *En*
étude (f) d'une route *Fr*

Straßenplanung (f) ***De***
road planning *En*
programmation (f) des routes *Fr*

Straßenreinigung (f) ***De***
street cleaning/cleansing *En*
nettoyage (m) des rues *Fr*

*** see/siehe/voir: Introduction page IX**

Straßenreinigung (f), -fegen (nt) *De*
street sweeping *En*
ébouage (m) des rues *Fr*

Straßenschild (nt), Verkehrszeichen (nt) *De*
road sign *En*
signal (m) routier *Fr*

Straßensperrung (f) *De*
road closure *En*
barrage (m) de la route *Fr*

Straßenverkehr (m) *De*
road traffic *En*
circulation (f) routière *Fr*

Straßenverkehrsordnung (f) *De*
traffic regulations *En*
règlements (m.pl) sur la circulation *Fr*

strategic plan *En*
plan (m) de développement *Fr*
strategischer Plan (m) *De*

strategic planning *En*
stratégie (f) urbaine *Fr*
strategische Planung (f) *De*

stratégie (f) corporative *Fr*
Unternehmensstrategie (f) *De*
corporate strategy *En*

stratégie (f) de développement économique *Fr*
Konjunkturentwicklungsplan (m) *De*
economic development strategy *En*

stratégie (f) de l'habitat *Fr*
Wohnstrategie (f) *De*
housing strategy *En*

stratégie (f) économique *Fr*
langfristige Konjunkturpolitik (f) *De*
economic strategy *En*

stratégie (f) hasardeuse *Fr*
risikoreiche Strategie (f), Risikostrategie (f) *De*
high risk strategy *En*

stratégie (f) industrielle *Fr*
industrielle Strategie (f) *De*
industrial strategy *En*

stratégie (f) régionale *Fr*
Regionalstrategie (f) *De*
regional strategy *En*

stratégie (f) urbaine *Fr*
strategische Planung (f) *De*
strategic planning *En*

strategische Planung (f) *De*
strategic planning *En*
stratégie (f) urbaine *Fr*

strategischer Plan (m) *De*
strategic plan *En*
plan (m) de développement *Fr*

street cleaning/cleansing *En*
nettoyage (m) des rues *Fr*
Straßenreinigung (f) *De*

street lighting *En*
éclairage (m) des rues *Fr*
Straßenbeleuchtung (f) *De*

street sweeper (machine) *En*
balayeuse (f) de rues (machine) *Fr*
Straßenkehrmaschine (f) *De*

street sweeper (person) *En*
balayeur (m) de rues (personne) *Fr*
Straßenfeger (m) *De*

street sweeping *En*
ébouage (m) des rues *Fr*
Straßenreinigung (f), -fegen (nt) *De*

Streik (m) *De*
strike *En*
grève (f) *Fr*

streng vertraulich (adj) *De*
private and confidential (adj) *En*
secret et confidentiel (adj) *Fr*

Streß (m) *De*
stress *En*
tension (f) nerveuse *Fr*

stress *En*
tension (f) nerveuse *Fr*
Streß (m) *De*

strike *En*
grève (f) *Fr*
Streik (m) *De*

strittige Fragen (f.pl) *De*
controversial issues *En*
questions (f.pl) controversables *Fr*

Strombedarf (m) *De*
electricity demand *En*
demande (f) de l'électricité *Fr*

Stromverbrauch (m) *De*
electricity consumption *En*
consommation (f) de l'électricité *Fr*

structural engineer *En*
ingénieur (m) constructeur *Fr*
Hochbauingenieur/-in (m/f) *De*

structure (f) des prix du voyage *Fr*
Fahrpreisgefüge (nt) *De*
fare structure *En*

structure (f) économique *Fr*
Wirtschaftsstruktur (f) *De*
economic structure *En*

structure plan *En*
plan (m) d'occupation des sols *Fr*
Strukturplan (m) *De*

structure planning *En*
établissement (m) du plan d'occupation des sols *Fr*
Strukturprogramm (nt) *De*

Strukturplan (m) *De*
structure plan *En*
plan (m) d'occupation des sols *Fr*

Strukturprogramm (nt) *De*
structure planning *En*
établissement (m) du plan d'occupation des sols *Fr*

Strukturwandlung (f) *De*
economic change *En*
changement (m) économique *Fr*

student *En*
étudiant (m) (-ante f.) *Fr*
Student/-in (m/f) *De*

Student/-in (m/f) *De*
student *En*
étudiant (m) (-ante f.) *Fr*

Student/-in (m/f) *De*
undergraduate *En*
étudiant (m) (-ante f.) qui prépare la licence *Fr*

student accommodation *En*
logement (m) des étudiants *Fr*
Studentenwohnungen (f.pl) *De*

student grant *En*
bourse (f) d'études *Fr*
Studienbeihilfe (f) *De*

Studentenwohnungen (f.pl) *De*
student accommodation *En*
logement (m) des étudiants *Fr*

(Studien)beihilfe (f); Zuschuß (m); Subvention(f) *De*
grant (noun) *En*
bourse (f) *Fr*

Studienbeihilfe (f) *De*
student grant *En*
bourse (f) d'études *Fr*

*** see/siehe/voir: Introduction page IX**

studieren (vb) *De*
study (vb) *En*
étudier (vb) *Fr*

study (vb) *En*
étudier (vb) *Fr*
studieren (vb) *De*

Stundenplan (m) (Schule) *De*
timetable (school) *En*
emploi (m) du temps (école) *Fr*

stützen (vb) *De*
underpin (vb) *En*
étayer (vb) *Fr*

sub-contractor *En*
tâcheron (m) *Fr*
Subunternehmer (m) *De*

sub-letting *En*
sous-location (f) *Fr*
Untervermietung (f) *De*

sub-standard (adj) *En*
de qualité inférieure (adj) *Fr*
unzulänglich (adj) *De*

sub-committee *En*
sous-comité (m) *Fr*
Unterausschuß (m) *De*

sub-contract (noun) *En*
sous-traité (m) *Fr*
Untervertrag (m) *De*

sub-contract (vb) *En*
sous-traiter (vb) *Fr*
(an) Subunternehmer vergeben (vb) *De*

sub-let (vb) *En*
sous-louer (vb) *Fr*
untervermieten (vb) *De*

subsidence *En*
abaissement (m) (du terrain) *Fr*
Senkung (f) *De*

Subsidiarität (f) *De*
subsidiarity *En*
subsidiarité (f) *Fr*

subsidiarité (f) *Fr*
Subsidiarität (f) *De*
subsidiarity *En*

subsidiarity *En*
subsidiarité (f) *Fr*
Subsidiarität (f) *De*

subsidise (vb) *En*
subventionner (vb) *Fr*
subventionieren (vb) *De*

subsidy *En*
subvention (f) *Fr*
Subvention (f) *De*

subsistence allowance *En*
indemnité (f) journalière *Fr*
Aussendienstzulage (f) *De*

subsoil *En*
sous-sol (m) *Fr*
Untergrund (m) *De*

Subunternehmer (m) *De*
sub-contractor *En*
tâcheron (m) *Fr*

Subunternehmer; an — vergeben (vb) De
sub-contract (vb) En
sous-traiter (vb) Fr

suburb/suburbia *En*
banlieue (f) *Fr*
Vorort (m); Vororte (m.pl) *De*

suburban (adj) *En*
de banlieue (adj) *Fr*
Vorort- *De*

subvention (f) *Fr*
Sponsorschaft (f) *De*
sponsorship *En*

subvention (f) *Fr*
Subvention (f) *De*
grant aid *En*

subvention (f) *Fr*
Subvention (f) *De*
subsidy *En*

Subvention (f) *De*
grant aid *En*
subvention (f) *Fr*

Subvention (f) *De*
subsidy *En*
subvention (f) *Fr*

subvention (f) de bâtiment industriel *Fr*
Steuerfreibetrag (m) für gewerbliche Gebäude *De*
industrial building allowance *En*

subvention (f) de l'Etat *Fr*
Pauschalsubvention (f) *De*
block grant *En*

subvention (f) de l'Etat *Fr*
Sondersubvention (m) *De*
specific grant *En*

subvention (f) de réhabilitation *Fr*
Ausbesserungszuschuß (m) *De*
repair grant *En*

subvention (f) des impôts locaux (en GB) par l'Etat *Fr* *
Kommunalsteuersubvention (f) (in GB) *De*
rate support grant (GB) *En*

subvention (f) destinée à la modernisation *Fr*
Modernisierungsbeihilfe (f) *De*
home improvement grant *En*

subvention (f) destinée à la réhabilitation *Fr*
Renovierungszuschuß (m) *De*
improvement grant *En*

subvention (f) d'investissement *Fr*
Investitionszuschuß (m) *De*
investment grant *En*

subvention (f) pour le réaménagement du centre ville *Fr*
Stadtbeihilfe (f) *De*
urban aid *En*

subventionieren (vb) *De*
subsidize (vb) *En*
subventionner (vb) *Fr*

subventionierte Schule (f) (in GB) *De* *
grant maintained school (GB) *En*
collège (m) subventionné par l'Etat (en GB) *Fr*

subventionner (vb) *Fr*
bewilligen (vb) *De*
grant aid (vb) *En*

subventionner (vb) *Fr*
subventionieren (vb) *De*
subsidize (vb) *En*

subventions (f.pl) spécifiques *Fr*
Investitionszuschüße (m.pl) *De*
capital grants *En*

Subventionsgebiet (nt) *De*
assisted area *En*
zone (f) subventionnée *Fr*

subway *En*
passage (m) souterrain *Fr*
Unterführung (f) *De*

summons *En*
citation (f) *Fr*
Vorladung (f) *De*

summons (vb) (to appear in court) *En*
citer (vb) (quelqu'un à comparaître) *Fr*
(gerichtlich) vorladen (vb) *De*

*** see/siehe/voir: Introduction page IX**

summons (noun); issue a —. En
lancer (vb) une assignation *Fr*
eine Vorladung beantragen (vb) *De*

summons (noun); serve a —. En
faire (vb) une assignation à quelqu'un *Fr*
jmdm eine Vorladung zustellen (vb) *De*

sundry expenses En
frais (m.pl) divers *Fr*
verschiedene Ausgaben (f.pl) *De*

superannuation En
retraite (f) par limite d'âge *Fr*
Rente (f) *De*

superannuation benefit En
pension (f) de retraite *Fr*
Rentengeld (nt) *De*

superannuation contribution En
retenue (f) pour la retraite *Fr*
Beitrag (m) zur Rentenversicherung *De*

superannuation fund En
caisse (f) des retraités *Fr*
Rentenfonds (m) *De*

superficie (f) Fr
Grund-. Bodenfläche (f) *De*
floor area *En*

supervise (vb) En
diriger (vb) (une entreprise) *Fr*
beaufsichtigen (vb) *De*

supervision En
direction (f) (d'une entreprise) *Fr*
Aufsicht (f) *De*

supervision order En
mandat (m) de surveillance *Fr*
Aufsichtspflicht (f) *De*

supervisory staff En
cadre (m) de maitrise *Fr*
Aufsichtspersonal (nt) *De*

supplément (m) Fr
Zuschlagsgebühr (f) *De*
extra charge *En*

supplementary rate En *
impôt (m) local supplémentaire (en GB) *Fr*
zusätzliche Gemeindesteuern (f.pl) *De*

supplier En
fournisseur (m) *Fr*
Lieferant (m) *De*

supply (vb) En
fournir (vb) (qn de qch) *Fr*
liefern (vb) *De*

supply and demand En
offre (f) et la demande *Fr*
Angebot (nt) und Nachfrage (f) *De*

support En
soutien (m) *Fr*
Unterhalt (m) *De*

suppression (f) des taudis Fr
Slumsanierung (f) *De*
slum clearance *En*

surcharge En
débours (m) injustifié porté à la charge du responsable *Fr*
Zuschlag (m) *De*

surcharge (vb) En
faire supporter (vb) (au responsable) une erreur de paiement *Fr*
Zuschlag erheben (vb) *De*

surface drain En
tranchée (f) à ciel ouvert *Fr*
Gully (m) *De*

surface (f) synthétique Fr
Plastikbelag (m) *De*
synthetic surface *En*

surface water En
eau (f) superficielle *Fr*
Oberflächenwasser (nt) *De*

surplus land En
surplus (m) de terrain *Fr*
überschüssiges Land (nt) *De*

surplus (m) de terrain Fr
überschüssiges Land (nt) *De*
surplus land *En*

surreprésentation (f) Fr
Überrepräsentation (f) *De*
over-representation *En*

sursis (m) Fr
Straferlaß (m) *De*
remission (of sentence) *En*

surveillée; en liberté (f) —. Fr
(auf) Bewährung (f) *De*
(on) probation *En*

surveiller (vb) Fr
kontrollieren (vb) *De*
monitor (vb) (performance etc) *En*

survey (vb) En
faire (vb) le levé (d'une ville, d'un édifice etc) *Fr*
inspizieren (vb) *De*

survey (noun) (construction) En
levé (m) *Fr*
(Bau)inspektion (f) *De*

survey (for rating) En
cadastre (m) *Fr*
Begutachtung (f), Gutachten (nt) *De*

surveyor (of property) En
architecte (m.) expert *Fr*
Gutachter (m) *De*

susmentionné (adj) Fr
obenerwähnt (adj) *De*
above-mentioned (adj) *En*

suspended sentence En
condamnation (f) avec sursis *Fr*
Strafe (f) mit Bewährung *De*

sustainable development En
réalisation (f) possible *Fr*
haltbare Entwicklung (f) *De*

Süßwasser (nt) De
fresh water *En*
eau (f) douce *Fr*

syllabus En
programme (m) (d'un cours) *Fr*
Lehrplan (m) *De*

sylviculture (f) Fr
Forstwirtschaft (f) *De*
forestry *En*

syndic (m) de faillite Fr
Konkursverwalter/-in (m/f) *De*
receiver *En*

syndicaliste (m/f) Fr
Gewerkschaftler/-in (m/f) *De*
trade unionist *En*

syndicat (m) de logement/copropriétaires Fr
Wohnstiftung (f) *De*
housing trust *En*

syndicat (m) ouvrier Fr
Gewerkschaft (f) *De*
trade union *En*

syndicat (m) professionnel Fr
Fachverband (m) *De*
trade association *En*

syndicat (m) régional des transports en commun Fr
regionales Amt (nt) für Verkehr *De*
regional transport authority *En*

*** see/siehe/voir: Introduction page IX**

synthetic language (computer) *En*
langage (m) synthétique *Fr*
synthetische Sprache (f) *De*

synthetic surface *En*
surface (f) synthétique *Fr*
Plastikbelag (m) *De*

synthetische Sprache (f) *De*
synthetic language (computer) *En*
langage (m) synthétique *Fr*

system building *En*
préfabrication (f) *Fr*
Systembauweise (f) *De*

system built (adj) *En*
préfabriqué (adj) *Fr*
vorgefertigt (adj) *De*

System (nt) der degressiven Kosten *De*
economies of scale *En*
économies (f.pl) de grande échelle *Fr*

Systemanalyse (f) *De*
systems analysis *En*
analyse (f) de systèmes *Fr*

Systemanalytiker (m) *De*
systems analyst *En*
analyste (m/f) de systèmes *Fr*

Systembauweise (f) *De*
system building *En*
préfabrication (f) *Fr*

système (m) d'égouts *Fr*
Kanalisation (f) *De*
drainage *En*

système (m) d'incitations monétaires *Fr*
Anreizsystem (nt) *De*
incentive scheme *En*

système (m) d'informations financières *Fr*
Finanzinformationssystem (nt) *De*
financial information system *En*

système (m) d'informatique de gestion *Fr*
Management-Informationssystem (nt) *De*
management information system *En*

système (m) de circulation giratoire *Fr*
Kreisverkehr (m) *De*
gyratory system *En*

système (m) de garanti d'emprunt *Fr*
Kreditbürgschaftsprogramm (nt) *De*
loan guarantee scheme *En*

système (m) de gestion de fichiers *Fr*
Datenspeichersystem (nt) *De*
file management system *En*

système (m) de limitation de dépenses (en GB) *Fr* *
Regelveranlagung (f) (in GB) *De*
Standard Spending Assessment (SSA) *En*

système (m) électoral *Fr*
Wahlsystem (nt) *De*
electoral system *En*

Système (m) Européen Monétaire *Fr*
Europäisches Währungssystem (nt) *De*
European Monetary System *En*

système (m) informatique *Fr*
Informationssystem (nt) *De*
information system *En*

systems analysis *En*
analyse (f) de systèmes *Fr*
Systemanalyse (f) *De*

systems analyst *En*
analyste (m/f) de systèmes *Fr*
Systemanalytiker (m) *De*

*** see/siehe/voir: Introduction page IX**

T

tableau (m) comparatif de performances ***Fr***
Ergebnisanalyse (f) *De*
performance analysis *En*

tableur (m) ***Fr***
Arbeitsblatt (nt), Tabellenkalkulation (f) *De*
spreadsheet *En*

tâcheron (m) ***Fr***
Subunternehmer (m) *De*
sub-contractor *En*

tâches (f.pl) évaluées (à l'école en GB) ***Fr*** *****
Beurteilungsaufgaben (f.pl) *De*
standard assessment tasks *En*

tachograph ***En***
tachygraphe (m) *Fr*
Fahrtschreiber (m) *De*

tachygraphe (m) ***Fr***
Fahrtschreiber (m) *De*
tachograph *En*

Tagesarbeit (f) ***De***
daywork *En*
travail (m) à la journée *Fr*

Tagesmutter (f) ***De***
child minder *En*
assistante (f) maternelle *Fr*

Tagesordnung (f) ***De***
agenda *En*
ordre (m) du jour *Fr*

Tagesstempel (m) ***De***
date stamp *En*
dateur (m) *Fr*

tageweise Freistellung (f) (zur Fortbildung) ***De***
day release *En*
jour (m) de permission accordé pour la formation professionnelle *Fr*

take-home pay ***En***
salaire (m) net *Fr*
Nettolohn (m) *De*

take-over bid ***En***
offre (m) de rachat *Fr*
Übernahmeangebot (nt) *De*

tap water ***En***
eau (f) du robinet *Fr*
Leitungswasser (nt) *De*

tarif (m) de stationnement ***Fr***
Parkgebühr (f) *De*
parking charge *En*

tarif (m) réduit ***Fr***
ermäßigter Tarif (m) *De*
concessionary fare *En*

tarif (m) uniforme ***Fr***
Einheitssatz (m) *De*
flat rate *En*

Tarifpolitik (f) ***De***
fares policy *En*
politique (f) des prix du voyage *Fr*

Tarifverhandlung (f) ***De***
pay bargaining/negotiation *En*
négotiation (f) salariale *Fr*

Tarifverhandlungen (f.pl) ***De***
collective bargaining *En*
convention (f) collective *Fr*

tarmacadam ***En***
tarmacadam (m) *Fr*
Makadam (m) *De*

tarmacadam (m) ***Fr***
Makadam (m) *De*
tarmacadam *En*

(tar)macadamiser (vb) ***Fr***
makadamisieren (vb) *De*
tarmacadam (vb) *En*

tarmacadam (vb) ***En***
macadamiser (vb) *Fr*
makadamisieren (vb) *De*

task force ***En***
force (f) tactique *Fr*
Sonderkommando (nt) *De*

Tastatur (f) ***De***
keyboard (computer) *En*
clavier (m) *Fr*

Tätigkeitsbericht (m) ***De***
progress report *En*
rapport (m) périodique *Fr*

Tätigkeitsbeschreibung (f) ***De***
job description *En*
description (f) de la fonction *Fr*

taudis (m) ***Fr***
Slum (m) *De*
slum *En*

Tauglichkeits-, Eignungsstudie (f) ***De***
feasibility study *En*
étude (f) de faisabilité *Fr*

taux (m) d'abonnement à l'eau ***Fr***
Wassergebühren (f.pl), -geld (nt) *De*
water rate *En*

taux (m) d'accidents ***Fr***
Unfallziffer (f) *De*
accident rate *En*

taux (m) d'inflation ***Fr***
Inflationsrate (f) *De*
inflation rate *En*

taux (m) d'intérêt ***Fr***
Zinssatz (m) *De*
rate of interest *En*

taux (m) d'intérêts ***Fr***
Zinssatz (m) *De*
interest rate *En*

taux (m) de change flottant ***Fr***
flexibler Wechselkurs (m) *De*
floating exchange rate *En*

taux (m) de fertilité ***Fr***
Fruchtbarkeitsziffer (f) *De*
fertility rate *En*

*** see/siehe/voir: Introduction page IX**

taux (m) de l'impôt *Fr*
Steuersatz (m) *De*
tax rate *En*

taux (m) de la mortalité *Fr*
Sterblichkeitsziffer (f), Sterberate (f) *De*
death rate *En*

taux (m) de mortalité *Fr*
Mortalität (f) *De*
mortality rate *En*

taux (m) de rendement *Fr*
Gewinnsatz (m) *De*
rate of return *En*

taux (m) de réponse *Fr*
Antwortsrate (f) *De*
response rate *En*

taux (m) de salaire *Fr*
Lohnsatz (m) *De*
pay rate *En*

taux (m) des salaires *Fr*
Lohnsatz (m) *De*
wage rate *En*

taux (m) du crime *Fr*
Kriminalitätsrate (f) *De*
crime rate *En*

taux (m) officiel de l'escompte *Fr*
Diskontsatz (m) *De*
bank rate *En*

taux (m) syndical *Fr*
Gewerkschaftsbeitrag (m) *De*
trade union rate *En*

taux (m) variable *Fr*
schwankender Kurs (m) *De*
fluctuating rate *En*

tax *En*
impôt (m); taxe (f) *Fr*
Steuer (f) *De*

tax (vb) *En*
imposer (vb) *Fr*
besteuern (vb) *De*

tax allowance *En*
abattement (m) personnel (sur l'impôt) *Fr*
Steuerfreibetrag (m) *De*

tax benefit/concession/relief *En*
abattement (m) d'impôt *Fr*
steuerliche Vergünstigung (f) *De*

tax credits *En*
déductions (f.pl) fiscales *Fr*
Steuerguthaben (nt) *De*

tax cut *En*
réduction (f) d'impôt *Fr*
Steuersenkung (f) *De*

tax deductible (adj) *En*
déductible des impôts (adj) *Fr*
(steuerlich) absetzbar (adj) *De*

tax exemption *En*
éxonération (f) d'impôt *Fr*
Steuerfreiheit (f) *De*

tax free (adj) *En*
exonéré (adj) d'impôts *Fr*
steuerfrei (adj) *De*

tax incentive *En*
incitation (f) fiscale *Fr*
Steueranreiz (m) *De*

tax office *En*
bureau (m) des contributions *Fr*
Finanzamt (nt) *De*

tax paid (adj) *En*
net d'impôt (adj) *Fr*
nach Abzug der Steuern; netto (adj) *De*

tax rate *En*
taux (m) de l'impôt *Fr*
Steuersatz (m) *De*

tax reform *En*
réforme (f) fiscale *Fr*
Steuerreform (f) *De*

tax threshold *En*
seuil (m) d'imposition *Fr*
Steuergrenze (f) *De*

taxable income *En*
revenu (m) imposable *Fr*
steuerpflichtiges Einkommen (nt) *De*

taxation *En*
imposition (f) *Fr*
Besteuerung (f) *De*

taxe (f) à la valeur ajoutée (TVA) *Fr*
Mehrwertsteuer (f) (MWSt) *De*
value added tax (VAT) *En*

taxe (f) de consommation locale *Fr*
örtliche Umsatzsteuer (f) *De*
local sales tax *En*

taxe (f) de vente *Fr*
Verkaufssteuer (f) *De*
sales tax *En*

taxe (f) professionnelle *Fr*
einheitliche Geschäftsgebühr (f) *De*
unified business rate *En*

taxe (f) professionnelle *Fr*
Gewerbesteuer (f) *De*
business rate *En*

taxe (f) professionnelle *Fr*
Gewerbesteuer (f) *De*
non domestic rate *En*

taxe (f) professionnelle *Fr*
Handelsrate (f) *De*
commercial rate *En*

taxpayer *En*
contribuable (m/f) *Fr*
Steuerzahler (m)/-zählerin (f) *De*

teach (vb) *En*
enseigner (vb) *Fr*
unterrichten (vb) *De*

teacher education/training *En*
éducation (f) professionnelle de l'enseignement *Fr*
Lehrerausbildung (f) *De*

teacher (primary) *En*
instituteur (m) (-trice f.) *Fr*
Lehrer/-in (m/f) *De*

teacher (secondary) *En*
professeur (m) *Fr*
Lehrer/-in (m/f) *De*

teaching *En*
enseignement (m) *Fr*
Lehrberuf (m) *De*

teaching aid/material *En*
matériel (m) pédagogique *Fr*
Lehrmittel (nt) *De*

teaching hospital *En*
centre (m) hospitalier universitaire *Fr*
Ausbildungskrankenhaus (nt) *De*

teaching method *En*
méthode (f) d'enseignement *Fr*
Lehr-/Unterrichtsmethode (f) *De*

teaching profession *En*
corps (m) enseignant *Fr*
Lehrberuf (m) *De*

technical college *En*
collège (m) technique; lycée (m) technique *Fr*
Fachhochschule (f) *De*

*** see/siehe/voir: Introduction page IX**

technical services *En*
services (m.pl) techniques *Fr*
technischer Dienst (m) *De*

technician *En*
technicien (m) (-ienne f.) *Fr*
Techniker/-in (m/f) *De*

technicien (m) (-ienne f.) *Fr*
Techniker/-in (m/f) *De*
technician *En*

technicien (m) de la circulation *Fr*
Verkehrsplaner/-in (m/f) *De*
traffic engineer *En*

Technik (f) *De*
engineering *En*
ingénierie (f) *Fr*

Technik (f) *De*
technology *En*
technologie (f) *Fr*

Techniker/-in (m/f) *De*
technician *En*
technicien (m) (-ienne f.) *Fr*

technique (f) de la circulation *Fr*
Verkehrsplanung (f) *De*
traffic engineering *En*

technique (f) opérationnelle *Fr*
Know-how (nt) *De*
know-how *En*

technisch (adj) *De*
technological (adj) *En*
technologique (adj) *Fr*

technische Innovation (f) *De*
technological innovation *En*
innovation (f) technologique *Fr*

technische Veränderungen (f.pl) *De*
technological change *En*
changements (m.pl) technologiques *Fr*

technische Zeichnung (f) *De*
engineering drawing *En*
dessin (m) de mécanique *Fr*

technischer Dienst (m) *De*
technical services *En*
services (m.pl) techniques *Fr*

technological (adj) *En*
technologique (adj) *Fr*
technisch (adj) *De*

technological change *En*
changements (m.pl) technologiques *Fr*
technische Veränderungen (f.pl) *De*

technological innovation *En*
innovation (f) technologique *Fr*
technische Innovation (f) *De*

technologie (f) et travaux (m.pl) manuels *Fr* *
Werken (nt), Gestaltung (f) und Technologie (f) *De*
Craft Design and Technology (CDT) *En*

technologie (f) *Fr*
Technik (f) *De*
technology *En*

technologie (f) nouvelle *Fr*
neue Technologie (f) *De*
new technology *En*

Technologiepark (m) *De*
science park *En*
campus (m) scientifique *Fr*

Technologiepark (m) *De*
technology park *En*
campus (m) technologique *Fr*

technologique (adj) *Fr*
technisch (adj) *De*
technological (adj) *En*

technology *En*
technologie (f) *Fr*
Technik (f) *De*

technology park *En*
campus (m) technologique *Fr*
Technologiepark (m) *De*

teenager *En*
adolescent (m) (-ente f.) (de 13 à 19 ans) *Fr*
Teenager (m) *De*

Teenager (m) *De*
teenager *En*
adolescent (m) (-ente f.) (de 13 à 19 ans) *Fr*

Teilzeitarbeit (f) *De*
part-time work *En*
travail (m) à temps partiel *Fr*

telecommunication *En*
télécommunication (f) *Fr*
Fernmeldewesen (nt) *De*

télécommunication (f) *Fr*
Fernmeldewesen (nt) *De*
telecommunication *En*

téléconference (f) *Fr*
Telekonferenzen (f.pl) abhalten *De*
teleconferencing *En*

teleconferencing *En*
téléconference (f) *Fr*
Telekonferenzen (f.pl) abhalten *De*

téléfax (m); télécopie (f) *Fr*
Faksimileübertragung (f), Fax (nt) *De*
facsimile transmission (fax) *En*

Telefonist/-in (m/f) *De*
telephone operator, telephonist *En*
téléphoniste (m/f) *Fr*

Telefonnummer (f) *De*
telephone number *En*
numéro (m) de téléphone *Fr*

Telekonferenzen (f.pl) abhalten *De*
teleconferencing *En*
téléconference (f) *Fr*

telephone directory; phone book *En*
annuaire (m) des téléphones *Fr*
Fernsprechbuch (nt) *De*

telephone exchange *En*
central (m) téléphonique *Fr*
Fernmeldeamt (nt) *De*

telephone number *En*
numéro (m) de téléphone *Fr*
Telefonnummer (f) *De*

telephone operator; telephonist *En*
téléphoniste (m/f) *Fr*
Telefonist/-in (m/f) *De*

téléphoniste (m/f) *Fr*
Telefonist/-in (m/f) *De*
telephone operator, telephonist *En*

teletext *En*
télétexte (m) *Fr*
Teletext (m) *De*

Teletext (m) *De*
teletext *En*
télétexte (m) *Fr*

télétexte (m) *Fr*
Teletext (m) *De*
teletext *En*

telex *En*
télex (m) *Fr*
Telex (nt) *De*

*** see/siehe/voir: Introduction page IX**

télex (m) *Fr*
Telex (nt) *De*
telex *En*

Telex (nt) *De*
telex *En*
télex (m) *Fr*

telex (vb) *En*
télexer (vb) *Fr*
telexen (vb) *De*

telexen (vb) *De*
telex (vb) *En*
télexer (vb) *Fr*

télexer (vb) *Fr*
telexen (vb) *De*
telex (vb) *En*

teller (at election) *En*
scrutateur (m); recenseur (m) *Fr*
Stimmenzähler/-in (m/f) *De*

témoigner (vb) *Fr*
Zeuge/-gin sein; bestätigen (vb) *De*
witness (vb) *En*

témoin (m) *Fr*
Zeuge/-gin (m/f) *De*
witness (noun) *En*

temporary accommodation *En*
logement (m) provisoire *Fr*
provisorische Unterkunft (f) *De*

temporary basis (on a) (adv) *En*
provisoirement (adv) *Fr*
provisorisch (adj) *De*

temporary employment/work *En*
emploi (m) (à titre) provisoire *Fr*
vorübergehende Anstellung (f) *De*

temporary measures *En*
mesures (f.pl) provisoires *Fr*
provisorische Maßnahmen (f.pl) *De*

temporary staff *En*
personnel (m) (à titre) provisoire *Fr*
Aushilfe (f), Aushilfskräfte (f.pl) *De*

tenancy agreement *En*
contrat (m) de location *Fr*
Mietvertrag (m) *De*

tenancy *En*
location (f) *Fr*
Mietverhältnis (nt) *De*

tenant *En*
locataire (m/f) *Fr*
Mieter/-in (m/f) *De*

tenants' association *En*
association (f) de locataires *Fr*
Mieterausschuß (m) *De*

tenants' rights *En*
droits (m.pl) du tenancier *Fr*
Mieterrechte (nt.pl) *De*

tender (vb) for a contract *En*
soumissionner (vb) à une adjudication *Fr*
ein Angebot für einen Vertrag einreichen (vb) *De*

tenement block *En*
maison (f) de rapport divisée en appartements *Fr*
Wohnblock (m) *De*

tenement *En*
appartement (m) *Fr*
Mietshaus (nt) *De*

tenir (vb) qn au courant *Fr*
aktualisieren (vb) *De*
update (vb) *En*

tension (f) nerveuse *Fr*
Streß (m) *De*
stress *En*

tenu en propriété perpétuelle et libre (adj) *Fr*
Eigentums- *De*
freehold (adj) *En*

tenue (f) des livres *Fr*
Buchhaltung (f) *De*
bookkeeping *En*

tenure *En*
(période de) jouissance (f) *Fr*
Besitz (m); Amtszeit (f) *De*

tenure (f) à bail *Fr*
gepachtet, gemietet (adj) *De*
leasehold *En*

tenure (f) flexible *Fr*
flexible Anstellung (f) *De*
flexible tenure *En*

Termin (m) *De*
appointment (meeting) *En*
rendez-vous (m) *Fr*

terminal care *En*
soins (m.pl) terminaux *Fr*
Pflege (f) für unheilbar Kranke *De*

Terminkalender (m) *De*
diary *En*
agenda (m) *Fr*

terminus (m) *Fr*
Endstation (f) *De*
rail terminus *En*

terms of payment *En*
conditions (f.pl) de paiement *Fr*
Zahlungsbedingungen (f.pl) *De*

terms of reference *En*
mandat (m) *Fr*
Anweisungen (f.pl) *De*

terraced houses *En*
rangée (f) de maisons de style uniforme *Fr*
Reihenhäuser (nt.pl) *De*

terrain (m) affecté au logement *Fr*
Wohngebiet (nt) *De*
housing land *En*

terrain (m) constructible *Fr*
Bauland (nt) *De*
building land *En*

terrain (m) constructible résidentiel *Fr*
Wohnbebauungsland (nt) *De*
residential land *En*

terrain (m) de décharge *Fr*
Müllkippe (f) *De*
dump (noun) (refuse) *En*

terrain (m) de jeux/sports *Fr*
Sportplatz (m) *De*
playing field *En*

terrain (m) industriel *Fr*
Industrielandschaft (f) *De*
industrial land *En*

terrain (m) scolaire *Fr*
Schulgelände (nt) *De*
school grounds *En*

terrain (m) vague *Fr*
nicht bewirtschaftetes Land (nt) *De*
derelict land *En*

terrain (m) vague *Fr*
unbebautes Gelände (nt) *De*
vacant land/site *En*

terrain (m) vièrge *Fr*
Bauplatz (m) im Grünen *De*
green field site *En*

terrains (m.pl) bâtissables *Fr*
Erschließungsgebiet (nt) *De*
development land *En*

terre (f) agricole *Fr*
Ackerland (nt) *De*
agricultural land *En*

*** see/siehe/voir: Introduction page IX**

terre (f) agricole *Fr*
Ackerland (nt) *De*
farmland *En*

terre (f) végétale *Fr*
Mutterboden (m) *De*
topsoil *En*

tertiärer Bildungsbereich (m) *De*
tertiary education *En*
enseignement (m) technologique *Fr*

tertiary college *En*
lycée (m) *Fr*
Schule (f) für den tertiären Bildungsbereich *De*

tertiary education *En*
enseignement (m) technologique *Fr*
tertiärer Bildungsbereich (m) *De*

text processing *En*
traitement (m) de textes *Fr*
Textverarbeitung (f) *De*

Textverarbeitung (f) *De*
text processing *En*
traitement (m) de textes *Fr*

Textverarbeitung (f) *De*
word processing *En*
traitement (m) de textes *Fr*

Textverarbeitungssystem (nt) *De*
word processor *En*
machine (f) de traitement de textes *Fr*

Theodolit (m) *De*
theodolite *En*
théodolite (m) *Fr*

theodolite *En*
théodolite (m) *Fr*
Theodolit (m) *De*

théodolite (m) *Fr*
Theodolit (m) *De*
theodolite *En*

théorie (f) politique *Fr*
politische Theorie (f) *De*
political theory *En*

Therapie (f) *De*
therapy *En*
thérapie (f) *Fr*

thérapie (f) *Fr*
Therapie (f) *De*
therapy *En*

therapy *En*
thérapie (f) *Fr*
Therapie (f) *De*

thermal energy *En*
énergie (f) thermique *Fr*
thermische Energie (f) *De*

thermal insulation *En*
isolation (f) thermique *Fr*
Wärmeisolierung (f) *De*

thermal unit *En*
unité (f) thermique *Fr*
thermochemische Einheit (f) *De*

thermische Energie (f) *De*
thermal energy *En*
énergie (f) thermique *Fr*

thermochemische Einheit (f) *De*
thermal unit *En*
unité (f) thermique *Fr*

third age *En*
troisième age (m) *Fr*
Alter (nt) *De*

third party *En*
tierce personne (f) *Fr*
Dritte(-r) (m/f) *De*

third party insurance *En*
assurance (f) au tiers *Fr*
Haftpflichtversicherung (f) *De*

third world *En*
tiers monde (m) *Fr*
dritte Welt (f) *De*

through traffic *En*
circulation (f) directe *Fr*
Durchgangsverkehr (m) *De*

tied accommodation/housing *En*
logement (m) de fonction *Fr*
Gesindehaus (nt); Dienstwohnung (f) *De*

tier (of government etc) *En*
niveau (m) (de gouvernement etc) *Fr*
Rang (m) (Regierung usw) *De*

tierce personne (f) *Fr*
Dritte(-r) (m/f) *De*
third party *En*

tiers monde (m) *Fr*
dritte Welt (f) *De*
third world *En*

tight schedule *En*
horaire (m) minute *Fr*
sehr knapper Zeitplan (m) *De*

Tilgungsfonds (m) *De*
sinking fund *En*
fonds (m) d'amortissement *Fr*

time clock *En*
enregistreur (m) de temps *Fr*
Stechuhr (f) *De*

time limit (for payment) *En*
délai (m) de paiement *Fr*
Frist (f) *De*

time management *En*
organisation (f) du temps *Fr*
Zeitplanung (f) *De*

time sheet *En*
feuille (f) de présence *Fr*
Stechkarte (f) *De*

timetable (commerce) *En*
plan (m) de mise en exécution (commerce) *Fr*
Zeitplan (m) *De*

timetable (school) *En*
emploi (m) du temps (école) *Fr*
Stundenplan (m) (Schule) *De*

tip (noun) *En*
dépotoir (m) (d'ordures etc) *Fr*
Müllkippe (f) *De*

tip (vb) *En*
débiter (vb) des foutaises *Fr*
Müll/Schutt abladen (vb) *De*

Tippfehler (m) *De*
typing error *En*
faute (f) de frappe *Fr*

tipping *En*
décharge (f) (d'ordures etc) *Fr*
Schuttabladen (nt) *De*

tirage (m) par offset *Fr*
Offsetdruck (m) *De*
offset printing *En*

titres (m.pl) *Fr*
Wertpapiere (nt.pl) *De*
securities *En*

to whom it may concern *En*
à qui de droit *Fr*
an alle, die es angeht *De*

Todesschein (m) *De*
death certificate *En*
acte (m) de décès *Fr*

*** see/siehe/voir: Introduction page IX**

toll *En*
droit (m) de passage *Fr*
Straßengebühr (f) *De*

toll bridge *En*
pont (m) à péage *Fr*
gebührenpflichtige Brücke (f) *De*

toll road *En*
route (f) à péage *Fr*
gebührenpflichtige Straße (f) *De*

topsoil *En*
terre (f) végétale *Fr*
Mutterboden (m) *De*

tort *En*
délit (m) civil *Fr*
Delikt (nt) *De*

tory *En*
conservateur (m) (-trice f.) *Fr*
Tory (m), Konservative(-r) (m/f) *De*

Tory (m), Konservative(-r) (m/f) *De*
tory *En*
conservateur (m) (-trice f.) *Fr*

Totgeburt (f) *De*
stillbirth *En*
mortinaissance (f) *Fr*

Totgeburtenzahl (f) *De*
stillbirths rate *En*
mortinatalité (f) *Fr*

tourism area *En*
région (f) touristique *Fr*
Touristengebiet (nt) *De*

tourism *En*
tourisme (m) *Fr*
Tourismus (m) *De*

tourisme (m) *Fr*
Tourismus (m) *De*
tourism *En*

Tourismus (m) *De*
tourism *En*
tourisme (m) *Fr*

tourist *En*
touriste (m/f) *Fr*
Tourist/-in (m/f) *De*

tourist board *En*
service (m) de tourisme *Fr*
Fremdenverkehrsamt (nt) *De*

Tourist/-in (m/f) *De*
tourist *En*
touriste (m/f) *Fr*

touriste (m/f) *Fr*
Tourist/-in (m/f) *De*
tourist *En*

Touristengebiet (nt) *De*
tourism area *En*
région (f) touristique *Fr*

tower block *En*
immeuble-tour (m) (pl. immeubles-tours) *Fr*
Hochhaus (nt) *De*

town *En*
ville (f) *Fr*
Stadt (f) *De*

town and country planning *En*
aménagement (m) urbain et rural *Fr*
Stadt- Landschafts- planung (f) *De*

town centre *En*
centre (m) ville *Fr*
Stadtmitte (f) *De*

town clerk *En*
secrétaire (m/f) de la municipalité *Fr*
Stadtdirektor (m) *De*

town council *En*
conseil (m) municipal *Fr*
Stadtrat (m) *De*

town gas *En*
gaz (m) de ville *Fr*
Stadtgas (nt) *De*

town hall *En*
hôtel (m) de ville; mairie (f) *Fr*
Rathaus (nt) *De*

town plan *En*
plan (m) de développement de la ville *Fr*
Stadtplan (m) *De*

town planner *En*
urbaniste (m/f) *Fr*
Stadtplaner/-in (m/f) *De*

town planning *En*
urbanisme (m) *Fr*
Stadtplanung (f) *De*

toxic material *En*
matière (f) toxique *Fr*
Giftstoff (m) *De*

toxic waste *En*
déchets (m.pl) toxiques *Fr*
Giftmüll (m) *De*

toxicomane (m) *Fr*
Drogensüchtige(-r) (m/f) *De*
drug addict *En*

toxicomanie (f) *Fr*
Drogenabhängigkeit (f) *De*
drug dependence *En*

trade *En*
commerce (m) *Fr*
Handel (m); Gewerbe (nt) *De*

trade (vb) *En*
faire (vb) le commerce (de/en qch, avec qn) *Fr*
Handel treiben (vb) *De*

trade association *En*
syndicat (m) professionnel *Fr*
Fachverband (m) *De*

trade balance *En*
balance (f) commerciale *Fr*
Handelsbilanz (f) *De*

trade barrier *En*
barrière (f) commerciale *Fr*
Handelsschranke (f) *De*

trade fair *En*
foire (f) commerciale *Fr*
Messe (f) *De*

trade gap *En*
déficit (m) du commerce extérieur *Fr*
Handelsbilanzdefizit (m) *De*

trade mark *En*
marque (f) de commerce *Fr*
Handelsmarke (f) *De*

trade mark (registered) *En*
marque (f) déposée *Fr*
(eingetragenes) Warenzeichen (nt) *De*

trade secret *En*
secret (m) de fabrique *Fr*
Geschäftsgeheimnis (nt) *De*

trade union *En*
syndicat (m) ouvrier *Fr*
Gewerkschaft (f) *De*

trade union rate *En*
taux (m) syndical *Fr*
Gewerkschaftsbeitrag (m) *De*

trade unionist *En*
syndicaliste (m/f) *Fr*
Gewerkschaftler/-in (m/f) *De*

*** see/siehe/voir: Introduction page IX**

trading standards department *En*
direction (f) des normes de conformité *Fr*
Gewerbeordnungsabteilung (f) *De*

trading standards *En*
règlement (m) du commerce *Fr*
Gewerbeordnung (f) *De*

traffic *En*
circulation (f) (routière) *Fr*
Verkehr (m) *De*

traffic calming *En*
limitation (f) de vitesse *Fr*
Verkehrsberuhigung (f) *De*

traffic capacity/volume *En*
capacité (f) d'écoulement de trafic *Fr*
Verkehrsaufkommen (nt) *De*

traffic census/count *En*
recensement (m) de la circulation *Fr*
Verkehrszählung (f) *De*

traffic congestion *En*
encombrement (m) de circulation *Fr*
(Verkehrs)stau (m) *De*

traffic control *En*
contrôle (m) de la circulation *Fr*
Verkehrskontrolle (f) *De*

traffic diversion *En*
déviation (f) *Fr*
Umleitung (f) *De*

traffic engineer *En*
technicien (m) de la circulation *Fr*
Verkehrsplaner/-in (m/f) *De*

traffic engineering *En*
technique (f) de la circulation *Fr*
Verkehrsplanung (f) *De*

traffic flow *En*
écoulement (m) de la circulation *Fr*
Verkehrsfluß (m) *De*

traffic island *En*
refuge (m) (pour piétons) *Fr*
Verkehrsinsel (f) *De*

traffic lights *En*
feux (m.pl) de circulation *Fr*
(Verkehrs)ampel (f) *De*

traffic management *En*
gestion (f) de la circulation *Fr*
Verkehrsregelung (f) *De*

traffic regulations *En*
règlements (m.pl) sur la circulation *Fr*
Straßenverkehrsordnung (f) *De*

traffic warden *En*
contractuel (m) (-elle f.) *Fr*
Hilfspolizist/-in (m/f); Politesse (f) *De*

trafic (m) voyageurs *Fr*
Personenverkehr (m) *De*
passenger traffic *En*

Tragkonstruktion (f) *De*
framed construction *En*
bâtiment à (m) structure discontinue *Fr*

train (vb) *En*
former (vb) *Fr*
ausbilden (vb) *De*

train (m) à grande vitesse (TGV) *Fr*
Hochgeschwindigkeitszug (m) *De*
high speed train *En*

trainee *En*
stagiaire (m/f) *Fr*
Trainee (m/f) *De*

Trainee (m/f) *De*
trainee *En*
stagiaire (m/f) *Fr*

training *En*
formation (f) *Fr*
Ausbildung (f) *De*

training centre *En*
centre (m) de formation *Fr*
Ausbildungszentrum (nt) *De*

training officer *En*
responsable (m/f) de la formation *Fr*
Ausbildungsoffizier (m) *De*

training policy *En*
politique (f) de formation *Fr*
Ausbildungspolitik (f) *De*

training scheme *En*
programme (m) de formation *Fr*
Ausbildungsprogramm (nt) *De*

traite (f) bancaire *Fr*
Banktratte (f) *De*
banker's draft *En*

traité (m) *Fr*
Vertrag (m) *De*
treaty *En*

traitement (m) *Fr*
Gehalt (nt) *De*
salary *En*

traitement (m) curatif *Fr*
Heilbehandlung (f) *De*
remedial treatment *En*

traitement (m) d'informatique *Fr*
Datenverarbeitung (f) *De*
data processing *En*

traitement (m) de textes *Fr*
Textverarbeitung (f) *De*
text processing *En*

traitement (m) de textes *Fr*
Textverarbeitung (f) *De*
word processing *En*

traitement (m) intermédiaire *Fr*
Zwischenbehandlung (f) *De*
intermediate treatment *En*

traitement (m) médical *Fr*
ärztliche Behandlung (f) *De*
medical treatment *En*

traitement (m) thermique *Fr*
Wärmebehandlung (f) *De*
heat treatment *En*

tranchée (f) à ciel ouvert *Fr*
Gully (m) *De*
surface drain *En*

transfert (m) de fonds *Fr*
Banküberweisung (f) *De*
credit transfer *En*

transformation (f) d'utilisation *Fr*
Alternativmöglichkeit (f) *De*
alternative use *En*

transmission (f) des données *Fr*
Datenübertragung (f) *De*
data transmission *En*

transparence (f) *Fr*
freie Regierungsform (f) *De*
open government *En*

transport (m) *Fr*
Beförderung (f), Transport (m) *De*
transport *En*

transport *En*
transport (m) *Fr*
Beförderung (f), Transport (m) *De*

transport (m) aérien *Fr*
Luft(fracht)verkehr (m) *De*
air transport *En*

*** see/siehe/voir: Introduction page IX**

transport costs *En*
frais (m.pl) de transport *Fr*
Beförderungs-, Transportkosten (pl) *De*

transport (m) d'enfants *Fr*
Schultransport (m) *De*
school transport *En*

transport (m) (de marchandises) *Fr*
Fracht (f) *De*
freight *En*

transport (m) de marchandises *Fr*
Güterverkehr (m), -transport (m) *De*
goods traffic/transport *En*

transport (m) de marchandises par chemin de fer *Fr*
Gütertransport (m) *De*
rail freight *En*

transport (m) par chemin de fer *Fr*
Eisenbahnbeförderung (f) *De*
rail transport *En*

transport (m) par voie d'eau *Fr*
Flußtransport (m) *De*
river freight/transport *En*

transport (m) routier *Fr*
Fracht (f) *De*
commercial transport *En*

transport management *En*
gestion (f) de transport *Fr*
Transportleitung (f) *De*

transport planning *En*
programmation (f) de transport *Fr*
Transportplanung (f) *De*

transport policy *En*
politique (f) de transport *Fr*
Beförderungspolitik (f) *De*

Transportleitung (f) *De*
transport management *En*
gestion (f) de transport *Fr*

Transportplanung (f) *De*
transport planning *En*
programmation (f) de transport *Fr*

transports (m.pl) en commun *Fr*
öffentliche Verkehrsmittel (nt.pl) *De*
public transport *En*

transports (m.pl) en commun *Fr*
Personenbeförderung (f) *De*
passenger transport *En*

transports (m.pl) en commun gratuits *Fr*
kostenloser öffentlicher Personenverkehr (m) *De*
free public transport *En*

transports (m.pl) routiers *Fr*
Spedition (f) *De*
road haulage *En*

transports (m.pl) routiers *Fr*
Straßengüterverkehr (m) *De*
road transport *En*

Trauschein (m) *De*
marriage certificate *En*
acte (m) de mariage *Fr*

travail (m) *Fr*
Arbeit (f) *De*
labour *En*

travail (m) *Fr*
Arbeit (f) *De*
work *En*

travail (m) à la journée *Fr*
Tagesarbeit (f) *De*
daywork *En*

travail (m) à temps partiel *Fr*
Teilzeitarbeit (f) *De*
part-time work *En*

travail (m) de bureau *Fr*
Büroarbeit (f) *De*
clerical work *En*

travail (m) de nuit *Fr*
Nachtarbeit (f) *De*
night work *En*

travail (m) fait à domicile *Fr*
Heimarbeit (f) *De*
outwork *En*

travail (m) manuel *Fr*
manuelle Tätigkeit (f) *De*
manual labour *En*

travail (m) par équipes *Fr*
Schichtarbeit (f) *De*
shift work *En*

travail (m) saisonnier *Fr*
Saisonarbeit (f) *De*
seasonal work *En*

travail (m) volontaire *Fr*
freiwillige Arbeit (f) *De*
voluntary work *En*

travailleur (m) indépendant *Fr*
Selbständige(-r) (m/f) *De*
self-employed person *En*

travailleur (m) manuel *Fr*
Hand-, Schwerarbeiter (m) *De*
manual worker *En*

travailleur (m) saisonnier *Fr*
Wander-, Gastarbeiter (m) *De*
migrant worker *En*

Travaux (m.pl) d'Intérêt Général (TIG) *Fr*
Sozialdienst (m) *De*
community service *En*

travaux (m.pl) de voirie *Fr*
Straßenarbeiten (f.pl) *De*
road works *En*

travaux (m.pl) en terre *Fr*
Erdarbeiten (f.pl) *De*
earthworks *En*

travaux (m.pl) extérieurs *Fr*
Außenarbeiten (f.pl) *De*
external works *En*

travaux (m.pl) préparatoires sur un terrain *Fr*
Geländearbeiten (f.pl) *De*
site works *En*

travaux (m.pl) publics *Fr*
Hoch- und Tiefbau (m) *De*
civil engineering *En*

travel concession *En*
prix (m) réduit du voyage *Fr*
Reisekonzession (f) *De*

traveller's cheque *En*
chèque (m) de voyage *Fr*
Reisescheck (m) *De*

travelling expenses *En*
frais (m.pl) de voyage *Fr*
Reisekosten (pl) *De*

travelling people *En*
nomades (m.pl) *Fr*
fahrendes Volk (nt) *De*

travers; à — le programme d'études *Fr*
quer durch das Pensum (nt) *De*
cross-curricular (adj) *En*

treasurer *En*
trésorier (m) *Fr*
Leiter/-in (m/f) der Finanzverwaltung *De*

treaty *En*
traité (m) *Fr*
Vertrag (m) *De*

tree felling *En*
abattage (m) (des arbres) *Fr*
Baumfällung (f) *De*

tree planting *En*
plantage (m) (des arbres) *Fr*
Baumpflanzung (f) *De*

tree preservation order *En*
protection (f) réglementaire (d'un arbre) *Fr*
Baumschutzanweisung (f) *De*

trésor (m) public *Fr*
Einnahmen (f.pl) *De*
revenue account *En*

trésorier (m) *Fr*
Leiter/-in (m/f) der Finanzverwaltung *De*
treasurer *En*

trespass *En*
violation (f) de propriété *Fr*
unbefugtes Betreten (nt) *De*

Treuhandgesellschaft (f); Treuhänderschaft (f) *De*
trust; trusteeship *En*
fidéicommis (m) *Fr*

Treuhandvermögen (nt) *De*
trust fund *En*
fonds (m) de dépôts *Fr*

trial by jury *En*
jugement (m) par jury *Fr*
Schwurgerichtsverfahren (nt) *De*

tribunal *En*
tribunal (m) *Fr*
Gericht (nt) *De*

tribunal (m) *Fr*
Gericht (nt) *De*
court *En*

tribunal (m) *Fr*
Gericht (nt) *De*
tribunal *En*

tribunal (m) criminel *Fr*
Strafgericht (nt) *De*
criminal court *En*

tribunal (m) d'instance *Fr*
Schiedsgericht (nt) *De*
magistrates' court *En*

tribunal (m) industriel *Fr*
Arbeitsgericht (nt) *De*
industrial tribunal *En*

tribunal (m) pour enfants et adolescents *Fr*
Jugendgericht (nt) *De*
juvenile court *En*

tribunaux (pl) de première instance *Fr* *
Grafschaftsgericht (nt) *De*
county court *En*

Trinkwasser (nt) *De*
drinking water *En*
eau (f) potable *Fr*

troisième age (m) *Fr*
Alter (nt) *De*
third age *En*

trottoir (m) *Fr*
Bürgersteig (m) *De*
pavement *En*

truancy *En*
absentéisme (m) scolaire *Fr*
unentschuldigtes Fernbleiben (nt); Schuleschwänzen (nt) *De*

trunk road *En*
grande route (f) *Fr*
Fernstraße (f) *De*

trust fund *En*
fonds (m) de dépôts *Fr*
Treuhandvermögen (nt) *De*

trust; trusteeship *En*
fidéicommis (m) *Fr*
Treuhandgesellschaft (f); Treuhänderschaft (f) *De*

trustee *En*
membre (m) du conseil d'administration (d'une fondation) *Fr*
Kurator/-in (m/f); Verwalter/-in (m/f) *De*

tunnel (m) trans-Manche *Fr*
Kanaltunnel (m) *De*
channel link/tunnel *En*

turnover *En*
chiffre (m) d'affaires *Fr*
Umsatz (m) *De*

tutor *En*
directeur (m) (-trice f.) des études (d'un groupe d'étudiants) *Fr*
(Privat)lehrer/-in (m/f) *De*

tuyau (m) *Fr*
Rohr (nt) *De*
pipe *En*

tuyau (m) d'eau *Fr*
Wasserrohr (nt) *De*
water pipe *En*

twin town *En*
ville (f) jumelle *Fr*
Partnerstadt (f) *De*

twinning *En*
jumelage (m) *Fr*
Zwillingsverbindung (f) *De*

type (vb) *En*
écrire (vb) à la machine *Fr*
(auf der) Schreibmaschine schreiben (vb) *De*

typewriter *En*
machine (f) à écrire *Fr*
Schreibmaschine (f) *De*

typing *En*
dactylographie (f) *Fr*
Maschineschreiben (nt) *De*

typing error *En*
faute (f) de frappe *Fr*
Tippfehler (m) *De*

typing pool (room) *En*
salle (f) des dactylos *Fr*
Schreibbüro (nt) *De*

typing pool (staff) *En*
équipe (f) de dactylos *Fr*
Schreibkräfte (f.pl) *De*

typist *En*
dactylo(graphe) (m/f) *Fr*
Schreibkraft (f) *De*

*** see/siehe/voir: Introduction page IX**

Überbesetzung (f) *De*
overmanning *En*
avoir un personnel trop nombreux *Fr*

Überführung (f) *De*
flyover *En*
passage (m) supérieur *Fr*

Übernahme (f) *De*
adoption (of road by council) *En*
prise (f) en charge d'une rue par la municipalité *Fr*

Übernahmeangebot (nt) *De*
take-over bid *En*
offre (m) de rachat *Fr*

überprüfen (vb) *De*
vet (vb) *En*
analyser (vb) *Fr*

Überprüfung (f) der Bedürftigkeit *De*
means test *En*
enquête (f) sur les ressources familiales *Fr*

Überprüfung (f) der Politik *De*
policy review *En*
évaluation (f) des politiques *Fr*

Überrepräsentation (f) *De*
over-representation *En*
surreprésentation (f) *Fr*

überschüssiges Land (nt) *De*
surplus land *En*
surplus (m) de terrain *Fr*

Überstunden (f.pl) *De*
overtime *En*
heures (f.pl) supplémentaires *Fr*

übertragen (vb) *De*
vire (vb) *En*
virer (vb) *Fr*

üdertragen (vb); (Verantwortung usw) *De*
devolve (vb) powers (to) *En*
déléguer (vb) des pouvoirs (à) *Fr*

ultra vires (adj) *De*
ultra vires (adj) *En*
au delà des pouvoirs (adj) *Fr*

ultra vires (adj) *En*
au delà des pouvoirs (adj) *Fr*
ultra vires (adj) *De*

Umbau (m) *De*
house conversion *En*
aménagement (m) d'une maison *Fr*

Umbau (m) *De*
rebuilding *En*
reconstruction (f) *Fr*

Umbauten (m.pl) *De*
converted buildings *En*
bâtiments (m.pl) aménagés *Fr*

(Umgebung usw) verschönern (vb) *De*
enhance (vb) (environment etc) *En*
améliorer (vb) (l'environnement etc) *Fr*

Umgehungsstraße (f) *De*
by-pass *En*
route (f) d'évitement *Fr*

Umgehungsstraße (f) *De*
ring road *En*
boulevard (m) périphérique *Fr*

umgestalten (vb) *De*
redesign (vb) *En*
redessiner (vb) *Fr*

Umleitung (f) *De*
diversion *En*
déviation (f) *Fr*

Umleitung (f) *De*
traffic diversion *En*
déviation (f) *Fr*

Umorganisation (f) *De*
reorganization *En*
réorganisation (f) *Fr*

umorganisieren (vb) *De*
reorganize (vb) *En*
réorganiser (vb) *Fr*

umquartieren (vb) *De*
rehouse (vb) *En*
reloger (vb) *Fr*

Umquartierung (f) *De*
rehousing *En*
relogement (m) *Fr*

Umsatz (m) *De*
turnover *En*
chiffre (m) d'affaires *Fr*

umschulen (vb) *De*
retrain (vb) (staff) *En*
recycler (vb) (personnel) *Fr*

Umschulung (f) *De*
retraining *En*
recyclage (m) *Fr*

umstrukturieren (vb) *De*
restructure (vb) *En*
réorganiser (vb) *Fr*

Umstrukturierung (f) *De*
restructuring *En*
réorganisation (f) *Fr*

Umverlegung (f) *De*
redeployment *En*
reconversion (f) *Fr*

Umwelt (f) *De*
environment *En*
environnement (m) *Fr*

(Umwelt)gesundheitsdienst (m) *De*
environmental health *En*
salubrité (f) publique *Fr*

(Umwelt)verschmutzung (f) *De*
pollution *En*
pollution (f) *Fr*

umweltbewußtes Gebiet (nt) *De*
environmentally sensitive area *En*
région (f) d'importance écologique *Fr*

*** see/siehe/voir: Introduction page IX**

Umwelterziehung (f) *De*
environmental education *En*
éducation (f) à l'environnement *Fr*

umweltfreundlich (adj) *De*
environmentally friendly *En*
qui ne nuit pas à l'environnement *Fr*

Umweltkontrolle (f) *De*
environmental control *En*
contrôle (m) de l'environnement *Fr*

Umweltplanung (f) *De*
environmental planning *En*
programmation (f) de l'environnement *Fr*

Umweltschäden (m.pl) *De*
environmental damage *En*
dégats (m.pl) à l'environnement *Fr*

Umweltschutz (m)/-politik (f) *De*
environmental conservation/policy *En*
protection (f) de l'environnement *Fr*

Umweltschützer/-in (m/f) *De*
conservationist *En*
partisan (m) (-ane f.) de la conservation *Fr*

Umweltschützer/-in (m/f) *De*
environmentalist *En*
écologiste (m/f) *Fr*

Umweltschutzgruppe (f) *De*
environmental group *En*
groupe (m) écologiste *Fr*

Umweltschutzleitung (f) *De*
environmental management *En*
gestion (f) de l'environnement *Fr*

Umweltschutzorganisation (f) *De*
environmental services *En*
services (m.pl) de l'environnement *Fr*

Umweltverbesserung (f) *De*
environmental improvement *En*
amélioration (f) en matière d'environnement *Fr*

Umweltverschmutzung (f) *De*
environmental pollution *En*
pollution (f) de l'environnement *Fr*

unadopted road *En*
chemin (m) privé *Fr*
Privatweg (m), -straße (f) *De*

unbebautes Gelände (nt) *De*
vacant land/site *En*
terrain (m) vague *Fr*

unbefugtes Betreten (nt) *De*
trespass *En*
violation (f) de propriété *Fr*

unbenutztes Gebäude (nt) *De*
redundant building *En*
bâtiment (m) en surnombre *Fr*

unbewohnbare Unterkunft (f) *De*
unfit dwelling/housing *En*
logement (m) inhabitable *Fr*

under fives *En*
enfants (m/f pl) au-dessous de cinq ans *Fr*
Kinder (nt.pl) unter fünf Jahren *De*

underfunding *En*
sousfinancement (m) *Fr*
Unterfinanzierung (f) *De*

undergraduate *En*
étudiant (m) (-ante f.) qui prépare la licence *Fr*
Student/-in (m/f) *De*

underground railway *En*
chemin (m) de fer souterrain; métro (m) *Fr*
Untergrundbahn; U-bahn (f) *De*

underpass *En*
passage (m) souterrain *Fr*
Unterführung (f) *De*

underpayment *En*
rémunération (f) insuffisante *Fr*
Unterbezahlung (f) *De*

underpin (vb) *En*
étayer (vb) *Fr*
(ab)stützen (vb) *De*

underprivileged (adj) *En*
défavorisé (adj) *Fr*
unterprivilegiert (adj) *De*

underspending *En*
dépenses (f.pl) en dessous des chiffres prévus dans le budget *Fr*
Budgetunterschreitung (f) *De*

understaffed (to be) *En*
manquer (vb) de personnel *Fr*
(an)Personalmangel leiden *De*

unearned income *En*
rente (f) *Fr*
Kapitaleinkommen (nt) *De*

uneinbringliche Schulden (f.pl) *De*
bad debts *En*
mauvaises dettes (f.pl) *Fr*

unemployed; unwaged (adj) *En*
en chômage (adj) *Fr*
arbeitslos (adj) *De*

unemployed/unwaged person *En*
chômeur (m) *Fr*
Arbeitslose(-r) (m/f) *De*

unemployment *En*
chômage (m) *Fr*
Arbeitslosigkeit (f) *De*

unemployment benefit *En*
indemnité (f) de chômage *Fr*
Arbeitslosengeld (nt) *De*

unentschuldigtes Fernbleiben (nt); Schuleschwänzen (nt) *De*
truancy *En*
absentéisme (m) scolaire *Fr*

Unfähigkeit (f) *De*
incompetence *En*
incompétence (f) *Fr*

unfair dismissal *En*
destitution (f) sans cause *Fr*
ungerechtfertigte Entlassung (f) *De*

Unfallziffer (f) *De*
accident rate *En*
taux (m) d'accidents *Fr*

unfit dwelling/housing *En*
logement (m) inhabitable *Fr*
unbewohnbare Unterkunft (f) *De*

unfurnished (adj) *En*
non meublé (adj) *Fr*
unmöbliert (adj) *De*

unfurnished accommodation *En*
logement (m) non meublé *Fr*
unmöblierte Wohnung (f) *De*

Ungebühr (f) vor Gericht *De*
contempt of court *En*
outrage (m) au tribunal *Fr*

ungelernt (adj) *De*
unskilled (adj) *En*
inexperimenté (adj) *Fr*

ungelernter Arbeiter (m), Hilfsarbeiter (m) *De*
unskilled worker *En*
ouvrier (m) (-ière f.) non qualifié (-e) *Fr*

*** see/siehe/voir: Introduction page IX**

ungerechtfertigte Entlassung (f) ***De***
unfair dismissal *En*
destitution (f) sans cause *Fr*

ungesetzlich (adj) ***De***
unlawful (adj) *En*
illégal (adj) *Fr*

Ungleichheit (f) zwischen den Rassen ***De***
racial inequality *En*
inégalité (f) raciale *Fr*

unification (f) ***Fr***
Vereinigung (f) *De*
amalgamation *En*

unified business rate ***En***
taxe (f) professionnelle *Fr*
einheitliche Geschäftsgebühr (f) *De*

unit cost ***En***
coût (m) de l'unité *Fr*
Kosten (pl) pro Einheit *De*

unité (f) centrale de traitement ***Fr***
Großrechner (m) *De*
mainframe computer *En*

unité (f) de visualisation ***Fr***
Bildschirmgerät (nt) *De*
visual display unit (VDU) *En*

unité (f) monétaire ***Fr***
Währung (f) *De*
currency *En*

unité (f) thermique ***Fr***
thermochemische Einheit (f) *De*
thermal unit *En*

Universität (f) ***De***
university *En*
université (f) *Fr*

université (f) ***Fr***
Universität (f) *De*
university *En*

university ***En***
université (f) *Fr*
Universität (f) *De*

unlawful (adj) ***En***
illégal (adj) *Fr*
ungesetzlich (adj) *De*

unlawful assembly ***En***
attroupement (m) *Fr*
verbotene Versammlung (f) *De*

unlawful dismissal ***En***
destitution (f) illégale *Fr*
gesetzwidrige Entlassung (f) *De*

unmöbliert (adj) ***De***
unfurnished (adj) *En*
non meublé (adj) *Fr*

unmöblierte Wohnung (f) ***De***
unfurnished accommodation *En*
logement (m) non meublé *Fr*

unofficial (adj) ***En***
non officel (adj) *Fr*
inoffiziell (adj) *De*

unprofitable (adj) ***En***
sans profit (adj) *Fr*
unvorteilhaft (adj) *De*

unskilled (adj) ***En***
inexperimenté (adj) *Fr*
ungelernt (adj) *De*

unskilled labour ***En***
main-d'oeuvre (f) non qualifiée *Fr*
Hilfsarbeit (f) *De*

unskilled worker ***En***
ouvrier (m) (-ière f.) non qualifié(e) *Fr*
ungelernter Arbeiter (m), Hilfsarbeiter (m) *De*

unsocial hours ***En***
heures (f.pl) indues *Fr*
ausserhalb der normalen Arbeitszeiten (f.pl) *De*

unter Depression leidendes Gebiet (nt) ***De***
depressed area *En*
région (f) touchée par la crise *Fr*

Unterausschuß (m) ***De***
sub-committee *En*
sous-comité (m) *Fr*

Unterbezahlung (f) ***De***
underpayment *En*
rémunération (f) insuffisante *Fr*

Unterbrechung (f) der Berufstätigkeit ***De***
career break *En*
interruption (f) dans la carrière *Fr*

unterbringen (vb) ***De***
accommodate (vb) *En*
loger (vb) *Fr*

unterbringen (vb) ***De***
house (vb) *En*
loger (vb) *Fr*

Unterfinanzierung (f) ***De***
underfunding *En*
sousfinancement (m) *Fr*

Unterführung (f) ***De***
subway *En*
passage (m) souterrain *Fr*

Unterführung (f) ***De***
underpass *En*
passage (m) souterrain *Fr*

Untergrund (m) ***De***
subsoil *En*
sous-sol (m) *Fr*

Untergrundbahn/U-bahn (f) ***De***
underground railway *En*
chemin (m) de fer souterrain; métro (m) *Fr*

Unterhalt (m) ***De***
support *En*
soutien (m) *Fr*

unterhalten, instandhalten (vb) ***De***
maintain (vb) *En*
entretenir (vb) *Fr*

Unterhaltsbeihilfe (f) ***De***
maintenance grant *En*
bourse (f) d'entretien *Fr*

Unterhändler (m) ***De***
negotiator *En*
négociateur (m) (-trice f.) *Fr*

Unterkunft (f) ***De***
accommodation *En*
logement (m) *Fr*

Unterkunft (f) ***De***
lodging *En*
hébergement (m) *Fr*

Unterkunft (f) ***De***
residential accommodation *En*
logement (m) *Fr*

Unternehmen (nt) ***De***
enterprise *En*
entreprise (f) *Fr*

Unternehmensberater (m) ***De***
management consultant *En*
conseil (m) en gestion *Fr*

Unternehmensbewertung (f) ***De***
project appraisal/evaluation *En*
évaluation (f) du projet *Fr*

Unternehmensbewertung (f) ***De***
project co-ordination *En*
coordination (f) des projets *Fr*

Unternehmensforschung (f) De
operational research *En*
recherche (f) opérationnelle *Fr*

Unternehmensstrategie (f) De
corporate strategy *En*
stratégie (f) corporative *Fr*

Unternehmer/-in (m/f) De
entrepreneur *En*
entrepreneur (m) *Fr*

unternehmerisch (adj) De
entrepreneurial (adj) *En*
qui a l'esprit d'entreprise *Fr*

Unternehmerorganisation (f) De
enterprise agency *En*
agence (f) de promotion de l'entreprise *Fr*

Unternehmungs-, Unternehmerinitiative (f) De
enterprise initiative *En*
initiative (f) d'entreprise *Fr*

unterprivilegiert (adj) De
underprivileged (adj) *En*
défavorisé (adj) *Fr*

Unterricht (m) in den Naturwissenschaften De
science education *En*
enseignement (m) scientifique *Fr*

Unterricht (m) (in) der Muttersprache De
mother tongue teaching *En*
enseignement (m) de la langue maternelle *Fr*

unterrichten (vb) De
teach (vb) *En*
enseigner (vb) *Fr*

unterstützen (vb); (einen Antrag —.) De
second (vb) (a motion) *En*
appuyer (vb) (une proposition) *Fr*

Unterstützung (f); nach Bedurftigkeit gestaffelte —. De
means tested benefit *En*
indemnité (f) allouée après enquête sur les ressources familiales *Fr*

Untersuchung (f) De
inquiry *En*
enquête (f) *Fr*

Untersuchungsausschuß (m) De
committee of enquiry *En*
commission (f) d'enquête *Fr*

Untersuchungsgefängnis (nt) De
remand centre *En*
maison (f) de detention provisoire *Fr*

Untersuchungshaft (f) De
remand (noun) *En*
détention (f) préventive *Fr*

untervermieten (vb) De
sub-let (vb) *En*
sous-louer (vb) *Fr*

Untervermietung (f) De
sub-letting *En*
sous-location (f) *Fr*

Untervertrag (m) De
sub-contract (noun) *En*
sous-traité (m) *Fr*

unvorteilhaft (adj) De
unprofitable (adj) *En*
sans profit (adj) *Fr*

unzulänglich (adj) De
sub-standard (adj) *En*
de qualité inférieure (adj) *Fr*

update (noun) En
rapport (m) périodique *Fr*
Lagebericht (m) *De*

update (vb) En
tenir (vb) qn au courant *Fr*
aktualisieren (vb) *De*

upgrade (vb) (building) En
améliorer (vb) un batiment *Fr*
verbessern, ausbauen (vb) *De*

upgrade (vb) (staff) En
avancer (vb) (personnel) *Fr*
befördern (vb) *De*

upgrading En
avancement (m) *Fr*
Verbesserung (f); Beförderung (f) *De*

urbain (adj) Fr
städtisch (adj); Stadt- *De*
urban (adj) *En*

urban (adj) En
urbain (adj) *Fr*
städtisch (adj); Stadt- *De*

urban aid En
subvention (f) pour le réaménagement du centre ville *Fr*
Stadtbeihilfe (f) *De*

urban area En
secteur (m) urbain *Fr*
Stadtbezirk (m) *De*

urban centre En
centre (m) urbain *Fr*
Stadtmitte (f) *De*

urban conservation En
sauvegarde (f) d'un quartier *Fr*
Städteerhaltung (f) *De*

urban decay/decline En
délabrement (m) urbain *Fr*
Verslumung (f) *De*

urban design En
architecture (f) urbaine *Fr*
Städtebau (m) *De*

urban development area En
zone (f) d'aménagement concerté (ZAC) *Fr*
Urbanisationsgebiet (nt) *De*

urban development En
développement (m) des villes *Fr*
städtebauliche Erschließung (f) *De*

urban planning En
urbanisme (m) *Fr*
Stadtplanung (f) *De*

urban policy En
politique (f) urbaine *Fr*
Städtepolitik (f) *De*

urban renewal En
réhabilitation (f) urbaine *Fr*
Stadterneuerung (f) *De*

urbanisation En
urbanisation (f) *Fr*
Urbanisierung (f) *De*

urbanisation (f) Fr
Urbanisierung (f) *De*
urbanisation *En*

urbanisation (f) contrôlée Fr
Baulückenschließung (f) *De*
infill; infilling *En*

Urbanisationsgebiet (nt) De
urban development area *En*
zone (f) d'aménagement concerté (ZAC) *Fr*

*** see/siehe/voir: Introduction page IX**

Urbanisierung (f) *De*
urbanisation *En*
urbanisation (f) *Fr*

urbanisme (m) *Fr*
Grundstücksverwaltung (f) *De*
land management *En*

urbanisme (m) *Fr*
Planung (f) *De*
planning *En*

urbanisme (m) *Fr*
Stadtplanung (f) *De*
town planning *En*

urbanisme (m) *Fr*
Stadtplanung (f) *De*
urban planning *En*

urbaniste (m/f) *Fr*
Planer/-in (m/f) *De*
planner *En*

urbaniste (m/f) *Fr*
Stadtplaner/-in (m/f) *De*
town planner *En*

Urkunde (f) *De*
deeds *En*
acte (m) *Fr*

Urlaubanspruch (m) *De*
holiday entitlement *En*
congé (m) statutaire *Fr*

Urteil (nt) *De*
judgement *En*
jugement (m) *Fr*

Urteils- und Entscheidungssammlung (f) *De*
law report *En*
rapport (m) juridique *Fr*

Urteilssache (f) *De*
matter of judgment *En*
question (f) de jugement *Fr*

user friendly (adj) *En*
à la portée de l'utilisateur/ "facilement utilisable" *Fr*
benutzerfreundlich (adj) *De*

usine (f) *Fr*
Fabrik (f) *De*
factory *En*

usine (f) à gaz *Fr*
Gaswerk (nt) *De*
gas works *En*

usine (f) d'incinération des déchets *Fr*
Feststoffentsorgungsanlage (f) *De*
solid waste transfer station *En*

usine (f) d'incinération *Fr*
Müllhalde (f) *De*
refuse transfer station *En*

usine (f) de distribution de l'eau *Fr*
Wasserwerk (nt) *De*
waterworks *En*

usure (f) normale *Fr*
natürliche Abnutzung (f) *De*
wear and tear *En*

utilisation (f) des terrains *Fr*
Bodennutzung (f) *De*
land use *En*

utilities *En*
services (m.pl) publics *Fr*
(öffentliche) Versorgungsbetriebe (m.pl) *De*

V

vacancy (staff) *En*
poste (m) vacant *Fr*
freie Stelle (f) *De*

vacant accommodation/dwelling *En*
logement (m) inoccupé *Fr*
leerstehende Wohnung (f) *De*

vacant land/site *En*
terrain (m) vague *Fr*
unbebautes Gelände (nt) *De*

(with) vacant possession *En*
libre possession (f) *Fr*
bezugsfertig (adj) *De*

vagabond (m) *Fr*
Land-, Stadtstreicher/-in (m/f) *De*
vagrant *En*

vagabondage (m) *Fr*
Land-, Stadtstreicherei (f) *De*
vagrancy *En*

vagrancy *En*
vagabondage (m) *Fr*
Land-, Stadtstreicherei (f) *De*

vagrant *En*
vagabond (m) *Fr*
Land-, Stadtstreicher/-in (m/f) *De*

valeur (f) ajoutée *Fr*
Mehrwert (f) *De*
added value *En*

valeur (f) immobilière *Fr*
Immobilienwert (m) *De*
property value *En*

valeur (f) locative imposable *Fr*
steuerbarer Wert (m) *De*
rateable value *En*

valeur (f) marchande *Fr*
Marktwert (m) *De*
market value *En*

valeurs (f.pl) disponibles *Fr*
flüssige Mittel (nt.pl) *De*
liquid assets *En*

valuation *En*
évaluation (f) *Fr*
Schätzung (f) *De*

value added tax (VAT) *En*
taxe (f) à la valeur ajoutée (TVA) *Fr*
Mehrwertsteuer (f) (MWSt) *De*

valuer's department *En*
direction (f) des bâtiments *Fr*
Schätzungsabteilung (f) *De*

vandal *En*
vandale (m/f) *Fr*
Rowdy (m) *De*

vandale (m/f) *Fr*
Rowdy (m) *De*
vandal *En*

vandalism *En*
vandalisme (m) *Fr*
Vandalismus; Wandalismus (m) *De*

vandalisme (m) *Fr*
Vandalismus; Wandalismus (m) *De*
vandalism *En*

variable cost *En*
coût (m) variable *Fr*
variable Kosten (pl) *De*

variable Kosten (pl) *De*
variable cost *En*
coût (m) variable *Fr*

variation order *En*
changement (m) d'instructions *Fr*
Änderungsauftrag (m) *De*

variations (f.pl) démographiques *Fr*
demographische Veränderung (f) *De*
demographic change *En*

Vaterschaftsurlaub (m) *De*
paternity leave *En*
congé (m) de paternité *Fr*

véhicule (m) industriel *Fr*
Last(kraft)wagen (m) *De*
heavy goods vehicle *En*

véhicule (m) industriel *Fr*
Nutzfahrzeug (nt) *De*
goods vehicle *En*

vendeur (m) (-euse f.) *Fr*
Verkäufer/-in (m/f) *De*
shopworker *En*

vente (f) aux enchères *Fr*
Versteigerung (f) *De*
auction sale *En*

vente (f) des HLM *Fr*
Verkauf (m) von Sozialwohnungen *De*
council house sales *En*

vente (f) du terrain *Fr*
Grundstücksverkauf (m) *De*
land disposal *En*

venture capital *En*
capitaux (m.pl) spéculatifs *Fr*
Beteiligungs-, Risikokapital (nt) *De*

verabschieden (vb); (einen Gesetzentwurf — .) *De*
pass (vb) (a law) *En*
voter (vb) (une loi) *Fr*

Veränderungsmanagement (nt) *De*
managing change *En*
gérer (vb) le changement *Fr*

verantwortlich (adj) *De*
accountable (adj) *En*
responsable (adj) *Fr*

Verantwortlichkeit (f) *De*
accountability *En*
responsabilité (f) *Fr*

(Verantwortung usw) übertragen (vb) *De*
devolve (vb) powers (to) *En*
déléguer (vb) des pouvoirs (à) *Fr*

verarbeitende Industrie (f) *De*
manufacturing industry *En*
industrie (f) de fabrication *Fr*

*** see/siehe/voir: Introduction page IX**

verbessern, ausbauen (vb) *De*
upgrade (vb) (building) *En*
améliorer (vb) un batiment *Fr*

Verbesserung (f) *De*
improvement *En*
amélioration (f) *Fr*

Verbesserung (f); Beförderung (f) *De*
upgrading *En*
avancement (m) *Fr*

Verbesserung (f) der Wohnverhältniße *De*
housing improvement *En*
amélioration (f) du logement *Fr*

verbieten (vb) *De*
ban (vb) *En*
interdire (vb) *Fr*

Verbindlichkeit (f); ohne — . *De*
without prejudice *En*
sous toutes réserves (f.pl) *Fr*

Verbindlichkeiten (f.pl) *De*
liabilities *En*
obligations (f.pl) *Fr*

Verbindungsstraße (f) *De*
link road *En*
route (f) d'accès *Fr*

Verbot (nt) *De*
ban (noun) *En*
proscription (f) *Fr*

verbotene Versammlung (f) *De*
unlawful assembly *En*
attroupement (m) *Fr*

Verbotsbestimmung (f) *De*
prohibition order *En*
arrêté (m) d'interdiction *Fr*

Verbraucher (m) *De*
consumer *En*
consommateur (m) (-trice f.) *Fr*

Verbrauchsabgabe (f) *De*
excise duty *En*
droit (m) sur la consommation *Fr*

Verbrauch(s)steuer (f) *De*
excise duties *En*
droits (m.pl) de régie *Fr*

Verbrennung (f) *De*
incineration *En*
incinération (f) *Fr*

Verbrennungsanlage (f) *De*
incinerator *En*
incinérateur (m) *Fr*

Verdienst (m) *De*
earnings *En*
revenu(s) (m/m.pl) *Fr*

Verdrehung (f) *De*
misrepresentation *En*
fausse déclaration (f) *Fr*

Vereinigung (f) *De*
amalgamation *En*
unification (f) *Fr*

verfahrensmäßige Angelegenheit (f) *De*
procedural matter *En*
question (f) de procédure *Fr*

Verfall (m) *De*
dilapidation *En*
dégradation (f) *Fr*

verfallenes Gebäude (nt) *De*
derelict building *En*
bâtiment (m) en état d'abandon *Fr*

Verfallstermin (m) *De*
deadline *En*
date (f) limite *Fr*

Verfassung (f) *De*
constitution *En*
constitution (f) *Fr*

Verfassungsrecht (nt) *De*
constitutional law *En*
droit (m) constitutionnel *Fr*

Verfassungsreform (f) *De*
constitutional reform *En*
réforme (f) constitutionnelle *Fr*

verfolgen (vb); stafrechtlich — . *De*
prosecute (vb) *En*
poursuivre (vb) qn en justice répressive *Fr*

verfolgung (f); strafrechtliche — . *De*
prosecution *En*
poursuites (f.pl) judiciaires *Fr*

verfügbares Einkommen (nt) *De*
disposable income *En*
revenu (m) disponible *Fr*

Verfügung (f) *De*
injunction *En*
injonction (f) (à qn de s'abstenir de faire qch) *Fr*

Verfügung (f) *De*
writ *En*
assignation (f) *Fr*

verge *En*
accotement (m) (de la route) *Fr*
Bankette (f) *De*

verhaltensgestörtes Kind (nt) *De*
maladjusted child *En*
enfant (m/f) à problème *Fr*

Verhaltenskodex (m) *De*
code of conduct *En*
code (m) de déontologie *Fr*

Verhältnis (nt) zwischen Bevölkerungsgruppen *De*
community relations *En*
intégration (f) sociale locale *Fr*

Verhältniswahlsystem (nt) *De*
proportional representation *En*
représentation (f) proportionnelle *Fr*

verhandeln (vb) *De*
negotiate (vb) *En*
négocier (vb) *Fr*

Verhandlung (f) *De*
hearing (court) *En*
audience (f) *Fr*

Verhandlung (f) *De*
negotiation *En*
négociation (f) *Fr*

vérification (f) de comptes *Fr*
Rechnungsprüfung (f) *De*
audit *En*

vérifier et certifier (vb) *Fr*
prüfen (vb) *De*
audit (vb) *En*

vérifier (vb) un projet de procès-verbal/rapport *Fr*
Entwürfe überprüfen (vb) *De*
check (vb) draft minutes/report *En*

Verkauf (m) von Sozialwohnungen *De*
council house sales *En*
vente (f) des H.L.M. *Fr*

Verkäufer/-in (m/f) *De*
shopworker *En*
vendeur (m) (-euse f.) *Fr*

Verkaufssteuer (f) *De*
sales tax *En*
taxe (f) de vente *Fr*

Verkehr (m) *De*
traffic *En*
circulation (f) (routière) *Fr*

(Verkehrs)ampel (f) *De*
traffic lights *En*
feux (m.pl) de circulation *Fr*

*** see/siehe/voir: Introduction page IX**

Verkehrsaufkommen (nt) ***De***
traffic capacity/volume *En*
capacité (f) d'écoulement de trafic *Fr*

Verkehrsberuhigung (f) ***De***
traffic calming *En*
limitation (f) de vitesse *Fr*

Verkehrseinrichtungen (f.pl) für Radfahrer ***De***
cycle facilities *En*
pistes (f.pl) cyclables *Fr*

Verkehrsfluß (m) ***De***
traffic flow *En*
écoulement (m) de la circulation *Fr*

Verkehrsinsel (f) ***De***
traffic island *En*
refuge (m) (pour piétons) *Fr*

Verkehrskontrolle (f) ***De***
traffic control *En*
contrôle (m) de la circulation *Fr*

Verkehrsplaner/-in (m/f) ***De***
traffic engineer *En*
technicien (m) de la circulation *Fr*

Verkehrsplanung (f) ***De***
highway planning *En*
programmation (f) des ponts et chaussées *Fr*

Verkehrsplanung (f) ***De***
traffic engineering *En*
technique (f) de la circulation *Fr*

Verkehrsregelung (f) ***De***
traffic management *En*
gestion (f) de la circulation *Fr*

Verkehrssicherheit (f) ***De***
road safety *En*
prévention (f) routière *Fr*

(Verkehrs)stau (m) ***De***
traffic congestion *En*
encombrement (m) de circulation *Fr*

Verkehrsunfall (m) ***De***
road accident *En*
accident (m) de la route *Fr*

Verkehrszählung (f) ***De***
traffic census/count *En*
recensement (m) de la circulation *Fr*

Verkehrszeichen (nt), Straßenschild (nt) ***De***
road sign *En*
signal (m) routier *Fr*

Verlängerung (f) ***De***
extension *En*
extension (f) *Fr*

Verlängerung (f) einer Zahlungsfrist ***De***
extension of credit *En*
prolongation (f) d'un crédit *Fr*

Verletzung (f) einer Hauptpflicht ***De***
breach of condition notice *En*
avis (m) de non-accomplissement de contrat *Fr*

Verleumdung (f) (schriftliche) ***De***
libel *En*
diffamation (f) *Fr*

Verlust (m) ***De***
forfeiture *En*
déchéance (f) *Fr*

Verlust (m), Schulden (f.pl) abschreiben (vb) ***De***
write off (vb) (a debt, a loss) *En*
amortir (vb) (une dette, une perte) *Fr*

Vermessungsingenieur/-in (m/f) ***De***
chartered surveyor *En*
cadastreur (m) *Fr*

Vermieter (m), Hausbesitzer (m) ***De***
landlord *En*
propriétaire (m) *Fr*

Vermittlung (f) ***De***
mediation *En*
intervention (f) *Fr*

Vermittlung (f) ***De***
operator *En*
opérateur (m) (-trice f.) *Fr*

Vermögen (nt) ***De***
assets *En*
avoirs (m.pl) *Fr*

Vermögensanlage (f) in Industriewerten ***De***
industrial investment *En*
investissement (m) industriel *Fr*

Vermögensfinanzierung (f) ***De***
capital finance *En*
investissement (m) *Fr*

Vermögenssteuer (f) ***De***
property tax *En*
impôt (m) foncier *Fr*

Vermögenszuteilung (f) ***De***
capital allowance *En*
déductions (f.pl) fiscales sur les investissements *Fr*

Vernachlässigung (f) der Berufspflichten ***De***
professional negligence *En*
négligence (f) professionnelle *Fr*

Verordnung (f) ***De***
byelaw *En*
arrêté (m) municipal *Fr*

Verpachtung (f), Vermietung (f) ***De***
letting *En*
location (f) *Fr*

Verpächter/-in (m/f) ***De***
lessor *En*
bailleur (m) bailleresse (f) *Fr*

Verpackung (f) in Container ***De***
containerization *En*
conteneurisation (f) *Fr*

versagen (vb) ***De***
default (vb) *En*
faire (vb) défaut *Fr*

Versammlung (f); Besprechung (f) ***De***
meeting *En*
réunion (f) *Fr*

verschiedene Ausgaben (f.pl) ***De***
sundry expenses *En*
frais (m.pl) divers *Fr*

Verschmutzung (f) durch die Industrie ***De***
industrial pollution *En*
pollution (f) industrielle *Fr*

verschönern (vb); Umgebung usw —. ***De***
enhance (vb) (environment etc) *En*
améliorer (vb) (l'environnement etc) *Fr*

Verschmutzungskontrolle (f) ***De***
pollution control/monitoring *En*
contrôle (m) de la pollution *Fr*

Verschönerungsgebiet (nt) ***De***
general improvement area *En*
zone (f) d'embellissement général *Fr*

Versendung (f) ***De***
consignment *En*
expédition (f) *Fr*

*** see/siehe/voir: Introduction page IX**

verser (vb) les prestations *Fr*
(Beihilfe) auszahlen (vb) *De*
pay out (vb) benefits *En*

Versetzung (f) *De*
relocation (staff) *En*
redéploiement (m) du personnel *Fr*

Versicherung (f) *De*
insurance *En*
assurance (f) *Fr*

Versicherungsgesellschaft (f) *De*
insurance company *En*
société (f) d'assurance(s) *Fr*

Versicherungspolice (f) *De*
insurance policy *En*
police (f) d'assurance *Fr*

Versicherungsprämie (f) *De*
insurance premium *En*
prime (f) d'assurance *Fr*

Versicherungsschein (m) *De*
insurance certificate *En*
certificat (m) d'assurance *Fr*

Versicherungsurkunde (f) *De*
certificate of insurance *En*
certificat (m) d'assurance *Fr*

Verslumung (f) *De*
urban decay/decline *En*
délabrement (m) urbain *Fr*

verstaatlichter Wirtschaftszweig (m)/verstaatlichte Industrie (f) *De*
nationalised industry *En*
industrie (f) nationalisée *Fr*

Versteigerung (f) *De*
auction sale *En*
vente (f) aux enchères *Fr*

Vertrag (m) *De*
contract *En*
contrat (m) *Fr*

Vertrag (m) *De*
treaty *En*
traité (m) *Fr*

(Vertrag usw) aufsetzen (vb) *De*
draw up (vb) (contract etc) *En*
préparer (vb) le projet d'un contract *Fr*

vertraglicher Anspruch (m) *De*
contractual claim *En*
créance (f) contractuelle *Fr*

Vertragsbedingungen (f.pl) *De*
conditions of contract *En*
cahier (m) des charges *Fr*

Vertragsbruch (m) *De*
breach of contract *En*
rupture (f) de contrat *Fr*

Vertragseinhaltung (f) *De*
contract compliance *En*
exécution (f) de contrat *Fr*

Vertragsform (f) *De*
form of contract *En*
modèle (m) de contrat *Fr*

Vertragsrecht (nt) *De*
contract law *En*
droit (m) des obligations *Fr*

Vertragsrecht (nt) *De*
law of contract *En*
droit (m) des obligations *Fr*

Vertragsvorbemerkungs-vordruck (m) *De*
standard contract preamble *En*
modèle (m) de préliminaires de contrat *Fr*

Vertragsvorschriften (f.pl) *De*
contract regulations *En*
dispositions (f.pl) d'un contrat *Fr*

Vertrauen (nt) der Öffentlichkeit *De*
public confidence *En*
confiance (f) publique *Fr*

Vertrauensmann (m) *De*
shop steward *En*
délégué (m) syndical *Fr*

Vertrauenssache (f) *De*
matter of trust *En*
question (f) de confiance *Fr*

Vertraulichkeit (f) *De*
confidentiality *En*
caractère (m) confidentiel *Fr*

verurteilen (vb) *De*
sentence (vb) *En*
prononcer (vb) une condamnation (contre quelqu'un) *Fr*

verwalten (vb) *De*
administer (vb) *En*
administrer (vb) *Fr*

Verwaltung (f) *De*
administration *En*
administration (f) *Fr*

Verwaltungsbeamte(-r)/-beamtin (m/f) *De*
administrator *En*
administrateur (m) *Fr*

Verwaltungsrecht (nt) *De*
administrative law *En*
loi (f) de l'administration *Fr*

Verwaltungszentrum (nt) (einer Stadt) *De*
civic centre *En*
centre (m) civique *Fr*

Verweigerung (f); Ablehnung (f) *De*
refusal *En*
refus (m) *Fr*

vet (vb) *En*
analyser (vb) *Fr*
überprüfen (vb) *De*

vêtements (m.pl) protecteurs *Fr*
Schutz(be)kleidung (f) *De*
protective clothing *En*

viabilité (f) commerciale *Fr*
wirtschaftliche Lebensfähigkeit (f) *De*
commercial viability *En*

viable proposition *En*
proposition (f) praticable *Fr*
durchführbares Projekt (nt) *De*

vice (m) de construction *Fr*
Defekt (m) *De*
defect (in building) *En*

vice-chair/-chairman/chairperson *En*
vice-président (m) (-ente f.) *Fr*
stellvertretende(-r) Vorsitzende(-r) (m/f) *De*

vice-président (m) (-ente f.) *Fr*
stellvertretende(-r) Vorsitzende(-r) (m/f) *De*
vice-chair/chairman/chairperson *En*

victim of child abuse *En*
enfant (m/f) martyr(-e) *Fr*
Opfer (nt) der Kindesmißhandlung *De*

victim support *En*
soutien (m) des victimes du crime *Fr*
Opferhilfe (f) *De*

vidange (m) (ordinateur) *Fr*
Dumping (nt) *De*
dumping (computer) *En*

*** see/siehe/voir: Introduction page IX**

vignette (f) *Fr*
Kraftfahrzeugsteuer (f) *De*
road tax *En*

ville (f) *Fr*
Stadt (f) *De*
town *En*

ville (f) en plein développement *Fr*
expandierende Stadt (f) *De*
expanding town *En*

ville (f) jumelle *Fr*
Partnerstadt (f) *De*
twin town *En*

ville (f) nouvelle *Fr*
neue Stadt (f) *De*
new town *En*

ville; municipalité (f) *Fr* *
(Stadt)gemeinde (f), Bezirk (m) *De*
borough *En*

violation (f) de propriété *Fr*
unbefugtes Betreten (nt) *De*
trespass *En*

violence (f) contre les enfants *Fr*
Kindesmißhandlung (f) *De*
child abuse *En*

vire (vb) *En*
virer (vb) *Fr*
übertragen (vb) *De*

virement *En*
virement (m) *Fr*
Budgetüberweisung (f) *De*

virement (m) *Fr*
Budgetüberweisung (f) *De*
virement *En*

virer (vb) *Fr*
übertragen (vb) *De*
vire (vb) *En*

Visitenkarte (f) *De*
business card *En*
carte (f) d'affaires *Fr*

visual display unit (VDU) *En*
unité (f) de visualisation *Fr*
Bildschirmgerät (nt) *De*

visual handicap *En*
diminution (f) visuelle *Fr*
Sehbehinderung (f) *De*

visually handicapped (adj) *En*
malvoyant (adj) *Fr*
sehbehindert (adj) *De*

vocational education/training *En*
éducation (f) professionnelle *Fr*
Berufserziehung (f), /-ausbildung (f) *De*

vocational guidance *En*
orientation (f) professionnelle *Fr*
Berufsberatung (f) *De*

voeux (m.pl) du comité *Fr*
Auschußbeschluß (m) *De*
committee resolution *En*

void *En*
maison (f) inoccupée *Fr*
Wohnungsleerstand (m) *De*

voie (f) rapide *Fr*
Schnellstrasse (f) *De*
expressway *En*

voisin (m) (-ine f.) *Fr*
Nachbar/-in (m/f) *De*
neighbour *En*

voisinage (m) *Fr*
Gegend (f) *De*
neighbourhood *En*

voiture (f) de pompiers *Fr*
Löschfahrzeug (nt) *De*
fire engine *En*

voiture (f) de secours *Fr*
Hilfsfahrzeug (nt) *De*
emergency vehicle *En*

voiture (f) des boueurs *Fr*
Müllwagen (m) *De*
dustcart *En*

voix (f) prépondérante du président *Fr*
ausschlaggebende Stimme (f) *De*
casting vote (of chairman) *En*

vol (m) *Fr*
Raub (m) *De*
robbery *En*

vol (m) à l'étalage *Fr*
Ladendiebstahl (m) *De*
shoplifting *En*

Völkerrecht (nt) *De*
international law *En*
droit (m) international *Fr*

Volksabstimmung (f), Referendum (nt) *De*
referendum *En*
référendum (m) *Fr*

Volkszählung (f) *De*
census of population *En*
recensement (m) de la population *Fr*

Volkszählung (f), Zensus (m) *De*
census *En*
recensement (m) *Fr*

Vollstreckungsbenachrichtigung (f) *De*
enforcement notice *En*
avis (m) d'application (d'une loi etc) *Fr*

volontaire (m) *Fr*
freiwillige(-r) Helfer/-in (m/f); Freiwillige(r) (m/f) *De*
voluntary worker/volunteer *En*

voluntary agency/organisation *En*
organisation (f) bénévole *Fr*
Freiwilligenverband (m) *De*

voluntary aided school *En* *
école (f) confessionnelle *Fr*
Konfessionsschule (f) *De*

voluntary sector *En*
secteur (m) non-gouvernemental *Fr*
freiwilliger Sektor (m) *De*

voluntary service *En*
service (m) volontaire *Fr*
freiwilliger Dienst (m) *De*

voluntary work *En*
travail (m) volontaire *Fr*
freiwillige Arbeit (f) *De*

voluntary worker/volunteer *En*
volontaire (m) *Fr*
freiwillige(-r) Helfer/-in (m/f); Freiwillige(-r) (m/f) *De*

(von) Gemeinsinn zeugend (adj) *De*
public spirited (adj) *En*
dévoué au bien public (adj) *Fr*

Voranschlag (m) *De*
estimate *En*
devis (m) *Fr*

Vorarbeiter (m) *De*
foreman *En*
contremaître (m) *Fr*

(Voraus)planung (f) *De*
projection *En*
prévision (f) *Fr*

Voraussage (f), Prognose (f) *De*
forecasting *En*
pronostication (f) *Fr*

*** see/siehe/voir: Introduction page IX**

Vorauszahlung (f) De
advance payment *En*
paiement (m) par anticipation *Fr*

Vorbesprechung (f) De
pre-meeting *En*
réunion (f) préparatoire *Fr*

vorderster; in — Linie De
forefront (in the) *En*
(au) premier plan *Fr*

Vordruck (m) eines Bauvertrages De
standard form of building contract *En*
modèle (m) de contrat de construction *Fr*

vorgefertigt (adj) De
system built (adj) *En*
préfabriqué (adj) *Fr*

vorgefertigter Beton (m) De
precast concrete *En*
béton (m) prémoulé *Fr*

vorgeladen werden; auftreten (vb) De
appear (vb) (in court) *En*
comparaître (vb) en justice *Fr*

vorhersagen (vb) De
forecast (vb) *En*
prévoir (vb) *Fr*

Vorkaufsrecht (nt) De
option to purchase *En*
possibilité (f) d'achat *Fr*

Vorladung (f) De
summons (noun) *En*
citation (f) *Fr*

(eine) Vorladung beantragen (vb) De
summons (noun) (to issue a —) *En*
lancer (vb) une assignation *Fr*

Vorlesung (f) De
lecture *En*
conférence (f) *Fr*

(eine) Vorlesung halten (vb) De
lecture (vb) *En*
faire (vb) une conférence *Fr*

Vormund (m) De
guardian *En*
gardien (m) *Fr*

Vorort- De
suburban (adj) *En*
de banlieue (adj) *Fr*

Vorort (m); Vororte (m.pl) De
suburb/suburbia *En*
banlieue (f) *Fr*

Vorrang (m); Priorität (f) De
priority *En*
priorité (f) *Fr*

Vorschlag (m) De
proposal *En*
proposition (f) *Fr*

Vorschrift (f); Regelung (f) De
regulation *En*
règlement (m) *Fr*

Vorschulerziehung (f) De
nursery education *En*
enseignement (m) préélémentaire *Fr*

Vorschußkredit (m) De
bridging loan *En*
crédit (m) provisoire *Fr*

vorsichtige Schätzung (f) De
conservative estimate *En*
évaluation (f) prudente *Fr*

Vorsitz (m) De
chairmanship *En*
présidence (f) *Fr*

Vorsitzende(-r) (m/f) De
chair/chairman/chairperson *En*
président (m) (-ente f.) *Fr*

Vorstand (m) De
board of directors *En*
conseil (m) d'administration *Fr*

Vorstand (m) De
governing board/body *En*
conseil (m) d'administration *Fr*

Vorstandssitzung (f) De
board meeting *En*
réunion (f) du conseil *Fr*

Vorstellungsgesprächsleiter (m), Interviewer (m) De
interviewer *En*
intervieweur (m) *Fr*

Vorstellungsgespräch (nt), Interview (nt) De
interview *En*
interview (f) *Fr*

Vorstrafen (f.pl) De
police record *En*
casier (m) judiciaire *Fr*

vorübergehende Anstellung (f) De
temporary employment/work *En*
emploi (m) (à titre) provisoire *Fr*

vorübergehend versetzt sein De
seconded (to be seconded) *En*
hors cadre (être mis hors cadre) *Fr*

vorübergehende Versetzung (f) De
secondment *En*
détachement (m) *Fr*

Vorurteil (nt) De
prejudice *En*
préjugés (m.pl) *Fr*

vorzeitiger Ruhestand (m) De
early retirement *En*
retraite (f) prématurée *Fr*

vote (noun) En
vote (m) *Fr*
Stimme (f) (m/f) *De*

vote (m) Fr
Stimme (f) (m/f) *De*
vote (noun) *En*

vote (vb) En
voter (vb) *Fr*
wählen (vb) *De*

voter En
électeur (m) (-trice f.) *Fr*
Wähler/-in (m/f) *De*

voter (vb) Fr
wählen (vb) *De*
vote (vb) *En*

voter (vb) le budget Fr
(das Budget) bewilligen (vb) *De*
pass (vb) the budget *En*

voter (vb) une loi Fr
(einen Gesetzentwurf) verabschieden (vb) *De*
pass (vb) a law *En*

voyou (m) Fr
Hooligan (m), Rowdy (m) *De*
hooligan *En*

voyouterie (f) Fr
Hooliganismus (m), Rowdytum (nt) *De*
hooliganism *En*

*** see/siehe/voir: Introduction page IX**

Wächter (m) *De*
security guard *En*
gardien (m) *Fr*

wage *En*
salaire (m) *Fr*
Lohn (m) *De*

wage bargaining *En*
négotiation (f) salariale *Fr*
Lohntarifverhandlung (f) *De*

wage freeze *En*
blocage (m) des salaires *Fr*
Lohnstopp (m) *De*

wage rate *En*
taux (m) des salaires *Fr*
Lohnsatz (m) *De*

wage restraint *En*
contrainte (f) sur les salaires *Fr*
Zurückhaltung (f) bei Lohnforderungen *De*

Wahl- *De*
electoral (adj) *En*
électoral (adj) *Fr*

Wahl (f) *De*
election *En*
élection (f) *Fr*

Wahlbezirk (m) *De*
electoral ward *En*
circonscription (f) électorale *Fr*

Wahlbezirk (m) *De*
ward (constituency) *En*
circonscription (f) électorale *Fr*

wählen (vb) *De*
vote (vb) *En*
voter (vb) *Fr*

Wähler (m.pl), Wählerschaft (f) *De*
electorate *En*
corps (m) électoral *Fr*

Wähler/-in (m/f) *De*
constituent *En*
électeur (m) (-trice f.) *Fr*

Wähler/-in (m/f) *De*
elector *En*
électeur (m) (-trice f.) *Fr*

Wähler/-in (m/f) *De*
voter *En*
électeur (m) (-trice f.) *Fr*

Wählerverzeichnis (nt) *De*
electoral register/roll *En*
liste (f) électorale *Fr*

Wahlfreiheit (f) *De*
freedom of choice *En*
liberté (f) de choix arbitraire *Fr*

Wahlkabine (f) *De*
polling booth *En*
isoloir (m) *Fr*

Wahlkampf (m); Agitation (f) *De*
electioneering *En*
manoeuvres (f.pl) électorales *Fr*

Wahlkosten (pl) *De*
election expenses *En*
frais (m.pl) de l'élection *Fr*

Wahlkreis (m) *De*
constituency *En*
circonscription (f) électorale *Fr*

Wahlleiter/-in (m/f) *De*
returning officer (in election) *En*
directeur (m) (-trice f.) du scrutin *Fr*

Wahllokal (nt) *De*
polling station *En*
bureau (m) de vote *Fr*

Wahlrecht (nt) *De*
electoral law *En*
droit (m) électoral *Fr*

Wahlrecht (nt) *De*
franchise (political) *En*
droit (m) de vote *Fr*

Wahlreform (f) *De*
electoral reform *En*
réforme (f) électorale *Fr*

Wahlsystem (nt) *De*
electoral system *En*
système (m) électoral *Fr*

Währung (f) *De*
currency *En*
unité (f) monétaire *Fr*

(Währungs)abwertung (f) *De*
devaluation *En*
dévaluation (f) *Fr*

waiting list *En*
liste (f) d'attente *Fr*
Warteliste (f) *De*

Wandalismus; Vandalismus (m) *De*
vandalism *En*
vandalisme (m) *Fr*

Wander-, Gastarbeiter (m) *De*
migrant worker *En*
travailleur (m) saisonnier *Fr*

ward (constituency) *En*
circonscription (f) électorale *Fr*
Wahlbezirk (m) *De*

ward (hospital) *En*
salle (f) d'hôpital *Fr*
Station (f) *De*

ward of court *En*
pupille (m/f) sous tutelle judiciaire *Fr*
Mündel (m) (unter Amtsvormundschaft) *De*

warehouse *En*
entrepôt (m) *Fr*
Lager (nt) *De*

warehousing (customs) *En*
entreposage (m) (de marchandises) *Fr*
Lagerung (f) *De*

Warenbestandkontrolle (f) *De*
stock control *En*
contrôle (m) des stocks *Fr*

*** see/siehe/voir: Introduction page IX**

Wärmebehandlung (f) *De*
heat treatment *En*
traitement (m) thermique *Fr*

Wärmeisolierung (f) *De*
thermal insulation *En*
isolation (f) thermique *Fr*

Warmwasseranlage (f) *De*
hot water system *En*
installation (f) d'eau chaude *Fr*

Warmwasserversorgung (f) *De*
hot water supply *En*
arrivée (f) d'eau chaude *Fr*

warrant (arrest) *En*
mandat (m) d'arrêt *Fr*
Haftbefehl (m) *De*

warrant (travel) *En*
feuille (f) de route *Fr*
Erlaubnis (f), Genehmigung (f) *De*

Warteliste (f) *De*
waiting list *En*
liste (f) d'attente *Fr*

Wassergebühren (f.pl) *De*
water charge *En*
redevance (f) de l'eau *Fr*

Wassergebühren (f.pl), -geld (nt) *De*
water rate *En*
taux (m) d'abonnement à l'eau *Fr*

Wasserrechnung (f) *De*
water bill *En*
quittance (f) d'eau *Fr*

Wasserreinigung (f) *De*
water purification *En*
épuration (f) de l'eau *Fr*

Wasserrohr (nt) *De*
water pipe *En*
tuyau (m) d'eau *Fr*

Wasserschutz (m) *De*
water conservation *En*
conservation (f) de l'eau *Fr*

Wasserturm (m) *De*
water tower *En*
château (m) d'eau *Fr*

Wasserverschmutzung (f) *De*
water pollution *En*
pollution (f) de l'eau *Fr*

Wasserversorgung (f) *De*
water supply *En*
service (m) des eaux *Fr*

Wasserversorgungsamt (nt) *De*
water authority *En*
service (m) des eaux *Fr*

Wasserwerk (nt) *De*
waterworks *En*
usine (f) de distribution de l'eau *Fr*

Wasserzähler (m), -uhr (f) *De*
water meter *En*
compteur (m) à eau *Fr*

waste *En*
déchets (m.pl) *Fr*
Abfall (m), Müll (m) *De*

waste collection *En*
ramassage (m) des ordures *Fr*
Müllabfuhr (f) *De*

waste disposal *En*
élimination (f) des déchets *Fr*
Abfallbeseitigung (f) *De*

waste paper basket *En*
corbeille (f) à papiers *Fr*
Papierkorb (m) *De*

waste paper *En*
papier (m) de rebut *Fr*
Papierabfall (m) *De*

waste recovery *En*
récuperation (f) des déchets *Fr*
Abfallrückgewinnung (f) *De*

waste recycling *En*
recyclage (m) des déchets *Fr*
(Abfall)wiederaufbereitung (f); Recycling (nt) *De*

water authority *En*
service (m) des eaux *Fr*
Wasserversorgungsamt (nt) *De*

water bill *En*
quittance (f) d'eau *Fr*
Wasserrechnung (f) *De*

water charge *En*
redevance (f) de l'eau *Fr*
Wassergebühren (f.pl) *De*

water conservation *En*
conservation (f) de l'eau *Fr*
Wasserschutz (m) *De*

water main *En*
conduite (f) d'eau *Fr*
Hauptwasserleitung (f) *De*

water meter *En*
compteur (m) à eau *Fr*
Wasserzähler (m), -uhr (f) *De*

water pipe *En*
tuyau (m) d'eau *Fr*
Wasserrohr (nt) *De*

water pollution *En*
pollution (f) de l'eau *Fr*
Wasserverschmutzung (f) *De*

water purification *En*
épuration (f) de l'eau *Fr*
Wasserreinigung (f) *De*

water rate *En*
taux (m) d'abonnement à l'eau *Fr*
Wassergebühren (f.pl), -geld (nt) *De*

water supply *En*
service (m) des eaux *Fr*
Wasserversorgung (f) *De*

water tower *En*
château (m) d'eau *Fr*
Wasserturm (m) *De*

waterworks *En*
usine (f) de distribution de l'eau *Fr*
Wasserwerk (nt) *De*

wear and tear *En*
usure (f) normale *Fr*
natürliche Abnutzung (f) *De*

Wechsel (m) *De*
bill of exchange *En*
lettre (f) de change *Fr*

Wechselkurs (m) *De*
exchange rate *En*
cours (m) du change *Fr*

Wegerecht (nt) (zu einem Haus) *De*
right of entry *En*
droit (m) d'entrée *Fr*

Wegweiser (m) *De*
signpost *En*
poteau (m) indicateur *Fr*

weighbridge *En*
pont-bascule (m) (pl.ponts-bascules) *Fr*
Brückenwaage (f) *De*

weight limit/restriction *En*
limite (f) de poids *Fr*
Gewichtbeschränkung (f) *De*

weights and measures *En*
poids (m.pl) et mesures (f.pl) *Fr*
Masse und Gewichte (pl) *De*

weiterbildende Schule (f) *De*
further education college *En*
lycée (m) professionnel *Fr*

*** see/siehe/voir: Introduction page IX**

Weiterbildung (f) *De*
further education *En*
enseignement (m) postscolaire *Fr*

weitere Auskunft (f) *De*
further information *En*
renseignements (m.pl) complémentaires *Fr*

welfare policy *En*
politique (f) sociale *Fr*
Wohlfahrtspolitik (f) *De*

welfare state *En*
état (m) providence *Fr*
Wohlfahrtsstaat (m) *De*

welfare work *En*
assistance (f) sociale *Fr*
Sozialarbeit (f) *De*

welfare worker *En*
assistant (m) (-ante f.) social(e) *Fr*
Sozialarbeiter/-in (m/f) *De*

well woman clinic *En*
centre (m) de soins gynécologiques *Fr*
Frauenklinik (f) *De*

Werbekampagne (f) *De*
advertising campaign *En*
campagne (f) de publicité *Fr*

Werbekampagne (f) *De*
marketing campaign *En*
campagne (f) de commercialisation *Fr*

werben (vb) *De*
canvass (vb) (vote etc) *En*
solliciter (vb) (la voix etc) *Fr*

Werbung (f) *De*
advertising *En*
publicité (f) *Fr*

Werbung (f) *De*
promotion (commerce) *En*
promotion (f) (commerce) *Fr*

Werft (f) *De*
dockyard *En*
chantier (m) de construction des navires *Fr*

Werft (f) *De*
shipyard *En*
chantier (m) naval (pl. chantiers navals) *Fr*

Werken (nt), Gestaltung (f) und Technologie (f) *De* *
Craft Design and Technology (CDT) *En*
technologie (f) et travaux (m.pl) manuels *Fr*

Werkstatt (f) *De*
workshop *En*
atelier (m) *Fr*

Wertpapiere (nt.pl) *De*
securities *En*
titres (m.pl) *Fr*

Wertzuwachsabgabe (f) *De*
betterment levy *En*
impôt (m) sur les plus-values *Fr*

Wettbewerb (m) *De*
competition *En*
concurrence (f) *Fr*

Wettbewerbsfreiheit (f) *De*
deregulation *En*
marché (m) libre *Fr*

wharf *En*
quai (m) *Fr*
Kai (m) *De*

wheel clamp *En*
sabot (m) de Denver, pince (f) d'immobilisation *Fr*
Parkkralle (f) *De*

wheelchair *En*
fauteuil (m) roulant *Fr*
Rollstuhl (m) *De*

wheeled bin *En*
poubelle (f) roulante *Fr*
Mülltonne (f) auf Rädern *De*

wholesale trade *En*
commerce (m) en gros *Fr*
Großhandel (m) *De*

wiederverwerten (vb) *De*
recycle (vb) *En*
recycler (vb) *Fr*

width restriction *En*
limitation (f) de largeur *Fr*
Breitenbeschränkung (f) *De*

Wiederaufbereitung (f) *De*
reprocessing *En*
recyclage (m) *Fr*

Wiedergewinnung (f) *De*
reclamation *En*
mise (f) en valeur *Fr*

Wiederherstellung (f) *De*
reinstatement *En*
réintégration (f) *Fr*

Wiederinbesitznahme (f) *De*
repossession *En*
rentrée (f) en possession *Fr*

wind up (vb) (debate etc) *En*
résumer (vb) (un débat etc) *Fr*
(Debatte usw) beschließen (vb) *De*

window envelope *En*
enveloppe (f) à fenêtre *Fr*
Fensterbriefumschlag (m) *De*

Wirkungsanalyse (f) *De*
impact analysis *En*
analyse (f) des résultats (d'une politique/action etc) *Fr*

Wirtschaft (f) *De*
economy *En*
économie (f) *Fr*

wirtschaftliche Entwicklung (f) *De*
commercial development *En*
développement (m) commercial *Fr*

wirtschaftliche Lebensfähigkeit (f) *De*
commercial viability *En*
viabilité (f) commerciale *Fr*

wirtschaftliches Entwicklungsgebiet (nt) *De*
commercial improvement area *En*
zone (f) d'amélioration commerciale *Fr*

wirtschaftliches Fördergebiet (nt) *De*
enterprise zone *En*
zone (f) d'entreprise *Fr*

Wirtschaftlichkeit (f) *De*
cost-effectiveness *En*
coût (m) et efficacité (f) *Fr*

Wirtschaftsanalyse (f) *De*
economic analysis *En*
analyse (f) économique *Fr*

Wirtschaftserklärung (f) *De*
financial statement *En*
état (m) de finances *Fr*

Wirtschaftsförderer (m) *De*
economic development officer *En*
responsable (m) du développement économique *Fr*

Wirtschaftsgebiet (nt) *De*
economic area *En*
secteur (m) économique *Fr*

*** see/siehe/voir: Introduction page IX**

Wirtschaftsinitiativen (f.pl) *De*
economic initiatives *En*
initiatives (f.pl) économiques *Fr*

Wirtschaftskrise (f) *De*
depression *En*
crise (f) économique *Fr*

Wirtschaftslage (f) *De*
economic climate *En*
état (m) économique *Fr*

Wirtschaftsmodell (nt) *De*
economic model *En*
modèle (m) économique *Fr*

Wirtschaftsplanung (f) *De*
economic planning *En*
programme (m) de développement économique *Fr*

Wirtschaftspolitik (f) *De*
economic policy *En*
politique (f) économique *Fr*

Wirtschaftsstruktur (f) *De*
economic structure *En*
structure (f) économique *Fr*

Wirtschaftswachstum (nt) *De*
economic growth *En*
croissance (f) économique *Fr*

Wirtschaftswissenschaften (f.pl) *De*
economics *En*
sciences (f.pl) économiques *Fr*

Wirtschaftswissenschaftler/-in (m/f) *De*
economist *En*
économiste (m) *Fr*

wissenschaftliche Sehenswürdigkeit (f) *De*
Site of Special Scientific Interest (SSI) *En*
espace (m) naturel sensible *Fr*

without prejudice *En*
sous toutes réserves (f.pl) *Fr*
ohne Verbindlichkeit (f) *De*

witness (noun) *En*
témoin (m) *Fr*
Zeuge/-gin (m/f) *De*

witness (vb) *En*
témoigner (vb) *Fr*
Zeuge/-gin sein; bestätigen (vb) *De*

Wochenpflege (f) *De*
maternity care *En*
soins (m.pl) de maternité *Fr*

Wohl (nt); das öffentliche — . *De*
public good *En*
bien (m) public *Fr*

Wohlfahrtspolitik (f) *De*
welfare policy *En*
politique (f) sociale *Fr*

Wohlfahrtsstaat (m) *De*
welfare state *En*
état (m) providence *Fr*

Wohlstand (m) *De*
prosperity *En*
prosperité (f) *Fr*

Wohltätigkeit (f) *De*
charity *En*
charité (f) *Fr*

Wohnantrag (m) *De*
housing application *En*
demande (f) de logement *Fr*

Wohnbebauungsland (nt) *De*
residential land *En*
terrain (m) constructible résidentiel *Fr*

Wohnbedingungen (f.pl) *De*
housing condition *En*
condition (f) des maisons *Fr*

Wohnberatungsbüro (nt) *De*
housing advice centre *En*
centre (m) de conseil résidentiel *Fr*

Wohnblock (m) *De*
block of flats *En*
immeuble (m) *Fr*

Wohnblock (m) *De*
tenement block *En*
maison (f) de rapport divisée en appartements *Fr*

Wohndichte (f) *De*
housing density *En*
densité (f) du logement *Fr*

Wohngebiet (nt) *De*
housing land *En*
terrain (m) affecté au logement *Fr*

Wohngebiet (nt), -gegend (f) *De*
residential area *En*
quartier (m) residentiel *Fr*

Wohngeld (nt) *De*
housing benefit *En*
aide (f) personnalisée au logement *Fr*

Wohnhaus (nt) *De*
residential property *En*
propriété (f) résidentielle *Fr*

Wohnheim (nt) *De*
hostel *En*
foyer (m) *Fr*

Wohnkollektiv (nt) *De*
housing co-operative *En*
société (f) coopérative de logement *Fr*

Wohnraumbedarf (m) *De*
housing demand *En*
demande (f) en logement *Fr*

Wohnrechte (nt.pl) *De*
housing rights *En*
droits (m.pl) du logement *Fr*

Wohnsiedlung (f) *De*
housing estate (council) *En*
groupe (m) de HLM *Fr*

Wohnsiedlung (f) *De*
residential development *En*
aménagement (m) urbain *Fr*

Wohnstiftung (f) *De*
housing trust *En*
syndicat (m) de logement/copropriétaires *Fr*

Wohnstraße (f) *De*
residential road *En*
rue (f) résidentielle *Fr*

Wohnstrategie (f) *De*
housing strategy *En*
stratégie (f) de l'habitat *Fr*

Wohnung (f) *De*
dwelling *En*
habitation (f) *Fr*

Wohnung (f) *De*
flat *En*
appartement (m) *Fr*

Wohnungbauzuschuß (m) *De*
housing grant *En*
aide (f) au logement *Fr*

Wohnungen (f.pl) *De*
housing *En*
logement (m) *Fr*

Wohnungen (f.pl) für Behinderte/Senioren *De*
sheltered accommodation *En*
logement (m) pour personnes handicapées *Fr*

Wohnungsamt (nt) *De*
housing agency *En*
agence (f) immobilière *Fr*

Wohnungsamt (nt) *De*
housing authority/department *En*
service (m) du logement *Fr*

*** see/siehe/voir: Introduction page IX**

Wohnungsanpassung (f) *De*
housing adaptation *En*
adaptation (f) des maisons *Fr*

Wohnungsbau (m) *De*
house building *En*
entreprise (f) de bâtiments *Fr*

Wohnungsbau (m) für Kleinverdiener *De*
low income housing *En*
logement (m) pour personnes à revenus modestes *Fr*

Wohnungsbaugesellschaft (f) *De*
development company *En*
société (f) d'exploitation *Fr*

Wohnungsbaugesetz (nt) *De*
housing law *En*
droit (m) de logement *Fr*

Wohnungsbauinvestition (f) *De*
housing investment *En*
investissement (m) immobilier *Fr*

Wohnungsbauprogramm (nt) *De*
housing programme *En*
programme (m) de logement *Fr*

Wohnungsbestand (m) *De*
housing stock/supply *En*
parc (m) de logements *Fr*

Wohnungsinstandhaltung (f) *De*
housing maintenance *En*
entretien (m) du logement *Fr*

Wohnungsmarkt (m) *De*
housing market *En*
marché (m) immobilier *Fr*

Wohnungsnot (f) *De*
housing need *En*
besoin (m) en logement *Fr*

Wohnungspolitik (f) *De*
housing policy *En*
politique (f) du logement *Fr*

Wohnungsvermittlung (f) *De*
accommodation agency *En*
agence (f) immobilière *Fr*

Wohnungsverwaltung (f) *De*
housing management *En*
gestion (f) du logement *Fr*

Wohnviertel (nt) mit Sozialwohnungen *De*
council estate *En*
groupe (m) de HLM *Fr*

Wolkenkratzer (m) *De*
sky-scraper *En*
gratte-ciel (m) (pl. grattes-ciel) *Fr*

women's group *En*
groupe (m) qui est partisan du MLF *Fr*
Frauengruppe (f) *De*

women's liberation *En*
mouvement (m) pour la libération de la femme (MLF) *Fr*
Frauenemanzipation (f); Frauenbewegung (f) *De*

women's refuge *En*
asile (m) pour femmes *Fr*
Frauenhaus (nt) *De*

women's rights *En*
droits (m.pl) de la femme *Fr*
Frauenrechte (nt.pl) *De*

word processing *En*
traitement (m) de textes *Fr*
Textverarbeitung (f) *De*

word processor *En*
machine (f) de traitement de textes *Fr*
Textverarbeitungssystem (nt) *De*

work *En*
travail (m) *Fr*
Arbeit (f) *De*

work experience *En*
stage (m) de pratique professionnelle *Fr*
Arbeitserfahrung (f) *De*

work force *En*
main-d'oeuvre (f) *Fr*
Arbeiterschaft (f), Belegschaft (f) *De*

work sharing *En*
partage (m) du travail *Fr*
Job-sharing (nt) *De*

work station *En*
station (f) de travail *Fr*
Arbeitsplatz (m) *De*

work study *En*
étude (f) du travail *Fr*
Arbeitsstudie (f) *De*

worker *En*
ouvrier (m) (-ière f.) *Fr*
Arbeiter/-in (m/f) *De*

worker co-operative *En*
coopérative (f) ouvrière de production (COOP) *Fr*
Produktivgenossenschaft (f) *De*

worker director *En*
gérant-ouvrier (m) *Fr*
dem Vorstand angehöriger Arbeitnehmer (m) *De*

workers' rights *En*
droits (m.pl) de la main-d'oeuvre *Fr*
Arbeiterrechte (nt.pl) *De*

working capital *En*
fonds (m.pl) de roulement *Fr*
Betriebskapital (nt) *De*

working conditions *En*
conditions (f.pl) de travail *Fr*
Arbeitsbedingungen (f.pl) *De*

working drawing *En*
dessin (M) de construction *Fr*
Konstruktionszeichnung (f) *De*

working hours *En*
heures (f.pl) de travail *Fr*
Arbeitszeit (f) *De*

working majority *En*
majorité (f) suffisante *Fr*
handlungsfähige Mehrheit (f) *De*

working paper *En*
document (m) de travail *Fr*
Bericht (m) *De*

working party *En*
groupe (m) de travail *Fr*
Arbeitsgruppe (f) *De*

working week *En*
semaine (f) de travail *Fr*
Arbeitswoche (f) *De*

working woman *En*
femme (f) professionnelle *Fr*
berufstätige Frau (f) *De*

workload *En*
programme (m) de travail *Fr*
Arbeitslast (f) *De*

workplace nursery *En*
crèche (f) au lieu de travail *Fr*
(betriebseigene) Kinderkrippe (f) *De*

workshop *En*
atelier (m) *Fr*
Werkstatt (f) *De*

writ *En*
assignation (f) *Fr*
Verfügung (f) *De*

write off (vb) (a debt, a loss) *En*
amortir (vb) (une dette, une perte) *Fr*
(Schulden, Verlust) abschreiben (vb) *De*

* see/siehe/voir: Introduction page IX

youth centre *En*
foyer (m) des jeunes *Fr*
Jugendzentrum (nt) *De*

youth custody *En*
garde (f) à vue (pour les mineurs) *Fr*
Jugendstrafe (f) *De*

youth employment *En*
admission (f) des jeunes au travail *Fr*
Anstellung (f) Jugendlicher *De*

youth organisation *En*
organisme (m) de jeunesse *Fr*
Jugendorganisation (f) *De*

youth service *En*
service (m) de la jeunesse *Fr*
Jugendarbeit (f) *De*

youth training scheme *En*
éducation- formation (f) des jeunes *Fr*
Ausbildungsprogramm (nt) für Jugendliche *De*

youth unemployment *En*
chômage (m) des jeunes *Fr*
Jugendarbeitslosigkeit (f) *De*

youth work *En*
éducation-formation (f) des jeunes *Fr*
Jugendarbeit (f) *De*

youth worker *En*
éducateur-formateur (m) auprès des jeunes *Fr*
Jugendfürsorger/-in (m/f) *De*

*** see/siehe/voir: Introduction page IX**

Z

Zahlungsbedingungen (f.pl) De
terms of payment *En*
conditions (f.pl) de paiement *Fr*

Zählungsbezirk (m) De
enumeration district *En*
secteur (m) de recensement *Fr*

Zahlungsbilanz (f) De
balance of payments *En*
balance (f) des paiements *Fr*

Zahnarzt/-ärztin (m/f) De
dentist *En*
dentiste (m/f) *Fr*

Zahnmedizin (f) De
dentistry *En*
dentisterie (f) *Fr*

Zahnpflege (f) De
dental care *En*
soins (m.pl) dentaires *Fr*

zebra crossing *En*
passage (m) pour piétons *Fr*
Zebrastreifen (m) *De*

Zebrastreifen (m) De
zebra crossing *En*
passage (m) pour piétons *Fr*

Zeichner/-in (m/f) De
draughtsman *En*
dessinateur (m) (en architecture) *Fr*

Zeichnungen (f.pl) De
drawings *En*
dessins (m.pl) *Fr*

Zeilenbauweise (f) De
ribbon development *En*
extension (f) urbaine en bordure de route *Fr*

Zeitplan (m) De
timetable (commerce) *En*
plan (m) de mise en exécution (commerce) *Fr*

Zeitplanung (f) De
time management *En*
organisation (f) du temps *Fr*

Zeitungsausschnitt (m) De
press cutting *En*
coupure (f) de journal *Fr*

Zensus (m); Volkszählung (f) De
census *En*
recensement (m) *Fr*

Zensusdaten (nt.pl) De
census data *En*
résultats (m.pl) du recensement *Fr*

Zentrale (f) De
head office *En*
siège (m) *Fr*

Zentralisierung (f) De
centralization *En*
centralisation (f) *Fr*

Zentralregierung (f) De
central government *En*
gouvernement (m) central *Fr*

Zentrum (nt) für Informationstechnik De
information technology centre *En*
centre (m) de traitement de l'information *Fr*

zero based budgeting *En*
budgétisation (f) à base zéro *Fr*
auf Null basierender Haushalt (m) *De*

zero rating *En*
imposition (f) nulle *Fr*
Befreiung (f) von der Mehrwertsteuer *De*

Zeuge/-gin (m/f) De
witness (noun) *En*
témoin (m) *Fr*

Zeuge/-gin sein; bestätigen (vb) De
witness (vb) *En*
témoigner (vb) *Fr*

Zeugnis (nt), Bescheinigung (f) De
certificate *En*
certificat (m) *Fr*

Zickzackmarkierung (f) De
zig zag marking *En*
marquages (m.pl) en zigzag *Fr*

Ziele (nt.pl) De
aims and objectives *En*
but (m) *Fr*

Ziele (nt.pl) De
attainment target *En*
évaluation (f) de progrès *Fr*

Ziele (nt.pl) De
objectives *En*
buts (m.pl) *Fr*

Zielformulierung (f) De
policy formulation/making *En*
élaboration (f) des politiques *Fr*

zielorientiertes Management (nt) De
management by objectives *En*
direction (f) par objectifs *Fr*

Zielplanung (f) De
policy planning *En*
planification (f) des politiques *Fr*

zig zag marking *En*
marquages (m.pl) en zigzag *Fr*
Zickzackmarkierung (f) *De*

Zigeunerlager (nt) De
gipsy site *En*
aire (f) de stationnement pour nomades *Fr*

Zinsfreibetrag (m) De
interest relief *En*
allégement (m) des intérêts *Fr*

Zinssatz (m) De
interest rate *En*
taux (m) d'intérêts *Fr*

Zinssatz (m) De
rate of interest *En*
taux (m) d'intérêt *Fr*

*** see/siehe/voir: Introduction page IX**

zirkulieren (vb); Akten usw — lassen. *De*
circulate (vb) papers etc *En*
distribuer (vb) les papiers etc *Fr*

Zivilrecht (nt) *De*
civil law *En*
droit (m) civil *Fr*

Zivilschutz (m) *De*
civil defence *En*
protection (f) civile *Fr*

Zoll (m) *De*
customs *En*
douane (f) *Fr*

Zoll (m) *De*
duties (customs) *En*
droit(s) (m/m.pl) de douane *Fr*

Zollabfertigung (f) *De*
customs clearance *En*
dédouanement (m) *Fr*

zone (f) centrale de commerce *Fr*
Geschäftszentrum (nt) *De*
central business district *En*

zone (f) d'amélioration commerciale *Fr*
wirtschaftliches Entwicklungsgebiet (nt) *De*
commercial improvement area *En*

zone (f) d'amélioration *Fr*
Erschließungsgebiet (nt) *De*
improvement area *En*

zone (f) d'aménagement concerté (ZAC) *Fr*
Bebauungsplangebiet (nt) *De*
simplified planning zone *En*

zone (f) d'aménagement concerté (ZAC) *Fr*
Prioritätserschließungsgebiet (nt) *De*
special development area *En*

zone (f) d'aménagement concerté (ZAC) *Fr*
Urbanisationsgebiet (nt) *De*
urban development area *En*

zone (f) d'embellissement général *Fr*
Verschönerungsgebiet (nt) *De*
general improvement area *En*

zone (f) d'entreprise *Fr*
wirtschaftliches Fördergebiet (nt) *De*
enterprise zone *En*

zone (f) d'expansion industrielle *Fr*
Industrieverbesserungsgebiet (nt) *De*
industrial improvement area *En*

zone (f) d'exploitation *Fr*
Entwicklungsgebiet (nt) *De*
development area *En*

zone (f) de développement *Fr*
Erschließungsgelände (nt) *De*
development site *En*

zone (f) de réhabilitation *Fr*
Sanierungsgebiet (nt) *De*
redevelopment area *En*

zone (f) franche (de commerce) *Fr*
Freihandelszone (f) *De*
free trade zone *En*

zone (f) industrielle *Fr*
Industriegelände (nt) *De*
industrial area/estate *En*

zone (f) non nucléaire *Fr*
atomwaffenfreie Zone (f) *De*
nuclear free zone *En*

zone (f) piétonne *Fr*
Fußgängerzone (f) *De*
pedestrian area/precinct/zone *En*

zone (f) prioritaire *Fr*
Prioritätszone (f) *De*
priority area *En*

zone (f) protégée *Fr*
Naturschutz-, Landschaftsschutzgebiet (nt) *De*
conservation area *En*

zone (f) subventionnée *Fr*
Subventionsgebiet (nt) *De*
assisted area *En*

zone (f) verte *Fr*
Grüngürtel (m) *De*
green belt *En*

zoning (school catchment areas) *En*
sectorisation (f) *Fr*
bezirksgebundene/stadtteilgebundene Einteilung (f) *De*

Zufahrtsstraße (f) *De*
access road *En*
route (f) d'accès *Fr*

Zufahrtsstraße (f) *De*
approach road *En*
route (f) d'accès *Fr*

Zugang (m) zu Informationen *De*
access to information *En*
droit (m) à l'information *Fr*

zugreifen (vb) auf *De*
access (vb) *En*
accéder (vb) à *Fr*

Zukunftsplanung (f) *De*
forward planning *En*
planification (f) stratégique *Fr*

zur Begleichung vorgelegte Rechnung (f) *De*
account rendered *En*
compte (m) rendu *Fr*

Zurückhaltung (f) bei Lohnforderungen *De*
wage restraint *En*
contrainte (f) sur les salaires *Fr*

zurücktreten (vb) *De*
resign (vb) *En*
démissionner (vb) *Fr*

zusammenarbeiten (vb) *De*
liaise (vb) *En*
faire (vb) la liaison *Fr*

zusätzliche Gemeinde-steuern (f.pl) *De*
supplementary rate *En*
impôt (m) local supplémentaire (en GB) *Fr*

zusätzliche Hilfe (f) zum Lebensunterhalt *De*
income support *En*
complément (f) de revenu *Fr*

zusätzliche Leistungen (f.pl) *De*
fringe benefits *En*
compléments (m.pl) de salaire en nature *Fr*

Zuschlag (m) *De*
surcharge *En*
débours (m) injustifié porté à la charge du responsable *Fr*

Zuschlag erheben (vb) *De*
surcharge (vb) *En*
faire supporter (vb) (au responsable) une erreur de paiement *Fr*

Zuschlagsgebühr (f) *De*
extra charge *En*
supplément (m) *Fr*

Zuschlagstoffe (m.pl) *De*
aggregates (civil eng.) *En*
granulats (m.pl) *Fr*

*** see/siehe/voir: Introduction page IX**

Zuschuß (m) zu den Lebenshaltungskosten *De*
cost of living allowance *En*
maintien (m) du pouvoir d'achat *Fr*

Zustellung (f) einer Verfügung *De*
delivery of a writ *En*
signification (f) d'un acte *Fr*

zustimmen (vb) *De*
adopt (vb) (minutes of council) *En*
approuver (vb) le procès-verbal d'une séance du conseil *Fr*

Zustimmung (f) *De*
adoption (of council minutes) *En*
approbation (f) du procès-verbal d'une séance du conseil *Fr*

Zustimmung (f) *De*
consent *En*
consentement (m) *Fr*

Zuteilung (f) *De*
apportionment *En*
partage (m) *Fr*

zuviel ausgeben (vb) *De*
overspend (vb) *En*
dépenser (vb) au delà des moyens *Fr*

Zuweisung (f) der Mittel *De*
allocation of resources *En*
répartition (f) des moyens *Fr*

zweispurige Straße (f) *De*
dual carriageway *En*
route (f) jumelée *Fr*

Zweizweckgebäude (nt) *De*
dual use building *En*
bâtiment (m) partagé *Fr*

Zwillingsverbindung (f) *De*
twinning *En*
jumelage (m) *Fr*

Zwischenbehandlung (f) *De*
intermediate treatment *En*
traitement (m) intermédiaire *Fr*

zyklisch (adj) *De*
cyclic (adj) *En*
cyclique (adj) *Fr*

*** see/siehe/voir: Introduction page IX**

Select Bibliography

British Chambers of Commerce, Six Language Business Dictionary (Colt Books)

Cassell Business Companions series: France, Germany, Italy, Spain (ed. Haltern and Neuhaus)

Cassell Language Guides series: French, German, Italian, Spanish. (Series ed. Worth-Stylianou)

Dictionary of Acronyms for European Community Action Plans and Programmes (Commission of the European Communities)

EURODICAUTOM – Computerized language database (Commission of the European Communities)

European Municipal Directory (ed. Ellis, published by European Directories Ltd)

European Treaties Vocabulary Parts I and II (Commission of the European Communities)

Meeting Industry Terminology (Commission of the European Communities and International Association of Professional Congress Organizations)

The Structure of Local Government in Europe (ed. Eileen Harloff, International Union of Local Authorities)